AFRICAN AMERICAN DRAMATISTS

AFRICAN AMERICAN DRAMATISTS

AN A-TO-Z GUIDE

Edited by
Emmanuel S. Nelson

GREENWOOD PRESS
Westport, Connecticut • London

Library of Congress Cataloging-in Publication Data

African American dramatists : an A to Z guide / edited by Emmanuel S. Nelson.
    p. cm.
  Includes bibliographical references and index.
  ISBN 0-313-32233-3 (alk. paper)
    1. American drama—African American authors—Dictionaries. 2. American
drama—African American authors—Bio-bibliography—Dictionaries. 3. African American
dramatists—Biography—Dictionaries. 4. African Americans—Intellectual life—Dictionaries.
5. Dramatists, American—Biography—Dictionaries. 6. African Americans in literature—
Bibliography. I. Nelson, Emmanuel S. (Emmanuel Sampath), 1954–
PS338.N4A69 2004
812.009'896073'003—dc22   2004052652

British Library Cataloguing in Publication Data is available.

Library of Congress Catalog Card Number: 2004052652
ISBN: 0-313-32233-3

First published in 2004

Greenwood Press, 88 Post Road West, Westport, CT 06881
An imprint of Greenwood Publishing Group, Inc.
www.greenwood.com

Printed in the United States of America

The paper used in this book complies with the
Permanent Paper Standard issued by the National
Information Standards Organization (Z39.48-1984).

10   9   8   7   6   5   4   3   2   1

CONTENTS

Preface   xi

Ira Aldridge (1807–1867)   1
   Linda M. Carter

James Baldwin (1924–1987)   7
   Robin Jane Lucy

Amiri Baraka (1934–)   17
   Darcy A. Zabel

Marita Bonner (1898–1971)   33
   Loretta G. Woodard

Arna Bontemps (1902–1973)   40
   Linda M. Carter

William Blackwell Branch (1927–)   45
   Laverne Luster

William Wells Brown (1814–1884)   51
   Linda M. Carter

CONTENTS

Elizabeth Brown-Guillory (1954–)   56
Loretta G. Woodard

Ed Bullins (1935–)   64
Ladrica Menson-Furr

Ben Caldwell (1937–)   78
Cristi A. Fox

Vinnette Carroll (1922–2002)   88
Kimberly K. Harding

Pearl Cleage (1948–)   96
Gwendolyn S. Jones

Kathleen Conwell Collins (1942–1988)   102
Chandra Tyler Mountain

J(oan) California Cooper (?–)   109
Tarshia L. Stanley

Kia Corthron (1962–)   115
Deborah Gleason-Rielly

Ossie Davis (1917–)   125
Lean'tin L. Bracks

Thomas Covington Dent (1932–1998)   133
James L. Hill

Owen Dodson (1914–1983)   140
Louis J. Parascandola

Alice Moore Dunbar-Nelson (1875–1935)   148
Loretta G. Woodard

Lonne Elder III (1931–1996)   154
Justin Brodeur

Rudolph Fisher (1897–1934)   167
Helen R. Houston

J. e. Franklin (1937–)   172
Ymitri Jayasundera

CONTENTS

Charles Gordone (1925–1995)   177
  Yolanda W. Page

Shirley Graham (1896–1977)   182
  Leela Kapai

Micki Grant (1941–)   188
  Kimberly K. Harding

Angelina Weld Grimké (1880–1958)   196
  Terry Novak

William Harrison Gunn (1934–1989)   200
  Jessie N. Marion

Lorraine Hansberry (1930–1965)   208
  Loretta G. Woodard

Leslie Pinckney Hill (1880–1960)   217
  Valleri Robinson Hohman

Pauline Elizabeth Hopkins (1859–1930)   223
  Terry Novak

Langston Hughes (1902–1967)   226
  Karl L. Stenger

Zora Neale Hurston (1891–1960)   247
  Rhonda Harvey

Georgia Douglas Johnson (1880?–1966)   253
  Loretta G. Woodard

Samuel L. Kelley (1948–)   260
  Joel Shatzky

Adrienne Kennedy (1931–)   265
  Steven Carter

May Miller (1899–1995)   283
  Joyce Russell-Robinson

Ron Milner (1938–2004)   289
  Freya M. Mercer

CONTENTS

Loften Mitchell (1919–2001)   300
Harish Chander

Barbara Molette (1940–)   311
Gwendolyn S. Jones

Richard Bruce Nugent (1906–1987)   316
Linda M. Carter

Robert O'Hara (1970–)   321
Johnny Woodnal

OyamO (1943–)   330
Rochell Isaac

Suzan-Lori Parks (1964–)   336
Sharon M. Brubaker

Louis Stamford Peterson (1922–1998)   347
James L. Hill

Aishah Rahman (1937–)   352
Suzanne Hotte Massa

Willis Richardson (1889–1977)   358
Harish Chander

Sonia Sanchez (1934–)   371
Sharon Glazier Hochstein

Victor Sejour (1817–1874)   382
Ladrica Menson-Furr

Ntozake Shange (1948–)   387
Carrie J. Boden

Ted Shine (1931–)   408
Joyce Russell-Robinson

Anna Deavere Smith (1950–)   417
Kimberly Rae Connor

Eulalie Spence (1894–1981)   429
Yvonne Shafer

CONTENTS

Wallace Thurman (1902–1934) 435
  Linda M. Carter

Eugene (Jean) Pinchback Toomer (1894–1967) 440
  Emma Waters Dawson

Joseph A. Walker (1935–) 451
  Emmanuel S. Nelson

Douglas Turner Ward (1930–) 456
  Kristina A. Clark

Samm-Art Williams (1946–) 464
  Rochell Isaac

August Wilson (1945–) 472
  Karen C. Blansfield

Charlayne Woodard (1955–) 491
  Christine M. Lemchak

Richard Wright (1908–1960) 498
  Robert Felgar

Marvin X (1944–) 503
  Michael E. Idland

Selected Bibliography 515

Index 517

About the Contributors 523

PREFACE

The central purpose of this reference work is to introduce readers to the lives and works of sixty-one representative African American playwrights of the last 150 years. Each chapter offers reliable, thorough, and up-to-date biographical, critical, and bibliographic information on an individual dramatist. Collectively, the sixty-one chapters provide a historical overview of the African American theatrical tradition as well as scholarly assessments of influential figures, seminal texts, and crucial moments in the development of that tradition. Advanced scholars will find this sourcebook a foundational research tool; its user-friendly style, format, and level of complexity, however, make it accessible to a much wider audience that includes undergraduate students and even general readers. Each chapter begins with relevant biographical information on the playwright, then it offers an interpretive commentary on his or her major texts and provides a succinct overview of the critical reception accorded, and then it concludes with a selected bibliography that lists, separately, the playwright's primary works and secondary sources. To facilitate cross-referencing, whenever a writer who is also the subject of a chapter in this volume is first mentioned within a chapter, an asterisk appears next to his or her name.

If performativity is the defining criterion of drama, then the African American dramatic tradition began in 1619 with the first recorded arrival of Africans in America. Prototheatrical elements were a salient feature of the ceremonies, rituals, stories, songs, and dance that the early Africans brought with them. Those social practices gradually began to assume quasi-formal status as the displaced people sought to preserve their indigenous traditions and later, sometimes under duress, to provide entertainment to white audiences. In 1816, however, African American theater made its formal debut when the Caribbean-born William Henry Brown founded the African Company, an all-black theatrical group. In 1821, he established the African Grove Theatre in New York City and the African Company actors, under the directorship of Brown himself, staged numerous plays that included Shakespearean classics as well as contemporary skits and sketches. Brown's *The Drama of King Shotaway*—a play about an anticolonial insurrection on a Caribbean island—was produced there in 1823. Later that year, however, the African Grove Theatre closed down and it was not until after the Civil War that other all-black theater companies began to emerge. Though dozens of black actors did participate in numerous white-controlled minstrel shows, revues, pageants, and musicals throughout the nineteenth century, their roles were often severely limited in range and complexity.

By the 1920s, with the advent of the Harlem Renaissance, African American theater began to emerge. Black actors as well as plays by black playwrights began to appear with considerable regularity on Broadway. Predominantly black colleges and universities, with their own on-campus theater companies and stage productions, began to nurture the talents of aspiring actors as well as playwrights. During the 1930s, the Federal Writers' Project—a Depression-era program instituted under President Franklin Roosevelt's Works Progress Administration—gave substantial, though short-lived, impetus to African American drama. By the 1960s, African American plays and playwrights had become an entrenched part of the American theater scene. The works of dramatists such as Langston Hughes, Eulalie Spence, Lorraine Hansberry, Loften Mitchell, William Blackwell Branch, and James Baldwin had ensured black presence and visibility from Broadway to small campus and community theaters. And the Black Theater Movement, which began in the mid-1960s and lasted well into the 1970s, witnessed the emergence of many angry young playwrights whose often intensely political and polemical plays were designed to advance a revolutionary social agenda. During that time there was a spectacular proliferation of black companies; prominent among them were the Negro Ensemble Company, the National Black Theatre, the Black Arts Repertory Theatre and School, the New Heritage Theatre, the Black Theatre Alliance, the Free Southern Theatre, and the Spirit House. These companies were able to showcase the works of a host of new playwrights, such as Amiri Baraka, Ed Bullins, Vinnette Carroll, Micki Grant, Joseph A. Walker, and Alice Childress, among others. By the closing decades of the twentieth century, African American drama had begun to edge its way to the very center of the American stage. Playwrights—such as Charles Gordone, August Wilson, Suzan-Lori Parks, and Charles H. Fuller, Jr.—had won every major theatrical award including the Pulitzer Prize for Drama.

PREFACE

A goal of this reference volume is to document the extraordinary story of the evolution of African American drama from marginal performance spaces to the very heart of Broadway. But this sourcebook does not claim to be comprehensive in its coverage; nor is it engaged in the dubious enterprise of constructing a canon. It does, however, facilitate a gathering of representative African American playwrights whose works have helped build one of the world's great dramatic traditions. This sourcebook offers a scholarly map of their individual journeys and celebrates their monumental collective achievement.

IRA ALDRIDGE
(1807 – 1867)

Linda M. Carter

BIOGRAPHY

Ira Frederick Aldridge, acclaimed as the Tragedian of Color and the African Roscius, was born on July 24, 1807, in New York City, to Daniel and Luranah Aldridge. He attended the African Free School No. 2, a Manhattan institution for free black American youth where he won oratory prizes. His father, a lay preacher and a straw vendor who was undoubtedly impressed with his younger son's elocution skills, wanted him to become a minister. When his mother died and his father remarried, Aldridge ran away from home and worked briefly on a ship. When the ship docked in North Carolina, a slave dealer offered the captain $500 for Aldridge. The captain refused the offer, and Aldridge later returned to New York City.

Aldridge became fascinated with the theater. He worked backstage at the Chatham and Park theaters around 1816 or 1820 and gained acting experience with the African Company, a group founded and managed by William Henry Brown; James Hewlett, the African Company's leading actor; and other blacks. The group built the African Grove Theatre, the first resident African American theater in the United States, in 1821. Aldridge made his acting debut as Rolla, a Peruvian character in Richard Brinsley Sheridan's adaptation of August von Kotzebue's *Pizarro*, and had additional minor roles in other productions of the African Company. He may have played the male lead in *Romeo and Juliet*.

Aldridge, seventeen years old and cognizant that America offered few opportunities for aspiring African American actors, sailed to Liverpool, England, in 1824. He attended the University of Glasgow for approximately eighteen months while he developed a performance repertoire.

The first African American actor to establish himself professionally in a foreign country, Aldridge made his European debut on October 10, 1825, at London's Royal Coburg Theatre (now known as the Old Vic) in the lead role of Oroonoko in *The Revolt of Surinam, or A Slave's Revenge*; this play was an adaptation of Thomas Southerne's *Oroonoko*. The playbill listed Aldridge's surname as Kean. Thus, Aldridge observed a common theatrical practice of assuming an identical or similar nomenclature to that of a celebrity (in this case, Edmund Kean, who was regarded as one of the outstanding actors of his time) in order to garner attention. Aldridge resumed use of his birth name sometime between 1831 and 1835. During his six-week engagement at the Royal Coburg, the young actor starred in five melodramas and earned admiration from his audiences while most critics emphasized Aldridge's lack of stage training and experience. A number of critics were infuriated that a black man audaciously pursued an acting career.

Aldridge left London in order to refine his craft in the English provinces. His popularity continued to grow as he toured for seven years. His first provincial appearance was at Brighton's Theatre Royal where, in December 1825, he starred in *Oroonoko* and *Othello*, his first Shakespearean performance in Europe. During these years away from London, Aldridge also performed in Liverpool, which was a major United Kingdom center for the slave trade.

Aldridge was an abolitionist. Sometimes at the end of performances, he played a guitar and sang antislavery songs. In 1829, on the final nights of his engagements, Aldridge began delivering farewell addresses that focused on slavery's injustices and hope for the liberation of the enslaved. He contributed significant amounts of money to the antislavery movement and, from 1830 to 1861, to the Negro State Conventions.

During Aldridge's tour of the British Isles, he starred in tragedies as well as a few comedies and sometimes performed as many as sixteen roles in less than two weeks. His performance as Othello at the Covent Garden Theatre in April 1833, marked his return to the London stage after his seven-year tour of the provinces. Aldridge then toured the provinces for the next nineteen years. His acting style was described as dignified and realistic without ranting, exaggeration, or gimmicks. He was known for his power to captivate audiences. Aldridge was the first U.S.-born actor to gain popularity and ultimately critical acclaim on the European stage. He began playing nonblack characters after he exhausted the limited number of black roles. Whites portrayed black characters; now Aldridge, wearing wigs and white makeup, reversed the theatrical practice by portraying such characters as King Lear, Shylock, Richard III, Hamlet, and Macbeth.

On July 14, 1852, Aldridge left England and began his first tour of the Continent; his travels included Cologne, Frankfurt, Leipzig, Vienna, Berlin, and other cities in the German Federation, as well as Prague, Brunn, and Budapest. He returned to London in the spring of 1855. Three years later, he traveled to Russia for the first time. Aldridge, who became a British citizen in 1863, never returned to America although he initiated negotiations for performances in New York shortly before his death.

Aldridge was scheduled to perform in Lodz, Poland, in 1867. After his arrival, rehearsals were discontinued when his health deteriorated. He died on August 7, 1867, and was buried two days later in Lodz's Evangelical Cemetery. He was preceded in death by his first wife Margaret (née Gill), and survived by his second wife, Amanda Pauline (née von Brandt) and children. Aldridge received many awards and honors including a commission in the Army of Haiti in the Seventeenth Regiment of the Grenadiers, the Prussian Gold Medal of the First Class of the Academy, Switzerland's White Cross, the Imperial Jubilee de Tolstoy Medal, Austria's Medal of Ferdinand; Russia's the Golden Cross of Leopold; and the title Knight of Saxony presented by the state of Saxe-Coburg-Gotha, whose *Almanac*, according to Aldridge biographers Herbert Marshall and Mildred Stock "was the most exclusive aristocratic social register ever known" (335). These tributes offer verification that Ira Aldridge's talents, courage to pursue an acting career regardless of the numerous racist obstacles, and perseverance did not go unnoticed during his lifetime. Aldridge's most prestigious posthumous honor is the Ira Aldridge Memorial Chair at the Shakespeare Memorial Theatre at Stratford-on-Avon.

MAJOR WORKS AND THEMES

Ira Aldridge performed at least forty roles during his forty-two years as a professional actor. As a result of the difficulty of finding suitable roles, he adapted two plays. The first, *The Black Doctor* (1847), is based on Auguste Anicet Bourgeois and Paul Dumanoir's *Le Docteur Noir* (1846). It is the story of Fabian, a former slave, who becomes an eminent physician; saves Pauline Reynerie, the daughter of his former master; falls in love and elopes with her; is sent to the Bastille; goes mad; is released from prison; and sacrifices his life in order to save his beloved Pauline. The drama depicts a society that is quick to acknowledge the black doctor's skills yet cannot accept his marriage to a white woman. To reflect better *The Black Doctor*'s theme, the play's subtitle, *A Romantic Drama in Four Acts*, should be changed to *A Romantic, Interracial Drama in Four Acts*.

During the nineteenth century, melodrama was a prevalent genre in England, and *The Black Doctor* employs stock melodramatic characteristics such as the conflict between good and evil (the moral and upright Fabian is separated from the virtuous Pauline because of two evil characters: Pauline's mother and her former fiancé, Chevalier St. Luce), the villain's harassment of the hero (St. Luce has Fabian imprisoned), and an appeal to the audience's emotions (pity for Fabian and Pauline because they cannot be together, horror when it appears that Fabian and Pauline will perish as the sea rises higher and higher on the rock where they have just confessed their love to each other before their elopement, and moral indignation that the only reason the couple cannot be together is racism). At the end of *The Black Doctor*, pity, horror, and moral indignation are evoked again as a gunman aims at Pauline and Fabian rushing forward, receives the bullet, and dies.

Aldridge's second play was an adaptation of Shakespeare's *Titus Andronicus* (1594). The original, Shakespeare's first and most violent tragedy, was regarded as too grim for theater audiences. Aldridge could not stage the original *Titus Andronicus* because it was incompatible with his objective "of offering to the 'respectable world' only such productions as were suitable for all the family and without offence even to the most sensitive religious feelings" (Marshall and Stock 170). Therefore Aldridge and his collaborator, C. A. Somerset, made major revisions; they deleted horror scenes such as Lavinia's triple misfortune: rape, cutting out of her tongue, and chopping off of her hands; and added a scene from *Zaraffa, The Slave King*, a play written for Aldridge. However, of greater significance is the transformation of Aaron the Moor from villain to hero. Aldridge and Somerset's adaptation (1849) marked *Titus Andronicus*'s revival; the play had not been produced for 128 years.

CRITICAL RECEPTION

Ira Aldridge's contributions to the theater have not received adequate scholarly attention. Most research focuses on his life and acting career. To date Marshall and Stock's 1958 biography, reprinted in 1993, remains the one book-length study of Aldridge, while Bernth Lindfors's article (1999) seems to be the most recent one on Aldridge published in a literary journal.

Aldridge's two adaptations have never been widely available in print. *The Black Doctor* was first published in 1870, twenty-three years after its creation; it was republished in 1880. Its inclusion in James Hatch and Ted Shine's *Black Theatre USA* (1996) marks *The Black Doctor*'s only twentieth-century publication. It appears that Aldridge's *Titus Andronicus* has never been published. Although Aldridge did not write original plays, he is recognized as the third African American playwright (Pawley 17; Peterson 26).

Commentary concerning *The Black Doctor* and *Titus Andronicus* is even more scarce than Aldridge's biographical information.

Bernard Peterson identifies Aldridge's first adaptation, *The Black Doctor*, as the "second recorded play in English by a black American playwright" (26). According to Hatch and Shine, Aldridge's description of his protagonist, Fabian, as a mulatto may have been an indication to "white audiences that the term 'black' included shades other than charcoal" (4). Hatch and Shine also suggest that there are autobiographical elements in *The Black Doctor:* "Perhaps the tragedian's situation was akin to the Black doctor's in the play: his color sometimes provoked hostility, but his talent was so in evidence that his detractors could not hold the field. Like Fabian, he married a white Englishwoman . . . and enjoyed honors, property . . ." (4). There is consensus among the critics that Fabian is a dignified, noble character. Aldridge's search for additional "strong black leading roles for inclusion in his repertoire" led him to *Titus Andronicus* (Peterson 25). He rewrote the Shakespearean play to present Aaron as a lofty character and to make the play more tolerable for audiences. Errol Hill asserts that Aldridge was always cognizant that he was viewed as a representative of the African race whenever he was on a stage. Such awareness "had a profound effect on the interpretation Aldridge brought to his roles. He was not content simply to deal with the fictive conflict of his stage character. He remained conscious of the social and racial problems underlying the society beyond the immediate concerns of the play" (xiv).

It is obvious that Ira Aldridge, the forefather of generations of African American actors and playwrights, merits further scholarly attention.

BIBLIOGRAPHY

Dramatic Works by Ira Aldridge

"The Black Doctor." 1847. *Black Theatre USA, Plays by African Americans: The Early Period, 1847–1938*. Eds. James V. Hatch and Ted Shine. Rev. ed. New York: Free Press, 1996. 3–24.

(With C. A. Somerset). Titus Andronicus. 1849. Unpublished.

Studies of Ira Aldridge's Dramatic Works

Hatch, James V., and Ted Shine, eds. *Black Theatre USA, Plays by African Americans* (rev. ed.). New York: Free Press, 1996.

Hill, Errol. Introduction. *Ira Aldridge: The Negro Tragedian*. Ed. Herbert Marshall and Mildred Stock. 1958. Washington, DC: Howard University Press, 1993.

Isaacs, Edith J. *The Negro in the American Theatre*. New York: Theatre Arts, 1947.

Lindfors, Bernth. "'Mislike Me Not for My Complexion . . .': Ira Aldridge in White-face." *African American Review* 33 (1999): 347–354.

Marshall, Herbert, and Mildred Stock, eds. *Ira Aldridge: The Negro Tragedian*. 1958. Washington, DC: Howard University Press, 1993.

Pawley, Thomas D. "The First Black Playwrights." *Black World* 21 (1972): 16–24.

Peterson, Bernard L., Jr. "Ira Aldridge." *Early Black American Playwrights and Dramatic Writers: A Biographical Directory and Catalog of Plays, Films, and Broadcasting Scripts*. Westport: Greenwood, 1990. 25–26.

JAMES BALDWIN
(1924–1987)

Robin Jane Lucy

BIOGRAPHY

James Baldwin was born in Harlem on August 2, 1924, to Emma Berdis Jones. Three years later, Emma married David Baldwin and subsequently had eight additional children. David was a factory laborer and a storefront preacher. Baldwin's relationship with his stepfather was a troubled one: emotionally distant, if not abusive, Baldwin's stepfather exercised an "arbitrary and puritanical discipline" rooted in his fundamentalist beliefs and his personal frustration at the racism and poverty that confronted his family (Leeming 5).

In early adolescence, Baldwin was taken in hand by a white schoolteacher, Orilla (Bill) Miller, who first exposed him to theater, an Orson Welles production of *Macbeth*, with an all-black cast, at the Lafayette Theatre in Harlem. In his essay, "The Devil Finds Work," Baldwin parallels the experience of being in the audience with his religious conversion a year later, at the age of fourteen. The theater, like the church, was a ritual experience of communion, a type of transubstantiation, in a secular setting: one is "responding to one's flesh and blood: in the theater, we are recreating each other. . . . [W]e are *all* each other's flesh and blood" (501). The actors represented for Baldwin the existential challenge of living an authentic life of risk, love, and the creation and assertion of personal and communal identities, choices that often conflicted with the "safety" of God and the church ("Down" 296): "For, they were themselves, these actors. . . . They could *be* Macbeth only because they were themselves: my first real apprehension of the mortal challenge" ("Devil" 504). Baldwin's religious conversion was incorporated into his first novel, *Go Tell It on the Mountain* (1953); the crisis of leaving the church and the "theatre" of the pulpit—he became a "Young Minister" at the age of seventeen ("Down" 308) and of becoming a "witness" in a secular vocation (Baldwin, "Sweet" 758) are addressed in *The Amen Corner*, written while his novel was being published.

Baldwin left the church and home in 1941 but returned to Harlem when David was hospitalized with tuberculosis. When David died in 1943, Baldwin moved to Greenwich Village to write; there, he also experienced the relative freedom to live out his homosexuality. In 1944, Baldwin met Richard Wright* who helped him secure a writing fellowship. In 1948, the last of a second writing grant financed his relocation to Paris, though Baldwin returned regularly to the United States during the 1950s. In 1957, he made his first trip to the Deep South. In 1957–1958, Baldwin worked on an adaptation of his novel *Giovanni's Room* (1956) for Lee Strasberg's Actors Studio; he met Lorraine Hansberry* at a workshop production of his script in May 1958. In the summer of that year, Baldwin apprenticed on two theatrical productions with the director Elia Kazan.

In the 1960s, Baldwin became increasingly involved with civil rights activism and worked with, among others, Medgar Evers, Malcolm X, and Martin Luther King, Jr. According to W. J. Weatherby, Baldwin was involved in orchestrating a face-to-face talk between King and Malcolm X, but Malcolm X was assassinated two days before the scheduled meeting (263). Baldwin's film script of *The Autobiography of Malcolm X* (1964) begins with Malcolm X's drive to the Audubon Ballroom and, through a series of flashbacks, tells his life story.

Baldwin spent the last twenty years of his life in Paris, Istanbul, Africa, and, finally, at his house in St. Paul-de-Vence in the south of France. At his death of cancer in St. Paul on December 1, 1987, Baldwin was working on several plays. Over five thousand people attended Baldwin's memorial service at St. John the Divine in New York.

MAJOR WORKS AND THEMES

The Amen Corner, written in 1953, was performed on Broadway in April 1965, a year after the production of *Blues for Mister Charlie*. The play had a short run under the direction of Owen Dodson* at Howard University in 1955 and was produced in Los Angeles a few years later by Frank Silvera (Collier 29), who would play Luke on Broadway, where it ran for forty-eight performances.

Set in the home and church of the pastor Sister Margaret, *Blues for Mister Charlie* covers a week between and including Sunday services. A decade earlier, at the death of her second child, Margaret left her husband Luke, a jazz musician, to raise her young son David alone and pursue her religious "vision" (122), which is revealed in the course of the play as a "hiding place" from life itself (88). Margaret controls her congregation with what Baldwin describes in his introduction as her "merciless piety" and is a "tyrannical matriarch" to both it and her son (xvii). Her favorite biblical passage is "Set thine house in order, for thou shalt die and not live." The return of Luke, who is ill, upsets this imposed order; Margaret refuses to care for him and departs for Philadelphia, leaving David to tend to his father.

Luke's return precipitates a crisis for the congregation and David. The church members begin to question both Sister Margaret's piety—the materialization of her forgotten husband proves she was a sexual woman and "ain't nothing but flesh and blood, like all the rest of us" (49)—as well as her spending habits. David discusses his love of music with Luke and that as soon as he began to play with a group of jazz musicians, he "stopped praying . . . stopped believing . . ." (61). Luke passes on his hard-won knowledge that music is but one expression of love and that no person knows who he or she is "inside . . . without somebody [loving] him" (63). This is one of Baldwin's major themes: that love and sexuality are essential to both day-to-day and spiritual life, that they are deeply implicated in one's identity. When Margaret, back from Philadelphia, overhears a recording of Luke's music as she stands before her congregation, her response ironically demonstrates this fact. She commands the congregation to "[k]neel down" and pray for "a clean heart and a clean mind . . ." (81). While she is vilifying the music and its message, she is at a deeper level, paying obeisance. At the end of act 2, Luke articulates the challenges that face David and Margaret respectively: Luke will no longer let Margaret keep David "safe" nor is it his, but Margaret's, "soul we been trying to save" (91).

In act 3, David declares his break from both the church and his mother: "It's time you let me be a man" (120). He also affirms his secular vocation, his music: "Maybe I can say something . . . in music that's never been said before" (120–121). Luke's presence and his music also work on Margaret, who recounts her vision in very different terms: "I just remember that it was dark and I was scared and my baby was dead and I wanted Luke, I wanted Luke, I wanted Luke" (122). After Luke dies, and with his trombone's mouthpiece pressed against her breast, Margaret delivers her final sermon to a congregation that has deposed her: "To love the Lord is to love all His children—all of them, everyone!—and suffer with them and rejoice with them and never count the cost!" (134). Baldwin writes in his introduction that "she has lost everything, [but] also gains the keys to the kingdom. The kingdom is love, and love is selfless, although only the self can lead one there" (xvii–xviii).

Blues for Mister Charlie opened on Broadway in April 1964—after a turbulent rehearsal period—as an Actors Studio production directed by Burgess Meredith; the play was published by Dial Press at the same time. Ticket prices were kept low to, as the producer stated, "make it possible for a subway audience to come" and this contributed to the fact that the audience was often predominantly African American (Weatherby 242). The ticket prices, and the controversy that surrounded the play, took a financial toll. Posted to close after a one-month run, Baldwin mounted a successful media campaign to keep the play on stage for several more months; it finally closed on August 23.

Blues is based on the 1955 lynching of Emmett Till and the subsequent acquittal of his murderers by an all-white jury. Dedicated to Medgar Evers and the children of the Birmingham bombing, killed in 1963, Baldwin wrote in his introduction that the play was "one man's attempt to bear witness to the reality and the power of light" (xv). To witness, however, entailed a brutal confrontation on the part of his audience with the disease of racism and an unexamined Christianity that supported it in "Plaguetown, U.S.A." (xv).

The set is literally divided. Whitetown and Blacktown, the black church and the courthouse, are on opposite sides of the color line. The black residents of the community are engaged in a civil rights struggle that is met with violence. The play opens with the murder of Richard Henry, the son of the black minister Meridian, at the hands of a white storekeeper, Lyle Britten. Richard, a musician, has returned south after battling drug addiction in New York City. The personal and political struggle between love and hate, nonviolent and violent resistance, is a major theme in the play. In a series of flashbacks, we learn of Richard's life in New York and the event that instigated his move north: the murder of his mother at the hands of white men and the fact that Meridian did not avenge her death. Richard's confrontation with his father over this fact is followed, somewhat incongruously, by the surrender of his gun to Meridian. This does, however, dramatize both the conflict between violence and nonviolence and Meridian's confrontation with a Christianity that is also a compensation: "Since I wasn't a man in men's eyes, then I could be a man in the eyes of God" (38). Act 1 concludes with Meridian's moral challenge to the white liberal, Parnell James, who has pushed for the trial of Britten but is unwilling to do what his friend, the pastor, asks: to confront Lyle with the question of his guilt.

In act 2, which is set in Whitetown, the audience is witness to the event that leads to Lyle's murder of Richard: in Lyle's store, Richard engages in a series of ritual insults directed at Lyle's sexual prowess. This moment is embedded in an act that lays bare the highly sexualized power—but sometimes loving—relations between black and white individuals: Lyle has pursued, or raped, countless black women and has already killed one black man; Parnell had loved a black woman but the plague of racism prevented love's actualization; Jo Britten, Lyle's wife, is subject to patriarchal control of her sexuality while, at the same time, the men in her community hold her up as the epitome of inviolate white womanhood. Of the murderer Britten, Baldwin writes in his introduction: "It is we who have locked him in the prison of his color . . . to protect the honor and purity of his tribe" (xiv–xv).

The final act, at the courthouse, departs from the realism of the earlier acts; each major character, before his or her public testimony, engages in a soliloquy that reveals a deep element of character. Juanita describes her lovemaking with Richard, her "lover made of flesh and blood" (94). This love is implicitly compared to, in keeping with the metaphor of the plague of racism, diseased sexualities like those detailed in the second act. Ultimately, Jo Britten lies on the stand, detailing a sexual assault by Richard that never happened and Parnell lacks the courage to point out her inconsistencies when he testifies. Britten is found not guilty, but outside the courthouse, under questioning from Meridian and Parnell, he admits to the killing. The play ends with a return to the scene of Richard's murder and invokes two choices for the plague's cure. Meridian, who has hidden Richard's gun in his pulpit, ponders the possibilities of the righteous vengeance of "the Bible *and* the gun"; there is irony, however, in his declaration that it is the conjoining of these in American experience that has made especially virulent the plague of racism (120; emphasis added). At the same time, Juanita and the other young people are on their way to another march for civil rights; when Parnell asks to join her, her reply is guarded, its implications not completely clear: "we can walk in the same direction . . ." (121).

Baldwin would return to these issues in his script on the life of Malcolm X. Begun as a theater project with Alex Haley and Elia Kazan, Baldwin produced a screenplay under contract with Columbia Pictures when the producer Marvin Worth bought the rights to *The Autobiography* in 1968. Near the end of Baldwin's work for Columbia, the studio insisted he work with scriptwriter Arnold Perl. In "Devil," Baldwin writes that Perl's "translations" resulted in scenes in which "all meaning was being siphoned out of them" (552). Early in 1969, Baldwin walked out on the project; he published his script, without Perl's revisions, in 1972. Spike Lee chose the Baldwin–Perl collaboration as the basis of his script for his 1992 film on Malcolm X, writing that it was "the best script" of four other versions then under option to Warner Brothers (27). Lee never mentions having read Baldwin's 1972 screenplay.

CRITICAL RECEPTION

Critics of *The Amen Corner* have primarily responded to the issue of religion in the play. Carlton Molette, who saw the play several times, emphasizes the effect the "black church ritual" at its core had on an audience that, he argues, is assumed to be black: the play operates from a place of cultural familiarity and, as he describes it, drew the audience into an experience of communion marked by love between the family on stage and extending into the "congregation" of actors and theatergoers (184). Darwin Turner also focuses on the issue of audience: "Freeing himself from the need to create characters familiar to white spectators, Baldwin projected individuals who are known within the Black culture" (193). Louise Pratt, writing at the same time as Molette and Turner, focuses on the "illusion and self-deception" (84) that has become "religion" for Sister Margaret and how each member of her family re/discovers essential elements of identity when she abandons her fixation. Pratt also insists that the play is a *"whole* drama of conflict" and not limited to issues of race and religion, both of which define for her a reductive or essentialist reading of Baldwin's art; she argues for both an irreducible cultural specificity in African American literature and a universality that is recognizable to a diverse audience (83).

Recent criticism has more fully acknowledged the ambivalence and contradictions in Baldwin's presentation of religion in the play. Both Michael Lynch and Barbara Olson view *Amen* as an "essential corollary" of his first novel (Lynch 34). Olson argues that "[t]he play was the young Baldwin's attempt to make *Mountain*'s ambiguous criticism of the faith he had abandoned more explicit, more pointed" (297). However, Olson, like Carolyn Sylvander, points to the irony that Baldwin's use of a black church idiom—specifically, its power to invoke the experience of communion that Molette describes—worked to dilute his critique and appears to vindicate the church. Olson points to Margaret's final sermon, which seems to make Christianity "self-corrective" (299). Lynch, however, argues for a "religious dialectic" in the play (45), one that mediates Baldwin's commitment "to both the critique and the mystery of faith" (58). David embodies this tension when he "quits the community on the grounds of its own values but also internalizes them as he seeks to make his contribution to the church of the larger world" (58). Baldwin wrote of his ambitions as a playwright in his introduction to *Amen*: "I knew that out of the ritual of the church . . . comes . . . the *communion* which is the theatre. . . . [W]hat I wanted to do in the theatre was to recreate moments I remembered as a boy preacher, to involve the people, even against their will, to shake them up, and, hopefully, to change them" (xviii).

Saadi Simawe's article invokes music in the play—whether it is David's and Luke's jazz or church music as it is played "under everything" (*Amen* 3), specifically "under" the Word as it is spoken or sung—that testifies to "the undercurrent and more genuine life of the characters" and "unlimited humanistic love" (Simawe 20). In Lynch's and Simawe's criticisms, the writer or musician—the latter, Simawe argues, is Baldwin's figure of "the supreme artist" (12)—are "virtual secular minister[s]" (Lynch 40).

The critical response to *Blues for Mister Charlie* both passionately defends and vehemently critiques the play and its perceived message. Eugenia Collier's article is an excellent summary of the range of critical writing before 1979. She argues that there is a discernible difference in the response of black and white critics, the latter generally far less favorable than the former. For example, both Toni Cade [Bambara] and Calvin Hernton saw the play. Cade writes that though blacks were not uncritical of aspects of the play, "[i]t was a rally. It was a fire. It was energetic, vital, relevant, cathartic, upsetting. . . . It was the beginning . . . of polarization on stage and in the house" (136). Hernton writes that because the play examined "the sexual variable . . . involved in racism" (109), many white audience members appeared visibly uncomfortable while blacks "seemed to be enthralled . . . to see for the first time the true nature of their lives, and their plight, played back to them with dignity and no beating around the bush" (110). While it is dangerous to draw too absolute a conclusion, it is instructive to contrast these responses to that of the drama critic Robert Brustein's admonition that the play was "an inflammatory broadside of race hatred which will profit nobody but the author" (37) or Philip Roth's pronouncement that *Blues* was ultimately propaganda in which "the real hero of these last two acts is blackness, as the real villain is whiteness" (41).

The factors that produced these widely divergent readings are complex, but by the mid-1960s, as David Van Leer writes, Baldwin had made a "full commitment to a political reading of the black self" and moved away from "[t]he vaguely existential aestheticism of his earlier work" points to one source (7). This shift also produced a rhetoric of criticism that is both disturbingly maculinist and implicitly homophobic. Edward Margolies emphasizes the apocalyptic rhetoric of his political writings "translate[d] . . . into concrete social terms" in *Blues* (74–75), but dismisses Richard as a character who is "highly neurotic, obstreperous, and disagreeable. . . . His heroism—if that is what it may be called—lies in his ability to articulate all the venom and bitterness he feels toward whites" (75). He concludes his essay with markedly ambivalent praise for Baldwin's "new found [sic] virility. . . . He recognizes the virtues of rage as well as its evils. . . . [O]ne wonders whether, as an artist, he may not now possibly consume himself in his recently recovered Jehovah-like rage" (76). Calvin Hernton echoes this description in more positive, but nonetheless problematic, terms, arguing that the author of *Blues* "is an aggressive, a masculine Baldwin" (109). These characterizations take on additional irony when considered in the context of the virulent heterosexism, the masculinist rhetoric, and the consequent dismissal of Baldwin's work in contemporary essays by Norman Mailer and Eldridge Cleaver. Collectively, the tenor of this commentary supports Van Leer's view that there must continue to be an ongoing critical reevaluation of Baldwin's work, one that is able to both "divorce his personality from the racial, political, and sexual stereotypes others imposed on him" and "effect a similar divorce of those stereotypes . . . from the literature he wrote—to see him clearly as an author" (12).

The issue of sexuality also emerges in analyses of the play itself. Roth was offended by what he took to be both the play's obsession with the black phallus and the "banality" of both Richard and Lyle (43) who "give evidence to . . . the narcissistic, pompous, and finally ridiculous demands made by the male ego when confronted by moral catastrophe" (42). Pratt considers Richard to be prey to "the black male sex mystique" (92); Cade echoes this in her description of an audience skeptical of "the over-sharped cliche of black virility—white impotency" (136). In the spirit of Michael Lynch, who emphasizes Baldwin's focus on sexuality in his work as a whole as playing a "positive, potentially sanctifying role . . . in human relations" (54–55), Sherley Williams focuses on how Richard changes through his love for Juanita and is, ultimately, restored to the "group rhythm" of his black community (150). Williams's metaphor also links Richard to the figure of the musician who, though often a figure of "alienation and estrangement" in Baldwin's work (147), comes to be a member of the "[B]lacktown chorus" by coming to terms with a "group tradition"—of which music, and particularly the blues, is an expression—that embodies not "docility and passivity" but survival, endurance, and power (154).

BIBLIOGRAPHY

Dramatic Works by James Baldwin

The Amen Corner. 1968. New York: Laurel–Dell, 1990.
Blues for Mister Charlie. 1964. New York: Dial, 1964. New York: Vintage–Random, 1992.
One Day, When I Was Lost: A Scenario Based on Alex Haley's The Autobiography of Malcolm X. 1972. New York: Laurel–Dell, 1992.
Lee, Spike, and Ralph Wiley. *By Any Means Necessary: The Trials and Tribulations of Making* Malcolm X . . . , *including the Screenplay* [by James Baldwin, Arnold Perl, and Spike Lee]. New York: Hyperion, 1992.

Works on Drama by James Baldwin

"The Devil Finds Work: An Essay." 1976. *James Baldwin: Collected Essays*. Ed. Toni Morrison. New York: Library of America, 1998. 477–572.
"Down at the Cross." *The Fire Next Time*. New York: Dial, 1963. Rpt. of "Letter from a Region in My Mind." *New Yorker* 17 Nov. 1962. Ed. Toni Morrison. New York: Library of America, 1998. 296–347.
"Sweet Lorraine." 1969. Ed. Toni Morrison. New York: Library of America, 1998. 757–761.

Studies of James Baldwin's Dramatic Works

Abramson, Doris. *Negro Playwrights in the American Theater, 1925–1959*. New York: Columbia University Press, 1969.

Bigsby, C. W. E. "The Committed Writer: James Baldwin as Dramatist." *Twentieth Century Literature* 13 (Apr. 1967): 39–48.

Bloom, Harold, ed. *James Baldwin*. New York: Chelsea, 1986.

Brustein, Robert. "Everybody's Protest Play." *New Republic* 16 May 1964: 35–37.

Cade [Bambara], Toni. "Black Theater." *Black Expression: Essays by and about Black Americans in the Creative Arts*. Ed. Addison Gayle, Jr. New York: Waybright, 1970. 134–143.

Campbell, James. *Talking at the Gates: A Life of James Baldwin*. New York: Viking-Penguin, 1991.

Collier, Eugenia. "Baldwin's Plays: A Criticism of the Critics." *MAWA Review* 5.2 (1990): 29–34.

Driver, Tom F. "*Blues for Mister Charlie*: The Review That Was Too True to Be Published." *Negro Digest* 13 (Sept. 1964): 34–40.

Hernton, Calvin C. "A Fiery Baptism." *James Baldwin: A Collection of Critical Essays*. Ed. Keneth Kinnamon. Englewood Cliffs: Spectrum–Prentice, 1974. 109–119.

Kinnamon, Keneth, ed. *James Baldwin: A Collection of Critical Essays*. Englewood Cliffs: Spectrum–Prentice, 1974.

Leeming, David. *James Baldwin: A Biography*. New York: Knopf, 1994.

Lynch, Michael F. "Staying Out of the Temple: Baldwin, the African American Church, and *The Amen Corner*." *Re-viewing James Baldwin: Things Not Seen*. Ed. Quentin Miller. Philadelphia: Temple University Press, 2000. 33–71.

Margolies, Edward. "The Negro Church: James Baldwin and the Christian Vision." *James Baldwin*. Ed. Harold Bloom. New York: Chelsea, 1986. 59–76.

Miller, Quentin, ed. *Re-viewing James Baldwin: Things Not Seen*. Philadelphia: Temple Univeristy Press, 2000.

Molette, Carlton. "James Baldwin as a Playwright." *James Baldwin: A Critical Evaluation*. Ed. Therman B. O'Daniel. Washington, DC: Howard University Press, 1977. 183–188.

Neal, Larry. "Into Nationalism, Out of Parochialism." *Performance* 1.2 (1972): 32–40.

O'Daniel, Therman B., ed. *James Baldwin: A Critical Evaluation*. Washington, DC: Howard University Press, 1977.

Olson, Barbara K. " 'Come-to-Jesus Stuff' in James Baldwin's *Go Tell It on the Mountain* and *The Amen Corner*." *African American Review* 31.2 (1997): 295–301.

Phillips, Louis. "The Novelist as Playwright." *Modern American Drama: Essays in Criticism*. Ed. William E. Taylor. Deland: Everett/Edwards, 1968. 145–162.

Pratt, Louis H. *James Baldwin*. Boston: Twayne–Hall, 1978.

Roth, Philip. "Blues for Mister Charlie." *James Baldwin*. Ed. Harold Bloom. New York: Chelsea, 1986. 37–43.

Silvera, Frank. "Towards a Theater of Understanding." *Negro Digest* 18 (Apr. 1969): 33–35.

Simawe, Saadi A. "What Is in a Sound?: The Metaphysics and Politics of Music in *The Amen Corner*. *Re-Viewing James Baldwin: Things Not Seen*. Ed. Quentin Miller. Philadelphia: Temple University Press. 12–32.

Standley, Fred L. "James Baldwin as Dramatist." *Critical Essays on James Baldwin*. Ed. Fred L. Standley and Nancy V. Burt. Boston: Hall, 1988. 298–302.

Sylvander, Carolyn Wedin. *James Baldwin*. New York: Ungar, 1980.

Tedesco, John L. *"Blues for Mister Charlie:* The Rhetorical Dimension." *Players: The Magazine of American Theatre* 50.1–2 (1975): 20–23.

Turner, Darwin T. "James Baldwin in the Dilemma of the Black Dramatist." *James Baldwin: A Critical Evaluation*. Ed. Therman B. O'Daniel. Washington, DC: Howard University Press. 189–194.

Van Leer, David. "James Baldwin." *African American Writers*. Ed. Valerie Smith. 2nd ed. Vol. 1. New York: Scribner's–Gale, 2001. 1–13.

Weatherby, W. J. *James Baldwin: Artist on Fire*. New York: Fine, 1989.

Weixlmann, Joe. "Staged Segregation: Baldwin's *Blues for Mister Charlie* and O'Neill's *All God's Chillun Got Wings*. *Black American Literature Forum* 11.1 (1977): 35–36.

Williams, Sherley Anne. "The Black Musician: The Black Hero as Light Bearer." *James Baldwin: A Collection of Criticals Essays*. Ed. Keneth Kinnamon. Englewood Cliffs: Spectrum–Prentice, 1974. 147–1954.

AMIRI BARAKA
(1934–   )

Darcy A. Zabel

BIOGRAPHY

Born on October 7, 1934, in Newark, New Jersey, Everett Leroy Jones, who in 1953 would change his name to LeRoi Jones and then later in 1968 to Amiri Baraka, was the firstborn son of Coyt Leroy Jones and Anna Lois Jones. Originally from the agrarian South, Baraka's parents moved North to the urban cities of New Jersey in the 1920s. His mother, a Tuskegee and Fisk University educated woman, worked in a clothing factory as a piecework stitcher until her appointment in 1941 to the United States Office of Dependency Benefits as a social worker. Like the character Court Royal in Baraka's 1967 play, *Great Goodness of Life: A Coon Show*, Baraka's father worked for the United States Postal Service and in 1951 was promoted to the status of postal supervisor.

Baraka and his younger sister, Sandra Elaine, grew up in the racially mixed middle-class neighborhoods of Newark. Graduating with honors from a predominantly white preparatory school, Jones attended Rutgers University for one year before transferring to Howard University in Washington, DC, in 1952. It was at Howard, between his sophomore and junior years, that Everett Leroy Jones changed his name to LeRoi Jones, legally adopting for his first name the French spelling of his middle name, meaning "The King." Discontent with college life, Baraka left Howard University at the end of his junior year and joined the United States Air Force.

His first permanent assignment was at Ramey Air Force Base, in Puerto Rico, as a B-36 right rear gunner for the 73rd Strategic Reconnaissance and Bombardment Squadron. In his second year of service, an anonymous letter sent to his superiors accused Baraka of being a communist. Though not a communist, following a yearlong investigation, Baraka's security clearance was revoked and he received an undesirable discharge. Thus, at the age of twenty-two, Baraka was free to move to Greenwich Village to become a writer.

His first job in the Village was as the shipping manager for a small jazz magazine, and he was hired by the woman who would one day become his first wife, a white Jewish woman from Brooklyn, named Hettie Cohen. Baraka explains in his 1984 autobiography (*The Autobiography of LeRoi Jones*) that in contrast to the wild Village life, Hettie seemed calm, orderly, clean, and being with her gave him a sense of well-being (146). And yet, their relationship did not progress smoothly. The two had very different notions of what raising a mixed-race child in the 1950s might entail. The issue of parenting mixed-race children is one that Baraka would later grapple with in his 1964 play *The Slave*.

Following a tumultuous two-year courtship, the two married in 1958 in a Manhattan Buddhist temple. In April 1958, the two published the first edition of *Yugen*, a twenty-four-page, hand-stapled journal edited by LeRoi Jones. It also contained Baraka's first published poem. That same year, at age twenty-four, Baraka published his first essay, a defense of the Beats, in the *Partisan Review*. Inspired by the Beats, particularly Allen Ginsberg and Frank O'Hara, Baraka began to write many autobiographical poems. While some critics label this period of Baraka's work (1957–1962) his "Beat Period," to do so is to ignore his political works also written during this time. In 1959, in honor of rebel guerilla leader Fidel Castro's takeover of Cuba, Baraka published a celebration of Castro's triumph, an essay that resulted in an invitation from the new government in Cuba, in 1960, to visit Cuba.

This trip to Cuba was a turning point in Baraka's personal life and in his career. In Cuba, the twenty-six-year-old Baraka found himself criticized by young Latin American intellectuals for writing apolitical art, and according to his autobiography, Cuba was where Baraka first met "youth not just turning on and dropping out, not just hiply cynical or cynically hip, but using their strength and energy to change the *real* world" (166). Back in the United States, with Diane di Prima, Baraka started a new literary magazine, the *Floating Bear*, in which Baraka's first play, *The Eighth Ditch*, was published. This play about an individual's loss of value when conscripted by the United States Army first appeared in 1961 and became one of the layers of hell in Baraka's longer work "The System of Dante's Hell," completed in 1965.

But in October 1961, Baraka, now age twenty-seven, was arrested by the FBI for sending obscenity through the mail because of the language used in volume nine of the *Floating Bear*. The obscene material in question was an excerpt from William Burroughs's *Naked Lunch* and an excerpt from Baraka's continuing drama *Dante*. When the case went to trial, Baraka defended himself by quoting passages of James Joyce's masterpiece *Ulysses*, a classic of Irish literature once labeled "obscene," and quoted from the presiding judge's ruling on the obscenity charges regarding *Ulysses*; Baraka's case was dismissed.

Reunited with his wife after the trial, in 1962, Baraka moved his family to Cooper Square, a move that placed them directly over the Ezra Lasley Acting School. That spring, the student director in Lee Strasberg's master class at the Actors Studio staged Baraka's play about interracial homosexuality, *The Toilet*. *Dutchman*, a play in which an older white woman seduces and then kills a young black intellectual on a subway train, was workshopped here before its first commercial performance in March 1964. That year, when Baraka was thirty, *Dutchman* won the Obie Award for Best Play of 1964. This success was followed by the 1964 productions of *The Baptism*, a play in which a black preacher and a homosexual devil barter for the soul of a young black man; *The Slave*, a play about a black revolutionary who goes to the home of his white ex-wife to take back his children; and *The Toilet*, a play in which Baraka again returns to the theme of interracial homosexuality, but this time, set in an urban high school.

In February 1965, Malcolm X was assassinated, and two days later, Baraka moved out of the home he shared with Hettie Jones and into a rented brownstone in Harlem. Though Hettie Jones refused to agree to a divorce, Baraka went to Mexico, the following year, where the divorce was granted. Meanwhile, Baraka and his associates in Harlem, founded a new theater school, the Black Arts Repertory Theatre/School (BARTS). The aim of BARTS, according to Baraka, was "to create an art that would be a weapon in the Black Liberation Movement" (*Autobiography* 215). That same year, Baraka won a Guggenheim Fellowship and the next year, in 1966, a grant from the National Endowment for the Humanities. With this federal grant to start a summer arts and culture program, Baraka and his companions brought new music, poetry, dance, and theater to the streets of Harlem including Baraka's *Experimental Death Unit #1* (in *Four Black Revolutionary Plays*), a play in which a black prostitute and her two white johns are executed by a black military unit, and *J-E-L-L-O*, a parody of the Jell-O gelatin company sponsored *The Jack Benny Show*.

In response to complaints about the government funding of antiwhite propaganda, federal funding for the BARTS summer program was dropped, and the theater in Harlem closed. With community support in Newark, New Jersey, however, Baraka opened Spirit House, a theater and cultural center providing self-help classes and social activities along with plays, poetry readings, and concerts specifically designed for urban African Americans. Along with the 1966 opening of Spirit House, Baraka founded his own publishing company, Jihad Publications.

That same year, at age thirty-two, Baraka met the woman who would become his second wife and lifelong partner, Sylvia Robinson, the actress and dancer who appeared in his 1966 production of *Black Mass* (in *Four Black Revolutionary Plays*), Baraka's parody of Mary Shelley's *Frankenstein*, in which the white man is the monster. Baraka was arrested again, this time for allegedly producing pamphlets instructing readers how to make Molotov cocktails, but was again cleared of all charges.

In the spring of 1967, Baraka was offered a one-year job as a visiting professor at San Francisco State College to teach poetry and playwrighting, and his play *Madheart* (in *Four Black Revolutionary Plays*),was first produced at the college. In San Francisco, he met black nationalist leader Ron Karenga. Inspired by Karenga's theories of cultural nationalism, Baraka wrote *Slave Ship*, with much of the play's dialog in Yoruba; a second book of fiction, *Tales;* and an anthology of essays on jazz, *Black Music*. Returning home to Newark, at the end of the school year, 1967 also saw the production of *Arm Yourself, or Harm Yourself* and *Great Goodness of Life: A Coon Show* at Baraka's Spirit House. In between an arrest for his part in a summer riot in Newark and a January 1968 court date at which he would be found innocent of all charges, Baraka produced the play *Home on the Range*, and Robinson and Baraka wed in a Yoruba marriage ceremony.

After his acquittal, Baraka devoted himself full-time to politics, and as a result of his increasing interest in the ideas of the Sunni Muslims, a group who had supported him during his trial, at the age of thirty-four, he adopted a new name, Ameer Barakat, Arabic for "the blessed prince." Baraka modified the spelling of the name to Amiri Baraka when he had his name legally changed from LeRoi Jones. His wife took a new name as well, Amina, meaning "faithful."

In 1969, Baraka published *Black Magic*, a collection of political poems, and his first classical full-length play, *Resurrection of Life*, was produced in Harlem and New York City. For the next ten years, Baraka would average writing one Off-Broadway play each year, many of which were performed at Spirit House. In 1970, however, Baraka was again thrust into the political spotlight for his part in organizing CFUN, an umbrella organization of black political associations dedicated to electing a black candidate for mayor of the largely black Newark. Baraka followed up on this local victory by turning his attention to the national political arena as a public speaker and political organizer for the Congress of Afrikan Peoples, and, in 1972, served as coconvener at the first National Black Political Convention, representing the convention and their National Black Agenda at the Democratic Party's national convention.

After two years in the mainstream political arena, Baraka became concerned that "the old cultural nationalist positions we upheld were insufficient" (*Autobiography* 305). Though Baraka tried to, in his own words, "square Marxism with cultural nationalism," he no longer believed in the "back to Africa" ideology (308). To test his hypothesis, in 1974, he and his seven-year-old son traveled to Tanzania for a meeting of the Pan-African Congress, where Baraka was to give a speech on the future of Pan-African culture. The experience solidified for Baraka the real "African reality," and he came home with the realization that the "never-neverland Africa of nationalist invention" was nothing like the "real thing" (309). Though Africa was "more beautiful than our words," it was also, Baraka says, "much more ugly as well" (310). By going to Tanzania, Baraka writes, he came to realize "that the US was my home. As painful and complicated as that was . . . I was no longer a nationalist. . . . It was clear to me that only socialism could transform society" (311).

Following this transformative experience, Baraka, now age forty, taught for one year at Yale University followed by a year at George Washington University, before joining the Africana Studies Department of the State University of New York at Stony Brook. In 1980, at age forty-six, Baraka was awarded the Life Achievement Award by the American Book Awards Committee, and, in 1981, a Poetry Award from the National Endowment for the Arts. This was followed in 1982 with an award from the New Jersey Council for the Arts, and with wife Amina Baraka, in 1983, Amiri Baraka coedited *Confirmation: An Anthology of African-American Women*, for which the couple received an award in 1985 from the Before Columbus Foundation. Popular as a guest lecturer and speaker, Baraka continued to work as a professor in the State University of New York system until his sixty-fifth birthday, and retired from teaching in 1999. In 2001, Baraka was inducted by a jury of his literary peers into the prestigious American Academy of Arts and Letters.

In May 2002, the now sixty-eight-year-old Baraka was named poet laureate of New Jersey. New Jersey Republicans later mounted a campaign to remove Baraka from his position when his poetry came under attack as a result of a poem he wrote reflecting on the terrorist attacks of September 11. The governor of New Jersey requested Baraka's resignation from the post; Baraka refused. After ten unsuccessful attempts to fire Baraka as poet laureate, in December 2002, the New Jersey Senate State Government Committee voted to eliminate the position. Though frustrated by the attempts to silence his poetry, and lamenting the state of New Jersey's attempts to legalize a political maneuver that, in Baraka's words, would "repress and stigmatize independent speakers everywhere," Baraka remains an active part of African American cultural life (qtd. in Trotta, par. 7). Through his voluntary participation in many free social and cultural events in Harlem and Newark designed to bring African American art, music, and theater directly into the community, despite political controversy, Baraka has maintained his connection to the people of New York and New Jersey. With over thirty plays written between the years 1958 and 1983, innumerable published poems written over the course of a fifty-year career as a poet, and countless political and academic essays, Baraka's contribution to the fields of the arts, literature, education, music, and politics cannot be silenced. Brilliant, irreverent, often controversial, and always passionate, Baraka's power to mold language and to challenge others to enter into an ongoing and ever-changing conversation about America, reverberates throughout all his essays, poetry, and plays.

MAJOR WORKS AND THEMES

Primarily regarded as a poet in the twenty-first century, Amiri Baraka's most well-known and popularly anthologized dramatic works were first written and produced in the 1960s. While Baraka continues to produce plays sporadically, his more recent plays, performed both in Harlem community theaters and at Spirit House, are not readily available in print form for the general reader. Of all of Baraka's plays, *Dutchman*, written in 1964, was the play that first brought Baraka critical acclaim as a playwright and is still the most frequently anthologized, written about, and taught of all Baraka's dramatic works. Set in the subways of New York, Lula, a thirtysomething white woman with flaming red hair, stalks twentysomething college-educated young black men, engages them in verbal foreplay, and then when they assert their masculinity, stabs them in an attempt to birth what Ralph Ellison refers to as the white man's desire for a "blackless" America in which "blackness" is "banished . . . from the nation's bloodstream, from its social structure, and from its conscience and historical consciousness" (578). In the play, Lulu's first target for the evening is a young man named Clay. She attempts to mold Clay into an image of black masculinity she can accept, and when she cannot get him to agree to be one of the only two clichés about black men white America embraces—the caricature of the black man as sexualized animal or the black man as invisible—she kills him. "We'll pretend people cannot see you," Lula offers; and when this does not appeal to him, she tries "the gritty grind, like you ol' rag-headed mammy. Grind till you lose your mind. Shake it, shake it. OOOOweeeeeeee! Come on Clay, Let's do the choo-choo train shuffle" (2132–2136). Clay refuses, rejects Lula, she stabs him, and the play ends with Clay's body being thrown from the train, and Lula's approach to another young black man in his twenties.

While the critics often do not agree about what exactly Clay's death signifies, they do agree that the play showcases the major themes of Baraka's dramatic productions during his Black Nationalist period. Sex does not heal, love between the races is not the answer, and, as George Piggeford suggests, the play, like many of Baraka's plays in the 1960s "functions as a warning" both to whites and blacks, that physical violence, for too long, has been the prerogative of the white man and that the time has come, as Craig

Werner reads Baraka, for "the black everyman" to "kill them in the name of life" (Piggford 75; Werner 38).

The usual critical assessment of *The Baptism*, also produced in 1964, is that it is a "flaw[ed] but important play" (Brady 32). In the play, several different allegorical characters vie for possession of the soul of the main character, "the boy," who has committed a sexual sin and seeks redemption. The bohemian women of the assimilationist chorus want to have sexual relations with the boy to signify the liberal and all-embracing nature of white middle-class America. The effeminate white homosexual character offers the boy the witty intellectual life of an artist, while the old woman in the play offers a sort of false back-to-Africa promise that she cannot really give him. The Minister wants the boy to be a savior for "his" people, and when the boy rebels, the entire congregation decides to sacrifice him so that they can keep their illusions about who he should be for them, as he is not entitled to a life of his own. To free himself, the boy kills the congregation (although the homosexual character does not die—symbolic of Western civilization, he is too aloof to die), and thus, the boy's baptism into manhood is through the mass shedding of blood instead of through the "sin" of sexual procreation. Manhood requires the destruction of those who would try to destroy the boy before he can assert his own identity as a man.

More widely anthologized than *The Baptism* are Baraka's other two plays from 1964, *The Toilet* and *The Slave*. Set entirely in a high school restroom, the characters' motivation for the violent action of *The Toilet* centers on the secret offstage love affair between Ray, or Foots as he is called by his friends, who is the well-built, physically fit leader of a black gang, and Karolis, a skinny, unattractive but well-spoken white boy. A sexually graphic love letter from Karolis to Foots/Ray has been intercepted, and Foots/Ray is compelled to fight Karolis to prove to his friends that he is not gay. The two boys are terribly mismatched in terms of size and physical strength, but Karolis refuses to deny his attraction to Ray. In addition to the physical difference between the two boys, before the fight even begins, Foots/Ray's friends have already badly beaten Karolis for his presumptive love.

As the two boys square off, with Karolis barely able to stand, Foots/Ray tries to call the fight off, but Karolis insists, saying, "No. You have to fight me. I sent you a note, remember. That note saying I loved you. The note saying you were beautiful. You remember that note, Ray?" (114). Karolis then says that it was in this very same "filthy toilet" that he and Ray first met, and exchanged names and caresses. As the conversation, and the fight escalates, Karolis demands, "Are you Ray or Foots, huh?" (114). Despite the mismatch in size, following Karolis's identification of Foots by his real name, Ray, refuses to fight and it appears as if Karolis may actually succeed in choking the life out of Ray, until one of Ray's friends leaps into the fight, breaking the spell, and knocking Ray and Karolis apart. The crowd of boys watching the fight "surges into the center punching the fallen Karolis in the face" (115) and when he passes out, they drape him with wet toilet paper. The play ends with all of the characters leaving the stage except the fallen Karolis.

When Karolis is alone on the stage, Ray comes back, "looks quickly over his shoulder, then runs and kneels before the body, weeping and cradling the head in his arms" (116). While it is tempting to read the play with Karolis as the hero and Ray as a sort of antihero who is not strong enough to embrace his true sexual identity in the face of his social group's expectations about true manhood, when examined in the context of Baraka's other work from the 1960s, the white homosexual character usually represents a well-intentioned liberal intellectual who, nevertheless, by "loving" black men, seeks to control them, separate them from the black community, isolate them, name or rename them with an honorable white name, and unconsciously emasculates them and renders them ineffectual.

In his own discussion of the plays in his autobiography, Baraka says that "Clay, in *Dutchman*, Ray in *The Toilet*, and Walker in *The Slave* are all victims" and that it is his intention to "show victims so that their brothers in the audience will be better able to understand that they are the brothers of victims, and that they themselves are victims" but that this theater, "which is now peopled with victims, will soon begin to be people with new kinds of heroes" and that "these new men, new heroes" will be the stars of a new "theatre of assault" and that the play "will be called THE DESTRUCTION OF AMERICA" (211–215). Or as Kathryn Seidel reads it, the purpose of the play, and by extension, Baraka's other works from the 1960s including plays such as "'The Baptism' (1964), 'The Slave' (1964), 'The Toilet' (1964), 'Experimental Death Unit #1' (1966) and 'JELLO' [*sic*] (1966), and 'Arm Yourself or Harm Yourself: A Message of Self-Defense for Black Men' (1967)" are designed to show how "white America has preyed upon the best of black men" (88).

This theme is well articulated in Baraka's third play of 1964, *The Slave*, which is divorce, mixed-race children, and revolution, produced a month and a half before Baraka's six-year marriage to Hettie Cohen Jones ended. The prologue to the play, which is really an epilogue in terms of chronology, has the main character, Walker, now aged, much older than his character in the play itself, dressed as an old field slave. Walker tells the audience that it has been his experience that at the "core of our lives" is "deceit" and that in the process of lying to everybody else, we also lie to ourselves and to "possible lovers" as a result of "a stupid longing not to know which is automatically fulfilled" (98–99). He then tells his listeners that ideas are more than just harmless thoughts, and that ideas "need judging" because there is nothing that is "too righteous to question" (99). The character then "assumes the position he will have when the play starts" and an explosion rocks the stage (100–101).

In brief, Walker is a black freedom fighter accused of murder who has left his white wife and his two children by her and gone to join a black army preparing for revolution. When the play begins, Walker has broken into the home of his ex-wife, Grace, and her new husband, Brad, a former family friend and professor, to take his children away. During the course of the evening, Brad reveals himself to be a racist despite "a liberal education, and a long history of concern for minorities and charitable organizations" and Grace calls her former husband a "nigger" (104–106). With forced "cynical hilarity," Walker reminds Grace "only you and your husband are white in this house. Those two lovely little girls upstairs are niggers. You know, circa 1800, one drop makes you whole" (107). At this, Grace runs at Walker and attacks him, and Walker pushes her away.

Holding a gun on Brad and Grace, Walker tells them that he has already been upstairs to see his children, to take them away, but that he decided to "wait to say hello to the mommy and stepdaddy" (110). As the play rushes headlong toward its climax, there is a sense of both a binge and a purge as the characters continue to drink alcohol and spit out cruel truths at one another. After the initial name-calling, the discussion settles on what is best for the two girls upstairs. Grace argues that it is better for the children to grow up with her than to have the girls watch their father gunned down in some failed revolution; Walker asserts that his dramatic death would still be "better than being freakish mulattoes in a world where your father is some evil black thing you can't remember" (116). Both of them end up screaming at each other, insisting that each is "rescuing" the children from the other parent's vision of what it means to be black in America (116).

It is at this point that Grace tells Brad to kill Walker if he can. Brad jumps Walker, and Walker shoots him dead. Grace realizes then that Walker planned to kill Brad from the beginning, take the children away from her, and leave her alone as retribution for what she had done to him when she took the children and left. By now, the revolution is just outside the door and explosions rock the stage. Grace demands to know if he is taking the girls, and Walker shakes his head, but before she can be sure whether his nod meant yes or no, the house collapses on top of them. Walker is able to break free of the debris, but Grace is not. She urges him to go and rescue the children, but again, he shakes his head. This time, he tells her that they are dead. As the explosions continue to tear through the rubble, Walker shouts, "They're dead Grace!" and slowly, Grace dies (129). There is silence, Walker exits, "and then there is a child heard crying and screaming as loud as it can" (129).

Bernard Dukore notes that Baraka's play is written in such a way that several different interpretations of the ending are possible, just as the Delphic Oracle in the Yeats poem Walker quotes as his own "gives accurate but ambiguous prophecies" (785). Some critics believe that Walker has killed his two sleeping children, or has attempted to kill them both, but failed as indicated by the scream of "a child" not two children (*Slave* 129). Others believe that Walker has not killed or attempted to kill the children and simply "lied in order to hurt his wife, in which case the question of the survival in black America of integrated human beings, and of some sort of integration itself, is open" (Dukore 786). Still others believe that up until the very end of the play it was certain that either Grace or Walker would die, so that the girls would not be destroyed by the revolution, whether it succeeded or failed, they would emerge with either one identity or the other, and could live with a "sense of wholeness of self" (Brady 99). Another hypothesis is that Walker knows the girls are not dead, but tells Grace they are so that she can let go and die easy, a strange gift of sorts, from Walker to his ex-wife, revealing, yet again, Walker's "self-divided" and fragmented nature (Brady 101).

Baraka again returned to this theme of the fragmented nature and self-divided sense of self that so afflicted members of the black middle class in his 1966–1967 play *Great Goodness of Life: A Coon Show*. First performed at Spirit House, and dedicated to his father, Coyt Leroy Jones, this play tells the story of Court Royal, a postal supervisor, with a wife named Louise, and a man who likes nothing better than a nice evening of bowling, who finds himself on trial for the sins of his revolutionary son. Offered freedom if he is willing to "prove" his innocence by shooting his son in the head with a gun made of diamonds and gold, Court Royal at first questions the decision of the court, but is promised a return to his everyday normal life should he comply (154). After shooting his son, he will be permitted to go back to his "natural reality. Without guilt. Without shame. Pure and blameless" with his "soul washed white as snow" (155). Charmed by this promise of a return to everyday normalcy, Court Royal shoots his son in the face. The play ends with Court Royal looking for his bowling bag now that the trial is over, the son executed, and the father found innocent of all guilt with his "soul as white as snow" and his life "a beautiful thing" (156).

Baraka's later plays begin to combine an increasingly articulated under-standing of the part class plays in structuring social opportunities. While race is still very much a theme, plays such as *What Was the Relationship of the Lone Ranger to the Means of Production: A Play in One Act* (1979) and *Money: A Jazz Opera* (1982), a collaborative production with music provided by white Swiss-born jazz pianist George Gruntz for the Paris Opera with a workshop version produced for the stages of the Off-Broadway theater LaMama, demonstrate Baraka's evolving political consciousness to include gender and class alongside race as a determinant of one's experience of the human condition. In *Boy & Tarzan Appear in a Clearing* (1981), for example, Baraka asserts that having learned how to abuse power from white imperi-alists, present-day African leaders are just as corrupt and greedy as their for-mer white oppressors. Greed makes villains of the African characters in the play and avarice is condemned as a vehicle of slavery no matter what race or color the character may be. A distrust of race is replaced by a growing awareness of class as an important and often unjustly limiting determinant of human experience.

While most literary critics continue to focus on the dramas from Baraka's Black Nationalist period, the plays from his Marxist–Leninist period are fascinating extensions of Baraka's understanding of the slave master culture of the nineteenth century updated for the modern world in which class more than race creates or constrains cultural experiences. In the 1970s and 1980s, Baraka's dramas increasingly demonstrated that skin color was not a trustworthy determinant of political correctness and that truly revolutionary and transformative theater undermines bourgeois values, whether black bourgeois or white, American or international. Baraka's aesthetic shift reflects his political change of perspective and allegiances.

Throughout the 1990s and the early part of the twenty-first century, Baraka has focused his writing talents on oratory poetry, which is meant to be read and performed aloud. While his themes continue to explore the contradictions and paradoxes of American history, the treatment of black Americans in the United States, the contributions of black Americans to American art and history, they increasingly focus on the importance of the rebel-hero, the individual man who is willing to stand alone in the face of what appears to be an unconquerable foe. Quite often the forces of opposition are embedded in the culture itself, a culture based on theories of consumption against which the hero must struggle. And this battle to overcome evil, Baraka concludes, is not color or race specific. Rather, this, and this alone, is the great human universal.

CRITICAL RECEPTION

Critical reception of Amiri Baraka's plays includes theater production reviews from the 1960s and 1970s when his plays were first reviewed by theater critics, and also academic reviews written by literary scholars from the 1970s through today. The original critical reception of Baraka's early plays was mixed. *Dutchman*, for example, won the Obie Award for the Best American Play of 1964, and yet many critics agreed with theater critic John Simon who dismissed the play as "merely propaganda" of the worst sort (424). Langston Hughes, a successful writer in his own right criticized "that boy LeRoi" for tasteless obscenity, while critics such as Elizabeth Hadley Freydberg saw later plays such as Baraka's 1970 *Junkies Are Full of Shhh . . .* or his 1970 *Bloodrites* as "failures" that "despite the rhetoric of self-determination and freedom from the influences of whites" were insulting to black audiences because the works seemed to suggest "that Blacks require didactic works free of all subtlety in order to be reached" and that the moral message could be reduced to this: "blacks who align themselves in any way with whites are morally decrepit scoundrels, and as deserving of nothing whatsoever—or, more precisely, as deserving of death" (28). Other critics, such as Werner Sollors, however, championed the originality and spirituality of

Jones/Baraka's creation of the secularized black messiah figure who "is only the physical victor in the end of the play; spiritually she has been exorcised" (131), while other critics simply ignored the racial issues and urged their readers to do so as well. Tom Reck, for example, in his 1970 scholarly review of Baraka's *Dutchman* insisted that the play was "only symbolic of white versus black" and that Jones/Baraka felt "pity" for the "white world" (67–68). Reck insisted that the message of the poem was Emersonian, that a man should never "submit to imitation" for imitation is "death" and should "be true to his own nature" (68). In fact, a 1967 production of the play in Poland, produced by Andrzej Ceynowa, with an all-white cast emphasized that exact point: "Free from being conditioned to see a racial problem, the Polish theatergoers saw *Dutchman* as a play about honesty towards oneself and the wages of betraying one's people" (qtd. in Ursu par. 26).

Later critics have both celebrated and castigated Baraka's controversial plays from his Black Nationalist period, some seeing them as accurate reflections of a facet of American life middle-class white Americans too often ignore, while others, such as George Piggford have been disturbed by Baraka's "misogynistic and homophobic discussion of the gender/race system" (80). Critics such as Sandra Richards have insisted that the antihomosexual, anti-Jewish, antiwhite, and "woman-hating" nature of the plays cancelled out any redeeming artistic or social merit (233). Current critical analysis of Baraka's plays now focuses primarily on his Black Nationalist plays of the 1960s and, throughout the 1990s, the plays have been anthologized in numerous college textbooks including *Stages of Drama* published by St. Martin's Press in 1991 and the 1998 *Norton Anthology of American Literature*. Critics continue to make exhaustive studies of Baraka's use of Christian symbolism, black liberation theology, jazz semiotics of style, and epic myth, and his denunciation of western European cultural arrogance as demonstrated by both the form and the content of his plays.

Theater critics and literary scholars have been less enthusiastic about Baraka's later class-based, Marxist–Leninist plays, suggesting that these later plays fail because Baraka's focus shifted from a depiction of social realism with the intention that the theatergoers would then map out an approach to social change to an advocacy for a very specific kind of anticapitalist-, prolabor-mapped-out vision for social change. By becoming prescriptive instead of merely descriptive, Baraka's new style of dramaturgy was less popular with both theater and literary critics.

Written over thirty-five years ago, Baraka's *Dutchman* is still performed, and the play still provokes heated discussions about race relations in America, and many viewers are still offended by the play. "They can't give us reasons; they just say they're offended," explains Ralph Remington, the actor playing Clay in the 1998 Minnesota run of the play (qtd. in Ursu par. 21). Baraka himself attempted to explain such a reaction in his 1966 essay "The Revolutionary Theatre," saying that "the liberal white man's objection to the theatre of revolution" will be that he can clearly see that such theater "will be out to destroy them and whatever they believe is real. American cops will try to close the theatres where such nakedness of the human spirit is paraded . . . because this is a theatre of assault" (Jones 210–215).

As a writer of the twenty-first century, Baraka is now primarily a poet. His early experiences with theater, however, continue to have a profound impact on his poetry. As a poet who came of age during the Beat Generation, who then became a dramatist, a political activist, an essayist, a teacher, and, now in retirement, a poet once more, Baraka's experiences as a playwright, producer, and political orator and activist have greatly influenced his current poetics, infusing much of it with power of theater and the form of a dramatic monologue. Baraka's poetry is written to be read aloud, and, quite often, public recitations involve physical actions, sounds, music, and motion. Baraka's early success in the world of theater and continued involvement with Black Arts and Spirit House as both a director and a producer continue to make him a powerful and dynamic dramatic poet.

BIBLIOGRAPHY

Dramatic Works by Amiri Baraka

America More or Less. 1976. Unpublished.
Arm Yourself, or Harm Yourself: A Message of Self-Defense to Black Men. Newark: Jihad, 1967.
The Baptism. 1964. New York: Grove, 1980.
"*Bloodrites*." 1970. *Black Drama Anthology*. Ed. Woodie King, Jr., and Ron Milner. New York: New American Library, 1971. 21–29.
Board of Education. 1968. Unpublished. Performed at Spirit House, Newark, New Jersey.
Boy & Tarzan Appear in a Clearing. 1981. Unpublished.
Columbia: The Gem of the Ocean. 1973. Sound recording/nonmusic. Boulder: Alternative Radio.
"*The Coronation of the Black Queen*." 1970. *Black Scholar* 1.8: 11–16.
Dante. 1961. Also performed as *The Eighth Ditch* (1961). *Floating Bear* 9, 1961. Grove: Floating Bear, 1965.
"*The Death of Malcolm X*." 1969. *New Plays from Black Theatre: An Anthology*. Ed. Ed Bullins. New York: Bantam, 1969.
Dim Cracker Party Convention. 1980. Unpublished.
"*Dutchman*." 1964. The *Selected Plays and Prose of Amiri Baraka/LeRoi Jones*. Ed. Imamu Amiri Baraka. New York: Morrow, 1979. 70–96.
The Election Machine Warehouse. New York: Simon, 1997.
Four Black Revolutionary Plays: All Praises to the Black Man, by LeRoi Jones/Amiri Baraka. New York: Bobbs, 1969. [Includes *Experimental Death Unit #1*, *A Black Mass*, *Great Goodness of Life: A Coon Show*, and *Madheart*.]

"*General Hag's Skeezag*." 1992. *Black Thunder: An Anthology of Contemporary African American Drama*. Ed. William Brank. New York: Mentor, 1992.

A Good Girl Is Hard to Find. 1958. Unpublished.

"*Great Goodness of Life: A Coon Show*." 1966–1967. *The Selected Plays and Prose of Amiri Baraka/LeRoi Jones*. Ed. Imamu Amiri Baraka. New York: Morrow, 1979. 140–156.

"*Home on the Range*." 1968. *A Sourcebook of African-American Performance: Plays, People, Movements*. Ed. Annemarie Bean. New York: Routledge, 1999.

Insurrection. 1968. Unpublished.

"*Jack Pot Melting*." *Voices of Color: Scenes and Monologues from the Black American Theater*. Ed. Woodie King, Jr. New York: Applause, 1994.

J-E-L-L-O. 1966. Chicago: Third World, 1970.

"*Junkies are Full of Shhh . . .*" 1970. *Black Drama Anthology*. Ed. Woodie King and Ron Milner. New York: New American Library, 1971. 11–23.

Money: A Jazz Opera. 1982. Music by George Gruntz. New York: Grove, 1982.

The Motion of History. 1977. Draft available from the Archival Materials Department of the University of Virginia–Charlottesville.

"*The New Ark's A-Moverin*." 1974. Introduction by John Yau. *Grand Street 39*. New York: Grand Street, 1991. 28–40.

"*Police*." (1968) *A Sourcebook of African-American Performance: Plays, People, Movements*. Ed. Annemarie Bean. New York: Routledge, 1999.

Primitive World. 1984. Unpublished.

A Recent Killing. 1973. Unpublished. Performed at the New Federal Theater, New York.

"*Resurrection of Life or BA-RA-KA*." 1969. *Spontaneous Combustion*. Ed. Rochelle Owens. New York: Winter House, 1972. 41–88.

The Sidnee Poet Heroical or If in Danger of Suit, The Kid Pet Heroical. 1975. New York: Reed, 1979.

"*The Slave*." 1964. *The Selected Plays and Prose of Amiri Baraka/LeRoi Jones*. Ed. Imamu Amiri Baraka. New York: Morrow, 1979. 97–156.

"*Slave Ship: A Historical Pageant*." 1967. *Crosswinds: An Anthology of Black Dramatists in the Diaspora*. Ed. William Branch. Bloomington: Indiana University Press, 1993.

S-1. 1976. *The Motion of History and Other Plays*. New York: Morrow, 1978.

Song: A One Act Play about the Relationship of Art to Real Life. 1983. Newark: Cabaret, 1984.

"*The Toilet*." 1964. *Grove Press Modern Drama: Six Plays by Brecht, Baraka, Feiffer, Genet, Mrozek, Ionesco*. Ed. John Lahr. New York: Grove, 1975. 95–116.

Weimar 2. 1981. Unpublished.

What Was the Relationship of the Lone Ranger to the Means of Production: A Play in One Act. 1979. New York: Anti-Imperialist Cultural Union, 1978.

Studies of Amiri Baraka's Dramatic Works

Bergesen, Eric, and William Demastes. "The Limits of African-American Political Realism: Baraka's *Dutchman* and Wilson's *Ma Rainey's Black Bottom*." *Realism and the American Dramatic Tradition*. Ed. William Demastes. Tuscaloosa: University of Alabama Press, 1996. 218–234.

Bigsby, C. W. E. "The Theatre and the Coming Revolution." *Conversations with Amiri Baraka*. Ed. Charlie Reilly. Jackson: University Press of Mississippi, 1994. 130–138.

Brady, Owen Edward. "This Consciousness Epic: LeRoi Jones's Use of African Myth and Ritual in *The Baptism, The Toilet, Dutchman, The Slave*, and *A Recent Killing*. Diss. University of Notre Dame, 1973.

Casimir, Louis. "*Dutchman:* The Price of Culture is a Lie." *The Binding of Proteus: Perspectives on Myth and the Literary Process*. Ed. Marjorie McCune, Tucker Oribson, and Philip Withim. Lewisburg: Bucknell University Press, 1980. 298–310.

Ceynowa, Andrezej. "The Dramatic Structure of *Dutchman*." *Black American Literature Forum* 17.1 (1983): 15–18.

Dukore, Bernard. *Seventeen Plays: Sophocles to Baraka*. New York: Crowell, 1976. 783–805.

Duval, Elaine. "Reasserting and Raising Our History: An Interview with Amiri Baraka." *Obsidian II* 3.1 (1988): 1–19.

Freydberg, Elizabeth Hadley. "The Concealed Dependence upon White Culture in Baraka's 1969 Aesthetic." *Black American Literature Forum* 17.1 (1983): 27–29.

Hughes, Langston. "That Boy, LeRoi." *Anthology of the American Negro in the Theater: A Critical Approach*. Ed. Lindsay Patterson for The Association for the Study of Negro Life and History. New York: The Association for the Study of Negro Life and History, 1967.

Jones, LeRoi/Amiri Baraka. "The Revolutionary Theater." *Home: Social Essays*. New York: Morrow, 1966. 210–215.

Lacey, Henry. *To Raise, Destroy, and Create: The Poetry, Drama, and Fiction of Imamu Amiri Baraka*. Troy: Whiston, 1981.

Levesque, George. "LeRoi Jones' *Dutchman*: Myth and Allegory." *Obsidian* 5.3 (1979): 33–40.

Ogunyemi, Chikwenye Okonjo. "Iconoclasts Both: Wole Soyinka and LeRoi Jones." *African American Literature Today*. Ed. Eldred Durosimi Jones. New York: Africana/Heinemann, 1978. 25–38.

O'Sullivan, Maurice. "Dutchman's Demons: Lula and Lilith." *Notes on Modern Literature* 10.1 (1986): 4–6.

Patsalidis, Savas. "Discipline and Punish: The Case of Baraka's *Dutchman*." *North Dakota Quarterly* 6.2 (1992): 101–113.

Piggford, George. "Looking into Black Skulls: Amiri Baraka's *Dutchman* and the Psychology of Race." *Modern Drama* 40.1 (1997): 74–85.

Reck, Tom. "Archetypes in LeRoi Jones' *Dutchman*." *Studies in Black Literature* 1.1 (1970): 66–68.

Richards, Sandra. "Negative Forces and Positive Non-Entities: Images of Women inthe Dramas of Amiri Baraka." *Theatre Journal* 34.2 (1982): 233–240.

Seidel, Kathryn Lee. "The Lilith Figure." *Weber Studies* 10.2 (1993): 85–94.

Shannon, Sandra. "Amiri Baraka on Directing." *Conversations with Amiri Baraka*. Ed. Charlie Reilly. Jackson: University Press of Mississippi, 1994. 230–238.

Simon, John. "*Dutchman*." *Hudson Review* 17.3 (1964): 424.

Sollors, Werner, and Maria Diedrich. *The Black Columbiad*. Cambridge: Harvard University Press,1994.

Sonnega, William. "*Dutchman* De-Stablized: Ideology and Multicultural Discourse." *Theatre Studies* 38.1 (1993): 5–15.

Ursu, Anne. "Back in Black." *Citypages.com: The Online News and Arts Weekly of the Twin Cities* 19.917 (1998): 27 pars. 13 Apr. 2003 <http:/www.citpages.com/artsfeature/archive/baraka>.

Werner, Craig. "Brer Rabbit Meets the Underground Man: Simplification of Consciousness in *Dutchman* and *Slaveship* [*sic*]." Obsidian 5.1–2 (1980): 35–40.

Additional Materials

Baraka, Amiri. *The Autobiography of LeRoi Jones*. New York: Freundlich, 1984.

Bernotas, Bob. *Amiri Baraka: Black Americans of Achievement*. New York: Chelsea, 1991.

Ellison, Ralph. "What America Would Be Like Without Blacks." Ed. John Callahan. *The Collected Essays of Ralph Ellison*. New York: Random, 1995. 577–584.

Funkhouser, Chris, Webmaster. "Official WWW Outpost for Amiri Baraka" (n.d.). 13 Apr. 2003 <http://www.amiribaraka.com>.

Jones, Hettie. *How I Became Hettie Jones.* New York: Dutton, 1990.

"State Poet Asked to Resign for Criticizing Israel." *Pravda Online News*. 1 Oct. 2002: 2 pars. 13 Apr. 2003 <http://english.pravda.ru/main/ 2002/10/01/37555.html>.

Trotta, Liz. "Politicians Quarrel in New Jersey over Its Poet Laureate." *Washington Times* 2 Feb. 2003: 21 pars. 13 Apr. 2003 <http:// www.washingtontimes.com>.

MARITA BONNER
(1898–1971)

Loretta G. Woodard

BIOGRAPHY

Playwright, short-story writer, and essayist Marita Odette Bonner was born in Boston, Massachusetts, on June 16, 1898, to Joseph Andrew and Mary Anne (Noel) Bonner. The youngest of four children—his siblings were Bernice, Joseph, and Andrew (who died young)—Bonner grew up in a second-generation New England family in a middle-class community. She was educated in the public schools at Boston's Brookline High School, where she excelled in musical composition, writing, and German. While contributing regularly to the *Sagamore*, a student magazine, it was her faculty adviser who encouraged her to study writing at Radcliffe College.

In 1918, Bonner entered Radcliffe College, in Massachusetts, and majored in English and comparative literature. She took such upper-level English courses as the History of English Literature, the Lives and Characters of English and American Men of Letters, Anglo-Saxon, and Shakespeare (Chick 22), which firmly grounded her education in the classics and provided source materials for her own writing. Admitted into the highly competitive writing seminar of Charles T. Copeland, Bonner was cautioned not to be a "bitter" writer, but his reprimand, which she called "a cliché to colored people who write" (Roses and Randolph 180), further fueled her determination to become a writer, to protest the social ills of America. As she contemplated on her writing career, she also continued her studies in German literature, which may have made a tremendous impact on her playwriting (Hatch and

Shine 206), and musical composition, for which she won two music song-writing competitions, in 1918 and 1922. In her senior year at Radcliffe, probably for monetary reasons, Bonner began her vocation as a teacher at Cambridge High School in Boston. After graduating with an A.B. in 1922, she taught for two years in Bluefield, West Virginia, at Bluefield Colored High School. Then, in 1924, she moved to Washington, DC, where she taught for eight years at Armstrong Colored High School, the first manual training school for African Americans.

During Bonner's stay in Washington, DC, she attended poet and playwright Georgia Douglas Johnson's* famous S Street Salon, a weekly writers' group, where she was encouraged and inspired to write plays by playwrights Zora Neale Hurston,* May Miller,* Langston Hughes,* Willis Richardson,* Jean Toomer,* and her close friend and mentor Johnson. Though much of Bonner's literary career would be devoted to fiction, sometimes writing under the pseudonym Joseph Maree Andrew, it was during this period that she wrote three plays that voiced her concern for the racial, class, and gender inequities blacks faced living in America. *The Pot Maker (A Play to Be Read)* (1927) was published in *Opportunity*, and both *The Purple Flower: A Phantasy That Had Best Be Read* (1928) and *Exit, An Illusion* (1929) were published in *Crisis*. The latter two one-act plays won the $200 first prize for Best Play in the 1927 *Crisis* magazine contest. *Muddled Dreams*, her fourth play, has not been located.

Although Bonner joined the Washington Krigwa Players, the company did not produce her prize-winning plays. Even Krigwa member Willis Richardson was unaware that Bonner, like himself, was a playwright. As the subtitles of Bonner's first two plays suggest, she apparently intended them to be read, which may account for why they were never produced in her lifetime. Critics speculate that they were never staged because they were too avant-garde, setting them apart from the plays of her contemporaries, and because of the numerous technological challenges to stage them. Nevertheless, they were read and appreciated by a number of the artists of the Harlem Renaissance and were most influential to later writers like Toni Morrison, Alice Walker, Gloria Naylor, Toni Cade Bambara, and Gayl Jones (Roses and Randolph 166).

In 1930, Bonner married accountant William Almy Occomy, a Rhode Island native and Brown University graduate, and moved to Chicago. After her marriage, she ceased writing drama to raise three children—William Almy, Jr., Warwick Gale Noel, and Marita Joyce—and to focus exclusively on writing fiction, for which she received literary recognition in *Crisis* and *Opportunity*. Sometime around 1941, Bonner stopped writing to teach school in Chicago: first at the Phillips High School and then, between 1950 and 1963, at the Doolittle School for education-challenged children. Aside from family commitments and teaching, some critics note that she abandoned her writing to devote much of her time and energy to the Christian Science Church.

On December 6, 1971, Bonner died in Chicago as a result of injuries she sustained in a fire in her apartment. Like Alice Dunbar-Nelson, Bonner's literary output was small in terms of her plays, but she was one of the most versatile and talented figures in the theater movement in the 1920s. An innovator in form and thesis, she was a woman ahead of her time and critics have noted that she anticipated later playwrights like Adrienne Kennedy* and Ntozake Shange.*

MAJOR WORKS AND THEMES

In her autobiographical essay, "On Being Young—A Woman—and Colored,"published in *Crisis* in December 1925, Marita Bonner sets the tone for all of her works, including her plays. This social commentary discusses a host of themes that concerned her throughout her life: the plight of blacks, the disempowerment of women, race relations, and segregation. Introducing innovative elements—the structure of a one-act morality play, second-person narration, to direct the reader-viewer's focus and responses, elaborate stage directions, and a plot development, which generally relies on a dominant metaphor—Bonner used the stage as a platform to address a wide range of social issues precipitated by gender, class, and especially race.

The Pot Maker (A Play to Be Read) (1927) is written in dialect with vivid characterizations, lots of dramatic tension, and a rural and simple setting, which suggests a strong naturalistic influence of Georgia Douglas Johnson. Set in a small cabin, it makes an indictment against infidelity in oppressive, poverty-ridden conditions and centers on Lucinda Jackson, a young woman who is totally disheartened with her marriage and her ruthless mother-in-law, Nettie Johnson. Using the pot as a symbol, Bonner reveals the many cracks or flaws of her characters. Since Lucinda's husband Elias has been called by God from the cornfields to preach to his brothers and sisters, his blindness or insensitivity to his wife's needs leaves her feeling forsaken or "devalued" as a woman. Her only salvation is to take a lover, Lew Fox, a friend of the family. While rehearsing for his first sermon, Elias tries to inform Lucinda in his parable about the pot maker, that he knows of her affair, and that her sins can be forgiven by God and by him. After the parable, Lew leaves the house and Lucinda attempts to follow him, but her mother-in-law stops her. Then Lucinda seizes the moment and candidly criticizes her husband for his many failures. "Fools can't preach. . . . If you was any kind of a man you'd get a decent job and hold it and hold your mouth shut and move me into my own house. Ain't no woman so in love with her man's mother she wants to live five years under the same roof with her like I done" (qtd. in Shafer 429). When Lew sneaks around to see Lucinda, he falls into a well and Elias refuses to help save him. Enraged by his hypocritical actions, she runs to Lew and falls in the well. Bonner reveals that during his own epiphany, Elias realizes that he has cracks too, and he runs to save Lucinda but is pulled into the well. As Elizabeth Brown-Guillory* notes, "Though not condoning Lucinda's affair, Bonner apparently could sympathize with a woman who felt trapped and helpless in a marriage in which the male seemed oblivious to her emotional and financial needs" ("Marita" 2).

Acknowledged as her best work, Bonner's *The Purple Flower: A Phantasy That Had Best Be Read* (1928) is a historical allegory of race relations in America that focuses on the plight of blacks. Without humor, the setting takes place in a nonexistent world, where white people, called the "White Devils," live in Somewhere, and the black people, a group called "Us's," live below the valley that lies between Nowhere and Somewhere. By challenging the conventional symbol of the flower, of all that is pure and fair (Chick 21), Bonner's the purple Flower-of-Life-at-Its-Fullest, is a symbol of race, wealth, power, opportunity, and freedom that belongs solely to the White Devils. While the Us's of all shades do everything humanly possible to attain their freedom, by following the philosophies of Booker T. Washington (hard work), W. E. B. Du Bois (education), the religion/God, or money philosophies, the Us's recognize they will never have access to the purple flower. By the end of the play, Bonner asks the question: "Is it time?" She suggests, as in Lorraine Hansberry's *What Use Are Flowers?* (1962) and *Les Blancs* (1970), that only a violent revolution in a racist America or even in another country will ensure that the NEW MAN survives. According to Nancy Chick, Bonner's play differs from the conventional genre, for the battle is not to save souls, as in traditional morality plays (25). Written three decades before the turbulent 1960s, critics note that Bonner's *The Purple Flower* signals a vast change in America and sets the stage for such contemporary writers as Lorraine Hansberry,* Amiri Baraka,* Sonia Sanchez,* and Ed Bullins* (see, for example, Brown-Guillory, *Their Place* 18).

In Bonner's brief last play, *Exit, An Illusion* (1929), she probes the issue of light-skinned blacks "passing" for white, as in Alice Dunbar-Nelson's *Gone White*. Bonner focuses on the plight of a black woman, Dot, who can pass for white, but who is unable to deal with her circumstances. She loves Buddy, a jealous black man, who allows his suspicion and hatred of her to become a detrimental force in the black community. Dot's date with Exit Mann, whom Buddy believes is white, makes him furious and he threatens to shoot both of them. Unable to admit that he loves her, Dot goes to Exit and in a blind rage, Buddy fires a shot that hits a light. Buddy fails to recognize that it is not the white lover, but death, the "hollow eyes and fleshless cheeks," an actual force personified as the mysterious lover Exit, that is lingering for Dot. When Buddy awakes as if from a dream, he realizes that she is dead and declares his love for her. By combining a "Pirandellian theatrical self-reflexivity," Bonner not only penetrates to the heart of gender relations and color consciousness in America, but she explores the nature of theater itself (Burton xxxix).

CRITICAL RECEPTION

During the initial publication of Marita Bonner's noteworthy plays, they brought her widespread recognition, but not much beyond the Harlem Renaissance. Over the past two decades, however, more critical works have been written to assess the importance of Bonner's literary contribution. In 1987, her writing was first collected in the posthumous publication of Joyce Flynn and Joyce Occomy Stricklin's *Frye Street and Environs*, which did much to reestablish her as "the most interesting black woman dramatist during the years of the Harlem Renaissance" (McKay 129).

Critics note how *The Pot Maker* differs from that of other plays by women of the period in Bonner's treatment and depiction of women. Will Harris contends that "Lucinda's direct criticism of her husband Elias violates the rule of silence on the subject of black men held by other female salon playwrights. Lucinda's affair results in her own death, her lover's, and her husband's" (205). Brown-Guillory observes that Bonner depicts "poor and middle class black women who defend themselves against gender-based, societal constraints" ("Marita" 2). With this work, Brown-Guillory believes Bonner influenced the work of future writers such as Flannery O'Connor whose "Christocentric" fiction of the 1950s "resembles . . . [and emphasizes] redemption and saving grace" (2).

The first of the playwrights among her contemporaries to use surrealism, Bonner's 1928 publication of *The Purple Flower* garnered rave reviews. Praised for its unique allegorical style, critics called it her "masterpiece," and her most "ambitious . . . effort to represent a black quest for 'Life-At-Its-Fullest'" (Gilbert and Gubar 1577). It was also described as "non-realistic," "expressionistic," or "allegorical" (Kelly 309) and "perhaps the most provocative" as well as "one of the most unusual plays ever written" (Wilkerson and Hill, qtd. in Kelly 309). According to Sally Burke, "Bonner pressed the boundaries of the drama, providing new ways, of depicting age-old struggles. Because these struggles continue, her timeless allegory speaks even now with all its power" (98).

Noting the play's influence, Esther Beth Sullivan claims "Bonner's use of the allegorical form closely approximates modern art forms such as expressionism and symbolist drama (309–317). The play also responds to the call by Du Bois to develop drama that is "propagandistic with a vengeance" (qtd. in Sullivan 309–317). Nellie McKay seems to think Bonner mastered this with "her view of the inevitability of a racial revolution, and her placement of "black American oppression within the framework of world oppression based on the hierarchy of race" (129). Brown-Guillory also credits Bonner's "preoccupation with the destructiveness of the rural South and the urban North in her writings" as a probable source of influence for Richard Wright* and other Chicago Renaissance writers of the 1940s and 1950s (1).

BIBLIOGRAPHY

Dramatic Works by Marita Bonner

"*Exit, An Illusion*." *Crisis*. 36 (Oct. 1929): 335–336, 352.
"*The Pot Maker (A Play to Be Read)*." *Opportunity* 5 (Feb. 1927): 43–46.
"*The Purple Flower: A Phantasy That Had Best Be Read*." *Crisis* 35 (Jan. 1928): 9–11, 28, 30.

Studies of Marita Bonner's Dramatic Works

Abramson, Doris E. "Angelina Weld Grimké, Mary T. Burrill, Georgia Douglas Johnson, and Marita O. Bonner: An Analysis of Their Plays." *SAGE* 2.1 (Spring 1985): 9–13.

Berg, Allison. "Marita Odette Bonner (1898–1971)." *American Women Writers, 1900–1945: A Bio-Bibliographical Critical Sourcebook*. Ed. Laurie Champion. Westport: Greenwood, 2000. 39–44.

Berg, Allison, and Meredith Taylor. "Enacting Difference: Marita Bonner's *Purple Flower* and the Ambiguities of Race." *African American Review* 32.3 (1998): 469–480.

Brown-Guillory, Elizabeth. *Their Place on the Stage: Black Women Playwrights in America*. Westport: Greenwood, 1988.

———, ed. and comp. "Marita Bonner (1899–1971)." *Wines in the Wilderness: Plays by African American Women from the Harlem Renaissance to the Present*. Westport: Greenwood, 1990. 1–10.

Burke, Sally. *American Feminist Playwrights: A Critical History*. New York: Twayne, 1996. 65–99.

Burton, Jennifer, ed. *Zora Neal Hurston, Eulalie Spence, Marita Bonner, and Other Plays: The Prize Plays and Other One-Acts Published in Periodicals*. New York: Hall, 1996.

Chick, Nancy. "Marita Bonner's Revolutionary Purple Flowers: Challenging the Symbol of White Womanhood." *Langston Hughes Review* 13.1 (1994–1995): 21–32.

Flynn, Joyce. "Marita Bonner Occomy." *Dictionary of Literary Biography: Afro-American Writers from the Harlem Renaissance to 1940*. Ed. Trudier Harris. Vol. 51. Detroit: Gale, 1987. 222–228.

Flynn, Joyce, and Joyce Occomy Stricklin, eds. *Frye Street and Environs: The Collected Works of Marita Bonner*. Boston: Beacon, 1987.

Gavin, Christy, ed. *African American Women Playwrights: A Research Guide*. New York: Garland, 1999. 3–11.

Gilbert, Sandra, and Susan Guber, eds. *The Norton Anthology of Literature: The Traditions of English*. 2nd ed. New York: Norton, 1996.

Harris, Will. "Early Black Women Playwrights and the Dual Liberation Motif." *African American Review* 28.2 (1994): 205–221.

Hatch, James V., and Ted Shine, eds. *Black Theatre USA: Plays by African Americans, 1847 to Today*. Rev. ed. New York: Free Press, 1996. 206–212.

Hill, Errol. "The Revolutionary Tradition in Black Drama." *Theatre Journal* 38 (Dec. 1986): 408–426.

Kelly, Katherine E., ed. *Modern Drama by Women, 1880s–1930s: An International Anthology*. London: Routledge, 1996.

McKay, Nellie. "'What Were They Saying?': Black Women Playwrights of the Harlem Renaissance." *The Harlem Renaissance Re-examined*. Ed. Victor A. Kramer. New York: AMS, 1986. 129–147.

Miller, Jeanne-Marie. "Black Women Playwrights from Grimké to Shange: Selected Synopses of Their Works." *But Some of Us Are Brave: Black Women's Studies*. Ed. Gloria T. Hull, P. B. Scott, and Barbara Smith. New York: Feminist Press, 1982. 280–290.

Roses, Lorraine E., and Ruth E. Randolph. "Marita Bonner: In Search of Other Mothers' Gardens." *Black American Literature Forum* 21.1–2 (Spring–Summer 1987): 165–183.

Shafer, Yvonne. "Marita Bonner (1899–1971)." *American Women Playwrights, 1900–1950*. New York: Lang, 1995. 428–432.

Sullivan, Esther Beth. "Marita Bonner and the Harlem Renaissance." *Modern Drama by Women, 1880s–1930s: An International Anthology*. Ed. Katherine E. Kelly. London: Routledge, 1996. 309–317.

Wilkerson, Margaret B., ed. *Nine Plays by Black Women*. New York: New American Library, 1986.

ARNA BONTEMPS
(1902 – 1973)

Linda M. Carter

BIOGRAPHY

Author, librarian, and educator Arnaud (Arna) Wendell Bontemps was born in Alexandria, Louisiana, on October 13, 1902, to Paul and Maria Bontemps. His father was a brick mason, and his mother was a teacher. Three years later, the family moved to California to escape southern racism. Although Bontemps's father was Catholic and his mother was Methodist, the family became Seventh-Day Adventists after their move West. After graduating from San Fernando Academy, a predominantly white boarding school run by the Seventh-Day Adventist Church, Bontemps attended the University of California at Los Angeles, and he graduated from Pacific Union College in 1923 with a bachelor of arts degree. Bontemps took graduate courses at UCLA while he worked in a Los Angeles post office along with his friend Wallace Thurman.* During this period, Bontemps began to write poetry.

After his poem "Hope" was published in *Crisis* in 1924, Bontemps moved to New York. He accepted a teaching position at the Seventh-Day Academy of Harlem and later became principal of the school. Bontemps studied at Columbia University, New York University, and City College of New York. He was heralded as one of the Harlem Renaissance's most talented younger writers as he wrote prose as well as poetry. Bontemps, husband and father of a growing family that eventually included six children, was forced to leave Harlem for economic reasons.

For approximately the next twenty years, he lived in several locations as he pursued educational and writing careers. While serving as principal of the Shiloh Academy in Chicago, he joined the South Writers' Group, an organization founded by Richard Wright,* in 1936, and two years later, Bontemps was appointed editorial supervisor of the Federal Writers Project of the Illinois Works Progress Administration. He received a master's degree in library sciences from the University of Chicago in 1943.

In 1943, Bontemps was appointed a professor of creative writing and head librarian at Fisk University, and from 1964 to 1965, he served as acting librarian as well as director of university relations at Fisk. From 1966 to 1969, Bontemps was a professor of English at the University of Illinois–Chicago Circle. While in Chicago, he suffered a stroke, yet he was able to resume his professional activities after his recovery. Bontemps then served as a lecturer at Yale University and as curator of the university's James Weldon Johnson Memorial Collection in the Beinecke Library from 1969 to 1971. He returned to Fisk and was writer in residence until 1973. Bontemps was a prolific writer. He wrote four novels including *Black Thunder* (1936), which is considered his best novel and is based on a slave revolt in Virginia. Bontemps also authored short stories such as the most frequently anthologized "A Summer Tragedy" (1932). Four decades later, twelve of his stories were collected and published as *The Old South: "A Summer Tragedy" and Other Stories of the Thirties* (1973). Poetry remained of interest to Bontemps as he compiled/edited *Golden Slippers: An Anthology of Negro Poetry for Young Readers* (1941) and with Langston Hughes* compiled and edited *The Poetry of the Negro* (1949), *American Negro Poetry* (1963), and *Hold Fast to Dreams* (1969); and he authored *Personals* (1963). Turning his attention to nonfiction, Bontemps ghostwrote composer and musician W. C. Handy's autobiography, *Father of the Blues* (1941) and edited *Great Slave Narratives* (1969) and *The Harlem Renaissance Remembered* (1972). In addition, Bontemps wrote children's novels as well as histories and biographies for juveniles during the 1950s and 1960s. He was writing his autobiography at the time of his death in 1973.

Arna Bontemps, who began his career as an author during the Harlem Renaissance, diligently wrote about black life for nearly half a century. Also of note is Bontemps's role as a preserver of the African American literary tradition. Arthur P. Davis credits Bontemps's anthologies with increasing understanding and appreciation of African American literature: "In these days when everybody is printing or reprinting 'black' material, we should remember that Bontemps (along with Hughes, Sterling Brown, and a few other critics and anthologists) kept flowing that trickle of interest in Negro American literature—that trickle which is now a torrent" (89).

MAJOR WORKS AND THEMES

Arna Bontemps authored seven plays with four collaborators, and to date, only two of the plays have been published: *St. Louis Woman* (with Countee Cullen; written in 1933, published in 1973), and *When the Jack Hollers, Or Careless Love* (with Langston Hughes; written in 1936, published in 2002), *Creole* (n.d.), Bontemps's collaboration with producer and drama critic Schulyer Watts, is the only one of Bontemps's seven plays that has never been produced. *The Conjure Man Dies* (1936) is Bontemps and Countee Cullen's adaptation of Rudolph Fisher's* novel *The Conjure Man Dies: A Mystery Tale of Dark Harlem*; although Fisher is usually credited as the playwright, he had been dead for more than a year by the time the play opened (Peterson 1990; Woll 1983). Bontemps and Hughes's *When the Jack Hollers* is a folk comedy about black and white sharecroppers in the Mississippi Delta region. Their second dramatic collaboration, *Cavalcade of the Negro Theatre* (1940), is a historical pageant that highlights black contributions from Dion Boucicault's *The Octoroon* to 1940s Chicago jazz and singing (Hatch and Abdullah 23). Bontemps and Hughes's third dramatic work, *Jubilee: A Cavalcade of the Negro Theatre* (1941), is a radio play that was adapted from their 1941 script. Bontemps's last play was *Free and Easy: Blues Opera* (1959), which Harold Arlen adapted from Bontemps and Cullen's *St. Louis Woman*.

St. Louis Woman, Bontemps's most well-known dramatic work, is an adaptation of his novel *God Sends Sunday* (1931) with music by Harold Arlen and lyrics by Johnny Mercer. It was produced on Broadway at the Martin Beck Theatre from March 30 to July 6 and ran for 115 performances. Among the actors in the cast were Harold Nicholas as Little Augie; Harold's brother, Fayard Nicholas, as Barney; Ruby Hill as Della Green; Rex Ingram as Biglow Brown; and Pearl Bailey as Butterfly. Capitol Records released an original cast recording in 1946; it was reissued one year later. After its Broadway run, a successful road tour was arranged. *St. Louis Woman*, a musical comedy, takes place in the late 1890s and is centered around Little Augie, a jockey who believes he will always have good luck at the track and elsewhere because he was born with a caul over his eye. Fame and fortune are his as he frequents bars and balls in celebration of his victories. He is led to believe that good luck has "left him" after he becomes romantically involved with Della, a woman of questionable character, and he is accused of murdering Biglow, Della's former boyfriend. Little Augie loses race after race, and Della leaves Little Augie because she believes she is the source of his misfortune. After Lila, another former girlfriend of Biglow, confesses she murdered Biglow, Little Augie ultimately realizes that luck is insignificant. The theme of return, prevalent in Bontemps's poetry is present in *St. Louis Woman* (Davis 85). Little Augie ". . . disappears for a period of regeneration, after which he is able to overcome superstition, reclaim the hand of the woman he loves, and win again" (Jones, "Arna Bontemps" 15).

CRITICAL RECEPTION

St. Louis Woman's hit song "Come Rain or Come Shine" has received more attention than the play itself. Kirkland Jones comments that the play received mixed reviews, was frequently compared with *Porgy and Bess*, and judged less favorably than *Porgy and Bess* (*Renaissance Man* 116).

Although older members of the Harlem Renaissance such as W. E. B. Du Bois encouraged the younger writers to focus on the success of the black middle class, Bontemps and Cullen wrote about people who were not among the "talented tenth." E. Quita Craig asserts that Bontemps and Cullen "show that all blacks do not fit any single mold: the black community, like any other, consists of human beings, good, bad, and indifferent" (45). Loften Mitchell reveals that *St. Louis Woman* inspired African American playwrights who "believed a new day was about to dawn for the black theatre worker" (128–129).

Arna Bontemps has not received the critical attention bestowed on his other Harlem Renaissance contemporaries, Langston Hughes and Zora Neale Hurston.* The critical studies of Bontemps's works tend to ignore or merely mention Bontemps's dramatic contributions. Jones's excellent biography of Bontemps, *Reaissance Man from Louisiana* (1992), will hopefully serve as a starting point for further research on Bontemps's plays as well as his other works.

BIBLIOGRAPHY

Dramatic Works by Arna Bontemps

Cavalcade of the Negro Theatre (with Langston Hughes). 1940. Unpublished.
"*The Conjure Man Dies*" (with Countee Cullen). 1936. Unpublished.
Creole (with Schulyer Watts). n.d. Unpublished.
Free and Easy: Blues Opera (with Countee Cullen and Harold Arlen). 1959. Unpublished.
Jubilee: A Cavalcade of the Negro Theatre (with Langston Hughes). 1941. Unpublished.
"*St. Louis Woman*" (with Countee Cullen). 1933. *Black Theater: A Twentieth Century Collection of the Work of Its Best Playwrights*. Ed. Lindsay Patterson. New York: New American Library, 1973. 1–70.
"*When the Jack Hollers, Or Careless Love*" (with Langston Hughes). 1936. *The Plays to 1942: Mulatto to The Sun Do Move*. Vol. 5 of *The Collected Works of Langston Hughes*. Columbia: University of Missouri Press, 2002. 333–406.

Studies of Arna Bontemps's Dramatic Works

Craig, E. Quita. *Black Drama of the Federal Theater Era: Beyond the Formal Horizon*. Amherst: University of Massachusetts Press, 1980.
Davis, Arthur P. "Arna Bontemps." *From the Dark Tower: Afro-American Writers, 1900–1960*. 1974. Washington, DC: Howard University Press, 1982. 83–89.

Hatch, James V., and Omanii Abdullah, eds. "Arna Bontemps." *Black Playwrights, 1823–1977: An Annotated Bibliography of Plays*. New York: Bowker, 1977. 22–23.

Jones, Kirkland C. "Arna Bontemps." *Afro-American Writers from the Harlem Renaissance to 1940*. Vol. 51 of *Dictionary of Literary Biography*. Ed. Trudier Harris and Thadious M. Davis. Detroit: Gale, 1987. 10–21.

———. *Renaissance Man from Louisiana: A Biography of Arna Wendell Bontemps*. Westport: Greenwood, 1992.

Mitchell, Loften. *Black Drama: The Story of the American Negro in the Theatre*. New York: Hawthorn, 1967.

Peterson, Bernard L., Jr. "Arna (Wendell) Bontemps." *Early Black American Playwrights and Dramatic Writers: A Biographical Directory and Catalog of Plays, Films, and Broadcasting Scripts*. Westport: Greenwood, 1990. 35–37.

Sanders, Leslie C. *The Development of Black Theater in America: From Shadows to Selves* Baton Rouge: Louisiana State University Press, 1988.

Woll, Allen. "St. Louis Woman." *Dictionary of the Black Theatre: Broadway, Off-Broadway, and Selected Harlem Theatre*. Westport: Greenwood, 1983. 142–143.

WILLIAM BLACKWELL BRANCH (1927–)

Laverne Luster

BIOGRAPHY

William Blackwell Branch—playwright, journalist, media producer, son of a Methodist minister—was born in New Haven, Connecticut, but grew up in various towns along the eastern seaboard, including New York City, Washington, DC, and Charlotte, North Carolina. He received his bachelor of science degree from Northwestern University in 1949. After serving in the army, Branch attended graduate school at Columbia University where received his M.F.A. in dramatic arts in 1958. He later spent a year as a resident fellow in screenwriting at the Yale School of Drama. Branch performed briefly as a stage actor and in radio and television. From his brief performances, Branch became convinced that only African Americans could truthfully write and produce theater about African Americans. Since that time, he has written, directed, and produced extensively for the stage, television, radio, and his own media consulting and production firm. Not only is Branch an accomplished playwright, he is an educator as well. He has served as visiting professor at the University of Maryland and the University of Ghana, and visiting playwright, scholar, and guest lecturer at numerous other colleges and universities. A resident of New Rochelle, New York, Branch is currently professor of Theatre, Dramatic Literature, and Communications at the Africana Studies and Research Center at Cornell University.

In addition to scholarly accomplishments, Branch has received numerous awards and honors. They include a Guggenheim Fellowship in playwriting; a

Yale University–American Broadcasting Company Fellowship in screenwriting; a Robert E. Sherwood Television Award; and a citation from the National Conference of Christians and Jews (NCCJ)—the latter two are for his NBC television drama *Light in the Southern Sky* about the African American educator Mary McLeod Bethune. Other honors include an American Film Festival Blue Ribbon Award and an Emmy nomination shared with fellow producer William Greaves for the PBS documentary film *Still a Brother: Inside the Negro Middle Class* and an NCCJ Citation for his PBS drama *A Letter from Booker T*, which starred Ossie Davis and Ruby Dee.

MAJOR WORKS AND THEMES

William Blackwell Branch's first play, *A Medal for Willie*, written when he was twenty-seven, was produced by the Committee for the Negro in the Arts and directed by Elwood Smith. The play opened at Harlem's Club Baron in October 1951, and it ran through January 1952. The day after the opening of the play, Branch was inducted into the United States Army.

A Medal for Willie, a short play, is about the ironies of a memorial service and presentation ceremony for Corporal Willie Jackson, an African American soldier, who has been killed in battle. The play's setting is the auditorium of the all-black Booker T. Washington High School in Midway, a small southern town.

The play opens in the Jackson's household with Willie's sister, Lucy Mae, styling her mother's hair in preparation for the presentation ceremony. Critic Doris E. Abramson notes Mrs. Jackson's apprehension for the "honor" that will soon be bestowed on her son, the same boy who was labeled "no count" by her husband and ignored by society (178). Mrs. Jackson recalls her son's struggles in life and the incident that led to his stubbornness and his decision to shine shoes rather than return to school. She remembers how the town willfully failed Willie when he needed help; because of these thoughts, she cannot muster the enthusiasm that such an honor deserves. She does acknowledge the good deed, but ponders its futility. The gesture, it seems, is a little too late for him now.

In *A Medal for Willie*, Branch explores grief and the loss of a loved one. This play deals with the place and the recognition of the African American in pre–civil rights America. He points to the irony of the black soldier fighting for the freedom of others in another country and yet being denied those same basic freedoms and rights in his own country. The issue of racism is clearly delineated in this play as Branch constructs the scene between the mayor of Midway and the general who is to present the medal. The scene mirrors the larger society in America. It is during this scene that the mayor instructs the general to minimize his commendation about Corporal Jackson, so as to not offer too much encouragement to the Negroes. However, a

Jewish captain who is from the North does not understand and disagrees, but he is quickly outvoted by the others. In another scene, Branch permits another character, the barber, to acknowledge that there is something dreadfully wrong with Willie fighting and dying for a country that refuses "to see" him, but in his death "sees" him. In opposition to this perspective, Branch presents the typical view of the southern whites through a customer who remarks that there is no valor in his death because he "ain't nothing but another dead nigger." This statement speaks voluminously to the attitudes and views of white America at that time. Branch continues to illustrate the racial bias in the scene in which, ironically, the son of the customer in the barbershop verbally accosts Willie's girlfriend, Bernice, because she rejects his attention, and it results in a brief physical altercation.

Branch also highlights the various images that were and are often associated with African Americans both within and outside of the race. He portrays Mr. Torrence, the high school principal, as the Uncle Tom as he is viewed by some members of his faculty and Mrs. Jackson. Mr. Torrence rationalizes his actions as those that are good for the school, and he expects others to have that same perspective and accept his actions without questions. Dramatically, Branch ends the play with Mrs. Jackson rejecting the hypocrisy of both Mr. Torrence and Midway as she refuses to read the prepared speech and exits the stage.

In the next play, *Baccalaureate: A Drama in Three Acts*, Branch addresses the issues of feminism, civil rights, and family relationships. This play focuses on the struggles of a young African American woman, her attempts to gain advancement through education, and her battle for self-fulfillment. In the pursuit of these goals, Angela must rely on the generosity of her sister and her husband. This generosity is not limited to monetary support but also to emotional support. Angela finds herself, like many young people, with dreams that cannot be fulfilled without the assistance of the family, but with a strong desire to remain independent, as this help is needed, and these goals are accomplished. Angela understands this sacrifice, yet she is unwilling to permit her sister Martha into her private affairs until it becomes absolutely necessary. Martha, on the other hand, understands her sister's dilemma and the advantages that a college education provides and the successes that await her, but she is still determined to breach that wall. Branch gives Martha those characteristics and opinions that were prevalent among middle-class women during that time period. Angela, on the other hand, represents the new era and believes that there is too much emphasis placed on the middle class and its controversial values.

Branch explores other values that are associated with the middle class through the character Roger Sampson, the young attorney who has just been made a partner with a major law firm. His involvement with Angela is good until he discovers her secret—an abortion—and then he is ready to abandon the relationship. His first inclination is to leave because he is determined to avoid any damage to him and his career. He quickly recognizes his insensitivity and offers understanding, but Angela knows the system and lets him go. The male desire for the "unblemished" woman is an another issue that Branch addresses in this play. It is at this point that Angela realizes that she has in some way been chasing something, which may or may not exist.

Branch also explores the issues of race and injustice through the character Kenny, who mirrors one of the young civil rights workers killed near Greenville, Mississippi, in 1963. Kenny represents the attitudes and feelings of those in the 1960s who believed in asserting blackness and resisting racial injustice. It is because of his strong desire to change the system that he refuses to make a commitment to Angela, and then he journeys to Mississippi where he meets his unfortunate fate.

Later in the play, Branch introduces the idea that a woman must pay "in kind for assistance or service rendered." Doc, Martha's husband, has a strong attraction to Angela and a fierce jealousy of her relationships with other men; he eventually forces her to yield sexually to him for a repayment of a $300 loan. We are led to believe it with this encounter with Doc that Angela becomes pregnant, and she has to have an abortion. It is precisely this situation that she has been trying to avoid. Her submission to Doc has caused irreparable damage to her, and the untold secret would cause even more for her sister and her family. This act has changed how she will eventually see herself and how she will handle the challenges that life will present to her.

In Splendid Error was written while Branch was stationed in Germany. The play's original title was *Frederick Douglass*, but he retitled it after his discharge from the army in 1953. The title change is appropriate because the play is not just about Frederick Douglass but John Brown as well. The play opened at the Greenwich Mews on October 26, 1954, and ran through January 1955. According to critic Doris Abramson, Branch, while stationed in Europe, came into possession of several books, which served as impetus for the play. Those texts were *The Life and Times of Frederick Douglass* (1892); Shirley Graham's *There Was Once a Slave* (1947), a fictionalized biography of Douglass; and *God's Angry Men* (1932), a novel about John Brown by Leonard Ehrlich.

The action of *In Splendid Error* takes place in the home of Frederick Douglass in Rochester, New York, between 1859 and 1860. Here, Branch reflects on slavery by presenting two dominant personalities and their perspectives as to how this horrible act can be abolished. John Brown, alias Nelson Hawkins, believes that freedom can only be attained through guerilla warfare, while Frederick Douglass believes that freedom must be attained through a national mandate. The play draws attention to the special relationship that exists between the two men whose individual fight for freedom will be decidedly different. This notwithstanding, their mutual respect and desires make them steadfast compatriots in their fight to rid the country of slavery.

Branch opens the play in the parlor of Douglass's home with a hearty discussion between Frederick Douglass and several prominent white gentlemen on the issue of slavery and its evils. It is in this discussion that Branch first introduces the alliance between Douglass and John Brown. From the beginning, it is obvious that the two white gentlemen do not appreciate John Brown, who is himself white. To them, his actions could stall the cause of freedom. It is here that Frederick Douglass attempts to explain Brown's position and actions both of which preach bloodshed for freedom. Even so, he advocates for Brown's successes, which are to be achieved by different tactics. Then he proceeds to explain his perspective on the horrors of slavery and its political ramifications.

John Brown's plan is to create an escape route from New Hampshire to Florida and Maryland to Missouri with a trained militia. With trained men and the mountainous terrain, John Brown hopes to steal the slaves from their masters and then channel them through the Blue Ridge Mountains into Canada by way of the Underground Railroad. By this action, he hopes to strike a major blow to slavery, in the pockets of the slaveholders. Douglass, on the other hand, sees the risk involved in this plan and tries to dissuade him, but to no avail. Douglass believes that his mission like John Brown (Nelson Hawkins) is to fight for freedom but in a venue where he can succeed.

In act 2, Frederick Douglass's refusal to go along with John Brown results in a heated exchange between the two. Brown is convinced that his plan is a sure success where Douglass sees the imminent danger that exists for all those involved. According to Abramson, Brown taunts Douglass as he leaves his friend disappointed that he will not be a part of this great moment, but later acknowledges after his capture that Douglass's decision was the best one. He should live to fight in other ways.

This kinship between Frederick Douglass and John Brown was based on mutual respect even though they had different ideologies and beliefs as to how to achieve the same results. The title of the play reflects the unlikely and uncommon valor between two revoluntaries whose lives were intertwined, but the paths that were chosen sealed their destinies. Brown's legacy lies in his "splendid error" to meet death head on, while Douglass's "splendid error" is his legacy to alter the course of history through the written word.

CRITICAL RECEPTION

There is very little critical review of William Blackwell Branch as a playwright and limited critical review of his works. He is apparently a talented writer who has kept true to his philosophy that only African Americans can truly tell the African American story. In this regard, the cultural imagination embodied in his works, with all of the accompanying subtleties and nuances, deliver very powerful messages. His themes have a resonance that is gentle yet overpowering.

BIBLIOGRAPHY

Dramatic Works by William Blackwell Branch

Baccalaureate: A Drama in Three Acts. 1954. Unpublished.
To Follow the Phoenix. 1956. Unpublished.
A Medal for Willie. New York. 1951. Unpublished.
In Splendid Error. 1954. Unpublished.
A Wreath for Udomo. 1957. Unpublished.

Studies of William Blackwell Branch's Dramatic Works

Abramson, Doris E. *Negro Playwrights in the American Theatre, 1925–1959*. New York: Columbia University Press, 1969. 171–188.

Mitchell, Loften. "Three Writers and a Dream." *Crisis* 72 (1965): 219–233.

Tarver, Australia. "William Blackwell Branch." *The Oxford Companion to African American Literature*. Ed. William L. Andrews et al. New York: Oxford University Press, 1997. 95.

Williams, Clara Robie. "William Blackwell Branch." *Dictionary of Literary Biography*. Ed. Thadius M. Davis and Trudier Harris. Vol. 76. Detroit: Gale, 1987. 8–10.

Williams, Melvin G. "William Branch's *In Splendid Error*." *Black American Literature Forum* 12.3 (Fall 1978): 110–112.

WILLIAM WELLS BROWN
(1814–1884)

Linda M. Carter

BIOGRAPHY

William Wells Brown, abolitionist and the first African American author of belles lettres, was born near Lexington, Kentucky, in 1814. His mother was a slave, and his father was a relative of his master. In 1816, Brown's master moved his family and slaves to the Missouri Territory. He worked various jobs and dreamed of living in Canada with his family. However, his sister was sold to a new owner before Brown and his mother attempted an escape in 1833. After they were caught in Illinois, Brown's mother was sent to a New Orleans plantation, and he was sold to a new owner, from whom he escaped on January 1, 1834.

Brown worked for nine years on Lake Erie steamboats and ferried many slaves to freedom. From May to December 1842, for example, he transported sixty-nine fugitive slaves across Lake Erie to Canada. Brown began lecturing for antislavery societies in 1843. When he moved to Boston in 1847, he was recognized as a leading antislavery orator and became a professional writer. His landmark publications include his first autobiography, *Narrative of William W. Brown, A Fugitive Slave, Written by Himself* (1847); the first full-length African American novel, *Clotel, or the President's Daughter: A Narrative of Slave Life in the United States* (1853); his second autobiography, which is also the first travel book by an African American, *The American Fugitive in Europe, Sketches of Places and People Abroad* (1855); one of the first volumes of African American history, *The Black Man: His Antecedents, His Genius, and*

His Rebellion (1863); the first military history of African Americans, *The Negro in the American Rebellion* (1867); and his third autobiography, *My Southern Home: Or the South and Its People* (1880).

Brown traveled to England in 1849 and attended the International Peace Conference in Paris. The Fugitive Slave Law was enacted in 1850; consequently, he remained in England until his freedom was purchased in 1854, and then he returned to America. Two years later, Brown wrote his first play, *Experience, or, How to Give a Northern Man a Backbone*. Although he was not the first black dramatist, he was one of the earliest African American playwrights. With the publication of *The Escape; or, A Leap for Freedom*, in 1858, Brown became the first African American playwright to be published in the United States. He practiced medicine in the 1860s, yet he continued to write and lecture.

Brown died on November 6, 1884, at his Chelsea, Massachusetts, home. He devoted most of his adult life to the antislavery movement. His works reflect his commitment to freedom and African American progress.

MAJOR WORKS AND THEMES

By 1856, the year William Wells Brown wrote *Experience, or, How to Give a Northern Man a Backbone*, he was a prominent lecturer at antislavery events and the author of four published works (two autobiographies, a volume of song-poems, and a novel) that focused on slavery's evils. Brown began writing drama because he "had learned by experience that in order to win and hold the attention of possible converts to the antislavery cause, he must vary from time to time the form in which he presented his antislavery arguments" (Farrison, *William Wells Brown* 277). John Ernest adds that Brown was aware that he could raise more money for abolitionism by reading a play instead of lecturing (Introduction x).

Brown read *Experience* to many audiences in New England, New York, Ohio, and Pennsylvania. The three-act drama is his satirical response to Rev. Dr. Nehemiah Adams's proslavery work, *A South Side View of Slavery; or, Three Months at the South, in 1854*. In *Experience*, a Boston minister, Jeremiah Adderson, condones slavery. During his second trip to the South, he is kidnapped and enslaved. When Adderson regains his liberty, he condemns slavery and returns to Boston. He meets Marcus, a fugitive slave, who persuades Adderson to help him reach Canada. Thus, Adderson, the former Southern sympathizer and former slave, becomes an agent on the Underground Railroad. To date, Brown's script, recognized as the first play by an African American playwright to use American slavery as a theme (Peterson 42), has not been found, and *Experience* remains unpublished as well as unproduced.

Inspired by the generally favorable public approval of *Experience*'s blending of an antislavery message with entertainment, Brown wrote *The*

Escape; or, A Leap for Freedom, and read it to audiences. The five-act melodrama is centered around two slaves, Glen and Melinda, who, unbeknownst to their masters, are married. In Brown's preface to *The Escape*, he writes, "The main features in the drama are true. Glen and Melinda are actual characters, and still reside in Canada. Many of the incidents are drawn from my own experience of eighteen years [in] the South" (37). Among the autobiographical incidents in *The Escape* are the slave child being identified by a visitor to the plantation as the master's "white" son, the master's efforts to continue to profit as a slave speculator, and the transporting of fugitive slaves across the Niagara River into Canada.

Although slavery is *The Escape*'s issue of concern, a second institution—marriage—affects the plot. Melinda's master, Dr. Gaines, and his wife are more concerned with financial gain and status than the state of their marriage. Miscegenation is prevalent in their community, and Gaines, the father of a slave who "looks so much like his papa" (50), tells Melinda he loves her and will free her, provide her with a cottage and "dress [her] like a lady" if she will be his mistress (51). When Melinda tells Gaines she is married to his brother-in-law's slave, he has Glen imprisoned. After Glen escapes, he flees to Canada and freedom with Melinda. Prior to Glen and Melinda's escape, Gaines sells Sam, and he is sent "down the river." Mrs. Gaines forces Sam's wife, Hannah, to marry Cato, a slave who Dr. Gaines allows to act as a doctor to slaves. In addition to Brown's derision of the Gaines's marriage and Hannah and Cato's "marriage," he satirizes Mrs. Gaines's piety. She states that she will "skin [Hannah] from head to foot" in the same breath she tells a minister to continue his "heavenly conversation" (42). After Mrs. Gaines realizes that her husband is in love with Melinda and he refuses to sell her, she tries to convince Melinda to commit suicide. Brown also ridicules Dr. Gaines's dedication to the medical profession. He longs for an outbreak of yellow fever or cholera, and as previously mentioned, he avoids providing direct medical assistance to blacks. *The Escape*, a "story of black self-determination" (Ernest, Introduction xli) and "the first extant play by a black playwright to dramatize the problems of American slavery" (Peterson 42), remained unproduced for 113 years until it was staged in December 1971 at Emerson College in Boston (*The Escape* 37).

CRITICAL RECEPTION

William Wells Brown's dramas have not received the consistent scholarly attention that his autobiographies and novels have generated. In fact, *Experience* remained a forgotten play until William Edward Farrison's 1958 article, "Brown's First Drama." Although Farrison acknowledges that *Experience* and *The Escape* "have contributed to the dramatization of the anti-slavery crusade" (104) and discusses both plays in his subsequent publications, other critics generally continue to ignore *Experience*. As far as *The Escape* is concerned, earlier twentieth-century critics have not offered extended commentary. Sterling Brown describes The Escape as "a hodge-podge with some humor and satire and much melodrama" (109). J. Saunders Redding adds, "It is doubtful that in the writing of his novels, plays . . . [Brown] saw beyond the cause. . . . *The Escape* . . . shows clearly that Brown knew nothing of the stage. Loosely constructed according to the formula of the day and marred by didacticism and heroic sentimentality, its chief characters are but pawns in the hands of Purpose" (26–28). Three decades after Sterling Brown's and J. Saunders Redding's comments, Loften Mitchell opines that Brown's "comic scenes, unfortunately, are close to blackface minstrelsy, much more so than the author's personal slave experiences should have permitted" (34).

Recent critics have offered more favorable assessments of Brown's plays. James Hatch and Ted Shine point out that *The Escape* "deserves to be read for more than the gratuity that 'William Wells Brown was the first Negro. . . .' The play is a well-structured melodrama" (*The Escape* 36). According to Ronald Takaki, *The Escape* provides Brown with an opportunity "to do in a symbolic way what he had failed to do in his past. As a slave he had wanted to . . . protect . . . his sister and his mother. . . . Through Glen and Cato, existing in the fantasy of his fiction, Brown was able to assert his own manhood violently and to protect black women against libidinous white despoilers" (222). John Ernest cites *The Escape* as a drama of "self-redefinition" ("Reconstruction" 1112) and adds that the play is important for Brown's exploration of "the complexities of United States culture in the late 1850s, an era when tensions between the North and the South were threatening to explode into civil war" (Introduction x). Bernard Peterson asserts that "Brown's plays, like those of the three earliest playwrights, did not alter the course of black theatre history in America, but they do mark the beginning of a truly indigenous black American drama, which did not develop or flourish until well into the twentieth century" (6). Peterson (1990), Paul Gilmore (1997), Ernest (1998, 2001), and Harry Elam (2001) are among the scholars who offer the most recent discussions of Brown's plays; hopefully they will be joined by others who will add to the reader's understanding of *Experience* and *The Escape*.

BIBLIOGRAPHY

Dramatic Works by William Wells Brown

"*The Escape; or, A Leap for Freedom.*" 1858. *Black Theatre USA, Plays by African Americans: The Early Period, 1847–1938.* Ed. James V. Hatch and Ted Shine. Rev. ed. New York: Free Press, 1996. 37–60.
*Experience, or, How to Give a Northern Man a Backbone.*1856. Unpublished.

Studies of William Wells Brown's Dramatic Works

Abramson, Doris M. "William Wells Brown: America's First Negro Playwright." *Educational Theatre Journal* 20 (1968): 370–375.

Bond, Frederick W. *The Negro and the Drama*. Washington, DC: Associated, 1940.

Brown, Sterling. *Negro Poetry and Drama and the Negro in American Fiction*. 1937. New York: Atheneum, 1969.

Candela, Gregory L. "William Wells Brown." *Afro-American Writers before the Harlem Renaissance*. Vol. 50 of *Dictionary of Literary Biography*. Ed. Trudier Harris and Thadious M. Davis. Detroit: Gale, 1986. 18–31.

Dorsey, Peter A. "William Wells Brown." *Antebellum Writers in the South* Vol. 248 of *Dictionary of Literary Biography*. Ed. Kent P. Ljungquist. Detroit: Gale, 2001. 31–37.

Draper, James P., ed. "William Wells Brown." *Black Literature Criticism: Excerpts from Criticism of the Most Significant Works of Black Authors over the Past 200 Years*. Vol. 1. Detroit: Gale, 1992. 292–306.

Elam, Harry J., Jr. "The Black Performer and the Performance of Blackness: *The Escape; or, A Leap to Freedom* by William Wells Brown and *No Place to Be Somebody* by Charles Gordone." *African American Performance and Theater History: A Critical Reader*. Ed. Harry J. Elam, Jr. and David Krasner. New York: Oxford University Press, 2001. 288–305.

Ellison, Curtis W., and E. W. Metcalf, Jr. *William Wells Brown and Martin R. Delany: A Reference Guide*. New York: Hall, 1978.

Ernest, John. Introduction. *The Escape; or, A Leap for Freedom*. 1858. Knoxville: University of Tennessee Press, 2001. ix–li.

———. "The Reconstruction of Whiteness: William Wells Brown's *The Escape; or, A Leap to Freedom*." *PMLA* 113 (1998): 1108–1121.

Farrison, William Edward. "Brown's First Drama." *CLA Journal* 2 (1958): 104–110.

———. "*The Kidnapped Clergyman* and Brown's Experience." *CLA Journal* 18 (1975): 507–515.

———. *William Wells Brown: Author and Reformer*. Chicago: University of Chicago Press, 1969.

Gilmore, Paul. "'De Genewine Artekil': William Wells Brown, Blackface Minstrelsy, and Abolitionism." *American Literature* 69 (1997): 743–780.

Mitchell, Loften. *Black Drama: The Story of the American Negro in the Theatre*. New York: Hawthorn, 1967.

Pawley, Thomas D. "The First Black Playwrights." *Black World* 21 (1972): 16–24.

Peterson, Bernard L., Jr. "William Wells Brown." *Early Black American Playwrights and Dramatic Writers: A Biographical Directory and Catalog of Plays, Films, and Broadcasting Scripts*. Westport: Greenwood, 1990. 40–41.

Redding, J. Saunders. *To Make a Poet Black*. Chapel Hill: University of North Carolina Press, 1939.

Takaki, Ronald H. "Violence in Fantasy: The Fiction of Williams Wells Brown." *Violence in the Black Imagination: Essays and Documents*. New York: Putnam, 1972. 215–230.

Trudeau, Lawrence J., and Linda M. Ross, eds. "William Wells Brown." *Drama Criticism*. Vol. 1. Detroit: Gale, 1991. 31–48.

ELIZABETH BROWN-GUILLORY (1954–   )

Loretta G. Woodard

BIOGRAPHY

One of the nation's foremost contemporary African American playwrights is Elizabeth Brown-Guillory, director, performing artist, author, educator, critic, and lecturer, who was born on June 20, 1954, in Lake Charles, Louisiana. She is the daughter of Leo Brown, Sr., who served in the United States Army during World War II, and Marjorie Savoie Brown. She grew up in rural Church Point, Louisiana, with her seven siblings, John, Mary Lelia, Oakley Ann, Theresa, Roy, Leo Brown, Jr., and Ronnie, and with parents and grandparents who spoke Creole or a French patois. Through the eighth grade, she attended Our Mother of Mercy Catholic School. At age thirteen, Elizabeth, a shy farm girl, who had never seen or attended a play, wrote her first play for the high school's students at the request of her first male teacher. She states: "He saw talent I didn't even know I had. . . . He said I had a creative spirit" (Coutinho par. 3). Though she does not recall what the play was about, it was a success. In 1972, she graduated from Church Point High School with honors and her interest in the theater grew as she went on to attend college in Louisiana and Florida.

Brown-Guillory attended the University of Southwestern Louisiana, where she earned a B.A. and an M.A. in English in 1975 and 1977, respectively. While at USL, she studied playwriting under the direction of Paul Nolan, an English professor and founder of The Eavesdrop Theatre. In 1976, her first college-level production, *Bayou Relics*, was first produced at the theater. She received a Ph.D. in English and American literature, with an emphasis on African American literature, from Florida State University in 1980. After earning her degree, she joined the faculty at the University of South Carolina as an assistant professor of English. Two years later, she taught as an assistant professor of English at Dillard University until 1988. On August 6, 1983, she married Lucius M. Guillory, a middle school principal, with whom she had one daughter, Lucia Elizabeth.

During her tenure at Dillard University, Brown-Guillory began her prolific career as a playwright. She wrote and produced several one-act comedies: *Somebody Almost Walked Off with All of My Stuff* (1982); *Bayou Relics* (1983); *Marry Me, Again* (1984), which won first prize in a statewide playwriting competition and garnered a commendation from the mayor of New Orleans that same year; and *Snapshots of Broken Dolls* (1987). All of Brown-Guillory's plays were produced at Dillard University and various other locations in Louisiana and throughout the United States. The Contemporary Drama Service of Colorado Springs published *Bayou Relics* and *Snapshots of Broken Dolls* in 1987. The latter was produced Off-Broadway at the Lincoln Center in New York City in October 1986.

Brown-Guillory joined the faculty at the University of Houston, in 1988, where she is a professor of English and associate dean of the College of Liberal Arts and Social Sciences. She also teaches graduate and undergraduate courses in African and Caribbean literature, African American literature, and modern American drama. While continuing to write for the stage, she published her groundbreaking critical work of essays on American authors, *Their Place on the Stage: Black Women Playwrights in America* (1988). Two years later, she edited the anthology *Wines in the Wilderness: Plays by African American Women from the Harlem Renaissance to the Present* (1990), a title inspired by Alice Childress's (her favorite writer) play *Wine in the Wilderness*. After the publication of her landmark critical works, she produced her full-length plays, *Mam Phyllis* (1990) and *Just a Little Mark* (1992).

In 1992, because of her "passion" for the theater and the stage, director and adviser Brown-Guillory founded The Houston Suitcase Theater (THST), a student troupe of over seventy members, based on Langston Hughes's own Harlem Suitcase Theatre, that produces and promotes theater and dance by people of color. Frequently, Brown-Guillory or other playwrights of color create original works for faculty, staff, and students who act in the theater. The first production of THST was Brown-Guillory's two-act, award-winning play, *Just a Little Mark*, which premiered November 4, 1992, to an audience of seven hundred people at the Houston University Cullen Performance Hall and later won the Houston Theatre Ensemble's Out of the Shadows Playwriting Contest. After the successful opening of *Just a Little Mark*, Brown-Guillory wrote *Saving Grace* (1993), also staged by the THST, with Amiri Baraka* (formerly LeRoi Jones), the leading playwright of the black arts movement and author of *Dutchman* and *The Toilet*, attending the premiere and reading from his award-winning works after the November 18 performance. Three years later, Brown-Guillory revisited the theme of the mistreatment of the elderly in a nursing home and produced *Missing Sister* (1996).

On a grant from the University of Houston, Brown-Guillory studied black women's theater at the Schomburg Center for African-American Culture in Harlem and became even more engrossed in the theater. In the summer of 1999, she made her debut at the Tulsa Council Chautauqua as an Oklahoma Chautauqua Scholar/Artist, portraying her favorite character, Madam C. J. Walker, an entrepreneur, activist, and philanthropist. During the summer of 2002, she portrayed Sissieretta J. Jones, a major black concert and theatrical pioneer on the American stage. In addition, she has performed one-woman shows, based on the life of entertainer and activist Josephine Baker, presented excerpts from her own plays. Within the last few years, Brown-Guillory has continued to captivate her audiences with her more recent plays. In the fall of 2000, *La Boucherie* was given a staged reading by THST, and on February 27, 2001, *La Bakair*, a play based on the life of entertainer and activist Josephine Baker, premiered to Houston audiences for two performances at the University of Houston Cullen Performance Hall. Directed by Chuck Smith, the ETA Creative Arts Foundation, a professional theater group in Chicago that showcases the work of black writers and actors, performed *When Ancestors Call* from May 1 to June 15, 2003. Her most recent play, *The Break of Day* (2003), with its first all-male cast, was directed and produced by Brown-Guillory on the University of Houston campus by THST from April 9 to 11, 2003, starring Christopher Stafford, a junior finance major, as Tory; Shayne Lee, an assistant professor of sociology, as Thomas; Lucius Guillory, Brown-Guillory's husband, in the role of Michael; and Brown-Guillory's two longtime friends, John Lewis as Ron and James Stelly as Paul.

Assessing Brown-Guillory's accomplishments in the theater, poet and author Margaret Walker Alexander said, "The decade of the '80s is truly the decade of black women in American Literature. . . . It is this decade to which Elizabeth Brown-Guillory belongs" (xiv). Since the 1980s to the present, the sensitive, talented playwright Brown-Guillory has written and produced a total of thirteen plays, three of which have been published. Now, along with her "mother" playwrights, she has taken her place among contemporary black female literary artists.

MAJOR WORKS AND THEMES

Like her contemporaries Alice Childress, Lorraine Hansberry,* and Ntozake Shange,* Elizabeth Brown-Guillory's plays are about ordinary people. Mostly one-act comedies, they center on the themes of aging, reconciliation, redemption, betrayal, love, ambition, child abuse, legal and illegal drug abuse, family relationships, and healing, exploring with pathos and comedy the lives of her characters. Brown-Guillory comments: "It seems as if every play I've written in the last 10 years keeps coming back to reconciliation, resolving conflicts" (Schiche par. 4). "I try to put a mixture of pathos and comedy in all my plays. . . . We know that these are serious issues, but we have to have the ability to laugh at ourselves as well" (Schmidt and Lim par. 8). According to Violet Harrington Bryan, Brown-Guillory's plays "are all to some extent comic social commentary on the people and culture of Southwest Louisiana" (55), as she attempts to "preserv[e] the rich heritage of Louisiana" (55).

Brown-Guillory uses humor and pathos in *Bayou Relics* (1987), a long one-act comedy, to address the inhumane treatment of senior citizens in a nursing home in southwest Louisiana. Containing twists in plot suspense, asides, screen scenes, and repartee, Brown-Guillory makes the pertinent point that the elderly are, indeed, still productive citizens, who are wise, energetic, humorous, and sometimes pensive. Most significant, like *Missing Sister* (1996), she depicts how regardless of their age, the elderly still desperately yearn for what young people also want: mutual respect, friendship, love, support, and even healthy relationships. In a world that has virtually forgotten about the needs of the elderly and taken them for granted, Brown-Guillory brings to the forefront the serious issue of health care versus human or quality care in America's facilities for the elderly.

In her award-winning *Marry Me, Again* (1984), Brown-Guillory uses humor and pathos to discover how a newlywed couple learns to adjust to each other's idiosyncrasies. It is the talking pieces of furniture that give a commentary on its owners and insight into its own problems. For instance, "Loveseat" is chauvinistic, while "Armchair" is an instigative motormouth and "Bookshelf" is haughty. In *Snapshots of a Broken Doll* (1987), humor and pathos are used to combat the pain of old wounds as three generations of women, all broken dolls, or "cracked pots," find the courage to face their fears while waiting for the birth of the fourth generation in the labor room of a hospital.

Brown-Guillory's *Mam Phyllis* (1990), her first full-length comedy and most ambitious play, relies heavily on humor and pathos and offers a compelling look at how the culture of the Creoles of color is important in America. Specifically, the culture of Brown-Guillory's characters reveals their strong emphasis on Catholicism and Hoodoo, hospitality and food as a social institution, intraracial biases, special relationships with Cajuns, and their emphasis on education and good humor (Brown-Guillory 187–188). Brown-Guillory brilliantly and skillfully examines these elements through her two powerful, fully developed, and witty characters. Mam Phyllis, the central character, is the matriarch of the community. She is a nurse/midwife, guardian, friend, grandmother, and an unselfish Christian servant respected and loved by all. One of her major concerns throughout the play, while working as a nurse/midwife on both sides of the track, is to secure an education for Helena, the first in four generations to go to college. When Helena announces her plans to marry before she completes her education, the entire community is hurt. Her fair-skinned best friend, Sister Viola, best exemplifies the emphasis on intraracial biases and hospitality. Though she is hospitable, she is a cynical, gossiping woman, prejudiced against both dark-skinned blacks and whites and as the play unfolds, she never misses an opportunity to make offensive comments about Mam Phyllis's shortcomings and those of the community. Ultimately, these so-called shortcomings are the "strengths" and "conventions" of a group of people whose culture is their lifeline.

Two of her innovative plays, *Just a Little Mark* (1992) and *When the Ancestors Call* (2003) use pathos, comedy, spirituality, old Louisiana folklore, magical realism, and family history to center on the problems of her characters, as they begin their journey to wholeness. In *Just a Little Mark*, the central character, Caroline Mark, is a young female medical doctor who is under the care of her therapist, Bill, to find healing for her repressed fears and anger, which have made her emotionally imbalanced and cause her to doubt her sanity. Her healing begins with the help of other family members' experiences: the two ancestral ghosts—her grandmother, Granny Vi, a mean woman in her early seventies, and her great-grandmother, Gertrude, the proud matriarch of the family, as well as her living grandfather, Mr. Ernest, Caroline's hateful sister Jackie, and her conjuring aunt Taunt who wails constantly. In *When the Ancestors Call*, most of the same characters reappear as Brown-Guillory traces the root of Caroline's traumatic experience, which is not disclosed in *Just a Little Mark* and explores the world of child abuse of two sisters. Caroline continues with her therapy, while her sister Jackie denies any childhood trauma and chooses to drown her pain with beer and vodka. Her only wish is to get her Grandpa (Pop) to sell his home and live with her, but he still mourns his deceased wife of six months, Granny Vi. In the end, it is Granny Vi's ghost or spirit that helps the sisters deal with their painful past. *Like Snapshots of Broken Dolls*, each character in these plays has a secret pain or demon that only an ancestral spirit can rid them of in order for them to survive.

Drawing on her own experiences and those of people she knows, *The Break of Day*, is Brown-Guillory's first play with all males. She states: "A local actor I know asked me when I was going to write a play with men's roles. . . . I told him all my plays had men in them. But with this play, I wanted to create a play to speak to men's issues" (qtd. in Schmidt and Lim par. 10). Covering a brief span of time on Mardi Gras Day in Louisiana, Brown-Guillory uses humor and pathos in *The Break of Day* to chronicle the interactions between three generations of men in the Day family whose resentments are finally in the open. The key character, Paul, lives in a house with Michael, his father, a recently retired night watchman, and his two sons, Thomas and Tory. A Tulane graduate, the first son works as a pizza deliveryman and the latter, a college dropout, works as a singer and exotic dancer. Paul's old friend is Ron Dixon. Like Manly in *Marry Me Again*, the men are unable to communicate, until the day of the Mardi Gras when they release all of their inhibitions. Paul feels unworthy and dislikes his father for the verbal abuse he suffered as a child. Likewise, Paul's two sons resent him for being a workaholic bank executive who virtually abandoned them. Reminiscent of the characters in *Snapshots of Broken Dolls*, *Just a Little Mark*, *Saving Grace*, and *When Ancestors Call*, Brown-Guillory's insightful psychological probing of her characters' thoughts reveals their bittersweet painful honesty and their slow journey to recovery.

CRITICAL RECEPTION

Since most of Elizabeth Brown-Guillory's plays have not been published and since they have been mainly performed on college campuses, at churches, and at local theaters, critical assessments of her works are very limited. However, ten more of her plays will be published by the Alexander Street Press, as part of one of the largest collections of plays by black, African and Caribbean writers ever, which will be accessible online to universities, libraries, and other research centers. As Brown-Guillory's plays become more available to a wider audience, they will undoubtedly elicit more scholarly interest.

According to Violet Harrington Bryan, Brown-Guillory points out "the strengths of the people and their conventions but criticizes their limitations with humor" (56). She further notes that Brown-Guillory "presents us with a sense of the language, habits, and values of the religious, race-conscious, Cajun/Creole small town community in which she grew up in" (56). Bryan also points out that Brown-Guillory "shows a particular fascination with old people, especially old women of Southwest Louisiana" (55). Of one of her own recurring leading characters, Viola, in *Mam Phyllis* and *Snapshots of Broken Dolls* (as well as *Just a Little Mark* and *When Ancestors Call*), Brown-Guillory acknowledges, "Sister Viola is a blend of both of my grandmothers and a few great aunts in my little town. I hear their voices, which are so rich that I feel compelled to keep them alive. . . . In a strange way, they're helping me to grow—to live—though they are dead" (qtd. in Byran 56).

Speaking of *Just a Little Mark*, her first play staged by The Houston Suitcase Theater, Brown-Guillory claims, "This is the best play I have written. . . . [It] is a play about triumph, about working through the tough spots in order to appreciate the goodness and greatness of this thing called life [and] [t]he students have taken to this play and made a commitment to it" (Cachola par. 2). Although Everett Evans of the *Houston Chronicle* writes that "it's a string of melodramatic outbursts and long-winded monologues that never quite add up to a play," he, nevertheless, credits the play with "[g]ood intentions and some colorful descriptive passages," and further admits that "the dedicated cast gives its all" and the ghostly ancestors, "even manage to muster some moments of credibility" (4).

Critic Tom Williams of *Chicago Stage Talk* comments that *When Ancestors Call* is "a riveting look at the world of child abuse" and it is "a powerful, finely paced, well-written" play (par. 1), "with elements of mystery and spirituality that I found engrossing" (par. 4). He further states Brown-Guillory sees the connection between calling on ancestors for guidance and professional therapy for African Americans (par. 6). Of her latest play, *The Break of Day*, Brown-Guillory declares, "The play is a serious one that deals with very important issues, but it has lighter moments as well" (Schmidt and Lim par. 13).

BIBLIOGRAPHY

Dramatic Works by Elizabeth Brown-Guillory

La BaKair. 2001. Produced by The Houston Suitcase Theater (THST) at the University of Houston Cullen Performance Hall.

Bayou Relics. 1983. Colorado Springs: Contemporary Drama Service, 1987.

La Boucherie. 2000. A staged reading by THST at the University of Houston Cullen Performance Hall.

The Break of Day. 2003. Directed by Elizabeth Brown-Guillory. Produced at the University of Houston Cullen Performance Hall, April 9–11, 2003.

Just a Little Mark. 1992. Directed by Elizabeth-Brown Guillory. Assistant director Travis-Jon Mader. Produced by THST at the University of Houston Cullen Performance Hall, November 7–8, 1992; Baton Rouge in 1994. Directed by Ron Jones and produced by the Town Art Center Repertory Theatre, October 27–29, 1995.

"*Mam Phyllis*." 1990. *Wines in the Wilderness: Plays by African American Women from the Harlem Renaissance to the Present*. Ed. Elizabeth Brown-Guillory. Westport: Greenwood, 1990. 191–227.

Marry Me, Again. 1984. Produced at Dillard University, March 1984.

Missing Sister. 1996. Produced by THST at the University of Houston Cullen Performance Hall.

Saving Grace. 1993. Produced by THST at the University of Houston Cullen Performance Hall.

Snapshots of Broken Dolls. 1987. Colorado Springs: Contemporary Drama Service, 1987. Produced at Dillard University, fall 1986. Produced Off Broadway at New York's Lincoln Center, October 1986.

Somebody Almost Walked Off with All of My Stuff. 1982. Unpublished.

When Ancestors Call. 2003. Directed by Chuck Smith. Produced by the ETA Creative Arts Foundation in Chicago, May 1–June 15, 2003.

Studies of Elizabeth Brown-Guillory's Dramatic Works

Alexander, Margaret Walker. Foreword. *Their Place on the Stage: Black Women Playwrights in America*. Westport: Greenwood, 1988. xiii–xiv.

Brown-Guillory, Elizabeth, ed. "Elizabeth Brown-Guillory (1954–). *"Wines in the Wilderness: Plays by African American Women from the Harlem Renaissance to the Present*. New York: Praeger, 1990. 185–227.

Bryan, Violet Harrington. "Evocations of Place and Culture in the Works of Four Contemporary Black Louisiana Writers: Brenda Osbey, Sybil Kein, Elizabeth Brown-Guillory, and Pinkie Gordon Lane." *Louisiana Literature* (Fall 1987): 49–60.

———. Personal interview. 13 Aug. 1986.

Cachola, Leonard M. "Making a *Mark*: Ensemble Performs UH Professor's Play." 5 May 2003: 6 pars. 18 Aug. 2003 http://www.stp.uh.edu/vol61/951025/7ahtml>.

Coutinho, Juliana. "'La BaKair' Author Discusses Career, Goals." 5 May 2003: 9 pars. 18 Aug., 2003 <http://www.stp.uh.edu/vol66/106/news/news3.html>.

Evans, Everett. "Shapeless 'Just a Little Mark' Misses the Mark, Repeatedly." *Houston Chronicle* 30 Oct. 1995, 2 Star ed.: 4.

Peterson, Bernard L., Jr., ed. "Elizabeth Brown-Guillory." *Contemporary Black American Playwrights and Their Plays: A Biographical Directory and Dramatic Index*. Westport: Greenwood, 1988. 76–78.

Schiche, Ericka. "Play Focuses on Family's Healing Process." 6 Nov. 1992: 14 pars. 19 Aug. 2003 <http://www.stp.uh.edu/vol58/92-11-06.html>.

Schmidt, Christian, and Pin Lim. "Class Act: UH Professor Pushes Imaginative Envelope on Stage." 8 May 2003: 17 pars. 7 Apr. 2003 <http://www.stp.uh.edu/vol68/127/news/news2.html>.

Williams, Tom. "*When Ancestors Call*." *Chicago Stage Talk*. 11 May 2003: 7 pars. 22 Aug. 2003 <http://www.chicagocritic.com/html/more_may.html>.

ED BULLINS
(1935-   )

Ladrica Menson-Furr

BIOGRAPHY

Ed Bullins was born in (north) Philadelphia, Pennsylvania, on July 2, 1935. Privy to both an urban and suburban primary education, Bullins's adolescent years found him in an inner-city middle school and later in street gangs. After dropping out of high school, Bullins joined the navy where he became a lightweight boxing champion. After completing a tour, Bullins realized that "he was not as well equipped for the world as he had previously thought" (Hay 21). So he returned to Philadelphia in 1955 to complete his secondary education and begin his formal education as a writer. During this time, Bullins enrolled at the William Penn Business Institute and met an instructor by the name of Mr. Jason whom Bullins's literary biographer Samuel Hay says "can be blamed for pushing Bullins in the direction of theatre" (22). Although Bullins began to complete his studies in Philadelphia, it was not until he migrated west to California where he would complete his general education degree studies in 1959 and begin to compose plays. Bullins enrolled at Los Angeles City Community College and began his interaction with the stage and the major arm of the black power movement, the Black Panther Party. It is from these two influences that the Ed Bullins of American and African American theater would come into existence.

Bullins began to write plays in 1964 after enrolling in the creative writing program at San Francisco State College. His partnership with the playwright Marvin X* would result in the establishment of the short-lived Black

House and the 1966 production of Bullins's *It Has No Choice*. It was not until 1967, after several years of searching for theater companies to produce his plays and his ousting as the Black Panther Party's minister of arts, that Bullins's works would find a home and support back on the East Coast at the New Lafayette Theatre. Bullins was invited to serve as the playwright in residence at the New Lafayette Theatre by Robert Macbeth. One year later, in 1968, Bullins's first plays were produced by the New Lafayette Theatre and billed under the title *Three Plays by Ed Bullins* (*The Electronic Nigger, A Son Come Home, and Clara's Ole Man*). *Three Plays* was well received and garnered Bullins the Vernon Rice Award, which would be the first of numerous awards to come. Bullins's tenure with the New Lafayette Theatre catapulted his dramatic career and landed him into various playwright in residence positions, a decadelong staff position with the New York Public Theatre's New York Shakespeare Festival, two Guggenheim Fellowships, two Rockefeller grants, and Obie Awards for the plays *In New England Winter*, *The Fabulous Miss Marie*, and *The Taking of Miss Janie*. It is also during his time with the New Lafayette Theatre that Bullins's "twentieth-century-cycle" dramas would begin to emerge.

After the closing of the New Lafayette Theatre in 1973, Bullins became the playwright in residence at the American Place Theatre. Here, he would continue to compose works that were part of the twentieth-century cycle, and write his most critically successful play *The Taking of Miss Janie*. Earning Bullins a Drama Critics Award for Best American Play, *The Taking of Miss Janie* exemplifies Bullins's mastery of dramatic technique and characterization, and exemplifies his mastery of the presentations of the complexities of human interaction, especially when the issue of race is central to the discussion.

Although quite successful during the latter 1960s and the 1970s, Ed Bullins continues his relationship with theater today. Presently on faculty at Northeastern University in Boston, Massachusetts, Bullins continues to write dramas and instruct burgeoning playwrights in the art of dramatic writing.

MAJOR WORKS AND THEMES

Ed Bullins has composed over one hundred plays that deal with the African American as both victim and perpetuator of the various "-isms" that affect American society. His most important works appear to be those written between 1968 and 1975, particularly those plays that he identifies as part of his twentieth-century cycle. Bullins's twentieth-century-cycle plays—*In the Wine Time*, *In New England Winter*, *The Duplex*, *The Fabulous Miss Marie*, *Clara's Ole Man*, and the unpublished *Daddy*—"deal with an extended family of modern African Americans from the underclass of America's ghettos" (Hay 67). As famed playwright August Wilson is presently doing and Eugene

O'Neill set out to do with his plays, Bullins has also attempted to present the stories of the "underworld" of the African American culture. Bullins explains that these works "are an attempt to illuminate some of the lifestyles of the previous generations of the black underclass, and some of whom were the forbears of today's crack, ice, and substance-abuse victims" (qtd. in Hay 67). His twentieth-century-cycle plays were also designed to prove that in spite of the numerous instances of self-imposed victimization, many members of the black underclass did "intentionally and unwittingly . . . escape the cycle of destruction with dreams of building a better tomorrow" (Hay 67).

Bullins's dramaturgy is best exemplified in the works that comprise his twentieth-century cycle. Like Eugene O'Neill and August Wilson, Bullins envisioned a collection of plays that would examine the lives of a small group of persons within the black underclass. *In the Wine Time* (1968), *The Duplex* (1970), *In New England Winter* (1971), *The Fabulous Miss Marie* (1974), *Home Boy* (1977), *Daddy* (1977), and *Boy x Man* (1995) comprise the world that these persons exist in as Bullins attempts to offer African Americans "some impressions and insights into their own lives in order to help them consider the weight of their experience of having migrated from the North and the West, from an agricultural to an industrial center" (Bullins, qtd. in Hay 258). Moreover, in this cycle of plays, Bullins states that he wishes to explore the lives of those black persons typically excluded from mainstream and middle-class African American thought. This group would be led by and visited often by one of Bullins's most legendary characters, Steve Benson, but would trace the lives of several other characters connected through kinship and friendship.

The plays of Bullins's twentieth-century cycle not only reflect his adherence to the tenets of the black aesthetic/black theater movements through their subject matter or even their specific audiences, but also through the important messages that Bullins attempts to send to African Americans themselves. For example, the alcohol abuse that is present in the majority of these seven plays, particularly in *In the Wine Time*, blatantly points out the downfalls that the persons within the culture place on themselves. This is an illustration of the way Bullins defines *revolution* in these works—it means to get African Americans to realize that they are guilty of crimes against themselves and one another, mainstream culture has little to do with their problems.

At this writing, approximately seven of the twenty plays planned for this twentieth-century cycle have been written and staged. It will be interesting to see how and if Bullins will complete his proposed cycle, or will he, like Tennessee Williams, abandon this goal.

In the Wine Time, the first play of Bullins's twentieth-century cycle, delves into the heart of the black underclass as it exposes the intoxicated lives and the deferred dreams of what may be considered the members of the generation X of the 1950s. Cliff and Lou Dawson, Ray, their nephew, Bunny Gillette, Doris,

Red, Bama, and Tiny are all members of this subculture of the larger African American world whose lives are bordered by "The Avenue" and the steps of the Dawson home. It is on these steps that the nightly wine times, the communal gathering of this motley crew, take place. The steps serve as the seats, the soapboxes, and the end tables upon which the members of this group define their individual realities, which are not strong enough to separate them from the common link of alcoholism, unemployment, and indifference that so often plagues the members of this world. The gallons of cheap wine that the members share each night symbolically represent the sameness of their lives and the impossibility of escape, for no one is strong enough to leave the confines of the group, that is, except the youngest member of the group, Ray.

It is in Ray that Bullins implants the possibility of a life that does not exist within the wine times of his family and friends. Ray, "adopted" by his aunt Lou and uncle Cliff upon the institutionalizing of his mother, also an alcoholic, has been an unwitting victim of the wine times since his youth. Although only sixteen, he is able to drink as much as any adult around him, and he is just as familiar with smoking and women as the men are he has befriended. Hence, with the exception of age, he is just as much an adult member of this family as are the other members who frequent the Dawson home nightly. However, present in Ray's youthfulness is the chance for escape from the confines of the wine times. Ray aspires to join the navy, yet he is legally too young to join without the consent of his guardian, Lou. His uncle Cliff says "I'll sign for you" and encourages Ray to go, for he wants him to see the world and have a chance to get beyond The Avenue. Lou, on the other hand, opposes Ray's enlistment for fear of losing him and the even greater fear that he will return just as Cliff has, an unemployed drunk, who as he says "refuses to work for a dollar" (21).

The argument over Ray's fate stems from Cliff and Lou's unconscious attempts to live their unfulfilled dreams through Ray, who is essentially their last chance at success. Lou, who loves Cliff, is disappointed in the choice she has made in him. She claims to have only married him to have kept him out of the brig and compares his slovenly state to that of her hardworking father. Yet, she continues to live with him and support him in spite of the fact that he abuses her verbally and physically, and he sleeps around with their female friends and other women in the community. She defends his antics to their group, and willingly walks around hearing and seeing none of the evil that Cliff does. Her hopes are for Ray to be a better man than his uncle is; hence, she does not approve of his camaraderie with and participation in the male rituals that Cliff teaches and encourages Ray to participate in.

Cliff, however, should not only be viewed as the notorious, insensitive ringleader of this group. Yes, he holds court nightly on his steps, and he is training his protégé, Ray, but Bullins creates Cliff with a complex mixture of street intelligence and academic intelligence that may leave a reader-viewer confused as to how to judge him. Cliff is a former navy enlisted man who spent more time in the brig than he did on duty. After the completion of his tour, he returned home and utilized the GI Bill to attend college to study business. This plan sounds and is admirable for a person from the black underclass to aspire to; however, instead of forging toward this goal, Cliff continues to set himself back with his abuse of alcohol, what Bullins calls "the drug of choice" (67) for the black working class of the 1950s.

It is the potent mixture of alcohol and academics that makes Cliff a dangerous entity in this world, for he has the natural leadership abilities and the "smarts" to motivate others, yet he uses these talents to continue the characteristic antics of members of this sector of the African American world—drinking, smoking, spousal abuse, promiscuity, swearing, and un-employment. Hence, Lou and Ray and all of the other members of the wine time imitate and perpetuate what they believe are the expected norms of the black underclass.

The climax of the play occurs as Cliff "jumps into" a fight between Ray and Red. In this brawl, Red turns out to be the unlucky victim at the hands of Cliff or Ray, but when the police arrive it is Cliff who martyrs himself so that his nephew may forge a new path through the navy and "escape the cycle of destruction" Bullins discusses in this cycle of plays (67). Before exiting the play and the wine times for jail, Cliff asks Lou to let Ray go. This last request settles the debate of Ray's fate, for his uncle Cliff, who is seemingly selfish and insensitive to others, sacrifices his free-dom for the life of Ray.

In the Wine Time offers a look into those trapped in the lives of the black underclass and the one that manages to escape. It is with the suggestion of Ray's escape that Bullins proves that the cycle can be broken, even from within by those very persons, those Cliffs, who appear to be responsible for the imprisonment of others.

In the Wine Time includes many presentations of the lives of the black underclass that are unappealing to many members of the black middle-class and mainstream audiences. For example, the vulgar language the characters use, the alcohol abuse, and the "party house" on the block are images of black America that many African Americans and mainstream audiences wish to eradicate. However, Bullins points them out without censure, for these images were and remain a reality for many persons residing in African American ghettos.

New York Times theater critic Lindsay Patterson applauded Bullins's *In the Wine Time* and spoke to its universal quality, although all of the charac-ters in the play are black: "'In the Wine Time' . . . should be seen by white as well as black audiences. It is not only relevant to the black experience, but to all experience. It has a quality called universality" (7). Patterson's entire re-view of the play is interesting, for she points out that during the time of this play, 1968, most black playwrights were writing against white America and forgetting about their own culture as relevant material while white playwrights were composing works that were identifying "black heroes"; however, Bullins's *In the Wine Time* contradicts that antimainstream focus and focuses on the black culture:

That is why it is particularly pleasing to see a play by a young black author that makes little or no mention of whitey, but presents a slice of black life as it is actually lived; and in a curious way, Ed Bullins' "In The Wine Time" turns out to be a far more serious indictment of white society than any polemic on the subject. (7)

Patterson continues in this review to compare Bullins's playwrighting to Eugene O'Neill, but also points out that Bullins "has quite a lot going for himself on his own terms. He has a deep sensitivity, love and understanding for his characters that enable him to present a rare thing, a truthful presentation of ghetto dwellers" (7).

Patterson's only criticism of *In the Wine Time* was its ending: ". . . Mr. Bullins must have been thinking of a different play or, more likely, he did not trust his own instinct to let the play flow to a natural conclusion. He chooses suddenly to become melodramatic, and the shift does not fit the piece" (7). I concur with this critique for although Cliff becomes the hero of the piece, it comes at the expense of a Ralph Ellison–styled "battle-royal" scene between Cliff's hopes and dreams and the reality of the lifestyle that he has chosen. By confessing to his nephew's crime, Cliff defers his dreams so that the next generation may have a chance.

The second installment in Bullins's twentieth-century cycle follows the path of Steve Benson, the character many critics believe to be Bullins's stage persona, from one side of the country to the other and in two different time periods. Steve is found in this play alongside his half brother, Cliff Dawson, introduced in the first play of this cycle, *In the Wine Time*. A further examination into the character of Cliff, *In New England Winter* begins at the end of things, in 1960, with an AWOL Steve hiding out in the apartment of his partially insane girlfriend, Liz. Bullins then inserts the flashback technique, as the reader-viewer encounters the familiar character of Cliff Dawson, Steve, and a childhood friend Bummie in 1955 planning the robbery of a finance company.

Again, alcohol, violence, and illegal actions permeate the background of this discussion of the black underclass; however, Bullins inserts the problem of self-hatred possessed by many members of this class. This self-hatred, as discussed by Richard Scharine, is illustrated by Steve throughout the play as he attempts and succeeds, for the most part, to destroy all those things that strike him as being more powerful than he, or simply put all those things white (106). According to Scharine this contempt for both whom he is—a black man—and whom he wishes to be—white or powerful—are demonstrated from his initial act of forcing Bummie to dress in pink female mask and blond wig during the rehearsal of the robbery, to his slaying of Bummie for telling Cliff about his affair with Cliff's Lou (remember Lou is pregnant in *In the Wine Time*), and the possibility that he, Steve, is the father of her child (106). As stated by Scharine:

To be white means, in Steve's terms, to be favored in all things—from the love of Liz, who lapses into insanity dreaming of a baby, white "like the winter's face," to being the first and favored son in place of Cliff": You know I always win, Cliff. . . . One day even mom will like me more than you." The New England winter is a vivid metaphor for white America, and, as Steve half-consciously realizes, for death as well: It's snowing up there now. Snowing. . . . Big white, white flakes. Snow. Silent like death must be." It is Steve's tragedy that both betrayal and murder have been pointless, but Cliff's forgiveness [he already new about Steve and Lou's affair] has at least brought him to self-revelation: "You love me so much . . . and I hate both of us." (106)

A depressing play from beginning to end, *In New England Winter* reflects the emotions of many members of the black underclass as they lash out against each other while they pretend to lash out against what or whom they really despise the most, the mainstream culture that they believe ostracizes them and prevents them from full participation in life. *In New England Winter* also sets out to prove to the members of this world that self-pity is not the answer to their discouragement, and mainstream America is not the only, or always, the problem. As proven by Steve's actions, oftentimes members of this group are their own enemies who limit themselves to the confines of the black underclass and its rites of passage and methods of survival. Both Steve and Cliff had the navy and its opportunities as their way out; however, they cannot pull themselves far enough away from the black underclass. There is no point of no return for them, for they restrict their own barriers on themselves.

The Fabulous Miss Marie (1974), the fourth installment in Bullins's twentieth-century cycle, places its readers-viewers in the middle of an urban party. Continuing what appears to be Bullins's knack for mixing various personalities, this party, hosted by Miss Marie, represents a cross section of this underclass culture. Again featuring the character of Steve Benson, Bullins continues to follow this young man's life through his various trials and tribulations.

The Fabulous Miss Marie picks up where Bullins's *The Duplex* leaves off, not as a neat sequel to the play, but rather as a continued docudrama into the lives of the characters. Set within a modest middle-class, suburban home and among a medley of twentysomething and fortysomething individuals, *The Fabulous Miss Marie* presents another side of the black underclass found in Bullins's twentieth-century cycle: the aspiring middle class that cannot escape its dark, or rather "niggerish," past.

The play begins in the midst of a three-day Christmas party at the home of Bill and Marie Horton. A pornographic film, bottles of alcohol, a dog in heat, and a sleazy, but festive, atmosphere greet the reader-viewer as he or she meets the world of the fabulous Miss Marie. The inhabitants of this world, however, are not those persons whom one would typically find in attendance at this type of party. Instead, Bullins's guest list for this blasphemous celebration of Jesus' birth includes Miss Marie, the hostess and a Negro club woman; her parking attendant husband, Bill; Bud, a junior high school math teacher; Toni, his social worker wife; Ruth, a commercial seamstress; and Wanda, Marco, Gafney, and Steve, all university students (at one time or another). These character types are those who W. E. B. Du Bois called for and appreciated as representations of the way blacks should be presented; however, he would have been incensed by the "reality" that Bullins calls their lives.

Samuel Hay compares the characters and plot of this play to a jazz composition with Marie Horton, the titular character, being the band's leader who introduces each character and his or her respective monologue/solo. He observes that "[e]ach singer [speaker], additionally, helps to develop Miss Marie's character by telling stories that connect the soloist to Miss Marie . . ." (191). The first solo is her own, of course, where she discusses her affinity for Ambassador scotch and her wild life as a "slick little chick" (*Fabulous* 15) growing up in Buffalo. She only discusses this portion of her life, but it is Wanda, her niece, who tells the rest of Miss Marie's life story from her illegitimate birth to her marriage to Bill:

> WANDA. She had quite a reputation for being wild. . . . They said that her mother died in childbirth, she being the child and nobody knowing who was the daddy. . . . And Aunt Marie was brought up by her mother's mother . . . who was one of the first colored teachers in Pottstown, Pa. And they said that Aunt Marie was very spoiled from receiving almost anything that she wanted. . . . They said that Aunt Marie used to drink corn whiskey and smoke cigarettes in public and cuss and race in cars with their tops rolled back and she wouldn't go to school. . . . "Look what school did for my poor little mamma," she would say. And she was a showgirl and went to Philly and New York . . . and somethin' happened that nobody ever talks about and she ended up out here with Bill. (50)

Although Miss Marie's story does not completely unfold from her mouth, the stories of the other characters and their dealings with Marie (directly or indirectly) unfold upon her calling. Hay's analysis of *The Fabulous Miss Marie* as a jazz ensemble proves how each character's life is affected and connected to Marie. Each person's narrative is a self-contained unit but also serves as an orchestral piece. In each monologue/solo the ugly "reality" of these seemingly middle-class persons' true stories and perspectives unfolds, thus proving what Wanda says near the plays end: "Ahhh . . . this is such a miserable, mean existence" (49). Hay contends that the body of this musical composition called *The Fabulous Miss Marie* "elaborates the theme, which is that mankind's search for self-completion is an infinite cut-throat game" (190). This is proven as the solos unfold and we learn of the adultery, deceit, incest, and psychological and physical abuses these middle-class characters use in order to attempt to make themselves and their lives complete.

Critically, *The Fabulous Miss Marie* faired well in the eyes of Mel Gussow. He found the play to be "probably the most composed of the [twentieth-century-] cycle" plays and "more of a comedy than its predecessors" (C16). Moreover, he notes how *The Fabulous Miss Marie* and its examination of the black middle class is an interesting one and that the play's characters trace the evolution of African Americans from the black underclass to the black middle class:

Before the breed vanishes, Bullins captures it completely, as if for a time capsule. In each play of his cycle—I have seen two and read two—the playwright is viewing a different area of black society. The style varies; the author is stretching his estimable talent. These are works progressing towards something cumulative: a composite, yet highly individualized, portrait of black America. (C16)

The Duplex (the third play in the twentieth-century cycle) should be regarded as one of Bullins's best plays. Set within a duplex, Bullins tells a tale of the interwoven lives of its tenants and their visitors with a complexity that proves that even this substrata of urban, African American life has a defined order and set of rules that must be followed and acknowledged. Similar to *In the Wine Time*, *The Duplex* has a group of characters who navigate through life together. Drinking, eating, partying, and advising one another, this amalgamation of different personalities finds itself in the midst of a constant chaos that, again, the character of alcohol allows chances them to escape.

The Duplex was also one of the reasons for Bullins's controversial position in American theater. The Lincoln Center presentation of *The Duplex* caused Bullins to separate himself from the work, for its director did not stage the play the way Bullins intended it to be staged. Clive Barnes observed that this production of Bullins's work was a good one, and he praised Bullins's talent for dialogue and his keen observations of humanity: "Mr. Bullins is a playwright with his hand on the jugular vein of people. He writes with a conviction and sensitivity, and a wonderful awareness of the way the human animal behaves in his human jungle" ("Humanity" 46).

Home Boy, the fifth play in Bullins's twentieth-century cycle, continues to explore the idea of the African American victim, but moves the primary setting of the cycle from the city to the country. Bullins uses his trademark flashback playwrighting style to move the play between the 1950s and 1960s, and the North and the South. Featuring two main characters, Dude and Jody, *Home Boy* follows their decision to move to the North from the South and the migration's effect on them and the people around them.

Gussow found the work to fall short of Bullins's cycle plays, especially in comparison to *The Fabulous Miss Marie*. Dude and Jody, in Gussow's opinion, were merely "sketched" in "outline" and did not leave the audience (in this case critic) wanting to know more about them and "the people who touch their lives" (qtd. in Hay 335). Gussow also notes the resemblance of Jody and a secondary character, Uncle Clyde, to "a character in one of his [Bullins's] other plays" and to Cliff Dawson (qtd. in Hay 335). With this observation, I concur and contend that although Bullins moves his discussion of the black underclass victim from an urban setting to a rural setting, he remains true to his cycle by presenting visages of past characters. As he traces the evolution of African Americans from the underclass to the middle class, or in this case from South to North, he reminds his readers-viewers that all classes of the African American culture are related.

In *Daddy*, Bullins focuses his plot lens on the African American absentee father. Bullins uses the work to indict black men who walk away from their families under the guise of bettering themselves, the men who replace them in the home through the what we now call "common-law marriages," and I contend to point out how the broken black family is not just a self-imposed black problem, but a direct by-product of racism (particularly economic) in America. However, in true Bullins style, he writes this play for an audience who experience this problem everyday—the black audience.

Thomas Lask did not find any merit in *Daddy*, except for Bullins's "natural way with black speech patterns" infused into the drama's dialogue (C10). He says that the play fails because it appears unclear if Bullins was "torn between making a play and making a point" (C10).

Bullins's themes are the core of the contrary nomenclature given to him by Hay and his more severe critics. Dealing with issues and characters that are the stereotypical images found in African American dramas, Bullins presents the persons who inhabit the "netherworld" of the African American community. According to Hay, Bullins's early works turned the tables against many African American playwrights as he chose to "all but ignore the theme found in most of his contemporaries' plays, that all whites are enemies of African Americans" (27). His themes are not made up, but come from the challenges that human beings face daily. Actually, Bullins's themes are universal themes that range from, as he states, "people's needs for sexual satisfaction, safety, economic security, family, self-esteem, and self-improvement" (Hay 27). Bullins tells Anthony DeGaetani that he also examines the theme of "You can't go home again" in which he examines "the breakdown of communications among loved ones, and misunderstanding among good intentions" (41). Hay quotes Bullins as saying that his themes and characters are disliked because they address contemporary issues that many in the theatrical world do not wish to see or experience: "the establishment has no desire to recognize the contemporary black urban experience as subject for great literature . . ." (28).

Two themes that Bullins is highly criticized for are his treatment of violence and rape. He defends the use of these themes to DiGaetani as he contends that the violence in his plays is used to "startle and shock" his audience members and to highlight those issues in the play that he deems important. He uses "violence" and the violence of rape metaphorically to represent "some race relations and pseudo-race relations" and to explore another way in which people can acquaint themselves with one another:

. . . In addition, I've been interested in some of the ways that these people could touch one another to get to know one another, or even just move one another. One of those ways is through violence, and that violence can be verbal or physical. But also violence is an exciting spectacle in the theater. (DiGaetani 41)

Bullins contends that he uses rape in his plays as a metaphoric framework, particularly in the highly controversial play *The Taking of Miss Janie*. To Bullins, rape is more than an act of violence, it is also "a mind trip. It's someone who invades someone's mind and that person's psyche" (41). Of course theater critics and feminists alike reacted negatively to these rape-themed plays; however, Bullins never recanted his dramatic thoughts. Instead, he again lived up to his contrary reputation in mainstream theater and defied traditional dramatic conventions.

It is from these same characterizations and themes that the plots of Ed Bullins's black America come into existence. Also, it is from these same characterizations (when combined with Bullins's plots and themes) that the argument of this discussion evolves. It appears that because Bullins has chosen to depict a blunt version of contemporary society in his dramas that he remains on the periphery of theater. Of course, many persons could argue against this interpretation of Bullins's position, for he has received numerous awards and accolades from various dramatic organizations and his work has even been introduced at the famous Lincoln Center; yet these same persons must also acknowledge the fact that Bullins is not, nor has been, as well-known, discussed, or celebrated as his protégé August Wilson.

CRITICAL RECEPTION

Critically, as presented in the prior section along with a discussion of some of his more important works, Ed Bullins has faired well. Although many mainstream critics may not be in complete agreement with his subjects, they have not been able to ignore his theatrical talents and penetrating themes. Take, for example, Bullins's most critically successful drama, *The Taking of Miss Janie*. Beginning after the rape of the titular character Janie (Miss Janie) by her platonic black, male friend, Steve, the plot is relayed through Bullins's signature theatrical flashback scenes. *The Taking of Miss Janie* revisits the events leading up to Janie's "taking" by Monty, and concludes with her "retaking" by Monty. Rape, the most politically and morally charged action Bullins uses, is the central focus of much of the criticism surrounding this work, particularly from feminist critics of the play. Hay discusses how *Village Voice* critic Julius Novick echoes Erika Munk (a woman Bullins is rumored to have had an affair with) as she interprets the rape of Janie as Bullins's fantasy. Hay quotes Munk as saying of *The Taking of Miss Janie*:

Is it possible that this moral indignation of mine conceals a psychological hang up? Was I made angry by Miss Janie because I suspect [that] humiliating women really is a satisfying and rewarding thing to do, and that I may be missing something by not trying it? Perhaps, a little; I think most men have a rape fantasy down in there somewhere. (The question is what we do, or don't do about it.) Or could I really be angry because Mr. Bullins celebrates a black man humiliating a white woman? Am I really reacting as a racist? Again, perhaps; but frankly I doubt it. And if I am a racist, it seems clear that Mr. Bullins is even more of one, and [a] particularly vicious sexist to boot. (50)

While Novick focuses on the sexist and racist content of the play, *New York Times* critics Walter Kerr and Clive Barnes focus on the structural incongruity of the work. In Kerr's review titled "A Blurred Picture of a Decade," he discusses the "wandering" recollection of the 1960s that Bullins offers in *The Taking of Miss Janie* and notes that the play raises the question of the purpose of Janie's rape:

. . . we are left wondering why Janie's "taking" should be made to serve as summary of a decade's mishaps and misapprehensions. Is physical conquest the only answer to the thousand questions raised; was "rape" the resolution the '60s ought to have been seeking? Or is Janie no more than a nitwit, making impossibly childish demands in a situation too grave for children? (1)

Kerr observes that the rationale for the rape is not justified or even explained by the play's disjointed structure (1). Barnes agrees with Kerr's assessment of the complex structure of *The Taking of Miss Janie* but commends Bullins's writing, especially for the characters of the play: "Each of the characters has a soliloquy—chiefly satirical in tenor, particularly when it comes to whites, who are depicted as even more stupid and venal than the blacks—and these, and the quick dissolving scenes, do offer the image of a period seen through the distorting glass of a special mind ("Miss" 5). This mixed response to *The Taking of Miss Janie* is typical of the reception that Bullins's plays in general have elicited. His work remains the stuff of controversy.

BIBLIOGRAPHY

Dramatic Works by Ed Bullins

"Blk Commercial #2." *The Theme Is Blackness:* The Corner *and Other Plays*. New York: Morrow, 1973. 131–134.

"The Box Office." *Black Theatre* 3 (1969): 17–19.

"City Preacher." *New/Lost Plays by Ed Bullins: An Anthology*. Ed. Ethel Pitts Walker. Aiea, HI: That New, 1993. 171–243.

"Clara's Ole Man." *Five Plays*. New York: Bobbs, 1969. 249–282.

"The Corner." *Black Drama Anthology*. Ed. Woodie King, Jr. and Ron Milner. New York: Columbia University Press, 1972. 77–89.

"Death List." *Four Dynamite Plays*. New York: Morrow, 1972. 17–38.

"Dialect Determinism." *The Theme Is Blackness:* The Corner *and Other Plays*. New York: Morrow, 1973. 17–37.

The Duplex: A Black Love Fable in Four Movements. New York: Morrow, 1971.

"The Electronic Nigger." *Five Plays*. New York: Bobbs, 1969. 215–248.

The Fabulous Miss Marie. New York: Anchor, 1974.

"The Gentleman Caller." *A Black Quartet: Four New Plays by Ben Caldwell, Ronald Milner, Ed Bullins, and LeRoi Jones*. Ed. Ben Caldwell, Ronald Milner, Ed Bullins, and LeRoi Jones. New York: New American Library, 1970. 117–139.

"Goin' a Buffalo." *Five Plays*. New York: Bobbs, 1969. 1–100.

"The Helper." *The Theme Is Blackness:* The Corner *and Other Plays*. New York: Morrow, 1973. 56–77.

"High John da Conquerer: The Musical." *New/Lost Plays by Ed Bullins: An Anthology*. Ed. Ethel Pitts Walker. Aiea, HI: That New, 1993. 77–121.

Home Boy. 1977. Unpublished.

How Do You Do: A Nonsense Drama. San Francisco: Illumination, 1967.

"I Am Lucy Terry: An Historical Fantasy for Young Americans." *New/Lost Plays by Ed Bullins: An Anthology*. Ed. Ethel Pitts Walker. Aiea, HI: That New, 1993. 17–69.

"In New England Winter." *New Plays from the Black Theatre*. New York: Bantam, 1969. 511–556.

"In the Wine Time." *Five Plays*. New York: Bobbs, 1969. 101–184.

"It Bees Dat Way." *Four Dynamite Plays*. New York: Morrow, 1972. 1–16.

"It Has No Choice." *The Theme Is Blackness:* The Corner *and Other Plays*. New York: Morrow, 1973. 38–55.

"Jo Anne!!!" *New/Lost Plays by Ed Bullins: An Anthology*. Ed. Ethel Pitts Walker. Aiea, HI: That New, 1993. 245–310.

"Malcolm '71, or Publishing Blackness." *Black Scholar* (June 1975): 84–86.

"The Man Who Dug Fish." *The Theme Is Blackness:* The Corner *and Other Plays*. New York: Morrow, 1973. 85–97.

"A Minor Scene." *The Theme Is Blackness:* The Corner *and Other Plays*. New York: Morrow, 1973. 78–83.

"One Minute Commerical." *The Theme Is Blackness:* The Corner *and Other Plays*. New York: Morrow, 1973. 138–140.

"Pig Pen." *Four Dynamite Plays*. New York: Morrow, 1972. 39–118.

"The Play of the Play." *The Theme Is Blackness:* The Corner *and Other Plays*. New York: Morrow, 1973. 183.

"Salaam, Huey Newton, Salaam." *Best American Short Plays of 1990*. Ed. Howard Stein. New York: Applause Theater Books, 1991. 48–51.

"A Short Play for a Small Theater." *The Theme Is Blackness:* The Corner *and Other Plays*. New York: Morrow, 1973. 182.

"*A Son Come Home.*" *Five Plays*. New York: Bobbs, 1969. 185–214.

"*State Office Bldg. Curse: A Scenario to Ultimate Action.*" *The Theme Is Blackness:* The Corner *and Other Plays.* New York: Morrow, 1973. 136–137.

"*A Street Play.*" *The Theme Is Blackness:* The Corner *and Other Plays.* New York: Morrow, 1973. 141–143.

"*Street Sounds.*" *The Theme Is Blackness:* The Corner *and Other Plays.* New York: Morrow, 1973. 144–181.

"*The Taking of Miss Janie.*" *Black Thunder: An Anthology of Contemporary African American Drama*. Ed. William B. Branch. New York: Mentor 1992. 416–451.

"*The Theme Is Blackness.*" *The Theme Is Blackness:* The Corner *and Other Plays*. New York: Morrow, 1973. 84.

To raise the dead and foretell the future. New York: New Lafayette Theatre, 1970.

"*We Righteous Bombers*" (under the pseudonym of Kingsely B. Bass). *New Plays from the Black Theatre*. New York: Bantam, 1969. 557–625.

Studies of Ed Bullins's Dramatic Works

Barnes Clive. "Humanity in *The Duplex*." *New York Times* 15 Mar. 1972: 46.

———. "Miss Janie." *New York Times* 5 May 1975, sec. 2: 5.

DeGaetani, Anthony. "Ed Bullins' Best Play." *Village Voice* 10 May 1975: 41.

Gussow, Mel. "Black Festival in Bullins's *Miss Marie*." *New York Times* 31 May 1979: C16.

Hay, Samuel. *Ed Bullins: A Literary Biography*. Detroit: Wayne State University Press, 1998.

Jeffers, Lance. "Bullins, Baraka, and Elder: The Dawn of Grandeur in Black Drama." *CLA Journal* 7 (Sept. 1972): 32–48.

Kerr, Walter. "A Blurred Picture of a Decade." *New York Times* 12 May 1975, sec. 2: 1.

Lask, Thomas. "Stage: Black to White." New York Times 17 June 1977: C10.

Novick, Julius. "The Taking of Miss Cegenation." *Village Voice* 8 May 1975 : 87–89.

Patterson, Lindsey. "New Home, New Troupe, New Play." *New York Times* 22 Dec. 1968, sec. 2: 7.

Sanders, Leslie. " 'Like Niggers': Ed Bullins' Theater of Reality." *The Development of Black Theater in America: From Shadows to Selves*. Baton Rouge: Louisana State University Press, 1988. 176–228.

Schraine, Richard G. "Ed Bullins Was Steve Benson." *Black American Literature Forum* (Fall 1979): 103–109.

Smitherman, Geneva. "Ed Bullins/Stage One: Everybody Wants to Know Why I Sing the Blues." *Black World* (Apr. 1974) 4–13.

Tener, Robert L. "Pandora's Box: A Study of Ed Bullins' Dramas." *CLA Journal* 19 (June 1976): 533–544.

BEN CALDWELL
(1937–   )

Cristi A. Fox

BIOGRAPHY

Ben Caldwell was born in Harlem on September 24, 1937. His parents moved from the South to New York City two years prior to his birth. Caldwell grew up in a large family—he is the seventh of nine children. In his youth, he displayed a natural talent and attraction to the arts. He showed promise as a painter and a writer, attempting to write a novel about the Civil War when he was only eleven. Caldwell was cautious, however, of choosing the arts as a career path. He was not convinced that he would be able to become economically successful as a black artist.

Caldwell was encouraged by his middle school guidance counselor to enroll in the School of Industrial Arts in New York City. There, his guidance counselor felt Caldwell could focus his artistic abilities toward a career by studying commercial illustration and industrial design. During his first year of high school, Caldwell's father died. His death forced Caldwell to abandon school in 1954 in order to find employment to help support his family. During this time, Caldwell continued his artistic interests, painting and drawing, as well as writing plays and essays. His efforts were largely directed at improving his craft and clarifying issues in his own mind. Some of his paintings and drawings netted Caldwell a supplementary income, but he did not have a strong intention to publish any of his writing. This changed, however, after fellow playwright LeRoi Jones (now known as Amiri Baraka*) read some of Caldwell's plays and gave him reason to seriously consider publication.

Caldwell joined a group of fellow artists and writers, including Jones, in Newark, New Jersey. For eighteen months spanning 1965 and 1966, Caldwell lived and wrote there, later referring to this time as his "Newark Period." It was during this period that he wrote what would become his most well-known and acclaimed play, *Militant Preacher* (later titled *Prayer Meeting, or the First Militant Minister*). First performed in 1967 at the Spirit House in Newark, this play was included in the 1970 publication A Black Quartet, accompanying plays by Ron Milner,* Ed Bullins,* and LeRoi Jones/Amiri Baraka. Caldwell had previously shared print with these three playwrights, as well as Larry Neal, Jimmy Garrett, John O'Neal, Sonia Sanchez,* Marvin X,* Woodie King, Jr., Bill Gunn, and Adam David Miller, in the summer 1968 special issue *4 Plays* of *Drama Review*, which spotlighted black theater. In this issue, which has come to define the black arts movement, four of Caldwell's acerbic plays were published—*Riot Sale, or Dollar Psyche Fake Out*; *The Job*; *Top Secret, or a Few Million after B.C.*; and *Mission Accomplished*. With experience and maturity guiding him, Caldwell wrote *The King of Soul, or the Devil and Otis Redding* and *All White Castle (After the Separation)*—both performed in 1973 at the New Federal Theatre in New York City—and *Birth of a Blues!*, published in 1989 in a collection edited by Woodie King, Jr. titled *New Plays for the Black Theatre*.

Caldwell's talent and efforts were recognized with the Harlem Writer's Guild Award in 1969 and the Guggenheim Fellowship for Playwriting in 1970. In 1982, Caldwell produced *World of Ben Caldwell* at the New Federal Theatre. Although running for only twelve days, this sketch-comedy and monologue collection brought Caldwell the most critical response since *Prayer Meeting*. Caldwell now focuses more attention on the fine arts, although he still writes plays and essays. Much of Caldwell's work, however, has returned to its original intent—intrinsic expression for the creator.

MAJOR WORKS AND THEMES

The black arts movement that provided a platform for Ben Caldwell's work sprung amid the black power movement of the 1960s. Writers who were part of this artistic movement produced and performed works specifically for the black audience, seeking not to entertain but to shame them for their acquiescence to the conditions imposed on them by white America. In his introduction to *A Black Quartet*, Clayton Riley describes the movement as "an artistic motion to adjourn all former misunderstandings . . . histories of false assumption. Plays designed to further a spirit of newness. Further it. Bring the thing down front where we all can see what it wants to mean. *Has* to mean" (vii). To this movement, Caldwell contributed his particularly relentless style of satire in the form of short one-act plays, consisting mostly of only a few characters and minimal props. The plays contain very specific stage directions and many have subtitles or alternate titles attached to them, sharpening the satirical edge of the work. "Of Caldwell's work," continues Riley, "it must be said that he pursues, at all times, his total commitment to the cause of Black Nationalism and the complete devotion to militancy that cause implies" (xvi). Caldwell's broad humor is draped over a strong satirical backbone that, at close range, slices into the white-veiled myths and stereotypes the black community perpetuates at the expense of dignity and empowerment.

The militant political message of the black power movement is dramatized in *Prayer Meeting, or the First Militant Minister*. As an Uncle Tom preacher arrives home, he unknowingly thwarts a burglary. Hearing the preacher approach, the burglar hides behind the dresser in the preacher's lavish bedroom and listens to the preacher pray for help and guidance. As the preacher wonders aloud how he can keep his congregation from reacting violently to the death of a black man at the hands of a white police officer, the burglar begins to speak his mind. The preacher believes him to be the voice of God and the burglar uses this to fill the preacher with the spirit of black power.

Throughout the play, Caldwell blasts the role of the preacher, illuminating him as a tool of the white man. The preacher tells the Lord, "I tried to show them where it was really brother Jackson's fault fo' provokin' that off'cer" (30). But the preacher is not concerned about the Lord's reaction: "The mayor said if I can't stop them there'll be trouble" (31). The burglar helps the audience see through the preacher's concerns, telling the preacher, "You worried 'bout what's gon' happen to you if something happens to your people" (31). The meticulous stage directions that Caldwell provides help establish the preacher's character as insincere, pathetic, and weak.

Many of the burglar's charges against the preacher are intended for the audience. Caldwell consistently tells them throughout the play that blacks do not question their situation. He tries to shame them into heightened racial consciousness: "those like you who're so comfortable they've forgot they're victims" (34). Caldwell's attack on materialism persists with his ironic humor as the minister says "[t]his is a heavy burden you place upon my shoulders" (34). The burglar responds, "I feel like I'm takin' some of your burdens away" as he is literally removing the contents of the preacher's bedroom (34). Caldwell intends to show the burdens of complacency and materialism as a hindrance to the genuine emancipation of African Americans. The play ends with the now-militant preacher addressing his congregation—and the audience—proclaiming, "the time has come to put an end to this murder, suffering, oppression, exploitation to which the white man subjects us. The time has come to put an end to the fear that, for so long, suppressed our actions. The time has come" (36).

Caldwell continues his attack on materialism in *Riot Sale, or Dollar Psyche Fake Out*. The setting is a late-night standoff between an armed black crowd and heavily armed white police officers. Again, the impetus for the protest is the death of a fifteen-year-old black boy. The police force attempts to pacify the crowd with warnings to submit before anyone is injured. As expected, the surrender of arms is required of only the black mob. Unable to convince the crowd to retreat, the police resort to their "master plan." A vehicle brings in a large cannon and fires its charges at the crowd. As the store-lined streets light up, the crowd sees the cannon's ammunition is money—millions of dollars. The revolutionary atmosphere is quickly dispersed as the crowd grabs armfuls of money and heads to the stores to make purchases. The play concludes with the police officers laughing at how "the black bastards go after that money" (42).

The white man's antipoverty solution presented in *Riot Sale* is juxtaposed to the control white America has over the black economic standard as set forth in *The Job*. The setting of this play is the New York Office for N.O., which stands for Project Negro Opportunities. Caldwell sarcastically abbreviates Negro Opportunities as N.O. in order to show the lack of employment opportunities for blacks. *The Job* is a literal representation of the white man keeping the black man "in line." Six interviewers wait a lengthy time in line to meet with the white interviewer of a government assistance program created to enhance employment opportunities for the black community. The interviewer is a metaphor for the white attitudes and assumptions that perpetuate black stereotypes by devaluing black education, condescendingly offering training for skills already possessed, and granting jobs in only a few selected categories. The sixth black man to meet with the interviewer, however, represents the Black Nationalists and is not in the office to find employment. Instead, he delivers Caldwell's sermon as he attacks and kills the interviewer:

All niggers should be doing this! Instead of begging and being killed. Kiss your ass when they should be kicking your ass! And trying to be like you! Hoping you'd treat us as men. Hoping you'd stop killing us. Hoping you'd accept us! But all you offer is jobs! We want our freedom and all you offer is jobs and integration! You've turned us wrongside out! You forced me into this role! Your clothes don't fit me! Your ways don't fit me! (46)

As the revolutionary walks out, a seventh job seeker enters the office. The curtain closes on this man waiting in line.

Generational differences in philosophy are highlighted in *Family Portrait, or My Son the Black Nationalist*. As Caldwell relates the scenario, he names the father "farthest from truth," the mother "nowhere near truth," and the son "sunshine on truth." The breakfast table conversation falls back onto what seems to be an exchange that has occurred many times before—between these characters as well as millions of other fathers and sons. In the opening lines, the father says to "stay out of trouble. That's the way to get ahead. We've got to show the white-man that we are ready and good enough to live with him. We have to prove we are just as good as he is" (190). The son immediately retaliates with the statements of the new generation stating that "we've got to show the white-man . . . that we resent the treatment we've received from him—the conditions he's imposed on us—and prove to him that we won't let him get away with it any longer" (191). The banter goes back and forth with tensions escalating until the son leaves the house in anger. The father and mother are the symbols of the gullible and materialistic, emulating blacks who will not give up their comfort status for any revolutionary ideals. The son embodies the Black Nationalist spirit, attempting to incite his family into gaining their freedom. All cultures and generations see rifts in their philosophies, but Caldwell's play speaks for an entire race and an ideal that must be sought in order to "repossess" the African identity. The son speaks for the black power movement.

Mission Accomplished delves into the past, re-creating a scene from the colonization of Africa. A colonial missionary and two nuns descend on a peaceful kingdom in the heart of late-nineteenth-century Africa. The translator is the comedian of the show, sarcastically interpreting the priest's message of God as, "Mgoon mwan ngold nresources nland! Mgive ugoda" (51). The African king easily sees the insincerity of the missionary and does not submit to his wishes. Attempting to convince the "savages," the nuns take out their hymnbooks and, according to Caldwell's stage direction, "go into a burlesque-type song-dance, with the most vulgar, obscene bumps and grinds, in their habits" (52). When the king still does not accept Christianity, the nuns overwhelm the king's guards—called "aces"—and the priest uses his cross to knock the king unconscious. The king is bound in chains and considered "saved." The priest concludes the colonial game saying, "I think it was Christ who said, 'don't take any chances with a king and two aces, unless you can beat the king and cover the aces'—or was it the Pope who said that" (52). Caldwell's reminder of the origins of slavery is meant to leave a bitter taste in the mouths of his audience.

Almost all of Caldwell's plays contain all or primarily black characters, but *Top Secret, or a Few Million after B.C.* is one exception. This all-white-cast play enacts a mock meeting of the president of the United States, an air force general, an army general, and three cabinet members. The group has come together to discuss the "nigger problem! Nigger trouble; nigger unrest; nigger demands; nigger population" (47). Together they try to come up with a solution for the increasing number of blacks in the country. After a few suggestions, one of which being genocide, a plan is hatched that brings to light the subtitle of the play—birth control (B.C.). Cabinet member Mc-Nack, a dated reference to Secretary of Defense Robert McNamara, arrives at the idea:

I've got it! I'VE GOT IT! The ideal solution! We can not only kill the niggers without their knowing it, we can kill them in advance and make them think we're doing them a favor! Niggers love to fuck—we can't stop that, and their women are the most fertile in the universe. We can use this particular, animalistic trait of theirs to our advantage. Let 'em fuck all they want. How do we stop the resulting babies? Birth control is the answer. (49)

The plan is further explained, pointing out that it would be easy to attract black women to the idea since the black man has already been rendered unable to provide for his family. It would also be sold as a way to imitate the typical, white two-child family. It is made very clear, however, that a certain number of blacks must be maintained to fill specific jobs, especially in entertainment.

The whole meeting is presented as a hilarious slam against the U.S. government, in particular the Johnson administration. The president is presented as an arrogant, disheveled redneck and the generals play with toy tanks and airplanes. And though the mockery is of the white governmental structure, Caldwell's aim is to expose the gullibility of many blacks. He criticizes their unquestioning consent to many of the government-sponsored programs directed toward assisting the black community. Caldwell also condemns the ease with which blacks fall victim to the idea that they must emulate whites.

Another play focusing on two white main characters is *All White Castle (After the Separation)*—a science fiction story set after the Third World War in which the blacks successfully overthrew the whites and subsequently returned to Africa. A white prison guard is escorting a white prisoner to his new "cell"—a run-down apartment in Harlem. As if waking from a coma, the prisoner questions the guard about his incarceration. The guard explains to the former writer that the white supporters and sympathizers of the Black Nationalist cause prior to the war must now fill the roles left empty by the black emigration to Africa. Like *Top Secret*, Caldwell uses the white characters to augment his criticism of the life that is allotted to and accepted by blacks. The prisoner can obtain only menial service jobs, earn a salary barely sufficient on which to survive, and live under the control of the government. Caldwell blasts the blacks' materialistic penchant for Cadillacs by turning the cars into items raffled to the prisoners for a "little luxury in the midst of all this abject poverty" (391). He sardonically ends the play with the white guard instructing a black guard that if the prisoner "resigns himself to his fate, get the guitar and teach him some 'blues'" (397).

The figure of the black entertainer is present in both *The King of Soul, or the Devil and Otis Redding* and *Birth of a Blues!*, the former based on the exploitation and death of Otis Redding and the latter based on the pervasive stereotype of the ill-conceived martyrdom of the blues entertainer. Otis Redding, a popular soul singer of the 1960s, died in a plane crash at the age of twenty-six just as his career began to peak. Caldwell's play dramatizes Otis at different ages meeting the devil in many disguises along the way. Masked as a music company's A&R man (responsible for finding and recruiting new talent), the devil persuades Otis to abandon his father's church choir and sell his soul in order to obtain wealth and fame. Caldwell makes the connection between the music contract and a contract with the devil. True to life, Otis achieves fame and begins to argue with the music company and assert control over his earnings and his voice. Caldwell suggests this as a possible cause of Otis's unfortunate death, portraying the devil as both the airplane salesman and the mechanic of the fated craft. The charges Caldwell asserts are dramatic, but necessary to drive home the message that black entertainers are the moneymakers for the white-owned industries.

Birth of a Blues! is an uproarious sketch of a street-corner "blues man." The play revolves around an elderly black man, decked out in the worn garb and shades "uniform" of the blues singer. A naïve white television reporter is interviewing him for a "series on all the great blues singers of the 20th century" (38). The man, however, is obviously not what would be considered a "great blues singer." The reporter asks questions of the man named B.B.B.B.B. King that call out many of the stereotypes of "the blues" and of blacks. When asked if he is related to Dr. Martin Luther King, Jr., the singer indignantly responds with the loaded statement, "[t]here's a whole host of King's I'm not related to" (39). The word *host* invokes Christianity, suggesting the religion that was imposed on Africans by the missionaries; by not being related to kings, Caldwell is implying that black Americans cannot relate to their African roots. Christianity professes that suffering will lead to redemption, but throughout his plays, Caldwell continuously states that the suffering of blacks is imposed, sometimes subtly, by the white power structure. The reporter refers to his white audience as "blues aficionados" and the singer retorts, "[i]f they appreciate the blues, they must not have ever had 'em" (39). Later in the play, however, it is discovered that tight shoes and hurting feet are the cause of this man's suffering. If this seems absurd, it is—but only superficially. The shoes are a symbol of the clothing and the life that was forced on the black man. By resorting to singing "the blues" instead of taking control over his situation, the black man has further accepted the roles placed on him by whites by becoming profit-making entertainment. Caldwell's intention is to expose this tendency and the impotence of the black community.

In its short run in 1982, *World of Ben Caldwell* caught the most attention from critics since *Prayer Meeting*. The play's subtitle, *A Dramatized Examination of the Absurdity of the American Dream and Subsequent Reality*, provides insight into the collection of stand-up comedy routines and one-act skits. The production featured such actors as Morgan Freeman and Saturday Nite Live alumnus Garrett Morris. Portrayals of comedians such as Richard Pryor, Bill Cosby, and the late John Belushi were delivered between sketches about adultery, capitalism, and the black American experience—many of the themes Caldwell endeavors to explore.

CRITICAL RECEPTION

In the eyes of his peers, Ben Caldwell is considered to be among the most gifted and powerful writers of the black arts movement. The goal of his plays suspends entertainment value, focusing on changing the attitudes of the black community. In their introduction to *Black Drama Anthology*, Woodie King and Ron Milner describe Caldwell's writing as having a "blunt blade" (x). In addition, Clayton Riley says, "Caldwell's work hurts, when looked at and listened to carefully. Hurts because he nearly always explores that painful break between the young who are Black, and their elders—parents—who were not allowed to be" (xvi). Riley praises Caldwell's insights into how "perilous the journey into manhood" can be, discussing this theme specifically in *Family Portrait* and *Prayer Meeting*. Of this latter play, Larry Neal says, "Caldwell twists the rhythms of the Uncle Tom preacher into the language of the new militancy" (197). Among his fellow black arts authors, Caldwell feels the journey into manhood for blacks must be achieved through revolutionary measures.

Writing on the satire of the authors of the black arts movement, Charles Peavy says the works are designed to supply "the Black Consciousness or Black Pride which will free the black man from the psychological enslavement he has endured for more than two centuries in an essentially racist, white society" (40). Peavy cites Caldwell's work as "typical of the satire of contemporary black drama," highlighting the plays *Riot Sale* and *Top Secret*. According to some critics, Caldwell's immersion in this political agenda weakened his later production of *World of Ben Caldwell*.

After viewing the production, Stanley Crouch felt Caldwell had overshot his target, calling the ideas "old hat" and claiming that the play's "satiric power is consistently drained off by noble savage muckraking or Marxist salt-of-the-earth ploys" (104). He praises Caldwell's ability to "stitch together fabrics of rhetoric ranging from bureaucratic to black bottom barber shop," which is evident in many of his other plays, as well (104). Crouch ultimately blasts Caldwell saying that "like all the worst agitprop writers, when he moves to the sermon his work sounds from a rotted pulpit" (104).

Lionel Mitchell gave a more favorable judgment of *World of Ben Caldwell*, but did not give it "anything near a rave" (33). Mitchell called some of the humor hard and crude, facilitating an X rating and causing several audience members to leave the theater in disgust. He alludes to Caldwell's blunt blade, saying there "definitely was a cutting edge in all of the skits, forcing his audience to be more aware and look at things differently" but it was at times "too hard and obviously offended many of the squeamish" (33). But that is Caldwell's intent—to make his audience uncomfortable and encourage them to view themselves critically.

Caldwell's plays do not necessarily provide resolutions to the issues presented. Ronald Ladwig says, "By setting both sides against the other, Caldwell goads more by implication than by sermon" (91). The subtle satire of plays like *Top Secret* and *All White Castle* depends on the strength of such implications. Ladwig feels Caldwell is "in total seriousness when he examines the imperfections of his own background. By drawing heavily upon the history of his Black peers, he places himself in a position to examine through comedy the mistakes of Blacks, and reminds us that it is only through honest sophistication and maturity that we all can laugh at our own follies" (91). It is an excellent and necessary reminder for everyone.

BIBLIOGRAPHY

Dramatic Works by Ben Caldwell

All White Castle (After the Separation). *Black Drama Anthology*. Ed. Woodie King, Jr. and Ron Milner. New York: Signet, 1971. 389–397.
Birth of a Blues! New Plays for the Black Theatre. Ed. Woodie King, Jr. Chicago: Third World Press, 1989. 37–44.
4 Plays (*Riot Sale, or Dollar Psyche Fake Out*; *The Job*; *Top Secret, or a Few Million after B.C.*; and *Mission Accomplished*). *Drama Review* 12 (Summer 1968): 40–52.
The King of Soul, or the Devil and Otis Redding and *Family Portrait, or My Son the Black Nationalist*. *New Plays from the Black Theatre*. Ed. Ed Bullins. New York: Bantam, 1969. 176–194.
Militant Preacher. Spirit House, Newark. Retitled and published as *"Prayer Meeting, or the First Militant Minister."* *A Black Quartet*. Ed. Clayton Riley. New York: Signet, 1970. 27–36.
World of Ben Caldwell: *A Dramatized Examination of Absurdity of the American Dream and Subsequent Reality*. New Federal Theatre, New York.

Studies of Ben Caldwell's Dramatic Works

Crouch, Stanley. "Satireprop." *Village Voice* 27 Apr. 1982, 104.
Grant, Nathan L. "Ben Caldwell." *The Oxford Companion to African American Literature*. Eds. William L Andrews, Frances Smith Foster, and Trudier Harris. New York: Oxford University Press, 1997. 116–117.
Ladwig, Ronald V. "The Black Black Comedy of Ben Caldwell." *Players* 51 (Feb.–Mar. 1976): 88–91.
Mitchell, Lionel. "Ben Caldwell's Crazy World Unsettles Audience." *New York Amsterdam News* 24 Apr. 1982, 33.
Neal, Larry. "The Black Arts Movement." *Within the Circle: An Anthology of African American Literary Criticism from the Harlem Renaissance to the Present*. Ed. Angelyn Mitchell. Durham: Duke University Press, 1994. 184–198.

Peavy, Charles D. "Satire and Contemporary Black Drama." *Satire Newsletter* 7 (Fall 1969): 40–49.

Riley, Clayton, ed. *A Black Quartet*. New York: Signet, 1970.

Walker, Robbie Jean. "Ben Caldwell." *Afro-American Writers after 1955: Dramatists and Prose Writers*. Vol. 38 of *Dictionary of Literary Biography*. Eds. Thadious M. Davis and Trudier Harris. Detroit: Gale, 1985. 61–66.

VINNETTE CARROLL
(1922–2002)

Kimberly K. Harding

BIOGRAPHY

Vinnette Jestina Carroll was born in New York City's Harlem Hospital on March 11, 1922, to Florence Morris Carroll and Dr. Edgar C. Carroll, a dentist. Named Vinnette after her father's mentor in Jamaica and Jestina after her paternal grandmother, bearing the same name, Carroll later dropped the "a," changing Jestina to Jestin (McClinton 14). Along with her sister Dorothy, her senior by one year, Carroll spent her formative years (from three to ten) with her maternal grandmother, Jem Morris, in Falmouth, Jamaica. It was in Jamaica where Carroll was exposed to plays, concerts, and excursions to art museums, and these experiences developed in her a deep and abiding interest in literature, art, and music. In 1933, while most of the nation was in the throes of the Great Depression, the Carroll sisters returned from Jamaica to their parents' spacious new lodgings in Harlem's affluent Sugar Hill district, where Dr. Carroll was able to rear his daughters in relative comfort, thanks to a prosperous, home-based dental practice (McClinton 15).

Because of her mother, whose passion and love of the arts inspired Vinnette to call her a "culture vulture" (Moritz 55), education for the Carroll sisters was liberal and included piano lessons for Dorothy and violin and viola lessons for Vinnette (McClinton 15). Carroll graduated from Wadleigh High School in 1940, and urged by a somewhat demanding father (Katz 72), she entered Long Island University in 1940 as a psychology major and earned a B.A. in 1944. Upon completing the requirements for the B.A., Carroll enrolled in New York University's master's program in clinical psychology, earning an M.A. in 1946. She completed all the requirements for the doctorate in clinical psychology except the dissertation and left Columbia to pursue a career in theater.

While a psychologist with the New York City Bureau of Child Guidance, she began her theatrical career. Carroll explains, "I got a scholarship with Erwin Piscator at the New School. I took night classes while I was a psychologist in the day. And that's how [my career in the theater] started" (qtd. in Mitchell 196). After leaving clinical psychology in the late 1940s to immerse herself fully in theater, Carroll studied with Lee Strasberg at the Actors Studio from 1948 to 1950 and with Stella Adler from 1954 to 1965. She supplemented the income she made from acting by teaching for several years at the High School of the Performing Arts in New York City and it was there she realized she wanted more from the theater: "At P.A. I learned for sure that I wanted most to direct and that I loved working with young people and I didn't want to act anymore. Later on, I began to see that what I wanted was my own company" (qtd. in Katz 74). In 1964, she left teaching at the high school and later transitioned to the head of a nonprofit company—the Ghetto Arts Program of the New York State Council on the Arts.

From the early 1960s through the mid-1970s, Carroll served as organizer and artistic director of the Urban Arts Corps in Greenwich Village, which provided actors of color a forum to perform roles not usually available to them in "mainstream" theaters and where many of her shows were first presented in workshop format. It is also where her collaborations with lyricist, composer, and playwright Micki Grant* would garner national and international acclaim. Together they created *Croesus and the Witch* (1971), *Bury the Dead* (1971), *Step Lively Boy* (1973), *The Ups and Downs of Theophilus Maitland* (1974), and *I'm Laughing but I Ain't Tickled* (1976); and they brought three works to the Broadway stage: *Don't Bother Me, I Can't Cope* (1972), *Your Arms Too Short to Box with God* (1976/1980), and *Alice* (1977) (originally titled *But Never Jam Today*). All works were conceived and directed by Carroll.

Carroll never really gave up her career in acting. Her stage credits include *Outside the Door* (1949), *A Streetcar Named Desire* (1956), *Small War on Murray Hill* (1957), *The Crucible* (1958), *Jolly's Progress* (1959), *The Octoroon* (1961), and *Moon on a Rainbow Shawl* (1962). She also had appearances in television's *All in the Family* and the film *One Potato, Two Potato*, among others. However, the racism in the industry that greeted Carroll manifested itself in her resolve to contribute mightily to the African American dramatic tradition. She has definitely made contributions. Her directing and playwright credits are legion, and the more outstanding works include *Trumpets of the Lord* (1963), *But Never Jam Today* (1969/1979), *Don't Bother Me, I Can't Cope* (1972), *The Ups and Downs of Theophilus Maitland* (1974), *Your Arms Too Short to Box with God* (1976/1980), and *When Hell Freezes Over, I'll Skate* (1979) ("Vinnette," *Women* 2–3).

In the 1980s, Carroll moved to Fort Lauderdale, Florida. There she would found the Vinnette Carroll Repertory Company where she remained artistic director and producer until her failing health forced her retirement in 2001. On November 5, 2002, Vinnette Carroll passed away, leaving behind legendary contributions to American theater. Her work has and will continue to inspire young artists for a lifetime.

MAJOR WORKS AND THEMES

Frustrated by the portrayal of blacks onstage, Vinnette Carroll set out to expand the African American canon of plays to include more positive images. She believed that critics who did not understand or appreciate African American culture devalued black theater as an art form. She valued the opportunity to work without the influence of commercial voyeurism. Hence, feeling the freedom to create and develop her own work in a nonprofit environment she was unburdened to make prominent the essential dignity of blacks, the basic equality of all humans, and the ever-present possibility for the transformation of the human condition. To realize her vision, Carroll puts to good use the "song-play" genre that relies heavily on the arts of music, dance, and poetry, as well as spirituality.

In the 1960s, Vinnette Carroll seemingly followed the examples of theoreticians such as Jerzy Grotowski and Antonin Artaud who questioned the relationship of the written text to the performability of a work. These theater artists combined dance, music, and the spoken word in a creation that relied little on a written book but heavily on the impact of performance. Such is the tradition of Vinnette Carroll's song-play that she isn't so much a writer of plays than she is a creator of theatrical events.

Carroll pioneered the song-play genre while conceptualizing staging for her 1961 directorial debut of Langston Hughes's* *Black Nativity*. Having enjoyed some critical recognition in her 1961 directorial debut, this mix of song, dance, drama, and spirituality would become her signature—a staple incorporated in all of her conceptualized pieces and adaptations of nondramatic works.

Carroll returned in 1963 as conceiver and director of *Trumpets of the Lord*, a work that she adapted from James Weldon Johnson's *God's Trombones* (1927) (Peterson 100). In *Trumpets*, the theater audience members participate as congregants as Carroll's show moves from sermon to song. Like Johnson's work, *Trumpets* celebrates African Americans through the lyrical beauty of the black vernacular sermon. Like Johnson, Carroll makes heroic the image of the black preacher often lampooned in American popular culture. The loosely connected songs are more united by music-induced moods than plot and action, a style characteristic of the song-play genre and associated with Carroll's aesthetic vision (Woll 195). Her vision would often incorporate literary text taken from poems and sermons relative to the lives of blacks.

Likewise, the 1972 revue *Don't Bother Me, I Can't Cope* blends song, dance, poetry, and a prayer, providing, in the process, meaningful commentary about "black and universal problems of coping with life" in all of its many ups and downs (Peterson 101). Initiating the now-legendary pairing of Carroll and Grant, *Cope* was billed as a "musical entertainment." Though the play bears the authorship of lyricist/composer Grant, Carroll "authored" the concept of stringing Grant's compositions together, thusly creating a dramatic work. In the notes on the production that come at the end of the play, Carroll sums up what *Cope*'s intended effect should be, its reason for being produced: "Above all [the play] must be done with taste, affection, and the realization that two Black women wanted young Black artists to have material on which to sharpen their instruments and watch as their grandparents sit in the audience and say 'Amen' " (65).

In her aim to connect race, gender, class, and generational lines, Carroll, in conceptualizing this song-play, creates black characters that raise pertinent issues about dreams deferred, relationships, gender inequality, and human pride and dignity. Integral to her theatrical project is the creation of positive black male characters. In a section of *Cope* entitled "They Keep Coming," the stage directions indicate a dance for "the glorification of maleness" (33), as characters Edmund, Steve, and Robert acknowledge that they can perform manual labor as well as perform open-heart surgery, sit on the Supreme Court, write literary classics, and sing Verdi and Puccini. By listing noteworthy things already done by black men, the play elevates black maleness to counter the many negative stereotypes about them. Critical reaction to *Cope* was mostly positive and the song-play garnered a Tony Award nomination and was the winner of the Outer Critics' Circle Award, two Obie Awards, two Drama Desk Awards, and an NAACP Image Award.

Encouraged by the success of *Cope* and cognizant of the scarcity of roles for black actors, Carroll revisited an earlier project *But Never Jam Today*, loosely basing it on Lewis Carroll's novels *Alice in Wonderland* and *Through the Looking Glass* but placing it within a black context. The 1979 version was reworked as a result of bad reviews for the original 1969 version and for equally bad reviews for the second remake in 1977 under a new title *Alice*. Although *But Never Jam Today* and its several rewrites flopped three times, it was the outstanding success of Carroll's 1976 song-play *Your Arms Too Short to Box with God* that put Carroll, Grant, and the Urban Arts Corps back on the cultural map. It received rave reviews in Italy and established Carroll as the first African American Woman to direct on Broadway.

The idea of *Your Arms Too Short to Box with God* resonated with theatergoers already wowed by the highly successful musicals *Godspell* (1971) and *Jesus Christ Superstar* (1971) that ushered in the Jesus movement and its flower children–inspired Christian rock music. However, Carroll, consistently wedded to her aesthetic vision, approached her telling of the Christ story by setting it in an atmosphere of gospel celebration. Freely based on the Book of Matthew, the song-play opens with members of the cast entering onstage as parishioners of a congregation. The minister, who proclaims to the audience "We're gonna have a good time," begins to narrate the story of Christ's death by crucifixion and his resurrection on the third day. As the story ensues, the choir becomes the cast of characters needed for the reenactment of the story. They change into biblical attire and join in the events being chronicled by the minister, and through contemporary and traditional gospel singing, rock, and calypso music, and the dance, they give life to this age-old biblical story. The story begins in the ancient past and ends in the present, as cast members return to their original roles. The second act bursts into a joyous gospel revival paying homage to some of the great gospel singers of the past. The play does not go without acknowledging, as one song states, "Everybody Has Their Own Way" of worshipping—an attempt to drive home one of the play's universal themes.

Carroll's *Your Arms Too Short to Box with God*, champions an art that speaks to issues of racial pride and uplift although she found dwelling on issues of mistreatment due to racism too "encumbering to [her] technique and to [her] work to dwell on that" (Mitchell 199). Noteworthy about this work was Carroll's insistence that in this all-black production Christ would have to be black. In the souvenir brochure from the 1980 Broadway run of the play, Carroll explained her motivation thus: "It was vitally important to do this show with a black Christ figure. In recent years, as black awareness has grown and black people have begun to like themselves better, we, as a people, have been able to deal with the serious concepts of black self-images. On another level, speaking to all people, having a black Jesus in the show only heightens the universality of the Christ figure." Carroll explains further that the color of her characters makes no difference to the telling of the story; therefore, culturally diverse audiences should be able to identify with the message. Critics recognized the success of Carroll's "total-theatre" concept, citing positively the play's strong musical numbers and staging. However, most were ambivalent in their assessment of her plot, character development, and originality.

Several weeks before *Your Arms Too Short to Box with God* was slated to open on Broadway, the Urban Arts Corps Theater premiered Carroll's *The Ups and Downs of Theophilus Maitland* on November 1, 1976. In this West Indian folktale that Carroll adapted for the stage, the play's hero and namesake is introduced to the audience as an aging widower. Upon seeing the beautiful villager Rosa, Theophilus falls head over heels in love with her; however, he discovers during their courtship that he is impotent. His happiness threatened, taunted by both lovers' families and the other Jamaican villagers because of his problem, he consults an obeah woman who gives him a potion that will make him virile again. Eagerly, he gulps down her potion all at once and goes blind. However, after much singing and dancing, the hero's vision and virility are restored and the play ends happily (Hughes 81).

Reminiscent of *Cope*, Carroll's *When Hell Freezes Over, I'll Skate* again employs her tried-and-true song-play format as the aesthetic vehicle for reflecting on the positive and negative aspects of the black experience in America through poetry, song, and dance. Using the poetry of Paul Laurence Dunbar, lindamichellebaron, Countee Cullen, Langston Hughes, and others, this exuberant, vivacious musical celebrates the sheer joy—and survival—of black music, song, and poetry since the days of America's Civil War. Employing styles that run the gamut from gospel to disco and from slave quarter sermons to contemporary black poetry, the poems provide their own dramatic pacing and propels along the loosely constructed plot. As the title suggests, the hell of racism and sexism so oppress people of color and women that one cannot move beyond basic survival mode until such a hell . . . "freezes over." Carroll revisits a theme that she repeatedly addresses in all of her works: whether one can positively self-identify as black, particularly in a country where blackness is always scrutinized, sensationalized, then trivialized.

CRITICAL RECEPTION

Clifford Mason, a playwright and critic who interviewed Vinnette Carroll for a *New York Times* article, was intrigued by the fact that the very talented director of such Broadway hits as *Cope* and *Your Arms Too Short* had not done more mainstream, typically constructed plays. Carroll's response reveals a major problem with how capitalism may dictate and (in some cases) warp an artist's aesthetic vision: ". . . the chief reason that I do so many musicals is that white producers won't pick up anything intellectual by us, no matter how good it is. They only want the singing and the dancing. It's where the quick money is" (D4).

Carroll's choice of the song-play as the vehicle for her theatrical works *Trumpets*, *Cope*, *Your Arms Too Short*, and *Skate* proved a hit with the critics, whose reception to the plays ensured and secured for them a successful run on Broadway. *Trumpets* received national and international success. *New York Times* critic Lewis Funke describes the 1963 production as "richly and beautifully embellished" with gospel music (qtd. in "Vinnette," FAMU 4). It ran for 161 performances Off Broadway at the Astor Place Theatre and was selected to represent the United States at the Theatre des Nations festival in Paris. Recognizing the infectiously entertaining appeal of *Cope* and *Your Arms Too Short*, Clive Barnes of the *New York Times* wrote, "Miss Carroll earlier conceived the long-running musical *Don't Bother Me I Can't Cope*, and something of the same energy runs through this present show. But *Your Arms Too Short* . . . has an onrushing vitality that practically pins you to your seat" (qtd. in Hughes 28).

Her adaptations of other works, however, did not fare as well. Although the critics uniformly praised the musical talent of the cast for *But Never Jam Today*, the play's conceptualization and the writing met with strong negative reactions. The *New York Times*'s Mel Gussow dubbed it "a case of missed opportunities," while Clive Barnes of the *New York Post,* when proposing whether the musical was worth doing, answered with a "resounding No!" However, the harshest criticism came from Glenne Currie in an August 8, 1979, review in the United Press International: "The staging and direction are unimaginative, the choreography—uninventive, the costumes—like 95 per cent [*sic*] of the book—downright silly" (qtd. in Hughes 13).

Likewise, overall reaction to another Carroll adaptation, *Theophilus Maitland*, was negative, and Richard Eder of the *New York Times*, though acknowledging the musical's delightful opening, pans it in the closing sentences of his review: "The play plays out; the humor gets coarser and triter. By the time it ends, with someone proclaiming the tired double entendre— 'You can't keep a good man down'—the life has vanished and we wish we had" (qtd. in Hughes 81).

In her use of the song-play, Carroll always strove to address the ironies present in the United States: the so-called differences between whites and blacks versus the actual similarities of all humans; the stereotypes of blacks versus the ideal (and often real images that she knew; and the seduction of racism, sexism, and other forms of human exploitation versus the power of transformation and transcendence in the willing human. Her critics found in her works—unlike how they usually assessed the works of Amiri Baraka* and Ed Bullins*—an emphasis on healing rifts rather than separating because of them. Although she often received negative reviews, the critics always found in her works a sense of human goodwill and black affirmation, yet rarely if any anger.

BIBLIOGRAPHY

Dramatic Works by Vinnette Carroll

Alice (with Micki Grant). 1977. Unpublished.
All the Kings Men. 1974. Unpublished.
Beyond the Blues. 1964. Unpublished.
Bury the Dead (with Micki Grant). 1971. Unpublished.
But Never Jam Today. 1969/1979. Unpublished.
Croesus and the Witch (with Micki Grant). 1971. New York: Broadway Play Publishing, n.d.

Don't Bother Me, I Can't Cope (with Micki Grant). New York: French, 1972.
Don't Bother Me I Can't Cope. Broadway original cast album. LP. Polydor, 1972.
I'm Laughing but I Ain't Tickled (with Micki Grant). 1976. Unpublished.
Love Power. 1974. Unpublished.
Step Lively Boy (with Micki Grant). 1973. Unpublished.
Trumpets of the Lord. 1963. Unpublished.
The Ups and Downs of Theophilus Maitland (with Micki Grant). 1974. Unpublished.
What You Gonna Name That Pretty Little Baby. 1978. Unpublished.
When Hell Freezes Over, I'll Skate. 1979. Unpublished.
When Hell Freezes Over, I'll Skate. By Vinnette Carroll. Dir. Vinnette Carroll and Emile
    Ardolino. Perf. Jeffrey Anderson-Gunter, Brenda Braxton, Lynne Clifton
    Allen, Cleavant Derricks, Clinton Derricks-Carroll, Reginald Vel Johnson, Lynne
    Thigpen, and Marilyn Winbush. Videocassette. A presentation of Thirteen/WNET
    New York, Great Performances. Broadway Theatre Archives, 1979.
Your Arms Too Short to Box with God (with Micki Grant). 1976/1980. Unpublished.
Your Arms Too Short to Box with God. Broadway original cast album. LP. MCA, 1977.

Studies of Vinnette Carroll's Dramatic Works

Hughes, Catharine. "Your Arms Too Short to Box with God." *American Theatre Annual:
    1976–77*. Ed. Catherine Hughes. Vol. 1. Detroit: Gale, 1977.
Katz, Judith. *The Business of Show Business: A Guide to Career Opportunities behind
    the Scenes in Theatre and Film*. New York: Barnes, 1981.
Mason, Clifford. "Vinette Carroll Is Still in There Swinging." New York Times 19 Dec.
    1976: D4.
McClinton, Calvin A. *The Work of Vinnette Carroll: An African American Theatre Artist*.
    Lewiston: Mellen, 2000.
Mitchell, Lofton. *Voices of the Black Theatre*. Clinton: White, 1975.
Moritz, Charles. *Current Biography Yearbook, 1983*. New York: Wilson, 1983.
Peterson, Bernard L., Jr. "Vinnette Carroll." *Contemporary Black American Play-
    wrights and Their Plays: A Biographical Directory and Dramatic Index*. West-
    port: Greenwood, 1988. 99–102.
Robinson, Alice M., Vera Mowry Roberts, and Milly S. Barranger, eds. "Vinnette Car-
    roll." *Notable Women in the American Theatre: A Biograhical Dictionary*. New
    York: Greenwood, 1989: 111–114.
"Vinnette Carroll." FAMU Literature Resource Center (Apr. 2003): 1–11. 12 Apr. 2003
    <.../LitRC?c=1&ai=16185&ste=6&docNum=H1000016084&bConts=
    4196511&tab=1&vrsn=04/12/2003>.
"Vinnette Carroll." *Women of Color, Women of Word: Female Playwrights* (Sept.
    2002): 1–5. 25 Sept. 2002 <http://www.scils.rutgers.edu/~cybers/carroll2.html>.
Woll, Allen. "Vinnette Carroll." *Dictionary of the Black Theatre: Broadway, Off-Broad-
    way, and Selected Harlem Theatre*. Westport: Greenwood, 1983. 194–195.

PEARL CLEAGE
(1948–)

Gwendolyn S. Jones

BIOGRAPHY

Pearl Cleage is a prolific writer in a variety of art forms: drama, poetry, short fiction, novels, and essays. This writer has also earned success in such professional pursuits as playwright in residence, educator, artistic director of communications, performer, contributor to periodicals and journals, and editor. Ms. Cleage, a resident of Atlanta, Georgia, is currently enjoying the status of full-time writer; she has an August 2003 publication date for her next novel (personal interview).

Born in Springfield, Massachusetts, in 1948, Cleage grew up in Detroit, Michigan. Her father founded and developed Black Christian Nationalism and established an influential secessionist church, The Shrine of the Black Madonna. She credits him with having "a profound influence on her life and her work" (Ollison par. 6). Books and storytelling played a large role during her childhood, no doubt influenced by the fact that her mother was a reading specialist. Described as an academically gifted student in high school, Cleage acknowledged Naomi Long Madgett, nationally known poet, as "having first recognized her talent and encouraged her to consider a writing career" ("Madgett" par. 4). Influenced by the political and intellectual unrest of the 1960s and 1970s, many themes appearing in her writings are reflections of events occurring during those times.

Cleage completed part of her undergraduate studies at Howard University (1966–1969). While there, she studied playwriting and had two one-act plays produced: *Hymn for Rebels* and *Duet for Three Voices*. She spent short periods of study at Yale University and at the University of West Indies before earning a bachelor of arts degree in drama from Spelman College in Atlanta, Georgia, in 1971. There, she had a one-act play, *The Sale*, produced. She completed her graduate courses at Atlanta University.

Her career choices have included a variety of positions in the media. She has held such positions as director of communications for the city of Atlanta; staff writer, interviewer, and executive producer with Atlanta television stations; and founding editor of *Catalyst*, a literary magazine. Cleage has also published poetry, including books entitled *We Don't Need No Music* and *Dear Dark Faces: Portraits of a People*; best-selling novels, including *What Looks Like Crazy on an Ordinary Day* and *I Wish I Had a Red Dress*; and collected essays, including *Mad at Miles: A Black Woman's Guide to Truth* and *Deals with the Devil and Other Reasons to Riot*.

A cofounder of Just Us Theater Company in Atlanta, Cleage received increased recognition when she became playwright in residence. Here, she wrote and produced *puppetplay*, *Good News*, and *Essentials*. These productions in the early 1980s probably marked the beginning of her career as a dramatist.

MAJOR WORKS AND THEMES

In her plays, Pearl Cleage blends personal experiences and observations with a feminine perspective. With the overriding theme of the liberation of African Americans, particularly African American women, her works lend themselves to social-political discussion and to literary analysis. Believing that the black woman's voice must be heard and that black women must empower themselves, her works explore the conditions of African American women, treating such topics as sexism, race, racism, love, and violence against women in the African American community. For example, *Chain* deals with the impact of drugs; *puppetplay* relates the conflicts evident in marriage. Two actors, representing ambivalence, portray the wife; the husband is represented by a seven-foot marionette. *Hospice* displays the need for strong relationships: between women. Here, a mother and daughter have a dysfunctional relationship: each is suffering in her own personal pain. Alice, the mother, an ex-patriot poet, has terminal cancer; Jenny, the daughter, now pregnant, was abandoned as a child for Alice's career and freedom. This misery is expressed with compassion and humor. In *Late Bus to Mecca*, a prostitute offers love and support to another African American woman.

Another characteristic of Cleage's work is that the characters she develops are working people who in their everyday lives may have lived through periods of historic significance. What the audience sees and hears are their reactions to these events and to the public figures and celebrities who also experienced these events. This feature of her writing is seen in *Flyin' West*, *Blues for an Alabama Sky*, and *Bourbon at the Border*, each based on historical fact. They were commissioned by Kenny Leon, artistic director of the Alliance Theatre Company. In each of these plays, the events are presented through the eyes of ordinary people who are regular, working people. Celebrities and public figures are discussed by the characters but are not presented in the plays.

Flyin' West is the most widely produced of the three. The story line was influenced by the writings of Ida B. Wells. Set in 1898 in an all-black town in Kansas, a family of black women joined the migration in the late 1800s from the South to the West. The issues presented are contemporary and include economics, spousal abuse, women controlling their own lives, intraracial dynamics, and gender dynamics. *Flyin' West* depicts the close relationships of women, their bonding, and their collective strength.

Set at the end of the Harlem Renaissance, the questions raised in *Blues for an Alabama Sky* are also contemporary: topics include birth control, abortion, sexual freedom, duty to self, duty to community, and black-on-black violence. A social issue that is dramatized is that of "new family groupings"; this happens when people migrate, then acquire new "family" members in the new location. *Blues for an Alabama Sky* is Cleage's first play in which a black woman did not triumph at the end.

Bourbon at the Border is a civil rights drama and treats the aftermath of yet another historical event. The young activists, Charlie and May, who went south to help register voters, are now middle aged. They are two wounded survivors of the Mississippi Freedom Summer of 1964. The action takes place in 1995, but Charlie and May are still not able to cope with the traumatic events of thirty years ago. Another conflict is that there is a gap in the understanding of the events between the participants and their now-adult children.

CRITICAL RECEPTION

Pearl Cleage enjoys consistent production in diverse venues, including regional theaters; many plays also appear in print. She "first gained widespread recognition as a playwright with the production of *puppetplay* by the Negro Ensemble Company in 1983" (Giles, "Motion" 709). Her plays reflect social, political, and economic situations; her style is forthright, and the black woman's voice is heard. She is articulate, possesses real talent, and exudes energy ("Madget" par. 6). Woodie King, Jr. says that it is obvious that she (and other black writers) love black people (iii).

Blues for an Alabama Sky received mixed reviews. Mark Turvin sees a valid and important viewpoint being presented, but sees "a behemoth of a script . . . which drags its feet and is preachy and repetitive" (par. 2). What Winston Barclay sees is "vivid characters with desires and dreams" (par. 8).

Paul Harris reflects the sentiments of a number of critics when he says it "explores a wide range of human emotions; the dialogue is lively and succinct; it is relevant to today's audiences . . ." (par. 6). He goes on to say it "loses its edge at the finale" (par. 8).

Darwin Turner describes *Flyin' West* as a "powerful and captivating play" (667). Chris Jones says that Pearl Cleage crafts an "awful plot," but with "appealing and credible characters" and with "humor in the script" (par. 3). That her work is critically acclaimed can be seen in the number of grants and awards received from such organizations as the National Endowment for the Arts, the Arts Council of Georgia, and AT&T On Stage Program.

Hospice won five AUDELCO (Audience Development Committee) Recognition Awards for Best Play, Best Playwright, and outstanding achievement Off Broadway (King 45). Arlene McKanic, of the *New York Amsterdam News*, thought that *Hospice* may not be the best, but it is interesting and worthwhile (22).

BIBLIOGRAPHY

Dramatic Works by Pearl Cleage

Banana Bread. Videotaped and premiered as part of local PBS series *Playhouse 30*, Atlanta, Georgia, 1982.

Blues for an Alabama Sky. First produced at the Alliance Theatre Company, Atlanta Georgia, 1994.

Bourbon at the Border. First produced at the Alliance Theatre Company, Atlanta Georgia, 1997.

"Chain" (one-act play). First produced Off Broadway by Women's Project and Productions and the New Federal Theater, 1992. Published in *Playwrighting Women: Seven Plays from the Women's Project*. Ed. Julia Miles. Portsmouth: Heinemann, 1993. 62–81.

Duet for Three Voices (one-act play). First produced at Howard University, Washington, DC, 1968.

Essentials. First produced at Just Us Theater Company, Atlanta, Georgia, 1985.

Flyin' West. First produced at Alliance Theatre Company, Atlanta, Georgia, 1992.

Good News. First produced at Just Us Theater Company, Atlanta, Georgia, 1984.

Hospice. First produced Off Broadway at Henry Street Settlement's New Federal Theater, 1983. Published in *New Plays for the Black Theatre*. Ed. Woodie King, Jr. Chicago: Third World, 1989; and in *Callaloo* 10.1 (Winter 1987): 40–62

Hymn for the Rebels (one-act play). First produced at Howard University, Washington, DC, 1967.

Late Bus to Mecca. First produced at Judith Anderson Theatre, New York City, 1992. Published in *Playwrighting Women: Seven Plays from the Women's Project*. Ed. Julia Miles. Portsmouth: Heinemann, 1993.

Porch Songs. First produced at Phoenix Theater, Indianapolis, 1985.

PR: A Political Romance (with Walter J. Huntley). First produced at Just Us Theater Company, 1985.

puppetplay. First produced at Just Us Theater, Atlanta, Georgia, 1981.

The Sale. First produced at Spelman College, Atlanta, Georgia, 1972.

Studies of Pearl Cleage's Dramatic Works

Andrews, William L., Frances Smith Foster, and Trudier Harris, eds. "Cleage, Pearl." *The Oxford Companion to African American Literature*. New York: Oxford University Press, 1997. 156–157.

Barclay, Winston. "Iowa Summer Rep2002 Offers Change of Pace with Cleage Readings." 5 July 2002: 18 pars. 5 Apr. 2003 <http://www.uiowa.edu/~ournews/2002/july/0705cleagereadings.html>.

Bell-Scott, Patricia. *Life Notes: Personal Writings by Contemporary Black Women*. New York: Norton, 1994. 345–347.

"Blues for an Alabama Sky." *American Theatre* 13 (1996): 21. Alabama Virtual Library Remote Access. Info Trac One File.

"Blues for an Alabama Sky by Pearl Cleage." 29 Aug. 2002: 7 pars. 5 Apr. 2003 <http://www.kckcc.edu/theatre/blues_for_an_alabama_sky/>.

Carroll, Rebecca. *I Know What the Red Clay Looks Like: The Voice and Vision of Black Women Writers*. New York: Southern, 1994. 49–62.

Cleage, Pearl. Personal interview. 4 Apr. 2003.

"Cleage, Pearl." *African-American History and Culture*. 10 Feb. 1999: 18 pars. 7 Apr. 2003 <http://www.fofweb.com/Onfiles/Afhe/AFHCSearchDetail.asp?>.

"Cleage, Pearl Michelle." *Who's Who Among African Americans*. 11th ed. Detroit: Gale, 1998. 244.

Giles, Freda Scott. "In Their Own Words: Pearl Cleage and Glenda Dickerson Define Womanist Theatre." *The Womanist*. Spring 1997: 51 pars. 7 Apr. 2003 http://www.uga.edu/~womanist/giles2.1.htm>.

_____. "The Motion of Herstory: Three Plays by Pearl Cleage." *African American Review* 31 (1997): 709–711.

_____. Rev. of *Bourbon at the Border*, by Pearl Cleage. *African American Review* 31.4 (1997): 725.

Harris, Paul. "Blues for an Alabama Sky." An Arena Stage, Alliance Theatre Company, and Hartford Stage Company presentation of a play in two acts by Pearl Cleage. 6 July 1999: 12 pars. 9 Apr. 2003 <http://www.variety.com/index.asp?layout=print_review&reviewid=VE1117911327&categoryid=31>.

Jones, Chris. "Flyin' West." An Alabama Shakespeare Festival presentation of a play in two acts by Pearl Cleage. 9 Feb. 2001: 9 pars. 9 Apr. 2003 <http://www.variety.com/index.asp?layout=print_review&reviewid>.

King, Woodie Jr., ed. *New Plays for the Black Theatre*. Chicago: Third World, 1989.

Kinsman, Clare D., ed. "Lomax, Pearl Cleage." *Contemporary Authors: A Bio-Bibliographical Guide to Current Authors and their Works*. Detroit: Gale, 1974. 383.

"Madgett, Naomi Long." *African-American History and Culture*. 3 Jan. 1999: 16 pars. 8 Apr. 2003 <http://www.fofweb.com/Onfiles/Afhc/AFHCSeaarchDetail.asp?>.

Malinowski, Sharon, ed. "Cleage, Pearl (Michelle) 1948– (Pearl Cleage Lomax)." *Black Writers: A Selection of Sketches from Contemporary Authors*. 2nd ed. Detroit: Gale, 1994. 131–132.

McKanic, Arlene. "'Hospice' Shows Compassion." *New York Amsterdam News*. 22 May 2002: 22.

Madison, Cathy. "Home Sweet Homestead." *American Theatre* 9 (1992): 11.

Ollison, Rashod. "A Writer Feels Free to Follow Her Heart." *Philadelphia Inquirer* 1 Aug. 2001: 9 pars. 6 Apr. 2003. <http://web9.epnet.com/delivery.asp?>.

"Pearl Cleage." 8 Mar. 2001: 9 pars. 8 Apr. 2003. <http://www.africanpubs.com/Apps/bios/0456Cleage Pearl.asp?pic=>.

"pearl cleage." *Women of Color Women of Word—African American Female Playwrights—Pearl Cleage*. 18 Feb. 1999: 12 pars. 8 Apr. 2003. <http://www.scils.rutgers.edu/~cybers/cleage2.html>.

"Pearl (Michelle) Cleage." Literature Resource Center. 2 Oct. 2000: 7 pars. 8 Apr. 2003 <http://galenet.galegroup.com/servlet/LITC?c=6&ste=32&printer>.

Perkins, Kathy A., and Roberto Uno. *Contemporary Plays by Women of Color: An Anthology*. New York: Routledge, 1996.

Rush, Theressa Gunnels, ed. "Lomax, Pearl Cleage." *Black American Writers Past and Present: A Biographical and Bibliographical Dictionary*. Vol. 2. Metuchen: Scarecrow, 1975. 497–498.

Turner, Darwin T. *An Anthology: Black Drama in America*. 2nd ed. Washington, DC: Howard University Press, 1994. 667–724.

Turvin, Mark S. P. "Slow but Silky Blues." 7 Feb. 1999: 6 pars. 9 Apr. 2003 <http://www.goldfishpublishers.com/BluesforanAlabamasky_ATC.html>.

Warfield, Carolyn. "Candescent Pearl: Detroit-Born Playwright: One of America's Hottest Writers." ProQuest Information and Learning. <http://enw.softlineweb.com/record.asp?msel_from=100&msel_to>.

KATHLEEN CONWELL COLLINS (1942–1988)

Chandra Tyler Mountain

BIOGRAPHY

Kathleen Conwell Collins (also known as Kathleen Conwell or Kathleen Collins Prettyman) was born in Jersey City, New Jersey, on March 18, 1942, to Frank and Loretta Conwell. During the forty-six years of her short life, she managed to change the face and content of black womanist film. Her father worked as a mortician and then became the principal of a high school that is now named after him. He later became the first African American state legislator in New Jersey. After graduating from Skidmore College in Sarasota Springs, New York, Collins followed her father's political lead and became involved in the Student Nonviolent Coordinating Committee's (SNCC) thrust to help register voters in the South.

After obtaining her degree in philosophy and religion in 1963, Collins furthered her education at the Sorbonne in Paris, France. There she became interested in telling stories through film. She completed the master of arts degree in 1966 through the Sorbonne's Middlebury graduate program. She then returned to the United States and began her writing career while working on the editorial and production staff of WNET Radio in New York.

Collins's first short stories reflected her experiences in SNCC and France as well as the dilemmas of a young married woman. In 1974, shortly after her marriage to Douglass Collins ended, Kathleen joined the faculty of City College at the City University of New York as a professor of film history and screenwriting. In fact, it was her students, particularly Ronald Gray, who encouraged her to pursue a script she had previously abandoned. Adapting Jewish writer Henry H. Roth's fiction to film, Collins became the first African American woman to write, direct, and produce a full-length feature film. The screenplay-turned-film, *The Cruz Brothers and Mrs. Malloy*, about the struggle of three Puerto Rican brothers to survive in a small country town, won first prize in the Sinking Creek Film Festival.

Losing Ground followed in 1982 and won first prize at the Figueroa da Foz International Film Festival in Portugal. Other films to her credit include *Madame Flor* (1987) and *Conversations with Julie* (1988). Her films have been shown on the Learning Channel and the Public Broadcasting Station.

Among her plays are *In the Midnight Hour* (1981); *The Brothers* (1982), which was a finalist for the Susan Blackburn International Prize in Playwriting and voted one of the Best Plays of 1982 by the AUDELCO (Audience Development Committee) Awards Committee; and *The Reading* (1984), a one-act play about the conflict between white and black women, commissioned by the American Place Theatre. She also penned *Begin the Beguine* (1985), a collection of one-act plays produced at the Richard Allen Center for Culture and Arts in New York, a play about the first black aviatrix, Bessie Coleman; *Only the Sky Is Free* (1985), *While Older Men Speak* (1986), and *Looking for Jane* (1986). In 1987, Collins married Alfred E. Prettyman and completed her screenplay *Madame Flor*. In the spring of 1988, Conwell completed a novel, *Lollie: A Suburban Tale*, and in the summer of that year, she completed another screenplay, *Conversations with Julie*, about a mother and daughter coming to terms with separation.

In 1983, Collins was reacquainted with Alfred Prettyman, whom she had met years earlier. The two married four years later. Within one week of their marriage, Collins learned that she had cancer. She died in 1988, survived by her husband; her daughter, Nina; her two sons, Asa Hale and Emilio; a step-daughter, Meryl Prettyman; and a stepson, Evan Prettyman.

Although Collins wrote and produced a number of plays and films in her lifetime, one gets the feeling that she was only just beginning when she succumbed to cancer. Her influence extends to other black filmmakers such as Euzhan Palcy and Julie Dash both of whom honor her fearlessness and presence as a writer and filmmaker. Her work has been described as postmodern, iconoclastic, and experimental (Williams 39).

MAJOR WORKS AND THEMES

Many of Kathleen Conwell Collins's plays are no longer in print. Readily available at many university libraries are the screenplay *Losing Ground* and the dramas published in other anthologies, *The Brothers* and *In the Midnight Hour.* Her plays employ such themes as marital malaise, male dominance and impotence, freedom of expression, and the unglorified plight of the black middle class. Her protagonists are typically self-reflective women who move from a state of subjugation to empowerment. Collins's plays followed the "Blaxploitation" era and a number of plays and films that focused on the rise of blacks from poverty or "ghetto" life. She met a great deal of criticism because many feel that her plays have not been black centered or have lacked the requisite positive representations of black life. Despite such disapproval, Collins continued to write about the complexities of black life, some of which has little, if anything, to do with race.

The original screenplay *Losing Ground* led to the first independent feature film by an African American woman filmmaker. The "comedy drama," as the author describes it, is set in New York and centers around a married couple, Sara, a professor of Western philosophy, and her artist husband, Victor. Sara is a consummate philosophy professor, fixated on examining ecstasy from a rational perspective while her husband Victor is more concerned about ecstasy in a more experiential manner. Sara's students point out to her how lucky she is to have a husband in addition to her other good qualities. While Victor is a "genuine Negro success" (130), Sara struggles against becoming the stereotypical tragic mulatto. Sara is orderly, straightforward, practical, and logical. Victor counts on that. He is passionate, irreverent, and vulgar. Though Sara knows that her husband is a flirt and engages in extramarital affairs, she claims, in conversation with her mother, that she is jealous of his freedom, his ability to let go without inhibition and not the fact that he inserts his "thing" inside other women. This declaration is dismantled when Sara becomes annoyed and then enraged by Victor's flirtations with Celia, a young and vivacious Puerto Rican woman, in her presence.

Sara's students convince her to step out of her conventional box and play Frankie, in an archetypal reinterpretation of the Frankie and Johnnie story. It is through the drama, that Sara begins to grapple seriously with her practical, rational, philosophical leanings and begins to seek in a realistic way the ecstasy that up until now she only writes about.

The philosophy Sara pursues in the classroom and in her scholarship undergirds the drama, and the lessons the protagonist learns comes out of a realization that she has operated both in the classroom and in her home in a masculinist and limiting world. She resists both when she figuratively shoots Johnnie in the play-within-a play at the end of the drama.

The Brothers, named by Theatre Communications Groups as one of twelve outstanding plays of the 1982 season, was first presented at the American Place Theatre on March 31, 1982, under the direction of Billie Allen. The temporal scheme of the drama runs from February 1, 1948 (the assassination of Mahatma Gandhi), to April 5, 1968 (the assassination of Martin Luther King, Jr.). The play opens with Gandhi's assassination and the decision of thirty-one-year-old two-time Olympic champion Nelson, the youngest of the brothers, to remain in his bed forever. He declares that the "Negro life is a void" (302). The Edwards brothers—Lawrence, Franklin, Jeremy, and Nelson—and the one sister, Marietta, were reared to be proud and unlimited by the fact of their blackness. They were coached by their cruel and unrelenting father to pursue "whiteness" and white dreams.

The Brothers is a complex drama centered on the Edwards men, but focused on the Edwards women. For although entitled *The Brothers*, it is the women who take center stage and are involved in all of the action of the play. The men are only glimpsed through the women's comments and remembrances, and the men are so endowed with the speed, tenacity, and will of the Edwards men that their presence fills a room even though they are never seen on stage. We meet them off camera, in snatches of the others' conversation, but we know them as intimately as their wives know them.

The brothers are central and essential in the women's lives. The wives' and sister's conversation, actions, and attitudes are all restricted to the brothers' needs, wants, and dispositions. One Edwards wife, Caroline, works as a maid to put her husband, Lawrence, through school. Lawrence is an unscrupulous real estate agent who will stop at nothing to get the deal he wants. He treats Caroline no better for it. Their marriage is unstable and unpredictable, made worse by the loss of their child, Laura. Lillie, Franklin's first wife, dies from an unnamed disease; she wastes her potential by sitting by the phone waiting for calls of death, for at the time of her death, Franklin is a mortician studying to become a teacher; later, he becomes a politician. To avoid having his mother-in-law gain custody of his children, Franklin marries Letitia, a thirty-eight-year-old virgin when they meet, whom he belittles and embarrasses because she does not measure up to Lillie's stature or grace. Witty Danielle, Nelson's wife, used to the high life of partying and drinking, cannot forgive Nelson for breaking his promise to give her the world. We never meet Aurora, Jeremy's wife, because, as Letitia points out, he's the only one who had the sense enough to get away from them. There is only one sister in the Edwards family, Marietta; she is unmarried because she believed her father would find her love interest too black in skin color and in aspiration.

The wives are sexually repressed and dissatisfied. Their frustrated potential is dwarfed by their husband's needs, wants, and expectations. The brothers are so caught up in brooding over what being a Negro means, and Marietta is so caught up in her brothers, that they take no note of the history taking place all around them. They make little notice of Gandhi's or King's assassinations, and one gets the sense that they have wasted the last twenty years on themselves.

In the Midnight Hour is an unusual drama with a twelve-hour time span. Set in 1962 Harlem, the drama focuses on the Daniels' family members and their own personal dreams (literal and figurative). Each family member—Ralph, Lillie, Anna, and Ben—wishes to paint a canvass with his or her memories and hold forever with him or her the good times in the family parlor where they talked, danced, and entertained and were entertained by their regular guests: Floyd, a rejected priest turned itinerant philosopher, and Chips, a pianist.

Ralph, the father, is obsessed with finding the truth. Recovering from years of depression and rage, he firmly believes that, as his psychiatrist teaches, anger is the only truth. He carves figurines, tables, chairs, dollhouses, and so on out of wood, believing that one can carve out the right life in the same manner that he skillfully carves with a carving knife.

Lillie, good-natured wife and mother, lives in the past of her own dreams, to an extent. She forgives Ralph for the years he psychologically absents himself from their marriage and determines to affect the perfect disposition for the perfect mother and wife for picture-perfect moments with her family and its closest friends.

Twenty-year-old Anna, nurtured for greatness, has just been introduced to the civil rights movement and is enthralled by the idea of doing something magnanimous to help others.

Ben, the eighteen-year-old son, rides an emotional roller coaster, possibly spun into action by his memories of racial awareness when he was a teenager, when he and his father were "ace boon coons" but he had not been taught that there were "Negro reasons" for some of the things he experiences. Ben and Anna marshal Christine, a young Barnard student from Boston, into their lives and she serves to balance out and lend something a little more grounded, mundane, and ordinary to the Daniels household.

In the middle of the play—in the middle of the night—the playwright ushers us into a scene that takes place in both the present and the far future. In the illusory, derivative properties of dream, by the end of this scene we are slightly disoriented but are given insight to the future for this family of dreamers—Ralph's therapist-god commits suicide and topples Ralph's progress; Lillie has lost her son, thus the good times and perfect picture she wants to create; Anna, in searching for the genuine trust and love she shared with her brother and in her quest to do something spectacular and different, has gone through several marriages and babies to end up lonely and cynical. Each family members' fate punctuates Ben's "present" story that he relates to Christine about his experience with Bucky Rogers and Walter Duffy, his private-school classmates, whose visit to Harlem when they were fifteen made him painfully aware of their differences.

In the closing scene of the drama, after Ben upsets Christine by foolishly jumping from a pier, we are left with a sense that it is Ben's anger that will ultimately lead to his and the family's ruin in the future.

Inspired by Lorraine Hansberry's* aesthetic, Collins wrote life as she saw it and did not allow herself to be fettered by constraints placed on African American writers. She looked at African Americans as human subjects not race subjects. When her plays did focus on issues of race, she rendered what she felt were honest portrayals of black life and not portrayals that exaggerated or posed overly positive aspects of black existence in America while ignoring the often negative and daunting realities. Rather than seeing black problems as simple manifestations of white oppression, through her writing, Collins suggests that much of it has to do with the internal dialogue and pressures we impose on ourselves. Her plays are deeply psychological in nature. She integrates certain elements of her personal life into her plays and invites us to go beyond the surface meaning of things and think about the values and the attitudes imposed on us by society and how we choose to deal with them.

CRITICAL RECEPTION

Though Kathleen Conwell Collins's plays deal with some of the deeper, psychological issues involved in individuals' lives and though she has won numerous awards and fellowships for her work, there has been little critical commentary on her plays. There is no doubt that she is a pioneering African American filmmaker and playwright, ushering in an era of black women filmmakers such as Julie Dash, who was her student at City University of New York, and Euzhan Palcy. John Williams mentions her influence in his exploration and review of black women filmmakers. He points out that though critical reception was less than positive in regard to much of Collins's work, she paved the way for a generation of black women filmmakers. He contends that Collins wrote dramas and produced feature films that wrote against what she saw as the "phallo-centric conventions of white Hollywood cinema" (Williams 38). He also writes that the few critics who "deigned to comment on [*Losing Ground*] were less than receptive to its originality (39). He further argues that most critics "simply did not know how to comment on *Losing Ground*'s subversive vision of black culture." Some even took issue with the very notion of a "black female philosophy professor" as entailing "too much of a willing suspension of disbelief" (39).

Mark Reid, like Williams, acknowledges Collins's work and its influence. He reads *Losing Ground* as a womanist text and notes that "Collins speaks of an 'imperfect synthesis' of the African American condition" (386).

Frank Rich in his *New York Times* review of *The Brothers*, while commenting on the weaknesses of the play's dialogue and limiting form, writes, "Miss Collins is a promising writer. She is capable of passions both tender and angry; she can be funny; she is also, to borrow a line from her text, 'fond of the sound of words' " (C13).

The fact that there has been little critical attention to Collins's work does not diminish the quality of her work. She was a playwright writing life as she saw it, perhaps a bit ahead of her critical moment.

BIBLIOGRAPHY

Dramatic Works by Kathleen Conwell Collins

Begin the Beguine. 1985. Unpublished.

"The Brothers." 1982. *Nine Plays by Black Women*. Ed. Margaret B. Wilkerson. New York: Mentor, 1986. 293–346.

"In the Midnight Hour." 1981. *The Women's Project*. Ed. Julia Miles. New York: Performance Arts Journal Publications and American Place Theatre, 1980. 35–83.

Looking for Jane. 1986. Unpublished.

"Losing Ground: An Original Screenplay." 1982. *Screenplays of the African American Experience*. Ed. Phyllis Rauch Klotman. Bloomington: Indiana University Press, 1991. 119–185.

Only the Sky Is Free. 1985. Unpublished.

The Reading. 1984. Unpublished.

While Older Men Speak. 1986. Unpublished.

Studies of Kathleen Conwell Collins's Dramatic Works

Brown, Janet. *Taking Center Stage: Feminism in Contemporary U.S. Drama*. Metuchen: Scarecrow, 1991.

Campbell, Loretta. "Reinventing Our Image: Eleven Black Women Filmmakers." *Heresies* 4.4 (1983): 58–62.

Nicholson, David. "A Commitment to Writing: A Conversation with Kathleen Collins Prettyman." *Black Film Review* 5.1 (1988–1989): 6–15.

Reid, Mark A. "Dialogic Modes of Representing Africa(s): Womanist Film." *Black American Literature Forum* 25.2 (Summer 1991): 375–388.

Rich, Frank. "Theatre: Black Anguish in 'Brothers'." *New York Times* 6 Apr. 1982: C13.

Williams, John. "Re-creating Their Media Image: Two Generations of Black Women Filmmakers." *Cineaste* 20.3 (Summer 1993): 38–42.

J(OAN) CALIFORNIA COOPER (?–   )

Tarshia L. Stanley

BIOGRAPHY

J. California Cooper's adamant refusal to name the year of her birth is not only reflective of the fierce way in with she guards her personal life, but also bespeaks the passion she has for her work. Born to Joseph and Maxine Lincoln Cooper in Berkeley, California, she remains a prolific and important African American writer. Often recognized for the strong moral themes in her work, Cooper values privacy, family, and intimacy. She is said to have been a "secret writer" whose work was pushed to new levels by her mother's refusal to let her continue to play with paper dolls after she was seventeen. Cooper maintains that the way in which she imagined paper dolls to speak to one another, "he said, she said," naturally led to her fascination with dialogue. Since she could no longer have her dolls act out the scenes she fantasized, she wrote them down, and thus gave birth to her first incarnation as a playwright.

J. California Cooper was married and a mother soon after she graduated from high school. She does not speak about her personal life except to say that her daughter, Paris A. Williams, is at the center of it, and that her mother is the source from which her fascination with wisdom sprang. Cooper maintains that her relationship with her mother was so effectual and passionate that she wanted to protect the name her mother gave her—keep it for herself in some way—and professionally uses only her first initial. She is connected to her birthplace and the birthplace of her father (Marshall, Texas) in ways that are reinforced throughout her writings. Subsequently, she adopted the name California and spent many years living in the small town of Marshall. The rural area in Texas was, for many years, crucial to her writing, because it provided the right balance of privacy and connection. There, Cooper was able to hear her writing voice and connect to her spiritual roots, if not to the townspeople. She says that no one knew her in Marshall and that the isolation was necessary. Critics often note the anomalousness of one who is so fervent about connection in her writing but who must dwell in isolation to produce it.

In 1984, Alice Walker launched Wild Trees Press, by publishing Cooper's first collection of stories, *A Piece of Mine.* Cooper credits Walker with encouraging her to write fiction and giving her a venue from which to present it. Walker called Cooper's work reminiscent of Zora Neale Hurston* and Langston Hughes* and describes it as deceptively simple. In the early 1990s, Cooper moved back to California to be close to her daughter and has continued to write powerful collections of short stories and novels. She has been called one of the most influential African American writers of the twentieth century and continues to be most widely known for her short stories and novels.

MAJOR WORKS AND THEMES

Interviews with J. California Cooper are filled with her delightful and unconventional anecdotes about life and living. She not only has a love and a desire for wisdom but an insatiable need to share it through her work. While Cooper is best known for her fiction, her beginning as a playwright is what first garnered her critical recognition. In the 1970s, the Berkeley Black Repertory Theatre, under the direction of Nora Vaughan, began producing Cooper's plays. Cooper's plays were performed in local theaters, on college campuses, and on public television. Cooper has seventeen plays to her credit, and it is apparent, even in these early works, that she is concerned with illustrating daily life in "parable" form. She makes a great show of presenting moral choices and is unafraid to make value judgments about her characters.

One of Cooper's recurring themes involves the lives of women. Her work is concerned about the ways in which her female characters are often complicit in their own destruction, as well as articulating the ensuing reverberations for these women, their families, and their communities. For example, in *How Now?* (1973), a mother has grown used to receiving welfare benefits for her handicapped child. The woman has become not only accustomed, but also pathologically complacent, as she encourages her crippled daughter to get pregnant in order that they might remain on government assistance. Cooper's style is a bit dictatorial because of its obviousness, but is nonetheless potent because of her mastery of character and dialogue. Cooper returns often to this thematic in work such as *The Mother*. In this play the principle character abandons her three children in search of a better life bathed in city lights. When she returns a quarter of a century later, her children are not children, and she must deal with disillusioned adults and the seeds she has sown.

Cooper's treatises do not stop at mothering and the powerful responsibility it engenders. The idea of women's sacrifice is also at the heart of her work. Both the protagonists in *Loved to Death* and *Killing of Kindness* are young women who are undone by their virtue. Seemingly honorable attributes such as love and kindness end by killing the women because they don't know how to mete them out, and often forget to include themselves in the dosage.

However, Cooper's women are not all self-effacing and self-sacrificing. In *Not One of a Kind* and *One for the Money,* it is the protagonists' inability to think of anyone but themselves that is their ruin. Particularly, in *One for the Money* the author begins a discourse on drug abuse, which she will return to in her fiction, as a kind of self-centeredness on the part of the abuser, rather than solely a victimization.

Not all of Cooper's work is so bleak in terms of the choices the principle characters make or the situations in which they find themselves. Many of her early themes include narratives by and about elder folk. Contrary to much of current societal notions about aging, several of Cooper's plays are about the life lessons older people have learned and that they try to share with younger people. This is the case in *Say What You Willomay*. *Too Hep to Be Happy* features an octogenarian discussing the shortcomings of her male friend. In keeping with this thematic, it was for her 1978 play *Strangers* that Cooper earned the Black Playwright of the Year Award. *Stranger* is about a couple, who after having been married for more than fifty years, struggle to redefine themselves and their union.

As a kind of griot, Cooper strives to connect generations, and reinforce through her dramas the importance of knowledge that has been handed down. Their understanding of and reliance on this wisdom is directly proportional to the ability of her characters to choose the more advantageous paths in life.

When Cooper writes about the sexual lives of her characters, she is more writing about their need for connection than the act itself. *Everytime It Rains* is a controversial look at a woman who manages to talk a would-be rapist out of attacking her. In the ensuing drama, she comes to understand his aggression as in many ways a manifestation of her own loneliness and the two marry. One reviewer of Cooper's protagonist in *The Unintended* compares it to the work of Tennesee Williams. The central character, who is thirty-five and still a virgin, suddenly involves herself in a sexual relationship. Abandoned and robbed by a con artist, she turns to a "gentle hunchback" who provides the money she needs to pay for her room at the motel, in exchange for sex. This trafficking eventually becomes affection and the craftsmanship of Cooper is once again apparent. Cooper continues to examine love and sex in *One Hour or Forever*. This is an experimental play and is staged in darkness as a cover for an illicit affair. The audience is made privy to what it costs these covert lovers to be together, and again Cooper is pointing to choices made out of emotion rather responsibility.

Although most of her characters are troubled and in trouble, Cooper drives to the heart of their matters. She unearths loneliness, the desire for connection, the often desperateness of their situations, and offers the audience the opportunity to watch the characters make choices for or against their dilemmas.

While much of her work is centered on the lives of women, Cooper does, indeed, have male protagonists in her early work. Both *Loners* and *System, Suckers, and Success* illustrate the lives of two young men who pursue the American Dream and financial success only to return to family and connection as the real essence of accomplishment. The theme is much the same in *Weight of Clay*, except that she returns to the female protagonist in order to discuss the ways in which real happiness must spring from internal sources, rather than popular designs for success. *Shed a Tear* takes place at the funeral of a man whose illegitimate son is the only one who grieves, and even then, much of the sadness if for what might have been. Throughout her work, Cooper returns to the familiar thematic in which life is full of choices, and the correct ones are never made based solely on selfish desires.

Like the fable writer or the storyteller, Cooper weaves life lessons in her dramas. Her characters are pensive or self-interested, passionate or self-effacing, but they are more than anything emblematic of the human condition. Apparent in all of Cooper's plays is her own belief in right and wrong and her fascination with gaining wisdom. According to Cooper in a Rebecca Carroll interview:

My writing is an accumulation of information from things I've read, things I've seen and observed. My mother used to tell me: "Any fool can get some fun, you need to get some sense." . . . Since I was a little girl, I have always liked wisdom. (66)

While the subject matter of Cooper's work is most often intense, she did author a play called *Moments* that is described as "a light musical," and *Monologues* that is, of course, a series of soliloquies. Yet, Cooper the dramatist remains passionate in her convictions about truth and lies, right and wrong, and sees life not as the pursuit of happiness, but wisdom. For Cooper, true wisdom will, by design, yield happiness.

CRITICAL RECEPTION

While there have been numerous articles and book reviews written about J. California Cooper's fiction, the scholarly work on her plays is virtually nonexistent. Eileen Joyce Ostrow's *Center Stage: An Anthology of Twenty-One Contemporary Black-American Plays* contains only one of Cooper's plays—*Loners*. There is also a very brief biographical sketch in which Nora Vaughn of the Berkeley Black Repertory Theatre is given credit for "discovering" J. California Cooper. Indeed, it is quite difficult to find any of Cooper's plays. Most of the plays have never been officially collected into an anthology or written about in a critical context. There are several investigations that examine her work on the whole and may briefly mention her dramatic work.

Since many of Cooper's plays are, in many ways, forerunners to her fiction, it may be feasible to extrapolate some of the theories about her novels and short stories to her playwriting. Barbara Jean Marshall's essay, "Kitchen Table Talk: J. California's Use of Nommo-Female Bonding and Transcendence," is specifically about Cooper's short stories, which she wrote immediately after her plays. Given her popularity in circles of fiction and the current relative obscurity in which she resides as a playwright, there is, at the moment, a dearth of scholarship surrounding Cooper's dramatic work.

BIBLIOGRAPHY

Dramatic Works by J(oan) California Cooper

Everytime It Rains. Written and performed 1970s–mid-1980s. Unpublished.
How Now? 1973. Unpublished.
Killing of Kindness. Written and performed 1970s–mid-1980s. Unpublished.
"Loners." 1991. *Center Stage.* Champaign: University of Illinois Press, 1991.
Loved to Death. Written and performed 1970s–mid-1980s. Unpublished.
Moments (Musical). Written and performed 1970s–mid-1980s. Unpublished.
Monologues. Written and performed 1970s–mid-1980s. Unpublished.
The Mother. Written and performed 1970s–mid-1980s. Unpublished.
Not One of a Kind. Written and performed 1970s–mid-1980s. Unpublished.
One for the Money (one-act play). Written and performed 1970s–mid-1980s. Unpublished.
One Hour or Forever (one-act play). Written and performed 1970s–mid-1980s. Unpublished.
Say What You Willomay. Written and performed 1970s–mid-1980s. Unpublished.
Shed a Tear. Written and performed 1970s–mid-1980s. Unpublished.
Strangers. 1978. Unpublished.
System, Suckers, and Success. Written and performed 1970s–mid-1980s. Unpublished.
Too Hep to Be Happy. Written and performed 1970s–mid-1980s. Unpublished.
The Unintended. 1983. Unpublished.

Studies of J(oan) California Cooper's Dramatic Works

Carroll, Rebecca, ed. "J. California Cooper." *I Know What the Red Clay Looks Like*. New York: Crown, 1994. 63–80.

Marshall, Barbara Jean. "Kitchen Table Talk: J. California Cooper's Use of Nommo-Female Bonding and Transcendence." *Language and Literature in the African-American Imagination*. Ed. Carol A. Blackshire-Belay. Westport: Greenwood, 1992. 91–102.

Ostrow, Eileen Joyce. *Center Stage: An Anthology of Twenty-One Black-American Plays*. Champaign: University of Illinois Press, 1991. xi–xiii, 17–27.

KIA CORTHRON
(1962–)

Deborah Gleason-Rielly

BIOGRAPHY

Kia Corthron was born and raised in Cumberland, Maryland, very close to the border of West Virginia and Pennsylvania. As a child, she witnessed the crushing inequities of racism and working-class poverty in the foothills of her small town. Corthron's father worked at the local paper mill, sometimes for thirteen-day stretches without a day off, and he frequently trained young white men who would eventually become his bosses. As Corthron's hard-working father was passed over for promotions, Kia attended a mostly white grade school where she was one of the few students of color. Thus, she developed a keen sense of the injustices suffered in the workplace, the small town, the schoolhouse, and in society at large.

Perhaps it is understandable then that Ms. Corthron should become a writer desperately concerned with social issues and political themes. She remembers being encouraged to write since the second grade when her sister went away to school, leaving Kia to amuse herself with only clothespins and stick figures. Corthron began telling stories and creating dialogue to pass the time as a lonely, country child. Still, she did not immediately turn to writing in her college years. She began at the University of Maryland majoring in communications, but in her senior year, she took a playwriting course and found her calling. One assignment was for students to write a fifteen-minute play and prepare it for the class. Corthron wrote a piece about Vietnam and was deeply affected when one woman in the class began sobbing quietly in the background during the reading. According to Corthron, that moment, when she was able to communicate on such a deep level with her classmates, made her realize that she wanted to touch people like this again, to share and awaken feelings about important issues (Reiter 77). Corthron then spent a year attending a playwriting seminar with Lonnie Carter at George Washington University and then moved to Columbia University for her M.F.A., studying under Howard Stein, Glenn Young, and Lavonne Mueller and graduating in 1992.

Since this auspicious beginning, Corthron has continued to invite notice; she has garnered multiple awards and commissions including a National Endowments for the Arts/TCG grant, a Callaway Award, and the Delaware Company's first Connections Award. Corthron wrote one of her first plays, *Catnap Allegiance* (1992), as the first recipient of the Manhattan Theatre Club's Van Lier Playwriting Fellowship. Ten of her seventeen plays have been commissioned by various organizations, including the Long Wharf Theater in New Haven, the Mark Taper Forum in Los Angeles, Second Stage in New York, the Royal Court Theatre in London, the Goodman Theater in Chicago, and the Alabama Shakespeare Festival. At present, Corthron is working on a Royal Court commission, a play that examines the problems of conformity and protest while following several generations of a black family during the McCarthy era and beyond.

In addition to Corthron's fervent desire to pack her plays with sociopolitical issues, she has also been lauded for her ability to fashion language into a distinctive, punctuated urban poetry. She has been compared to such greats as August Wilson* and David Mamet for moving audiences with her rhythmical diction. Corthron states, "I like writers who fiddle with the language and you have to keep up" (Shewey 5). The unique quality of her prose most likely owes something to the combination of southern, mid-Atlantic, and working-class dialects she was exposed to growing up in Cumberland. Yet, Corthron's work is nothing if not acutely thematic. She always uses her poetic and lyrical gift with language to tackle a variety of serious themes at once, earning her intense criticism for being fragmented as well as strong praise for her honest, cutting voice. Despite this obvious political commitment, she wants to distance herself from writers who write "agitation propaganda." Corthron admits, "I consider myself a political writer with a political point of view, [but] I don't write agit-prop because I think the point gets across much stronger if the audience feels something rather than being told something intellectually. But every play of mine starts from a socio political [*sic*] issue" (qtd. in Shewey 5).

To pull off this blend of politics and artful speech, Corthron usually does extensive specific research on an issue before she sits down to write. As a result, Corthron's plays often instruct and expand the audience's awareness. She began writing *Breath, Boom* (2000) after she taught a playwriting course at Riker's Island prison; and for *Seeking the Genesis* (1997), Corthron attended many lectures on biomedical technology. Because she lumps so many issues into one play, Corthron's endings are hardly neat, a point for which she is frequently criticized. However, she also keeps in mind a tenet of director Augusto Boal's: always leave the audience with some element of hope so that they will be inspired to create solutions to social problems (Shewey 5). Ever hopeful herself, Corthron has lived in New York City for thirteen years, seven of them in Harlem, and she continues to speak out against injustice, through both direct protest and the indirect arena of the stage.

MAJOR WORKS AND THEMES

Kia Corthron began her career on a high note when a play she had written at Columbia University, *Come Down Burning* (1993), won the Joe A. Callaway Playwriting Award and was published in the 1993–1994 edition of *Best American Short Plays*. Rooted in Corthron's Cumberland background, the play tells the story of two sisters facing racism, poverty, and motherhood in a small mountain town. Yet, as always, Corthron enriches and complicates her play with more: Skoolie, the main character, is paralyzed from a childhood accident and supports herself as a hairdresser and by performing abortions. Still, there is no brazen sentimentality here; Skoolie is quite capable of taking care of her sister, Tee, and Tee's two children. Skoolie helps Tee stand up to her daughter's racist teacher and cares for Tee after a botched self-performed abortion, even as Tee helps Skoolie come to terms with her disability and her limitations. *Come Down Burning* is Corthron at her best: short, punctuated phrases fit the tight subject matter, but underneath it all, Skoolie and Tee are loving sisters and their humanity shines through.

Most of Corthron's early plays continue to deal with various facets of racism with family as a backdrop. *Wake Up Lou Riser* (1991) portrays a family attempting to turn the tables and avenge their brother's murder at the hands of the Ku Klux Klan, while in *Catnap Allegiance* (1992), a Gulf War soldier struggles to break the cycle of war and racism and to turn out differently than his bitter Vietnam-veteran father. Of *Digging Eleven* (2000), Corthron says, "This is actually my most personal play. My father worked in paper mills all of his life, and, unlike any other play of mine, a character is based on somebody I know, my grandmother. This play is literally like family to me" (Kerkhoff par. 3). Like her previous work, *Digging Eleven* deals with a poor, working-class man, Io, who works in a factory while raising his one-year-old sister, Ness. Yet, again, Corthron is not content to deal merely with poverty, racism, and inequality; she adds homosexuality, senility, coming of age, and adultery into the fray.

While Corthron typically employs realism, sometimes shockingly combining theme upon theme, several of her plays also take on a surreal bent. *Cage Rhythm* (1993), another of her highly acclaimed and anthologized plays, takes place in a correctional facility, where a group of women of color grapple with being in confinement, isolated further from their families and children because of their race and circumstance. Written in response to the Rockefeller drug laws that have resulted in countless numbers of minority women imprisoned and out of touch with their families, the women in this play deal with the smallness of their lives inside by reaching out, some to one another, and some through astral projection. Likewise, Corthron draws on the bizarre in *Life by Asphyxiation* (1995) in which a death row resident is visited by the ghost of the girl he raped and murdered and again in *The Venus de Milo Is Armed* (2001) as landmines go off during a family reunion in America. Still, even amid these absurdist touches, Corthron continues to pepper these plays with political topics such as the death penalty and corporate responsibility.

Corthron continued to expand her repertoire of social themes into the scientific realm in 1996. In her plays *Splash Hatch on the E Going Down* (1996) and *Seeking the Genesis* (1997), Corthron exposes serious ethical dilemmas in science, all the while continuing to utilize her trademark rhythmical urban vernacular. *Splash Hatch*'s main character, Thyme, starts out urbane enough, as a pregnant teenager who lives with her teenage husband and her parents in Harlem. However, Corthron dispels any stereotypes quickly: Thyme is articulate, bright, and consumed with concern over the environmental state of the world. As Thyme works to deliver her baby in water naturally, a "Splash Hatch," she ironically misses the signs of her husband's occupationally induced lead poisoning. Later, after losing her husband and giving birth to her child, Thyme gazes at the night sky and echoes Corthron's poignant message: "[S]till most of the people in the world'll just look up tonight and peg another star on the map. Just comfortably believe in that perpetualness, that permanence, security that they can just peer into the sky any night and there it'll be, that funny fuzzy star just floating in the cup of the Big Dipper. Forever" (58). While scientific slang imbues every part of this play, the symbolic references to stars, water, birth, and earth emphasize the greater human meaning.

Likewise, in *Seeking the Genesis*, commissioned by the Goodman Theater, Corthron mixes the social problems of an urban family with scientific debate. Stemming from Corthron's concern over research done in universities that would seek to locate a gene for violence, the play centers around a six-year-old inner-city boy aptly named Kite. Kite's mother, C Ana, must face a devastating decision: does she listen to the teacher and the professor who see Kite's hyperactivity as detrimental to his education and symptomatic of his predisposition to violence, placing Kite on medication for life, or does she give in to her own doubts as she watches her creative, playful child turn into a passive, dutiful student? As with *Splash Hatch*, *Seeking the Genesis* does not just focus on the medication debate, but rather Corthron includes in her plot aspects of the urban ghetto violence as well as poverty, failing schools, and racism, always through her trademark staccato lyricism.

Recently, Corthron has continued to explore the cyclical problem of violence in the inner city. In *Breath, Boom* (2000) and *Force Continuum* (2001), she again uses the idea of the urban "family," this time to address gangs and police brutality. Interestingly, *Breath, Boom* was commissioned by the Royal Court Theatre in London. Audiences there found the play quite exotic because it follows not just gangs, but girl gangs in the Bronx. Corthron's rhythmical, harsh Bronx dialects pierce through the images of blood, violence, and survival. The main character, Prix, having grown up with a drug addict mother and a stepfather who molests her, becomes the abrasive leader of a female gang by the age of sixteen. *Breath, Boom* shows how Prix survives in and out of prison until she is forced into gang retirement at the age of thirty. What keeps Prix going is her fascination with fireworks, a magical display that ends with a "boom" and leaves only calm. Once again, Corthron does not supply a tidy ending; rather, she spills a glimmer of life-affirming force into her acidic story.

Force Continuum takes a similar stance on police brutality. Corthron writes in response to the Abner Louima scandal, but she does not frame the violent incident as merely white-on-black police brutality. *Force Continuum* refers to the police dictum of assessing how much force is necessary to subdue a suspect. Yet, the title also denotes the legacy that has been passed down to the main character, Dece, a black cop, from his mother, father, and grandfather, also black police officers in New York City. Dece, like his mother, father, and grandfather before him, must deal with racism, profiling, and the pressure to use brutal force, eventually coming face to face with his own decision to use force, black-on-black style. As with *Breath, Boom*, Corthron gives the audience a glimmer of hope in *Force Continuum*, advocating the power of community policing and increased recruitment of minorities to change the harsh realities of the present. Always political, always jarringly expressive, Corthron continues to write about what concerns her. At present, she has a short play *Somnia* (2001) on the Internet in response to U.S. sanctions against Iraq and she is working on a new play, *Slide, Glide the Slippery Slope*, that addresses biomedical engineering, cloning, and heredity.

CRITICAL RECEPTION

Kia Corthron has been hailed as one of the brightest contemporary playwrights and, at the same time, as a playwright who is too political and too subjective, who tries to bundle too many issues into one play. This is perhaps the essence of Corthron's work: her politics and her clear perspective, as well as her insistence on assaulting the audience with many compelling subjects at once, may confound critics but it is this blend of talents that also puts Corthron into the forefront of great playwrights. For example, Corthron's controversial play *Splash Hatch on the E Going Down* was hailed by Benedict

Nightingale as "the less accomplished but the meatier" (n.p.) play on the bill for the London Donmar Theatre in 1996. Likewise, Alvin Klein of the *New York Times* called Thyme, the main character of *Splash Hatch*, "one of those compulsive blubberers for a cause" and "a self-serving soapbox" ("Girls" CT15). Similarly, critics did not take kindly to *Digging Eleven*, again because of the variety of weighty subject matter addressed, including homosexuality, senility, poverty, adolescence, unionism, and racism. Despite these objections to some of Corthron's early work, critics also acknowledged that Corthron's language is always poetic and rhythmical and her ability to up-end stereotypes as well as her refusal to shy away from difficult questions show evidence of great promise.

Similarly, Corthron's more recent plays have also opened to mixed reviews. *Force Continuum*, Corthron's highly pertinent play about police brutality, was criticized for being "a distinctly messy play" (Isherwood, "Breath" 26). Once again, critics lamented Corthron's need to cover many issues and to create characters who are mouthpieces for her views, rather than real human beings. Yet, critics went further with this play, denouncing the confusing time shifts and lack of narrative structure. Frequently, it has been suggested that Corthron's plays would be better suited to television or film because of this fragmented structure. Still, critics could not help but admire the adeptness with which Corthron uses honest urban poetics to craft serious arguments. According to Elyse Sommer, *Force Continuum*, "at its best . . . [l]ooks squarely and fairly at uncomfortable problems and engages the audience's emotions sufficiently to abet intelligent post-theater discussions" (par. 12). Michael Feingold agreed: "Her language is all her own, an elliptical blend of street talk and modernist blur, scarred by media babble, stuck with sharp pins of journalistic fact, and wrapped around ominous lumps of theory and statistical data" ("Fire" 69). Likewise, with *Seeking the Genesis*, Ben Brantley acknowledged both the problems with the weighty play and also the potential genius of Corthron's language and intent: "Ms. Corthron affectingly plays on the juxtaposition of traditional images of idyllic innocence with those of squalor and mayhem. . . . If she raises too many big and complex topics, she also considers them without oversimplification. And she makes expressive use of a language that is surreally brisk and fragmented, as if shaped by the chaos and urgency of its characters' surroundings" ("Hyperactivity" C18).

Perhaps Corthron's best reviews have come from plays that deal with mostly female casts such as *Breath, Boom*. While still attempting to tackle many issues in the same play, Corthron is able to develop complex human characters who carry razors in their mouths while putting together scrapbooks. Again, Corthron's use of urban language is praised: "[W]ith its mix of high-flying poetry, street-corner obscenities, hip-hop lingo and almost ritualized pain and violence, Corthron give us our own very recognizable tragedy in a play that detonates with tremendous force" (Weiss par. 5). According to

Charles Isherwood, "Although her subject is sensational, Corthron's writing never is; it's rich with humor, terse vernacular strength and gritty detail, and she manages to turn each of the play's many characters into a real personality rather than a generic type" ("Breath" 26).

As in *Breath, Boom*, which is somewhat limited in subject matter, for Corthron that is, *Cage Rhythm* also elicited quite good reviews, perhaps because the play focuses on the injustices of prison life for minority women. Sydne Mahone wrote that in *Cage Rhythm*, Corthron "breaks down the politics and sociology into very poignant, fast-paced, emotionally taut scenes that turn on a dime. Two levels of reality—one physical and one spiritual—are rendered as absolute truth" (xxvii). *Cage Rhythm* was one of Corthron's early plays and the first to win the New Professional Theatre Playwriting Award. In the same vein, *Come Down Burning*, one of Corthron's early works that focused on two women, was also anthologized and received favorable reviews for Corthron's ability to interweave grave themes into a story of very human characters while treating the audience to a feast of artfully fragmented language. Despite Corthron's ups and downs with the critics, it seems that her desire to venture into new, shocking themes coupled with her genius for language will serve the theater and her audience well for some time to come.

BIBLIOGRAPHY

Dramatic Works by Kia Corthron

Anchor Aria. New York: New Dramatists Play Service, 1997.

"Breath, Boom." 2000. *Leading Women: Plays for Actresses II*. Ed. Eric Land and Nina Shengold. New York: Vintage, 2002. 131–214.

"Cage Rhythm." 1993. *Colored Contradictions: An Anthology of Contemporary African-American Plays*. Ed. Harry J. Elam, Jr. and Robert Alexander. New York: Penguin, 1996. 32–83.

Catnap Allegiance. New York: New Dramatists Service, 1992.

"Come Down Burning." 1993. *Colored Contradictions: An Anthology of Contemporary African-American Plays*. Ed. Harry J. Elam, Jr. and Robert Alexander. New York: Penguin, 1996. 417–450.

Digging Eleven. New York: New Dramatists Service, 2000.

Force Continuum. 2001. New York: Dramatists Play Service, 2002.

"Life by Asphyxiation." *Black Ink*. New York: New Dramatists Play Service, 1995.

Light Raise the Roof. New York: New Dramatists Service, n.d.

"Safe Box." *Urban Zulu Mambo*. New York: New Dramatists Service, 1999.

Seeking the Genesis. 1997. New York: Dramatists Play Service, 2002.

"Somnia." *Voices in the Wilderness: A Campaign to End the Economic Sanctions against the People of Iraq*. 19 Nov. 2001. 28 Mar. 2003 <http://www.nonviolence.org/vitw/old_site/Resources5.html>.

Splash Hatch on the E Going Down. 1996. New York: Dramatists Play Service, 2002.

Suckling Chimera. New York: New Dramatists Play Service, 1998.

Up. New York: New Dramatists Play Service, 2000.

The Venus de Milo Is Armed. New York: New Dramatists Play Service, 2001.

Wake Up Lou Riser. 1991. New York: New Dramatists Play Service, 1992.

Studies of Kia Corthron's Dramatic Works

Brantley, Ben. "Hyperactivity Is the Least of This Boy's Problems." Rev. of *Seeking the Genesis*, by Kia Corthron. *New York Times* 18 June 1997, late ed–final ed.: C18.

———. "Rich Voices Paint a Path to Paradise." Rev. of *Urban Zulu Mambo*, by Kia Corthron. *New York Times* 26 Feb. 2001: E1.

———. "Social Detectives for Life's Confusions." Rev. of *Force Continuum*, by Kia Corthron. *New York Times* 9 Feb. 2001, late ed (East Coast): E5.

Clay, Carolyn. "Girl Trouble." Rev. of *Breath, Boom*, by Kia Corthron. *Boston Phoenix* 9 Mar. 2003. 22 Mar. 2003 <http://www.bostonphoenix.com/boston/arts/theater/documents/02766125.htm>.

Coen, Stephanie. "Kia Corthron: Taking Sides." Interview with Kia Corthron. *Dramatists Guild Quarterly* (Winter 1997): 22–25.

Daniels, Robert. Rev. of *Seeking the Genesis*, by Kia Corthron. *Variety* 23 June 1997: 102.

Feingold, Michael. "Boom Times." Rev. of *Breath, Boom*, by Kia Corthron. *Village Voice* 46.25 (2001): 74.

———. "Fire Power." Rev. of *Force Continuum*, by Kia Corthron. *Village Voice* 46.7 (2001): 69.

———. "Manila Envelops." Rev. of *Urban Zulu Mambo*, by Kia Corthron. *Village Voice* 46.10 (2001): 69.

———. "Sade but True." Rev. of *Black Ink*, by Kia Corthron. *Villiage Voice* 40.50 (1995): 85.

———. "Somber Queries." Rev. of *Seeking the Genesis*, by Kia Corthron. *Village Voice* 42.25 (1997): 95.

Fitzgerald, Jason. "Curtain Call." Rev. of *Breath, Boom*. *Arts Editor* 15 Mar. 2003. 22 Mar. 2003 <http://www.artseditor.com/html/sublevels/curtaincall.shtml>.

Gardner, Elysa. "Message of 'Zulu Mambo' Totally Lost in the Translation." Rev. of *Urban Zulu Mambo*, by Kia Corthron. *USA Today* 26 Feb. 2001: D4.

Gener, Randy. "Kia Corthron's *Force Continuum* Reveals Trials of Black NYC Cops." Rev. of *Force Continuum*, by Kia Corthron. *Broadway Online* 7 Feb. 2001. 13 Mar. 2003 <http://www.theatre.com/news/public/newsprint.asp?newsid=10039>.

Giuliano, Mike. Rev. of *Splash Hatch on the E Going Down*, by Kia Corthron. Center Stage, Baltimore. *Variety* 22 Dec. 1997: 73.

Gutman, Les. Rev. of *Breath, Boom*, by Kia Corthron. Playwrights Horizon Studio, New York. *CurtainUp* 8 June 2002. 14 Mar. 2003 <http://www.curtainup.com/breathboom.html>.

———. Rev. of *Seeking the Genesis*, by Kia Corthron. Manhattan Theater Club Stage II, New York. *CurtainUp* June 1997. 3 Apr. 2003 <http://www.curtainup.com>.

———. Rev. of *Splash Hatch on the E Going Down*, by Kia Corthron. Center Stage Theater, Baltimore. *CurtainUp* Nov. 1997. 4 Apr. 2003 <http://www.curtainup.com>.

Hickman, Christopher. "Disarming Drama." *American Theatre* Feb. 2003: 8. *Master-FILE Select*. EBSCO Host. 22 Mar. 2003.

Hofler, Robert. "Drama Club." *Harper's Bazaar* (Mar. 2001): 334.

———. Rev. of *Urban Zulu Mambo*, by Kia Corthron. Signature Theater Co., New York. *Variety* 5 Mar. 2001: 53.

Isherwood, Charles. "Breath, Boom." Rev. of *Breath, Boom*, by Kia Corthron. *Variety* 18 June 2001: 26.

———. Rev. of *Force Continuum*, by Kia Corthron. Atlantic Theater, New York. *Variety* 12 Feb. 2001: 46.

Jones, Chris. "Southern Writers Festival of New Plays." *Variety* 3 Mar. 2003: 71.

———. "Tyros on Parade." *Variety* 16 Dec. 2002. *MasterFILE Select*. EBSCO Host. 3 Apr. 2003.

Kerkhoff, Ingrid. *Contemporary American Drama*. Bremen University. 13 Mar. 2003: 47 pars. 18 Aug. 2003 <http://www.fb10.uni-bremen.de/anglistik/kerkhoff/ContempDrama/Corthron.htm>.

King, Robert L. "Life in the Theater." *North American Review* 284.2 (1999): 45–48. *Literature Online*. ProQuest. 25 Mar. 2003.

Klein, Alvin. "Girls with a Death Obsession." Rev. of *Breath, Boom*, by Kia Corthron. Yale Repertory Theater. *New York Times* 10 Nov. 2002: CT15.

———. "Sheer Terror? When Polemics Overtake the Magic." Rev. of *Splash Hatch on the E Going Down*, by Kia Corthron. *New York Times* 1 Feb. 1998, sec. 14: CN12.

Lowry, Mark. "Female Playwrights Are Hitting the Mark." *Fort Worth Star-Telegram* 18 Feb. 2002: C3.

Mahone, Sydne. Introduction. *Moon Marked and Touched by Sun*. New York: Theatre Communications Group, 1994.

Nightingale, Benedict. "Food for Thought: Parcel from America." *Times of London* 22 Feb. 1999. Dialog@Carl Database. 25 Mar. 2003.

Raskin, Sarah. *Synchrotheatre*. 22 Mar. 2003. 19 Aug. 2003 <http://www.synchrotheatre.com/pressclippings-breath-interview.htm>.

Reiter, Amy. "Kia Corthron: Giving the Voiceless a Voice." *American Theater* (Oct. 1994): 77.

Renner, Pamela. "Talking Shop (which Takes in the World)." Interview with Kia Corthron. *New York Times* 25 Feb. 2001, late ed. (East Coast): sec. 2, 16.

Shewey, Don. "A Playwright Who's Unafraid to Admit She's Political." Interview with Kia Corthron. *New York Times* 4 Feb. 2001, late ed. (East Coast): sec. 2, 5.

Siegel, Ed. "Girls Interrupted: In 'Breath, Boom,' Gang Members Face Violence, Drugs, and Dreams Denied." Rev. of *Breath, Boom*, by Kia Corthron. *Boston Globe* 14 Mar. 2003: C15.

Sommer, Elyse. Rev. of *Force Continuum*, by Kia Corthron. Atlantic Theater, New York. *CurtainUp* Feb. 2002: 12 pars. 14 Mar. 2003 <http://www.curtainup.com/forcecontinuum.html>.

Stevenson, Sarah Lansdale. Rev. of *Breath, Boom*, by Kia Corthron. *Theatre Journal* 54.2 (2002): 291–294.

Taylor, Markland. Rev. of *Digging Eleven*, by Kia Corthron. Hartford Stage Co., Hartford. *Variety* 1 Feb. 1999: 73.

Weber, Bruce. "Girls of the Ghetto: Students of a Harsh Finishing School." Rev. of *Breath, Boom*, by Kia Corthron. *New York Times* 11 June 2001: E5.

Weiss, Hedy. "Sonic 'Boom': An Explosive Tale of Devastated Young Lives." *Chicago Sun Times* 6 Mar. 2003: 9 pars. 21 Aug. 2003 <http://www.suntimes.com/output/weiss/cst-ftr-breath06.html>.
Weisstuch, Liza. "Street Theater." *Boston Phoenix* (Feb.–Mar. 2003): C4.

OSSIE DAVIS
(1917–)

Lean'tin L. Bracks

BIOGRAPHY

Ossie Davis was born in 1917 in Cogdell, Georgia, to Kince Charles and Laura Cooper Davis. Davis, who was originally named after his paternal grandfather Raiford Chatman Davis, was affectionately called R.C. by his family. The stronghold of "Jim Crow," a racist institution at that time in the South, allowed the affectionate name of R.C. to be incorrectly recorded on Davis's birth certificate by a white county clerk—thus, the name Ossie. In those days, white county clerks in the South were not to be challenged. Growing up in Georgia, Davis, like many African American children, learned about life and community through the stories told to them by family. Both of Davis's parents would share with their nine children the African American oral tradition of storytelling, and it was Davis's father, a railroad worker and preacher, whose stories filled and strengthened the times they spent together. It is these stories and the power that language offered that fueled Davis's interest in creating his own narratives.

By the time Davis reached high school in 1930, he was eager to explore speech and language in new and different ways. He found great pleasure in reading Shakespeare and participating in plays and other theatrical productions. Motivated by a high school friend's experience of seeing a play in New York, Davis tried his hand at playwriting and wrote a play that was successfully produced in the school auditorium. Once graduating in 1934 from Central High School in Waycross, Georgia, Davis knew what he wanted to be—a playwright—but no great plan had presented itself regarding how. Even though he received scholarships to Tuskegee Institute and Georgia State College, he could not afford to utilize either because he had no funds for living expenses. Still determined to get an education, in 1935 Davis hitchhiked to Washington, DC, to stay with a host family and enroll in Howard University, where Davis's lifelong goals were realized.

Through the instruction of Professor Sterling Brown and his course in Negro literature at Howard University, Davis learned to understand and validate his cultural experiences as worthy and beautiful. He came to appreciate the stories shared by his family as creative oral texts and came to realize that the language of the blues was truly great poetry. It was from Alain Leroy Locke, a professor of philosophy at Howard and the first Negro Rhodes Scholar in America, that Davis got the most direct guidance regarding his goals. Locke encouraged Davis to go to Harlem after graduation, and explore the theater firsthand, if he truly was serious about being a playwright. Taking this advice to heart, Davis decided to leave Howard after only two years and pursue his playwriting aspirations in Harlem. His departure was slightly delayed, as he and his traveling companion found it imperative to be in attendance at the Lincoln Memorial on April 16, 1939. Marion Anderson, a world-renowned African American singer, was scheduled to give a concert on the steps of the memorial as a form of protest, because Anderson was denied permission to sing at Constitution Hall because of her race. This was the first of many protests in which Davis would participate. His sense of social consciousness and moral responsibility, brought him to the Lincoln Memorial, but it was also his personal commitment to effect social change that resulted in a clarification of his lifelong goals. In the autobiography of Davis and his wife, Ruby Dee, *With Ossie and Ruby: In This Life Together*, Davis reflected on the importance of this event in his life: "It married in my mind forever the performing arts as a weapon in the struggle for freedom. It was a proclamation and a commitment" (Davis amd Dee 86). This idea served as the motivation and inspiration for much of Davis's life and career.

Once arriving in Harlem, Davis made contact with the Rose McClendon Players who were managed by Dick Campbell and Muriel Rahn. Campbell saw Davis's potential for becoming a fine actor. Along with theater experiences with the Players, Davis took acting lessons to support his new craft. He supported his playwriting goals by reading and writing extensively and frequenting local libraries. With the advent of World War II, Davis put his career on hold and decided to join the army. He spent much of his tour of duty in West Africa and Liberia and was later transferred to special services where he was able to write and produce several plays. After Davis's discharge, he returned to New York and to the stage with a lead role in the play *Jeb* in 1946.

Acting had become a major factor in Davis's career as he was not only a fine actor, but found through it a lucrative way to care for his growing family.

After several successful acting roles, inclusive of a key role in *Anna Lucasta* (1946–1947), Davis completed and produced the play *Alice in Wonder* in 1952. Davis had since married fellow actor Ruby Dee in 1948, and they had begun their family. *Alice in Wonder* continued Davis's commitment to be involved in the events of the day, as the play focused on the McCarthy trials that caused many performers, including Davis and Dee, to be blacklisted. Despite some difficulties, Davis's acting career continued to be promising, and in 1955, he had the lead role in *The Emperor Jones*, by Eugene O'Neill. In 1960, he replaced Sidney Poitier in the highly acclaimed play *A Raisin in the Sun*, by Lorraine Hansberry.* By 1961, after five years of writing backstage and amid numerous distractions, the play *Purlie Victorious* was completed. *Purlie Victorious*, which offered laughter as a means toward change, was a satire about racism in the South and echoed the cultural ignorance and disrespect that segregation and racism have embedded in the American psyche. The play was so well received that after only a seven-month run, it was adapted into a movie entitled *Gone Are the Days*. In 1970, *Purlie Victorious* was reproduced as the Broadway musical *Purlie*.

The events of the 1960s continued to encourage Davis's ongoing activism in the fight against injustice, and for freedom, within his community and his career. Davis was active in the civil rights movement, from the March on Washington in 1963 to the boycotting of theatrical and commercial productions in which there were discriminatory practices and often no African Americans employed. Davis also testified before Congress regarding racial discrimination in the theater industry. His activism continued to play a major role in his creative choices as reflected in his writing, producing, and directing. In 1976, Davis wrote the historically based play *Escape to Freedom: A Play about Young Frederick Douglass*, which earned him an award from the American Library Association in 1979. This work was followed in 1982 by the play *Langston* that reflected on the life of the acclaimed African American poet, author, and playwright Langston Hughes.* In 1970, Davis received media attention as the director of the film *Cotton Comes to Harlem*, adapted from a novel of the same name by African American author Chester Himes. Davis's revisions to the screenplay were a crucial component in the success of the film. As an actor in the film industry, Davis often accepted roles in films that made strong social commentaries, such as *School Daze* (1988), *Jungle Fever* (1991), and *Get on the Bus* (1996), all written and directed by African American filmmaker Spike Lee. As a further extension of his overall involvement in the theatrical world on varied levels, Davis, Dee, and their three children, Nora, Guy, and LaVerne (Hasna after her conversion to Islam), formed Emmalyn II Enterprise in the 1980s to produce and distribute many of their creative projects.

Ossie Davis's commitment to the creative arts and social change has not gone without recognition, as he has received numerous awards including an honorary doctorate from Howard University; the American

Library Association Award, the Coretta Scott King Award, and the Jane Addams Children's Book Award in 1979 for his play *Escape to Freedom*; the Theater Hall of Fame Award in 1994; the Presidents National Medal of the Arts honoring both Davis and Dee in 1995; and three Emmy Award nominations for *Teacher, Teacher* (1969), *King* (1978), and *Miss Evers' Boys* (1997). Davis continues to write and produce and his most recent contribution to the theatrical world is the play *A Last Dance for Sybil* written over two decades that opened at the New Federal Theatre in New York City in January 2003. As a playwright, actor, director, and activist, Ossie Davis has made great contributions to the performing arts. His plays, children's books, poetry, articles, and other literary offerings have brought to life thoughtful and thought-provoking characters, who both entertain and enlighten, as rooted in the African American oral tradition of storytelling.

MAJOR WORKS AND THEMES

In 1939, Ossie Davis began his first professional play, *Leonidas Is Fallen* (1942), before leaving Howard University for the experiences of Harlem, New York. In coming to terms with his own struggle as a black man in America in the 1930s and the struggles of his character, a noble slave, Davis explored the dynamics of power. He recognized that power can oppress, but he also acknowledged that the oppressed may confront power through resistance. It thus became the challenge of giving his character a voice, reflective of this power—resistance—that fueled Davis's continued work as a playwright.

It was not until his play *Alice in Wonder* (1952) that Davis experienced his first professional production. This play brought attention to his emerging talent and was reflective of a theme of historical awareness and social consciousness that informed his own life experiences. *Alice in Wonder* utilized the theater to protest the struggles and injustices of the time. The main character, who is a popular African American entertainer, is called to testify in Washington, DC, against the activities of another African American entertainer. Mirroring the events surrounding Paul Robeson and the McCarthy trials, Davis makes a clear statement about the black man's continued victimization whether they are on trial, or made to play the role of informant.

In 1961, nine years after his first professional production, Davis wrote his most critically acclaimed play, *Purlie Victorious*. Davis uses the primary character, Purlie Victorious Judson, to reveal the injustices of black life, particularly in the South, and does so within the arena of comedy. The play ridicules conventional stereotypes while Judson, who needs a church to "preach freedom in the cotton patch," plays the cunning role of dealing with the white landowner while preaching a truer sense of justice to his audience. Davis gives his main character a voice that melded believability and a grandiose message with humor, while addressing socially challenging topics such as segregation and racism. He also successfully used the power of resistance, through the voice of Judson, against the oppressive circumstances that existed in the southern town. In many ways, the play was revolutionary because it allowed audiences to laugh with the black characters instead of laughing at them, which was the traditional and racist perspective of the time. Also, as noted by Ruby Dee, who was also Davis's closest confidant, Malcolm X, and a respected friend, much of the play made white America the focus of laughter, which was a new experience for theatergoers of that time. In 1963, *Purlie Victorious* was remade into the movie *Gone Are the Days*, with Davis as the screenwriter. In 1970, the play opened on Broadway as the musical *Purlie*, starring Melba Moore and Cleavon Little. Both Moore and Little won Tony Awards for their performances. Although Davis had also written the play *Curtain Call, Mr. Aldridge Sir* in 1963, which was produced in California, it did not receive the acclaim that *Purlie Victorious* had, which prompted Davis to turn his attention to historical plays.

Escape to Freedom: A Play about Young Frederick Douglass was produced in 1978, and was followed four years later by the play *Langston* in 1982. In *Escape to Freedom*, Davis presents the early years of the great African American Frederick Douglass who valiantly fought for the end of slavery and for justice and equality in America. *Langston* celebrates the poetry and artistic vision of Langston Hughes an acclaimed African American artist of the Harlem Renaissance and the twentieth century. Davis was greatly influenced by Hughes's poetry because it presented a true and honest portrayal of black life in America. Davis continues to use the theater as well as all artistic mediums to protest injustices and to bring to light topics that affect the African American community in particular. As an activist and in the arena of the stage, whether as playwright, screenwriter, or actor, Davis's work finds purpose in examining black history and culture, and confronting the social issues of the day. Ossie Davis's most recent play, *A Last Dance for Sybil* performed in 2003 at the New Federal Theatre in New York, continues that tradition.

CRITICAL RECEPTION

As a playwright, Ossie Davis's plays have been well received, but *Purlie Victorious* stands out as the work that had the broadest influence on the American audience. It was the possibility of this influence that originally had Davis concerned about the timing of his play:

The 1960's were a time of revolution. Black folk were determined to change the image by which we were perceived, to put folk humor aside and put on war paint, so that white folks should be under no illusion that we were joking. We had to present them with our sternest face. And that's the kind of play I had tried so long to write, but I had ended up with laughter instead of revenge. Was *Purlie Victorious*, with all its laughter, its gags, itsschtick, and one-liners, an act of betrayal? (Davis and Dee 291)

Recognizing that no event operates in isolation, Davis shared the script with colleagues and others in the community prior to its production. Bolstered by positive reviews, and an offer from Howard Da Silva, the director of *A Raisin in the Sun*, to direct Davis's play, *Purlie Victorious* was produced. The first live performance of the play before the Congress of Racial Equality received a lukewarm response, but the overall responses during the run of the play were extremely positive. Both W. E. B. Du Bois, noted African American scholar and leader, and Martin Luther King, Jr., leading advocate and activist of civil rights in America, came to see *Purlie Victorious*. Each offered positive responses regarding the production and congratulated Davis on his work. The play, referred to by Roy Wilkins, executive secretary of the NAACP, as "entertainment-with-a point" (qtd. in Funke 56), brought attention from the entertainment world, as well as the socially conscious, and the academically astute. Sylvester Leaks, an author and a reviewer of Davis's work as discussed in the article, "Purlie Emerges Victorious," uses the words of another writer, Maxim Gorky, to speak to the overall success of the play and how it adheres to the purpose of literature, which is:

[t]o help man to know himself; to fortify his belief in himself and support his striving after the truth; to discover the good in people and root out what is ignoble; to kindle shame, wrath, courage, in their hearts; to help them acquire a strength dedicated to lofty purposes and sanctify their lives with the holy spirit of beauty. (347)

Davis's main character, Purlie Victorious Judson, represented this idea and served as a hero, in that he was able to "succeed in accomplishing his goals on his own terms in an environment that is designed to make him a victim. Furthermore, he does so with wit and with panache" (Molette 453). The result of such a combination of consciousness and comedy earned Davis a nomination for the coveted Pulitzer Prize.

Although Ossie Davis is primarily recognized as an actor and playwright, his skill as a screenwriter is clearly realized in the film *Cotton Comes to Harlem*, presented in 1970, which Davis also directed. Arnold Perl was the originator of the screenplay as adapted from the novel of the same name written by Chester Himes. Davis's suggestions and revisions to the screenplay helped make the film a major success and also changed the perspective of Hollywood regarding black American audiences. The story, which takes place in Harlem, is centered around a back-to-Africa campaign by a local preacher, and two detectives who suspect that the whole project is an illegal scheme. Davis was asked to offer suggestions to the original screenplay to ensure that it was accurately portraying black life. After several suggestions, Davis was asked to do a full revision of the screenplay. As a result of this, and his acceptance as director of the film, "[t]he film has been credited with being the first commercial Hollywood film to prove that there was a considerable market for black films, even if white folks decided to stay away" (Davis and Dee 336). This realization, as ushered in by Davis's skill as a screenwriter and his commitment to culture and community, offered a new perspective and thus more expansive opportunities for the production of black films and the black audiences the films would attract. For Davis,

acting is a choice, but writing a compulsion. My response to things is to cast them inwords, to take complex systems and reduce them to morsels which can be easily digested. Art should help reduce things to manageable proportions, help extricate the complexities of life. (qtd. in Scasserra 12)

BIBLIOGRAPHY

Dramatic Works by Ossie Davis

Alice in Wonder. Performed at the Elk Theatre, New York, 1952.
Curtain Call, Mr. Aldridge, Sir. Performed at the Henry Hudson Hotel, 1963.
Escape to Freedom: A Play about Young Frederick Douglass. New York: Viking, 1976.
Langston. New York: Delacorte, 1982.
A Last Dance for Sybil. Performed at the New Federal Theatre, New York, 2003.
Leonidas Is Fallen. 1942. Unpublished.
Purlie Victorious. New York: French 1961.

Other Cited Material by Ossie Davis

With Ossie and Ruby: In This Life Together (with Ruby Dee). New York: Morrow, 1998.

Studies of Ossie Davis's Dramatic Works

Burdine Warren. "Let the Theatre Say 'Amen.'" *Black American Literature Forum* 25.1 (Spring 1991): 73–82.
Core, Richard. "The New Negro Dramatist." *Transition* 11 (Nov. 1963): 29–20.
Dodson, Owen. "Who Has Seen the Wind? Part III." *Black American Literature Forum* 13.2 (Summer 1980): 54–59.
Funke, Lewis. *The Curtain Rises: The Story of Ossie Davis* New York: Grosset, 1971.
Leaks, Sylvester. "Theatre: Purlie Emerges Victourious." *Freedomways* 1 (Spring 1961): 347.

Molette, Barbara J. "Black Heroes and Afrocentric Values in Theatre." *Journal of Black Studies* 15.4 (June 1985): 447–462.

"Opening Night Festivities." *Jet Magazine* 103.4 (20 Jan. 2003): 44.

"Purlie Victorious." *Ebony* 17.5 (Mar. 1962): 55–60.

Scasserra, Michael P. "Writing Wrongs." *American Theatre* 12.6 (July–Aug. 1995): 12.

Turner, Darwin T. "Past and Present in Negro American Drama." *Negro American Literature Forum.*2.2 (Summer 1968): 26–27.

Wiggins, William H., Jr. "'In the Rapture': The Black Aesthetic and Folk Drama." *Calllaloo* 2 (Feb. 1978): 103–111.

THOMAS COVINGTON DENT (1932–1998)

James L. Hill

BIOGRAPHY

Thomas Covington Dent, dramatist, poet, editor, journalist, cultural historian, educator, and civil rights activist, was born on March 20, 1932, at the Flint Goodridge Hospital in New Orleans, Louisiana. A child prodigy of a socially prominent and politically committed family, Tom Dent, as he usually preferred to be called, was groomed early in his life to become a successful black professional. His father, Dr. Albert Walker Dent, was president of Dillard University from 1941 to 1969; and a former concert pianist, his mother, Ernestine Jessie Covington Dent, was the first African American musician awarded a scholarship to Juilliard. Dent's grandfather was Dr. Jesse Covington, a leader in Booker T. Washington's National Negro Business League and one of the founders of the Riverside General Hospital, the first medical facility for blacks in Houston. His grandmother, Belle Covington, was an early leader in Texas interracial movements and one of the founders of the Blue Triangle YWCA.

Educated in the public and private schools of New Orleans, Dent graduated in 1947 from Gilbert Academy, a college preparatory school for black students, located on St. Charles Avenue. That same year, he enrolled in Morehouse College, and he graduated in 1952 with a B.A. in political science. Subsequently, he continued his education at the Syracuse University School of International Studies (Maxwell School of Citizenship from 1952 to 1956) and completed all of his coursework leading to the doctorate. From

1957 to 1959, Dent served in the United States Army. After he left the army, instead of returning to Syracuse to complete his credentials and pursue a promising academic career, Dent elected to become actively involved in the civil rights movement. Though he would later earn an M.F.A. in creative writing from Goddard University in 1974, he never really seemed suited for the life of the academy.

In 1959, Dent's relocation to New York became for him a cultural vista. Working as a reporter for the Harlem *New York Age* from 1959 to 1960 with Calvin Hicks, Tom Feelings, and Chuck Stone and associating with writers such as Raymond Patterson, Lloyd Addison, Calvin Hernton, David Henderson, and Langston Hughes* created new options for Dent. One of the first options he exercised was his own personal development as a writer. Although he had actually begun his career as a reporter for the *Houston Informer*, New York offered richer opportunities for his apprenticeship as a writer. In addition to the *Writer's Digest* correspondence course he had taken while in the army, Dent sought more formal training. He responded to a *New York Post* ad for a writers' class and was accepted in a creative writing course run by Lajos Egri, a Hungarian immigrant and author of the classic textbook *The Art of Dramatic Writing*. There he met other black writers with whom he became friends, particularly Walter Dean Meyers. Dent also made two important discoveries: that a writer can achieve a reputation without necessarily becoming wealthy and that black writers did not have to limit themselves to the literary and can become influential writers with fundamental ties to their community (Salaam 330). His discovery of these options prepared him for his role as a cultural nationalist, which became the central focus of his life and work. Evaluating his emerging sense of his role as a cultural nationalist and as a black writer, Dent later said, "I guess I was always looking for that" (qtd. in Salaam 330).

Dent's newfound nationalist ideology led him in two directions, cultural nationalism and political activism, which for him were often the same. With Calvin Hicks, Max Roach, Abbey Lincoln, Archie Shepp, LeRoi Jones/Amiri Baraka,* and Harold Cruise, he helped establish the intellectual discussion group On Guard for Freedom and a fledgling newspaper by the same name. On Guard was a transitory group, lasting for only about two years. Dent, Calvin Hernton, and Raymond Henderson still envisioned an organization to develop and publish writers. In 1962, they cofounded the New York–based Umbra Writers Workshop and *Umbra*, a poetry magazine, which became an important publication in the black arts movement. Umbra was collective of black artists, activists, and thinkers on the Lower East Side of New York City who explored the interface between politics, social activism, art, and literature. "The Umbra writers, continuing the trend popularized by the 'beat generation' poets of the 1950s," Lorenzo Thomas observed, "presented public poetry recitations that challenged audiences' preconceptions" ("Tom" 88). Dent later described the vitality of Umbra: "Just the idea of black poets reading and using the language black people speak, was unique—no other group had done that. Whenever the Umbra poets read, it sounded like a well-orchestrated chorus of deeply intimate revelations . . . the rich and varied impact of verbal black music" (Thomas, "Tom" 88).

Umbra, Dent recalled, "came from a search to find other black writers my age in New York," and he aggressively recruited other writers to join Umbra, including N. H. Pritchard, Joe Johnson, Ishmael Reed, Askia Muhammad Toure, and Lorenzo Thomas (qtd. in Salaam 329). In fact, Umbra became the medium for the crystallization of Dent's nationalist views. "Umbra was my introduction to the Black Arts Movement," he declared. "[I]t turned me into viewing reality through a black lens. Not that I didn't already know I was black, but the way a *writer* perceives reality is a trained response and carries with it a certain degree of consciousness and self-recognition" (Thomas, "Tom" 88). Umbra was also seminal in freeing him to find his own voice, writing style, and social commitment. "Each of us was challenged . . . ," he said, "to discover his or her own way of rendering and transforming those dominant ideas through our works, according to our personal vision" (Dent, "Lower" 597). With all of the Umbra writers, Dent realized that he shared one dominant, common, and consistent reality: the black experience.

Living and working in New York also provided a canvass for Dent's political activism. While he worked as a social services investigator for the Welfare Department from 1960 to 1961, he gained a firsthand knowledge of poverty in New York. The next two years, he worked as a press attaché for the NAACP and eventually became the public information director of the NAACP Legal Defense Fund, where he worked closely with and became a friend of Thurgood Marshall. He also participated in United Nations and other civil rights demonstrations. In 1965, at the beginning of what would become the black power movement, however, Dent made two fateful decisions: he decided to return to New Orleans, and he subsequently joined the fledgling Free Southern Theater (FST), a black community theater group of intellectuals and activists. Perhaps it was always Dent's fate that he return to New Orleans; but his relocation to the Big Easy was actually influenced by more mundane reasons. In 1965, he was having difficulty in New York, working only part time, and he was robbed. These circumstances and his father, who came to New York for a meeting, finally convinced him to return to New Orleans, which he never really left again.

When he departed New York in 1965, Dent became affiliated with the FST, and from 1966 to 1970, he was associate director. His association with the group lasted almost a decade, and during those days, he became a dramatist. Among the plays he published are *Snapshot* (1969), *Song of Survival* (1969), *Inner Blk Blues* (1972), and *Ritual Murder* (1978), and he is credited with several unpublished plays: *Negro Study*, *Riot Duty*, and *Feathers and Stuff*. *Snapshot*, *Song of Survival* (coauthored with Val Ferdinand [Kalamu ya Salaam]), and *Inner Blk Blues* were published in *Nkombo*. *Ritual Murder*, originally produced by the FST in 1967, was not published until 1978 in *Callaloo*, a literary journal Dent cofounded with Charles Rowell and Jerry Ward. Subsequently, after realizing the need for a southern prototype of Umbra, Dent founded an FST Writing Workshop group in 1968, which eventually became BLKARTSOUTH.

Under Dent's leadership, between 1968 and 1973, BLKARTSOUTH published the literary magazine *Echoes from the Gumbo*, coedited by Dent and Kalamu ya Salaam; it was later renamed *Nkombo*. Additionally, the group organized a touring ensemble that performed poetry and drama across the South. In 1969, with Gilbert Moses and Richard Schechner, Dent coedited *The Free Southern Theater*, a collection of poetry, journal entries, letters, and essays about FST's radical theater experiment in the South. Later, he founded the Southern Black Cultural Alliance to coordinate the activities of black artists in the South. Unfortunately, despite its achievements and enormous potential, the FST fell short of Dent's vision, eventually motivating his departure. Not only did the FST become mired in its members' philosophical differences about the role of the FST, but around 1967, it lost much of its funding and was forced to suspend its touring program. In 1976, two years after leaving the FST, Dent, with Lloyd Medley, founded the New Orleans–based Congo Square Writers Union, which published the journal *Bamboula*. Dent edited several issues of the group's newspaper, the *Black River Journal*.

Meanwhile, Dent maintained his literary and historical focus as a cultural historian of the South. From 1968 to 1970, he commuted to and taught at Mary Holmes College in East Point, Mississippi. In the early 1970s, he also contributed articles to a number of journals and magazines, for example, *Black Collegian*, *Freedomways*, and *Negro Digest*; and from 1971 to 1974, he served as the public relations director for the New Orleans antipoverty agency. An established poet, Dent also published two volumes of poetry: *Magnolia Street* (1976) and *Blue Lights and River Songs* (1982). From 1979 to 1981, he was the Marcus Christian Lecturer in Afro-American Literature at the University of New Orleans.

A relentless chronicler of history, Dent conducted oral history interviews with Mississippi civil rights workers between 1978 and 1985; and in 1984, he interviewed New Orleans and Arcadian musicians, both collections of which are located in the Amistad Research Center in New Orleans. From 1984 to 1986, he worked as a writer on Andrew Young's autobiography, *An Easy Burden*, and on the Mississippi Oral History Project on the civil rights movement with Jerry Ward. The next three years, 1987–1990, Dent served as executive director of the New Orleans Jazz and Heritage Foundation, which annually presents the New Orleans Jazz and Heritage Festival. In 1990, he resigned that position to begin work on what would be his last book, *A Southern Journey: A Return to the Civil Rights Movement*, published in 1997. One year later, on June 6, 1998, he died from a heart attack at Charity Hospital in New Orleans.

MAJOR WORKS AND THEMES

Although Thomas Covington Dent was primarily a poet, he became one of the three major playwrights for the FST. Like black arts movement agit-prop drama, his plays *Snapshot*, *Song of Survival*, *Inner Blk Blues*, and *Ritual Murder* are conscience-raising dramas written to confront African Americans with their actions within their communities. *Song of Survival* explores issues requisite to the survival of African Americans, while *Snapshot* dramatizes the conspicuous hypocrisies in the practice of black religion, especially imitations of the extravagances and trappings of white culture. *Inner Blk Blues*, like *Song of Survival* and *Snapshot*, is also an agitprop play written to prick the consciousness of black youths about resisting the brainwashing of white oppression. Set in New Orleans, it is a multimedia presentation of positive and negative black images using music, slides, and filmstrips to comment on the narrative. Joe Brown, the protagonist, dreams of becoming a famous musician, but lack of access to economic mobility defers and destroys his dream, eventually leading him to murder his best friend. In effect, *Inner Blk Blues* is poignant in its revelation of the effects of racial discrimination and oppression in African American communities: broken dreams, self-hatred, drugs, black-on-black crime, and other rituals of self-destruction.

Written to create more viable black drama for community theater, *Ritual Murder* is Dent's best known, if not his best, play. Like *Inner Blk Blues*, it is another of Dent's explorations of the theme of black-on-black crime. *Ritual Murder* also focuses on the life of a young black man, Joe Brown, who resides in the Desire Housing Project. An obvious use of irony in name, Desire is actually known as the most dangerous housing complex in the Big Easy; and just as Southside Chicago creates its Bigger Thomas in *Native Son*, Desire is responsible for Joe, who deliberately, irresponsibly, and senselessly murders his best friend. Structurally, the play is organized as a television documentary in which the narrator confronts all of the key individuals in Joe's life to discern the reason for the murder. Unable to explain Joe's murdering his friend, the other characters represent powerless beings who can only acknowledge their inability to change their environment. *Ritual Murder* is, therefore, Dent's comment on the pathology of life in Desire that produces black-on-black crime, and the play underscores the fact that young black men, denied self-esteem and upward mobility, most often turn inwardly on each other. In *Ritual Murder*, Dent hammers his audience with the idea that Joe's life is absent of hope and that lack of hope is really the murderer.

CRITICAL RECEPTION

Better known among civil rights activists, historians, and community theater groups than playwrights of the African American theater, Thomas

Covington Dent remains a marginal dramatist, even among literary scholars and critics. As a cultural nationalist, however, Dent was much more interested in community theater than Broadway and Off Broadway; and he believed that the South had the potential to develop a vital and culturally significant tradition in black theater paralleling that in black music ("Beyond" 17). Further, he concluded that it was only through viable community theater that such a tradition could develop, and the real test for him and other black dramatists was to offer "nothing that black people didn't feel was natural to them, that was foreign to our life-style, that did not have a use, a usefulness to our lives" ("Beyond" 20). The FST, Dent's model for community theater, had already spawned analogs across the South and toured many cities, including Houston, Prairie View, Little Rock, Bogulusa, Jackson, San Antonio, Tuskegee, and Albany. Unlike many of his contemporaries, therefore, Dent did not write for traditional theater; and since he did not publish in the traditional sources, critics have been less than diligent in searching out and writing about his plays.

It was in the medium of community theater, therefore, that Dent wrote and produced his plays; and *Snapshot*, *Song of Survival*, *Inner Blk Blues*, and *Ritual Murder* were written expressly for black community theater with the purpose of raising consciousness and engendering thought. A classic in New Orleans theater, *Ritual Murder* is Dent's best example of such community theater. Not only did Dent locate the FST's community theater in the Desire Housing Project area in New Orleans, but he also used the Desire Housing Project as the setting in *Ritual Murder*. Primarily, critics of Dent's plays were community theater audiences, not individuals who made their living writing. Even the community theater audiences, however, were often not prepared for the militant and realistic plays, and sometimes their responses were generational. "As I remember it," Dent recalled in an interview with Salaam, "generally when we performed in those situations, the older, settled respectable Blacks who thought they were coming to a pleasant 'cultural evening' were shocked and turned off—but the young people were turned on, and wanted to hang with us afterwards" (337).

Despite the unique achievements and potential of community theater, the FST in particular, Dent eventually came to believe that community theater in the South should be a part of the national theater movement. While the community theater movement in the South eventually attracted the attention of such critics as Hoyt Fuller and was occasionally included in the theater roundup in *Negro Digest/Black World*, the reviews were often written by the community theater activists, not by critics who came to see the productions. For community theater in the South to develop fully, Dent concluded, "[w]e need the analysis, criticism and inspiration from people in New York, Chicago, Newark and/or Detroit so that we can keep ourselves going . . ." ("Beyond" 24). As a dramatist and poet, Dent earned a considerable reputation, but his interest in the opinions of community theater audiences far exceeded that he showed in any recognition he garnered from professional theater critics. Dent appears to have been much more interested in cultural nationalism; and his enduring legacy will likely be his continuing efforts to create and sustain avenues for the organization and distribution of the writings and ideas of other black writers, not those of this own.

BIBLIOGRAPHY

Dramatic Works by Thomas Covington Dent

"*Inner Blk Blues*." 1972. *Nkombo* 8.4 (Aug. 1974): 26–42.
"*Ritual Murder*." 1978. *Callaloo* 2 (Feb. 1978): 67–81.
"*Snapshot*." 1969. *Nkombo* 2.4 (1969): 85–90.
"*Song of Survival*" (with Val Ferdinand [Kalamu ya Salaam]). 1969. *Nkombo* 2.4 (1969): 91–96.

Other Material by Thomas Covington Dent

"Beyond Rhetoric toward a Black Southern Theater." *Black World* (Apr. 1971): 14–24.
"Black Theater in the South: Report and Reflections." *Freedomways* 14 (1974): 247–254.
"The Free Southern Theater." *Negro Digest* (Apr. 1967): 41–48.
The Free Southern Theater by the Free Southern Theater. Ed. Tom Dent, Richard Schechner, and Gilbert Moses. Indianapolis: Bobbs, 1969.
"Lower East Side Coda." *African American Review* 27.4 (1993): 596–598.
"Umbra Days." *Black American Literature Forum* 14 (1980): 105–108.

Studies of Thomas Covington Dent's Dramatic Works

Bryan, Violet H. *The Myth of New Orleans Literature: Dialogues of Race and Gender*. Knoxville: University of Tennessee Press, 1993.
Salaam, Kalamu ya. "Enriching the Paper Trail: An Interview with Tom Dent." *African American Review* 27.2 (1993): 327–344.
Thomas, Lorenzo. "Dent, Tom." *The Oxford Companion to African American Literature*. Ed. William L. Andrews, Frances Smith Foster, and Trudier Harris. New York: Oxford University Press, 1997. 209–210.
———. "Tom Dent." *African American Writers after 1955: Dramatists and Prose Writers*. Vol. 38 of *Dictionary of Literary Biography*. Ed. Thadious M. Davis and Jerry Ward. Detroit: Gale, 1985. 86–91.
———. "Southern Black Aesthetics: The Case of *Nkombo* Magazine." *Mississippi Quarterly* 44 (Spring 1991): 143–150.

OWEN DODSON
(1914 – 1983)

Louis J. Parascandola

BIOGRAPHY

Owen Vincent Dodson was born in Brooklyn, New York, on November 28, 1914, the last of nine children of Nathaniel Barnett Dodson, a journalist, and Sarah Elizabeth Goode Dodson. The family was not wealthy but Nathaniel's position as director of the National Negro Press Association provided a steady income and brought such luminaries as Booker T. Washington, W. E. B. Du Bois, and James Weldon Johnson to the family's home. This would serve as an introduction for young Owen into the world of black letters, which he would pursue for the remainder of his life. Tragedy, however, also dogged the family. Both of Owen's parents succumbed to fatal illnesses before he was thirteen; and several of his siblings died at a young age. It is not surprising that Dodson once said, "There was a great scent of death in the garden when I was born" (Hatch 1). Dodson documents these early years of his life in his two semiautobiographical novels *Boy at the Window* (1951) and *Come Home Early, Child* (1977).

Despite his personal losses, Dodson excelled in school. His academic proficiency earned him a scholarship to Bates College in Lewiston, Maine, where some of his classmates and friends included the poet John Ciardi and the statesman Edmund Muskie. While in a freshman English class, he suggested that he could write sonnets as good as those by John Keats. This braggadocio resulted in the teacher having Dodson write a sonnet a week until he graduated in 1936. Owen also became coeditor of the college's literary magazine, the *Garnet*, in which he published poetry and verse drama.

After graduating from Bates, Dodson entered the Yale Drama School, where he received an M.F.A. in playwrighting in 1939. While there, he wrote several plays, including *Divine Comedy* (1938) and *Garden of Time* (1939). During these years, Dodson also established a network of influential friends including W. H. Auden, Harold Jackman, and Carl Van Vechten. Throughout his life, with his lively wit and generous nature, Dodson managed to build a coterie of supporters who helped him out when times got tough.

Upon receiving his M.F.A., Dodson was offered a position to teach speech and drama at Spelman College in Atlanta, where he worked from 1939 to 1941. He would go on to teach at a number of universities for the next forty years, interrupted by a two-year stretch in the navy from 1940 to 1942, when he wrote and produced a series of short radio documentaries of naval heroes, including *The Ballad of Dorrie Miller*, about a black messman who shot down four enemy planes at Pearl Harbor. After being discharged from the navy because of a severe asthmatic condition, Dodson became executive secretary of the Committee for Mass Education in Race Relations, where he labored to change images of ethnic minorities in America.

Dodson then resumed his teaching career, including a long stint at Howard University (1947–1970), where he, along with his colleagues Anne Cooke and John Butcher, helped foster an important training ground for African American theater. During his career at Howard, he helped cultivate the talents of such students as Toni Morrison, Roxie Roker, and Debbie Allen. His importance as a mentor and his willingness to extend himself to his students cannot be overestimated.

Dodson also wrote several plays while at Howard, including *Bayou Legend* (1948), loosely taken from Henrik Ibsen's *Peer Gynt*. In 1949, Dodson led a troupe of Howard drama students on a ten-week tour of Scandinavia and Germany, where they performed Ibsen's *The Wild Duck* and DuBose Heyward's *Mamba'a Daughters* to wide acclaim. This was the first black college group to be sponsored by the U.S. State Department. In addition to his plays, Dodson also published a volume of verse, *Powerful Black Ladder* (1946).

Dodson won a Guggenheim Fellowship in 1953, enabling him to spend a year in Italy, where he stayed in Auden's house in Ischia. The 1950s also saw Dodson directing a number of plays, including *Hamlet*, *Emperor Jones*, and the first production of James Baldwin's* *The Amen Corner* in 1955.

The 1960s were the most hectic years of Dodson's life. Between 1963 and 1965, for example, he wrote twenty-five theater reviews and directed twenty-one shows. The climax of this frenzied activity was an invitation to the White House in 1964 to visit with President Lyndon Johnson.

This was also the beginning of a period of heavy drinking. Dodson seemed somewhat out of touch with the rebelliousness of the new generation of black writers. He took exception to revolutionary writers such as

Baldwin and Amiri Baraka,* who he believed sacrificed their talents to their politics. Feeling himself an outsider, he began missing classes regularly, and in 1968, he was given a one-year leave of absence.

Dodson returned to Howard in the fall of 1969, but he soon was plagued by illness and needed a hip replacement. Administrators at the university, seeking to sever ties with him, urged Dodson to retire on disability. Free from teaching, Dodson took up several projects, including a sound recording *The Dream Awake* (1970), a narration for several film documentaries on the black experience. He also composed a volume of poetry, *The Confession Stone* (1960), later adapted for the stage.

Freedom from Howard also meant a decrease in Dodson's funds since he was unable to collect his pension until he turned sixty-five. He was forced to scramble for work. He would take short-term teaching positions at such schools as the City College of New York and York College, both branches of the City University of New York, but would soon lose these positions, causing him serious financial distress.

These were often lonely times for Dodson. He had long struggled with his sexual identity. Twice he had become engaged but never married, no doubt because of his preference for men. His homosexuality remained muted in his literary works. According to his biographer James V. Hatch," Estimates of Owen's love life by those who knew him ranged from busy to bleak" (183). In any event, Dodson seemed to live his whole life searching for a companion, someone to whom he could pour out his heart and soul. Despite his many friends and the devoted love of his sisters, Lillian and Edith, he never found this person. In his later years, in particular, he seemed to feel this void as is documented by one former lover, Hilton Als, in his autobiography *The Women* (1996).

Without the ready presence of the classroom, Dodson often would read his work and retell his stories to any audience he could find, whether by telephone or at dinner parties. His loneliness and crippling arthritis led him to rely more and more heavily on alcohol. There were, however, a number of happy moments in these dark times. In 1973, he gave a highly successful reading at the Library of Congress, incorporating dance with his poetry. And in 1974, a collage of his works, *Owen's Song*, assembled by two of Owen's former students, Glenda Dickerson and Mike Malone, was staged at the Kennedy Center in Washington. The same year, the Kennedy Center also staged his opera *Till Victory Is Won*, written with composer Mark Fax in celebration of the centennial of Howard University. In addition, he collaborated with visual artist Camille Billops and photographer James Van Der Zee in *The Harlem Book of the Dead* (1978). His poetic drama, *Life in the Streets*, was performed at New York City's Public Theatre in 1982. He also was awarded honorary doctorate degrees by Bates College and Lincoln University.

Despite these successes, Dodson became increasingly alienated in his later years. His sister Edith died early in 1983. This seemed to be the final blow to his spirit, and he died in New York City on June 21, 1983, of a heart attack. A week after his death, a celebration of his life at the Community Church in New York drew four hundred people, who remembered him from better days. Perhaps his spirit is captured best by Nathan L. Grant: "The best of the Owen Dodson that the world knew . . . was generous and courtly, and his aesthetic often rendered flashes of brilliance as it sought to interpret the personal tragedy that was the testament of his youth" (645). His ashes are interred in Evergreen Cemetery in Brooklyn.

MAJOR WORKS AND THEMES

Owen Dodson was a novelist and a poet of some renown. Drama, however, was his greatest love and he worked in the theater in numerous capacities, including writing, directing, acting, teaching, and stage managing. He said, "My particular experiences in life have been that of directing plays, of writing plays, and of writing plays with poems" (qtd. in Rowell 631). He wrote over thirty-five plays and operas and had some twenty-seven produced; however, only a handful of his plays have been published. A review of five of his pieces—*The Shining Town*, *Divine Comedy*, *Garden of Time*, *Bayou Legend*, and *The Confession Stone*—will serve to illustrate his main themes.

Dodson is not generally considered to be a writer of social criticism, but the one-act *The Shining Town* (1937) is an example of his more politically oriented works. The play, written while Dodson was at Yale, has yet to be performed, perhaps due to its controversial subject matter. Set during the Depression, the play powerfully evokes the stark poverty of black domestic workers, who are forced to work virtually for nothing. The place where the women assemble, a subway station in the Bronx, while awaiting their white employers, is little short of a slave market. The play is indicative of Dodson's sympathy for the oppressed.

Divine Comedy, like much of Dodson's best dramatic work, is written in verse. The play is in keeping with his belief in "total theatre . . . poetry, dance, drama, and music" ("Divine" 84). It was first staged at the Yale Drama School in 1938 and demonstrates the false allure of a religious figure such as Father Divine to people as lacking in hope as Harlemites during the Depression Era. There is strong sympathy evinced for those who have fallen under the sway of the preacher. Dodson's warning, however, is aimed not only at cult figures like Divine. The power of all prophets, even Christ, is seen as existing only within their followers. At the conclusion of the play, the chorus, in triumph, affirms that prophets are unnecessary and that the people themselves "*are* the miracle." The play reflects Dodson's own ambivalent feelings about religion. As Grant observes, Dodson "was often cynical about his faith, sorely tested as it was by the events of his upbringing, and it often served only as a vehicle for his most tortured negotiations between love and death" (640).

Garden of Time is an ambitious verse drama that has yet to be published but was first staged at Yale University in 1939. It was, as Dodson says, "an attempt to enlarge the theater, to let out the stops" (Peck 16). The sprawling story is taken from the classical story of Medea. In Dodson's play, however, Medea is black and Jason is white and the story is transported halfway through from Colchis and Greece to nineteenth-century Haiti and Georgia. The play won the Maxwell Anderson Verse Play Contest at Stanford University in 1940.

Bayou Legend, first produced at Howard University in 1948, is more than just an adaptation of Ibsen's *Peer Gynt* transplanted to a Louisiana bayou. Indeed, Dodson said that "the play is my own as much as Anouilh's *Antigone* is attached to Sophocles" (Hatch 147). This verse drama reflects Dodson's interest in African American folklore and culture. The loose plot, with over forty characters, concerns the rise and fall of the profligate Reve Grant, who eventually gains salvation through the faith of his Christian lover, Sophie-Louise. But as was often the case in Dodson's work, the story is less important than the poetry and pageantry.

The Confession Stone, published as a cycle of poems on the three days from Good Friday to Easter Sunday in 1960, was first staged at Carnegie Hall in New York City in 1970. The play dramatizes the lives of such biblical figures as Mary, Joseph, Pontius Pilate, and Judas. Unlike most of Dodson's other dramas, the play is stark in its setting, needing little in the way of lighting or costuming. This places the emphasis where Dodson wants it to be: on the songs themselves. *The Confession Stone* would be what Dodson considered to be his finest work. The narrative poems easily lent themselves to dramatic rendering and Dodson quickly adapted the work for the stage. He said of it: "*The Confession Stone* is not a dramatic work but a literary one, but if you listen, it will become a dramatic work, for within each of the characters whirls a tempest" (Hatch 247).

The majority of Dodson's papers and manuscripts are located at the Hatch–Billops Collection in New York City, in the Moorland–Spingarn Collection at Howard University, in the James Weldon Johnson Collection at Yale University, and in the Harold Jackman Collection at Atlanta University.

CRITICAL RECEPTION

Owen Dodson has been called "the best Negro poet in the United States" by distinguished author Richard Eberhart (qtd. in Hatch 234). He was given several prestigious awards, including a Rosenwald Fellowship (1944–1945), a Guggenheim Fellowship (1953–1955), a Rockefeller Grant (1969–1970), and an AUDELCO (Audience Development Committee) Outstanding Pioneer Award (1975). He has been recognized by his peers as an outstanding writer and director. Despite these accolades Dodson still has not achieved his proper place in the black literary and theatrical canon. James Hatch suggests several reasons for this relative neglect: that he had no real ties to any black literary movements, that he wrote in several genres, that he used traditional forms, that he simply was born at the wrong time, too late for the Harlem Renaissance and before the black arts movement. Hatch, in fact, has been the main authority on Dodson, including the authorized biography, *Sorrow Is the Only Faithful One*.

The majority of criticism of Dodson's dramas has come in the form of reviews. Mel Gussow, in commenting on a revival of *Divine Comedy*, declared that the "play is flawed and somewhat fragmentary. At times the verse is windily poetic. But this is an intriguing play on a fascinating subject" (33). Brenda Dixon-Stowell, in reviewing the same production, writes that despite some moments where the play "rambles," it is "truly inspired" (12).

Opinion on *Garden of Time* was generally mixed. Alain Locke called it "the most competent piece of playwriting that any of our young authors has yet turned out . . . a powerful and challenging play despite its occasional expressionistic mannerisms" (10). Joe Bostic writes that the theatergoer is left "thoroughly stimulated and terribly depressed" by the play (22). An anonymous reviewer in *Mademoiselle* felt the play "though honest and often beautiful, [was] a little sleep-making" ("Theatre" 240). Lewis Nichols also believed the play to be "a bit pretentious" and "pretty slow" (13). Wilella Waldorf concurs, feeling that the play was "tediously obvious," and that "the author is far more adept at poetic composition than he is at building a drama" (22).

Jay Carmody, in reviewing *Bayou Legend*, also feels that Dodson's plays are more poetry than drama. He suggests that Dodson "is an author who sees visions and loves words and whose blending of the two stimulates the imagination more than it satisfies any audience demand for the tidy or the terse" (B22).

Owen Dodson, as an author, director, and teacher, was a pivotal force in African American drama for fifty years. However, most of his plays remain unpublished, and are seldom revived or written about. This leaves a void in studies of the drama, one that it is hoped will be filled by future researchers.

BIBLIOGRAPHY

Dramatic Works by Owen Dodson

"The Ballad of Dorrie Miller." *Theatre Arts* 27 (July 1943): 18–28. Performed at Great Lakes Naval Training Station, Illinois, 1943.
"Bayou Legend." *Black Drama in America: An Anthology*. Ed. Darwin T. Turner. Greenwich: Fawcett, 1971. Performed at Howard University (1948); Hunter College (1950); Augusta, Georgia (1952); Howard University (1957); Amas Theatre,

New York (1975); Inner City Cultural Center, Los Angeles (1979); and Bermuda (1979).

"The Confession Stone." Black Theatre USA. Rev. ed. Ed. James V. Hatch and Ted Shine. New York: Free, 1996. Performed on London BBC TV (1964 and 1968; in New York City (1970); at the Philharmonic Civic Center (1972); at the National Arts Club (1972); at the RACCA Arts Consortium, New York (1978); at the Theatre Off Park, New York (1979); and at Karamu House, Cleveland (1980).

"Divine Comedy." Black Theater USA. Ed. James V. Hatch and Ted Shine. New York: Free, 1974. Performed at Yale Drama School, 1938; Atlanta University, 1938; Howard University, 1938; Hampton Institute, 1942; Jackson State College, 1952; YMCA, Harlem, 1956; Grambling College, 1970; and New Federal Theatre, New York, 1975.

"Everybody Join Hands." Theatre Arts 27 (Sept. 1943): 10–19. Performed at Great Lakes Naval Training Station, Illinois, 1943.

Garden of Time. Performed at Yale Drama School, 1939.

Life in the Streets. Performed at the Public Theatre, New York, 1982.

New World A-Coming. Performed at Madison Square Garden, New York, 1944.

"The Poet's Caprice." Garnet (Dec. 1935): 1–9.

"The Shining Town." The Roots of African American Drama. Ed. Leo Hamalian and James V. Hatch. Detroit: Wayne State University Press, 1990.

"Sonata." Garnet (May 1935): 15–28.

Till Victory Is Won (with Mark Fax). Performed in Bermuda (1965); at Howard University (1965); in Baltimore (1970); at the Kennedy Center, Washington, DC (1970); at Howard University (1970); at the Kennedy Center (1974); at Opera Ebony, New York (1979); at the Riverside Church (1982); and at Carnegie Hall Opera Ebony (1983).

Studies of Owen Dodson's Dramatic Works

Als, Hilton. *The Women*. New York: Farrar, 1996.

Bostic, Joe. " 'Garden of Time' Phantasy Stimulating Theatre Fare." *People's Voice* 17 Mar. 1945: 22.

Carmody, Jay. "Old Stars Dominate Film; Poetic Drama at Howard U." *Evening Star* (Washington, DC) 8 May 1948: B22.

Dixon-Stowell, Brenda. "Something Very Special." *Villager* (New York) 20 Jan. 1977: 12.

Grant, Nathan L. "Extending the Ladder: A Remembrance of Owen Dodson." *Callaloo* 20.3 (1998): 640–645.

Gussow, Mel. " 'Divine Comedy,' Play of Father Divine." *New York Times* 16 Jan. 1977: 33.

Hatch, James V. *Sorrow Is the Only Faithful One: The Life of Owen Dodson*. Urbana: University of Illinois Press, 1993.

Hatch, James V., Douglas A. M. Ward, and Joe Weixlmann. "The Rungs of a Powerful Long Ladder: An Owen Dodson Bibliography." *Black American Literature Forum* 14.2 (1980): 60–68.

Locke, Alain. "Dry Fields and Green Pastures." *Opportunity* 18 (Jan. 1940): 10.

Nichols, Lewis. "Uptown Jason." *New York Times* 10 March 1945: 13.

O'Brien, John, ed. "Owen Dodson." *Interviews with Black Writers*. New York: Liveright, 1973. 31–34.

Peck, Seymour. "Owen Dodson, New Writer." *P.M.* 7 Mar. 1945: 16.

Peterson, Bernard L. "The Legendary Owen Dodson of Howard University: His Contributions to the American Theatre." *Crisis* (Nov. 1979): 373–378.

Rowell, Charles H. "An Interview with Owen Dodson." *Callaloo* 20.3 (1998): 627–639.

"Theatre." *Mademoiselle* (May 1945): 240.

Waldorf, Wilella. "American Negro Theatre Gives 'Garden of Time.'" *New York Post* 12 Mar. 1945: 12.

ALICE MOORE DUNBAR-NELSON (1875–1935)

Loretta G. Woodard

BIOGRAPHY

Alice Ruth Moore, a playwright, poet, short story writer, journalist, activist, author, and educator, was born of African American, Native American, and Caucasian ancestry on July 19, 1875, in New Orleans, Louisiana. Alice was the youngest of two daughters in the family of Joseph Moore, a Creole merchant marine, and Patricia (Wright) Moore, a seamstress. Alice attended public school in New Orleans, and graduated from high school there in 1889. All during her girlhood, she participated in amateur theater, attended plays and movies regularly, and wrote and directed plays and pageants for various school, church, and community groups. Then at age fifteen, she entered a two-year teaching program at Straight University (now Dillard University), where she was encouraged to pursue English literature and the classics, trained as a stenographer, and was an accomplished violin-cellist and a mandolin player.

After graduation in 1892, she began her career as a teacher at the Old Marigny Elementary School in New Orleans. Four years later she moved north, first to Medford, Massachusetts, with her mother, sister, and brother-in-law, James Young. She relocated to Brooklyn, New York, in 1897, where she taught at Public School 83. She accepted a teaching position and assisted Victoria Matthews to found the White Rose Mission (later, the White Rose Home for Girls in Harlem), and then taught at Public School 66.

On March 8, 1898, over the objections of her family and friends, she married renowned black poet Paul Laurence Dunbar in a secret ceremony in New York City. After living briefly in Brooklyn, New York, where she taught in the public schools and worked as a teacher on New York's East Side, she joined her husband in Washington, DC, where their literary careers thrived. Their marriage and their literary collaboration ended in 1902 and he died of tuberculosis in 1904. She moved to Wilmington, Delaware, and was joined by her mother, divorced sister, and her sister's four small children. She worked first as an English and drawing instructor and later as head of the English Department at the Howard High School. While directing the seven summer sessions for in-service teachers at State College for Colored Students (now Delaware State College), she taught two years in the summer session at Hampton Institute. Also, she pursued further training at Cornell University, where she received an M.A., and Columbia University, the Pennsylvania School of Industrial Art, and the University of Pennsylvania, specializing in education testing and psychology.

In Wilmington, on January 19, 1910, Dunbar-Nelson secretly married her second husband, Henry Arthur Callis, a fellow teacher at Howard High School, twelve years her junior, and divorced a year later. On April 20, 1916, she married Robert "Bobbo" J. Nelson, a journalist and a widower with two children from Harrisburg, Pennsylvania. From 1920 to 1922, they published the *Wilmington Advocate* newspaper, were actively engaged in politics, and directed political activities among black women. She organized a much-publicized Flag Day parade, formed a local chapter of the Circle for Negro War Relief, and toured the South as a field representative of the Women's Committee of the United States Council of National Defense in 1918. She served on the State Republican Committee of Delaware in 1920. October of that same year, after eighteen years as head of the English Department at Howard High School, she lost her position, following an unapproved trip to Marion, Ohio, for Social Justice Day. From 1924 to 1928, she worked as a teacher and parole officer in Marshalltown, Delaware, with women from the State Federation of Colored Women to found the Industrial School for Colored Girls.

Between 1899 and 1920, Dunbar-Nelson's career flourished as a short fiction writer, journalist, poet, and anthologist. Her lifelong interest in drama led to the publication of her first play, *The Author's Evening at Home: The Smart Set* (1900), a one-act satire, which apparently relates to her own marriage to Dunbar, as it depicts the struggles between an author and his wife. In 1916, *An Hawaiian Idyll*, a three-act operetta, directed by Conwell Benton, was produced as a Christmas entertainment for her students at Howard High School. Prompted by her political activism, especially her World War I work, *Crisis* published Dunbar-Nelson's most popular play, *Mine Eyes Have Seen* (1918), which was "designed for the educational and moral edification of the students" (Hull, *Works* xlix) and performed at Howard High School. *Love's Disguise*, her typescript film scenario, was probably written around 1909–1916 (Hull, *Works* 218). Her three-act play, *Gone White*, was written sometime later and was not published or produced.

Although Dunbar-Nelson wrote very few plays for the theater, her plays were of grave significance for breaking new ground for those playwrights who followed (Shafer 387). Also, she was genuinely dedicated to the cause of improving the conditions of blacks, socially, politically, and educationally, and spent much of her later life traveling and speaking between 1928 and 1931, as the executive secretary of the American Friends Inter-Racial Peace Committee. After Robert was appointed to the Pennsylvania Athletic (Boxing) Commission in January 1932, she, along with her mother, sister, and her sister's children, moved to Philadelphia. Dunbar-Nelson died at the University of Pennsylvania Hospital on September 18, 1935, of coronary complications she had suffered from for three years.

MAJOR WORKS AND THEMES

Ora Williams notes that "in all her writings . . . Dunbar-Nelson is always direct. . . . Her concerns about racism, the roles of men and women in society, and the importance of love, war death, and nature appear as recurring themes. . . . Hers was one of the most consistent, secure, and independent voices of the black community" (227). In her only play of distinction, *Mine Eyes Have Seen* (1918), Alice Moore Dunbar-Nelson's patriotic play, which gets it title from the opening line of *The Battle Hymn of the Republic*, centers around a young black named Chris, who is about to be drafted into the army, and explores the depth of black citizens' dedication to a country in the midst of a war, where their own rights are constantly violated. Chris, his sister, Lucy, and Dan, his crippled brother, were raised in a beautiful home in the South that was burned by white men and they were forced to flee to the North. There was no justice, nor was there any for the murder of their father. Since the country in which they serve does not provide protection from violent acts of racism in their own communities, the overarching question concerns whether blacks even have a patriotic duty to their country during war. To many blacks it seems unconscionable to serve a country that allows these very same acts to prevail when they have toiled and sweated to build the fabric of this country. Essentially, the play denounces answering hate with hate, and it ends with characters expressing pride in being black while a passing band plays *The Battle Hymn of the Republic*.

Gone White, along with Marita Bonner's* *Exit, An Illusion*, focuses on the theme of passing where love is never attained. Allan, a very light-skinned black who can pass for white, wants to be an engineer, but he cannot get the job despite his exceptional qualifications. Once his aunt tells Anna, whom he wants to marry, that her dark skin will impede his career, she sacrifices her love for him for a rich man. Her marriage turns into a disaster and Allan fears that his white wife or his employers will discover his secret of passing for white. When they meet again, Allan pleads for Anna to run away with him to another country, but the meddling aunt suggests that he remain in his prestigious position and get Anna to become his mistress. Once Anna realizes how he has changed, she is able to save her marriage and to have a healthier relationship with her husband.

CRITICAL RECEPTION

Since the 1980s and 1990s, Alice Moore Dunbar-Nelson has been recognized as a key figure in the development of African American theater. Critics have often noted her compelling depictions of female characters; her focus on Louisiana settings and culture; and her sometimes conflicting attitudes toward race, class, and color. According to Elizabeth Brown-Guillory,* "Dunbar-Nelson's later writing, like Georgia Douglas Johnson's, reflects the voice of social protest that was probably shaped by three major factors: a severed attachment to the New Orleans Creoles of color, World War I, and the developing Harlem Renaissance" (8).

Jennifer Burton observes that in *Mine Eyes Have Seen* Dunbar-Nelson "combines elements of propaganda and black history" but unlike most plays of the period "ends on an upbeat note (literally), harking back to the optimism of black women's writings during the post-Reconstruction period" (xxvi–xxvii). James Hatch contends that the play is "a double-edged examination of the loyalty blacks owe to a nation that denies them equality" (qtd. in Roses and Randolph 88).

A few critics note the significance of Dunbar-Nelson's characters and development. Lorraine Elena Roses and Ruth Randolph point out that "[t]oo many characters overwhelm this short play . . . and the protagonist's sudden decision to answer a draft call is unconvincing" (88). Another critic acknowledges how "the characters are not developed through the use of dialect" and "the absence of characterization by means of dialogue weakens the drama and creates a rather strange effect . . . [but] the play is essentially a clear work of propaganda which was effective in its time, but whose message was questioned later" (Shafer 385–386).

Described as "a more ambitious play," Yvonne Shafer claims that *Gone White* "draws attention to several problems for African Americans by those of lighter skin" (387). Commenting on the specific characteristics of the play, Gloria Hull asserts that "[t]hough mostly poor, the characters are decent, respectable, and above all, well-spoken. There is no dialect here, no comedy, as Dunbar-Nelson tries to live up to her call for a broader, more realistic Afro-American drama" (*Works* 1).

BIBLIOGRAPHY

Dramatic Works by Alice Moore Dunbar-Nelson

"*The Author's Evening at Home: The Smart Set*." Sept. 1900. *The Works of Alice Dunbar-Nelson*. Ed. Gloria T. Hull. Vol. 3. New York: Oxford, 1988. 105–106.

"*Gone White*." 1910?–1922?. *The Works of Alice Dunbar-Nelson*. Ed. Gloria T. Hull. Vol. 3. New York: Oxford, 1988. ___–___.

"*Love's Disguise*." 1909?–1916?. *The Works of Alice Dunbar-Nelson*. Ed. Gloria T. Hull. Vol. 3. New York: Oxford, 1988. ___–___.

"*Mine Eyes Have Seen*." *Crisis* 15 (Apr. 1918): 271–275. Rpt. in *The Works of Alice Dunbar-Nelson*. Ed. Gloria T. Hull. Vol. 3. New York: Oxford, 1988. ___–___.

Studies of Alice Moore Dunbar-Nelson's Dramatic Works

Brown-Guillory, Elizabeth. *Their Place on Stage: Black Women Playwrights in America*. Westport: Greenwood, 1988.

Bryan, Violet Harrington. "Creating and Re-creating the Myth of New Orleans: Grace King and Alice Dunbar-Nelson." *Publications of the Mississippi Philological Association* (1987): 185–196.

———. "Race and Gender in the Early Works of Alice Dunbar-Nelson." *Louisiana Women Writers: New Essays and a Comprehensive Bibliography*. Ed. Dorothy H. Brown and Barbara C. Ewell. Baton Rouge: Louisiana State University Press, 1992. 122–138.

Burton, Jennifer. Introduction. *Zora Neale Hurston, Eulalie Spence, Marita Bonner, and Others: The Prize Plays and Other One-Acts Published in Periodicals*. Ed. Henry Louis Gates, Jr. New York: Hall, 1996. xxvi–xxvii.

Gates, Henry Louis, Jr. *Zora Neale Hurston, Eulalie Spence, Marita Bonner, and Others: The Prize Plays and Other One-Acts Published in Periodicals*. New York: Hall, 1996.

Hill, Patricia Liggins, ed. "Alice Moore Dunbar-Nelson." *Call and Response: The Riverside Anthology of the African American Literary Tradition*. Boston: Houghton, 1998. 616–621.

Hull, Gloria T. "Alice Dunbar-Nelson: A Personal and Literary Perspective." *Between Women: Biographers, Novelists, Critics, Teachers, and Artists Write about Their Work on Women*. Ed. Carol Ascher, Louise DeSalvo, and Sara Ruddick. Boston: Beacon, 1984. 105–111.

———. ed. *The Works of Alice Dunbar-Nelson*. Vol. 3. New York: Oxford University Press, 1988.

Ijeoma, Charmaine N. "Alice Dunbar-Nelson: A Biography." *Collections* 10 (2000): 25–54.

Roses, Lorraine Elena, and Ruth Randolph, eds. *Harlem Renaissance and Beyond: Literary Biographies of 100 Black Women Writers, 1900–1945*. Cambridge: Harvard University Press, 1997.

Shafer, Yvonne. *American Women Playwrights, 1900–1950*. New York: Lang, 1995. 383–387.

Whitlow, Roger. "Alice Dunbar-Nelson: New Orleans Writer." *Regionalism and the Female Imagination: A Collection of Essays*. Ed. Emily Toth. New York: Human Sciences, 1985. 109–125.

Williams, Ora. "Alice Moore Dunbar-Nelson." *Afro-American Writers before the Harlem Renaissance*. Vol. 50 of *Dictionary of Literary Biography*. Ed. Trudier Harris and Thadious M. Davis. Detroit: Gale, 1986. 225–233.

LONNE ELDER III
(1931 – 1996)

Justin Brodeur

BIOGRAPHY

Lonne Elder III is the type of person you would be happy to be seated next to for the duration of a trans-American journey on Greyhound or Amtrak. In his sixty-five years, he lived a life as varied as the genres he wrote across in his distinguished career as playwright, screenwriter, and scriptwriter, receiving awards and accolades for many of his principal works. At times critic, dockworker, numbers runner, phone clerk, and professional gambler, Elder settled into writing, as he told Liz Gant in a 1973 interview, "when I was about six or seven years old" (38), as a means of "writing to myself; it was a way of expressing feelings that I didn't know how to express in other ways, like talking" (38). Like the father in *Ceremonies in Dark Old Men*, who conveys his emotions and love for his departed wife through stories of what never was—fanciful retellings of either an invented past or a past revisited and changed in the telling—Elder too told stories, as William Bryan Hart observed, weaving his "multifaceted personal life into his plays" (qtd. in "Elder" par. 2).

Born in Americus, Georgia, to Lonne Elder II and Quincy Elder, Lonne Elder III and family made the move from rural Georgia to New York City while he was still an infant. After the death of his parents when he was ten, he moved in with a relative on a New Jersey farm where, dissatisfied with small-town life, he ran away so frequently that he was sent to live in Jersey City with an aunt and uncle (Cherry 98). A bright but nonetheless "restless student" (98), Elder dropped out of school before his nineteenth birthday: his education continuing for the next few years in various nonmatriculated courses and his eventual involvement with the black equality movement (98), until being drafted into the U.S. Army in 1952.

While stationed at Fort Campbell, Kentucky, Elder was introduced, as he tells Gant, to "[poet-teacher] Robert Hayden. Since I had done some writing—poems and short stories—I spent much time with Dr. Hayden. I gave him my work to read and he was very, very encouraging" (39). At that time, most of Elder's work was a "direct expression of [his] own anguish about the race situation. They made for great politics, but they were bad art" (39). From the hindsight of 1973, twenty-one years after his service in the army, Elder comments on this, noting:

When I was very, very young, I used to pose a lot of questions and try to answer them. Most of what I wrote at that time were political tracts, but as I look back on them, basically they were demeaning of the people I was trying to write about rather than taking situations, very common and very simple situations of people—you know, touch, feel—and exalting them to a place of nobility. That's not very easy to do, and I just hope that I can do it. (44)

Lonne Elder would never lose this underpinning of racial politics in his later works though he would weave it in more artfully, such that it seldom came off as preachy or overt: a balance he sought to maintain throughout his career.

After his discharge and move back to New York City, he moved in with writer and friend Douglas Turner Ward.* Through Ward he would come in contact with novelist John Killens who encouraged Elder to consider himself a writer, and proved supportive of his work through the years (39). It was at this time that Elder first began to "take [himself] seriously as a writer. [He] began to meet a lot of people in Harlem who were into something other than just standing on the corner" which until then, "was where [he] was" (39). It was through Ward and a recently written play that Elder, then "nineteen or twenty," thought that if a peer of his same age could do it, then he, who had never written more then "maybe a 15-page short story or a one-page poem" (40), could do it too. He found that he came to prefer the dramatic form of writing to his previous genres, as playwriting offered an "immediacy of expressing a feeling or emotion. . . . There was something about it that just got to me. And no mater what I saw, I thought I could do better" (40). It was also during this time that he "hustled," which, as he told Dan Sullivan in a 1975 interview, means, "really taking care of business. Like, I used to unload trucks. I was a dealer in a gambling house until somebody pulled a gun on me. I was an actor. I did what I had to do to get the time to write. I hustled!" (668).

A later role as Bobo in a 1959 Broadway production of Lorraine Hansberry's* *A Raisin in the Sun* provided Elder with not only the acting base he would need to "enhance [his] writing tremendously" (Gant 41), but also two years of stability in which he was able to produce "a greater volume of writing than [he] had ever been able to do before" (40). Of these is his first play worth noting, the as-yet-unpublished *A Hysterical Turtle in a Rabbit Race*. Though the plot is described as "convoluted," the characters as "undeveloped," and the dialogue as "stilted" (Cherry 98), Elder's play suggests themes that run throughout his later works: importance of family and race relations.

Two years after his Broadway run as Bobo, Elder married Betty Gross, and, in 1964, became a father to son David DuBois, probably named after author W. E. B. Du Bois whose writings, Elder says, have "had a great impact on [my] life" (Gant 44). Elder's first marriage, however, did not last longer then four years; he divorced Betty in 1967. The midpoint of his marriage marked the arrival of his first critically acclaimed play and "heralded Elder's professional debut as a playwright" (Cherry 100); *Ceremonies in Dark Old Men*, first performed at Wagner College, Staten Island, was later produced through the Negro Ensemble Company, running from 1967 to 1969, and featured Douglas Turner Ward in the lead role. The playwright was recognized with numerous awards including the Outer Critics' Circle Award, the Vernon Rice Drama Desk Award, the Stella Holt Memorial Playwrights Award, the Stanley Drama Award, the Los Angeles Drama Critics Award; and he placed second for the prestigious Pulitzer Prize in 1969.

A duet of one-act plays followed: *Kissing Rattlesnakes Can Be Fun* (1966) and *Seven Comes Up and Seven Comes Down* (1966). Though both remain unpublished and unproduced, they at turns "recall the game playing in *Hysterical Turtle*" and the "sleight-of-hand ending of the then unwritten *Charades on East Fourth Street*" (Cherry 101), Elder's next dramatic work of note.

Charades, another one-act play, was commissioned by the New York City Mobilization for Youth, and is noteworthy for its reference, in the words of Darwin T. Turner, as "a thesis drama . . . urg[ing] young blacks to combat the oppression of corrupt police by legal means rather than by violence" (qtd. in Peterson 161–162). Though the play was not received in the same way as *Ceremonies*, *Charades* is, nonetheless, a powerful drama that moves away from Elder's earlier ironic undertones into the realm of violence and hostility "that is missing from both *Hysterical Turtle* and *Ceremonies*" (Cherry 101).

Concurrent to *Charades*, *Seven*, and *Rattlesnakes*, Elder wrote profusely for the screen, both silver and television ranging from scripts for *N.Y.P.D.*, *Camera Three*, and *The Terrible Veil*, as well as various *McCloud* episodes. This large quantity of screen writings might explain the relatively few plays written, or even produced, since *Ceremonies*. Another factor in the author's move from playwright to screenwriter came when Elder decided in 1970 to move from the drama capital (New York) to the movie capital (Los Angeles), as "New York for me just became a mentally unbearable place to live in. I'm just not made of the stuff to walk around with daggers in my eyes and a clenched fist. I just can't live like that" (qtd. in Gant 41–42).

From his arrival to his death, Elder would have to learn how to "adjust to what he calls 'the whore mentality' that smogs the film–TV industry" (Sullivan 668): an assumption that producers will drop you like a bad habit the moment you fail to deliver what they desire (668). What they desired at that moment in time was, as Elder put it, for black actors to "talk black! Be black! Meaning, be foolish. Swagger around" (qtd. in Sullivan 668). It is this mentality that prompts both his move out West and his eventual founding of The Black Artist Alliance shortly after his arrival in California (Gant 48) because, as he tells it, "film and TV send 'information' into everybody's heads, not just into the relatively few heads that can be reached in the theater" (qtd. in Sullivan 668).

Two years after his arrival, he adapts, from William H. Armstrong's Newberry Award–winning children's story, what turns out to be the silver screen equivalent to *Ceremonies*: *Sounder*. He is nominated for an Academy Award for best-adapted screenplay, and though he does not win the award, the "nomination proved significant" (Cherry 102). Though other screenplays came out after *Sounder*—*Melinda* (1972), *Part 2, Sounder* (1976), and *Bustin' Loose* (1981)—only one other play, *Splendid Mummer* (1986), made it onto Elder's remarkably short list of dramatic works.

MAJOR WORKS AND THEMES

Of Lonne Elder III's six dramatic works, only two were widely produced: *Ceremonies* and *Charades*. Of those two, only *Ceremonies* was received with honors and is widely considered as his culminating dramatic work. Of *Ceremonies*, Elder says, "It was well received in New York and I felt that, in terms of what I had set out to do, I'd accomplished that out of my own experiences and I didn't have to do it any more. I said I wasn't going to write any more Black 'kitchen sink dramas'" (qtd. in Gant 41). This response is indicative of his later move away from the dramatic canon into screenwriting, and underscores why, after *Ceremonies*, only four other plays would follow. Despite these few representations of his dramatic works, Wilsonia Cherry writes that the "plays that he has written strongly emphasize his belief in the survival of a people traumatized both from without and from within" (98). This proves to be a central theme of his career as playwright.

Called by one critic "a Black Doctor Jeckyll and Mr. Hyde" and "the schizophrenic of the year" by another (Gant 43) for his alleged lack of consistency in his choice of themes and dramatic techniques, Elder responds that such criticism is reflective, as he tells Gant, of the perception that "Black people are not supposed to have a whole range of feelings to relate or project" (43). Because they have been typecast and pigeonholed into the very roles Elder sought to do away with in his written portrayals of blacks, "you get to the point where you know what to expect before you even go into the theater or pick a book up" (43). Though his refusal to have a "one-track mind" (43) or to "imitate [himself]" (43) has not won him points with some critics, he intends "for whatever [he] write[s] to be excellent" concluding that he will not "just shove things out" because others want him to (44).

Elder goes on to say that if "one theme rides throughout my work, I'm basically trying to deal with Black people in the fullest sense by trying to illustrate all the ways we've historically survived in the face of a physical and psychological brutality which completely denies survival, or sanity for that matter" (44). This theme runs throughout *Ceremonies in Dark Old Men*, represented in the many ways the Parker family attempts to survive between 125th and 124th streets in Harlem.

On the surface, *Ceremonies* is about a family whose three principal male figures struggle to reconcile their need to work, with their desire to avoid the menial jobs they are bound to find themselves in should they work. Supported by Adele, the sole breadwinner, Russell B. Parker and his sons, Bobby and Theo, shuffle through life until Adele threatens to expel them from their loft apartment. Unconvinced that her father can make a decent buck in his single chair barbershop, she is particularly strict and stringent with him, telling him at one point:

I am not going to let the three of you drive me into the grave the way you did Mama. . . . Mama killed herself because there was no kind of order in this house. There was nothing but her old-fashion love for a bum like you Theo, and this one [Bobby] who's got nothing better to do but shoplift every time he walks into a department store. And you, Daddy, you and those fanciful stories you're always ready to tell . . . the money you spent on the numbers you got from Mama. . . . In a way, you let Mama make a bum out of you—you let her kill herself! (24)

But, as Chester Fontenot writes in his essay "Mythic Patterns," "placing these restrictions does not resolve the source of conflict between moral turpitude and pragmatic action" (46); it simply introduces another means for the men to get by: Blue Haven, Black Hood and "Prime Minister of the Harlem De-Colonization Association" (*Ceremonies* 73), whose "aim is to drive Mr. You-Know-Who out of Harlem" (75). Of the character Blue, Elder says, "Blue Haven is just that for the family: a haven. But not one you go to. One that comes to you. Very appealing. The message, I guess, is that what looks safest and most appealing can be most dangerous and most terrifying" (qtd. in Sullivan 669). What Blue proposes is a bootleg and numbers running scheme that promises to both make the Parkers rich and stick it to the man, driving him out of the ghetto forever.

However, by turning the barbershop into a front for corn whiskey and numbers running, Mr. Parker introduces a new element into the mix: moral chaos, undermining the moral standards "Adele has sought to keep intact" (Fontenot 47). Once moral people, the Parkers slowly unravel: Mr. Parker begins to embezzle their new income; Bobby turns his quick fingers over to Blue in a shoplifting spree designed to close down white businesses in the neighborhood; and Theo is left to hold down the front with no help as he churns out case after case of bootleg whiskey (47). Ironically, it is Theo, who initially brought Blue into their lives, who begins to see through Blue's front and decides in the latter half of the play to try to bring the family back together and undo the damage. The play ends on a profoundly ironic and tragic note as the family begins to unite in preparation of confronting Blue, suggesting a resolution offset into an uncertain future.

Of the title, Elder comments that "the ceremonies . . . are rituals, ways of getting by" (qtd. in Sullivan 668) in a ghetto whose sole purpose was to provide a place for blacks to die. Elder asks:

How did we as black Americans survive for so many years the constant psychological and physical brutality perpetuated by American racism and yet remain a people, a glorious and beautiful lot? I would say that our most fervent desire was to survive, and that desire out of necessity was colored with style, ceremony, and ritual . . . these are the elements I tried to thrust into a soulful orbit . . . to cancel out the hazardous and interminable crime of *being black* and having to live in racist America in a black world built for them to die in. The ritual of survival by black men and women is merely survival, and they die anyway. (*Ceremonies* jacket)

The play ultimately suggests three methods of getting by: conform or sell out by working for the man in a thankless job; stick it to the man by running him out and claiming the world as your own; or stick together, maintaining what you can when you can. A telling interchange between Adele and Theo further highlights this central theme of not only *Ceremonies* but also Elder's dramatic works as a whole:

> THEO. No matter what you do, he's [Mr. Parker] gon' die anyway. This whole place was built for him to die in—so you bite, you scratch, you kick: you do anything to stay alive!
> ADELE. Yes, you bite! You scratch, you steal, you kick, and you get killed anyway! Just as I was doing, coming back here to help Momma. . . . Sure this place was built for us to die in, but if we aren't very careful, Theo—that can actually happen. (164–165)

Elder's choice of setting *Ceremonies* in a barbershop is highly symbolic and further forwards the central theme of the play: survival and getting by. In a 1979 essay on the topic, Trudier Harris writes that "the barbershop is the black man's way station, point of contact, and universal home. Here he always finds a welcome—a friendly audience as he tells his story . . ." (112). This is particularly true in *Ceremonies* when one considers that the Parker home is an extension of the shop, indeed to get into the actual living areas one has to enter through the shop before setting foot into the house proper. The barber-shop then serves not only as the Parker's living area, but the living area of the immediate black community. It is here, Harris writes, that Mr. Parker "can escape into a world in which he is king" (115); where he can reminisce about his days as a vaudeville dancer before his knees gave out and his wife died; where the past is present and tall tales and soft shoe are all that matter: "It becomes his fantasized ceremony or ritual for survival" (115). It is here too that the Parker sons, Theo and Bobby, as well as Mr. Jenkins come to cope with life between bouts with the outside world. "The barbershop," says Elder, "is symbolic of a whole lot of things in black culture. A lot of lies are told in barbershops. A whole lot of ceremonies happen" here (qtd. in Sullivan 669).

Not as complex a work as *Ceremonies*, *Charades on East Fourth Street*, Elder's third play and second produced, is a departure from the familial themes of the former, espousing a different set of themes entirely. This is largely because the play, unlike any of his other dramatic works, was commissioned as a means of portraying nonviolent solutions to police brutality. The play centers on a group of black and Hispanic adolescents who kidnap a white cop they believe to be responsible for the harassment and rape a fifteen-year-old girl. The gang is headed by the masked Adam who is clearly the brains of the outfit. Over the course of the play, the adolescents attempt to goad the nameless cop into confessing to the crime through a series of "games" that culminates with their setting him in a portable guillotine. Still the police officer refuses to confess to the crime that he obviously did not commit, repeating almost as a mantra: "I don't know what you're talking about . . ." (11). Somehow, as the others tinker with the failing guillotine, the officer manages to convince Adam of his innocence. Moments shy of the execution, Adam sends the others away for a basket to catch the severed head as an excuse to set the cop free. Alone, Adam literally drops the *charade* of his belief in the cop's innocence, revealing his true intentions: to punish and blame someone for the crime, even if that someone is innocent. Though the dialogue is stilted and the narration simplistic, recalling medieval morality plays and allegorical children's stories where the moral is clearly laid out before the reader, *Charades* makes its point through the violent final scene in which Adam reveals that it was *his* sister who was raped and proceeds to break the arms of the innocent cop. The others return to find the officer unconscious and on the verge of death. They stand in disbelief pondering their fates as the curtain falls. "I may go to jail tomorrow," one says, "but for now, I'm going to a dance" (40).

CRITICAL RECEPTION

"Critics hold that despite his many contributions to film and television, Elder's reputation as a dramatist is based chiefly on one work, *Ceremonies in Dark Old Men*" (Clurman 662). Of the numerous reviews written on Lonne

Elder III's dramatic writings, only one refers directly to his later works, *Splendid Mummer* and *Charades on East Fourth Street*. As for *Ceremonies*, though it had been read as early as 1965 in various workshops and colleges, its official production date and subsequent criticism center around its February 4, 1969, release by the then two-year-old Negro Ensemble Company at the St. Marks Playhouse in New York City. Prior to its opening, as Elder mentions in an interview shortly after the play's release, he had "earned about $8,000 off it" (Bigsby par. 24) from the various awards it had received. If this is any indication of the play's eventual success, then what follows is merely icing on the cake.

Called by one critic "the most successful black drama since *Raisin in the Sun*" (Sullivan 667), this sentiment is echoed in the later writings of Addell Anderson. Edith Oliver of the *New Yorker* goes a step further when she writes, "[I]f any American has written a finer [play] I can't think what it is" (90). "Mr. Elder," writes Tom Prideaux in *Life* magazine two months after the opening, "is more than a good playwright who deserves to be recognized. Now, on the basis of his first play alone, he is a recognized playwright who deserves to be rewarded" (14), and rewarded he is, though, as other critics add their voices to the growing ranks, dissension begins to rear its ugly head. A concern voiced by some is the play's length, best voiced by the double-edged criticism of Henry Hewes.

Hewes suggests that "although Elder has done a great deal of television writing, this is his first play"and is therefore flawed (29). He faults it with being "overlong," with "sequences that, because they are not essential to the plot" draw it out too much (29), making it longer then it need be. Another fault he points out is his perception that Elder relies too much on conflict, "not trusting his characters to hold our attention with their deeper emotional involvement in the action" (29). Despite this, we the audience, will ultimately "forgive him all this because of the trueness of his observation and the complete avoidance of self-pity in a situation that could very easily have played upon our guilt by indicting us for the misfortunes the play's characters suffer" (29). Overall, in Hewes opinion, Elder does an admirable job walking that fine line "between realism and entertainment" (29) in a play that could easily have gone over into the threads of "artificiality and melodrama" (29) inherent in the play. Jeanne-Marie A. Miller articulates a similar concern in her article for the *Journal of Negro Education*.

"*Ceremonies* ranges out of control because Elder packs too much into it—the story of a dark old man who dreams, lives off memories, and tries to squeeze a bit of love out of life before he dies" (Miller 396); coupled with his "matriarchal" daughter who wants nothing more than for her father and brothers to be "respectable" and not freeload off her; a brother who wants success without having to slave "for the white man"; and the younger brother whose talents lie in his quick fingers, creates numerous "structural problems," as Miller puts them, creating a play that lacks focus. However, despite this lack of control, Miller goes on to claim that "the drama is an enjoyable one both to read and to see performed" (397).

Elder, who admits that he reads all reviews of his work as "it causes me to think" (Bigsby par. 18), responded in detail to this specific criticism of length in a 1969 interview saying:

[One] of the things they said was that the play was long. I knew it was long but it wasn't long in terms of time. It was long in terms of the fact that the last act is very long. . . . The second act should really be another act but, in terms of what I was doing, the movement of the play, the rhythm, the move from one irony to another, I knew that if I made this another act, the last scene, the third act, it would kill what had gone before. . . . If I did it would kill the play. (Bigsby par. 20)

This criticism caused Elder, in response to these concerns, to do "some pruning" (Bigsby par. 22) when selling it to another producer for later production, though, as he notes, it is the longer, Negro Ensemble Company version, that was published.

Often critics seem to make the distinction between the writing of the play and its overall structure and its content, critiquing both on separate grounds, such that they can write about lackluster writing in the same breath that they praise him for the depth of character and theme. Harold Clurman, writing for the *Nation*, articulates this trend well when he says that "one may note some repetitiousness in the text and there were over-facile strokes for comic effect. The total impression, however, is without blemish. Even the crudities in the play's texture are of a kind which appear organic with the material, part of its reality" (665), adding of the central theme that

there is no special pleading: it pertains no thesis, espouses no cause, appeals for no largess. . . . There is no sensationalism, not even a "problem"—only the warp and woof of ordinary living: funny, crazy, frightening and somehow strangely innocent, heart-warming as much as heart breaking [*sic*]. The play, the first by a writer of 30, is a "little" comedy—much more telling than many that are ambitiously "significant." (665)

Clurman articulates the many elements of Elder's complex drama with verve and understanding, noting that even the flaws of writing allow the plot and characters to intermingle in as real a setting as is possible for a fiction. The play, he argues, is largely successful because it is "without a trace of rhetoric" (qtd. in Oliver 92), espousing the age-old adage "show, don't tell." This allows the Parkers, in all their "fallible, sweet, stupid, lovable" (Clurman 665), to come across as "always understandable folk" (665) who are "richly human and as such not easily subject to petty compromise in humdrum jobs at paltry wages" (665). "The Parkers," agrees Oliver, "are as close a family as you will ever see on a stage" (93). Because *Ceremonies* does not blare out its central theme, much as *Charades* later does, Elder's first play has often been labeled "naturalistic" by critics. This rankles the playwright to no end as he makes abundantly clear when he comments:

The critics said it was naturalism. It's naturalism to them mainly because they're unacquainted with the flow and the various colors of life in the black ghetto. . . . I definitely disagree with some of the critics who say that the play was naturalistic in the traditional or conventional sense of the word. It is naturalistic out of necessity in areas where it had to be. (qtd. in Bigsby par. 10)

If anything, Elder argued, it is more "akin to exalted realism" (Bigsby par. 10) as it "depends a great deal on language, on the tone, innuendo and rhythm of its language" (Bigsby par. 10). As Elder sees it, naturalism plays a small but necessary part to the whole of his vision, because, as he puts it, an overreliance "on the natural modes and habits of your characters and people" turns them into caricatures (Bigsby par. 10). A blending of forms allows for the writer to show aspects of characters or concepts that is "not always evident in the natural behavior of the people" (Bigsby par. 10).

One critic stands out from the others in his wholly scathing review of the play. Unlike other reviews that in the least mixed the good with the bad, Martin Duberman sees little merit in *Ceremonies*, finding "the relationships that contribute to its (the family's) collapse, especially the relationship between the two sons, are at once so incompletely and so predictably developed that the tale becomes an interminable cliché"; adding, "like all bad art, *Ceremonies* has interest only as sociology—and precious little even then" (par. 7). He also argues that had the play been written by a white it would have been dismissed and denounced "as a tissue of clichés and slanders" wherein black life is depicted as a "compound of middle-class hopes and aspirations sprinkled with dope, sex, and the rackets" (par. 8).

On a slightly different note, the apparently well meaning Clive Barnes, writing for the *New York Times*, says in his article:

We have known for decades that Negroes were natural actors; we are now busy discovering that they are also natural playwrights. Black writers are nothing new, but the existence of a developing black theater has provided them with totally new possibilities. . . . I hope he feels the wait was worthwhile, for this is a magnificent, breathtaking performance of a remarkable play. (par. 1)

He adds that, though the "play straggles a great deal—comes to indeterminate conclusions, changes directions, and loses the thread of its thought," it still manages to survive "beneath these failings, these tergiversations of dramatic prose" (par. 2). Jim Williams, responding in the spring issue of *Freedomways*, writes that "it would be self-defeating and dangerous to accept the well-intentioned but nonetheless patronizing Clive Barnes' discovery 'that blacks are natural actors and natural playwrights'" (par. 4). He argues for Elder and other African American playwrights, saying that theater writing is anything but the product of natural talent. It "represents the sternest of artistic disciplines requiring talent, tenacity . . . , assiduous study and the concomitant mastery of methods" that is taken away under Barnes's earlier claim (par. 4).

A few critics comment on the broad social issues at play in the heart of *Ceremonies*, moving beyond concerns of its language, length, and characterization into the murky waters of interpretation. Anderson, writing from the window afforded by over twenty years of hindsight, says that with *Ceremonies* "Elder joins the few playwrights able to demonstrate the realities of the impoverished of Black America and, specifically, the desperate, seemingly futile search of African-American males to attain a sense of dignity and financial independence" (par. 8). "Although the play is based on the daily ritual of survival in the black community," writes Miller, "this survival" (as Elder also states in the Bigsby interview) "[does not] necessarily have anything to do with black/white confrontation or any clenched fist anger" (397). "The critics did catch one thing," Elder adds, "[t]he play is really based on the daily ritual of survival in the black community. . . . They caught this" (qtd. in Bigsby par. 24). Others, according to Elder, did not, choosing instead to focus and react on his "black material" in an openly racist or asinine way, turning their criticism into a "personal attack on the substance of his material" (qtd. in Bigsby par. 24). Often the asinine comes from oversimplification of the issue, confusing or failing to understand the larger picture.

Two years after the release of *Ceremonies*, in the comfort of his California home, Elder adds to this earlier thought in a remark made in an interview with Dan Sullivan:

[T]he black man still exists in the media not as a man but as a problem. A headline. Or else a clown. . . . What it is, no one wants to really believe that black people are human. How *dare* a young black singing group think of singing anything other than soul music? How *dare* a black writer present his people as being complex? They're always ready to make a movie about black revolutionaries with submachine guns. That's less fearsome than a black character who falls into the realm of the poetic or the profound, like the father in *Ceremonies*. (668)

What *Ceremonies* essentially says for Lonne Elder III is, "Get rid of those old images in your head. Blacks aren't that simple. Never were" (Sullivan 668).

As for Elder's other plays, Addell Anderson, twenty-two years after the Montreal release of *Charades on East Fourth Street*, writes, "Elder's other dramatic works lack the craft and intense emotional impact of *Ceremonies*" (par. 13). Of the play, Anderson writes that *Charades* seems little more than "a vehicle to encourage young people to use legal means to protest against police brutality, however, the play seems little more than a vicarious means whereby an audience can experience the terrorization of a policeman" (par. 13).

When Elder finished *Charades* in 1971, it became little more than a footnote in a career that was quickly changing to television and film. In Liz Gant's 1973 interview, she asks Elder if he had given up on the stage, what with the release of two highly successful films and numerous television scripts that surpassed, in two years, what he had completed as a playwright over the preceding five. His response—"[O]h no. I really want to get back to the stage every three to four years . . . and see what happens" (47)—tells us that though he had found a different niche in Hollywood, his roots still called to him from time to time.

BIBLIOGRAPHY

Dramatic Works by Lonne Elder III

Bustin' Loose (screenplay). Adaptation by Universal Pictures, 1981.

Ceremonies in Dark Old Men. New York: Farrar, 1965.

Charades on East Fourth Street. 1971. Electronic Edition by Alexander Street Press, L.L.C., 2002. 10 Apr. 2003 <http://colet.uchicago.edu/cgi-bin/asp/bldr/navigate?/projects/artfla/databases/asp/bldr/fulltext/IMAGE/.281>.

A Hysterical Turtle in a Rabbit Race. 1958. Electronic Edition by Alexander Street Press, L.L.C., 2002. 10 Apr. 2003 <http://colet.uchicago.edu/cgi-bin/asp/bldr/navigate?/projects/artfla/databases/asp/bldr/fulltext/IMAGE/.147>.

Kissing Rattlesnakes Can Be Fun. 1966. Unpublished.

Melinda (screenplay). Metro-Goldwyn-Mayer, 1972.

Part 2, Sounder (screenplay). ABC, 1976.

Seven Comes Up and Seven Comes Down. 1966. Unpublished.

Sounder (screenplay). Adaptation by 20th Century Fox, 1972.

Splendid Mummer. 1986. Electronic Edition by Alexander Street Press, L.L.C., 2002. 10 Apr. 2003 <http://colet.uchicago.edu/cgi-bin/asp/bldr/navigate?/projects/artfla/databases/asp/bldr/fulltext/IMAGE/.398>.

Studies of Lonne Elder III's Dramatic Works

Anderson, Addell Austin. "Lonne Elder III: Overview." *Contemporary Dramatists*. 5th ed. (1993): 18 pars. 10 Apr. 2003 <http://www.galenet.com/servlet.LitRC?ste=1&vrsn=3&n=10&locID=cornell>.

Barnes, Clive. "Troubles of the Oppressed." *New York Times* 6 Feb. 1969, 7 pars. 10 Apr. 2003 <http://www.galenet.com/servlet.LitRC?ste=1&vrsn=3&n=10&locID=cornell>.

Bigsby, C. W. E., ed. "An Interview with Lonne Elder III." *Poetry and Drama*. Vol. 2 of *The Black American Writer* (1969): 42 pars. 10 Apr. 2003 <http://www.galenet.com/servlet.LitRC?ste=1&vrsn=3&n=10&locID=cornell>.

Black Drama 1850–Present. Alexandria: Alexander Street Press (2002): 6 pars. 10 Apr. 2003.<http://colet.uchicago.edu/cgibin/asp/bldr/authoridx.pl?docauthorid=A6321&showfull record=ON>.

Cherry, Wilsonia E. D. "Lonne Elder III." *Afro-American Writers after 1955: Dramatists and Prose Writers*. Vol. 38 of *Dictionary of Literary Biography*. Detroit: Gale, 1985. 97–104.

Clurman, Harold. "Ceremonies in Dark Old Men." *Achebe–Ellison*. Vol. 1 of *Black Literature Criticism*. Ed. James P. Draper. Detroit: Gale, 1992. 665–666.

Duberman, Martin. "Black Theater." *The Partisan Review* 36.3 (1969): 14 pars. 10 Apr. 2003 <http://www.galenet.com/servlet.LitRC?ste=1&vrsn=3&n=10&locID=cornell>.

"Elder, Lonne III." *Gale Group*. Online. (1999): 9 pars. 10 Apr.2003. <http://www.galenet.com/servlet/GLD/form?l=2>.

Fontenot, Chester J. "Mythic Patterns in 'River Niger' and 'Ceremonies in Dark Old Men.'" *MELUS* 7.1 (Spring 1980): 41–49.

Gant, Liz. "An Interview with Lonne Elder III." *Black World* 22 (Apr. 1973): 38–48.

Harris, Trudier. "The Barbershop in Black Literature." *Black American Literature Forum* 13.3 (Autumn 1979): 112–118.

Hewes, Henry. "Harlem on Our Mind." *Saturday Review* 52 (22 Feb. 1969): 29.

Jeffers, Lance. "Bullins, Baraka, and Elder: The Dawn of Grandeur in Black Drama." *CLA Journal* 16 (Sept. 1972): 32–48.

Miller, Jeanne-Marie A. "Ceremonies in Dark Old Men." *Journal of Negro Education* 40.4 (Fall 1971): 395–397.

Oliver, Edith. "Off Broadway. The First Hurrah." *New Yorker* 44 (15 Feb. 1969): 90–93.

Peterson, Bernard L., Jr., ed. *Contemporary Black American Playwrights and Their Plays*. Westport: Greenwood, 1988. 160–162.

Prideaux, Tom. "One Kind of Family Drama That Works." *Life* 66 (4 Apr. 1969): 14.

Sullivan, Dan. "What's a Nice Black Playwright Doing in a Place Like This?" *Black Literature Criticism*. Ed. James P. Draper. Vol. 1. Detroit: Gale, 1992. 667–669.

Williams, Jim. "Pieces on Black Theatre and the Black Theatre Worker." *Freedomways* 9.2 (Spring 1969): 15 pars. 10 Apr. 2003. <http://www.galenet.com/servlet.LitRC?ste=1&vrsn=3&n=10&locID=cornell>.

RUDOLPH FISHER
(1897–1934)

Helen R. Houston

BIOGRAPHY

Best known as a short story writer and novelist, Rudolph John Chauncey Fisher was born on May 9, 1897, in Washington, DC, to John W. (a minister) and Glendora Williamson Fisher. The family moved to New York in 1903 and to Providence, Rhode Island, in 1905 where Fisher engaged in his primary and secondary education. During this period, he won honors for his scholarship and showed a penchant for science and literature. He matriculated at Brown University where he earned both a B.A. and an M.A. degree. Fisher majored in biology and was elected to Phi Beta Kappa, Sigma Xi, and Delta Rho honor societies. Moreover, he won numerous prizes. Following Brown, Fisher entered Howard University Medical School in preparation for work as a radiologist. He graduated in 1924. The following year, the young physician married Jane Ryder, an elementary school teacher, and by 1926, he was the father of a son, Hugh, nicknamed "the New Negro." Rudolph Fisher died on December 26, 1934, of a stomach disorder.

Early in his education, Fisher had been recognized for his literary and musical talents. He pursued his love for jazz and writing while he was still a medical student. The would-be physician collaborated with Paul Robeson, consummate singer. "With Paul singing and Rudolph playing the piano and arranging, they toured the East Coast hoping to raise money for tuition" (McCluskey, "Rudolph" 280). Concurring with his academic recognitions, writers of the Harlem Renaissance such as Langston Hughes* commented on Fisher as the brightest among them for his genius, intellect, and wit—traits that are evidenced as Fisher combined his love for science, literature, and Harlem in his literary works.

MAJOR WORKS AND THEMES

During the last months of his life, Rudolph Fisher wrote three known plays. Two of them are unpublished and have no performance history, *Golden Slippers* and *The Vici Kid*. *Golden Slippers* is a Negro musical extravaganza—a mixture of light opera, revue, musical comedy, and melodrama—with the action occurring on several stages. "All the plots, counterplots, the chronology and divertissements, will be synchronized in the finale of each act" (Gable, "Annotated" par. 4) *The Vici Kid* was being prepared "for production on Broadway" and the "central character is . . . a slick-haired small-time gambler" (Gable, "Annotated" par. 6).

The third play is an adaptation of his novel *The Conjure-Man Dies: A Mystery Tale of Dark Harlem*, a detective story that until recently has been considered the first detective story by an African American. Due to the all-black setting of the novel and its black detective, it is seen as a forerunner to the fiction of Chester Himes, Valerie Wesley Wilson, Walter Mosley, and Barbara Neely. The play has not been published; however, there is a typescript copy of it in the Schomburg Center for Research. The play is titled *The Conjure Man Dies: A Play in Three Acts*. Under this heading are a "tentative cast" of performers (includes Thomas Poston and Theodore Ward) and the 105 pages of typescript of the dramatization. In places it is confusing and difficult to read. In spite of this, it is evident that the play does not deviate greatly from the novel.

The play begins with the discovery of a corpse and the pedantic Dr. Archer being called in to examine the body. The dead man is N'Ghana Frimbo, a fortune-teller/conjure man from West Africa, and a graduate of Harvard University with a master's degree in philosophy. Dr. Archer calls in his friend Perry Drake, one of the few black detectives in the New York Police Department. As they work toward solving this mystery, they match wits and philosophy. There is also an ex-veteran of the Department of Street Cleaners who has turned detective who is intent on unraveling the mystery because his friend stands accused of the murder of Frimbo. Part of the flavor and breadth of life in Harlem is exhibited through the dialogue of the characters:

> BUBBER. Me? I'm a—a detective.
> BART [*sic*]. Do—what?
> BUBBER. —'tective. Yes suh.
> DART. What kind of detective?

BUBBER. F-family detective.

DART. Family—?

BUBBER. Yes, suh. Hyar's my card. See?

DART. How long 've you been breaking the law like this?

BUBBER. What [ole] law, mistuh?

DART. You know you're not incorporated.

BUBBER. Oh—that I.N.C.? That's "ink"—means colored.

DART. Ex-veteran, D.S.C.—what Distinguished Service Cross did you ever win?

BUBBER. None, suh. That's Department of Street Cleanin'. Y'see, I was workin' for the City, but I got laid off. So I figured I'd go into business for myself. You know, monkey-business.

DART. What are you talkin' about?

BUBBER. Cheatin', backbitin', and all like o' that. Folks 'll pay to catch cheaters when they won't pay for nothin' else. I can catch cheaters as well as anybody else—jes' bust in on 'em and tell the judge what I seen. So that's why I had them cards printed. (3–5)

It is this reasoning and the vernacular that encouraged the audiences to howl and the critics to frown. As the play progresses, it is discovered that the dead man is not N'Ghana Frimbo, but his West African assistant, N'Ogo Frimbo. Thus, N'Ghana Frimbo is alive. He returns and tries to aid in the capture of "his murderer" and winds up being an actual corpse. The murderer and the motive are discovered by the time the play ends.

The first production of the play took place on March 11, 1936, almost two years after Fisher's death. It was staged at Harlem's New Lafayette Theatre by the Negro Unit as part of the Federal Theater Project and enthusiastically received by audiences. Between its March opening and its July 4, 1936, closing, it was reported "that some eighty-three thousand people viewed the play" (McCluskey, Introduction xxi). It was also produced by the Works Progress Administration traveling outdoor players in some New York parks and at the Cleveland, Ohio, Karamu House.

With a change in title from the first production, *The Conjure Man* was performed at the Henry Street Settlement in Manhattan in 2001 and directed by Clinton Turner Davis as a part of the 30th Anniversary Celebration of Woodie King's New Federal Theatre in New York City ("'Conjure Man Dies' Returns" par. 1). Joshua Tanzer says of this production, "The Harlem-Renaissance work shows its 1920s roots in its variety show style—there's a little mystery, a little singing, a little fighting, a little slapstick" (par. 2). The Kuntu Repertory Theatre at the University of Pittsburgh presented *The Conjure Man Dies* as part of its 2001–2002 season dedicated to mystery dramas.

There is a film adaptation of the novel in progress. However, there is no indication whether the available typescript will be used in the production of the film ("'Conjure-Man Dies' to Be" par. 1).

In spite of the fact that Fisher is known for his short stories and novels, a reading of his play indicates that he is still concerned with presenting the various sides of Harlem and Harlem life. The drama presents the educated and the ordinary man of the streets, and a real attention is given to verisimilitude as evidenced in the aforementioned excerpt. Fisher's characters are able to survive whole in the face of challenges presented by the city and its populace.

CRITICAL RECEPTION

Rudolph Fisher's reputation and reception as playwright rests solely on his unpublished but produced play, *The Conjure Man Dies*. Responses in 1936 and 2001 are similar since they indicate the play is verbose and suffers from the author's inability to edit. Doris Abramson's assessment of the 1936 production is "that 'Conjure Man Dies' needed cutting and rewriting during the rehearsal period" (61). Brooks Atkinson in his review "Harlem Mumbo Jumbo" says that "the plays seems like a verbose and amateur charade, none too clearly written and soggily acted" (qtd. in Abramson 63). Similarly, a reviewer of the 2001 production finds the drama "at 2 ½ hours with two ten minute intermissions . . . too long by at least half an hour and one intermission" (Sommer par. 7).

Regardless of the play's length and the need for editing, both audiences seem to have enjoyed the production. Atkinson says that "the Lafayette was bulging with family parties . . . who roared at the obese comedian, and howled over the West Indian accent of a smart Harlem landlady" (qtd. in Abramson 63). Tanzer says that the play "stands up today as an engrossing mystery and an amusing lark" (par. 5).

Critics who write about Fisher are generally indifferent to his career as a playwright. There are, however, occasional references to his dramatic work in the online *Rudolph Fisher Newsletter* that can be accessed at http://www.fishernews.org.

BIBLIOGRAPHY

Dramatic Works by Rudolph Fisher

The Conjure Man Dies: A Play in Three Acts. 1934. Manuscript held by Schomburg Center for Research in Black Culture, New York.
Golden Slippers. 1934. Unpublished.
The Vici Kid. 1934. Unpublished.

Studies of Rudolph Fisher's Dramatic Works

Abramson, Doris E. *Negro Playwrights in the American Theatre 1925–1959*. New York: Columbia University Press, 1969.

Bond, Frederick W. *The Negro and the Drama: The Direct and Indirect Contribution which the American Negro Has Made and the Legitimate Stage, with Underlying Conditions Responsible*. College Park: McGrath, 1969.

Bourne, St. Clair. "Murder Play at Lafayette." *New York Age* 21 Mar. 1936: 4.

"'Conjure Man Dies' Returns to Stage in 2001." *Rudolph Fisher Newsletter* 1.2 (2001): 3 pars. 27 Mar. 2003. <http://www.fishernews.org>.

"'Conjure Man Dies' to Be Turned into Film." *Rudolph Fisher Newsletter* 1.1 (2000): 4 pars. 11 Mar. 2003. <http://www.fishernews.org>.

"Fisher Bibliography in March 2000 Bulletin of Bibliography." *Rudolph Fisher Newsletter* 1.1 (2000): 3 pars. 28 Mar. 2003. <http://www.fishernews.org>.

Gable, Craig. *An Annotated Primary-Secondary Source Bibliography: The Drama of Rudolph Fisher*. 28 pars. 5 Feb. 2000. <http://www.fishernews.org/resources. htm#3>.

———. "Rudolph Fisher: An Updated Selected Bibliography." *Bulletin of Bibliography* 57.1 (2000): 13–19.

Garland, Robert. "Negro Theater Gives 'Conjure Man Dies.'" *New York World-Telegram* 12 Mar. 1936: 18

Mantle, Burns. "'Conjure-Man Dies' in Harlem." *Daily News* 13 Mar. 1936: 59.

Matthews, Ralph. "'The Conjure Man Dies' Is Good Entertainment, but Confusing Mystery Play." *Afro-American* 21 Mar. 1936: 10.

McCluskey, Joseph, Jr. Introduction. *The City of Refuge: The Collected Stories of Rudolph Fisher*. Columbia: University of Missouri Press, 1987. i–xxii.

———. "Rudolph Fisher." *The Oxford Companion to African American Literature*. New York: Oxford University Press, 1997.

Pullen, Glenn C. "Who-Done-It Play Offered by WPA Group." *Cleveland Plain Dealer* 13 Aug. 1936: 10.

Sommer, Elyse. "A CurtainUp Review: The Conjure Man Dies: A Mystery Tale of Dark Harlem." *CurtainUp: The Internet Theater Magazine of Reviews, Features, Annotated Listings* (2001): 8 pars. 11 Mar. 2003. <http://www.curtainup. conjuremandies.html>.

Tanzer, Joshua. "The Spirit Moves." *Offoffoff* 8 Feb. 2001: 5 pars. 10 Mar. 2003. <http://www.offoffoff.com/theater/2001/conjureman.php3>.

J. e. FRANKLIN
(1937 –   )

Ymitri Jayasundera

BIOGRAPHY

A native of Houston, Texas, Jennie Elizabeth Franklin is the eleventh of thirteen children. She grew up poor in a very strict household with both parents working, "one of them deep into the day, the other deep into the night" (Franklin 3). As a result, her brothers and sisters were responsible for each other. She had a very sheltered childhood, partly because she spent most of her time writing stories, filling many notebooks with her work, but she never envisioned becoming a playwright. She received her B.A. from the University of Texas at Austin in 1960, and she later studied at the Union Theological Seminary in New York for one year, 1972–1973. Franklin moved to Carthage, Mississippi, in 1964 to teach primary school. Her efforts to interest her students in reading led her to write plays, and her first full-length play, *A First Step to Freedom*, was performed at a community center there. In 1965, she moved to New York City, and she had various minor productions of her plays. For example, *The Prodigal Daughter* was performed at the Lincoln Center as a street theater project. *The In-Crowd* was performed at the Montreal Expo in 1967.

Franklin's major play *Black Girl*, for which she received the New York Drama Desk Most Promising Playwright Award in 1971, was first produced in 1971 at the New Federal Theater and then moved to the Theatre de Lys, both in New York City. It ran for the entire season to sold-out crowds. The play was later televised on public/educational television and then was made into a movie directed by Ossie Davis* and starring Leslie Uggams as Billie Jean, the title character. In her memoir, *Black Girl, from Genesis to Revelations*, Franklin discusses her coming-of-age as a writer and the difficulties she encountered converting the play into a television show and then adapting the play into a screenplay for the movie.

Since *Black Girl*, Franklin has written and had performances of several of her plays in regional theaters across the country and in New York City, mostly Off-Broadway. She has also dabbled in musical theater, writing the libretto for *The Prodigal Daughter*, renamed *The Prodigal Sister: A New Black Musical*; transforming a one-act play *The In-Crowd* into a full-length rock musical in 1977; and she returned to that genre in the 1980s in *Will the Real South Please Rise?* During this time, she also experimented with mime with *Guess What's Coming to Dinner*. She has received several major awards and grants indicating the extent of her talent: Media Women Award (1971), Institute for the Arts and Humanities Dramatic Arts Award from Howard University (1974), Better Boys Foundation Playwrighting Award (1978), National Endowment for the Arts Creative Writing Fellowship (1979), Rockefeller Grant (1980), and the Writer's Guild Award (1981). Franklin has incorporated her love of teaching by lecturing at various universities, notably Lehman College of the City University of New York from 1969 to 1975 and Brown University as a resident playwright from 1983 to 1989. In the 1990s, she was the director of the Zora Neale Hurston* Writer's Workshop of the New Federal Theatre in New York City. Franklin has become a transplanted New Yorker since she moved there in the mid-1960s. In her personal life, she has one daughter, Malika.

MAJOR WORKS AND THEMES

J. e. Franklin's work reflects her interest in the African American struggle for freedom and equality and the consequences of black–white racism within the African American family. In many of her plays, she explores the basic coming-of-age themes, the importance of gaining independence and realizing dreams from a female and a male point of view, as well as the parent–child and sibling conflicts within these domestic dramas. Although she has been a prolific playwright since her first play was produced in 1964, Franklin's reputation rests on her one major play, *Black Girl*. Set in Texas, it is a coming-of-age play about a seventeen-year-old girl named Billie Jean who wants to become a ballet dancer. She has not yet realized that "black" girls cannot become ballet dancers. Focusing on the family dynamics of sibling rivalry and a mother–daughter conflict, the play also includes elements of the *Cinderella* story with her two stepsisters and a foster mother who try to pressure her into a more conventional life. The larger sociological issues of black–white racism and intraracial oppression are subtly incorporated into the domestic drama, so Franklin argues that the play is not a tract about "whitey" (Parks 49). Stylistically, it is a conventional play, foregrounding the major characters but not experimenting with form, unlike, for example, Ntozake Shange's* 1976 choreopoem, *for colored girls who have considered suicide when the rainbow is enuf*.

Franklin examines several related themes in depth by writing a series of related plays. Although *The Prodigal Daughter* is not part of her octet of plays, it is her first incorporating biblical symbolism. Her second major full-length New York production, the play is a twentieth-century version of the prodigal son story in the Bible. An unwed teenage mother runs away from home to the big city, falls into the seamier side of life, and finally returns home to her welcoming parents. With Micki Grant* composing the music, she transforms the play into a musical by writing the libretto under the title *The Prodigal Sister*, which becomes one of very few black musicals in the country. She continues her biblical allegorical theme with a later play, *Christchild*, which is one of the plays from her octet of plays about the adolescent experience within the life of a black family in Houston. In the play, a young boy born with six fingers on one of his hands wrestles a bear to gain his father's approval. Set during the Depression, the play probes the consequences of abuse between an alcoholic father and his son and the impact of racism on African American men and within the family. In a sequel to *Christchild* within the same series, *Where Dewdrops of Mercy Shine Bright*, she continues the parent–child conflict theme in which an insensitive parent destroys his relationship with the second child.

Franklin does not limit herself to only writing domestic dramas. A civil rights activist, especially in the 1960s and 1970s, she is interested in art as a tool for educating the individual (Parks 50). She has written a series of articles investigating the "theological roots of racism" (Peterson 175), which reflects her theological background. The rock musical *The In-Crowd* incorporates a quasi-religious theme in which a youth gang kills their parents in effigy but later realizes the indestructibility of family bonds. Some of her plays directly examine the African American struggle for equal rights in the South, especially the racial division within southern college campuses. In *Throw Thunder at This House* a group of students desegregate a southern university and discover that freedom is a struggle and cannot be taken for granted. In *Cut Out the Lights and Call the Law* (1972), a group of black students at a white college must remain constantly vigilant in case they are attacked by white students.

CRITICAL RECEPTION

Black Girl earned J. e. Franklin her place in the canon of African American women playwrights of the 1970s. In many ways her play leads the decade that explodes with Ntozake Shange. Since *Black Girl*, Franklin has been a prolific playwright; however, her reputation rests on this one play. There have been several revivals of *Black Girl* in New York and across the country throughout the years, with the play becoming a popular and timeless classic. In one major revival, in 1995, Leslie Uggams, who had originally starred as Billie Jean in the 1971 stage production and then the movie, takes on the role of Mama Rosa, Billie Jean's foster mother. The *Village Voice* in its review of the production suggests that the play will "remain current as long as mothers fail their daughters and vice versa" (Kennedy 79).

Except for the occasional critic mentioning Franklin's name in passing as a late-twentieth-century African American woman playwright, there is no criticism of her work. Most of her plays are inaccessible to students and critics of literature since only *Black Girl* and *The Prodigal Sister* have been published. *Black Girl* is also included in her memoir *Black Girl, from Genesis to Revelations* in which she discusses her travails of transforming the play for the small and big screens. Franklin is included in various African American literary directories and encyclopedias, the most notable of which is the *Oxford Companion to African American Literature*. It points out that it is *Black Girl* that earned her the "acclaim and a following" (Houston 297). A more specialized directory, *Contemporary Black American Playwrights and Their Plays* provides brief descriptions of most of her dramatic works and also lists the major productions of some of the plays. Most of the directories, however, briefly list her biography and dramatic works. The one article on her in *Black World*, in 1972, is an assessment a year later of the production of *Black Girl*. It notes that "Blacks of all ages, political persuasions and economic strata . . . filled the house performance after performance" (Parks 49).

Although a critically neglected playwright, Franklin is part of a coterie of African American playwrights who came into their own in the 1970s, the most critically acclaimed are Sonia Sanchez* and Ntozake Shange.

BIBLIOGRAPHY

Dramatic Works by J. e. Franklin

Another Morning Rising. 1976. Unpublished.
Black Girl. Videocassette. Berkeley: University of California Extension Media Center, 1980.
Black Girl: A Play in Two Acts. New York: Dramatists Play Service, 1971.
Borderline Fool. 1988. Unpublished.
Christchild. 1989. Unpublished.
The Creation. 1975. Unpublished.
Crusader for Justice. 1975. Unpublished.
The Enemy. 1973. Unpublished.
A First Step to Freedom. 1964. Unpublished.
Four Women. 1973. Unpublished.

Grey Panthers: A Decatet of 10-Minute Plays. 1991. Unpublished.
The Hand-Me-Downs. 1978. Unpublished.
The In-Crowd. 1965. Unpublished.
MacPilate. 1974. Unpublished.
Mau Mau Room. 1969. Unpublished.
The Prodigal Daughter. 1965. Unpublished.
The Prodigal Sister: A New Black Musical (with Micki Grant). New York: French, 1975.
Throw Thunder at This House. 1993. Unpublished.
Under Heaven's Eye 'til Cockcrow. 1983. Unpublished.
Where Dewdrops of Mercy Shine Bright. 1983. Unpublished.

Other Cited Material by J. e. Franklin

Black Girl, from Genesis to Revelations. Washington, DC: Howard University Press, 1977.

Studies of J. e. Franklin's Dramatic Works

Beauford, Fred. "A Conversation with *Black Girl's* J. E. Franklin." *Black Creations* 3 (Fall 1971): 38–40.
Brantley, Ben. "Cinderella as Recast in Black for the 70's." *New York Times* 14 Nov. 1995: C14.
Hatch, Shari Dorantes, and Michael R. Stickland, eds. "Franklin, J. E. (Jennie Elizabeth)." *African-American Writers: A Dictionary*. Santa Barbara: ABC-CLIO, 2000. 124.
Henderson, Ashyia N., and Shirelle Phelps, eds. "Franklin, J. E." *Who's Who Among African Americans*. 12th ed. Detroit: Gale, 1999. 446.
Houston, Helen R. "Franklin, J. E." *The Oxford Companion to African American Literature*. Ed. William L. Andrews, Frances Smith Foster, and Trudier Harris. New York: Oxford University Press, 1997. 296–297.
Kennedy, Lisa. "Where's the Noise?" *Village Voice* 40 (5 Dec. 1995): 79.
Parks, Carole A. "J. E. Franklin, Playwright." *Black World* 12 Apr. 1972: 49–50.
Peterson, Bernard L., Jr. *Contemporary Black American Playwrights and Their Plays: A Biographical Directory and Dramatic Index*. Westport: Greenwood, 1988.
Woll, Allen. *Dictionary of the Black Theatre: Broadway, Off-Broadway, and Selected Harlem Theatres*. Westport: Greenwood, 1983.

CHARLES GORDONE
(1925–1995)

Yolanda W. Page

BIOGRAPHY

Born on October 12, 1925, in Cleveland, Ohio, Charles Gordone was reared in Elkhart, Indiana. Because his parents, William and Camille Morgan Gordone, chose to live on the white side of town rather than its black side, growing up in Elkhart was difficult for young Charles. He often found himself marginalized by both the town's white citizens and its black populace, which questioned his family's racial loyalty. Despite these problems, Gordone excelled academically and athletically as a student.

After graduating high school, Gordone began study at the University of California–Los Angeles, but left after a semester and served in the United States Air Force for a time, earning the rank of second lieutenant. After his stint in the air force, Gordone returned to California and studied music at Los Angeles City College. He eventually received a B.A. in acting in 1952 from Los Angeles State College (now California State University–Los Angeles).

Soon after receiving his degree, Gordone moved to New York to pursue an acting career despite the advice of a professor who told him that African American actors had no future in New York. His professor's counsel proved wrong, for soon after his arrival in New York, he was hired to play the part of Logan in Moss Hart's *Climate of Eden* on Broadway. He also appeared in Charles Sebree and Greer Johnson's *Mrs. Patterson;* John Steinbeck's *Of Mice and Men*, for which he won an Obie Award; and Jean Genet's *The Blacks*.

Gordone has said that Genet was a formative influence on his dramaturgy. In the article "From the Muthah Lode," he refers to *The Blacks* as a turning point for African Americans in legitimate theatre (95). Indeed, it was during his four-year stint with the play that he began writing *No Place to Be Somebody*.

MAJOR WORKS AND THEMES

In 1970 with *No Place to Be Somebody*, Charles Gordone became the first African American to win the Pulitzer Prize for Drama. Set in a New York City bar similar to one Gordone waited in while living in Greenwich Village, the play examines the thwarted ambitions of the bar's patrons that include hustlers, prostitutes, artists, and ex-cons and its owner, Johnny Williams. Like his customers, who all are searching for that person or situation that will help them realize their dreams of making it big, Johnny has been waiting for his big break. His break, as he sees it, is the release of his mentor Sweets Crane from prison, for before Sweets was imprisoned, he and Johnny had contrived a plan to commandeer a share of the neighborhood organized crime market. However, Johnny has had to postpone placing the plan into action for the past ten years while Sweets served his prison term. After Sweets is released, Johnny learns, though, that a now-reformed and ill Sweets wants no part of the scheme, and he must carry it out alone. Ultimately, the play culminates in Johnny's death as he attempts to implement the plan.

Johnny, however, is not murdered by the white crime bosses because of his attempt to usurp their power. He is killed by one of his bar patrons, Gabe Gabriel, a light-skinned black writer/actor. Like Johnny and the other characters, Gabe, too, is searching and waiting; he daily searches for work but finds himself unemployable because of the "dominant culture's definitions of blackness" (Elam 296): he is too light for African American roles and too dark for white ones. He also struggles to find racial identity. Because of his rejection by both the white and the African American worlds, Gabe, in several monologues throughout the play, exhorts that "they's mo' to bein' black than meets the eye!" In this way, Gabe becomes Gordone's spokesman. In addition to introducing each of the play's three acts, Gordone uses the humor and candor of Gabe's monologues to express the absurdity and tragedy of racism; he reminds the audience that they must look beneath the superficial, external sign of color.

Gordone Is a Muthah is a collection of five poems and a monologue story, which Gordone says "were written to be performed" (193). *Gordone Is a Muthah* was presented at Carnegie Recital Hall in May 1970, but never achieved the popularity of *No Place to Be Somebody*. Unlike *No Place to Be Somebody*, which explores a more universal subject, *Gordone Is a Muthah* focuses more on what Gordone refers to as the "the souls of black folk"

(193). Each work gives attention to a subject with which the masses would be familiar. For example, "A Child's Garden of Lessons—Dedicated to Black Castrated Fathers" depicts the cycle of black male social castration, and "A Black Woman's Brood" is a humorous description of a mother's preparation for a visit by the welfare lady.

Other unpublished plays include: *A Little More Light Around the Place* (1964), an adaptation of a novel by Sidney Easton of the same title; *Worl's Champeen Lip Dansuh an' Watah Mellon Jooglah*, which was performed at the Other Stage in 1969; *Baba Chops*, which was performed at the Wilshire Ebell Theatre in 1975; *The Last Chord* (1976) a melodrama about an African American church official who becomes involved with the mafia; *Anabiosis*, which was staged in 1979 by St. Louis's City Players; and *Roan Brown and Cherry* (1988).

In addition to the stage, Gordone also brought his dramaturgy talent to the community. He cofounded the Committee for the Employment of Negro Performers and was a member of the Commission on Civil Disorders and an instructor of Cell Block Theatre. In the late 1980s, he worked with Susan Kouyomjian to create a theater where actors of different ethnic origins were integrated into traditionally white roles without losing their unique identities as Latinos, African Americans, or Asians. Its aim was to dramatize a critical aspect of American society, that was not simply multiracial or multicultural but, more significantly, cross-cultural.

In 1987, Gordone was appointed distinguished lecturer in the Department of Speech Communication and Theatre Arts at Texas A & M University. He maintained this position until his death in 1995.

CRITICAL RECEPTION

Subtitled "A Black-Black Comedy," *No Place to Be Somebody* opened on Broadway to rave reviews. It was hailed for its brute and honest examination of the individual and communal struggle for identity. Though the play deals with the meaning of identity and community within a racial context, it also expands the frame of reference to the everyman. Dorothy Lee notes in "Three Black Plays: Alienation and Paths to Recovery" that "it shows the failure of *any* human relationship when individuals succumb to jealousy, greed or selfishness. . . . [I]t says that a person must accept himself but must also recognize the self's involvement in humanity" (403; emphasis added).

Critics also praised Charles Gordone's ability for characterization and dialogue; for example, "the language is exceptionally rough and exceptionally eloquent; it is proof of [his] immense talent that excrementitious gutterances of his large cast of whores, gangsters, jailbirds, and beat-up drifters stamp themselves on the memory as beautiful" (Oliver 112). Indeed, Gordone's use of language makes the character real. The audience actually finds itself sympathizing with the characters' plight, realizing that this motley crew can just as easily be them or someone they know at any given moment in time.

Criticism from African American reviewers was not so favorable. Many of them took offense to Gordone's refusal to be pigeonholed as black. Insisting that he was "part Indian, part French, part Irish and part nigger," he repeatedly defined himself as an American concerned with what he called "American Chemistry," the cross-cultural mixture of races and religions (Smith 167). Additionally, some stated they found evidence of self-hate, "a hint of contempt for black people in the play" (Smith 168). Even so, many of these critics had to concede that *No Place to Be Somebody* offers hope to all who are in despair.

In addition to the Pulitzer Prize for Drama, Gordone also received a Drama Desk Award and the Los Angeles Critics Circle Award for *No Place to Be Somebody*.

BIBLIOGRAPHY

Dramatic Works by Charles Gordone

Anabios. 1979. Unpublished.
Baba Chops. 1975. Unpublished.
"Gordone Is a Muthah." 1970. *The Best Short Plays of 1973*. Ed. Stanley Richards. Radnor: Chilton, 1973. 193–208.
The Last Chord. 1976. Unpublished.
A Little More Light Around the Place. 1964. Unpublished.
No Place to Be Somebody. Indianapolis: Bobbs, 1970.
Roan Brown and Cherry. 1988. Unpublished.
Worl's Champeen Lip Dansuh an' Watah Mellon Jooglah. 1969. Unpublished.

Studies of Charles Gordone's Dramatic Works

Barnes, Clive. Rev. of *No Place to Be Somebody*, by Charles Gordone. *New York Times* 5 May 1999: 265–266.
Elam, Harry J., Jr. "The Black Performer and the Performance of Blackness: *The Escape; or, A Leap to Freedom* by William Wells Brown and *No Place to Be Somebody* by Charles Gordone." *African American Performance and Theater History*. Ed. Harry J. Elam, Jr. and David Krasner. Oxford: Oxford University Press, 2001. 288–305.
"From the Muthah Lode." *Newsweek* 25 May 1970: 95.
Garland, Phyl. "Prize Winners." *Ebony* July 1970: 29+.
Gussow, Mel. Rev. of *The Last Chord*, by Charles Gordone. *New York Times* 17 May 1976: 287–288.

Hatch, Shari Dorantes, and Michael R. Strickland, eds. "Charles Gordone." *African American Writers: A Dictionary*. Santa Barbara: ABC-CLIO, 2000. 142.

Kerr, Walter. "Not Since Edward Albee . . ." *New York Times* 18 May 1969: 267–268.

Lee, Dorothy. "Three Black Plays: Alienation and Paths to Recovery." *Modern Drama* 19 (Dec. 1976): 397–404.

Leonard, Charles. "Charles Gordone." *The Oxford Companion to African American Literature*. Ed. William L. Andrews, Francis Smith Foster, and Trudier Harris. New York: Oxford University Press, 1997. 322–323.

O'Connor, John J. "The Theater." *Wall Street Journal* 6 May 1969: 266–267.

Oliver, Edith. "Off Broadway." *New Yorker* 44 (17 May 1969): 112+.

Peterson, Bernard L., Jr., ed. "Charles Gordone." *Contemporary Black American Playwrights and Their Plays: A Biographical Directory and Dramatic Index*. Westport: Greenwood, 1988. 196–198.

Ross, Jean W. "Charles Gordone." *Dictionary of Literary Biography*. Ed. John Mac Nicholas. Vol. 7. Detroit: Gale, 1981. 227–231.

Rush, Theresa, Carol Fairbanks Myers, and Ester Spring Arata, eds. "Charles Gordone." *Black American Writers Past and Present: A Biographical and Bibliographical Dictionary*. Metuchen: Scarecrow, 1975. 331–333.

Smith, Susan Harris. "Charles Gordone." *Speaking on Stage: Interviews with Contemporary American Playwrights*. Ed. Philip C. Kolin and Colby Kullman. Tuscaloosa: University of Alabama Press, 1996. 167–175.

Walcott, Ronald. "Ellison, Gordone and Tolson: Some Notes on the Blues, Style and Space." *Black World* 22 (Dec. 1972): 4–29.

SHIRLEY GRAHAM
(1896–1977)

Leela Kapai

BIOGRAPHY

Shirley Lola Graham was born on November 11, 1896, in Indianapolis, Indiana. Her father, Rev. David Graham, a preacher in the African Methodist Episcopal Church, was a man of principles who antagonized his superiors by his outspokenness. Consequently, though he was a well-read man and a respected preacher, his career never flourished, and he remained an itinerant preacher. A strong believer in education, he encouraged his talented daughter to excel in academics as well as music. After completing high school with honors in Spokane, Washington, Graham trained as a secretary. Her decision to marry young may have been an attempt to escape her father's rigid rules. However, taking care of her two sons and working to supplement the family income became equally constricting. She ended the marriage—a bold step for the daughter of a conservative preacher—and left her children with her mother as she explored different avenues to support her family.

Graham attempted to make a living with her skills as a secretary and a musician—as a music teacher at Morgan State College and then as a music librarian and secretary at Howard University. She went to Paris in 1926, took some classes at the Sorbonne, and for the first time heard music from the African subcontinent. In 1931, she entered Oberlin College and eventually received an A.B. in 1934 and an M.A. in 1935. Her master's thesis "The Survival of Africanism in Modern Music" was the first scholarly work of its kind.

Looking for a steady source of income, in 1935, Graham accepted the chairmanship of the department of Fine Arts at the Tennessee Agricultural & Industrial State College in Nashville. Lack of resources and inordinate demands on her time made it difficult for her to continue, so she moved to Chicago as the director of the local unit of the Federal Theater Project. In the next two years, in addition to fulfilling her administrative responsibilities, she was involved in writing and directing plays, designing sets, and composing musical scores. She collaborated with Charlotte Chopenning in producing a musical *Little Black Sambo* (1938). The production was derided by some African American critics and seen as a "giant leap backward" (Horne 76) but was liked by general audiences—it played in Cincinnati, Ohio, for six weeks and in Chicago for months. Another successful production during her tenure was *Swing Mikado*, a light comic opera, based on W. S. Gilbert and Arthur Sullivan's musical, that used African beats for its "swing tunes"—described as "having 'primitive' and 'jungle type sound'" (Perkins, "Unknown" 14).

Graham gradually grew disenchanted with her job. Often she was not accorded credit for her contributions. Furthermore, the success of the Federal Theater Project drew the ire of Broadway producers who resented government subsidies to their competition. Above all, the Federal Theater Project was coming under congressional scrutiny for sheltering communist writers and was expected to shut down. In 1938, Graham enrolled in the Yale School of Drama on a Rosenwald Fellowship. Though music was her specialty, she had written and produced several plays while at Morgan State and Oberlin, the years at Yale provided her with the theoretical underpinnings of playwriting. Most of the plays she authored were written or revised during these years and because of their generally favorable reception, she seriously considered pursuing the career of a playwright.

Graham left Yale in 1940, relinquishing the idea of completing requirements for a doctorate. During this period, she was considered one of the foremost African American dramatists of the period and was ranked with Langston Hughes* and Zora Neal Hurston* (Horne 84). Yet the lack of funds and support from producers made it impossible for her to dream of Broadway. Recognizing the insurmountable hurdles of racism and sexism, she gave up on her career as a playwright. After serving as the director of a YWCA theater group from 1940 to 1941 in Indianapolis, then as the director of a YWCA-USO camp at Fort Huachuca in Arizona—a job from which she was fired for her activism in defense of the rights of African American soldiers on their way to the war—she accepted the position of assistant field secretary of the NAACP. Her talents as a field organizer, an inspired speaker, and an untiring worker stood her in good stead in fulfilling her responsibilities. Instead of writing any more plays, she turned to penning biographies of noted African Americans. Their popularity brought her much-needed financial security.

Graham's marriage in 1951 to the renowned intellectual W. E. B. Du Bois, twenty-eight years her senior, whom she had known for many years, brought an end to the most productive period of her literary life. In 1952, when Dr. Du Bois came under the threat of imprisonment on the grounds of being an unregistered agent of a foreign country, the couple decided to leave the country. They moved to Ghana at the invitation of Kwame Nkrumah, the prime minister of the recently independent country, and, subsequently, became citizens of Ghana. Dr. Du Bois was entrusted with the responsibility of overseeing the ambitious project of compiling *Encyclopedia Africana*. Until the death of Dr. Du Bois in 1963, most of Graham's time and effort went into making his life comfortable. She remained a confidante of Nkrumah and served as his director of television until 1966, the year Nkrumah was deposed. She moved to Cairo and then to China where she resided until her death in 1977.

MAJOR WORKS AND THEMES

Shirley Graham's interest in dramatic arts had its genesis in W. E. B. Du Bois's call to playwrights to use theater to teach the African Americans "the meaning of their history and their rich emotional life" (Horne 56). He wanted a theater focused primarily on their community. As Kathy Perkins points out, Du Bois's words drew an enthusiastic response from aspiring African writers, particularly women (Introduction 3–4). Graham too heeded his call. The "Caravanzia" she produced at Oberlin, depicting the cultural contributions of fourteen nations, was clearly influenced by W. E. B. Du Bois's pageant *The Star of Ethiopia*. Her opera *Tom-Tom*, billed as an "An Epic of Music and the Negro," attempted to show the ties between the blues in Harlem and the music of Africa (Horne 58). In a wide sweep encompassing centuries, Graham transports the audience from the jungles of Africa before the freemen were enslaved to the plantations where they toiled, and then to scenes in Harlem. She even manages to introduce Marcus Garvey's back to Africa movement. With singers in the cabarets, dancers in African costumes, and the orchestra playing jazzy tunes, the production was an immense success.

Tom-Tom, the opera that brought national recognition to Shirley Graham, received mixed reviews. The black newspapers took pride in the success of one of their own; others praised the effort but pointed out several technical flaws in the production. A part of the appeal of *Tom-Tom* to its non–African American audience lay in the presentation of blacks as exotic and primitive (Perkins, "Unknown" 10), precisely the reason why it was criticized for perpetuating the racial stereotypes.

Graham's recognition as a playwright depends primarily on four plays produced during her years at Yale: *It's Morning* (1939), *Coal Dust* (1930; also presented as *Dust to Earth* [1941]), *I Gotta Home (or Elijah's Ravens)* (1939), and *Track Thirteen* (1940), the only play published during her lifetime. Most of these plays were revisions of works that had been produced in some form at Oberlin or at Cleveland's Karamu House or at an institution where she had taught. All deal with the lives of African Americans, but unlike many other contemporaries, she moved beyond the hearth to explore social, economic, and racial issues.

I Gotta Home is very likely the renamed and revised version of *Elijah's Ravens* (its manuscript has not been located) and is included in the anthology edited by Perkins. The setting is based on Graham's own experience of growing up in the home of a minister. Rev. Elijah J. Cobb, described by the author as the "last of a line of simple souls who, having heard 'the call' to preach does nothing else," his wife, and children suffer the tyranny of people like Dr. Caleb Green, the presiding elder, "one of those hierarchical leftovers from the days of overseers." The news that the reverend's sister, Mattie Cobb, is returning home rich with an inheritance sets in motion a comedy of errors, laying bare the hypocrisy of the church people and creating hilarious situations. Marked by vivid characterization and lively dialogue, the play is entertaining.

It's Morning, a one-act play set on a plantation on the eve of Emancipation, is reminiscent of a Greek tragedy. The slave women serve as the Greek chorus, describing the scene and then commenting on the developments. It deals with a theme that Graham had touched on in *Tom-Tom* and was reintroduced in *Beloved* by Toni Morrison—a mother murdering her young daughter rather than seeing her sold into slavery. The play was directed by Otto Preminger, who was on the faculty at Yale (Perkins, "Unknown" 15). Graham's growing expertise in composing and designing is reflected in her "Note on the Play" in which she explains the rationale of using different dialects and refers to her use of spirituals.

Track Thirteen, a radio play, is a suspenseful comedy about train porters and their superstitions and was broadcast over WICC Radio in New Haven, Connecticut, in 1940. The action takes place on train 27 out of Chicago that is rescheduled to leave on track 13. An African American porter waits for the impending disaster but as it turns out, number thirteen brings him luck, for he wins a $5,000 reward for his help in the capture of a disguised bank robber on board. *Track Thirteen* was the only play to be published during Graham's lifetime.

Dust to Earth—a revised version of her play *Coal Dust*, which was produced in 1930 at Morgan State College and revived at Karamu House in 1938—was produced at Yale in 1941. The play in three acts, set in a West Virginia mining town, deals with "issues such as illegitimacy, a brother–sister relationship, miscegenation, and class conflict" (Horne 82). One of the remarkable features of the production was the elaborate staging of a coal mine with a working elevator.

It is difficult to gauge the reception of Graham's plays in the absence of available contemporary reviews. References to these plays in the letters and other papers, mentioned in the works of Kathy Perkins and Gerald Horne, reveal that they were generally appreciated by the audience for their themes, lively dialogue, and deft use of dialect. She had her share of criticism as well, particularly by unsympathetic whites who felt that she was going beyond her capability in trying to depict characters other than African Americans.

CRITICAL RECEPTION

Though Shirley Graham published extensively during her lifetime—she wrote numerous articles for the *Crisis* and *Freedomways;* biographies of African American achievers such as George Carver, Paul Robeson, Frederick Douglass, and Phyllis Wheatley; and even a novel—she did not resume playwriting again. Until the resurrection of some of Graham's forgotten plays by James Hatch and Kathy Perkins in the1990s, few had heard of her as a playwright. She has been consistently ignored in the literary histories and rarely mentioned in even the recent reevaluations of the period. Her only claim to recognition seems to rest on her being the spouse of W. E. B. Du Bois.

Among the few critical essays discussing Shirley Graham's plays is Perkins's "The Unknown Career of Shirley Graham." An expanded version of this article is included in the *Dictionary of Literary Biography*. In *Race Woman: The Lives of Shirley Graham Du Bois*, Horne devotes two chapters to her career as a playwright and provides information based on her recently released personal papers. In the introductions to their anthologies, Perkins and Hatch provide some pertinent observations.

BIBLIOGRAPHY

Dramatic Works by Shirley Graham

"*Coal Dust*." Also presented as *Dust to Earth*. Unpublished. Shirley Graham Du Bois Papers.

"*I Gotta Home: A Comedy in Three Acts*." *Black Female Playwrights: An Anthology of Plays before 1950*. Ed. Kathy A. Perkins. Bloomington: Indiana University Press, 1990. 225–279.

"*It's Morning*." *Black Female Playwrights: An Anthology of Plays before 1950*. Ed. Kathy A. Perkins. Bloomington: Indiana University Press, 1990. 211–223.

"*Tom-Tom*." *Roots of African American Drama: An Anthology of Early Plays, 1858–1938*. Ed. Leo Hamalian and James V. Hatch. Detroit: Wayne State University Press, 1991. 238–286.

"*Track Thirteen*." *Lost Plays of Harlem Renaissance*. Ed. James V. Hatch and Leo Hamalian. Detrtoit: Wayne State University Press, 1996. 368–390.

Studies of Shirley Graham's Dramatic Works

Horne, Gerald. "On Her Journey Now" and " The Middle of Her Journey." *Race Woman: The Lives of Shirley Graham Du Bois*. New York: New York University Press. 52–70, 71–88.

Perkins, Kathy A. Introduction. *Black Female Playwrights: An Anthology of Plays before 1950*. Ed. Kathy A. Perkins. Bloomington: Indiana University Press, 1990. 3–16.

———. "Shirley Graham." *76: African American Writers, 1940–1955*. Vol. 76 of *Dictionary of Literary Biography*. Ed. Trudier Harris and Thadious M. Davis. Detroit: Gale, 1988. 66–75.

———. "The Unknown Career of Shirley Graham." *Freedomways* 25.1 (1985): 6–17.

MICKI GRANT
(1941 –   )

Kimberly K. Harding

BIOGRAPHY

Born Minnie Perkins in Chicago, Illinois, Micki Grant has enjoyed a stellar career in theater. In fact, it was her love for the movies that fueled her ambition to become an actress and a combination of her love for poetry and music that would mesh into a career as an author, lyricist, and composer for the theater.

Raised in near poverty, Grant always dreamed of a life in theater. It was her father, Oscar Perkins, a barber, who exposed her to movies at a young age. The disturbing African American images—ones that represented an accepted way for whites to look at blacks on the screen—that led the NAACP to protest may have introduced her to performance, but she never identified with these stereotypes. She saw in herself something far more humane (Flatley D6). These early years developed her love for performing and around the age of six, Grant made her onstage debut playing the "Spirit of Spring" in a community center production. By the age of eight, she began to write poetry and recite it for her family who listened with approval (Flatley D6).

Recognizing her penchant for the arts, Grant's father and mother—Gussie (Odessa)—sacrificed to buy musical instruments for her and her older sister. A piano was purchased for Lucy and a violin for Micki. At the age of nine, she learned the violin and spent the next several years studying music theory and harmony, and the double bass. "I wrote music for my own pleasure from the time I was fourteen or fifteen years old. I wrote compulsively; I couldn't help it. I'd sing my songs around the house and I always wanted to be in the the-atre," Grant expressed during a 1972 interview with Maurice Peterson for *Essence* (32). An accomplished musician, Grant played in the orchestras of every school she attended including the Chicago School of Music, where she studied on scholarship, and the University of Illinois (Grant interview).

To gain acting experience, Grant's first drama teacher, Porche Lawson, gave her free private lessons and, at eighteen, she began acting in a community theater group at the Wabash YMCA called the Center Aisle Players. Grant graduated from Englewood High School and enrolled in the journalism program at the University of Illinois. Passionate about writing, she felt constrained by journalistic rules and pursued a major in speech and drama and a minor in English instead (Grant interview). She moved to Los Angeles after the completion of her junior year to immerse herself fully in acting. While there she appeared in a production of *Fly Blackbird* and, in 1962, when the show moved east to the Off-Broadway district, Grant made her New York debut and took up residence in the city.

Throughout the 1960s, Grant worked as an actress, appearing in several stage shows, including *Tambourines to Glory*, *Jericho-Jim Crow*, *The Cradle Will Rock*, and *To Be Young, Gifted, and Black*. Entering the world of television soap operas, Grant set the record for the first African American contract player on a daytime serial. She played the role of attorney Peggy Nolan on NBC's *Another World* for seven years. Thirty years later, Grant still performs on and off Broadway and in regional theaters around the country. In 1997, she received the Helen Hayes Award as Outstanding Lead Actress for her portrayal of Sadie Delaney in *Having Our Say* at the Kennedy Center.

Aside from her performing endeavors, Micki Grant made her initial critical debut in the 1970s as a lyricist-composer for the Urban Arts Corps (UAC) in New York City. Founded by Vinnette Carroll,* the Urban Arts Corps Theater provided a space to nurture emerging playwrights and showcase their works. While at the UAC, Grant combined creative forces with Carroll, who conceived and directed UAC plays—a very talented collaboration that developed numerous works, including the Broadway smash hits *Don't Bother Me I Can't Cope* and *Your Arms Too Short to Box with God*.

Indeed, the most successful songwriter of UAC, Grant, as composer-lyricist-auteur for *Don't Bother Me I Can't Cope*, won a 1972 Grammy Award for Best Broadway Musical Album of the Year, two Drama Desk Awards for lyrics and performance, an Outer Circle Award, Obie Awards, the NAACP Image Award for Playwriting, the Mademoiselle Achievement Award, and three Tony nominations. With the late Alex Bradford, Grant developed the score of *Your Arms Too Short to Box with God*, which garnered a Grammy nomination.

Perhaps the first black women duo to find success on the Broadway stage, Grant's collaborations with Vinnette Carroll also include the Urban Arts Corps productions *Bury the Dead* (1971), *Croesus and the Witch* (1971), *Step Lively Boy* (1973), *The Ups and Downs of Theophilus Maitland* (1974), *I'm Laughing* *but I Ain't Tickled* (1976), and *Alice* (1977). Ever evolving, Grant continues to thrive as a lyricist-composer and can claim many other fruitful collaborations to her credit. Two projects include: J. e. Franklin's* *The Prodigal Sister: A New Black Musical* (1974) and, along with fellow songwriters, she received a Tony nomination for the score of the Stephen Schwartz musical *Working* (1978). Most recently, she has collaborated with Leslie Lee on *Phillis*, the story of the African American poet, Phillis Wheatley. Grant's body of work offers a plethora of good songs. They have been celebrated and preserved in two retrospectives, *Step Into My World* at the AMAS Repertory Theatre in 1989 and *Looking Back* produced by the New Federal Theatre in 1994. She continues to thrive and create in New York City.

MAJOR WORKS AND THEMES

Micki Grant, an artist with passionately optimistic views about universality and the brotherhood of mankind, writes African American–specific plays with humanist ideals. Though her plays use African American characters and idioms, she stresses their cross-cultural messages. "If a playwright wants to limit himself to a Black audience and a black community, he has the perfect right to do so, but I've always felt that the theater should be for the whole community" (qtd. in Flatley D6).

Concerned with social and political themes, much of her body of work looks probingly at American society. As the author, composer, and lyricist of *Don't Bother Me I Can't Cope*, the Broadway show in which she starred, Grant challenges conventional attitudes about political and social injustices without the harsh edge of the 1960s militant black theater movement. Instead, she diffuses hatred and infuses peace and love for mankind while insisting on the inherent dignity of black people.

Conceived and directed by Vinnette Carroll, *Cope* is not a conventional book musical. Though snippets of text appear occasionally, it is not dialogue driven. Instead, like the song-plays that Carroll pioneered and that rely heavily on music, dance, and ritual, Grant's compositions clearly shape the tone and style of her work. This makes her a lyricist-auteur of sorts—a storyteller who relies less on a conventionally written text instead creating and organizing actions in other dramatic ways. Grant interjects in a 1972 *Ebony* magazine interview, "I've come to realize that important things can be said through words set to music. More than being a diversion, songs can be an important and accessible form of communication, hence, my interest in musical theatre" ("Micki" 100). Indeed, *Cope* has something important to say.

The twenty-one songs in *Cope* actually serve as its book, whereas racism, war, sexism, poverty, and drug abuse provide some of the sources of lyrical content. Conversely, these song "scène lets" provide provocative commentary on the African American experience and universal issues. In her aim to develop variations on themes, Grant's lyrics well define character and mood. For example, the title song introduces myriad frustrated everyday folk whose rapid, rapping dialogue makes the piece engaging and energetic. The first character is further frustrated by an analyst who, unable to get to the root of her inability to cope, merely tells her so. Disgusted, the woman quips to her audience-therapists, "Do you think I'm paying you that kind of dough / For telling me something I already know / That's why I'm here fool, 'cause I can't cope" (15). Grant, in writing this song-play, dismisses the angry militant approach and creates joyous defiance. Conflict does not occur among her characters but against injustice or the complexity of human nature. It is then internalized and spills out as "song-liloquies," duets, or infectious rhythmic dialogue as the other cast members provide audience therapy. Through their various psychological and moral states, repeatedly, her characters bring home to the audience that amid human-induced horrors we can find humaneness.

While Grant exploits the opportunity to scold coyly the American culture, her compositions are dramatic and timeless. Employing styles that run the gamut from sacred to secular, she uses a mixture of blues, soul, folk, and gospel influences. In the 1972 production, Grant's performance of three songs in the second act was an integral part of the show's success. A talented acoustic guitarist, she accompanied her own conservative vocal delivery on "It Takes a Whole Lotta Human Feeling"—a thematically universal song that crossed over to mainstream appeal.

Having established themselves as a prolific team, Grant and Carroll continued UAC collaborations. Three years pass before they would have another show play on Broadway. Commissioned by the Italian government for the Spoleto Festival of Two Worlds, *Your Arms Too Short to Box with God* proved to be another commercial success for the pair. Conceived from the Book of Matthews, *Your Arms Too Short*, yet another retelling of the last days of Christ, boasts no less artistry than *Cope*. Carroll's conception brought both freshness and tradition to the gospel play, but its message is powerfully uplifted by the music of Alex Bradford and Micki Grant.

That Grant would find inspiration for a musical adaptation of the Book of Matthew comes as no surprise considering her own upbringing by parents who firmly believed in the Gospel. From "Beatitudes," a beautiful rendition of the oppressed whom Christ calls blessed, to "Something Is Wrong in Jerusalem," a lament sung by Mary, the mother of Christ, Grant's Christian roots and her consistent championing of human dignity and justice evince themselves in her lyrics. "The Sermon," which follows "We're Gonna Have a Good Time," the rollicking revival show opener, shows Grant's political subtlety by identifying Christ as one who upset the status quo. Identifying Christ as a radically righteous "thorn in the side of the establishment," she more than hints at those Christlike martyrs of the mid- and late 1960s such as John F. Kennedy, Malcolm X, Robert Kennedy, and, of course, Nobel laureate Dr. Martin Luther

King, Jr. These brave soldiers for justice and world peace led committed lives—ones made more challenging by the nagging reality that despite committing oneself to spiritual and virtuous ideals, people, for the most part, still exploit, oppress, and cheat one another. This sentiment is evident in Grant's style.

Called on to examine the enduring power and influence of a committed life, Grant became painfully aware that little has changed in human behavior since Christ walked on the earth. As Grant is committed to her vision of a moral utopia, she does not shy away from controversy and chose to partake in a controversial project that features a Jesus who is black and who "never says [or sings] a mumbling word." In fact, she helps, as author of several of the songs in the musical, to create a lyrical atmosphere in which Christ and Judas, the hero and the villain of the gospel, can be models to apply our everyday life lessons. For example, Grant's calypso-influenced "It's Too Late, Judas," reminds the audience that, like Judas, one may conceal one's crime from others but not from oneself.

Today, *Your Arms Too Short* stands as a gospel classic that enjoys generational resurgence. In 1980, while it returned to Broadway at the Ambassador Theater, a new musical written entirely by Grant—*It's So Nice to Be Civilized*—opened at the Martin Beck that same week. This was Grant's first commercial show that used a conventional book. In this work, Grant explores the themes of world peace and harmony as is obvious in "Pass a Little Love Around." The title song "It's So Nice to Be Civilized" was inspired by news events and became the germinal idea that spawned the musical. Of this musical Grant said in an April 14, 2003, telephone interview, "It's about all the little vagaries about what we call civilized living. It's not all so civilized." The story, which takes place over a weekend, contains several vignettes whose unifying thread revolves around a white social worker who attempts to persuade his inner-city adolescent charges to put their graffiti skills to more positive use and paint a mural. In that the musical addresses universal themes of human uplift and universals such as life, death, love, and loss, it bears Grant's signature philosophical stamp, and the show's opening song, "We're Going to Sing about Life," reveals Grant's ongoing commitment to producing art with social relevance.

The theme of human uplift also permeates Grant's most recent musical *Don't Underestimate a Nut*. Originally titled *Carver: Don't Underestimate a Nut*, Grant's tale unveils a musical version of the life of African American botanist/inventor George Washington Carver. Produced in 1994 by the Emmy Gifford Children's Theatre in Omaha, Nebraska, the show is written for adults to perform for children. Its cast of characters only includes one child, who plays the young Carver. Upon discovering his interest in plant life, young Carver's genius is revealed through the lyrics' "mystery and miracles." Pared down from a full-length endeavor, the sixty-minute, one-act play proclaims and praises Carver's discoveries through the lyrics "a goober is more than just a pea."

As in *Copes*, "They Keep Coming," a song that cites the achievements of African Americans that have "Overcome," *Don't Underestimate a Nut* makes heroic the image of a former slave. When asked in a telephone interview what message would Grant want the kids to get from this musical, she responded, "That the person who discovered and did all of these things with a nut was black and came from slavery, and that he helped change the economy, that he had a brilliant mind. It's about overcoming obstacles and succeeding."

CRITICAL RECEPTION

As is the case with many nonblack critics who judge artistic endeavors by blacks, critiques of Micki Grant's works, whether positive or negative, are, like other black works, categorized in one of two ways. The *Wall Street Journal* critic Edwin Wilson classifies ". . . black theater . . . as a tool of enlightenment and liberation, and nothing else . . . [or black theater that] allows a bit of entertainment to creep into it" (Marlowe and Blake 54). Such critics, whether in praise or condemnation, always position black theater as being serious and didactic, which may also read as militant and angry, or as affirmative and pleasurable—only occasionally moderately angry. The success or failure of African American works is often based on how comfortable or uncomfortable it leaves the white folks in the audience.

Most critics acknowledge Grant's lyrical and musical prowess, and Wilson's praise of the musical *Cope* ends his critique: "There is a place for purely educational black theater, but surely there is also a place for the message of 'Don't Bother Me.' It is one we hear all too seldom, and today need to hear more than ever, white and black alike" (qtd. in Marlowe and Blake 54). Opposed to Wilson's assessment is a review of the musical penned by *Women's Wear Daily* critic Joseph H. Mazo. Although Mazo snidely calls the musical "a commercial for black dignity," he criticizes it more so for being too preachy and for telling the audience things that it should already know. Mazo's "you're-preaching-to-the-choir" attitude to Grant's subtly political lyrics, does not prevent him from recognizing that "the show is blessed with some very strong moments." However, what Wilson calls Grant's "deep feeling," Mazo sees as "slickly liberal"; what Wilson sees as "great simplicity, strength, and warmth" Mazo calls a failed attempt to "make a commercial into a theatre piece" (qtd. in Marlowe and Blake 55).

Although Alex Bradford received top billing as the primary composer for *Your Arms Too Short*, Grant's contributions were substantial enough to merit critical attention. Although critic John Beaufort notes that the music contained "some unidentified assists by Micki Grant," he unknowingly praises her skills by noting that "the rich compilation of melody, harmony, and movement begins simply with 'Beatitudes,'" a piece written by Grant (qtd. in Marlowe and Blake 55). In the 1980 Broadway revival of the show, *New York Times* critic Mel Gussow praises Grant's mastery of her calypso style, and he cites "It's Too Late, Judas" and "We Are the Priests and Elders" as two songs worthy of special mention (qtd. in Marlowe and Blake 223).

Grant's *It's So Nice to Be Civilized*, her first commercial work as a solo writer, met with disastrous reviews. Perhaps its failure is predicated on Grant's book writing skills or the lack thereof, or the new ideas put forth from the commercial producers. In its embryonic form, the show extended its run at the AMAS Repertory Theatre due to popular demand, however, the AMAS show isn't fully what played Broadway. Critics praised the talent but condemned the book of the Broadway version. Gussow called it "a musical with first act trouble" (qtd. in Marlowe and Blake 221). Marilyn Stasio of the *New York Post* complains of the musical's lack of characterization and plot organization: "It would be much easier to love these aggressively lovable stereotypes if Grant had drawn them as characters and put them in a plotted play"(qtd. in Marlowe and Blake 221). Douglas Watt of the *Daily News* was more scathing in his assessment of her ability not only as a playwright but as a composer: "For the most part, the only interest in her music lies in its rhythmic variety—melodically and harmonically, her work is commonplace—and she obviously has no ability at all to construct a book" (qtd. in Marlowe and Blake 220). Despite mostly positive reviews of the lyrics and some excellent songs ("Look at Us" and "I've Still Got My Bite") and fine performances by Mabel King, Vivian Reed, and Obba Babatunde, critics lambasted the diffuse book and condemned it to a short run (Woll 90).

Grant's second book musical, *Don't Underestimate a Nut*, fared better in the press though one critic, Jim Delmont, was not effusively supportive: "[Carver] is meant to honor black history month. There couldn't have been a better choice." He went on to say, "The somewhat static spoken portions are enlivened from time to time with some good song and dance numbers, notably 'Togetherness,' and some nice ballads, including 'Miracles'" (F49).

In joining her personal philosophy to her art, Grant has successfully articulated many particularities of black life. Despite varied reactions from critics, most would concur that she places art before argument and human feeling before human politics. She has made, and continues to make, the black message universally accepted. She wants everyone, black and white alike, to see her works, not as black truths, but as human truths.

BIBLIOGRAPHY

Dramatic Works by Micki Grant

Alice (with Vinnette Carroll). 1977. Unpublished.
Bury the Dead (with Vinnette Carroll). 1971. Unpublished.

Croesus and the Witch (with Vinnette Carroll). New York: Broadway Play Publishing, n.d..

Don't Bother Me, I Can't Cope (with Vinnette Carroll). New York: French, 1972.

Don't Bother Me I Can't Cope. Broadway original cast album. LP. Polydor, 1972.

Don't Underestimate a Nut. 1994. Unpublished.

Hansel and Gretel in the 1980s. New York: Broadway Play Publishing, n.d.

I'm Laughing but I Ain't Tickled (with Vinnette Carroll). 1976. Unpublished.

It's So Nice to Be Civilized. 1980. Unpublished.

The Prodigal Sister: A New Black Musical (with J. e. Franklin). 1974. New York: French, 1975.

Step Lively Boy (with Vinnette Carroll). 1973. Unpublished.

The Ups and Downs of Theophilus Maitland (with Vinnette Carroll). 1974. Unpublished.

Working. 1978. Unpublished.

Working. Broadway original cast album. CD. Sony, 2001.

Your Arms Too Short to Box with God (with Vinnette Carroll). 1976/1980. Unpublished.

Your Arms Too Short to Box with God. Broadway original cast album. LP. MCA, 1977.

Studies of Micki Grant's Dramatic Works

Abdul, Raoul. *Famous Black Entertainers of Today*. New York: Dodd, 1974.

Delmont, Jim. "'Carver' Musical Honors Great Scientist." *Omaha World-Herald* 29 Jan. 1994: F49.

Flatley, Guy. "Don't Worry Micki Can Cope." *New York Times* 7 May 1972: D6.

Grant, Micki. Telephone interview. 14 Apr. 2003.

Green, Stanley. *Broadway Musicals Show by Show*. 1985. Milwaukee: Hal/Leonard, 1996.

Hughes, Catherine, ed. *New York Theatre Annual, 1977–78*. Detroit: Gale, 1978.

Marlowe, John, and Betty Blake, eds. *New York Theatre Critics' Reviews* 37 (1976): 54–56 and 41 (1980): 221–223.

"Micki Grant: She Can Cope." *Ebony* (Feb. 1973): 100.

Peterson, Maurice. "Theater: Micki Grant" *Essence* (Nov. 1972): 32.

Woll, Allen. *Black Musical Theatre: From "Coontown" to "Dreamgirls."* Baton Rouge: Louisiana State University Press, 1989.

ANGELINA WELD GRIMKÉ (1880–1958)

Terry Novak

BIOGRAPHY

Angelina Weld Grimké was born on February 27, 1880, in Boston, Massachusetts, to the mulatto Archibald Grimké and the white Sarah Stanley. Angelina Grimké Weld and Sarah Moore Grimké, famous abolitionists who turned their backs on their family's Southern plantation way of life to become Quakers in the North, were Angelina's great-aunts. Grimké's father, Archibald, was the product of a relationship between Grimké's slaveholding grandfather and one of his slaves. Upon the grandfather's death, Archibald and his siblings were seized as slaves by one of Grimké's white uncles. Once Archibald escaped from slavery, he was discovered and embraced by his aunts; Archibald Grimké named his daughter Angelina Weld Grimké, after his aunt Angelina Grimké Weld.

The young Angelina Weld Grimké lived a fairly sheltered childhood as the daughter of Harvard graduate lawyer Archibald Grimké and as a member of the prominent Boston Grimké family. Unfortunately, the family of her mother, Sarah Stanley, was unhappy with their daughter's marriage; by the time Angelina was seven, her mother had succumbed to the concerns of her own parents and abandoned her daughter to the care of Archibald. Sarah never saw Angelina again, although she did remain in contact with her. Despite this early unhappiness in her life, Angelina thrived in school, attending some of Boston's best institutions. As she grew older, she began to notice racism more and more in society, although she continued to live a fairly sheltered life herself. From 1902 to 1926 Angelina Weld Grimké made a living as an English teacher. She spent four summers of that time period studying at her father's alma mater, Harvard University. Grimké never found the fulfillment of a life partner, but she did indeed find solace in her prolific writings, which ranged from drama to short stories to poetry. While living in Washington, DC, she became part of a literary society that found its center at Howard University. Grimké moved to New York in the 1930s, after the death of her father. She was still living in New York when she died on June 11, 1958, at the age of seventy-eight.

MAJOR WORKS AND THEMES

Angelina Weld Grimké wrote two plays in her lifetime, only one of which was published and produced. *Rachel* was first produced on stage in March 1916 in Washington, DC; it opened in New York City in April 1917 and in Cambridge, Massachusetts, in May 1917. The play was published in 1920. *Rachel* is the story of the Loving family, which consists of mother Mrs. Loving and her children Tom and Rachel, who begin in the play as teenagers but who progress to young adults in the short three acts of the play. As the name intimates, the play revolves around Rachel's character. *Rachel* is often thought of as a "lynching play," and, in fact, the premise of the play does rest on the tragedy of lynching. In act 1, Rachel and Tom discover that the deaths of their father and half brother so long ago were violent lynching deaths, prompted by their father's outspoken social views in his newspaper. As Mrs. Loving puts it, "They—they—were lynched . . . by Christian people—in a Christian land. We found out afterward they were all church members in good standing—the best people" (145).

The ghosts of the father and son permeate the play, but the idea of troubled motherhood also becomes apparent. Rachel Loving goes from being a young woman dreaming of one day being a mother to many children to a woman far beyond her years in grief and worry, a woman who believes that bringing more "brown and black" babies to the world would be an injustice to them. Instead, she concentrates on trying to save the children who are already born, including the orphaned Jimmy, whom she has adopted. Shortly after Mrs. Loving's tale of the family deaths, Rachel declares, "Then, everywhere, everywhere, throughout the South, there are hundreds of dark mothers who live in fear, terrible, suffocating fear, whose rest by night is broken. . . . Why—it would be more merciful—to strangle the little things at birth. And so this nation—this white Christian nation— has deliberately set its curse upon the most beautiful—the most holy thing in life—motherhood!" (149).

Grimké uses her play to point out many instances of racism in society, including the problems in the public schools. She goes on to deal with the issues of the futility of education for most African Americans; many of Grimké's characters are well educated, but none holds the level of job his or her white counterpart is able to hold.

Grimké's second play, *Mara*, was never published or produced. The author's handwritten version of the finished play exists in the Angelina Weld Grimké collection at the Howard University Library in Washington, DC. *Mara* also has lynching themes as an underlying basis of the text. This play deals more specifically, however, with the rape of the black female protagonist by a white man. Perhaps it is this volatile premise that kept Grimké from pursuing—or gaining—publication or production of the play.

CRITICAL RECEPTION

Very little in the way of criticism exists concerning Angelina Weld Grimké's play *Mara*, although this seems destined to change. Phyllis Wood has written that this play shows a maturation of style that far exceeds *Rachel* in many ways (420). Wood's interest in the play has begun to spark other interest, all of which, to date, has been positive.

Much commentary exists regarding Grimké's play *Rachel*, which is overwhelmingly seen as the beginning of a "lynching play" movement. Although some of Grimké's own contemporaries were critical of the play because of its controversial theme, the play had a very successful run. In fact, production of *Rachel* was at first sponsored by the NAACP. Long before Grimké's death, appreciation for the play had fairly well disappeared. In recent decades, appreciation and interest have been revived, as has been the case with much African American literature. By 1991, Carolivia Herron was discussing *Rachel* in terms of the play's having set a major theme for most works in Grimké's canon (5). Judith L. Stephens also focuses on the theme of lynching in Grimké's play. Will Harris broadens the scope when he writes that "[i]n *Rachel*, Grimké brought into focus the themes of social inequality, hiring discrimination, the black frustration and familial erosion which resulted from economic strictures, and the pervasive, blighting effects of racism—in the process setting the pace for 'race' drama to come" (206).

Others have also dared to go beyond the theme of lynching in their discussion of *Rachel*. David Krasner believes that "[a]bove all, *Rachel* is a play about melancholy" (109). While Krasner understands and credits lynching as a main theme of the play, he finds the idea of Rachel's depression over the way life seems to be as also a major consideration in discussing the work. Again while honoring the theme of lynching, Angeletta K. M. Gourdine considers that "Grimké introduces the role of historical memory, and though her depiction of black maternity has drawn much negative evaluation, this facet of the story most manifests the use of *drama*" (538).

As the field of African American literary criticism continues to increase, especially for early works, one can expect that Grimké's plays will enjoy fresh perspectives and consideration in the future.

BIBLIOGRAPHY

Dramatic Works by Angelina Weld Grimké

Mara. Unpublished. Angelina Weld Grimké Collection. Howard University Library, Washington, DC.

"*Rachel*." 1920. *Selected Works of Angelina Weld Grimké*. Ed. Carolivia Herron. New York: Oxford University Press, 1991. 123–209.

Studies of Angelina Weld Grimké's Dramatic Works

Gourdine, Angeletta K. M. "The *Drama* of Lynching in Two Blackwomen's Drama, or Relating Grimké's *Rachel* to Hansberry's *A Raisin in the Sun*." *Modern Drama* 41 (1998): 533–545.

Harris, Will. "Early Black Women Playwrights and the Dual Liberation Motif." *African American Review* 28.2 (1994): 205–221.

Herron, Carolivia. Introduction. *Selected Works of Angelina Weld Grimké*. Ed. Carolivia Herron. New York: Oxford University Press, 1991. 3–22.

Krasner, David. *A Beautiful Pageant: African American Theatre, Drama, and Performance in the Harlem Renaissance, 1910–1927*. New York: Palgrave Macmillan, 2002.

Stephens, Judith L. "Lynching Dramas and Women: History and Critical Context." *Strange Fruit: Plays on Lynching by American Women*. Ed. Kathy A. Perkins and Judith L. Stephens. Bloomington: Indiana University Press, 1998. 3–20.

Wood, Phyllis. "Angelina Weld Grimké." *Notable Black American Women*. Ed. Jessie Carney Smith. Detroit: Gale, 1992. 416–421.

WILLIAM HARRISON GUNN (1934–1989)

Jessie N. Marion

BIOGRAPHY

Playwright, actor, novelist, scenarist, and pioneer black independent film director William Harrison Gunn was born on July 15, 1934, to William Harrison and Louise Alexander Gunn in Philadelphia, Pennsylvania. Raised in a comfortable, middle-class environment, Bill Gunn's family was one of the few African American families in his neighborhood who owned their own home. Gunn's home life and the quality education he received from a racially integrated Philadelphia public school system contributed to his successes later in life. In addition to the influences of this stability in his childhood, Gunn's development was also impacted by his parents' own creativity. Gunn's first taste for acting came from his mother, who was not only an actress, but was also a beauty contest winner, a cofounder of a self-help community service organization, and a leader of a theater group. Recognized as a songwriter ("Ball and the Jack"), musician, comedian, and unpublished poet, Gunn's father was an artistic influence as well. After high school, Gunn served in the United States Navy for a short time, only to leave the military to pursue the goal of becoming an actor that he had set early in life.

Unfortunately for Gunn, building a career as an African American actor in the 1950s and 1960s was not an easy task. Roles for black actors were extremely limited, for even the more significant roles available for the issue plays of the 1930s and 1940s, such as *Native Sun*, had begun to dwindle by the 1950s. Upon moving to the East Village in New York to pursue his career during this time period, Gunn found himself struggling both financially and ethically. At this time, most roles for African American actors were limited to stereotypical servant parts, leaving Gunn to grapple with the problem of compromising his artistic integrity for the sake of earning a living, a thought that is said to have left him with nightmares of being tossed penniless into the streets of Philadelphia and being made into a drug addict. A statement made by Gunn in a 1964 issue of *Variety* reflects this frustration over the casting practices for black actors in film and theater: "When a good part for a Negro actor comes along, they offer it to Sidney Poitier. If he turns it down, they rewrite it for a white actor" (qtd. in Leki 112).

Gunn's struggles as an actor influenced his eventual writings, which detail the "role of an artist in a materialistic and pitiless world," according to Ilona Leki in *Dictionary of Literary Biography* (114). However, in Gunn's own life he was able to overcome the odds and secure roles in both theater and on television throughout the 1950s and 1960s to the point that his earnings allowed him to study art, to purchase a historic house in New York, and to furnish his home with European art. Because of this degree of success and because of his frustration with the roles available to him, Gunn also began to develop his second career as a writer. Although Gunn's work has never become familiar to mass audiences, he gained the respect and admiration of critics, writers, and other artists in his lifetime. On April 5, 1989, Gunn died at the age of fifty-four of encephalitis arising from complications with meningitis in Nyack Hospital in New York. His death came one night before the opening of his play *The Forbidden City* at the Public Theater.

MAJOR WORKS AND THEMES

From novels to stage plays to screenplays, William Harrison Gunn's writings are largely autobiographical, for they are often built around a main character who is an artist from Philadelphia. His works address such issues as the problems of the black middle class, the struggles of the artist staying true to his art, and the difficulties that black artists, in particular, face "in a world structured and managed by whites" (Leki 111). Gunn is recognized today as a unique contributor to the African American literary tradition because of his exploration of race and the complicated way in which it is represented in his works. Many of Gunn's protagonists deal with issues outside of race alone, and instead are found surrounded by people of various races and nationalities who struggle with a wide variety of problems. However, these various characters cannot be pigeonholed, for as Gunn matured as a writer throughout his career, his protagonists reflected his own ever-changing and developing racial consciousness.

Gunn's first stage play, *Marcus in the High Grass*, for instance, was recognized as being more of a "white play" than as a "black" one. First produced with the Theatre Guild at the Westport Theatre in Connecticut in 1958 and later produced in New York City by the Theatre Guild in 1959, *Marcus in the High Grass* is a story about people in general and does not address any overtly racial issues. As a result, Gunn was first mistaken as a white author and was even hailed as Tennessee Williams's superior following the production of this play by columnist Dorothy Kilgallen, who believed he was white.

By the time Gunn produced his second play in 1966, however, there was evidence of his growing consciousness as a black artist. The one-act play *Johnnas*, which premiered in the Brooklyn Theatre Center, tackles the issues of race not addressed in *Marcus in the High Grass* through the exploration of the isolation and alienation of the black artist. Gunn suggests in this play, through the tragic life of his protagonist, Johnnas Gifford, that black society and American society in general are unprepared for the young black artist. In the play, Johnnas, a sensitive fourteen-year-old black artist, is shunned by his peers and society in general for not fulfilling the socially scripted role of an African American male adolescent. Instead of being found on the basketball court with other boys his age, Johnnas becomes an outcast because he is seen as being too sensitive and delicate, and is even taunted for being too "white." Although Johnnas is encouraged to write his beautiful poetry by both his mother and his white English teacher, Johnnas's rejection by society leads to his eventual suicide, for he jumps to his death from the ledge of a downtown office building into a crowd of insensitive, taunting onlookers. *Johnnas* was published in a special 1968 issue of *Drama Review* that focused on black theater, and in 1972, it was produced as a teleplay on NBC. The story's focus on society's rejection of the black artist reflects Gunn's own personal battles and became a theme that is built on in his later works.

Gunn's development of the theme of the struggling black artist continues into his next two plays that were produced: *Black Picture Show* (1975) and *Rhinestone* (1982). Just as in *Johnnas*, *Black Picture Show* outlines the life of a black artist who is unable to make it in a white-dominated society that is in no way sympathetic to artists. Alexander, the protagonist in *Black Picture Show*, was described by Jack Kroll in a 1975 edition of *Newsweek* as "a black artist who has to sell out to the devilish white culture in order to survive" (83). Unfortunately, Alexander is unable to succeed in his struggle to survive as an artist. The play opens with Alexander in a mental institution and then unfolds to portray the events in Alexander's life as a poet and writer that lead to his eventual breakdown. The questions presented in the play are further complicated by the presence of JD, Alexander's son, who is also an artist and is presented as his alter ego. While Alexander is driven mad by the exploitation and degradation of the black artist, JD finds his father overly idealistic about racial and artistic issues. Instead, JD calls himself a counterrevolutionary "whose interest lies not in freedom, but whose freedom lies in indifference toward the type of moral questions which drive his father insane and eventually kill him" (Leki 113). Because of the societal forces working against him, Alexander attempts to push aside his ideals in order to make money as his son has done, which is presented in a particularly memorable living room scene where Alexander and his second wife, Rita, attempt to entertain a white producer and his cocaine-sniffing wife in order to secure work. Alexander eventually succumbs to insanity, as a result of this sellout, rather than further degrade himself as a person and as an artist. As in *Johnnas*, Gunn's depiction of the black artist who is destroyed by the society that will not accept him in *Black Picture Show* reflects the playwright's personal experiences and beliefs that the society in which he lived was not ready for a successful black artist.

Gunn's next play to appear on stage was the 1982 production of the musical *Rhinestone*, adapted from his 1981 novel *Rhinestone Sharecropping*. According to Frank Rich, the work was "apparently inspired by [the author's] involvement with the 1976 Hollywood film biography of Muhammed Ali, *The Greatest*." The themes and events of *Rhinestone* build on the themes of Gunn's earlier works, and even include similar characters. Moreover, the protagonist, Sam Dodd, somewhat parallels Gunn himself, for he writes screenplays and is forced to deal with exploitive members of the film industry. As in his earlier plays, *Rhinestone*'s theme centers on the place of an artist of integrity in a world that is not accepting of artists, that exploits artists, and that only recognizes art as a vehicle for making money. Although Dodd's end is not as tragic as Gunn's other protagonists, his lack of success again reflects the humiliations and injustices suffered by the black artist.

Gunn's development of consciousness as an African American man and an artist was again reflected in his play *Family Employment*, produced by Joseph Papp in New York in 1985. In the three acts of this play, in which Gunn played the lead role, the events surround the life of an upwardly mobile middle-class black family, rather than a struggling black artist. Gunn's complex racial views are reflected in this play, in which the family members, some of whom are based on Gunn's own relatives, pursue the ideals of the African American middle class; this family has power and money, and one character in the play even temporarily passes as being white. However, as events unfold, we discover that the family's wealth has come largely from gambling and has been made through the exploitation of the black community. As a result, as Gunn states, the family becomes one that "self-destructs from within" (qtd. in Leki 114). In this way, although the family at the center of this play does not follow Gunn's pattern of black artist characters, the eventual destruction of its members again reveals Gunn's personal frustrations with race issues in America.

Although Gunn wrote a variety of other plays for stage that were never produced, including *The Owlight* (1961), *That's Gustavo* (1962), *Harmer Street Communion* (1989), and *Renaissance* (1989), his last stage play ever produced in theater was *The Forbidden City* (1989). Tragically, Gunn would never see this play produced, for he passed away one night before its opening in New York City. Despite numerous blockades and setbacks throughout his career, including the lack of a substantial black theatergoing audience, Gunn was able to work through his struggles as a black artist in order to achieve success as a playwright. Gunn's growth as an artist and as an African American man can be seen reflected through these works. They embody, then, not only Gunn's own personal struggles, defeats, and successes, but also those of the black artists whom they represent.

CRITICAL RECEPTION

When William Harrison Gunn's life labors and triumphs came to an end with his death at the age of fifty-nine, he had written more than twenty-nine dramatic scripts. His accomplishments covered the areas of stage, film, and television, and it is argued that when he reached the end of his life, he had "produced work the magnitude of which might have taken lesser artists several lifetimes to complete" (Williams 115). Gunn's accomplishments as an African American artist have also been acknowledged, and he is credited with being an influence on today's black artists, for his "iconoclastic spirit continues to animate the 'third' generation of Black 'indies' from Spike Lee to Euzhan Palcy" (Williams 115).

Throughout his lifetime, Gunn's plays/screenplays were highly praised, far more than even his other works of writing. Although his first play, *Marcus in the High Grass*, was not recognized as an African American dramatic work, Gunn was nevertheless commended for his writing. The play *Johnnas*, however, did deal with issues of race and is hailed as being "the simplest and most moving of Gunn's works" (Leki 114). In fact, when *Johnnas* was performed as a teleplay in Washington, DC, it won the 1972 Emmy Award for Best Teleplay. In addition to Gunn's Emmy Award for his teleplay, Gunn was also awarded Most Promising Playwright after the production of *The Celebration* in 1965.

The play *Black Picture Show* was also recognized as an exceptional work, winning Gunn the awards for Best Play of the Year and Best Director of the Year in 1975. However, *Black Picture Show* did receive mixed reviews from the critics. During its run of forty performances on Broadway, Gunn was praised for being an "obviously gifted" playwright (Gill 61), and the depiction of some of his characters was particularly noted, yet the play was criticized by many of the most influential theater critics as being full of flaws. Many critics had problems with "the mixture of biting and effective street language with occasional, less successful, bursts of verse and with the central issue of idealism and art versus money" (Leki 113). Critics Ted E. Kalem and Brendan Gill took issue with the theme Gunn presented in the play in particular, for both criticized the depiction of a writer's compromise with the Hollywood system. In the Janurary 30, 1975, issue of *Time*, for instance, Kalem questioned Gunn's depiction of his protagonist, Alexander, as a victim of exploitation: "No artist has ever been corrupted or humiliated by the quest for cash unless he was a willing accomplice" (76). And Gill, writing in the *New Yorker*, questioned, "Why is it worse for a black to sell out to a white than for a white to sell out to a white, or, for that matter, for a black to sell out to a black? Except on grounds of racial snobbery, with its implication that all blacks ought to be counted on to behave more honorably than all whites, why should the question of color arise?" (61). However, these same critics and others recognized and admired Gunn's obvious gift for writing and directing. In the end, *Black Picture Show* was acknowledged as being an award-winning accomplishment.

Gunn's 1982 musical *Rhinestone* also received negative criticism, though it did not achieve the same level of success as *Black Picture Show*. Unlike his previous work, Gunn received harsh criticism for his writing, rather than just his themes, from reviewers like Frank Rich, of the *New York Times*, who criticized the characterization of this production: "The hero and the other black characters are vaguely written martyrs or naifs; the moguls are absurdly caricatured racist villains. By Act III, there's little left for the two sides to do but scream at one another in a simplistically polarized debate that strains credibility to the breaking point" (11). Although race is not a recognizable issue in Gunn's earliest works, his production of *Rhinestone* was criticized, by John Simon of *New York*, for being "consumed with hate for . . . Hollywood" and "the whole white race" (51). He adds, "What, then, is left? The odd line flashing with honest anger, the occasional bit of searing sarcasm redolent of pain" (51). Despite these harsh assessments, critics did admit to Gunn's writing talent. Rich stated, "One finds good patches of writing [in *Rhinestone*] starting with a haunting opening monologue in which [the protagonist's] father . . . recounts how the producer David Belasco once exploited a Harlem vaudeville troupe during an earlier show-business era" (11).

Although Gunn received his share of criticisms for his work, unlike many of his characters, he was able to rise above the struggles of being a black artist to find success in his lifetime. Today, Gunn is recognized for his pioneering talent in theater, television, cinema, and literature, and he is hailed as being a major contributor to the African American literary tradition, particularly through his writing of plays/screenplays. Gunn's unique exploration of issues of race and art in American society marks him as "an innovator, well ahead of his time" (Splawn 196), but the depth of his contributions to American literature has yet to be recognized and explored.

BIBLIOGRAPHY

Dramatic Works by William Harrison Gunn

The Alberta Hunter Story, 1900–1950 (television script). 1982. Southern Pictures, BBC, London.

Black Picture Show. 1975. Performed at Vivian Beaumont Theater, Lincoln Center, New York.

The Celebration. 1965. Performed at Mark Taper Forum, Los Angeles.

Change at 125th Street. (television script). 1973. Ed Sullivan Productions.

Don't the Moon Look Lonesome (screenplay). 1970. Based on Don Asher novel. Chuck Barris Productions.

Fame Game (screenplay). 1968. Columbia Pictures. New York Shakespeare Festival Library.

Family Employment. 1985. Performed at New York Shakespeare Festival.

The Forbidden City. 1989. Performed at Public Theater, New York Shakespeare Festival.

Friends (screenplay). 1968. Universal Studios. New York Shakespeare Festival Library.

Harmer Street Communion. 1989. Performed at New York Shakespeare Festival.

"Johnnas." 1966. *Drama Review* 12 (Summer 1968): 126–138.

Johnnas (television script). 1972. Dir. Ray Williams. NBC.

The Last Cruise of the Spitfire (screenplay). 1985. Sam Waymon, R.U. Productions.

The Lena Horne Show (television script). 1985. Bill Cosby Productions.

The Life of Sojourner Truth (television script). 1973. CBS-TV: American Parade Series.

Marcus in the High Grass. 1958. Performed at Westport Theatre, Connecticut.

Men of Bronze (screenplay).1988. Danny Arnold, 4-D Productions. There City Cinema Archive, Oakland, California.

The Owlight. 1961. Unpublished.

Renaissance. 1989. Performed at New York Shakespeare Festival.

Rhinestone. 1982. Peformed at Richard Allen Cultural Arts Center, New York.

Territory (screenplay). 1985. Sam Waymon, Patterson International Pictures. New York Shakespeare Festival Library.

That's Gustavo. 1962. Unpublished.

Studies of William Harrison Gunn's Dramatic Works

Barnes, Clive. "Black Picture Show: A Tale of Corruption." *New York Times Theater Reviews* 7 Jan. 1975: 28.

Blum, Daniel, and John Willis, eds. "Black Picture Show." *A Pictorial History of Black Theatre: 1860–1976*. New York: Crown, 1977.

Brukenfeld, Dick. "Black Picture Show." *Village Voice* 3 Feb. 1975: 85.

Clurman, Harold. "Black Picture Show." *Nation* 25 Jan. 1975: 94.

Delaunoy, Didier. "Black Picture Show." *Encore* 17 Mar. 1975: 4.

Fabre, Genevieve. *Contemporary African American Theatre: Drumbeats, Masks, and Metaphor*. Cambridge: Harvard University Press, 1983.

Feingold, Michael. "Gloria in Excelsis: The Forbidden City." *Village Voice* 18 Apr. 1989: 97–98.

Frederick, Robert. "'The Owlight.' In Bill Gunn's Beef: If Sidney Poitier Can't Do It, They Rewrite It for a White Actor." *Variety* 4 Nov. 1964: 17.

Gale Group. "William Harrison Gunn." *Contemporary Authors Online.* 3 Dec. 1999. 4 May 2003 <http://libproxy.cortland.edu:2154/servlet/LitRC?c= 2&ai=37296&ste=6&doNum=H1000040493&bConts=8365&tab=1&vrsn=3& ca=1&tbst=arp&ST=gunn%2C+bill&srchtp=athr&n=10&locID=sunycort_ main&OP=contains>.

Gelb, Arthur. "Marcus in the High Grass." *New York Times Theater Reviews* 22 Nov. 1960: 38.

Gill, Brendan. "The Theatre Writing about Writing." *New Yorker* 20 Jan. 1975: 61–62.

Greer, Edward. "On and Off Broadway: Spring 1975." *Drama* 117 (Summer 1975): 34.

Guernsey, Otis, Jr., ed. *The Best of the American Theatre Series.* New York: Dodd, 1975.

Kalem, Ted E. "The Blame Game." *Time* 30 Jan. 1975: 76.

Kroll, Jack. "Black and White Picture." *Newsweek* 20 Jan. 1975: 83.

Leki, Ilona. "Bill Gunn." *Afro-American Writers after 1955: Dramatists and Prose Writers.* Vol. 38 of *Dictionary of Literary Biography.* Ed. Thadious M. Davis and Trudier Harris. Detroit: Gale, 1985. 109–114.

Loving-Sloane, Cecilia. "The Forbidden City." *Crisis* (May 1989): 4+.

"*Marcus in the High Grass*." "Negro Playwrights (Near Broadway)." *Ebony* (Apr. 1959): 100.

Peterson, Bernard L., Jr. *Contemporary Black Playwrights and Their Plays: A Biographical Directory and Dramatic Index.* Westport: Greenwood, 1988.

Peterson, Maurice. "Interview with Bill Gunn." *Essence* 4 (Oct. 1973): 27, 96.

Rich, Frank. "The Cutting Edge: *Rhinestone*." *New York Times Theater Reviews* 23 Nov. 1982: 11.

Simon, John. "Black Picture Show." *New York* 27 Jan. 1975: 51.

Sinclair, Abiola. "*The Forbidden City*: Season's Best." *New York Amsterdam News* 8 Apr. 1989: 24.

Splawn, P. Jane. "Bill Gunn." *Contemporary African American Novelists: A Bio-Biographical Critical Sourcebook.* Ed. Emmanuel S. Nelson. Westport: Greenwood, 1999. 192–197.

Williams, John. "Bill Gunn (1929–1989): Black Independent Filmmaker, Scenarist, Playwright, Novelist: A Critical Index of the Collected Film, Dramatic, and Literary Works." *Obsidian II: Black Literature in Review* 5.2 (1990): 115–147.

Willis, John. *Theatre World. Vol. 31: Season 1974–75.* New York: Crown, 1976.

Winer, Laurie. "*The Forbidden City* and *Member of the Wedding*." *Wall Street Journal* 7 Apr. 1989: 13.

LORRAINE HANSBERRY
(1930–1965)

Loretta G. Woodard

BIOGRAPHY

One of the most celebrated black playwrights in America to break the color barrier in the theater was activist and feminist Lorraine Vivian Hansberry, who was born into a middle-class family on May 19, 1930, in Chicago, Illinois. Both intellectuals and activists and natives of the South, her parents were Carl A. Hansberry, a prominent real estate broker and founder of one of Chicago's first black banks, and Nannie (Perry), a schoolteacher and later a ward committee woman. She was the niece of William Leo Hansberry, a Howard University professor of African history, who later became her mentor after her father's death. She was also the youngest of four children: Carl, Jr., Perry, and Mamie, her closest sibling. In 1938, when she was eight years old, Lorraine's family purchased a home in a restricted white, middle-class neighborhood, where they were subjected to racial hostility and discrimination. Her father challenged the city's Jim Crow housing laws and won an antisegregation case before the Illinois Supreme Court. These injustices would later impact her plays, especially *A Raisin in the Sun*, and before her theatrical career was cut short by cancer, she would become known worldwide as a renowned pioneer in protest theater.

Hansberry attended Betsy Ross Grammar School and then graduated in 1947 from Englewood High School, where she excelled in English and history and was elected president of her high school debating society. Upon seeing Howard Richardson and William Berney's folk musical *Dark of the Moon* and William Shakespeare's *The Tempest* and *Othello*, starring Paul Robeson, Hansberry was captivated by the theater. Her young creative imagination was also sparked during high school, by such eminent black leaders as W. E. B. Du Bois, Paul Robeson, Langston Hughes,* Jesse Owens, and Duke Ellington, who frequented her home. Of these luminaries, Hansberry was extremely impressed with Langston Hughes's poetry, especially how they reflected the lives of black people with a dream deferred, drying up like "a raisin in the sun." Not surprisingly, this line would inspire the title of her first play, *A Raisin in the Sun*.

As a protest against the segregation laws, Hansberry's parents sent her to public schools rather than private ones. She spent two years studying English, drama, art, and stage design at the University of Wisconsin at Madison, where she was active in the Henry Wallace campaign and president of the Young Progressives of America and the Labor Youth League, in 1949. While there, during the rehearsal of the Irish playwright Sean O'Casey's *Juno and the Paycock* (1924), she was extremely fascinated by the manner in which he portrayed oppressed people. She wrote: "The melody was one that I had known for a very long while. I was seventeen and I did not think then of writing the melody as I knew it—in a different key; but I believe it entered my consciousness and stayed there" (Hansberry 65). In the summer of 1949, Hansberry attended the University of Guadalajara art workshop in Ajijic, Mexico.

Hansberry moved to New York City in 1950 and began studying at the New School for Social Research. In 1951, she launched her career as a writer and worked full time as a reporter for Paul Robeson's *Freedom*, a radical black magazine, which provided her with numerous opportunities to broaden her understanding of the existing domestic and world problems. A year later she became an associate editor, taught classes at the Frederick Douglass School and traveled extensively. That same year, while covering a picket line at New York University, she met Robert B. Nemiroff, a white Jewish writer and activist, where he was a graduate student, engrossed in the works of American author Theodore Dreiser, literary criticism, and several social causes. For several months, they dated and participated in a number of political and cultural activities together. On June 20, 1953, they married in Chicago and moved to Greenwich Village. She left the *Freedom* staff in 1953 to devote more time to her writing. In the meantime, she worked odd jobs, studied African history with Du Bois and taught black literature at the Marxist-oriented Jefferson School for Social Sciences. Her experiences at the newspaper, her marriage to Nemiroff, and her study of African history continued to heighten her awareness of social justice. In 1956, she began writing *The Crystal Stair*, a line from Hughes's "Mother to Son," which eventually became *A Raisin in the Sun*.

In 1957, Hansberry read the first draft of *Raisin* to music publisher and friend Philip Rose, and he decided to publish it. Directed by Lloyd Richards, *Raisin* debuted on Broadway at the Ethel Barrymore Theatre on March 11,

1959, and had a run of 530 performances. That year, she was awarded the New York Drama Critics' Circle Award for Best Play of the Year, and was hailed the youngest playwright, the fifth woman, and the first black to win such a prestigious award. When the 1961 film version of the play opened, starring Sidney Poitier, Claudia McNeil, Ruby Dee, and Diana Sands, Hansberry received a special award at the Cannes Film Festival and was nominated for a Screen Writer's Guild Award for her screenplay. A second television adaptation of the play aired in 1989, starring Danny Glover, Esther Rolle, and Kim Yancey.

After completing the screenplay of *Raisin* and *Drinking Gourd*, Hansberry began work on several plays in the early 1960s. She began writing *Les Blancs* in 1960 and worked on the script until her death. In 1962, in response to Samuel Beckett's absurdist play *Waiting for Godot* (1952), she completed *What Use Are Flowers?* Although she became ill in April 1963, she continued most of her writing projects and political activities. Nemiroff and Hansberry were quietly divorced in Mexico on March 10, 1964, but they continued to collaborate on projects. She managed to complete her second play, *The Sign in Sidney Brustein's Window* (1964), which opened on Broadway on October 15, 1964, but after only 101 performances at the Longacre Theatre, the show closed on the evening of her death.

On January 12, 1965, Hansberry died of cancer of the pancreas at University Hospital in New York City, leaving behind several unfinished works. To keep her rich literary legacy alive, Robert Nemiroff, her ex-husband and the executor of her estate, adapted from Hansberry's writings and post humously published *To Be Young, Gifted, and Black*, which opened at the Cherry Lane Theatre in 1969. In 1971, it also appeared in book form. He completed *Les Blancs*, which was first presented on Broadway by Konrad Matthaei at the Longacre Theatre on November 15, 1970, and toured nationally for two years. *Les Blancs: The Collected Last Plays of Lorraine Hansberry* was edited and published in 1972 (included in the volume are *The Drinking Gourd*, *Les Blancs*, and *What Use Are Flowers?*). In 1973, Hansberry's first play was adapted into a musical entitled *Raisin* by Nemiroff and Charlotte Zaltzberg. The Tony Award–winning musical was revived in 1981.

Despite the brevity of Hansberry's theatrical life and despite the fact that only two of her plays were produced during her lifetime, she is, nevertheless, credited with making an invaluable contribution to American literature. As well, she is considered one of the most important female figures in African American literature. By protesting and validating the unfortunate circumstances of blacks in the United States, she became the voice of the people, using the stage as her platform, to ignite the social and political consciousness of all of her audiences, both black and white. In 1976, a documentary film entitled *Lorraine Hansberry*, was written and produced by Ralph J. Tangney. A special retrospective issue, *Lorraine Hansberry: Art of Thunder, Vision of Light*, was published by *Freedomways* magazine in 1979. Two plays based on Hansberry's life and works have appeared on stage: *Lovingly Yours, Langston and Lorraine* (1994) and *Love to All, Lorraine* (1995). Today, almost three decades later, Hansberry is still considered a phenomenal contemporary playwright who paved the way for other African American performers and dramatists such as James Baldwin,* Amiri Baraka,* and Ed Bullins.*

MAJOR WORKS AND THEMES

Using conventional twentieth-century social drama and realistically portraying black family life, all of Lorraine Hansberry's plays break new ground, as she reveals the struggles of blacks and whites in America. *A Raisin in the Sun* (1959), her best-known play, was inspired by Langston Hughes's poem *Harlem*, and based on firsthand knowledge of the working-class black tenants who rented from her father small apartments with their own kitchenette. As Hansberry breaks down racial stereotypes, she focuses largely on some of the more prevalent ideas of the Harlem Renaissance and anticipates those of the civil rights era, which were rare on the Broadway stage prior to now. In particular, she examines the crucial significance of the search for human dignity, the changing roles of women, the nature of marriage, the true worth of money, and African roots. Even more crucial, she addresses how far people should strive to attain white middle-class values, once freed from the shackles of discrimination (Cheney 58).

Like Louis Peterson's* *Take a Giant Step*, Hansberry's emotionally charged play chronicles the plight of the poor, black Younger family trapped in Chicago's South Side. They all have dreams and when the $10,000 insurance payment from Walter, Sr., arrives, Walter Lee's dream is to own a liquor store; Beneatha wants the money to pay for her medical school tuition. However, Walter Lee's wife, Ruth, and Lena, the matriarch of the family, want to escape the "rat trap" of the ghetto and buy a house where there is room for all, fresh air, and plenty of sunlight. Walter Lee is bitterly angry after she puts money down on a house, so she gives him the remaining amount, which he gives to Willy Harris as an investment for the liquor store. Meanwhile, the Younger family is offered a payoff by Mr. Lindner, a representative of the all-white neighborhood, to not move in, and Walter Lee learns that all of the money has disappeared. As tensions escalate between the black and the white characters, it seems as if the Younger family's dreams are deferred, but they find ways to spiritually and socially overcome their personal weaknesses and the barriers erected by the dominant culture. By the end of the play, Walter Lee makes a moving speech: "We have decided to move into our house because my father— my father—he earned it. We don't want to make no trouble for nobody or fight no causes—but we will try to be good neighbors" (Cheney 57). By "holding fast to [their] dreams," the play explores a universal theme of black families in search of freedom and the value of achieving their dreams.

The Sign in Sidney Brustein's Window (1964), a three-act comedy and Hansberry's second staged "play of ideas," examines a multiplicity of issues: family relationships, marriage, prostitution, homosexuality, politics, absurdist plays, abstract art, anti-Semitism, and racism (Cheney 72). A major concern is with the moral problems of Sidney Brustein, a Jewish intellectual in Greenwich Village, who becomes a burned-out, uncommitted idealist. His major flaws, an arrogant sense of superiority and his conceitedness, alienate him from his wife, Iris, a frustrated actress; Mavis, Iris's oldest sister; Gloria, Iris's younger sister; and Alton Scales, his friend. Sidney's false sense of self colors his illusory world. He is caught in the maze of modern society where he believes he has no choice but to conform to the institutions of an uncaring society. When Wally O'Hara, the local politician whom he supports with a sign in his window, wins an election, and turns out to be a phony, Sidney becomes disenchanted and finds promises of social reform empty. Realizing that he has been used because he was too aloof and uncommitted, the experience leaves him with a growing sense of self-awareness and he becomes an "American radical."

To Be Young, Gifted, and Black: A Portrait of Lorraine Hansberry in Her Own Words (1969), with rapid-shifting scenes and precise details, divulges facts, as the subtitle indicates, about Hansberry's life, her theory of romantic realism, her conception of art, and her attitude about politics (Cheney 134), which is strongly emphasized, revealing her increased social consciousness over the years. In some twenty episodes are excerpts from plays, screenplays, poems, interviews, speeches, essays, fiction, journals, memoirs, other writings, and unpublished works. What emerges by the end of the work is a powerful portrait of a private, often complex, contradictory woman, who was a romantic realist and a political activist. In essence, these are memories of an artist, of a young woman who wrote with ease about black life—black nationalism, slavery, financial problems, family squabbles, humor, cocktail parties, and the universal concerns of man's hopes and dreams (Cheney 133).

Adapted by Nemiroff, *Les Blancs* (1970), is a two-act historical drama set in Africa, which alludes to the title of Jean Genet's *The Blacks* (1959), and explores African heritage, colonialism, sexism, and racism. The young African intellectual, Tshembe Matoseh, leaves his white wife and child at home in England and returns home to Africa to attend his father's funeral. Once he returns, his countrymen are rebelling against the European colonials, their oppressors. Each brother's response to the conflict of colonialism is different. The burned-out nationalist, Tshembe, wishes to solve the conflict with petitions, delegations, and discussions; his brother Abioseh, a Catholic priest, uses his position to assist his people; and their younger half brother Eric, whose views are like those of the NEW MAN in Marita Bonner's* *The Purple Flower* (1928), strongly supports violence to rid the white settlers of control over his people. Though the liberal American journalist Charlie Morris sympathizes with the black African and naïvely hopes that change can occur without bloodshed, he has no personal alliances. Like Sidney Brustein,

Tshembe prefers not to be involved, and wishes for a peaceful resolution to his country's turmoil as well, but in the end he realizes, along with Eric, that a revolution is necessary in modern colonial Africa.

CRITICAL RECEPTION

The classic *A Raisin in the Sun* (1959) received rave reviews, and a *Time* reviewer hailed Lorraine Hansberry as a "fine, fresh playwriting talent" ("Theatre" 58). Struck by its universality and its candid statement about human activity and community, the play was hailed by Harold Stewart as an "institution . . . as one of the best plays ever written, black or white" and "this play will be read, performed, talked about and above all it will live on" (qtd. in Fletcher 16). It has perhaps "lived on" because Hansberry has crafted what Lewis Theophilus believes is a "social drama" that avoids "the pulpit, [the] social reformer, and the working politician" ("Theatre" 286–287). Speaking of Hansberry's success with characters, critic Jordan Y. Miller applauds her ability to keep the audience "interested in every one of them from the beginning," [while] each person is clearly individualized and none are able to dominate the others (161). Noting how far blacks have come in the theater, the reviewer for *Theatre Arts* affirms that the characters in *Raisin* are devoid of the stereotypes long typified in drama. The "happy" ending reflects "the age of improving but still imperfect relations" ("*A Raisin*" 22–23).

After *A Raisin in the Sun*, some critics accused Hansberry of abandoning the "black cause" and trying to win universal acclaim as a writer with *The Sign in Sidney Brustein's Window*. Others, however, disagreed and praised the work. According to Steven Carter, Hansberry continued her exploration of oppression "through the concept of the 'melting pot'" (Carter and Maclam 1). Some critics thought the play was "brilliant" (Killens 66), "provocative" (Barnes 44), and "a far more mature work" than *A Raisin in the Sun* (Holtan 222) with "skillfully etched scenes" (Lewis 758) and "superior dialogue" (Hewes 31). Recognizing that the play was ahead of its time, Julius Lester insists that "[t]he play was produced a year and a half before white liberal intellectuals were to be confronted by the spectre of black power. 'Sign' was a conscious warning" (46). As well, Lionel Mitchell believes "her view of the course of village liberalism . . . proved prophetic" (qtd. in Cheney 93).

Bernard Peterson, Jr. believes that *To Be Young, Gifted, and Black*, is "a unique self-portrait of the playwright as an artist, a black woman, and a spirited human being" (225). Anne Cheney agrees with Peterson and writes that "we are introduced to a young woman, brimming with hopes, disappointments, dreams, fears, and laughter. Not only does she become a vital human being, but she reveals—posthumously—the pattern of her entire career as a writer and a thinker" (134). In this work, Cheney concludes that Hansberry's "permanent debt to [Sean] O'Casey . . . becomes clear in . . . the play which is, more innovative in form than any other of the works of the young woman to whom it is both a memorial and an introduction" (150).

Les Blancs was perceived as "a timely and powerful work" that is "truthful as well as deeply haunting" (Cheney 18). It reflects Hansberry's abilities as "a brilliant geopolitical intelligence, a powerful moral imagination, and an emerging command of the great traditions of Western theatre" (Fuchs 93). Most impressive, according to Walter Kerr, is the play's language, which "achieves an internal pressure, a demand that you listen to it" (3). Of one of its characters, Kerr praises James Earl Jones "a Tshembe, who seizes the [language], toys with it, spits it back at the other players" (3). Jack Kroll sums up the play as dramatizing Hansberry's inner conflict as a black writer and observes that the playwright is "caught between the humanism that was natural to her and the violent militancy that she saw as inevitable and even right for black people" (122).

BIBLIOGRAPHY

Dramatic Works by Lorraine Hansberry

Les Blancs: A Drama in Two Acts. Adapted by Robert Nemiroff. New York: French, 1972.
"The Drinking Gourd." *Les Blancs: The Collected Last Plays of Lorraine Hansberry*. Ed. Robert Nemiroff. New York: Random, 1972.
A Raisin in the Sun: A Drama in Three Acts. New York: French, 1959.
The Sign in Sidney Brustein's Window: A Drama in Three Acts. New York: French, 1965.
To Be Young, Gifted, and Black: A Portrait of Hansberry in Her Own Words. Adapted by Robert Nemiroff. New York: French, 1971.
"What Use Are Flowers?" *Les Blancs: The Collected Last Plays of Lorraine Hansberry*. Ed. Robert Nemiroff. New York: Random, 1972.

Other Cited Material by Lorraine Hansberry

To Be Young, Gifted, and Black: Lorraine Hansberry in Her Own Words. Englewood Cliffs: Prentice, 1969.

Studies of Lorraine Hansberry's Dramatic Works

Adler, Thomas P. "Lorraine Hansberry: Exploring Dreams Explosive Drama." *American Drama, 1940–1960: A Critical History*. Ed. Thomas P. Adler. New York: Twayne, 1994. 181–200.
Barnes, Clive. "Stage: *Sidney Brustein*." *New York Times* 27 Jan. 27, 1972: 44.

Bernstein, Robin. "Inventing a Fishbowl: White Supremacy and the Critical Reception of Lorraine Hansberry's *A Raisin in the Sun*." *Modern Drama* 42.1 (1999): 16–28.

Brown-Guillory, Elizabeth. "Alice Childress, Lorraine Hansberry, Ntozake Shange: Carving a Place for Themselves on the American Stage." *Their Place on the Stage: Black Women Playwrights in America*. Ed. Elizabeth Brown-Guillory. Westport: Greenwood, 1988. 25–49.

Carter, Steven R. *Hansberry's Drama*. New York: Penguin, 1993.

Carter, Steven R., and Helen Maclam. "Inter-Ethnic Issues in Lorraine Hansberry's *The Sign in Sidney Brustein's Window*." *Explorations in Ethnic Studies* 11.2 (1988): 1–13.

Cheney, Anne. *Lorraine Hansberry*. Boston: Twayne, 1984.

Effiong, Philip Uko. *In Search of a Model for African-American Drama: A Study of Selected Plays by Lorraine Hansberry, Amiri Baraka, and Ntozake Shange*. Lanham: University Press of America, 2000.

Fletcher, Leah. "Black Theatre Alive and Struggling Hard." *Bay State Banner* 20 Mar. 1975: 16.

Friedman, Sharon. "Feminism as Theme in Twentieth-Century American Women's Drama." *American Studies* 25.1 (1984): 69–89.

Fuchs, Elinor. "Rethinking Lorraine Hansberry." *Village Voice* 15 Mar. 1988: 93, 98, 105.

Gavin, Christy, ed. *African American Women Playwrights: A Research Guide*. New York: Garland, 1999.

Hewes, Henry. "Broadway Postscript." *Saturday Review* 31 Oct. 1964: 31.

Holtan, Orley I. "Sidney Brustein and the Plight of the American Intellectual." *Players* 46 (June/July 1971): 222–225.

Kerr, Walter. "Les Blancs." *New York Times* 29 Nov. 1970: 3.

Killens, John Oliver. "Broadway in Black and White." *African Forum* 1.5 (1965): 66–68.

Kroll, Jack. "Between Two Worlds." *Newsweek* 76 (30 Nov. 1979): 122.

Lester, Julius. "The Politics of Caring." *Village Voice* 28 May 1970: 46.

Lewis, Theophilus. "Theatre." *America* 101 (2 May 1959): 286–287.

———. "Theatre: *The Sign in Sidney Brustein's Window*." *America* 11 (5 Dec. 1964): 758–759.

Marsh-Lockett, Carol P., ed. *Black Women Playwrights: Visions on the American Stage*. New York: Garland, 1999.

Miller, Jordan Y. "Lorraine Hansberry." *The Black American Writer: Poetry and Drama*. Ed. C. W. E. Bigsby. Vol. 2. Baltimore: Everett/Edwards, 1969. 157–170.

Nemiroff, Robert. "Critical Background." *Lorraine Hansberry: The Collected Last Plays*. Ed. Robert Nemiroff. New York: New American Library, 1983. 35–46.

Peterson, Bernard L., Jr. *Contemporary Black American Playwrights and Their Plays: A Biographical Directory and Dramatic Index*. Westport: Greenwood, 1988. 222–226.

Phillips, Elizabeth C. *The Works of Lorraine Hansberry: A Critical Commentary*. New York: Monarch, 1973.

"A Raisin in the Sun." *Theatre Arts* (May 1959): 22–23.

Roudané, Matthew C. *American Drama since 1960: A Critical History*. New York: Twayne, 1996.

"Theatre: *A Raisin in the Sun*." Time 73 (23 Mar. 1959): 58–59.

Washington, J. Charles. "*A Raisin in the Sun* Revisited." *Black American Literature Forum* 22.1 (1988): 109–124.

LESLIE PINCKNEY HILL
(1880–1960)

Valleri Robinson Hohman

BIOGRAPHY

Educator, poet, playwright, and civic leader Leslie Pinckney Hill was born in Lynchburg, Virginia, on May 14, 1880. His parents, Samuel Henry Hill, a stationary engine operator, and Sarah E. Brown Hill, a laundress, moved Leslie and his three siblings to East Orange, New Jersey, in the early 1890s. After Hill completed high school in New Jersey, he attended Harvard University, where he supported himself as a waiter in a fraternity house. At Harvard, he was a member of Phi Beta Kappa and the Harvard Debate Team. He received a bachelor's degree (cum laude) in 1903 and a master's degree in 1904. Upon completing his degrees, Hill embarked on his forty-seven-year teaching career when he accepted his first job teaching English and education under Booker T. Washington at the Tuskegee Institute in Alabama. In 1907, Hill married Jane Ethel Clark, with whom he had five daughters, and took a position as the principal of the Manassas Industrial Institute in Virginia. In 1913, Hill made his last career transition when he became the principal (and later the president) of the Institute for Colored Youth, a small private school in Cheney, Pennsylvania, later called Cheney State Teacher's College (1950).

Although Hill was primarily an educator, he also gained some recognition as a poet and playwright. He published his collection of poems, *The Wings of Oppression*, in 1921, and his play, *Toussaint L'Ouverture: A Dramatic History*, in 1928. In 1943, editor Rayford W. Logan commissioned Hill to write an essay for the collection *What the Negro Wants* (1944), a publication that became quite controversial despite the publisher's effort to present essays from conservative as well as liberal and radical African American intellectuals. Hill's essay, "What the Negro Wants and How to Get It: The Inward Power of the Masses," representing the more conservative stance, appeared with essays by Langston Hughes,* W. E. B. Du Bois, and Doxey A. Wilkerson, a member of the Communist Party.

Throughout his life, Hill remained active in civic life as an officer or member of important local and national organizations such as the Association of Negro Secondary and Industrial Schools, the Peace Section of the American Friends Service Committee, and the National Council of Student Christian Associations. He also founded the Pennsylvania Teachers Association, the West Chester Community Center, and the Pennsylvania State Negro Council and cofounded the Pennsylvania Association of Teachers of Colored Children.

Clearly, Hill dedicated his life to improving the quality of life for African Americans primarily through education. He urged that freedom and equality could be achieved only through education, interracial cooperation, and an unyielding faith in God and democracy in progress toward freedom and equality. As expressed in his essay, Hill believed that education was the "supreme task and challenge" of the leaders of the African American community (82). Of course, as a lifelong educator and largely conservative thinker, Hill had explicit views of what should comprise one's education. In addition to reading, writing, and arithmetic, Hill believed that the population should learn the ethics of responsibility and hard work, a philosophy of a universal human family, pride in their heritage, and faith in God. Importantly, Hill strongly believed in the importance of arts and literature in education:

Let our leaders teach the masses that we must clear our eyes to recognize and support the high spirits already in our midst, to hear their words, to look upon their work with reverence and to follow the paths they are blazing. Genius and talent give dignity to the life of the people and bring them to recognition. (88)

The desire to bring dignity and recognition to African Americans can be seen in Hill's poetry and drama as well as in his lifelong career as an educator. Hill served as the president of Cheney State Teacher's College until 1951, but he remained involved as the president emeritus until his death. He died following a stroke on February 16, 1960.

MAJOR WORK AND THEMES

Leslie Pinckney Hill's three major works include his book of poetry, *The Wings of Oppression* (1921); his play, *Toussaint L'Ouverture: A Dramatic History* (1928); and his essay, "What the Negro Wants and How to

Get It: The Inward Power of the Masses" (1944). While the works cover a range of topics and themes, several key ideas appear in each that express Hill's philosophy of life and human relations. First, as he stated directly in his 1944 essay, Hill believed in a universal brotherhood of all humanity, regardless of race or nationality: "Race and nation are only terms by which we distinguish in this one human family vast aggregates of its members who have similar or identical characteristics" (75). Second, Hill's writing consistently reflects his deep faith in a Christian God. In all of his work, Hill warns against flight from Christianity, the only true route to freedom. Finally, Hill continually expressed the necessity of art and literature for the elevation of the human spirit. For example, in his play and later in his essay, he encouraged the development of artistic and musical skills as essential human survival. These three ideas permeate Hill's literary works.

In his foreword to *Toussaint L'Ouverture*, Hill states that the work is not "a drama intended for the modern stage" (7). Rather, this play, written in blank verse, is presented as a dramatic poem recording the achievements of the Haitian leader in order to exalt him. In five parts consisting of thirty-five scenes, Hill dramatizes the major events between 1791 and 1802, covering L'Ouverture's rise to power as a great general in Haiti to his decline at the hands of the deceptive and corrupt French government. Hill does not follow a strict history of the events but is more interested in representing the spirit of the Haitian Revolution in distinct phases. As stated in his preface, Hill ultimately wrote the play as a means of countering the belief among black and white Americans "that the black race has no great traditions, no characters of world importance, no record of substantial contribution to civilazation" (8). He offers Toussaint L'Overture as a stark contrast to the popular image of the black buffoon or scaramouche (8). By telling this story in dramatic form and blank verse, Hill hoped to express the dignity and honor of his heroic character.

Hill centers the play on events that reveal the qualities of Toussaint L'Ouverture that make him a great leader, the kind of leader, in fact, that Hill exalts in his 1944 essay. Although L'Ouverture's vanity and misplaced trust ultimately lead to his downfall in the play, L'Ouverture possesses dignity, honesty, civility, and deep religious faith. He believes in the brotherhood of all humanity and strongly opposes the "Death to the whites" cry of some of his fellow leaders. Early in the play, L'Ouverture convinces others to abandon their separatist stance and to join with him and the Spanish army to overthrow the French, who have denied the black population its freedom. He urges his followers to overcome the evil of whites "with our good" (21). L'Ouverture also works with the mulatto general, Rigaud, for Haitian independence, although the French persistently inspire racial hatred between these men. L'Ouverture, espousing Hill's own philosophy, argues:

Throughout the universe I came to trace
A unity that bound all living things
In one coordinated whole; and man,
It seemed to me had but one proper task,
To learn the good and beauty of the world
And labor with his brother to increase
The benefit and happiness of all. (24)

This idea can be found in many of Hill's writings, such as the poem "The Ships" in *The Wings of Oppression*, which closes with the lines "And all shall learn at last to live / And labor for the sovereign good / Of universal brotherhood" (39).

In addition to representing a strong military and diplomatic leader dedicated to universal brotherhood, Hill has fashioned L'Ouverture as a loving husband and a stern but fair father. L'Ouverture's wife, Suzanne, and their sons, Isaac and Placide, appear intermittently in the play and allow Hill to depict L'Ouverture as a strong but caring family man. Two of the more interesting scenes in the play involve the Haitian leader and his son Isaac. In one scene, Isaac chooses to follow the French instead of his father, and L'Ouverture supports his son's decision. In a later scene, father and son are reunited in a silent and tender embrace.

Hill's L'Ouverture is also an unrelenting Christian. Early in the play, Toussant declares that he was "raised by God to know [his] calling," which is "to set [his] people free and make that world where black men live a safe and sure retreat for all the friends of freedom everywhere" (24). Throughout the play, he regularly prays to God for guidance. In two highly theatrical moments in the play, he spurns two voodoo women, who try to warn him of his downfall. Viewing them as sacrilegious, he hurls the talismans the women give him in disgust. In a significant, Christlike moment near the end of the play, when he is captured by the French, L'Ouverture cries, "God, why hast thou forsaken me!" (137). Later, facing death, his faith in God remains constant. Examples of unwavering faith in God abound in Hill's writing. He makes clear in his essay that he believes that faith in God is an essential component in the makeup of all people and expresses his regret that many leaders in his community dismiss religion.

CRITICAL RECEPTION

Leslie Pinckney Hill's work has drawn very little critical attention, and discussions of his play are limited, usually to just a few paragraphs. There are several reasons why scholars may have neglected his work. First, Hill worked and was viewed primarily as an educator rather than as a poet or playwright. In his lifetime, he drew attention as an African American leader because of his commitment to education, and few of his poems received critical acclaim or popularity for their literary value. Second, his works are largely didactic and conservative in form as well as idea and may seem reactionary in contrast with the works of leading African American literary figures of his era. Finally, there is no record of a performance of *Toussaint L'Ouverture*, which has kept this dramatic work from receiving scholarly attention.

In one of the more lengthy statements of Hill's writing in general, Benjamin Brawley, in *The Negro Genius*, stated:

In [Hill's] writing he is almost always conscious of his mission as a schoolmaster and mindful of the uncertain destiny of those before him. His verse may not reveal the greatest inspiration, but sometimes . . . his earnest feeling is embodied in memorable expression. (215)

Patsy B. Perry also offers a useful, brief overview of Hill's literary work in *Afro-American Writers from the Harlem Renaissance to 1940* in which she discusses "Hill's movement toward a world vision of one race under God in *Toussaint L'Ouverture*," as well as in *The Wings of Oppression* and his 1944 essay in *What the Negro Wants* (103). Despite limited critical attention, Hill's work offers insight into the complexity of the era in which he wrote. His play, *Toussaint L'Ouverture*, is certainly an important early model for writers who wanted to dispel popular, derogatory images of Africans, and their American descendents, in the American imagination.

BIBLIOGRAPHY

Dramatic Works by Leslie Pinckney Hill

Toussaint L'Ouverture: A Dramatic History. Boston: Christopher, 1928.

Other Cited Material by Leslie Pinckney Hill

"What the Negro Wants and How to Get It: The Inward Power of the Masses." *What the Negro Wants*. 1944. Ed. Rayford W. Logan. Notre Dame: University of Notre Dame Press, 2001. 70–82.
The Wings of Oppression. 1921. Freeport: Books for Libraries Press, 1971.

Studies of Leslie Pinckney Hill's Dramatic Works

Brawley, Benjamin. *The Negro Genius*. New York: Dodd, 1937.
James, Milton M. "Leslie Pinckney Hill," *Negro History Bulletin* 24 (Mar. 1961): 135–138.

Perry, Patsy B. "Leslie Pinckney Hill." *Afro-American Writers from the Harlem Renaissance to 1940*. Vol. 51 of *Dictionary of Literary Biography*. Detroit: Gale, 1987: 101–105.

Sanders, Mark A. "Leslie Pinckney Hill." *The Concise Oxford Companion to African American Literature*. Oxford: Oxford University Press, 2001. 199.

PAULINE ELIZABETH HOPKINS (1859–1930)

Terry Novak

BIOGRAPHY

Pauline Elizabeth Hopkins was born in Portland, Maine, in 1859 to Northrup Hopkins and Sarah A. Allen Hopkins. Soon after her birth, Hopkins's family moved to Boston, where they remained. Hopkins had an interesting family history: her father was a veteran of the Civil War, and the poet James Whitfield was her great uncle. Hopkins's family was a musical and theatrical one that made up the core of the Hopkins Colored Troubadours, a drama group that garnered enough local fame to have theater critics comment on Pauline's fine voice. This group also performed Hopkins's first play. Hopkins grew up under the privilege and safety of a middle-class household that encouraged reading and education.

Hopkins's first foray into the public eye as a writer was at age fifteen when she won an essay contest with a piece that focused on temperance, a favorite theme among socially concerned women of the nineteenth century. Hopkins moved from a focus on her writing to a focus on making a good living for herself in the 1890s, when she studied to become a stenographer. She succeeded at her studies and worked as a stenographer at several places, including the Massachusetts Institute of Technology. This does not mean that Hopkins abandoned her writing, however. In fact, she became a founding member of the periodical *Colored American Magazine*, editing the magazine from 1900 to 1904. Hopkins had several of her own writings published in the the magazine; in some instances she used her mother's name, Sarah A.

Allen, as a pseudonym, lest it seem her writing was taking over the magazine. The *Colored American* became a satisfying ground for Hopkins to write about her concerns as a social activist. She also found work lecturing on social issues occasionally.

Hopkins left her editorship of the *Colored American* when she began to suffer from ill health. She later contributed writings to the *Voice of the Negro* and even founded her own publishing company. Her professional activity slowed to a halt by 1920. Hopkins died on August 13, 1930, after suffering horrific burns in an accidental kitchen fire at her home.

MAJOR WORKS AND THEMES

Pauline Elizabeth Hopkins wrote two known plays during her lifetime; both were written early in her life. Her first play, *Slave's Escape; or the Underground Railroad*, was written in 1879. It was performed in Boston by the Hopkins Colored Troubadours. The play was later renamed *Peculiar Sam; or the Underground Railroad*. This was her first effort at drama and is a musical that celebrates the lives of historically important former slaves, such as Harriet Tubman and Frederick Douglass, who escaped their bondage and went on to become socially active and highly respected individuals. The play also has comedic elements, which is interesting for a topic such as the one Hopkins tackles here.

Hopkins's second play was written a few years later. Titled *One Scene from the Drama of Early Days*, it is a retelling of the biblical story of Daniel in the lion's den. It is unknown whether this play was ever produced. In any case, it is a certainty that Hopkins used these two plays to bring forth, even though in sometimes lighthearted ways, part of her social activism agenda. Hopkins celebrates the bravery and the intelligence of the African American in her plays; she also exhibits an underlying realization that the struggle for true freedom and equality is far from over.

CRITICAL RECEPTION

Peculiar Sam did enjoy some popularity when it was staged in 1880, although that could be attributed to the Boston public's appreciation of Pauline Elizabeth Hopkins's voice. By the end of her life, and indeed well into the second half of the twentieth century, Hopkins's writing, including her play, had been fairly well forgotten. With the renewed interest in the writings of earlier African American women writers that came in the 1970s, however, Hopkins's work finally began to be given its due. Anne Shockley is often credited with this revival of interest in Hopkins. Nellie McKay has written about the canon of Pauline Hopkins and sees her work as most useful to an understanding of nineteenth- and early-twentieth-century African American literature. Carol Allen reasons that Hopkins has not previously been taken as seriously as she should be "because critics have labeled middle-class black women like Hopkins, who wrote, lobbied, and seized the public forum during the Civil War and pre-Depression period, mere bourgeois strivers who wanted nothing more than to imitate their fellow white, middle-class, compatriots" (19). Allen argues that Hopkins's work needs to be seriously studied for what it is: a canon of high achievement and great interest to the development of the race.

It can be expected that, as literary critics continue to sift through the long-forgotten works of Hopkins and other writers, the plays of Pauline Hopkins will once again see some serious attention.

BIBLIOGRAPHY

Dramatic Works by Pauline Elizabeth Hopkins

One Scene from the Drama of Early Days. N.d. Unpublished.
Peculiar Sam; or the Underground Railroad. 1879. *The Roots of African American Drama*. Ed. Leo Hamalian and James V. Hatch. Detroit: Wayne State University Press, 1991. 100–123.

Studies of Pauline Elizabeth Hopkins's Dramatic Works

Allen, Carol. *Black Women Intellectuals: Strategies of Nation, Family, and Neighborhood in the Works of Pauline Hopkins, Jessie Fauset, and Marita Bonner*. New York: Garland, 1998.
Campbell, Jane. "Pauline Elizabeth Hopkins." *Black Women in America: An Historical Encyclopedia*. Ed. Darlene Clark Hine. New York: Carlson, 1993. 577–579.
McKay, Nellie Y. Introduction. *The Unruly Voice: Rediscovering Pauline Elizabeth Hopkins*. Ed. John Cullen Gruesser. Chicago: University of Illinois Press, 1996. 1–20.
Simmons, Simmona E. "Pauline Hopkins." *Notable Black American Women*. Ed. Jessie Carney Smith. Detroit: Gale, 1992. 515–518.

LANGSTON HUGHES
(1902–1967)

Karl L. Stenger

BIOGRAPHY

"My theory is, children should be born without parents—if born they must be," Hughes wrote to the South African playwright Richard Rive on March 27, 1962, not long before his untimely death (Rampersad, *Life* 1:4). In *The Big Sea*, the first volume of his autobiography, Hughes revealed that he hated his narrow-minded and bigoted father, resented his mostly absent mother, and did not get along with his strict and stern grandmother. Arnold Rampersad, Hughes's biographer, describes the damage that was inflicted on the boy, who "grew up a motherless and a fatherless child, who never forgot the hurts of his childhood," as follows: "He . . . paid in years of nomadic loneliness and a furtive sexuality; he would die without ever having married, and without a known lover or a child" (*Life* 1:4).

While Hughes presented a jovial and happy-go-lucky facade to the world, he was essentially a lonely man. When he chose the title *Laughing to Keep from Crying* for his first collection of short stories, Hughes uncharacteristically revealed his coping strategy. Although his gregarious personality won him many friends, none of them was able to pierce his thick armor. Even in his correspondence with Carl Van Vechten, a close friend and supporter with whom Hughes shared many interests, he revealed little about his intimate life. Emily Bernard, the editor of the letters, writes that "[a]t least in his letters, Hughes never shared with Van Vechten any more about his love life than he committed to public record" (xxiii). If anyone got too close to Hughes, he bolted. Although not averse to amorous advances of such women as Anne "Nan" Coussey, Sylvia Chen, and Elsie Roxborough, he pulled back as soon as marriage was mentioned, claiming that it would interfere with his life's goal to become a writer. Another reason for Hughes's reluctance to get married may have been his sexual orientation. While so far no definite proof has been found that his primary interest was in men, strong circumstantial evidence points in that direction. Emmanuel S. Nelson states: "There is overwhelming circumstantial and anecdotal evidence that Hughes, who never married or forged any significant relationship with women, was primarily homosexual in his orientation" (250). Alden Reimonenq explains the lack of irrefutable evidence as follows: "It should not be surprising to anyone who has tried to recapitulate the lives of literary figures during the pre-Stonewall America that finding physical traces of overt homosexuality is rare indeed. The closet, by the turn of the century, has been so firmly erected by heterosexism that the fear of coming out could last a lifetime, especially for public figures" (375). Reimonenq interprets the fact that Hughes kept mum as far as the oppression of homosexuals was concerned, while he vociferously fought political and racial discrimination, as a tell-tale sign: "As a gay man, Hughes lived that secret life silently in the confines of a very narrow, but well-constructed closet—one that still shelters him today" (374). Other scholars, however, have been reluctant to define Hughes's sexual orientation, given the dearth of clear evidence, and they have relegated him to a no-man's-land. A. B. Christa Schwarz, for example, states in her study *Gay Voices of the Harlem Renaissance* that Hughes's sexuality is "apparently indefinable" (142) and "that he did not perceive himself to be included in any category such as homo- or heterosexuality" (70).

It is clear that Hughes's biographers are in disagreement as far as his sexual orientation is concerned. Faith Berry is certain that Hughes was homosexual, whereas Arnold Rampersad, whose massive biography is considered definitive by many, strongly rejects the idea. Rampersad's "efforts to remove the homosexual label from Hughes," which have led Charles I. Nero to accuse the biographer of homophobia (195), are ultimately unconvincing. Rampersad, in fact, amasses a considerable amount of evidence that undercuts his purpose, such as Hughes's "first" homosexual encounter with a fellow crewman during a journey to Africa and his close association with numerous homosexual members of the Harlem Renaissance such as Alain Locke, Countee Cullen, Claude McKay, Wallace Thurman,* Richard Bruce Nugent,* and the already mentioned "honorary Negro" Carl Van Vechten. Rampersad stresses the fact that Hughes rejected amorous advances by Locke and Cullen; however, he fails to mention that the writer frequented well-known gay bars such as the Clam House. He also glosses over the fact that Hughes shared a rooming house with Wallace Thurman and his white male lover for a while, which Zora Neale Hurston* and Thurman dubbed

"Niggerati Manor," whose walls were adorned by brightly painted phalluses courtesy of the openly gay Nugent, and which soon "became famous for its hedonistic happenings" (V. Boyd 121). According to Hurston's biographer, "Zora had spent enough time with Hughes, Nugent, Thurman, and some of the other men of the Niggerati to be fully aware of the sexual ambiguity that characterized their lives. Thus, Zora's affection for Langston was friendly and big-sisterly; unlike several of their mutual male friends, she regarded him as a potential brother, not a potential lover" (V. Boyd 150).

Rampersad concedes that several of Hughes's intimates considered it a given that he was homosexual. Lebert "Sandy" Bethune, for example, a Jamaican-born poet whom Hughes had befriended in Paris, assumed that his friend had been a victim of a gay bashing when he visited him in the hospital during his final illness: "I don't know why, but I had assumed that Langston was gay, and I just imagined that he had been injured in some homosexual encounter, and that prostate trouble was a euphemism" (qtd. in Rampersad, *Life* 2:422). Similarly, the composer Jan Meyerowitz, Hughes's collaborator on the opera *The Barrier*, having been told by his homosexual colleague Virgil Thomson that Hughes was gay, found his assumption confirmed when he visited the writer: "I remember he had a picture on his desk of some black men in a chain gang, and one of the men was so unbelievably beautiful. Very beautiful. And Langston told me, 'I *love* him!' Now this man in the chain gang was very beautiful, and I would have loved him too. But the way Langston said it, it was too profound, too profound. I knew he was a homosexual" (qtd. in Rampersad, *Life* 2:177). Hughes not only surrounded himself with pictures of beautiful young men, he also sought out their company. Rampersad acknowledges that fact and even goes as far as to confirm that Hughes had a sexual fascination for young, dark-complexioned men (*Life* 2:336). One of the young men Hughes befriended was the handsome and shy actor Gilbert Price with whom the poet "seemed to fall in love. His feeling was reciprocated" (Rampersad, *Life* 2:373). During a trip to Africa, Hughes met Sunday Osuya, a young, dark-skinned policeman, and the two started to correspond with each other. Hughes made certain to visit his "African son" during subsequent Africa trips and left him a generous financial provision in his will (Rampersad, *Life* 2:362). Considering his fondness for these young men, it is not surprising that many of Hughes's acquaintances were convinced that he was homosexual. One man insisted in an interview with Rampersad that "[a]round the streets of Harlem in the sixties everyone knew that Langston Hughes was gay. We just took it for granted, as a fact. He was gay, and there was no two ways about it" (2:335).

Recently, Queer Studies scholars such as Gregory Woods, Anne Borden, and Alden Reimonenq have opened the door to Hughes's closet by identifying homoeroticism and other "gay markings" in poems such as "Young Sailor," "Trumpet Player," "Waterfront Streets," "Joy," "Desire," and especially "Café: 3 A.M." and "Tell Me" as well as the short story "Blessed Assurance." A. B. Christa

Schwarz has shown in her study *Gay Voices of the Harlem Renaissance* that Hughes "produces a multiplicity of meanings, works with an ambiguity of terms, and employs textual strategies, thereby opening up spaces also for gay readings" (72). Schwarz stresses that Hughes's "literary gay voice appears to have changed over the years" (87): while Hughes "construct[ed] a framework for same-sex experiences" (83) through his Whitmanesque depictions of sailors and life on the sea in his early works, he introduced stereotypical depictions of butch lesbians and effeminate gay men in his later plays, perhaps for commercial reasons. Some of Hughes's works have been included in gay anthologies. "Blessed Assurance" was included in *Black Like Us: A Century of Lesbian, Gay, and Bisexual African American Fiction* (2002) and four of Hughes's poems were reprinted in *Gay and Lesbian Poetry in Our Time* (1988). It is likely and desirable that future studies will dismantle Hughes's closet even further so that he "will take his place in literary history not just as a race and folk poet, but as one whose complex achievement includes battling oppression through his veiled homosexual expressivity. Then we will see that Hughes was not silent about his gayness after all" (Reimonenq 375).

He was born James Mercer Langston Hughes in Joplin, Missouri, on February 1, 1902, to James Nathaniel Hughes and Carrie Mercer Langston Hughes. The couple's first son had died two years earlier as an infant and the unnamed child had been buried in a pauper's grave. Soon after Langston's birth, his father left the family and moved to Mexico City, where he worked for the Pullman Company and later the Sultepec Electric Light and Power Company. His departure forced his wife into an unsettled and restless life; she moved from city to city in search of employment, leaving Langston mostly with her septuagenarian mother Mary Langston in Lawrence, Kansas. The boy did not get along with his strict grandmother and desperately missed his mother who would reappear for a short while, only to abandon him again. His grandmother instilled in Langston a sense of pride by telling him stories about her first husband, Lewis Sheridan Leary, who had been killed fighting alongside John Brown at Harper's Ferry, and her second husband, Charles Howard Langston, an abolitionist who was active in politics and publishing.

When Langston's grandmother died in 1915, he was joined by his mother; her new husband, Homer Clark; and his two-year-old stepbrother, Gwyn. Soon, however, the family was split up again when Carrie and Gwyn followed Homer to Lincoln, Illinois, leaving thirteen-year-old Langston with James and Mary Reed, a childless couple that "drenched Langston with love" (Rampersad, *Life* 1:15). Eventually the boy joined his family in Cleveland, Ohio, only to be abandoned again when his parents sought work in Chicago. Langston stayed behind, fending for himself and realizing that he could no longer count on his family to provide emotional and financial stability. He channeled his creative energy into writing poetry and short stories that appeared in his high school's magazine on a regular basis. Eventually, his now-prosperous father reappeared in his life and Langston agreed to visit him in Mexico. However, father and son soon clashed, one being as stubborn as the other. Langston realized that his opinionated and materialistic father expected him to study engineering in Germany or Switzerland once he had graduated from high school so that he could work alongside him in Mexico. James Hughes did not agree with his son's plan to attend Columbia University in New York with the goal of becoming a writer. Eventually, however, he relented and promised to pay at least one year's tuition provided that Langston attended engineering school. Langston's trip to Mexico not only secured his father's temporary financial support but it also inspired him to compose one of his most famous poems, "The Negro Speaks of Rivers." When he submitted the poem to *Crisis*, the official magazine of the National Association for the Advancement of Colored People, it was immediately accepted for publication. Additional poems and essays followed and "[i]n a few short months Hughes had become virtually the house poet of the most important journal in black America" (Rampersad, *Life* 1:48).

Langston's time at Columbia University, for which he had fought so hard, proved to be a disappointment. Besides experiencing discrimination, the young man was bored by his classes and tired of his demanding and nagging father. Soon he spent most of his time in theaters, where he enjoyed the greatest actors and plays of the day, and in Harlem, where he immersed himself in bohemian life. He later admitted that he "had come to New York to attend Columbia, but *really* why I had come was to see Harlem" (qtd. in Rampersad, *Life* 1:51). Even though Hughes had done fairly well during his freshman year, he decided not to return to Columbia University but to see the world instead. He was hired to work on the weatherbeaten freighter *West Hessetine*, which was bound for the west coast of Africa. In a symbolic act of liberation, Hughes threw his books, remnants of his old life, overboard into New York harbor. In an equally symbolic act, he saved his copy of Walt Whitman's *Leaves of Grass*. While Hughes was disappointed by Africa—he was flabbergasted when Africans considered him white—he was fascinated by Europe. During a trip to Holland, he jumped ship and spent several months exploring Paris and Venice. Subsequently moving to Washington, DC, Hughes took on menial jobs, composed more poems than ever before, and waited "for his ship to come in." Eventually, his patience paid off. When he entered the poem "The Weary Blues" in a prestigious contest organized by *Opportunity* magazine, he won first prize. During the awards banquet, Hughes made the acquaintance of the influential and flamboyant Carl Van Vechten who convinced Alfred Knopf to publish the young poet's first collection of poems. *The Weary Blues* appeared in 1925 with an introduction by Van Vechten to excellent reviews. Hughes's streak of good luck continued when several patrons agreed to underwrite further university study.

In January 1926, he entered Lincoln University, a prestigious black school near Philadelphia, where he achieved a prominent position and where he continued to hone his craft. It was there that he wrote "The Negro Artist and the Racial Mountain," his literary manifesto, for the *Nation*. In the essay, he asserted the need for "a true Negro racial art" and decried black poets like Countee Cullen who wanted to write like white poets. For Hughes, "the mountain standing in the way of any true Negro art in America" was the urge to be as little black as possible and to "pour racial individuality into the mold of American standardization" (Rampersad, *Life* 1:130). He called on black artists to celebrate the beauty of their race and to express their "individual dark-skinned selves without fear or shame." For Hughes, however, this did not mean an idealized and whitewashed depiction of black life and culture because "[w]e know we are beautiful. And ugly too" (Rampersad, *Life* 1:131). When he published his second collection of poetry, *Fine Clothes to the Jew*, in 1927, he not only celebrated the beauty of his race, but also included depictions of poverty (hence the book's title), prostitution, and spousal abuse. The critical response, especially from black critics, was devastating. Hughes was called a "sewer dweller" and the "poet low-rate of Harlem" and his book was characterized as "trash" and "a study in the perversions of the Negro" (Rampersad, *Life* 1:140). Similar criticism would be leveled at Hughes's work throughout his life.

At the same time that he had to endure the critics' wrath, his relationship with his most important patron, Charlotte Mason, deteriorated. "Godmother," as she liked to be called, clashed with Hughes more and more frequently over the content of his work and eventually severed her ties with him, feeling that he was a lost cause. Godmother was eventually supplanted by Noel Sullivan, one of San Francisco's "most prominent bachelors" (Rampersad, *Life* 1:238), who provided Hughes with financial and emotional stability and a safe haven where he could work without being disturbed. The break with Charlotte Mason together with racially explosive political events such as the Scottsboro case and the Angelo Herndon trial caused in Hughes a dramatic shift to the Left as did the devastating economic crisis that gripped the country. He became involved in various chapters of the John Reed Club, which was controlled by the Communist Party, and he published numerous poems and essays in *New Masses*, the party's official organ. In 1932, Hughes was invited along with twenty-one other black Americans to visit the USSR in order to participate in the production of *Black and White*, a film about the struggle of black steelworkers in Alabama against racism. Although the film never materialized, Hughes was able to immerse himself in Russian culture. He spent many evenings in Russian theaters, absorbing experimental stage techniques and meeting the innovative director Vsevolod Meyerhold, from whom he "acquired a number of interesting ways of staging plays" (*I Wonder as I Wander*, 199 f.). After one year in the USSR, Hughes returned to the United States, stopping in Tokyo and Shanghai on the way.

As the first black author to support himself exclusively through his writing, Hughes had to balance the need to publish financially profitable books with that of staying true to his artistic vision. Frequently, the exigencies of the publishing world forced him into becoming a "hack" and a "literary sharecropper," churning out anthologies and children's books, often juggling several projects at one time. "I am running a literary factory," he complained (qtd. in Rampersad, *Life* 2:231). Hughes supplemented his income by frequently going on the lecture circuit, where he experienced the adulation of African American crowds as well as the harassment by fundamentalists led by Aimee Semple McPherson who tried to exact revenge for having been mentioned by name in the controversial poem "Goodbye Christ." Hughes's attempt to break through Hollywood's discrimination against blacks was unsuccessful and, having failed to become a screenwriter, he bitterly complained. The commercial theater was equally resistant to black playwrights and plays and Hughes founded three small theater companies—the Harlem Suitcase Theatre, the New Negro Theatre in Los Angeles, and the Skyloft Players in Chicago—in order to be able to stage his works. He was more successful as a newspaper columnist; for the *Chicago Defender* he developed a series of columns featuring Simple, an uneducated but wise black man whose musings about racial inequality and current events became extremely popular. The newspaper carried the column for twenty-three years and Hughes collected Simple's stories in five volumes and used them as the basis for his musical play *Simply Heavenly* (in *Five Plays*).

Even though Hughes remained an inveterate traveler throughout his life, visiting such places as Barcelona, where he spent six months as a war correspondent during the Civil War, Paris, London, Germany, Italy, Jamaica, Nigeria, Uganda, Senegal, and Egypt, he eventually decided to settle down in Harlem, the place he had fallen in love with as a young man. In 1948, at the age of forty-six, he bought a brownstone row house on East 127th Street, where he would live with "Aunt" Toy Harper and "Uncle" Emerson Harper, his self-styled family, until the end of his life.

Having been haunted by his radical past for many years—in 1953, Hughes had to appear before Joseph McCarthy's House Committee on Un-American Activities where he was questioned by Roy Cohn—in his later years he was criticized by members of the civil rights movement for being too accommodating: "Langston's broad-minded attitude would soon be out of favor among the most vocal spokesmen" (Rampersad, *Life* 2:359). Hurt by the accusation that he had sacrificed his blackness in order to make it in the white man's world, which the Harlem *Liberator* leveled against him, and depressed by the rapid decline of his beloved Harlem as well as by the deaths of many of his close friends, Hughes considered moving to Paris: "To Langston, the whole world seemed to be going wrong. . . . His world seemed hopelessly stained by distrust, illness, violence, and death" (Rampersad, *Life* 2:415, 419). However, before he was able to travel to France, Hughes fell ill and after a prostate operation died on May 22, 1967, of septic shock and congestive heart failure. The unconventional funeral service was a fitting tribute to the writer who had loved jazz and blues throughout his life and who had fused it with his poetry. Lena Horne recalled: "There I was, tapping my toes and humming while y'all played, and I didn't know whether to cry for Langston or clap my hands and laugh" (qtd. in Rampersad, *Life* 2:425).

MAJOR WORKS AND THEMES

"If you want to die, be disturbed, maladjusted, neurotic, and psychotic, disappointed and disjointed, just write plays! Go ahead" (Rampersad, *Life* 2:251). Langston Hughes's warning to James Baldwin* in a letter dated July 25, 1956, reveals the playwright's ambivalence toward the world of theater. Hughes recognized the need for the serious treatment of black themes and he was determined "to render the stage a place of and for authentic black expression" (*Collected Works* 5:2). While Hughes is primarily known for his poetry and prose, he wrote forty plays independently and twenty-three collaboratively as well as numerous opera libretti; radio, film, and television scripts; and song lyrics. According to his biographer Faith Berry, drama, "second only to poetry, was his favorite genre" (99). Leslie Catherine Sanders goes even further when she states that "Hughes considered his plays his favorite and most important creations" (*Development* 65). He was understandably disappointed when his plays failed to be hits at the box office or when they were not even produced during his lifetime. In addition, Hughes had a falling out with his longtime friend Zora Neale Hurston over the play *Mule Bone* and his experiences with producers who failed to pay his royalties or made changes to his text without permission left him disillusioned. In short, "[t]heater was his love and his torment" (Rampersad in *Collected Works* 5:2).

Langston's love for the theater can be traced back to his childhood and to his mother's influence. Carrie Hughes longed to be on the professional stage and she took her young son to as many plays as she could. Soon, "the theater was in his blood" (Rampersad, *Life* 1:14). When Langston moved to New York in order to attend Columbia University, he spent more time on Broadway than in the classroom: "Langston liked few things better than sitting high in the balcony, dark and lonesome, with the stage across the footlights far below; he became a child in Kansas once again" (Rampersad, *Life* 1:55). It came as no surprise that one of the young man's first publications was a short play for children. *The Gold Piece: A Play That Might Be True*, which was published in *Brownie's Book* in 1921, is a moral fable about a Mexican peasant couple that selflessly sacrifices its only valuable possession, the gold piece, so that a poor woman's blind son can be cured. While clearly juvenilia, the play "shows certain thematic tendencies that would be expanded in Hughes's later dramatic works: folk culture, family relationships, and economic necessity" (McLaren, *Langston* 17).

Family relationships are at the center of Hughes's first major play, *Mulatto: A Play of the Deep South* (in Volume 5 of *Collected Works*), which he wrote in 1930 after graduating from Lincoln University and which he based on his poem "Cross." The drama revolves around the theme of the tragic mulatto. Robert, the son of white Colonel Norwood and his black housekeeper Cora Lewis, returns to the plantation after attending school in Atlanta. He not only physically resembles his father, he also shares his "fiery, impetuous temper" (Rampersad in *Collected Works* 5:18). Unlike his older brother and sisters, Robert challenges the existing order. He refuses to work in the fields, drives the colonel's car without permission, talks back insolently to the white people in town, and uses the front door in spite of Norwood's prohibition. He even insists on his rights as the son of the plantation owner: "Any-how, isn't this my old man's house? Ain't I his son and heir? Am I not Mr. Norwood, Junior?" (32). His challenge to the established order cannot be tolerated and he is banned from the plantation: ". . . to-night you'll get the hell off of this place and stay off. Get the hell out of this county" (40). When Robert defies his father yet again by insisting on leaving through the front door, a struggle ensues during which he strangles the colonel. Since "Robert's killing of Norwood is the ultimate assault on plantation order" (McLaren, *Langston* 65), its consequence can only be death. Before the lynch mob is able to string Robert from a tree, he shoots himself with his father's gun in his father's house. Having lost her son and her quasi husband, Cora's sense of reality disintegrates. The curtain falls on the mad woman surrounded by a roaring mob.

Leslie Catherine Sanders has shown that the play's perspective gradually shifts from that of the two men to Cora's until the story is told through her eyes: "Thus the house becomes hers, not only because as housekeeper, she has the keys, but because the audience comes to understand what has occurred through her experience of it. Her conquest of the stage, a pyrrhic victory at best, foreshadows elements in Hughes's later work and the conscious tactic of later playwrights, particularly Amiri Baraka" (*Development* 68). When *Mulatto* was presented at New York's Vanderbilt Theatre on November 11, 1935, it had been radically altered by its producer, Martin Jones. In an attempt to make the play a commercial hit, Jones had increased sex and violence in the drama by rewriting many of Hughes's lines and by adding the gratuitous rape of the protagonist's sister by a white overseer. Hughes watched helplessly from the sidelines, not daring to jeopardize the launch of his career as a playwright. In a letter to his friend Marie Short, he joked that "all the actors are happy because each one now either dies, kills, gets raped, or goes mad" (Rampersad, *Life* 1:313). He was devastated, however, when the reviewers praised the actors but questioned his competence as a playwright. Hughes's pleas to Jones about restoring the play to its original form fell on deaf ears. Moreover, the producer failed to pay the playwright and Hughes's attempts to recover his royalties turned into a lengthy legal battle. Despite the fact that *Mulatto* ran for 373 performances, second only to Lorraine Hansberry's* record-breaking *A Raisin in the Sun*, Hughes was disillusioned by his first foray into the world of the theater.

The disastrous collaboration with Zora Neale Hurston on *Mule Bone: A Comedy of Negro Life* did not help matters. Originally, the two friends had planned to write a jazz and blues opera, but when Theresa Helburn of the Dramatists Guild suggested to Hughes that he write a comedy because "practically all the plays by or about Negroes offered to the Guild were serious problem dramas," Hurston and Hughes accepted the challenge (*Mule Bone* 229). The play was to be based on "The Bone of Contention," a folk story that Hurston had been told as a child in Eatonville, Florida. In the story, two hunters, Dave Carter and Jim Weston, shoot a wild turkey and then argue over who killed the bird. Jim attacks Dave and knocks him unconscious with the hockbone of a dead mule, then absconds with the prize. When Dave accuses his opponent of assault and battery, Jim is tried and convicted on the basis of the biblical story about Samson slaying thousands with the jawbone of a donkey. Joe is banished from the town for two years. In the play, the central conflict was replaced at Hughes's suggestion by a dispute over the affections of Daisy Tailor, a "plump, dark and sexy domestic servant" who is fickle and aware of her appeal to men (*Mule Bone* 45). In addition, Dave and Jim became members of the Baptist and Methodist denominations and the trial turned into a struggle between the two religious camps.

At first the collaboration between Hughes and Hurston went smoothly. According to Hughes, they agreed "that I would do the construction, plot, whatever characterization I could, and guide the dialog. Miss Hurston was to put in the authentic Florida color, give the dialogue a true Southern flavor, and insert many excellent turns of phrase and 'wise-cracks' which she had in her mind and among her collections" (*Mule Bone* 230). Soon, however, Hurston became suspicious of Hughes's close relationship with their typist, Louise Thompson, and when Langston suggested a three-way split of any profits, Zora felt betrayed. According to her biographer Valerie Boyd, "[r]ather than express the full extent of her distress over the situation, Zora simply walked away from it" (202). She traveled to the South in order to do research for her folklore book, leaving Hughes with the impression that she was still working on the play. When Hughes visited his old friends Rowena and Russell Jelliffe, a white couple that ran the Karamu House in Cleveland, he discovered to his chagrin that *Mule Bone* was slated to be staged there and that Hurston had copyrighted the play in her name alone. Feeling betrayed in turn, Hughes contacted his lawyer and threatened Hurston with litigation. Several attempts to diffuse the situation failed and eventually the long-standing and close friendship between the two talented writers collapsed. Leslie Catherine Sanders has suggested that this collapse was unavoidable because both artists desperately strove to master the same territory: "Personal and professional jealousy may have been conscious motives, but an unconscious motive may have been the necessary separation of two headstrong, highly creative people who, in searching for their own voices, had found that they had to part ways" (*Development* 88). The Karamu House production of *Mule Bone* was cancelled and the play remained unperformed until New York's Lincoln Center produced it in 1991, giving both authors equal credit. Considering the innovative character of the play, namely, that of "depicting folk Afro-American life from the inside" through "a new dramatic technique based on the use of the black vernacular" (Manuel 88 f.), one must agree with Henry Louis Gates, Jr. when he writes that "[w]e can only wonder at the directions that black theatre might have taken in America had *Mule Bone* been produced and published" (*Mule Bone* xii).

After the *Mule Bone* disaster, Hughes temporarily turned away from comedy and concentrated on political plays. This change of focus reflected the playwright's dramatic shift to the left in the 1930s. He was especially affected by the Scottsboro case, which involved nine black teenagers who had been accused of raping two white women on a freight train bound for Mississippi in the spring of 1931. All nine were convicted despite the lack of solid evidence and all but the youngest were sentenced to death in the electric chair. When the NAACP hesitated to take on the defense of the young men, the International Labor Defense, the legal arm of the Communist Party, stepped into the breach. Hughes not only helped raise funds for the boys' legal fees, he even visited them in prison in Montgomery, Alabama, and read poems to them. He also poured his anger at the racist justice system into four poems ("Justice," "Scottsboro," "The Town of Scottsboro," and "Christ in Alabama") and the one-act play *Scottsboro, Limited*. The short play combines verse with agitprop techniques that Hughes had probably encountered at New York's Proletbuehne or at Jasper Deeter's innovative theater company, the Hedgerow Players, when he served as their playwright in residence in 1930. According to Leslie Catherine Sanders, *Scottsboro, Limited* is classic agitprop: "its concise analysis of its subject, rhythmic language and choreographed movement, audience involvement, and final call for action are all typical of the form" (in *Collected Works* 5:116). Hughes employs one white actor to play the multiple roles of sheriff, judge, prison keeper, and preacher and plants actors in the audience who represent the opposing views of those who want the boys convicted (Mob Voices) and those who want justice to be served (Red Voices). At the end of the play the boys smash the electric chair and join hands with the Red Voices while exhorting the members of the audience to join the fight:

ALL. Rise, workers, and fight!
AUDIENCE. Fight! Fight! Fight! Fight!

(Here the *Internationale* may be sung and the red flag raised above the heads of the black and white workers together.) (*Collected Works* 5:129)

It is not surprising that the first staging of the provocative play by the communist John Reed Club was prevented by the Los Angeles police. *Scottsboro, Limited* was eventually presented on May 8, 1932, during a mass rally in support of the Scottsboro boys.

During his lengthy stay in the USSR, Hughes was able to observe the innovative work of such constructivist directors as Vsevolod Meyerhold and Nikolai Okhlopkov and he integrated some of their techniques in his subsequent political plays. In *Harvest* (in *Political Plays*), a documentary play about the plight of farmworkers in California's San Joachim Valley, which Hughes wrote in collaboration with the leftist journalist Ella Winter, the playwright breaks the frame of the proscenium by using runways that reach into the audience space. The audience members are forced to take sides when Luther, the betrayer of the striking cotton pickers, hides among them and attacks the defenseless workers by throwing bricks. Susan Duffy writes, "His new physical position as part of the audience perpetuates an uncomfortable guilt by association. He becomes one of them, and they must find a way to dissociate themselves from him" (in *Political Plays* 67). As in *Scottsboro, Limited*, the audience is called to action in the final scene when one of the strikers holds up a banner that reads BLACK AND WHITE UNITE TO FIGHT. Hughes also uses a "newspaper curtain" between scenes, which reproduces portions of published reports of the strike, and suggests projections of original documents like "bits from the strikers' handbills, or from the Vigilantes' and growers' advertisements," techniques reminiscent of the Living Newspaper productions developed by the Federal Theater Project.

The simple set Hughes uses in his next political play, *Angelo Herndon Jones* (in *Political Plays*), was also influenced by the Russian productions he witnessed. The stage is divided into two parts by a wall on which a poster featuring the African American Communist organizer Angelo Herndon is prominently displayed. The two rooms separated by the wall "may be miles away, since the wall is only a symbolic barrier" (Rampersad in *Collected Works* 5:185). Lighting is used to indicate scene changes and to underline the symbolic role of Angelo Herndon: "Lights die out, come on flooding the Herndon poster on the wall. . . . The Herndon poster is bright under the street lights as the two lovers stop beneath it" (Rampersad in *Collected Works* 5:194). While Hughes uses agitprop techniques like the playing of the "Internationale" and Herndon's speech during which he exhorts "black and white unite to fight," he abandons the stylized and representative characters of *Scottsboro, Limited* and *Harvest* in favor of more realistic and differentiated ones. Though very short, the play succeeds in painting a vivid picture of the sad, poverty-stricken lives of two streetwalkers, Sadie Mae and Lottie; a young black worker, Buddy Jones; his pregnant girlfriend, Viola; and her mother, Ma Jenkins, and their fight against eviction from their homes. According to Leslie Catherine Sanders, the play has "more of the characteristics of social realism than of agitprop" (*Development* 97). Susan Duffy concurs when she writes that "*Angelo*

Herndon Jones more closely resembles a play of social criticism that offers a political solution than a play that overtly espouses a political ideology such as Communism" (in *Political Plays* 138).

Hughes moved away from agitprop techniques even further in *Don't You Want To Be Free?* He combined in this play, which according to Sanders is a "striking departure from his previous work" (in *Political Plays* 98), his poetry with music in order to chronicle the oppression of blacks through the ages. While not abandoning agitprop techniques entirely such as a bare stage, the use of audience space, active audience participation, and the call to action, Hughes created a new dramatic form that succeeded in "projecting the collective voice of black people and in creating the relationship between play and audience crucial to transforming both a black audience's relation to theater and a white audience's relation to plays about blacks" (Sanders, *Development* 99). To present this innovative play, Hughes founded the Harlem Suitcase Theatre in 1938. *Don't You Want To Be Free?* was an instant success. According to the playwright, it was "probably the most performed Negro play of our time, having had 135 performances in Harlem when it was done in 1937–38, and some 200 or more in various cities and at most of the Negro Colleges throughout the country" (qtd. by Rampersad in *Collected Works* 5:538). Hughes updated the play at least six times in order to reflect the changed political climate. In 1963, for example, "mention is made of freedom rides, sit-ins, and other landmark events of the civil rights movement" (Rampersad in *Collected Works* 5:539).

While moving away from the agitprop model and its serious political message, Hughes turned to the comedic presentation of black life, perhaps in an effort to reach a wider audience and to be commercially more successful. His shift to folk comedy, however, did not mean the end of his political involvement. The playwright stressed the social criticism inherent in his works when he stated in an interview, "To me most of my plays are similar in intent and purpose although the treatment may be lighter or heavier or melodramatic or comic" (Duffy in *Political Plays* 21). *Little Ham* (in *Five Plays*), the first comedy Hughes wrote for Cleveland's Karamu House, is set in the Harlem of the Depression years and focuses on the amorous entanglements of Hamlet Hambone (later Hitchcock) Jones, a diminutive, sporty, young shoe shiner. Both Mattie Bea and Tiny Lee, a hairdresser, fight over Little Ham in a scene reminiscent of Jim's and Dave's struggle over Daisy in *Mule Bone*. Eventually Tiny is victorious when it is revealed that Mattie is already married. Despite its farcical situations and colorful characters—the play is unique in its presentation of two gay characters, a "masculine lady" and an effeminate "youth" who leaves on the arm of the "hot stuff man"—*Little Ham* reminds the viewer of the economic trap the figures are caught in. To improve their lot, they play the number game that is controlled by white mobsters: "Only chance will release the inhabitants of the stage from the poverty and oppression that constrain them" (Sanders, *Development* 81). When *Little*

Ham opened on March 24, 1935, it was an instant hit. It appears that most viewers only saw the play's farcical surface and ignored the underlying social message. Most reviewers called *Little Ham* "a hilarious comedy," "side-splitting stuff," and "good clean humor" and only one critic recognized Hughes's serious message when he insisted that "underlying all that laughter you can hear at Karamu, there is the terrifying and tragic thread of life where there is no hope" (Rampersad, *Life* 1:325 f.). Even later critics such as Darwin Turner failed to perceive the play's social critique and Hughes felt compelled to stress in 1961 that "there is a serious undertone in *Little Ham*. There is in all my plays" (qtd. in Rampersad, *Life* 1:326).

When the Jack Hollers (included in Volume 5 of *Collected Works* [hereafter CW 5]), the next production of Karamu House's Gilpin Players, was co-written by Hughes and his close friend Arna Bontemps.* The play, which was originally called *Careless Love*, is set in the Mississippi delta and depicts the harsh life of black and white sharecroppers, albeit in a humorous vein. The play's title refers to the mating call of a mule as well as the various romantic relationships among the characters. *When the Jack Hollers* broke new ground because its "satiric and comic presentation of such grave topics as rural poverty, sexual exploitation, racism, and even the Ku Klux Klan ventured into areas that had not previously been addressed on stage in a comic vein" (Rampersad, *Life,* 2: 333). Perhaps because its social criticism was more obvious than that of *Little Ham*, *When the Jack Hollers* left the audiences cold and the reviewers unimpressed.

Hughes's next farce for the Gilpin Players, *Joy to My Soul* (in Volume 5 of *Collected Works*), was better received, especially by black audiences. It is set in Cleveland's Grand Harlem Hotel (Hughes later changed the setting to New York) in the 1930s and, like *Little Ham*, features a large cast of characters and numerous plots, revolving around Buster Whitehead, a naïve, wealthy black Texan who has come to Cleveland to meet his fiancée, whom he met through a newspaper column. He is beset by various con men and women and, having extricated himself from their schemes, he eventually finds true love. Compared to *Little Ham*, *Joy to My Soul* is darker and more sinister: "The background, thickly populated by con men, call girls, freaks, and a convention of the Knights of the Royal Sphinx, subtly offers a satirical, darker, at times even grotesque counterpoint to the lighter main action" (Rampersad, *Life* 1:336).

Hughes took the dark satire of *Joy to My Soul* even further in the short tragicomedy *Soul Gone Home* (in *CW* 5). The play, which Leslie Catherine Sanders characterized as "poignant and disturbing" (in *Collected Works* 5:266), opens with a mother mourning her dead son in a bare, ugly, and dirty tenement room. When she asks her son to come back from the dead, he actually does and berates her for neglecting him and contributing to his death. When the white ambulance attendants arrive, the boy returns to the realm of the dead and his mother gets ready to earn her living as a prostitute. While both characters are depicted in a comical way—the mother is mostly feigning her grief for show and the son is "slyly humorous" and "haunting his mother as much for fun as for spite"—the underlying message of racial and economic repression is devastating: ". . . both of them are hard-boiled marginal people, slum-shocked products of the rip tides of life" (in *Collected Works* 5:266).

No humor can be detected in *Front Porch* (in *CW* 5), the last play Hughes wrote for the Gilpin Players and a stark critique of the black bourgeoisie. Pauline Harper, a schoolteacher whose pretensions are signaled by her use of standard English instead of black vernacular, does her utmost best to disrupt the courtship of her oldest daughter, Harriet, by the warehouse worker and unionist Kenneth Mason. She wants her daughter to marry the educated and conservative Donald Butler instead. When Harriet becomes pregnant with Kenneth's child, class pretensions lead to tragedy. Mrs. Harper forces her daughter to have an abortion and Harriet dies as a result. Rowena Jelliffe, one of the directors of Karamu House, wrote an alternate ending for the play because Hughes was tardy in supplying the actors with the script. In this "happy" version, which completely undercuts Hughes's intentions, mother and daughter are reconciled. Despite its happy ending, *Front Porch* was not a success when it premiered on November 19, 1938. One of the reviewers called the play "tepid and non-descript" (qtd. in Rampersad, *Life* 1:365).

In the 1940s, Hughes's interest in integrating music into his plays, which had already been evident in *Don't You Want to Be Free?* and the comedies *Little Ham* and *Joy to My Soul*, became even more pronounced. In 1942, he wrote the music-play *The Sun Do Move* (in *CW* 5), a portrayal of slavery through gospel music. According to Leslie Catherine Sanders, the play reflects "Hughes's increasing interest in incorporating African American music into his dramatic work, bringing to the stage experimentation that had long been part of his poetry" (in *Collected Works* 5:591). Having provided the libretto for Kurt Weill's opera *Street Scene* (1947; in Volume 6 of *Collected Works* [hereafter *CW* 6]), which was based on Elmer Rice's play, Hughes collaborated with composer Jan Meyerowitz on *The Barrier* (1950; *CW* 6), an opera based on Hughes's play *Mulatto*. In 1957, he wrote the libretto for *Esther* (*CW* 6), an opera for which Meyerowitz again provided the score. Hughes's only historical play, *Emperor of Haiti* (1936; *CW* 5), which depicts the revolution in Haiti and the fate of the revolutionary leader Jean Jacques Dessalines, was transformed into the opera *Troubled Island* (1949; *CW* 6) by Hughes and the preeminent African American composer William Grant Still. Hughes also turned his comedy *Simple Takes a Wife* (1955; *CW* 6), which was based on the popular character Jesse B. Semple, into the musical *Simply Heavenly* (1957; in *Five Plays*), featuring songs by David Martin.

In the 1960s, Hughes created several gospel plays in which he combined two cornerstones of African black culture: black religion and black music (Sanders, *Development* 107). *Black Nativity* (1961; *CW* 6), according to Joseph McLaren, "is essentially a radical treatment of religious iconography because it rewrites the conventional Eurocentric imagery associated with the Nativity" by implying Christ's African origin ("From Protest" 51). *The Gospel Glory: From the Manger to the Mountain* (1962; *CW* 6), also called *Gospel Glow*, is a passion play, and in *The Prodigal Son* (1965; *CW* 6), Hughes retells the well-known biblical story through gospel music. *Jericho-Jim Crow* (1963; *CW* 6), a morality play, harkens back to *Don't You Want to Be Free?* and *The Sun Do Move* in its depiction of African American history.

Hughes's experiments with gospel plays culminated in *Tambourines to Glory* (1963; in *Five Plays*), "an urban-folk-Harlem-genre-melodrama" that combines elements of his urban comedies and his gospel plays and that revolves around "the old conflict between blatant Evil and quiet Good, with the Devil driving a Cadillac" (Rampersad, *Life* 2:255). Hughes used the theme of the black storefront church to illustrate this conflict: while Essie Belle Johnson gets involved in founding a church because of her deep faith, Laura Wright Reed's motive is financial greed. Hughes explained the theme of the play as follows: "Most of them are run by men of good will but there's an occasional bad seed that mars the record. Gospel singing is a feature of the store-front church, and it was with this idea that 'Tambourines' began" (qtd. in McLaren, "From Protest" 54). The playwright not only criticized certain aspects of the black church but he also got back at his archenemy Aimee Semple McPherson, the fundamentalist who had hounded him for years. At the beginning of the play Laura suggests to Essie, ". . . let's go make our fortune saving souls. Remember that white woman, that Aimee Semple McPherson what put herself on some wings, opened up a temple, and made a million dollars?" (*Five Plays* 192). When the play opened on November 2, 1963, it was not only its shoddy production that elicited a negative reception but also its critical view of some elements of the black church. Anna Arnold Hedgeman of the National Council of Churches, for example, berated Hughes when she wrote that it was tragic irony that he should present such a dreadful picture of the black church "when we so much need the truly significant religious story of the Negro to be presented" (Rampersad, *Life* 2:370). Recently, however, the assessment of *Tambourines to Glory* has changed and it is now generally considered to be among Hughes's best plays and the crowning glory of his dramatic career.

CRITICAL RECEPTION

Because Langston Hughes is primarily known as a poet and prose writer, scholars have concentrated above all on his poems, novels, short stories, and autobiographies until recently. An additional reason for the neglect of his plays is the fact that they remained unpublished until 1968 and that until then they were only accessible in manuscript collections. Webster Smalley rendered an invaluable service to Langston Hughes scholarship when he published *Mulatto, Soul Gone Home, Little Ham, Simply Heavenly*, and *Tambourines to Glory* as *Five Plays* in 1968 with a sympathetic and informative foreword. The publication was designed to stimulate "a vigorous Negro theatre movement" (xvi). The same year Darwin T. Turner published his essay "Langston Hughes as Playwright," a surprisingly negative assessment of Hughes's plays. Turner states that "Hughes never became outstanding as a dramatist" despite his extensive efforts (5) and he tries to prove this assertion through analyses of several plays. Turner concludes that Hughes "never developed the artistry of a Louis Peterson or Lorraine Hansberry" (15). The praise he is willing to mete out has a racist undercurrent. He states, for example, that "for a Negro writer [Hughes's achievements] were remarkable" (5) and he adds, "Least successful when he catered to the predictable taste of Broadway audiences, he was most artistic when he wrote simply and lyrically of the history and aspirations of Negroes" (15). It is unfortunate that Turner's negative assessment of the playwright's works remained largely uncontradicted until the 1980s when Catherine Daniels Hurst contributed an essay analyzing Hughes's dramatic work to the *Dictionary of Literary Biography* in 1981.

Leslie Catherine Sanders, who along with Joseph McLaren can be considered the foremost experts on Hughes's plays, dedicated a chapter to the author in her groundbreaking study *The Development of Black Theater in America* (1988). She discusses Hughes's dramatic oeuvre in great detail and divides it into the following two categories: "those that rely on conventional stage realism and those that experiment with dramatic presentation" (65). She comes to the conclusion that Hughes "brought to the stage figures from the black experience that had been stolen and abused by white artists in a racist stage tradition. His work was ultimately that of rehabilitating the stage for black audiences" (119). In three subsequent chapters, Sanders discussed Hughes's comedies, his gospel play *Tambourines to Glory*, and the influence of Russian theater on his later work.

In 1991, George Houston Bass and Henry Louis Gates, Jr. published the Hughes–Hurston collaboration *Mule Bone* and included much valuable information shedding light on the feud between the two former friends, such as relevant portions of Robert E. Hemenway's Hurston biography and Arnold Rampersad's Hughes biography as well as Hurston's and Hughes's correspondence. This edition has stimulated analysis of the play by such scholars as Lisa Boyd (1994–1005), Rachel A. Rosenberg (1999), and Carme Manuel (2001).

Next to *Mule Bone*, the play that has garnered considerable scholarly attention is *Mulatto*. Arthur P. Davis investigated the theme of the tragic mulatto in the play, the short story "Father and Son," and several poems in an essay published in 1955 and he stressed the autobiographical elements in Hughes's works: "In his handling of the theme he has found an opportunity to write out of his system, as it were, the deep feelings of disappointment and resentment that he himself felt as a "rejected" son" ("Tragic" 177). In

1986, Richard K. Barksdale compared *Mulatto* to Edward Sheldon's 1909 play *The Nigger* and concluded that "because Hughes, in his own life and career, had been close to the problem, his play has an emotional tautness and psychological intensity lacking in *The Nigger*. Sheldon had aesthetic distance from his subject, but this very fact robbed his play of the emotional intensity that differentiates good drama from melodramatic entertainment" (199). Germain J. Bienvenu investigated "intracaste prejudice" in *Mulatto* in a 1992 essay and demonstrated "how intracaste prejudice, as harbored and projected by Robert Lewis, the tragic mulatto of the play, contributes significantly to his tragic experience" (341).

Joseph McLaren published a detailed and informative study of Hughes as *Langston Hughes: Folk Dramatist in the Protest Tradition* in 1997, concentrating on the plays written between 1921 and 1943. McLaren concluded that Hughes's ultimate concern was to "revitaliz[e] black images through theatre of celebration, which presents models for African Americans and entertainment for general audiences without compromising political principles. He also reaffirmed that black music and humor could be effective masks of social protest" (170). In the essay "From Protest to Soul Fest," published the same year as his book, McLaren investigated Hughes's gospel plays, written after 1943.

Susan Duffy published four of Hughes's political plays (*Scottsboro, Limited; Harvest; Angelo Herndon Jones;* and *De Organizer*) in 2000 and contributed extensive and insightful studies of these plays. She proved that "[f]ew American artists were as articulate and as attuned to the political leanings of minority groups in the United States in the 1930s as Langston Hughes" (in *Political Plays* 202). The recent publication of Hughes's plays as part of the University of Missouri Press's monumental edition of his *Collected Works* (Volume 5: *The Plays to 1942: Mulatto to The Sun Do Move;* Volume 6: *The Gospel Plays, Operas, and Other Late Dramatic Work*), edited by Leslie Catherine Sanders who also provided brief yet insightful introductions to each play, should facilitate and stimulate further scholarly exploration of Langston Hughes's multifaceted and innovative dramatic oeuvre.

BIBLIOGRAPHY

Dramatic Works by Langston Hughes

The Ballad of the Brown King. Libretto by Langston Hughes, music by Margaret Bonds. New York: Fox, 1961.

The Collected Works of Langston Hughes. Vol. 5: *The Plays to 1942: Mulatto to The Sun Do Move*. Ed. and intro. Leslie Catherine Sanders. Columbia: University of Missouri Press, 2002.

The Collected Works of Langston Hughes. Vol. 6: *The Gospel Plays, Operas, and Other Late Dramatic Work*. Ed. Leslie Catherine Sanders. Columbia: University of Missouri Press, 2003.

Five Plays by Langston Hughes. Ed. Webster Smalley. Bloomington: Indiana University Press, 1963.

The Glory Round His Head. Libretto by Langston Hughes, music by Jan Meyerowitz. New York: Broude, 1953.

"*The Gold Piece: A Play That Might Be True*." *Brownie's Book* 2.1 (1921): 1–12.

Mule Bone: A Comedy of Negro Life (with Zora Neale Hurston). Ed. George Houston Bass and Henry Louis Gates, Jr. New York: Perennial, 1991.

The Political Plays of Langston Hughes. Intro. and anal. Susan Duffy. Carbondale: Southern Illinois University Press, 2000.

Scottsboro, Limited: Four Poems and a Play in Verse. New York: Golden Stair Press, 1932.

Troubled Island. Libretto by Langston Hughes, music by William Grant Still. New York: Leeds Music, 1949.

Studies of Langston Hughes's Dramatic Works

Abramson, Doris E. "'It'll Be Me': The Voice of Langston Hughes." *Massachusetts Review* 5 (Autumn 1963): 168–176. Rpt. in Tish Dace, ed., *Langston Hughes: The Contemporary Reviews*. Cambridge: Cambridge University Press, 1997. 682–687.

———. *Negro Playwrights in the American Theatre, 1925–1959*. New York: Columbia University Press, 1989.

Barksdale, Richard K. "Miscegenation on Broadway: Hughes's *Mulatto* and Edward Sheldon's *The Nigger*." *Critical Essays on Langston Hughes*. Ed. Edward J. Mullen. Boston: Hall, 1986. 191–199.

Bernard, Emily. *Remember Me to Harlem*. New York: Knopf, 2001.

Berry, Faith. *Langston Hughes: Before and Beyond Harlem*. New York: Wings, 1992.

Bienvenu, Germain J. "Intracaste Prejudice in Langston Hughes's *Mulatto*." *African American Review* 26.2 (1992): 341–353.

Borden, Anne. "Heroic 'Hussies' and 'Brilliant Queers': Genderracial Resistance in the Works of Langston Hughes." *African American Review* 28.3 (1994): 333–345.

Boyd, Lisa. "The Folk, the Blues, and the Problems of *Mule Bone*." *Langston Hughes Review* 13.1 (1994–1995): 33–44.

Boyd, Valerie. *Wrapped in Rainbows: The Life of Zora Neale Hurston*. New York: Scribner, 2003.

Clark, VeVe. "Restaging Langston Hughes's *Scottsboro Limited*." *Conversations with Amiri Baraka*. Ed. Charlie Reilly. Jackson: University Press of Mississippi, 1994. 157–167.

Coleman, Edwin Leon. "Langston Hughes as American Dramatist." Diss. University of Oregon, 1971.

Davis, Arthur P. "The Tragic Mulatto Theme in Six Works of Langston Hughes." *Phylon* 16 (1955): 195–204. Rpt. in *Five Black Writers: Essays on Wright, Ellison, Baldwin, Hughes, and Leroy Jones*. Ed. Donald B. Gibson. New York: New York University Press,1970. 167–177. Also rpt. in *Interracialism: Black–White*

Intermarriage in American History, Literature, and Law. Ed. Werner Sollors. Oxford: Oxford University Press, 2000. 317–325.

Emanuel, James A. *Langston Hughes*. Boston: Twayne, 1967.

Forbes, Ella. "Hughes as Dramatist." *Langston Hughes: The Man, His Art, and His Continuing Influence*. Ed. C. James Trotman. New York: Garland, 1995. 167–169.

Hay, Samuel A. *African American Theatre: A Historical and Critical Analysis*. Cambridge: Cambridge University Press, 1994.

Hicklin, Fannie Ella. "The American Negro Playwright, 1920–64." Diss. University of Wisconsin, 1965.

Hurst, Catherine Daniels. "Langston Hughes." In *Twentieth-Century American Dramatists, Part I: A–J*. Vol. 7 of *Dictionary of Literary Biography*. Ed. John MacNicholas. Detroit: Gale, 1981. 314–324.

King, Woodie, Jr. "Remembering Langston: A Poet of the Black Theater." *Negro Digest* 18.6 (1969): 27–32, 95–96.

Manuel, Carme. "*Mule Bone:* Langston Hughes and Zora Neale Hurston's Dream Deferred of an African-American Theatre of the Black Word." *African American Review* 35 (Spring 2001): 77–92.

Martinson, Deborah. "Langston Hughes." *Twentieth-Century American Dramatists*. 2nd Ser. Vol. 228 of *Dictionary of Literary Biography*. Ed. Christopher J. Wheatley. Detroit: Gale, 2000. 116–127.

McLaren, Joseph. "From Protest to Soul Fest: Langston Hughes' Gospel Plays." *Langston Hughes Review* 15.1 (1997): 49–61.

———. *Langston Hughes: Folk Dramatist in the Protest Tradition, 1921–1943*. Westport: Greenwood, 1997.

Mikolyzk, Thomas A. *Langston Hughes: A Bio-Bibliography*. Westport: Greenwood, 1990.

Miles, William. "Isolation in Langston Hughes' *Soul Gone Home*." *Five Black Writers: Essays on Wright, Ellison, Baldwin, Hughes, and Leroy Jones*. Ed. Donald B. Gibson. New York: New York University Press, 1970. 178–182.

Nelson, Emmanuel S. "Langston Hughes." *African American Authors, 1745–1945: A Bio-Bibliographical Critical Sourcebook*. Ed. Emmanuel S. Nelson. Westport: Greenwood, 2000. 249–258.

Nero, Charles I. "Re/Membering Langston: Homophobic Textuality and Arnold Rampersad's *Life of Langston Hughes*." *Queer Representations: Reading Lives, Reading Cultures*. Ed. Martin Duberman. New York: New York University Press, 1997. 188–196.

Ostrom, Hans. *A Langston Hughes Encyclopedia*. Westport: Greenwood, 2002.

Peterson, Bernard L., Jr. *Contemporary Black American Playwrights and Their Plays: A Biographical Directory and Dramatic Index*. New York: Greenwood, 1988.

Plum, Jay. "Accounting for the Audience in Historical Reconstruction: Martin Jones's Production of Langston Hughes's *Mulatto*." *Theatre Survey* 36 (May 1995): 5–19.

Rampersad, Arnold. "Langston Hughes." *African American Writers*. Ed. Valerie Smith. New York: Scribner's, 1991. 193–204.

————. *The Life of Langston Hughes*. Vol. 1: *1902–1941: I, Too, Sing America*. New York: Oxford University Press, 1986.

————. *The Life of Langston Hughes*. Vol. 2: *1941–1967: I Dream a World*. New York: Oxford University Press, 1988.

Reimonenq, Alden. "Langston Hughes." *The Gay and Lesbian Literary Heritage*. Ed. Claude J. Summers. New York: Holt, 1995. 374–375.

Rosenberg, Rachel A. "Looking for Zora's *Mule Bone:* The Battle for Artistic Authority in the Hurston–Hughes Collaboration." *Modernism/Modernity* 6.2 (1999): 79–105.

Sanders, Leslie Catherine. "'Also Own the Theatre': Representation in the Comedies of Langston Hughes." *Langston Hughes Review* 11.1 (1992): 6–13.

————. *The Development of Black Theater in America: From Shadows to Selves*. Baton Rouge: Louisiana State University Press, 1988.

————. "'Interesting Ways of Staging Plays.' Hughes and Russian Theatre." *Langston Hughes Review* 15.1 (1997): 4–12.

————. "'I've wrestled with them all my life': Langston Hughes's *Tambourines to Glory*." *Langston Hughes: Critical Perspectives Past and Present*. Ed. Henry Louis Gates, Jr. and K. A. Appiah. New York: Amistad, 1993. 197–204.

Schwarz, A. B. Christa. *Gay Voices of the Harlem Renaissance*. Bloomington: Indiana University Press, 2003.

Thurston, Michael. "Black Christ, Red Flag: Langston Hughes on Scottsboro." *College Literature* 22.3 (1995): 30–49.

Trotman, C. James. "'For All the Kids to Come': The Troubled Island of Grant Still and Langston Hughes." *Langston Hughes: The Man, His Art, and His Continuing Influence*. Ed. C. James Trotman. New York: Garland, 1995. 109–118.

Turner, Darwin T. "Langston Hughes as Playwright." *CLA Journal* (June 1968): 297–309. Rpt. in *Langston Hughes: Modern Critical Views*. Ed. Harold Bloom. New York: Chelsea. 5–15.

Woods, Gregory. *A History of Gay Literature: The Male Tradition*. New Haven: Yale University Press, 1998.

ZORA NEALE HURSTON (1891 – 1960)

Rhonda Harvey

BIOGRAPHY

During her lifetime, Zora Neale Hurston claimed to have been born on January 7, 1901, in Eatonville, Florida; however, legal records indicate that she was actually born in Notasulga, Alabama, in 1891. By the time young Zora was a year or two old, she and her family had moved from Alabama to Eatonville. This move was an extremely significant event in Hurston's life as living in the all-black community of Eatonville deeply affected Hurston and is reflected in most of her writing.

This new community provided opportunities for Hurston's father, John, who while working as a carpenter and preacher also became mayor of the town. When Zora was only three years of age, her mother Lucy died. John Hurston remarried, but, as is often the case, the woman he married did not get along well with his children. The stepmother made immediate arrangements to send Zora to a school in Jacksonville, Florida. When the family's economic situation no longer afforded such a luxury, Zora reluctantly returned home. However, it was clear that she was not welcome in her own home. In an attempt to put some distance between herself and her stepmother, Zora left home to work for a traveling theater company for a short while before finishing high school in Baltimore at Morgan Academy.

In 1920, Hurston began studies at Howard University. To support herself during the four years at Howard, she worked as a manicurist. It was at Howard that Hurston was first published. Her story appeared in the literary magazine at Howard, but it was very shortly after that time that another story was accepted by *Opportunity* magazine, which was located in New York City. Appropriately named, *Opportunity* provided a wonderful opportunity for twenty-three-year-old Hurston to move to New York, under the encouragement of many, including Charles S. Johnson, the editor of the magazine.

The bright Hurston was awarded a scholarship to Barnard College in New York where she studied anthropology with the renowned Ruth Benedict and Franz Boas, considered the founders of American anthropology. This study of people certainly influenced Hurston's writing—both her fiction and her drama.

While Hurston is best known for her fictional work, she certainly has made impressive contributions to the world of the theater. While in New York, Hurston met several members of the New Negro literary movement—of which she soon became a member. This movement, later named the Harlem Renaissance, produced some remarkable works of literature. One of Hurston's many contributions to the movement was the play *Color Struck*, which she had published in a short-lived magazine, *Fire!* The magazine was created in 1927 as the result of Hurston's collaboration with members of the Harlem Renaissance, including Langston Hughes.* During this time, she also wrote the play *Spears*, which, while winning honorable mention in a writing contest sponsored by *Opportunity*, has subsequently been lost.

In 1948, Hurston was arrested and charged with committing an immoral act with a ten-year-old boy. While the charges were later dropped when Hurston was able to prove that she was out of the country at the time of the alleged incident, the publicity that followed devastated Hurston. In 1950, she returned to Florida, where she worked as a cleaning woman. Later that year, she moved from Rivo Alto to Belle Glade, Florida, and attempted to restart her writing career. During her remaining years, Zora Neale Hurston worked as a newspaper reporter and as a substitute teacher. She died penniless in January 1960 after being forced to move into the Saint Lucie County (Florida) Welfare Home. She was buried in an unmarked grave at Fort Pierce's segregated cemetery, The Garden of the Heavenly Rest.

MAJOR WORKS AND THEMES

While Zora Neale Hurston is best known for her works of fiction such as *Their Eyes Were Watching God*, her dramatic works cannot be ignored. Using the theater as a creative outlet that also allowed her to make social commentary, Hurston wrote about problems within the black community as well as problems blacks had with whites. *Color Struck* was Hurston's first published play, and it deals with the issue of bigotry within the African American community—particularly the denigration of dark complexion and preference for lighter skin tones. Of this play and its title, critic Warren J. Carson writes:

By far the most outstanding feature of the play is its theme—color struck. As used in black communities, "color struck" is an ambiguous term, although [Hurston biographer Robert E.] Hemenway sees it only as "the intraracial color consciousness addressed by the bourgeoisie . . . [which] addresses those who envy whites biologically and intellectually. . . ." Lighter-hued blacks can be color struck by thinking they are superior to darker-skinned blacks because their skin color more closely approximates that of whites; dark-complexioned blacks can be color struck by thinking likewise, that lighter skin and straighter hair would somehow make them better and more acceptable. (126)

    Opportunity's editor Charles S. Johnson asked Hurston to contribute to his anthology of black writing, *Ebony and Topaz: A Collectanea*. Hurston chose her play *The First One: A Play in One Act* about Noah and his family after the flood. Like *Color Struck*, this play's major theme is color, although Hurston used a different approach to deliver her message—a biblical passage—and used this choice to make a point. Critic John Lowe writes:

Two things are worth noting about this play. First is that the origin of a race is in its founding father's joke. Second, the ending suggests that "The First [Black] One," a being who knows the true value of life, is superior to whites. Thus Hurston's playlet both embraces and inverts the traditional interpretation of the biblical passage upon which it is based. (67)

Warren S. Carson explains:

This short one-act play is actually a dramatization of the biblical story of Noah's curse on his youngest son, Ham, which resulted in Ham and his descendants being accursed with black skin and destined to be servants of mankind forever. . . . Hurston expands this [the biblical passage in Genesis] account in an effort to explore the age-old preoccupation with skin color, and she goes even further to establish the negative emotions that continue to be associated with the color black. (128)

    After the mild success of *The First One*, Hurston found herself a patron. Sponsored by a domineering Mrs. Osgood Mason, a wealthy woman who also sponsored Langston Hughes and Alain Locke, Hurston still found herself struggling to make ends meet. In 1931, she wrote for black musical revues, but she did not feel any reward in doing so, the characters felt superficial, the situations trite and contrived. After much begging by Hurston, Mrs. Mason provided financial backing for Hurston's play *The Great Day*, which debuted on January 10, 1932. Though the play attracted a good crowd and garnered favorable reviews, no producers came forward to offer an extended run. As a result, Mrs. Mason refused to allow Hurston to put on the play ever again as it was written. Hurston was able, however, to stage an edited version at Manhattan's New School on March 29, 1932. She retitled the performance *From Sun to Sun* and produced it in Florida, where it received good reviews. Like a phoenix rising from the ashes, the play was retitled a third time. This time,

Singing Steel was performed in Chicago and earned Hurston more than just good reviews. Officials from the Rosenwald Foundation offered to sponsor Hurston's return to Columbia to work on her Ph.D. in anthropology.

The most important play in Hurston's repertoire is said to be *Mule Bone*, which she wrote with Langston Hughes. This play was written in 1930, but the two authors had a falling out, and it was almost never produced. According to Hurston biographer Robert E. Hemenway:

Hughes claimed that he was to do the construction, plot, characterization and some dialogue, and that Hurston was to provide the authentic Florida color, give the dialogue a true southern flavor, and insert turns of phrase and "highly amusing details" from her collecting trips. (qtd. in Carson 122)

However, no one is exactly certain about which author wrote which part of the play. Carson writes, "There were numerous disputes over a proposed production, and the whole episode eventually ended with Hurston and Hughes actively avoiding each other for the rest of their lives" (122).

Hurston's *Polk County: A Comedy of Negro Life on a Sawmill Camp with Authentic Negro Music in Three Acts* is her only other full-length play. Like so many of her other works, *Polk County* is set in Florida. As in most of her pieces, Hurston wrote *Polk County* to show the real side of black life, complete with realistic characters, customs, and language.

Following *Polk County*, Hurston wrote a one-act play set, once again, in Florida, *The Fiery Chariot*. This play, like many of Hurston's other works, is based on an African American folktale. Adele Newson writes that this play ". . . supports both the well known motif of John the trickster and the stereotypical image of black men possessing superior physical speed" (qtd. in Carson 128).

While not best known for her dramatic works, Zora Neale Hurston used this genre to share her observations of the black community. Of this genre, Carson writes:

Clearly, the study of Hurston's few plays reinforces her insistence that black drama should be a sincere, realistic reflection of black life. The strong sense of place, the powerful imagery, the incorporation of music, dance, and spectacle, and the dramatic use of language are tributes not only to Hurston's immense and versatile talent, but underscore her philosophy regarding the ingenuity of black culture. (129)

CRITICAL RECEPTION

Zora Neale Hurston's dramatic works were both embraced and panned by critics. Members of the black community often criticized Hurston for her gritty, perhaps too authentic portrayal of African Americans. They criticized her characterizations and her dialogue and often complained about Hurston's use of humor.

In fact, *Mule Bone* was almost shelved, even after being "rediscovered" by Henry Louis Gates, Jr., who read the play while he was at Yale. Although Gates was moved by the play and encouraged others to support it, his efforts were met with animosity. In 1988, the play was read to a gathering of African American writers and theater personalities but many in the audience found it offensive because of its apparent use of some racial stereotypes. Three years later, the play, after some editorial changes, was staged in New York City. Its reception, however, was lukewarm.

Of Hurston's only other full-length play, *Polk County*, Lowe writes that ". . . like 'Mule Bone' it lacks a compelling story line, [but] it demonstrates that Hurston never gave up trying to achieve her dream of the 'real Negro theater'" (75). Lowe also writes that ". . . 'Polk County' is little known and, in some ways, represents a more intriguing turn in Hurston's dramatic career" (75). He further states, "Despite its many grimly realistic and naturalistic aspects, the play is by no means intent on slice-of-life theatrics. . . . The Hurston we see here is franker than she was in earlier works, especially about both racial attitudes and sexuality" (75).

While Zora Neale Hurston will never be known primarily as a playwright, her dramatic efforts must be acknowledged. Unfortunately, while she attempted to move away from the stereotypes so prevalent in the theater of her time, looking at her work in our world today shows that she did just the opposite. Of this, Lowe writes:

Hurston's fiction has taken a central place in the American literary canon, but it seems unlikely that her plays will be produced in the near future, largely because, for many readers, they seem to move uncomfortably close to stereotypes, even though Hurston felt she was doing just the opposite in her own day and time. In the more expansive mode of her fiction she was able to burst through into fully-fleshed characterizations, something that eluded her as dramatist. . . . Thus despite their many charms and innovations, Hurston's work for the theater appears headed for the "historical curiosity shelf." It seems likely, however, that her fiction and her own lively autobiography will continue to furnish subjects for the American stage. (78)

Not bad for the daughter of a preacher/carpenter from Eatonville, Florida. Not bad at all.

BIBLIOGRAPHY

Dramatic Works by Zora Neale Hurston

Color Struck. 1925. *Fire!* (1927): n.p.
The Fiery Chariot. 1933. Unpublished.

"The First One: A Play in One Act." 1926. *Ebony and Topaz: A Collectanea.* Ed. Charles S. Johnson. Freeport: Books for Libraries Press, 1977. 53–56.

The Great Day. 1932. Unpublished.

"Mule Bone: A Comedy of Negro Life" (with Langston Hughes). 1930. Ed. George Houston Bass and Henry Louis Gates, Jr. New York: Perennial, 1991.

Polk County: A Comedy of Negro Life in a Sawmill Camp, with Authentic Negro Music in Three Acts. 1944. Unpublished.

Studies of Zora Neale Hurston's Dramatic Works

Carson, Warren J. "Hurston as Dramatist: The Florida Connection" *Zora in Florida.* Orlando: University of Central Florida Press, 1991, 121–129.

Gates, Henry Louis, Jr. "Why the 'Mule Bone' Debate Goes On." *Critical Essays on Zora Neale Hurston.* Ed. Gloria L. Cronin. New York: Hall, 1998. 225–228.

Hemenway, Robert E. *Zora Neale Hurston: A Literary Biography.* Chicago: University of Illinois Press, 1977.

Lowe, John. "From Mule Bones to Funny Bones: The Plays of Zora Neale Hurston." *Southern Quarterly* 33.2–3 (1995): 65–78.

Pacheco, Patrick. "A Discovery Worth the Wait." *Critical Essays on Zora Neale Hurston.* Ed. Gloria L. Cronin. New York: Hall, 1998. 232–236.

Speisman, Barbara. "From 'Spears' to 'The Great Day': Zora Neale Hurston's Vision of a Real Negro Theater." *Southern Quarterly* 36.3 (1998): 34–46.

GEORGIA DOUGLAS JOHNSON (1880?–1966)

Loretta G. Woodard

BIOGRAPHY

The most prolific, successful, and influential of the black women play-wrights of the Harlem Renaissance was poet, journalist, and social activist Georgia Blanche Douglas Camp, who was born on September 10, 1880, to George and Laura Jackson Camp in Atlanta, Georgia. Educated in the pub-lic elementary schools of Atlanta, she then attended normal school from 1893 to 1896 at Atlanta University. While there, she taught herself to play the violin, and later studied piano, voice, composition, and harmony at Oberlin Conservatory of Music in Ohio and the Cleveland College of Music in the mid-1890s. After her return from Ohio, she taught music and worked as an assistant principal in the public schools of Atlanta.

Georgia Douglas Johnson met and married Henry Lincoln (Link) Johnson, an Atlanta attorney and politician, on September 28, 1903. They had two sons: Henry Lincoln, Jr. and Peter Douglas. In 1910, Georgia and Henry moved to Washington, DC, where he established a law practice and she studied musical composition at Howard University. Her husband's death from a third stroke in 1925 forced her to seek employment to main-tain the household and to raise her two sons, who would later attend Howard University, where they studied law and medicine. Johnson worked as a substitute public school teacher, librarian, file clerk for the Civil Ser-vice, and later conciliator for the U.S. Department of Labor for eight years. Though she maintained a busy schedule, she was a lecturer, journalist, and editor, and participated in civil rights activities. She also belonged to numerous organizations such as the Rendezvous Poetry Club, the Poetry Council of the National Women's Party, the Poetry Society of Washington, the Writer's League Against Lynching, the National Song Writer's Guild, the Poet Laureate League, the League of American Writers, the American Society of African Culture, the Negro Actor's Guild, and the Crisis Guild for Writers and Artists.

In the mid-1920s, at the invitation of Jean Toomer,* Johnson hosted literary gatherings in her home, which she called the Half-Way House, to provide a forum for intellectual stimulation and creativity to many of the prominent writers and artists of the Harlem Renaissance. Members of the literary salon, or Saturday Nighter's Club, included Langston Hughes,* Jean Toomer, Countee Cullen, Claude McKay, Bruce Nugent,* Zora Neale Hurston,* Alain Locke, Sterling Brown, W. E. B. Du Bois, James Weldon Johnson, Anne Spencer, Marita Bonner,* Mary P. Burrill, Angelina Grimké,* Lewis Alexander, Jessie Redmon Fauset, May Miller,* Owen Dodson, Willis Richardson,* E. C. Williams, Kelly Miller, Gwendolyn Bennett, Clarissa Scott Delaney, Alice Dunbar-Nelson,* and others. During this time, Johnson's own creativity flourished and she became motivated to write drama through her association with Du Bois, the white playwright Zona Gale, and the Krigwa Players. In the July 27 issue of *Opportunity* magazine, she commented of this genre: "Then came drama. I was persuaded to try it and found it a living avenue" (qtd. in Shafer 230).

From the mid-1920s to approximately 1940, Johnson wrote twenty-eight plays, which are listed in the "Catalogue of Writings" that she compiled in 1962–1963, but most of them are unavailable. Of the twenty-eight, only six were published. In 1925, she published *A Sunday Morning in the South*, followed by her one-act play *Plumes: A Folk Tragedy* (1927), which was awarded a $60 first prize in the 1927 *Opportunity* playwriting contest and produced by the Harlem Experimental Theatre in New York City. Her *Blue Blood* was performed by the Krigwa Players, starring May Miller and Frank S. Horne, in New York City during the fall of 1926, and at Howard University in 1933. It was published in *Fifty More Contemporary One-Act Plays* in 1927. Between 1935 and 1939, to reflect the apparent changes occurring across the country, she wrote social protest and historical plays, a form that she and her close friend, May Miller, popularized to teach young people, especially black children, about their own legacy (Brown-Guillory, "Black" 13). She wrote *Frederick Douglass*, *William and Ellen Craft*, and *Blue-Eyed Black Boy* in 1935. During the Federal Theater Project (1935–1939), Johnson submitted six of her plays, but since four were on the themes of lynching and rape, and the others on historical aspects of slavery, none of them were produced. Many of her unpublished plays, however, were produced in various schools, churches, and lofts throughout Washington, DC.

After the 1930s, Johnson did not write any more plays. Instead, she devoted the remainder of her life to writing and reading poetry, composing numerous musical compositions, and lecturing. According to Winona Fletcher, Johnson became "disheartened by the reception of her efforts to bring serious matters of the black life to the American stage" ("From Genteel" 40). Despite this reception, Johnson, who had a genuine love for the arts and for humanity, was an avid playwright whose literary career spanned into the mid-1960s. With May Miller at her bedside, she died of a stroke on May 28, 1966, almost one year after she received an honorary doctor of letters degree from her alma mater, Atlanta University. At the time, she was the oldest living graduate of the university.

MAJOR WORKS AND THEMES

Georgia Douglas Johnson's works, which include folk dramas and propaganda, serve as important vehicles to effect social progress and to show the tragic impact of racism on blacks in America. Often, due to her interracial background, Johnson's plays focus on the recurring themes of lynching, miscegenation, passing, black history, black folk life, and the empowerment or disempowerment of blacks (Brown-Guillory, "Georgia" 12). Johnson's plays are "finely structured" and "emotionally taut." Her folk plays offer glimpses into the lives of poor rural blacks, lives far removed from and much more common than the lives of those who frequented her salon" (Burke 92).

Since there was a great deal of controversy on the subject of lynching during the 1920s, Johnson wrote a number of lynching plays, including *A Sunday Morning in the South* (1925), *Safe* (1929), and *Blue-Eyed Black Boy* (1935). *Sunday Morning*, set in a kitchen next to a church in 1924, is one of Johnson's finest and her first drama in support of the antilynching campaign following World War I. While Sue Jones, the seventy-year-old grandmother, is having breakfast with her neighbor and her grandsons—Tom, nineteen, who aspires to be a minister, and Bossie, seven—the police appear and Tom is accused of committing rape the night before. Emotionally distraught, the young white woman is bullied into identifying him as her assailant, though he was home asleep in bed on the night in question. As the grandmother protests such a ludicrous false charge, the police arrest him anyway, and he is handed over to a mob to be lynched. By the time the grandmother seeks help from a white woman to intervene, it is too late. Tom is lynched and she falls in her chair, dying as the church choir is heard singing a hymn. *Safe* deals with a mother who strangles her newborn healthy son to protect him from the curse of a lynch mob when he grows up. *Blue-Eyed Black Boy* centers on a young man who faces a lynch mob because he allegedly brushed up against a white woman, but he is saved when his white father intervenes on his mother's behalf.

Blue Blood (1926), which won honorable mention in a contest held by *Opportunity*, is described as Johnson's only tragicomedy that explores the absurdities and sorrows of passing or the "mixing of the races" in the black community. It takes place shortly after the Civil War in Mrs. Bush's kitchen as preparations are being made for the marriage between May Bush and John Temple, two light-skinned characters. As the two mothers brag about their children, particularly in regard to the lightness of their skin color, Mrs. Bush reveals that May's father is Captain Winfield. Then Mrs. Temple informs Mrs. Bush that May cannot marry her son because she was raped by May's father, the captain. To keep John Temple from killing his white father and to protect him from the white men, they decide to tell the news to only May and Randolph Strong, her former suitor who still loves her. Unable to face the wedding guests or the intended groom, May runs off with Randolph to be married and to keep the secret.

Plumes (1927), Johnson's prize-winning play, is a folk tragedy set in the rural South that focuses on the impact of poverty and a poor education on the dilemma of a mother, Charity Brown, who has already lost two loved ones, and whose daughter, Emmerline, is seriously ill. Dr. Scott cannot assure her that her daughter will recover or even survive from the operation he wishes to perform. Tildy, Charity's friend, who assists her with her chores, advises her not to pay the doctor. As Tildy reads the coffee grounds in Charity's cup and foretells a big funeral, the doctor arrives to say he must operate, and Charity is torn between the operation and saving the $50 for an elaborate funeral with hacks, carriages, and horses wearing plumes if Emmerline dies. Charity's superstitious beliefs and her lack of faith in doctors convince her that Emmerline, whom she loves, is doomed to die. While she hesitates, the decision is taken out of her hands and her daughter dies. Charity gets her wish and looks out the window and cries, "My Lord! Ain't it grand! Look at them horses—look at their heads—plumes—how they shake 'em! Land o'mighty! It's a fine sight, sister Tildy" (qtd. in Shafer 76).

Johnson's historical play, *William and Ellen Craft* (1935), like *Frederick Douglass* (1935), deals with the slaves' attempt to escape via the Underground Railroad to freedom in the North. It seems Aunt Mandy is at first willing to put her trust and faith in Jesus and to hope for the best. William and Ellen, however, are unwilling to accept their plight and devise a plan of escape. Ellen, the light-skinned daughter of the master and a favorite house slave, who is trying to avoid exploitation by him, dresses as a white man and walks "biggity" like a white man, while her husband William walks behind her during the day, pretending that she is the servant. Tension mounts as Ellen tries to find clothes, cuts her hair, and toils over being able to pass as a white person. A more pressing problem is their encounter with Sam, who tries to empower himself by betraying slaves who want to escape. Without much choice, William kills Sam and they escape to freedom.

CRITICAL RECEPTION

Until recently, most critics generally agreed that Georgia Douglas Johnson's plays have been largely ignored by theater practitioners and scholars. Winona Fletcher writes, "Omitted from the most popular anthologies and textbooks, even when her black contemporaries gained admission, she was labeled 'minor' primarily because as a black woman of the genteel school she was over-shadowed by what J. Saunders Redding calls the "masculine literature of the 'New Negro'" ("Georgia" 153). Now, with the more recent publication of her plays, Johnson, like her contemporary, the revolutionary writer Marita Bonner, is considered one of the most significant figures in the development of African American literature.

In her earlier plays, critics have observed a number of her strengths. According to Yvonne Shafer, *A Sunday Morning in the South* is "a powerful play with richly developed characters and dialogue" (234). Elizabeth Brown-Guillory acknowledges "the manner in which the poor, rural folks band together in a crisis . . . [and how] the speech of these uneducated, humble characters is unpretentious, earthy, and alive" ("Black" 15). Noting the relationship between speech and performance, Megan Sullivan states that "the discourse—or talk—behind [black dialects] . . . reveals the ways in which women challenge hegemonic definitions of culture and rely on the solidarity of female relationships" (404). According to James Hatch and Ted Shine, the play "is not Johnson's most tightly structured drama . . . the plot is predictable and the conclusion inevitable, but the play's emotional impact is . . . powerful" (qtd. in Raynor 232). Jeanne-Marie Miller asserts that the "lynching plays anticipate the later social protest plays such as Theodore Ward's *Big White Fog* and Loften Mitchell's* *A Land Beyond the River*" (349).

Although Johnson's other plays have received limited critical attention, Gloria Hull suggests that "*Blue Blood* is an interesting creation, in that its essentially comic exterior is built upon a very un-funny substructure—the grim fact of miscegenation via the rape of black women by white men in the South shortly after the Civil War" (155). "Essentially," as Elizabeth Brown-Guillory states, "it is a play that demonstrates the powerlessness of black men and women" ("Georgia" 13). As Hull states, "Johnson in *Plumes* is as 'folk' as she is 'academic' in her poetry . . ." (170). Also speaking of the play, Brown-Guillory observes that "[t]he nobility of the characters is revealed by the facts that they can laugh at their own abject poverty while continuing to strive for a better future" ("Black" 15). Johnson's historical plays, one critic writes, "bring to life incidents from history and create an aura of excitement and actuality through vivid characterizations, dialogue, and action" (Shafer

239). Another critic claims Johnson's escape in *William and Ellen Craft*, is "quite telling" and "the device of disguise itself suggests the freedom reserved for white males" (Burke 93).

Assessing her craft as a playwright overall, Hatch and Shine credit Johnson with using such dramatic innovations as the innocence of the victim being established, and some type of resistance or retaliation being planned by the family or friends, which were pioneered by Angelina Grimké in *Rachel* (1916) and Mary P. Burrill in *Aftermath* (1919) (Raynor 233). Hull claims that Johnson "succeeded at . . . dramaturgy: undeniably, she knew how to write one-act plays" (155) that were "finely structured" and "emotionally taut" (Burke 93).

BIBLIOGRAPHY

Dramatic Works by Georgia Douglas Johnson

"*Blue Blood.*" 1926. *Georgia Douglas Johnson: The Selected Works of Georgia Douglas Johnson*. Intro. Claudia Tate. New York: Hall, 1997. 307–317.

"*Blue-Eyed Black Boy.*" 1935. *Black Female Playwrights: An Anthology of Plays before 1950*. Ed. Kathy A. Perkins. Bloomington: Indiana University Press, 1989.

"*Frederick Douglass.*" 1935. *Georgia Douglas Johnson: The Selected Works of Georgia Douglas Johnson*. Intro. Claudia Tate. New York: Hall, 1997. 333–352.

"*Plumes: A Folk Tragedy.*" 1927. *Opportunity* (July 1927): 200–201, 217–218.

"*Safe.*" 1929. *Wines in the Wilderness: Plays by African-American Women from the Harlem Renaissance to the Present*. Ed. and comp. Elizabeth Brown-Guillory. Westport: Greenwood, 1990. 26–32.

"*A Sunday Morning in the South.*" 1925. *Georgia Douglas Johnson: The Selected Works of Georgia Douglas Johnson*. Intro. Claudia Tate. New York: Hall, 1997. 385–393.

"*William and Ellen Craft.*" 1935. *Georgia Douglas Johnson: The Selected Works of Georgia Douglas Johnson*. Intro. Claudia Tate. New York: Hall, 1997. 353–376.

Studies of Georgia Douglas Johnson's Dramatic Works

Abramson, Doris E. "Angelina Weld Grimké, Mary T. Burrill, Georgia Douglas Johnson, and Marita O. Bonner: An Analysis of Their Plays." *SAGE* 2.1 (1985): 9–13.

Brown-Guillory, Elizabeth. "Black Theatre Tradition and Women Playwrights of the Harlem Renaissance." *Their Place on the Stage: Black Women Playwrights in America*. Ed. Elizabeth Brown-Guillory. Westport: Greenwood, 1988. 1–23.

———. "Georgia Douglas Johnson (1880–1966)." *Wines in the Wilderness: Plays by African American Women from the Harlem Renaissance to the Present*. Ed. Elizabeth Brown-Guillory. Westport: Greenwood, 1990. 11–37.

Burke, Sally. *American Feminist Playwrights: A Critical History*. New York: Twayne, 1996.

Dover, Cedric. "The Importance of Georgia Douglas Johnson." *Crisis* 59 (Dec. 1952): 633–636, 647.

Fletcher, Winona. "From Genteel Poet to Revolutionary Playwright: Georgia Douglas Johnson as a Symbol of Black Success, Failure, and Fortitude." *Theatre Annual* 40 (Feb. 1985): 40–64.

———. "Georgia Douglas Johnson." *Afro-American Writers from the Harlem Renaissance to 1940*. Vol. 51 of *Dictionary of Literary Biography*. Ed. Thadious M. Davis and Trudier Harris. Detroit: Gale, 1987. 153–164.

Gavin, Christy, ed. *African American Women Playwrights: A Research Guide*. New York: Garland, 1999.

Hull, Gloria T. *Color, Sex, and Poetry: Three Women Writers of the Harlem Renaissance*. Bloomington: Indiana University Press, 1987.

Marsh-Lockett, Carol P., ed. *Black Women Playwrights: Visions on the American Stage*. New York: Garland, 1999.

Miller, Jeanne-Marie A. "Georgia Douglas Johnson and May Miller: Forgotten Playwrights of the New Negro Renaissance." *College Language Association Journal* 33.4 (1990): 349–366.

Raynor, Sharon D. "The World of Female Knowing according to Georgia Douglas Johnson, Playwright." *CLA Journal* 45.2 (2001): 231–242.

Shafer, Yvonne. *American Women Playwrights: 1900–1950*. New York: Lang, 1995.

Sullivan, Megan. "Folk Plays, Home Girls, and Back Talk: Georgia Douglas Johnson and Women of the Harlem Renaissance." *College Language Association Journal* 38.4 (1995): 404–419.

SAMUEL L. KELLEY
(1948–   )

Joel Shatzky

BIOGRAPHY

Samuel L. Kelley was born on June 23, 1948, in Memphis, Tennessee, one of eight children. When he was almost six, his mother, Elnora Kelley, was already suffering from mental illness. His father, Booker T. Kelley, brought five of the eight children to live with his brother, Wesley Kelley, and his wife, Gertrude Kelley, in Marvell, Arkansas, in the spring of 1954. They lived on an eighty-acre farm that Wesley rented from a white lawyer.

This is where Sam Kelley spent his formative years. Kelley says, "I was bitten by the acting bug when my first and second grade teachers started me on the stage at M. M. Tate School in rural Marvell, Arkansas" (personal interview). One of his most memorable parts came at that time when he played a rooster to the barnyard hens. His aunt Gertrude kept the costume for many years. Kelley was active in theater and dramatic performance in schools and in his church in Arkansas.

His father died unexpectedly, following an operation for a brain tumor, when Kelley was ten. Plans to return to Memphis ended. His mother was moved around to relatives between Memphis, Marvell, and Jonestown, Mississippi, until she passed away during Kelley's senior year at college.

Kelley and his family chopped cotton for a livelihood and Sam was expected to do his share, although he later discovered that he was allergic to cotton and got asthma attacks when he worked in the fields. Still, all of the children were expected to do their share of work before they went to school. Although not an activist in his early youth, one of Kelley's older sisters was among the first black students to integrate Little Rock High School.

Kelley later attended college at the University of Arkansas at Pine Bluff (UAPB) where he majored in speech and drama, although he showed a great deal of interest in American and English literature. While at UAPB, he took on the role of Walter Younger in a production of *A Raisin in the Sun*, a harbinger of his own creative efforts in drama. Completing his studies in three and a half years in 1970, he taught briefly at Memphis Technical High School. Returning to Arkansas, he and his twin brother, who subsequently became a prominent doctor, enrolled in the graduate program at the University of Arkansas at Fayetteville where he received an M.A. in speech in 1971. He taught for two years at Vorhees College, a small black college associated with the Episcopal Church, in Denmark, South Carolina, and spent most of the rest of the decade at the University of Michigan, where he enrolled in the Ph.D. program in radio-TV-film. In 1979, he accepted a position as assistant professor in the Communication Studies Department at State University of New York (SUNY) College at Cortland. He is currently a professor there.

Determined to pursue the craft of playwriting, Kelley used his first sabbatical to enroll in the Yale School of Drama for one year in 1986. Two years later, he returned for a second year in the playwriting program where his best-known work, *Pill Hill*, was produced at the Yale Repertory Theatre, having been selected by Lloyd Richards, the legendary dean of the school, who also nurtured the work of August Wilson.*

Since he received his M.F.A. in playwriting from the Yale School of Drama in 1990, Kelley has been a prolific playwright, having had theater productions and readings of all of his plays in the last decade. Kelley presently lives in Cortland, a short walk from the SUNY campus where he is a popular teacher. A talented actor in his own right, Kelley has frequently performed, on the SUNY–Cortland stage and elsewhere, such Martin Luther King, Jr. speeches as "I Have a Dream" and "Letter from Birmingham Jail" as well as recitations of James Weldon Johnson's "The Creation" and "Go Down Death."

MAJOR WORKS AND THEMES

Unlike many of his contemporaries in Black theater, Samuel L. Kelley has explored other themes besides the "race issue" in his work. *Pill Hill* is about a group of black mill workers living in Chicago who meet over the years and compare how well they have done in life since they quit the mill. "Pill Hill" refers to the "legendary black upper-class neighborhood on Chicago's South Side, home of the 'pill-pitching doctors and wheeling and dealing lawyers,' that had come to epitomize the pinnacle of black achievement" (introduction, *Pill Hill* n.p.).

The most evident theme in this and all of Kelley's works is black people's need for a sense of location in a world in which they might find a way to fit in but cannot feel control over their lives. Kelley does not merely reveal identity crises but the whole dynamic of living in a "white man's world" without having become obsessed with it, which happens to many of the characters in August Wilson's work. Although most of Kelley's characters in his plays are black, their problems and issues can be recognized as those facing white people as well. This might be considered a harkening back to the Younger family in *A Raisin in the Sun*, but Kelley presents a contemporary view of the condition of trying to stay human, in the rapidly changing world of America, with a black perspective.

Even the play that Kelley adapted from a short story by Charles Chesnutt, *The Blue Vein Society* (1988), originally titled *The Wife of His Youth*, reveals his major focus: it is about a black man who is marrying a light-skinned black woman and is confronted by his dark-skinned wife of slavery times. The "Blue Vein" of the title refers to the snobbish attitude of light-skinned blacks who would not socially accept a black person whose skin was too dark to have visible the "blue vein" on the wrist.

Among Kelley's other plays, *White Chocolate* (1999) is about a middle-class family in which the father is about to be considered for a tenured position at his university. An added issue is that the teenaged daughter is dating a white boy. Unlike some plays about the black middle class, *White Chocolate* is not satirical but rather dramatizes a dilemma among members of the black bourgeoisie as to how far into assimilation they can move without losing their own sense of self-worth.

Thruway Diaries (DWB-Driving While Black) (2000) is a graphic depiction of what happens to a black family that is stopped on suspicion of carrying drugs, although their only crime is being black. The play does deal with racism, but Kelley makes the issue more complex as the two arresting policemen differ a great deal in their attitude toward the family they are terrorizing.

Kelley's latest work is a docudrama that he titled *Faith, Hope, and Charity: The Story of Mary McLeod Behune* (2002). In this one-woman show, Kelley explores the highlights in the life of one of the most influential black women of the twentieth century, an educator and founder of what is now Cook–Bethune College and a consultant on race relations to Eleanor Roosevelt.

CRITICAL RECEPTION

Although most of Samuel L. Kelley's plays are as yet not widely known, *Pill Hill* has had sixteen professional productions in the last ten years throughout the country, including Chicago, San Diego, Atlanta, Hartford, Philadelphia, and Yale. The play has been recognized with the Molly Kuhn Award as the Best Play at the Yale School of Drama (1990), the Kieffer Award for Best Production (Cleveland, 1993–1994) and the Joseph Jefferson Award for the Best Ensemble Performance (Chicago, 1994).

In his review of the production of *Pill Hill* by the Hartford Ensemble Company, Mel Gussow observes, "In confronting problems of rising black professionals, 'Pill Hill' raises issues similar to those in Richard Wesley's 'Talented Tenth' among other plays." Gussow concludes that "this is a play of substance with a great deal to say about the plight of even the most enterprising men. 'Pill Hill' has the aura of a shared life experience, truly told" (B8).

In another review of the play in the *Philadelphia Inquirer*, Cary M. Mazer notes, "The play is most interesting as a complex study of the human cost of economic mobility: financial and professional success inevitably generates new compromises, new betrayals and self-betrayals, and new, subtler forms of racism. And the goals themselves, which seemed straightforward, fail to provide the solutions the characters imagined" (C2).

Pill Hill has also been published in *New American Plays* (1992) and *Dramatic Publications* (1995). As well, two of the scenes from the play have been published in *Best Monologues for Male Actors* (1992).

Kelley's work has been performed at the Actors Theatre in Louisville, Kentucky (2002). In 2002, no less than three of his plays were presented at the Actors Theatre and the University of Louisville. Kelley has also been recognized both as the James Thurber Playwright-in-Residence and Playwright-in-Residence at Ohio State University while at the Thurber House (1998). Kelley has also had residencies at the Virginia Center for the Creative Arts in Mt. San Angelo (1997), the Mary Anderson Center for the Arts in Mt. St. Francis, Indiana (1997, 1998), and the Byrdcliffe Arts Colony in Woodstock, New York (1999).

BIBLIOGRAPHY

Dramatic Works by Samuel L. Kelley

The Blue Vein Society. 1988. Performed by Paul Robeson Company of the Performing Arts, Syracuse, New York.

Faith, Hope, and Charity: The Story of Mary McLeod Bethune. 2002. Performed by Actors Theatre, Louisville, Kentucky.

Pill Hill. 1988. New York: Heinemann, 1992.

Thruway Diaries (DWM-Driving While Black). 2000. Performed by Actors Theatre, Louisville, Kentucky.

White Chocolate. 1999. Performed by Paul Robeson Theatre Company, Syracuse, New York.

Studies of Samuel L. Kelley's Dramatic Works

Gussow, Mel. "Success and Failure in Black Struggle to Rise." Rev. of *Pill Hill*, by Samuel L. Kelley. *New York Times* 3 Dec. 1992: B8.

Kelley, Samuel L. Personal interview. 15 Oct. 2002.

Mazer, Cary. *"Pill Hill." Philadelphia Inquirer* 8 Feb. 1991: C2.

ADRIENNE KENNEDY
(1931 –   )

Steven Carter

BIOGRAPHY

Adrienne Kennedy was born Adrienne Lita Hawkins in Pittsburgh, Pennsylvania, on September 13, 1931. Her father, Cornell Wallace Hawkins, a graduate of Morehouse College, was executive secretary of the YMCA and a community leader. Her mother, Etta Haugabook Hawkins, a graduate of Spelman College, was a teacher. Middle-class professionals dedicated to the advancement of all blacks, her parents provided her with a comfortable middle-class childhood and encouraged her to have professional aspirations. They were pleased and supportive when Adrienne learned to read at the age of three and then became an avid reader. Her imagination and passion for reading inspired her to start writing fiction while very young.

When she was around four, her family moved to an ethnically diverse neighborhood in Cleveland, Ohio. There, among Italians, Jews, blacks, and others, she found an acceptance of cultural diversity that led her to believe that people from different cultural backgrounds could get along together, and her parents generally encouraged this belief. However, her mother also told her many stories about violence and prejudice directed toward blacks, and this helped her see that such harmony between cultures did not exist everywhere. Later, she came to feel that these stories and the way her mother told them were a major source for the violent imagery and tone of her plays The only actual violence that came near her during her generally idyllic childhood was a home invasion during which one of the burglars stuck a gun in her mother's side and took her wedding ring.

Christianity played an important role in Kennedy's childhood. She was told repeatedly in Sunday school that Jesus loved her and she accepted this, though much later when her parents divorced she began to have more disturbing images of Jesus that worked their way into her play *Funnyhouse of a Negro* (1962; in *Adrienne Kennedy Reader* [hereafter *AKR*]). In fourth grade, she was selected against her will to play Mary, the mother of Jesus, in the annual Christmas play, but found that she loved doing it, an experience that helped develop her love for drama.

She was also influenced by the movies. Named for the movie star Adrienne Ames, she was, at eleven, so moved by *Mrs. Miniver* that she restaged it with the neighborhood kids and fought with her best friend over who would play Mrs. Miniver. She was drawn to many types of movies, and several of them would form the background for her play *A Movie Star Has to Star in Black and White* (1976; *AKR*). One type that would have a strong impact on her work was the horror movie featuring monsters. She felt that the Wolf Man was the scariest monster of all, and the transformation of man into wolf imbued her with the conception of metamorphosis and change of identity that would become a major theme in her dramas.

Adrienne experienced a very unpleasant transformation in her world and in herself when she attended Ohio State. As one of the few black students on campus, she was subjected to racist hostility and discrimination. This terrible experience enraged her and probably engendered or at least encouraged her tendency to angry and violent imagery in her work, and one of her most autobiographical plays was significantly titled *The Ohio State Murders* (1992; *AKR*). Despite all obstacles and ugliness, she graduated with a B.A. in education from Ohio State. Two weeks later, on May 15, 1953, she married Joseph C. Kennedy.

Her husband was sent by the military to Korea within six months of their marriage and she waited for him and the arrival of their first child in her parents' home. While waiting, she made her first efforts at playwriting, modeling one play on Elmer Rice's *Street Scene* and another on Tennessee Williams's *The Glass Menagerie*. When Joseph returned, the two of them and their young son, Joseph C., Jr., moved to New York so that Joseph could do graduate studies at Columbia Teacher's College. Adrienne too studied, doing work on creative writing at Columbia University from 1954 to 1956 and at the American Theatre Wing in 1958.

In the fall of 1960, Adrienne, Joseph, and Joseph, Jr. traveled aboard the *Queen Elizabeth* to Europe and Africa. Various sights and experiences from that trip, such as the huge statue of Queen Victoria in front of Buckingham Palace and the murder of Patrice Lumumba, the African revolutionary, while she was in Ghana, had a powerful impact on Adrienne's imagination. They worked their way into her plays *Funnyhouse of a Negro* and *The Owl*

Answers (1963; *AKR*), which were originally conceived as one work and which she wrote in Rome while waiting for the birth of her second son, Adam, and for the arrival of Joseph who had remained in Nigeria to continue a research project. She completed *Funnyhouse* a week before Adam Patrice (named for Patrice Lumumba) was born, having been impelled by a sense that if she did not finish it then and before her thirtieth birthday she never would.

In 1962, while back in New York studying in Edward Albee's Circle-in-the-Square playwriting course, Kennedy finally saw one of her plays, *Funnyhouse of a Negro*, staged. The workshop cast included Diana Sands and Yaphet Kotto. Adrienne had been uncomfortable about showing so much of her inner feelings on the stage and many in the workshop had disliked it, but Albee told her she was doing just what a playwright ought to do: "A playwright is someone who lets his guts out on the stage and that's what you've done in this play" (qtd. in Kennedy, *Deadly* 101). In 1964, he coproduced her drama at the Off-Broadway East End Theatre, where it ran successfully and won an Obie Award for Distinguished Play.

Funnyhouse of a Negro had been a radical departure from traditional and realistic theatrical forms, including the ones by Elmer Rice and Tennessee Williams that she had imitated earlier. Having found her voice in it, Kennedy now felt free to follow her own instincts, and from 1963 to 1969, she had seven plays professionally produced. Of these, *The Owl Answers*, produced at the White Barn Theatre in Westport, Connecticut, in 1963, remains her personal favorite. Joseph Papp, who greatly admired the play, restaged it along with *A Beast Story* under the title *Cities in Bezique* for the New York Shakespeare Festival in 1969. While in London in 1967, Kennedy collaborated on a play based on Beatle John Lennon's poems and nonsense stories titled *The Lennon Play: In His Own Write* that was produced at Sir Laurence Olivier's National Theatre. In 1968, in response to a commission, she wrote *Sun: A Poem for Malcolm X Inspired by his Murder* for the Royal Court Theatre. (The published version is titled *Sun* [*AKR*] and dedicated to Malcolm X.) This difficult stage poem has perhaps been best described and interpreted by critic Genevieve Fabre who saw it as "a vision of a bloody world where the limbs and entrails of mutilated animals are tossed about" and the hope offered to the world by Malcolm X "explodes with his assassination" (122). Another play by Kennedy from this period was *A Rat's Mass* (1966; *AKR*), which was produced Off Broadway at the La Mama Experimental Theatre in 1969.

In 1966, Adrienne and Joseph divorced, though they have remained friendly, and Adrienne feels that he gave her vital support when she was first starting to write seriously. Following her divorce, she received a number of fellowships and grants that helped her continue writing. These included a Guggenheim Fellowship in 1968; Rockefeller Fellowships in 1969, 1973, and 1976; a National Endowment grant in 1973; and the Creative Artists Public

Service grant in 1974. She has also written commissioned plays, including her 1980 adaptations of *Orestes* and *Electra* (both in *AKR*) for the Juilliard Conservatory of Music and a 1980 fictionalized musical version of Charlie Chaplin's childhood titled *A Lancashire Lad* (in *The Alexander Plays*) for the Empire State Youth Theatre Institute. In addition, she has taught creative writing at Yale University, Princeton University, the University of California–Berkeley, the University of California–Davis, and Harvard University.

Her works have continued to develop in individual, experimental directions. Departing from the one-act form to which she had devoted herself after *Funnyhouse of a Negro*, Kennedy developed a three-scene play in *A Movie Star Has to Star in Black and White*, which was first produced as a work in progress at the New York Shakespeare Festival in 1976. In this drama, Kennedy blended scenes from three Hollywood films with scenes from the "real" life of a family, which included a character who seems modeled on herself and who quotes lines from Kennedy's previous dramas as if she had written them. Self-reflexive semiautobiography is similarly evident in a group of four works published together in 1992 as *The Alexander Plays* because they center around a character named Suzanne Alexander who shares much of Kennedy's own background and experience and who discusses the imagery and details of Kennedy's earlier dramas as if they were her own. In addition, Kennedy drew from her memoir, *People Who Led to My Plays* (1988), to create her musical drama *June and Jean in Concert (Concert of Their Lives)* (*AKR*), which premiered at the Signature Theatre Company, the Public Theatre, in New York in 1995. *June and Jean* earned Kennedy her second Obie Award, which she received in 1996.

Two of Kennedy's plays in the 1990s focused on the 1991 beating and arrest of her son Adam by a white officer who later claimed that Adam had struck him. The white officer's charges were dismissed and Adam won a civil suit, but the experience had a profound impact on both mother and son. Adrienne's play *Motherhood 2000* (*AKR*), staged by the McCarter Theater in Princeton, New Jersey, in 1994, was set in the near future and showed an unnamed mother reflecting on a son's beating and hitting the guilty policeman on the head with a hammer while he is performing the part of Christ in a passion play. *Sleep Deprivation Chamber*, presented by the Signature Theatre Company in 1996, was a collaborative effort by Adrienne and Adam. (Her other son Joseph had written the musical score for the 1981 Antioch College dual production of *Funnyhouse of a Negro* and *The Owl Answers*.) *Sleep* highlighted the responses of both mother and son to the son's beating and trial. By naming the mother Suzanne Alexander, Adrienne linked this play to the earlier Alexander plays and stressed its autobiographical connection. This powerful drama earned Adrienne and Adam an Obie Award for Best Play in 1996.

The year 2001 saw the publication of *The Adrienne Kennedy Reader*, an important collection that includes most of her major dramas and some significant prose. It provides readers with a valuable overview of her work, displaying the marvels and malignancies of her multifaceted mind, permitting patterns to be perceived, her dramatic range to be assessed, and her originality to shine forth. It makes one eager to see what she will do next.

MAJOR WORKS AND THEMES

Adrienne Kennedy is a writer who relies on her subconscious and her intuition to an extraordinary extent and this tends to make her plays dense, multilayered, difficult to interpret, poetic, and often profound. Her plays are allusive/elusive and nonlinear, depending heavily on images, symbols, repetitive dialogs and monologs, and fragments/figments of plot and character. She has learned to be true to her visions no matter how distressing or unreasonable they might be. Because of this, she has advised students that "you have to be careful about listening to other people because you don't want to get too logical. . . . You have to be careful with this material because it's very fragile" (qtd. in Hartigan N3). Critics have attempted to link her to surrealism, German expressionism, the theater of the absurd, and African theater, but have recognized that while links can be made she has her own distinctive approach.

Kennedy has acknowledged that "autobiographical work is the only thing that interests me" (qtd. in Bryant-Jackson and Overbeck ix), but she clearly did not mean this in a literal way. Her plays are often true to her psychological conflicts and inner torments rather than to outward, social circumstances. As Margaret B. Wilkerson has observed, "Adrienne Kennedy's plays are an expression of her 'self.' A sensitive woman, she views writing as 'an outlet for inner psychological confusion and questions stemming from childhood' and a creative way to figure out 'the "why" of things'" (164).

Her first major work, *Funnyhouse of a Negro*, is indeed both an expression of "self" and a probing into the "why" of things. The view of self taken in this play is, in some ways, similar to the ones taken by Luigi Pirandello in *Six Characters in Search of an Author* and Samuel Beckett in *Krapp's Last Tape*—that is, the self is fragmented, multiple, and discontinuous. What makes Kennedy's work distinctive is the nature of the fragmented selves in this play. The four "selves" of the protagonist listed among the characters as "Negro-Sarah" are Queen Victoria, the Duchess of Hapsburg, Jesus, and Patrice Lumumba. As the stage directions note, "*Funnyhouse of a Negro* is perhaps clearest and most explicit when the play is placed in the girl Sarah's room" (*AKR* 11). While other settings are indicated, such as the queen's chamber and the jungle, it is clear that nearly everything is really taking place inside Sarah's head.

Sarah's four selves imply multiple conflicts within her. It is significant, for example, that only one of the four selves—Negro-Sarah—is black, although he was widely viewed by Africans as a hero and a martyr for independence at the time of the play. In Sarah's mind, though, Lumumba seems to be associated with her father whom she condemns for being black and for having raped her light-skinned mother to produce her. Her father had been given a mission by his mother to go into the African jungle, preach Christianity to the Africans, and get the black race off the cross. However, Sarah's father, Sarah's Lumumba self, and Sarah's Christ self had all failed in this mission and Sarah herself remains on the cross of race—and self-hatred.

The fact that two of Sarah's selves are male and two are female suggests that she is androgynous. Thus, while the female selves express a deep-seated fear of being raped, the male selves become the would-be rapists. She is simultaneously victim and victimizer. Similarly, the "white" selves are afraid of the "black" selves, yet Sarah is both. She is being rent apart by the conflicts among her various selves.

Her choice of female selves, Queen Victoria and the Duchess of Hapsburg, implies another conflict: her love of a white European culture that looks down on and rejects blacks like her. Negro-Sarah, who writes poetry that imitates the works of mediocre British poets, longs for a refined, sophisticated, and elegant life that she believes upper-class Europeans enjoy. She also wants to be surrounded by white friends so that she will not have to think about her blackness too often.

Unable to mediate or resolve all the conflicts among her various selves, Sarah hangs herself. The irony hovering around her continues even after her death with the only two characters who are not part of her selves, her white landlady and her white Jewish lover, Raymond (also known as the Funnyhouse Woman and the Funnyhouse Man), laugh at her, mock her, and imply that they know more about her than she knew about herself.

While Sarah was not able to move beyond the conflicts that tormented her, Kennedy herself obviously could, simply by articulating them in this and subsequent plays so painfully, unflinchingly, and comprehensively. It should not be surprising that in her later plays centering on Suzanne Alexander she frequently refers to Frantz Fanon, the Martiniquean psychiatrist whose books *Black Skin, White Masks* and *The Wretched of the Earth* painstakingly probed the psychic wounds inflicted by colonialism, many of which had been exposed and explored so effectively in Kennedy's own work. It should also not be surprising that her work has come to take on political as well as psychological and philosophical dimensions.

Kennedy's next play after *Funnyhouse of a Negro*, *The Owl Answers*, deals with many of the same themes and issues that the earlier play did and at one time Kennedy thought of them as one play. The protagonist of *The Owl Answers*, Clara Passmore, like Sarah, has multiple selves but they have different components and function in a somewhat different way. Her name in the character list is SHE who is CLARA PASSMORE who is the VIRGIN MARY who is the BASTARD who is the OWL. The character is usually referred to as She throughout rather than as Clara Passmore, suggesting that Clara Passmore is simply one self alongside the other selves and equal to them rather than an integrating identity. She moves fluidly from one self to another throughout, though there are obvious conflicts between the selves, such as the one between her Bastard self and her Virgin Mary self. Other characters also have multiple selves, though in this play they are not additional selves belonging to She but separate selves belonging to people involved in She's life. These include Bastard's Black Mother who is the Reverend's Wife who is Anne Boleyn and Goddam Father who is the Richest White Man in the Town who is the Dead White Father who is Reverend Passmore. The cast even includes a nonhuman with multiple selves who stands in juxtaposition with She's Owl self, The White Bird who is Reverend Passmore's Canary who is God's Dove. At the same time, there are three figures from British culture and history, Shakespeare, Chaucer, and William the Conqueror, and a solitary figure designated only as the Negro Man.

As they were for Sarah in the previous play, race, culture, gender, and religion are all sources of conflict for She. Race for She has been a problem from birth since her father was a rich white man and her mother a black cook, though there is some confusion about this since Goddam Father who is the Richest White Man in the Town is also Reverend Passmore who is the black man that supposedly adopted and raised She. However, no matter whether her father is a white man or she merely wanted him to be a white man, She is clearly as wounded by being black as Sarah was.

As with Sarah, a large part of the reason She is distressed by her blackness is that she is rejected by the British culture that means so much to her. While the play essentially takes place in a subway car, it too, like Sarah's room, embraces other settings that include St. Peter's Chapel where She seeks to gain access to her Dead White Father and the Tower of London where she is held prisoner by Shakespeare, Chaucer, and William the Conqueror because she failed to answer their challenge—"If you are his ancestor why are you a Negro?" (*AKR* 30). Later in the play, She claims that she despises Shakespeare and the others who have imprisoned her. However, it is evident throughout that She has been rejected by the racist white British culture whose achievements have so profoundly moved her and that this has deeply hurt her.

She's problems with her gender and sexuality, like those besetting Sarah, have a lot to do with her parents. Having Bastard as one of her selves has made her highly insecure about sex. In addition, Bastard's Black Mother has led her to view sex as something bestial, perhaps something that can turn a human being into an owl, the presumed opposite of God's White Dove. While She cannot completely turn away from sex (neither could Sarah), She has ambivalent feelings toward it, seeking out black men on the subway to take home to her Harlem apartment and then trying to fight them off. She tells Chaucer and William the Conqueror that she begs black men to "take" her but that "something strange always happens" (*AKR* 37). The strange thing that happens at the end of the play when She brings the black man home is that She seems to be turning into an owl and it may be that this is what happens every time to her; it is probably a recurrent ritual.

While religion appears in *Funnyhouse of a Negro*, mainly in the form of Sarah's hunchback, yellow-skinned dwarf Jesus self, the savior who does not save, and Patrice Lumumba's failed mission to save the Africans through Christianity, it plays a major role in *The Owl Answers* as a sexual inhibitor. She remembers that "on my wedding day the Reverend's wife came to me and said when I see Marys I cry for their deaths, when I see brides, Clara, I cry for their deaths" (*AKR* 36). In her Virgin Mary self, She is, of course, expected to be forever pure, but in her Clara Passmore self she picks up strange men and then turns into her Owl self. This implies one possible meaning to her lament that "I call God and the owl answers." Shortly after She makes this lament, "the MOTHER, now part the black mother and part the REVEREND'S WIFE, in a white dress, wild kinky hair, part feathered" shows She the only sure way to St. Paul's Chapel, God, whiteness, and purity by stabbing herself to death (*AKR* 41). However, She remains impure, non-white, and an owl at the end.

Race, culture, gender, and religion come together again in *A Lesson in Dead Language*. The lesson is being given by a white dog (an actress costumed as a dog from the waist up) to seven girl pupils who, although the stage directions do not specifically identify them by race, have usually been played by blacks. Even without specifying the race of the pupils, the designation of a large white dog as teacher has racial overtones. In addition, the pupils are learning about Caesar, Calpurnia, and the Ides of March in a context that holds them accountable for the death of Caesar, thus inducing guilt in them and implying that they are not fit to be heirs to the European civilization that sprang in part from ancient Rome. They are told that they bleed for their responsibility in Caesar's death. Of course, they also bleed from menstruation, which evidently has just begun in them, and this makes them feel guilty as well for becoming women. The recurrent image in this play is the great circle of blood on the back of the white organdy dress that each of the pupils wears. Significantly, the pupils are surrounded by various Christian statues and are made to recite in unison, as in a catechism, that "this bleeding started when Jesus and Joseph and Mary, the two Wise Men, and my shepherd died, and now Caesar" (*AKR* 45). Clearly, like the other parts of their lesson, religion only serves to reinforce guilt and a sense of exclusion.

Although Kennedy has stated that *A Rat's Mass* is essentially a dramatized version of one of her dreams, the same issues predominate in it as in her previous plays, though in a somewhat different mixture and form. As in *A Lesson in Dead Language*, there is a white manipulator (like the white dog) who preys on those who are more naïve, vulnerable, and trusting than herself. This time the manipulator, a young girl named Rosemary who "wears a Holy Communion dress and has worms in her hair," convinces two black children who love her to commit incest on the lower part of a slide while she looks down on them from an "exalted" position at the top (*AKR* 47). Afterward, the two children, Brother Rat and Sister Rat (also named Blake and Kay), hold themselves responsible for what happened and do not blame Rosemary for the pregnancy that results. They even continue to accept Rosemary's spurious claim to moral and spiritual superiority, telling her that "if you do not atone us Kay and I will die." Rosemary's sweet, loving Christian response to this plea is "I will never atone you. Perhaps you can put a bullet in your head with your father's shotgun, then your holy battle will be done" (*AKR* 51).

Perhaps a large part of the hold Rosemary exerts over Brother Rat and Sister Rat is her firm position in a culture they can only aspire to. When they ask Rosemary about why she always goes to catechism, she tells them that she is a Catholic and proceeds to announce that the Virgin Mary, the Pope, and Julius Caesar are among her lofty ancestors. Achingly, Brother Rat and Sister Rat acknowledge their desire for such grand ancestry and reiterate their belief in Rosemary's beauty and holiness. Even after Sister Rat gives birth to the dead baby for which Rosemary had enacted the role of God/Mother, she and Brother Rat recall Rosemary as a loyal friend and teacher. Rosemary is even with them at the end when they are shot to death and tells Brother Rat/Blake that "it is our wedding, Blake. The Nazis have come" (*AKR* 53). Ironically, the Nazis whose arrival Brother Rat and Sister Rat have been dreading throughout the play also represent a significant part of European culture that has excluded them, though it is not a part they have aspired to.

It is, of course, sexuality that is the primary source of Brother Rat's and Sister Rat's guilt and, like She's conversion into an owl for similar reasons, it is what has turned them at least partly into animals. Brother Rat has the head and tail of a rat, though a human body, whereas Sister Rat has a rat's belly (presumably the part in her that has offended most by carrying an incestuous baby), a rat's tail, and a human head. They were presented as having been pure and innocent before their fall on the slide. Afterward, they are no longer part of the human community and dwell in an attic, where they hear the sounds of rats all around them. While the special nature of their sin is incest, their experience fits in with other depictions by Kennedy of sexuality itself as bestiality and this view of sex seems, as in the other plays, to be linked to religious attitudes about it.

Brother Rat and Sister Rat have obviously had religious longings for purity and holiness that have greatly augmented their sense of guilt, uncleanness, and exclusion from the human community. As previously noted, Rosemary refused to "atone" them, even though she provoked them into committing their sin. In addition, they are rejected by the most important figures in Christianity. At one point in the play, a procession consisting of Jesus, Joseph, Mary, two Wise Men, and a Shepherd (the same figures who appear in the procession in *A Lesson in Dead Language*) walk out on Brother Rat and Sister Rat, even though they plead desperately with these beloved religious figures not to leave them. The members of the procession announce that "we are leaving because it was Easter" when the two committed incest, and, when informed that it happened in June, they contend that "in our minds it was Easter" (*AKR* 51). Chillingly, when these religious figures finally return, they have turned into the long-expected Nazis bearing shotguns and it is they who kill Brother Rat and Sister Rat. The destructive effect of religion could not be presented more clearly—or more devastatingly.

Alongside her love for the great achievements of classical European culture, as shown in so many of her plays, Kennedy has always had an appreciation for popular culture, especially the movies. This appreciation is highlighted in her most anthologized drama, *A Movie Star Has to Star in Black and White*. As in *Funnyhouse of a Negro* and *The Owl Answers*, scenes take place in more than one setting at the same time, but in this play the settings for a drama about a black writer named Clara and her family are matched with characters and settings from three movies—*Now Voyager*, *Viva Zapata!*, and *A Place in the Sun*. The story involving Clara in many ways resembles Kennedy's life. Clara's middle-class parents come up from the South and live in Cleveland for many years. Then they divorce when Clara is grown and married, and her father remarries and moves back to the South. Shortly after Clara's marriage to Eddie, he is sent by the military to Korea and she has a miscarriage while waiting for him. Clara is the author of a play whose lines, when she quotes them, are those of *The Owl Answers*. Moreover, she announces that the next play she is writing will be titled *A Lesson in Dead Language*. After having one son with Eddie and expecting another, she divorces him. Then her brother gets in an accident and they all (father, mother, former husband, and Clara) meet at the hospital out of concern for him. At the end, it is learned that Clara's brother Wally will live but be brain damaged and paralyzed.

There are so many resemblances between the situations in Clara's life and those in Kennedy's that it is hard not to see Clara as a stand-in for Kennedy and the play as close to literal autobiography. What keeps it from being literal is the juxtaposition of movie scenes with real-life scenes and the fact that she has famous white actresses (stand-ins for Bette Davis, Jean Peters, and Shelley Winters) voicing Clara's thoughts and making many of Clara's speeches for her. These actresses had all been famous for starring in movies filmed in black and white that paid attention exclusively to whites. Now, however, these white actresses star in black and white by speaking a black woman's words and sometimes assuming a black woman's role.

In the play, Clara reveals that her former husband believes that "to me my life is one of my black and white movies that I love so . . . with me playing a bit part" (*AKR* 75). This would imply that she has lost herself in the movies and been dominated by them. On the other hand, it can be argued that she has made herself the star in her own movies by putting her lines in the mouths of actresses she has admired and making them perform in her life story. Given her desire to be a writer, a desire that she recognizes is especially complicated for a black writer in a predominantly white society that is hostile to her, this is an impressive feat of imagination.

The same themes that run through the previous dramas appear here too. In addition to the issue of how blacks are affected by white-centered movies, racial conflict is highlighted by the bitter memories of Clara's mother about living in the segregated South and in an ugly exchange of insults between Clara's divorced parents. Cultural conflict is, of course, shown in Clara's love for the movies and her sense of exclusion from them. Gender and racial conflict play a role in Clara's struggle to be a writer, especially since her former husband would rather have had her be a wife than a writer. Religious conflict emerges from the clash between the belief that God would tend to their needs and the many instances when God fails to do so, such as the divorce of Clara's parents, her own divorce, and the paralysis and brain damage of her brother, a situation that is paired with the drowning of Shelley Winters in *A Place in the Sun*. Significantly, the line Clara quotes most from her own plays is "I call God and the Owl answers" (*AKR* 73).

In *An Evening with Dead Essex*, first staged three years before *A Movie Star Has to Star in Black and White* but placed after that play in *The Adrienne Kennedy Reader* because it had been left out of the earlier collection *Adrienne Kennedy in One Act*, Kennedy makes her most explicit political statement. The "Essex" of the title is Mark Essex, a black man who in 1972 shot and killed several people, including three policemen, from the top of a motel as a protest against racism and the Vietnam War. The police, some of whom fired from helicopters, riddled his body with more than one hundred bullets. The play is presented as the last rehearsal for a play to be put on by a black director and a group of black actors with the only white a projectionist. In reviewing Essex's life for their project, the director and actors develop an increasing sense of identification with him and his rage. In a 1990 interview with editors Paul K. Bryant-Jackson and Lois More Overbeck for *Intersecting Boundaries*, Kennedy made it clear that she shared this identification. Acknowledging that she viewed Essex as "a victim and a hero," Kennedy further admitted, "I feel tremendous rage against American society. I feel like Mark Essex" (8).

Kennedy seems intent on probing the psychology underlying Essex's political violence. The actors and director talk about how he came from a Christian home and was very innocent toward nationalism and racism. They sing the patriotic songs they all grew up with and read the biblical verses that were part of their own youth. They also talk about the public events that changed his views, such as the Kennedy, King, and Kent State killings; the Vietnam War; and Nixon's lies. Summing up, the director says that he wants to show all the defining moments in Essex's life and how they shape his consciousness and his view of the world around him.

In *The Alexander Plays*, a cluster of dramas centering on African American writer Suzanne Alexander, Kennedy continues to link the political and the psychological, though this time her emphasis is more on healing the psychological wounds from political violence. In two of these works, *She Talks to Beethoven* and *Dramatic Circle*, Suzanne's husband, David, is endangered because of his close association with Frantz Fanon. As a psychiatrist in Algeria, Fanon had seen the psychological wounds of European colonialism firsthand and this had led him to take a revolutionary stance in favor of African liberation that had made numerous enemies for himself and his associates. In the first play, David hides out from these enemies to protect Suzanne, and, in the second, he is held prisoner by another one of Fanon's enemies. In both cases, Suzanne has to cope with his absence and her fear about what might have happened to him.

Ironically, Suzanne is enabled to get through her periods of intense fear and suffering in large part by Europeans—that is, by representatives of the same forces that had wounded Fanon's patients and placed his life and David's in peril. They also represent the cultures that had helped drive Sarah to suicide, turn Clara into an owl, and shoot down Brother Rat and Sister Rat. The Europeans who assist Suzanne are not viewed ambiguously but are seen as genuinely sympathetic healers.

In *She Talks to Beethoven*, the healer is Beethoven himself who magically appears to keep Suzanne company while she is waiting for news about David. She and David had been collaborating on a play about Beethoven at the time of David's disappearance and had argued because David felt that she was romanticizing the composer. Nevertheless, when Suzanne asks her returned husband whether he had sent Beethoven to her, David replies, in a voice "not unlike Beethoven's," that "I knew he would console you while I was absent" (*AKR* 150). However, no matter whether Suzanne hallucinated seeing Beethoven or David sent him to her through some magical spell or Beethoven's spirit came to her across time and space in response to her need, Suzanne is consoled by his presence not only because she has found his life intriguing enough to write about but also, more importantly, because of the similarities she sees between the two of them. Beethoven's remembrance of Napoléon's invasion of his country is a reminder that the rapacity and violence that Europeans exhibited toward Africans (and their white American descendents showed toward African Americans) have also been frequently directed by one group of Europeans toward another. In addition to experiencing this kind of anxiety, Beethoven, like Suzanne, has known an artist's fears of being rejected by the public, has been separated from a loved one, and has endured a physical affliction. He speaks to her both as one artist to another and one suffering person to another; race, nationality, and gender do not intervene between them.

The European who aids Suzanne in *Dramatic Circle*, Dr. Freudenberger, uses a work of European popular culture, *Dracula*, to help his patients cope with their psychological problems. By encouraging them to read together about terrifying experiences, he prepares them to face their inner demons. In Suzanne's case, once he learns that her husband has been held prisoner, he focuses on the section in *Dracula* in which Jonathan Harker suffers as a prisoner. He also appears several times at a distance with mysteriously whitened hair and a sudden limp to prepare her for the change in her husband from his captivity. Despite all his helpfulness, though, Freudenberger does not have the final word. The most significant message appropriately belongs to Fanon whom David quotes: "But the war goes on and we will have to bind up for years to come the many, sometimes ineffaceable, wounds that the colonialists have inflicted on our people" (*AKR* 196).

In *The Ohio State Murders*, Suzanne returns as a celebrated author to lecture on her student years at Ohio State University and, as requested, "to talk about the violent imagery in my work; bloodied heads, severed limbs, dead father, dead Nazis, dying Jesus," all staples of Kennedy's early work (*AKR* 152). The source of the imagery turns out to be twofold. One is gruesomeness and gore in the English literature she was drawn to, including such works as *Tess of the d'Urbervilles*, *King Arthur's Death*, and *Beowulf*, and in the movies she liked best, such as *Potemkin*, and *A Place in the Sun*. (All of these works are quoted or discussed in the play). The other is her excruciatingly painful experience at Ohio State.

Like Kennedy herself, Suzanne as a student faces racist hostility not only from her fellow students whose glares and giggles infuriate her but even worse from the faculty and the administration. Even though she excels in the study of literature and in writing, the English Department will not accept her as a major because black students were deemed unfit for the program. Thus, like Sarah and Clara Passmore, Suzanne is excluded from the culture she adored and is forced to study elementary education instead.

In addition to mirroring Kennedy's experiences at Ohio State, however, Suzanne also lives through a situation that would have fit well in a novel by Thomas Hardy. The young white English professor who teaches her *Tess of the d'Urbervilles* also seduces her, impregnating her with twin girls. Later, fearing exposure as the father of her children and, more damningly, a man who committed miscegenation, he kills the girls and then himself. Given all this, it is easy to see why Suzanne becomes a writer full of anger and bloody images.

In contrast to *The Ohio State Murders* and nearly all of Kennedy's other dramas, *June and Jean in Concert*, which is based on her autobiography *People Who Led to My Plays*, includes far more of the pleasant and positive experiences of her childhood and often seems as nostalgic and magical as Thornton Wilder's *Our Town*. The play recalls the delights of family rides in the car to get ice cream, the comfort of being told in church that Jesus loves you, the pride of watching someone receive an award for outstanding community service, the thrill of hearing Paul Robeson sing, and many other childhood joys. In fact, much of the play probably inspires most members of the audience with a longing to return to their own childhoods. However, Kennedy never overlooks the dark side of experience: the pleasure-giving car destroys a beloved brother's brain in an accident, the comforting Jesus of childhood turns cruel when parents divorce, the day the father receives his award is the day he tries to kill himself, and Robeson's singing career is cut short by a government that resents his fight against racial injustice. Nevertheless, for all its awareness of darkness, the play remains luminous—and illuminating.

Even though the play remains close to her autobiography, Kennedy, as always, adds an experimental dimension. She divides her experience between two twins, June and Jean. In *People Who Led to My Plays*, Kennedy mentions having known two twins with these names in kindergarten, adding "I walked as close as possible to them as possible so I could study these two people who looked exactly alike" (6). Jean becomes the author of Kennedy's plays. However, June's role is more dramatic, since, after reliving much of Kennedy's childhood, she dies and returns as a spirit. She and another spirit, Dead Aunt Ella, comment on the living and the dead and ultimately interact with the still living Jean. In this way, Kennedy's play resembles Latin American magic realism and Toni Morrison's fiction.

Sleep Deprivation Chamber, which Kennedy collaborated on with her son Adam, is also a realistic account of actual experience with some fantasy and imagination mixed in. While new names are given to the people involved, with Suzanne Alexander again taking on aspects of Adrienne's experience and Adam appearing as her son Teddy, a large part of the play seems almost a documentary of Adam Kennedy's unprovoked beating by a white police officer and his subsequent trial for allegedly assaulting the policeman who put him in the hospital. However, the addition of several sequences based on Suzanne's dreams, the interspersing of scenes from *Hamlet* and *The Ohio State Murders* (presented here as a work written by Suzanne Alexander), and the swift, cinema-like cutting between onchronological scenes for thematic and dramatic purposes greatly enhance the drama's depiction of racist brutality and its horrifying consequences. For example, the allusions to the governing rottenness in Denmark and the effects of institutionalized racism in *The Ohio State Murders* help the play take Adam's experiences—and Rodney King's and who knows how many others—and turn them into a powerful statement against institutionalized bias, abuse of authority, and racial injustice.

While Kennedy's extreme penchant for autobiography leaves little doubt the themes and content of her future work will depend in large part on what happens in her life as well as what she remembers, it is also clear that this new work will be remolded and given context and meaning by her creative imagination. The themes that she is not likely to leave behind, however, are her agonized awareness of the psychological vulnerability of individuals and the terrifying impact of racism, gender abuse, cultural conflict, religious and political lies, and any other form of discrimination and injustice.

CRITICAL RECEPTION

The critical reception to Adrienne Kennedy's work has generally been favorable, but there have been dissenting views. For example, *Funnyhouse of a Negro* garnered praise from most of the leading white critics as well as earned an Obie Award. Howard Taubman of the *New York Times* observed that "Kennedy explored 'relatively unknown territory' and dug 'unsparingly into Sarah's aching psyche'" and Michael Smith in the *Village Voice* "admitted that he did not know how to evaluate the play as art or craft, 'but as an obsessive, cruelly honest statement of self it is extraordinary and devastating'" (both qtd. in Wilkerson 166). Edith Oliver in the *New Yorker* called it a "strong and original" first play and Harold Clurman in the *Nation* felt that "the play . . . embraces far more than plays of similar theme" and that the "torment" of Sarah "parallels that of people who suffer the pathology of minorities" (both qtd. in Bryant-Jackson and Overbeck 24). Nevertheless, George Oppenheimer in *Newsday* spoke for a significant number of critics on this and later Kennedy dramas when he attacked the play as "bad theater of the absurd and a dismal 'charade,' a 'non-play' with a 'non-plot'" (qtd. in Bryant-Jackson and Overbeck 24). The most consistent negative criticisms that have plagued her work are that it is obscure, confusing, and lacking in plot and action.

Possibly because some members of the public have also found her plays difficult and confusing, Kennedy has not had widespread popular success, though Off-Broadway productions of her dramas have often attracted a cult following. While the lack of popularity has been disappointing to Kennedy, she has become resigned to it. As she told *Boston Globe* reporter Patti Hartigan in March 2000, "Sometimes I would become very, very sad—I think I was saddest in the 70s. . . . But over a period of time, it's become clear that my plays tend to be taught in colleges and are the subjects of dissertations and conferences [instead of being produced]. I've come to be happy and grateful for that because I could be just totally forgotten" (N2).

In 1970, Kennedy told interviewer James V. Hatch that when *Funnyhouse of a Negro* was first produced that black audiences "did not like it, and a controversy broke out in the Black press. Some considered *Funnyhouse* a laundering of 'dirty linen' because the racism of lighter Blacks against darker African Americans should not be aired in public" (Hatch and Shine 334). This was a criticism that would later be leveled against movie director Spike Lee for *School Daze*. The additional problem Kennedy faced is that many of her plays were produced at a time when most black playwrights were writing realistic plays and emphasizing black pride and nationhood, and in the eyes of some black nationalists she was not only outside their mainstream but represented a neurotic view of black life that was counterproductive. However, even then she found black critics and playwrights who admired her work. In 1967, Loften Mitchell* in his groundbreaking study *Black Drama: The Story of the American Negro in the Theatre* cited Kennedy as "a writer of considerable depth, quite introspective and quite knowledgeable of theatrical terms" (198), and in 1972, Paul Carter Harrison in *The Drama of Nommo: Black Theater in the African Continuum* deemed Kennedy "one of the most inventive black dramatists on the Babylonian scene" (216). In 1985, Margaret B. Wilkerson in "Diverse Angles of Vision: Two Black Women Playwrights" acclaimed Kennedy as "a poet of the theatre" and "one of the few accomplished black playwrights who employs the surrealistic mode of theatre" (qtd. in Bryant-Jackson and Overbeck 70, 68).

Nevertheless, as Kennedy herself suggested, her most appreciative audience may be students and scholars. In addition to the dissertations and conferences Kennedy cited with pleasure, a substantial number of scholars, including Herbert Blau, Ruby Cohn, Winona L. Fletcher, James Hatch, Linda Kintz, Robert L. Tener, and Toby Zinman, have written about her work. To date, however, there has only been one book-length study of her drama, *Intersecting Boundaries: The Theatre of Adrienne Kennedy*, edited by Paul K. Bryant-Jackson and Lisa More Overbeck. This book brings together the views of black and white scholars, such as bell hooks, Margaret B. Wilkerson, Kimberly W. Benston, Rosemary Curb, and Werner Sollors, and black and white directors of Kennedy's plays, such as Billie Allen, Robbie McCauley, Michael Kahn, Gaby Rodgers, and Gerald Freedman, and offers a startlingly wide range of perspectives. No matter whether the scholars and directors regard her as a surrealist, an absurdist, an expressionist, a creator in the African continuum, a theatrical poet, or an imagist, they all grant her the respect due to a major playwright.

As previously observed, there have been many attempts to interpret and sum up the significance of Kennedy's complex, experimental dramas. However, the best evaluation of her standing among contemporary playwrights seems to be that of Michael Feingold: "With Beckett gone, Adrienne Kennedy is probably the boldest artist now writing for the theater" (qtd. in *AKR* xv).

BIBLIOGRAPHY

Dramatic Works by Adrienne Kennedy

Adrienne Kennedy in One Act. Minneapolis: University of Minnesota Press, 1988.

The Adrienne Kennedy Reader. Minneapolis: University of Minnesota Press, 2001. Includes: *Dramatic Circle* (1992); *Electra* (Euripides) (1980); *An Evening with Dead Essex* (1973); *The Film Club (A Monologue by Suzanne Alexander)* (1992); *Funnyhouse of a Negro* (1962); *June and Jean in Concert (Concert of Their Lives)* (1995); *A Lesson in Dead Language* (1964); *Motherhood 2000* (1994); *A*

Movie Star Has to Star in Black and White (1976); *The Ohio State Murders* (1992); *Orestes* (Euripides) (1980); *The Owl Answers* (1963); *A Rat's Mass* (1966); *She Talks to Beethoven* (1989); and *Sun* (1968).

The Alexander Plays. Minneapolis: University of Minnesota Press, 1992.

Cities in Bezique (*The Owl Answers* and *A Beast Story*). New York: French, 1969.

"*The Lennon Play: In His Own Write*" (with John Lennon and Victor Spinetti). *Best Short Plays of the World Theatre: 1968–1973*. Ed. Stanley Richards. New York: Crown, 1973. 289–303.

Sleep Deprivation Chamber (with Adam Kennedy). New York: Theatre Communications Group, 1996.

Other Cited Material by Adrienne Kennedy

Deadly Triplets: A Theatre Mystery and Journal. Minneapolis: University of Minnesota Press, 1990.

———. *People Who Led to My Plays*. New York: Theatre Communications Group, 1988.

Studies of Adrienne Kennedy's Dramatic Works

"Adrienne Kennedy." *Contemporary Authors, New Revision Series, Vol. 26*. Detroit: Gale, 1989. 199–201.

"Adrienne Kennedy." *Contemporary Authors, Vol. 103*. Detroit: Gale, 1982. 256–258.

Bryant-Jackson, Paul K., and Lois More Overbeck, eds. *Intersecting Boundaries: The Theatre of Adrienne Kennedy*. Minneapolis: University of Minnesota Press, 1992.

Carter, Steven R. "Adrienne Kennedy." *The Oxford Companion to Women's Writing in the United States*. Ed. Cathy N. Davidson and Linda Wagner-Martin. New York: Oxford University Press, 1995. 456–457.

Fabre, Genevieve. *Drumbeats, Masks, and Metaphor: Contemporary Afro-American Theatre*. Cambridge: Harvard University Press, 1983.

Harrison, Paul Carter. *The Drama of Nommo: Black Theater in the African Continuum*. New York: Grove Press, 1972. 216–220.

Hartigan, Patti. "Adrienne Kennedy Is Fragile and Ferocious." *Boston Sunday Globe* 26 Mar. 2000: N2–N3.

Hatch, James V., and Ted Shine, eds. *Black Theatre USA: Plays by African Americans, The Recent Period, 1935 to Today*. Rev. and exp. ed. New York: Free, 1996.

Mitchell, Loften. *Black Drama: The Story of the American Negro in the Theatre*. New York: Hawthorn, 1967.

Page, James A., comp. *Selected Black American Authors: An Illustrated Bio-Bibliography*. Boston: Hall, 1977.

Peterson, Bernard L., Jr. *Contemporary Black American Playwrights and Their Plays: A Biographical Directory and Dramatic Index*. Westport: Greenwood, 1988.

Poland, Albert, and Bruce Mailman, eds. *The Off Off Broadway Book: The Plays, People, Theatre*. Indianapolis: Bobbs, 1972.

Robinson, Alice M., Vera Mowry Roberts, and Milly S. Barranger, eds. *Notable Women in the American Theatre: A Biographical Dictionary*. Westport: Greenwood, 1989.

Wilkerson, Margaret B. "Adrienne Kennedy." *Afro-American Writers after 1945: Dramatists and Prose Writers*. Vol. 38 of *Dictionary of Literary Biography*. Ed. Thadious Davis and Trudier Harris. Detroit: Gale, 1985. 162–169.

MAY MILLER
(1899–1995)

Joyce Russell-Robinson

BIOGRAPHY

May Miller was born on January 26, 1899, and died on February 11, 1995. She was the daughter of Annie Mae Butler Miller and Kelly Miller, the noted "race man" and prominent dean and professor of Howard University who upgraded the curriculum and made the study of African Americans a part of the curriculum. Kelly Miller's long tenure at Howard University (forty-four years) made it possible for May and her four siblings to grow up on the campus of Howard in the old John M. Langston House. Dean Miller's ties to Howard and his dedication to racial uplift caused his and the paths of his children to intersect with the paths of many African American scholars who, like Kelly, were dedicated race men and women. Thus, the Miller home welcomed frequent guests such as W. E. B. Du Bois, Carter G. Woodson, Alain Locke, and Booker T. Washington. Growing up in an atmosphere of intellectualism, and on a university campus, caused May to "cut her teeth" on literature and ideas.

Miller received her early education at the M Street School, the famous college preparatory institution in Washington, DC, which later became the Paul Laurence Dunbar High School. While attending M Street, Miller studied under the playwrights Mary P. Burrill and Angelina Grimké.* Burrill is best known for *They That Sit in Darkness*, a short play dealing with birth control, which was published in 1919. Grimké is best known for *Rachel*, a three-act play dealing with racial prejudice, which was first performed in

1916. The influence of these two early African American female playwrights on Miller is obvious, especially in the case of Burrill. It was she who encouraged Miller to write her very first play, *Pandora's Box* (1914), which was published in the *School Progress* magazine (Perkins 750). Later influences would be Locke—aesthetician, professor, and philosophical midwife of the New Negro movement—and Archibald MacLeish—a European American poet whom Miller would meet in 1950.

Miller graduated from M Street in 1916, and went on to enroll at Howard, where she majored in drama. After being awarded a B.A. degree in 1920, she began teaching at Frederick Douglass High School in Baltimore, Maryland.

Krigwa theater groups, founded by Du Bois, were popular in the 1920s, and, Miller, while in Baltimore, joined one of the groups. Being a Krigwa player enabled her to direct, act, and nurture her creativity by mingling with individuals who shared her artistic and literary interests, for example, artists such as poet Frank Horne and playwright Randolph Edmonds. Both were members of the Krigwa group to which Miller belonged (Perkins 750).

Poet-playwright Georgia Douglas Johnson* played a very significant part in Miller's development as an artist. From Baltimore, where she was teaching school, Miller made a weekly commute to Johnson's home in Washington, DC, to attend Johnson's weekly gathering of black literatti. Miller's connection to Johnson's S Street Salon, as the gatherings were called, resulted in a lifelong friendship between the two women. When Johnson died in 1966, Miller was at her bedside.

In the summers when Miller was not teaching, she studied playwriting at Columbia University. One of her instructors was Frederick Koch. He pointed out to her that her talents were quite suited for the development of African American folk characters and culture. Miller responded to Koch's observation by writing a number of plays employing African American folk materials, one of the more interesting ones being *Riding the Goat*, written in 1929, which I will discuss in the next section.

Miller retired from the Baltimore Public School System in 1944. That same year she turned away from plays and toward writing poetry. She believed that her disconnection from the schools left her no built-in platform from which her plays could be performed. Also in 1944, Miller returned to Washington, DC, where she had been born, reared, and educated. She was accompanied by her husband of three years, John Sullivan, a principal (later an accountant), who was always supportive of his wife's work.

Miller's achievements as a poet are just as significant as are her achievements as a playwright. As soon as she settled in Washington, she joined a poetry workshop. In her own words, "This workshop which was located at New Hampshire and S allowed [me] the opportunity to meet the great creative space with other poets and artists" (qtd. in Perkins 751). Playwright Owen Dodson* was one of the frequent participants of the poetry workshop, as was African American artist Charles Sebree.

Just one short year after Miller stopped writing plays and began concentrating on poetry, she received major recognition in a national magazine. The *Antioch Review* printed "Tally," which addresses the persona's fear about human reproduction. The poem had been written shortly after the bombing of Hiroshima and Nagasaki (Stoelting 245). In 1950, *Antioch* carried a second poem, "Hierarchy." *Poetry*, in 1948, carried three poems: "Measurement," "Instant Before Sleep," and "Brief Negro Sermon" (Stoelting 245). The quick publication of these early poems attested to Miller's abilities as a poet.

Although Miller retired from public school teaching in 1944, she later taught at different colleges and universities. She was poet in residence at Monmouth College in 1963, at the University of Wisconsin in 1972, and at West Virginia State College–Bluefield in 1974. Miller read her poetry at the inaugural ceremonies of Walter Washington, the first African American mayor of Washington, DC, and President Jimmy Carter.

MAJOR WORKS AND THEMES

Many of May Miller's plays have at their center social and political issues. Others (those written primarily for children), however, are concerned with positive image building. Then there are some that are intended to educate viewers, or readers, through the dramatizations of the lives of historical figures.

Politics and history are at the heart of *Christophe's Daughters* (1935), a play that evolves from and revolves around a moment of political unrest in Haiti. Henry Christophe, a ruler of Haiti, is about to be captured, and two of his three daughters demonstrate unflagging loyalty to him. The third, however, wavers and declares that she hopes not to be captured. She, in other words, manifests a love of life and prefers not to sacrifice herself for political reasons.

Graven Images (1929), set in 1490 B.C. Hazeroth, Egypt, was written for eighth grade students to give them a more positive image of themselves. The plot was inspired by a verse from the Hebrew scriptures: "Miriam and Aaron spoke against Moses because of the Ethiopian woman he married" (Num. 12.1). In Miller's story, Eliezer is a son of Moses. Eliezer and his Ethiopian wife are not accepted by those around them because of their complexion. Eliezer interrupts a children's game involving idol worship, and convinces the youngsters that he too—although of a darker complexion—is a child of God.

Miller's historical plays, *Sojourner Truth* (1935) and *Harriet Tubman* (1935), explore the lives of Sojourner Truth and Harriet Tubman. Of the two, *Sojourner Truth* is more artistic and creative. In it, Truth, through her arresting words about God, prevents a group of white youths from setting fire to the tent shelters at a religious campsite.

Riding the Goat is an important play because of its emphasis on the black community's value of lodges, secret organizations, and the like. The expression "riding the goat" once described the initiation of members joining a lodge. In Miller's play, Ant Hetty, preparing to attend a parade of a Baltimore lodge, states that the lodge played a significant part in the funeral services of her deceased husband. Ant Hetty is proud of the "Turnout" by the members. A Turnout, still held by some African American lodges today, is the name given to a public ceremony by members wearing their regalia. So the finery worn by the lodge members (including plumes and swords) and the candle-ringed coffin—all employed in the Turnout—were quite meaningful to Ant Hetty.

The conflict of *Riding the Goat* is built around Dr. William Carter, the fiancé of Ant Hetty's granddaughter Ruth. William does not wholeheartedly support lodges and does not understand what they mean to the black community: pride, unity, social interaction, prestige. When he refuses to participate in the parade, though he has been elected the grand exalted ruler, Ruth dons the regalia of her future husband, and marches in the parade in his place. Ruth's decision to take her husband's place indicates that she understands just how important the lodge is to her family and the community. In reality, Ruth shares William's views, specifically, that lodges do not necessarily enhance the community. In short, both she and her husband believe that such organizations are a waste of time.

Miller's known plays number fifteen. The most recent one to be published is *Stragglers in the Dust*.

CRITICAL RECEPTION

May Miller was a very productive writer, yet her name is frequently omitted from anthologies and scholarly texts. This omission is disturbing, as Miller's most fruitful period coincided with one of the best-known creative moments in African American literary history: the New Negro movement. Although a few individuals have produced a few articles here and there, Miller deserves much more attention.

Two of the most helpful treatments of Miller appear in two different volumes of the *CLA Journal*, the most recent, authored by Ethyl A. Young-Minor, praises Miller for writing a play that teaches black history from a female perspective. In the second *CLA* article, Jeanne-Marie A. Miller identifies what she perceives as flaws in the plays of Johnson and Miller. Simplicity and brevity, the critic suggests, make Miller's plays thin and uncomplicated. Critic Miller does intimate, however, that Miller's plays are superior to Johnson's as far as range and craftsmanship are concerned.

Kathy Ann Perkins drew attention to Miller in 1989 with the publication of *Black Female Playwrights: An Anthology of Plays before 1950*. Perkins's collection contains two plays by Miller, one of which—*Stragglers in the Dust*—had not been previously published.

Miller won many literary contests and received many honors during her lifetime. For example, in 1925, *The Bog Guide* won third prize in the Urban League's *Opportunity* contest. In 1926, *The Cuss'd Thing* received honorable mention in the *Opportunity* contest. And in 1986, Miller was the recipient of the very prestigious Mister Brown Award, named for William Wells Brown* who was the manager of the African Company in New York from 1816 to 1923 (Perkins 751). The award was given in recognition of Miller's achievements in drama and poetry and was presented by the National Conference of African-American Theatre at Morgan State University in Baltimore.

While it is clear that Miller was a prolific and talented playwright firmly situated in the New Negro movement, she nevertheless remains a neglected and marginalized figure. Her contributions to the development of African American drama need to be more fully studied.

BIBLIOGRAPHY

Dramatic Works by May Miller

"*The Bog Guide*." 1925. "The Opportunity Dinner." *Opportunity* (3 June 1925): 176.

"*Christophe's Daughters*." 1935. *Negro History in Thirteen Plays*. Ed. Willis Richardson and May Miller. Washington, DC: Associated, 1935. 241–264. Also published in *Black Female Playwrights: An Anthology of Plays before 1950*. Ed. Kathy A. Perkins. Bloomington: Indiana University Press, 1989. 166–175.

The Cuss'd Thing. 1926. Unpublished.

Freedom's Children on the March. 1943. Unpublished.

"*Graven Images*." 1929. *Plays and Pageants from the Life of the Negro*. Ed. Willis Richardson. Washington, DC: Associated. 1930. 109–137. Also published in *Black Theatre U.S.A.: Forty-Five Plays by Black Americans: The Early Period*. Ed. James V. Hatch and Ted Shine. New York: Free, 1996. 334–341.

"*Harriet Tubman*." 1935. *Negro History in Thirteen Plays*. Ed. Willis Richardson and May Miller. Washington, DC: Associated, 1935. 265–288. Also published in *Black Female Playwrights: An Anthology of Plays before 1950*. Ed. Kathy A. Perkins. Bloomington: Indiana University Press, 1989. 176–185.

Moving Caravans. 193?. Unpublished.

"*Nails and Thorns*." 1933. *The Roots of African American Theatre*. Ed. Leo Hamalian and James V. Hatch. Detroit: Wayne State University Press, 1972. 310–327.

"*Pandora's Box*." 1914. *School Progress* 1.3 (1915): 10–13.

"*Riding the Goat*." 1929. *Plays and Pageants from the Life of the Negro*. Ed. Willis Richardson. Washington, DC: Associated, 1930. 141–176. Also published in *Black Female Playwrights: An Anthology of Plays before 1950*. Ed. Kathy A. Perkins. Bloomington: Indiana University Press, 1989. 153–165.

"*Samory*." 1935. *Negro History in Thirteen Plays*. Ed. Willis Richardson and May Miller. Washington, DC: Associated, 1935. 289–311.

"*Scratches*." 1929. *Carolina Magazine* 59 (Apr. 1929): 1–14.

"*Sojourner Truth*." 1935. *Negro History in Thirteen Plays*. Ed. Willis Richardson and May Miller. Washington, DC: Associated, 1935. 314–333.

"*Stragglers in the Dust*." 1930. *Black Female Playwrights: An Anthology of Plays before 1950*. Ed. Kathy A. Perkins. Bloomington: Indiana University Press, 1989. 145–152.

Within the Shadows. 1920. Unpublished.

Studies of May Miller's Dramatic Works

Miller, Jeanne-Marie A. "Georgia Douglas Johnson and May Miller: Forgotten Playwrights of the New Negro Renaissance." *CLA Journal* 33.4 (1990): 349–366.

Parry, Betty. "Interview with May Miller Sullivan." *Truthtellers of the Times: Interviews with Contemporary Women Poets*. Ed. Janet Mullany. Ann Arbor: University of Michigan Press, 1998. 86–102.

Perkins, Kathy A. "May Miller." *Notable Black American Women*. Ed. Jessie Carney Smith. Detroit: Gale, 1992. 749–751.

Stoelting, Winifred L. *Dictionary of Literary Biography*. Ed. Thadious M. Davis and Trudier Harris. Vol. 41. Detroit: Gale, 1986. 241–247.

Young-Minor, Ethyl A. "May Miller's Harriet Tubman." *CLA Journal* 46.1 (2002): 30–47.

RON MILNER
(1938–2004)

Freya M. Mercer

BIOGRAPHY

Ron Milner was born in Detroit, Michigan, and grew up in "The Valley"—a downtrodden yet diverse area of pimps, hustlers, winos, Muslims, and Christian African Americans, and the home of Aretha Franklin (Smitherman 4). Milner is often referred to as "the people's playwright," and was greatly influenced by the social and political conditions of his native Detroit. As written in *Black Literature Criticism*, "Milner decided to become a writer after realizing that people on Hastings Street had a story to tell" (Draper 1402). In an interview with David Richards of the *Washington Star-News*, Milner stated, "The more I read in high school, the more I realized that some tremendous, phenomenal things were happening around me. What happened in a Faulkner novel happened four times a day on Hastings Street. I thought why should these crazy people Faulkner writes about seem more important than my mother or my father or the dude down the street. Only because they had someone to write about them. So I became a writer" ("Ronald" par. 1). Toward that end, Milner attended Highland Park Junior College for a short time after graduating high school.

He won a John Hay Whitney Foundation Fellowship in 1962 to finish a novel, *Life with Father Brown*. In 1964, he joined Woodie King, Jr. in the Concept East Theater in Detroit. Although attending college did not last long, Milner began teaching. He jokes, "I've taught at college more than I've attended," in an interview with Betty DeRamus of the *Detroit Free Press* (qtd. in Draper

1402). In 1966, while teaching at Lincoln University, he met Langston Hughes,* who had a great influence on his writing: "Langston taught me about simplicity and how to reach the people you're talking to" (qtd. in Draper 1402). Milner won a Rockefeller Foundation grant and joined a writing workshop at Columbia University. His first play, *Who's Got His Own*, was published shortly thereafter. With *Who's Got His Own*, and a fairly rapid succession of other plays including *The Monster, The Warning: A Theme for Linda*, and *M(ego) and the Green Ball of Freedom*, Milner established himself as a popular playwright of the black theater movement with important productions staged in New York. He also became an established academic because of campus performances of his works, guest lecturing, and positions as writer in residence. His plays of this time focus on urban characters, the disintegration of the family, and the need for stronger community. Unlike many of his contemporaries, Milner wrote quieter dramas about family and community, rather than railing at the injustices of being black in America. Sometimes criticized as a "preacher" writing "morality plays," Milner felt it was important for his works "to educate as well as entertain" ("Ronald" par. 7). Though he was writing during the volatile 1960s, Milner's works move beyond angry accusations.

In the 1970s, Milner began to publish essays. He wrote about the need for black artists to cultivate a black audience and of the important influence jazz musicians could have on the writer. He returned to Detroit to create the community-based theater he called for in his essays. Milner became interested in the "Jackson Five generation," young people influenced by music and popular culture. He also became concerned about the influence of pimps, drugs, sex, and money on these young people. He says of these youth, "They'd bought a system of values that says anything you do to get a car or money or clothes is all right" (Cunningham 203). *What the Wine-Sellers Buy*, produced in 1973, reflects this concern.

The 1980s marked a shift in Milner's writing. He began to write about the black middle class. Milner said about this change in his work:

For a long time, black writers dwelled on our negative history. They could never see any real victory. For them, the only victory lay in the ability to endure defeat. I was consciously trying to break that. I function a great deal on what I intuitively feel are the needs of the time. And the needs of the time are for the positive. ("Ronald" par. 3)

Ron Milner died on July 9, 2004 from complications of liver cancer.

MAJOR WORKS AND THEMES

It is obvious that Ron Milner has been greatly influenced by the world around him, particularly the disintegration of family and community. According to Amiri Baraka,* "Milner's work is characterized by its attention to

Afro-American social and psychological culture" (7). He writes about real people in real situations, paying close attention to the details of life. In *Who's Got His Own*, Milner portrays the troubled relationships of a mother, son, and daughter after the death of a domineering father. His most commercially successful play, *What the Wine-Sellers Buy*, focuses on pimp culture and the consequences of easy money on inner-city youth. *The Warning: A Theme for Linda* examines black manhood in the context of women's experiences. In *Checkmates*, Milner compares a retired African American couple with a young, upwardly mobile African American couple to show the intergenerational shift in values. One of his most recent plays, *Urban Transition: Loose Blossoms*, revisits the consequences of drugs and money on the family.

In *Who's Got His Own*, a title taken from the Billie Holiday tune, Milner studies the relationships of the Bronson family after the father's death and the impact of racism on black men. He uses the form of jazz to tell the story. Milner explains, "I just used the straight out old basic jazz form: an ensemble work, where someone steps down front and takes a solo; an ensemble, another solo. . . . And so on. I saw each of the characters as a particular musical instrument" (qtd. in King 12). No single character's story line can move ahead without support from the other characters. Each has his or her turn in the spotlight—pouring their souls into their solos, revealing the ugliness of human nature and the catharsis of sharing deep secrets.

Tim, Jr. and Clara have to come to terms with the tyrannical man who was their father, in light of their mother's revelations about him and their relationship. The tyrant who ruled the house with shouts and a belt is the same man Tim, Jr. saw hunched and defeated, cleaning white men's toilets. Tim cannot respect him because he never stood up for himself, because he let his boss treat him like dirt, yet he could beat and abuse them. He says, "Why couldn't he leave me one thing! One thing to remember and respect! Respect! Respect!—All this time that's all I've been lookin' for. Just one thing I could—just—that's all!" (138). Tim does not understand how his father struggled in his relationship with whites to keep from attacking a white man, or that it was Tim, Jr.'s legacy to resent white men, until his mother reveals a piece of his father's history. Tim, Sr. saw his own father beaten and killed by white men, then hanged and burned. Mrs. Bronson says of the incident, "Oh, yes, they had to do it all to him, everything they could think of. Out there in the yard, hollerin' and laughin' like—like devils in a dream. Lord, he was eight years old. Only eight years old!" (142). In addition to witnessing the brutal murder, Tim, Sr. lived in the same town and had to do business with those men. Mrs. Bronson says, "That's what broke him, Tim, Jr.! . . . Well, he was just a baby, but ever since then he couldn't stand to look at no white faces" (142). The hatred and racial tension predates Tim's attack on his white friend, Al; Clara's impregnation by a white man and subsequent abortion; and Tim, Sr.'s thankless job with insensitive, abusive bosses. Racism has destroyed the Bronson family. By trying to help her husband control his rage toward white men, Mrs. Bronson allowed him to beat and attack her, nearly killing her on a number of occasions. He beat his children, leaving a legacy of hatred and resentment. Milner examines what it means to be a black man in a racist society. The emasculation and rage at being subjugated by white men led Tim, Sr. to find an outlet for his anger—his family. The play ends with both children gaining an understanding of their father, mother, and society, and looking toward a future different from their past.

What the Wine-Sellers Buy is Milner's most autobiographical work. Influenced by the mean streets of Detroit, Milner writes a morality play about the influence of easy money on urban youth. It is the story of the temptation of a young man, Steve Carlton, to pimp his girlfriend, Mae, to support himself and his mother. The importance of money is clear from the play's opening. Steve says, "Sex and money! Gotta get 'em!" (197). In this didactic work, Milner juxtaposes the influence of the hustler, Rico, with characters representing morality, such as Mrs. Carlton, Mae, and Jim. Immediately after Rico tries poisoning Steve's mind, Mrs. Carlton launches into a diatribe against Steve's father:

Want it fast. Right now. Wait is a bad word. And work—work is for—for slaves! And fools. And—mule!—Uh-huh. Not me, Laura. They ain't gone run that trick on me. Workin' me till I'm bent over, never payin' me enough to get straightened-up, so I can be somethin'. Get somethin' for me. Naw, not me. 'Uh-huh. Naw, not for him. Not yo' daddy. He was goin' to outslick 'em. Just run up and snatch things from 'em. Take it. Uh-huh. I told him over and over. Just like I try to tell you. You have to be patient, work, an' plan. But, naw, not him. He had to try to thieve from the thieves. Outdog the dogs! (202)

Rico's influence is tempered by the influence of upright, respectable people. Steve has to choose between the illusion of easy money at the price of his girlfriend, and doing what is right, working hard for a living. As Addison Gayle writes, "The decision is ultimately a moral one with import for the entire Black community" (Gayle and Xavier 95). Mrs. Carlton and Jim become convinced Steve listens to Rico because he is a hustler, like Steve's dad. She tells Steve about the time his father was in jail and she was going to sleep with a lawyer to help him get out. His father wouldn't let her. Her story does affect him—he begins second-guessing the plan to earn money through Mae. In the end, Steve makes the right decision. He says to Mae, "If I sell you, what I'm gon' buy, baby, huh? . . . If I sell you what am I gonna buy?" (253). Milner digs deep into the foundations of hustling. Steve says, "See, to try to get in their game, Rico had to trade everything for money" (253). Steve's not ready to make that trade. He says that "it cost too much" to make easy money (253). Addison Gayle summarizes Milner's reasons for writing this play: "Like other contemporary Black playwrights, he has declared war on the twin evils which beset segments of the Black community, hedonism and sensationalism" (Gayle and Xavier 97). Though the play has been criticized for being too simplistically moralistic, it is a lesson Milner felt was needed at the time.

In *Urban Transition: Loose Blossoms*, Milner once again writes about the influence of easy money on youth. However, in this play the tempted young man, E.J., lives in a nice home in a middle-class neighborhood. As Anita Gates writes, "Whenever a drama's first scene depicts happy people celebrating and expressing affection, you can bet something bad is going to happen to them soon" (D3). The perfect middle-class household starts to crumble when Earl Carter, the father, injures his back. Earl cannot go back to his old job and refuses to be retrained on the computer. It is obvious he has made a living by working hard, and he's proud of it. The family starts to have money problems. E.J.'s fall into the hustler lifestyle is not nearly as dramatic as Steve's in *What the Wine-Sellers Buy*; there is no devil leading him astray. In fact, it is his idea to start doing work for Big John. When he gives his mother, Cheryl, some much-needed money, she becomes angry that he is hustling. She urges him to stop hustling but takes his money anyway. E.J. is triumphant: he feels that he has succeeded in establishing the legitimacy of his activities, at least partially, in his mother's eyes. Earl begins to suspect E.J. is hustling, but Cheryl and Gail, his sister, have become involved, knowing where the money is coming from, and conceal the truth from him. Soon they become used to the easy money and the things that come with it—furs, cars, designer clothes. Earl and Cheryl finally have a confrontation about E.J. dealing drugs when he notices a new mink coat. Earl says, "If it takes drug money to keep this house up . . . let the sonofabitch fall!" (130). Earl then confronts E.J. Practically crying, E.J. tells Earl that he had to do something, that he couldn't watch his family fall apart. E.J. asks, "What you want me to do?" (131). Earl replies, "Work! Like we did. Fight the bullshit, and make yo' way out!" (131). E.J. is moved by his father, but cannot see himself returning to the life of a child, relying on his father for money. Making easy money through drugs has killed E.J.'s ability to *consider* working, let alone to work for minimum wage flipping burgers. But Big John asks too much—he wants E.J. and his friend Eric to kill some other hustlers as a test of their loyalty. E.J. doesn't want to do it, and Eric shoots him. E.J. kills Eric and then dies. On the day of the funeral, Earl laments his blindness. He was as blinded by the money as E.J., Gail, and Cheryl were, so much so that he could not even admit to himself where it was coming from. Milner offers a moral similar to that in *What the Wine-Sellers Buy* in *Urban Transition* but with much more dire consequences. Whereas in *Wine-Sellers* the family remains intact and the child led astray does what is right, in *Urban Transition* a child and a family are destroyed because of the lure of easy money.

In *Checkmates*, Milner shifts his focus from inner-city working-class characters to middle-class characters. He shows the generation gap between an older couple who had no breaks, no education, and had to work hard to achieve middle-class status and a younger couple who grew up in a different world with opportunities. Lawrence Van Gelder explains that the Coopers:

[r]epresent black couples forged in the South of the Great Depression who migrated north, tasted prosperity and even equality in World War II, before struggling all over again to achieve financial security and a measure of tranquility in their lives and marriage. (Rev. of *Checkmates* C8)

The Williamses, on the other hand, "represent a generation reared in a world of expanded opportunities but grappling with new definitions of women's roles, redefined expectations of marriage and male insecurities at home and at work" (Van Gelder, Rev. of *Checkmates* C8).

Frank Cooper is portrayed as a bitter man, resentful of the opportunities and advantages the younger generation has had. He says of Syl Williams:

Him, lookin' down at me with his chest puffed out. Shoot, I'd a had the chances they got, I wouldn'a been workin' in no factory or office either. Woulda' owned factories and offices. Shoot, I mean, I woulda' had me something. You know how I was, Mattie: Quick and smart and handy. All them good ideas I had. Just couldn't get far enough ahead to work on 'em all. One thing's sure, I woulda' ended up with more than a construction company and two-three little piecea' houses." (44)

His wife tempers his bitterness, reminding him of all the good that has come from their marriage. Mattie is a "stand-by-your-man" woman, forgiving an affair, anger, and abuse.

Opportunity does not necessarily make things easier for the younger couple. They have the same struggles—maybe harder ones. Frank and Mattie have worked side by side raising four children and establishing themselves. Syl and Laura seem to be in competition over who can make the most money. Because they have money, they need to make more. But promotions and raises put a strain on Laura's and Syl's relationship. Laura decides to have an abortion without telling Syl she's pregnant because it is the wrong time for them to have a baby. She is trying to establish herself as a designer, and Syl is wrapped up in his work. He wants the traditional husband role—controlling and catered to—but cannot have it with the very modern Laura. Their relationship is not as strong as Frank's and Mattie's because they do not have a common struggle to build a life together. They could just as easily have comfortable lives on their own. In the end, that is what they choose to do.

Checkmates is a weak play that does not seem to have meaning beyond showing the difference between "old folks" and "young folks," which is not really all that different. It lacks the rich detail of Milner's urban settings—

there are no hustlers, pimps, or preachers to add color and character. There are no great psychological revelations beyond Syl's and Frank's insecurities about their manhood. There is not even a moral here, as in *What the Wine-Sellers Buy* and *Urban Transition*. There are some light moments, and some tough moments, but very few meaningful moments.

CRITICAL RECEPTION

Ron Milner is an important African American playwright who has been largely overlooked by critics. Amiri Baraka states, "Milner has never been accorded the acclaim that the quality and consistency of his work should command" (7). He suggests that it is precisely because of the quality and consistency of his work that Milner has been ignored by critics (7). In truth, Milner has not been ignored by critics—he has been lambasted in print. His prose has been found lacking, his attempts at edification discredited, his story lines deemed pointless. For every good review of his early plays, there are three or four poor ones. Positive critical reception is a new development for Milner. While almost every recent review mentions Milner's "best known for" plays, *What the Wine-Sellers Buy* and *Checkmates*, one might not realize that these two popular plays were panned by many critics.

In a *New York Times* review of a 1966 production of *Who's Got His Own*, Walter Kerr finds little merit in the play:

He would like to use the stage as though it were really a bear pit, with a point at the center where all angers must cross. He would like to make his play out of words, a hundred thousand harsh words and no window dressing. And he would like us to see his victims gored to death in full view, harried and helpless and beyond hope. (B9)

Kerr complains about the staging, which makes some dialogue hard to hear, but concedes that Milner may actually be trying to "make us listen." He feels Milner spends too much time dwelling on the past—never the future. Kerr also laments the unpoetic quality of the language, though he never explains why prose must be poetic.

On the other hand, Larry Neal, in an essay in *Drama Review* in 1968, writes, "Ron Milner's *Who's Got His Own* is of particular importance. It strips bare the clashing attitudes of a contemporary Afro-American family" (qtd. in Draper 1403). Despite the racism and abuse that fills the dialogue, Neal sees Milner as a writer whose "main thrust is directed toward unifying the family around basic moral principles, toward bridging the 'generation gap'" (qtd. Draper 1404). He sees *Who's Got His Own* as a positive piece that reveals and heals.

What the Wine-Sellers Buy has also received mixed reviews. In Milner's most popular and successful play, many critics had expected more. Walter

Kerr once again finds little to recommend Milner's work. He refers to the play as "Our Lesson for Today," comparing it to "street plays—exceedingly simple moralities in which Virtue and Vice contend for the souls of ghetto youngsters." He finds *What the Wine-Sellers Buy* to be no better than an after-school special admonishing kids to "stay clean." His chosen quotes do seem to illustrate this point. However, he concedes that Milner's writing of the character Mae, the girl who is almost led astray by her boyfriend, does not always follow the form of morality plays. After identifying the two scenes he feels do not follow form, he writes, "As Mr. Milner goes on with his work, he will do well to let impulse interrupt him oftener, let people speak for themselves instead of steadily saluting the evening's cause" (B9).

Nicholas Xavier does not understand all the fuss about this play, either:

The mission of art is to raise the level of political consciousness of the broad masses of the people to struggle against their oppression. Our artists, therefore, must project a vision of what the broad masses of the people must struggle *for*. . . . Is the question simply "to be or not to be a pimp"—which is the decision that Steve, a Black youth, has to make in the play? (Gayle and Xavier 95).

He complains that there is no universal question, nothing to struggle for. "The play, in short, does not rise to a vision of human grandeur—it does not unfold the creative capacities of man to move mountains" (95).

In contrast, Addison Gayle finds *Wine-Sellers* to be "Black domestic drama at its best" (Gayel and Xavier 95). He does not mind the moral lessons. In fact, Gayle thinks they are essential to the survival of the black community: "To choose intelligence over ignorance, perseverance over hustling, reality over illusion, is, finally, to choose life over death" (95). Gayle sums up his views of the play: "It is a total experience" (97).

The reviews of *Checkmates* are equally lackluster, despite Don Shirley's view that it "could thrust [Milner] into the role of the theater's primary chronicler of contemporary black middle class" (qtd. in "Ronald" par. 5). It is considered a crossover play—"his first effort to cross the line between black theater and theater whose players happen to be black" (Waltington B1). Frank Rich compares the play to *All in the Family* and *Three's Company*, bringing to mind images of cheap comedy in the juxtaposition of the staid, older Coopers and the upwardly mobile, young Williamses. He argues that the couples' race adds little to the story. Howard Kissell agrees, writing, "If *Checkmates*, a play about two black couples, one elderly and nostalgic, the other young and aggressive, were about whites, it probably wouldn't have been done" (qtd. in Draper 1408). Critics argue that there is a lack of movement in the story line: "The play's tedium, however, derives not so much from its bland content as from its lack of dramatic propulsion," writes Frank Rich. The best review, by Lawrence Van Gelder, calls the work "a modest, serviceable vehicle" (Rev. of *Checkmates* C8). However, he goes on to say

Checkmates "runs far too long, and its willingness to resort to irresolution in one of its conflicts condemns it to the realm of facile entertainments" (C8). Kissel ends his review:

Checkmates reflects an almost cynical economic awareness of a new black audience eager to come to Broadway. It has been shrewdly cast, handsomely mounted and well-directed. If only this effort had been expended on a real play." (qtd. in Draper 1408)

Jazz-set fares no better. Frank Rich writes, "*Jazz-set* looks like a play that has been rethought so many times that the author finally forgot what he was thinking about in the first place. It's full of half-baked ideas, blurry characters and fractured narrative lines that lead nowhere" (Rev. of *Jazz-set* B12). He finds the jazz foundation of the work to be sloppy, and the idea of "music is what's important" to be trite in light of the terrible experiences the characters reveal throughout the play: "The play gets better as it goes along only because each act—or "set"—is briefer than the one before" (B12).

Milner's more recent works have received better reviews. In his review of *Defending the Light*, Van Gelder states, "Potent history doesn't always make compelling drama, but in the case of *Defending the Light* the blood of the drama runs hot with issues and lessons that resonate across the decades of American life since the horrific events of the night of March 12, 1846." He finds the play "thought-provoking" and "interesting" (Rev. of *Defending* E2) Anita Gates finds *Urban Transition: Loose Blossoms* thought-provoking as well. She writes positively in her brief review about "Ron Milner's intelligent, incisive and all too believable new play about a black family in crisis" (D3).

Amiri Baraka writes of Milner, "His focus has been on the struggles and desires of the Black working class and the lower middle class, 'the people,' and out of these lives Milner has constructed a continuum of social and critical realist works, rooted in the dynamic heartbeat of Black life" (8). He blames Milner's lack of critical acclaim on the "narrow racist obloquy of bourgeois theater" (8).

BIBLIOGRAPHY

Dramatic Works by Ron Milner

"*Checkmates.*" 1987. *What the Wine-Sellers Buy Plus Three*. Detroit: Wayne State University Press, 2001. 22–74.
Crack Steppin'. 1981. Performed at Detroit Music Hall, Detroit.
Defending the Light. 2000. Performed at Performing Arts Center, New York.
Don't Get God Started. 1987. Performed at Longacre Theatre, New York.

Jazz-set. 1980. *What the Wine-Sellers Buy Plus Three*. Detroit: Wayne State University Press, 2001. 140–192.

"*M(ego) and the Green Ball of Freedom*." *Black World* 20 (1971): 40–45.

"*The Monster*." *Drama Review* 12 (Summer 1968): 94–105.

Season's Reasons: Just a Natural Change. 1976. Performed at Langston Hughes Theater, Detroit.

These Three. 1974. Performed at Concept East Theater, Detroit.

"*Urban Transition: Loose Blossoms*." 2002. *What the Wine-Sellers Buy Plus Three*. Detroit: Wayne State University Press, 2001. 76–137.

"*The Warning: A Theme for Linda*." 1969. *A Black Quartet*. Ed. Ron Milner, Amiri Baraka, Ed Bullins, and Ben Caldwell. New York: New American Library, 1970. 37–114.

"*What the Wine-Sellers Buy*." 1973. *What the Wine-Sellers Buy Plus Three*. Detroit: Wayne State University Press, 2001. 194–245.

"*Who's Got His Own*" 1966. *Black Drama Anthology*. Ed. Woodie King, Jr. and Ron Milner. New York: Signet, 1971. 89–145.

Work. 1978. Performed at Detroit Public Schools, Detroit.

Studies of Ron Milner's Dramatic Works

Anderson, Gary. "Ron Milner: Overview." *Comtemporary Dramatists*. Ed. K. A. Bernery. 5thed. Detroit: St. James, 1993. Literature Resource Center. Cortland College Library, Cortland, New York. 10 Apr. 2003. <http://libproxy.cortland.edu:2154/servlet/LitRC?c=1&ai=161089&ste=12&bConts=10927&tab=2&vrsn=3&ca=1&tbst=arp&ST=Ron+Milner&srchtp=athr&n=10&locID=sunycort_main&OP=contains>.

Baraka, Amiri. Foreword. "Ron Milner: The Artist as Cultural Worker." *What the Wine-Sellers Buy Plus Three*. By Ron Milner. Detroit: Wayne State University Press, 2001. 7–9.

Cunningham, Beunyce R. "Ron Milner." *Afro-American Writers after 1955: Dramatists and Prose Writers*. Vol. 28 of *Dictionary of Literary Biography*. Ed. Thadious M. Davis. Detroit: Gale, 1985. 201–207.

Draper, James, ed. "Ron Milner." *Black Literature Criticism*. Detroit: Gale, 1992. 1402–1409.

Gates, Anita. Rev. of *Urban Transition*, by Ron Milner. *New York Times* 22 Apr. 2002: D3.

Gayle, Addison, Jr., and Xavier Nicholas. "Two Views of 'Winesellers.'" *Black World* 25 (Apr. 1976): 95–97.

Kerr, Walter. Rev. of *What the Wine-Sellers Buy*, by Ron Milner. *New York Times* 24 Feb. 1974: B9.

———. Rev. of "Who's Got His Own." *New York Times* 13 Oct. 1966: C5.

King, Woodie, Jr. "No Identity Crisis: An Introduction to the Plays of Ron Milner." *What the Wine-Sellers Buy Plus Three*, by Ron Milner. Detroit: Wayne State University Press, 2001. 11–19.

Rich, Frank. Rev. of *Checkmates*, by Ron Milner. *New York Times* 5 Aug. 1988: C3.

———. Rev. of *Jazz-set*, by Ron Milner. *New York Times* 21 July 1982: Lexis-Nexis: B12.

"Ronald Milner." *Contemporary Authors Online*. Detroit: Gale, 2003: 8 pars. Litera-
    ture Resource Center. Cortland College Library, Cortland, New York. 10
    Apr. 2003.<http://libproxy.cortland.edu:2154/servlet/LitRC?c=1&ai=161089&s
    te=6&docNum=H1000069017&bConts=10927&tab=1&vrsn=3&ca=1&tbst=
    arp&ST=Ron+Milner&srchtp=athr&n=10&locID=sunycort_main&OP=
    contains>.
Smitherman, Geneva. "Ron Milner: People's Playwright." *Black World* 25 (Apr. 1976):
    4–19.
Van Gelder, Lawrence. Rev. of *Checkmates*, by Ron Milnder. *New York Times* 23 Apr.
    1996: C8.
———. Rev. of *Defending the Light*, by Ron Milner. *New York Times* 3 Mar. 2000: E2.
Waltington, Dennis. Rev. of *Checkmates*, by Ron Milner. *New York Times* 31 July
    1988: B10.

LOFTEN MITCHELL
(1919–2001)

Harish Chander

BIOGRAPHY

Loften Mitchell, African American playwright and theater historian, was born on April 15, 1919, in the small town of Columbus, North Carolina, the oldest son of Ulysses Sanford Mitchell and Willia Spaulding Mitchell. As Loften Mitchell relates in the introduction to his book *Black Drama: The Story of the American Negro in the Theatre* (1967), before he was one month old, his parents "left their rural North Carolina homeland to build a new life in the cold North" (5). His father was a maintenance man, and his mother was the manager of an apartment complex owned by whites. As he recalls in his essay, "Harlem My Harlem," his father was also "a master story-teller, who could spin "one yarn after another" (*Black Drama* 91). Mitchell had four siblings: three brothers—Melvin, Louis, and Clayton—and one sister, Gladys. In his novel, *The Old Stubborn Lady Who Resisted Change*, Mitchell writes about his parents' home at 28 West 131st Street, Harlem, remembering the sycamore tree in their yard, and the Mitchell children making wagons from baby carriage wheels and discarded boxes. In the novel, the unnamed narrator's mother seems to be speaking for Mitchell when she observes that like his father the narrator enjoys Harlem life, and considers the streets of Harlem "his own private social parlor" (20).

Mitchell's parents did not tolerate insults and humiliation from whites. He observes that his father did not "shuffle" before whites, nor did his mother "bow and bend" to them. His father punched a white school-teacher for mistreating his brother, and he ran after a car "to catch a white driver who had yelled insulting remarks at my mother" (*Black Drama* 2). Cast in the same mold, the Mitchell children retaliated when white gangs attacked them. Significantly, the dedication of Mitchell's *Voices of the Black Theatre* reads: "To the memory of my mother and my father" (v). In the essay "Harlem Reconsidered—Memories of My Native Land," in *Black Drama*, Mitchell remembers that white children told black children, "This country belongs to us more'n it does to youse" (468). To this remark, the black children retorted, "Our folks built this country and we gonna live in it, else you gonna die in it" (469).

Mitchell first attended Public School 68, which was popular with wealthy white families of Harlem. White children at this school, and later at Public Schools 89, 157, and 24, were hostile to Mitchell. In 1930, he was transferred to Cooper Junior High, but there faced a few racist teachers. A biology teacher ridiculed black speech, and another teacher directed a play that glorified the Confederacy (470–471). He attended DeWitt Clinton High School in the Bronx, graduating with honors in 1937.

As a child, Mitchell developed an interest in the theater when he attended vaudeville theaters in Harlem. He identified with the performances by black artists. As he observes in the introduction to *Black Drama*: "I saw in the theatre the elevation of human life and [projection of] the hopes, the aspirations of . . . the people I knew" (2). With the onset of the Depression in 1929, he found it hard to come by dimes to indulge his love for theatrical entertainment. He then started to sell newspapers, and made his "best sales backstage at Harlem theatres" (1).

In this way, he met famous artists and performers such as Ethel Waters, Fredi Washington, Dick Campbell, Muriel Rahn, Ralph Cooper, Eddie Green, Eddie Hunter, Johnny Hudgins, George Wiltshire, and Canada Lee. In *Voices of the Black Theatre* (1975), Mitchell calls Dick Campbell "a father figure," who taught him "what the theatre was all about" (89). Observing his enthusiasm for drama, Dick Campbell and others encouraged him to go into the theater. He started writing scripts for backyard shows, and later, as a high school student, he wrote dramatic sketches. His antiwar play *Shattered Dreams* was produced by the Pioneer Drama Group in 1938.

After his graduation from high school, Mitchell worked as an actor with the Rose McClendon Players in Harlem, while attending the City College of New York (now the City University of New York). As Mitchell reveals in his introduction to *Black Drama*, he "worked as an actor—between dishwashing, delivering lunch orders and standing in relief lines" (4). However, in 1939, an adverse critical verdict on his performance as Angel in Dennis Donohue's *The Black Messiah* had a negative impact on his enthusiasm for acting as a career (4). He decided to quit acting for some time, to undergo self-introspection and to concentrate on writing,

As Mitchell relates in the aforementioned introduction, through the influence of Andrew M. Burris, a youth club leader, he received a scholarship to study at Talladega College in Alabama. One September day, he packed his duffel bag and took the bus for the South on his first trip out of New York. In Richmond, Virginia, the bus stopped, and Mitchell was shocked as he saw for the first time signs separating "Colored" and "White" at the bus station.

At Talladega College, Mitchell's term paper for his freshman English class later became the basis of his book *Black Drama* (1967). In 1943, Mitchell graduated with honors, having majored in sociology, with a minor in creative writing. His father died that same year. Mitchell married actress Helen Marsh in 1948, and they had two sons—Thomas and Melvin. They were divorced in 1956, and Mitchell married Gloria Anderson in 1992.

During World War II, Mitchell served in the United States Navy as a seaman second class for two years. After the war, he began to write plays in earnest, enrolling in the graduate program in playwriting at Columbia University in 1947, where he studied playwriting with the famous drama critic John Gassner. One of his commercially successful plays, *Blood in the Night* (1946), was written during this period, In 1948, he accepted a job as a social investigator with the U.S. Department of Welfare, and continued his studies at Columbia University by attending evening classes. His experience as a social investigator later led to his heavily autobiographical novel titled *The Stubborn Old Lady who Resisted Change* (1973). As he states in *Black Drama*, from 1953 to 1958, he worked with the artist Romare Bearden in "administering public assistance grants to all people of Gypsy origin in the City of New York" (226). In *Stubborn Old Lady*, he tells the story of an old lady, Madeline Briggs, who lived in a very old ramshackle Harlem apartment but did not want to move out because of the associations it had with her gypsy lover, who had died a few days before their wedding. date. The year 1948 saw the production of Mitchell's *The Bancroft Dynasty*, which concerns an upper-middle-class Harlem family's struggle to resist the changing times. Mitchell received his master's degree from Columbia University in 1951. For his master's thesis, he wrote a history of the groups that had attempted to build a permanent art theater.

From 1950 onward, Mitchell wrote a number of plays. These include *The Cellar* (produced in 1952), *A Land Beyond the River* (produced in 1957), *The Phonograph* (produced in 1961), *Star of the Morning: Scenes in the Life of Bert Williams* (produced in 1965), *Tell Pharaoh* (produced in 1967), *The Final Solution to the Black Problem in the United States; Or, The Fall of the American Empire* (produced in 1970), *Sojourn to the South of the Wall* (produced in 1973), *Bubbling Brown Sugar* (produced in 1975), *Cartoons for a Lunch Hour* (produced in 1978), *A Gypsy Girl* (produced in 1982), and *Miss Waters, To You* (produced in 1983).

The Cellar was Mitchell's first commercially successful dramatic creation; it was presented by The Harlem Showcase, and ran from November

1952 to April 1953. It tells the story of a black blues singer who befriends a fugitive from southern justice, and her fiancé who hounds the fugitive. His civil rights era drama, *A Land Beyond the River*, presents the real-life struggle of the Rev. Joseph DeLaine to desegregate public schools in Clarendon County, South Carolina. This play turned out to be his most successful production, as it ran for nintey-six performances Off Broadway at the Greenwich Mews Theater. This play also led to his winning, in 1958, a Guggenheim Award for Drama. In his play *Star of the Morning* (1965), he recounts the trials and tribulations of the comedian Bert Williams during the years 1895 to 1910. *Tell the Pharaoh* is a concert drama depicting through spirituals the history of blacks in the United States. *Bubbling Brown Sugar* is a collage of black music and dance that celebrates over twenty-five years of Harlem life and nightlife. A 1970s couple is given a nostalgic tour of Harlem of yesteryear, from the early 1920s to the 1940s. This work was nominated for a Tony Award in 1976, and received London's Best Musical of the Year Award in 1977.

Apart from his creative writings, Mitchell wrote two books on the contributions of black theater artists: *Black Drama: The Story of the American Negro in the Theatre* (1967) and *Voices of the Black Theatre* (1975). With spicy humor and anecdotal narrative style, Mitchell surveys in *Black Drama* the history of black theater in the United States. "Theatre in America was," Mitchell observes, "virtually nonexistent until the middle of the eighteenth century" (14). Also, we learn that "[t]he Negro as subject matter was introduced to the American theatre in 1769," with Mungo, a West Indian clown in Isaac Bickerstaffe's comedy *The Padlock* (16). Mitchell reports that William Wells Brown's* *The Escape; Or, a Leap for Freedom* (1858) is "the first known play" by an African American. (34). Because the dominant white society rigidly circumscribed the roles of black people, blacks could traditionally only play stereotypical roles as comic buffoons, wretched freemen, tragic mulattos, and criminals. *Black Drama* recounts the black theater artists' struggle to avoid such a negative, demeaning portraiture, and their earnest efforts to be shown as they really are. The book dramatically recounts the history of black theatrical groups and the dramatic artists Mitchell personally knew.

Voices of the Black Theatre highlights the contributions of black actors, writers, directors, and producers to the American theater from the 1900s to the 1970s. Relying on taped interviews of seven dramatic artists—Eddie Hunter, Regina Andrews, Dick Campbell, Abram Hill, Frederick O'Neal, Vinnette Carroll,* and Ruby Dee—the volume brings together black theatrical pioneers so they can "tell their stories in their own words" (13). These artists recount how they became interested in the theater, who encouraged them, the social condition under which they worked, and the major issues dealt with in their plays. Dick Campbell, for example, tells the story of the beginning of the Negro People's Theatre in the 1930s, which he helped organize with the support of Rose

McClendon, and how when that theater folded, he founded the Rose McClendon Players, which was in existence until 1941. Campbell says that he did not object to staying Off Broadway because Broadway placed blacks in stereotypical roles, not permitting them to show their authentic selves. Ruby Dee recounts the difficulty she faced in being accepted as an actress, and observes that all black artists were perceived as having communist leanings in the McCarthy era. She is happy to observe that in the 1950s and 1960s, black playwrights began to deal with the "total humanity" of black people "telling the rest of the world: 'If you don't like it, you can lump it!'" (221).

Mitchell's other career highlights include actor, stage manager, and press agent of People's Theatre and Harlem Showcase, New York City, (1946–1952); writer of the NYCY-Radio weekly program *The Later Years* (1950–1962); writer of *Friendly Adviser* daily program (1954); adjunct professor of English, Long Island University (1969) and New York University (1970); professor, Department of Theater and Department of Afro-American Studies, State University of New York at Binghamton (1971–1985); and professor emeritus at State University of New York at Binghamton (1985–2001).

In addition to a 1958–1959 Guggenheim Fellowship Award, Mitchell received a Rockefeller Foundation grant for studying Broadway musical theater in 1961; the Harlem Cultural Special Award in 1969; the Special Award from the Church of Our Savior, Yonkers, New York, in 1972; and the Playwriting Award from the Research Foundation, State University of New York in 1974. In 1979, he was honored with the Outstanding Theatrical Pioneer Award from the Audience Development Committee (AUDELCO). In 1993, he was honored by the National Black Theater Festival in Raleigh-Durham, North Carolina, as a Living Legend of the Black Theater.

Loften Mitchell died on May 14, 2001, in St. Joseph's Hospital in Queens, New York, after a protracted illness. His papers are preserved at the State University of New York at Binghamton, the Schomburg Center for Research in Black Culture in New York, Talladega College in Alabama, and Boston University.

MAJOR WORKS AND THEMES

In his 1959 essay "The Negro Writer and His Materials," Loften Mitchell points out that white writers have portrayed blacks as inferior beings to keep them "in place." This denigration of blacks continued past the end of slavery. However, in the midst of World War I, some white writers like Ridgely Torrence and Eugene O'Neill began to write about blacks as central figures, but they "touched on a part of the truth but never on a whole truth" (285). It was therefore left to black writers to present their perspectives; however, they were hamstrung by the dominant society dictating "certain terms to the negro writer." These terms included showing at all times the need for "Negro–white unity," and having at least one "good" white person who "helped the Negro solve his problem" (285). It is, therefore, incumbent on the black writers to tell the whole truth as they see it. In his February 1965 *Crisis* essay, "Alligators in the Swamp," Mitchell declares that "the artist must seek the truth, communicate, educate and entertain" (85).

True to his own dictum, Mitchell presents the black experience without theatrical distortions to please white sensibilities. Bert Williams in *Star of the Morning* speaks for Mitchell, observing, "We're going . . . to do real theater, not *the typical colored show* they expect from us" (612; emphasis added). Broadly speaking, his themes fall into two categories: black protest against white racism, and truthful presentation of black history and heritage. Of Mitchell's published dramatic works, *A Land Beyond the River*, *Star of the Morning*, *Tell the Pharaoh*, and *Bubbling Brown Sugar* are the most important.

A Land Beyond the River is a plea for the equal education of all children regardless of race. It recounts the historic struggle of Rev. Joseph A. DeLaine on behalf of his parishioners' children for equal schools in Clarendon County, South Carolina. By 1950, with the support of the NAACP, Rev. De-Laine helped file the *Briggs v. Elliot* school desegregation lawsuit, which was combined with four other cases under *Brown v. Board of Education*, and decided in May 1954. In 1955, unknown assailants shot at the DeLaine home. Because DeLaine returned fire, he was charged with assault and battery with intent to kill, but he left South Carolina for New York. Well after his death in 1974, he was cleared of all charges (Chaney A3).

As the play opens, the audience's attention is drawn to the deplorable condition of the school building, with its floor caving in. Rev. Layne and community members Bill Raigen and Duff Waters begin to fix the floor, but are forced to yield because the wood is rotten beyond repair. Blacks live in a hostile environment, with whites intimidating blacks through threatening phone calls and letters, and by shooting at black homes. White employers force their employees to boycott black businesses. Duff reports that whole-sale merchants will not sell him goods for his store fearing a backlash from other whites (357). White ruffians severely beat the black child, Glenn Raigen, for his refusal to admit that he was "gonna look like a ugly ape sitting up in school side of white kids" (389). Mr. Cloud, the white superintendent of schools, dismisses Rev. Layne from his post as principal, and tries to bribe him by offering him a position as principal in a different school if the reverend can persuade his parishioners to withdraw their names from a petition for desegregation of the public schools. But the reverend and his wife, Martha, cannot be bought. Ultimately, the South Carolina Supreme Court decides in favor of separate but equal schools. In Layne's words, "The judges said segregation is legal, but the state has to make the schools equal" (382). To Layne, Bill, and Duff, the decision is a victory and an occasion for celebration, but to others, victory will only be complete when segregation is declared illegal.

Thematically, the play pits violence against nonviolence as methods of combating racism. Bill Raigen thinks that a nonviolent man feels like a coward before his own children. Rev. Layne explains that we should treat our enemies as if they were Prodigal children who will eventually come home. A corollary to this theme is the question of demanding immediate equality or accepting gradualism. While some favor gradualism, Martha Layne and the lawyer Ben Ellis know that black people have already waited too long (323). The play also emphasizes the key role women play in the movement for educational equality. It is because of Mary Raigen's concern for the education of her son, Glenn, and her insistence that he should not miss "one single solitary day of school" (332) that she forces Bill Raigan to help fix the floor after a long day's work.

Humor is an important element of this play. It helps the black characters cope with racism. Duff says that when he applied to the bank for a loan, he was denied because he belonged to Rev. Layne's church. J. C., a deacon in Rev. Layne's church, responds that there is "no danger of that happening this year 'cause you ain't been to church in so long . . ." (335). When Bill says that the taxman takes his money and "he don't put it in no back drawer," but he "integrates it" (330), he is exposing the hypocrisy of whites who oppose integration in public school education.

Star of the Morning traces the early dramatic career of Egbart Austin Williams (commonly known as Bert Williams), the great West Indian comic artist. Williams and George Walker performed vaudeville shows and musical comedy from 1895 to 1909. Mitchell dramatizes the social conditions and the state of American theater at the turn of the century. He also reproduces some of Bert Williams's trademark comic routines. The play depicts the two entertainers taking jobs at a San Francisco honky-tonk, replacing Oliver Jackson who will now be touring as a minstrel. Vaudeville shows of the period permitted blacks only stereotypical roles as shuffling, stealing clowns. Oliver says that minstrel shows of the day are no fun because the performers are themselves the butt of ridicule, whereas during slavery, slaves would put up minstrel shows to "poke fun at Old Master" (580). When their new boss addresses Williams and Walker as "boys," the offended Williams responds, ". . . [I]f you studied the human anatomy, you'd discover a remarkable difference between a boy and a man" (583). Thereupon, Ridge simply looks at him in wonder. This exchange reveals black entertainers' efforts to parry attacks on their dignity as artists and adults.

Williams does not want to lose his identity "behind a false face " (586), and resists using burned cork to blacken his face to conform to the stereotypical image of a black entertainer. The duo of Bert Williams and George Walker, ably assisted by their wives—Lottie Thompson Williams and Ada Overton Walker, respectively—had a command performance on the lawns of Buckingham Palace to celebrate the ninth birthday of the prince who later became Edward VIII. Always forthright in his satire, Williams says, "No one is happy in America, but every one [sic] pretends he is" (580). He tells black

Americans, "You've talked yourselves into buying a bill of goods that says anything all-black is wrong, inferior. You've got to get white approval to take a deep breath—even when that approval is cutting your insides" (622). For his penetrating understanding of people, places, and things, Bert Williams merits comparison with Shakespeare's Touchstone. Mitchell describes Bert Williams as "the funniest man I ever saw, the saddest man I ever knew" (636).

Mitchell's *Tell the Pharaoh* offers tribute to African and African American heritage in the wake of the 1954 Supreme Court decision in *Brown v. Board of Education*. The play celebrates Harlem as the hub of African American culture. This concert drama traces the history of Harlem, from its origins as Dutch Haarlem, to which a road was built in 1626 by eleven African slaves. After control of Manhattan passed to English hands, chattel slavery and rigid slave codes resulted. African Americans began migrating to Harlem in the late 1880s, gradually building it as a haven where blacks could "live like people and not be afraid" (30). The play follows Harlem through the eras of the Harlem Renaissance, the Depression, the McCarthy era, World War II, and civil rights. Mitchell recalls the Seventh Avenue of the 1920s. It was on this "Colored Folks' Broadway" where "you strolled those exciting afternoons" (37). You strolled with "your right leg dipping a bit, resembling a limp" (37). Mitchell laments the irony of the large number of black young men who went to fight in World War II, with each person "out there fighting for something he ain't got at home" (44). The play closes with the characters asking the Pharaoh to free those in bondage across the globe, so that "there be peace all over this earth" (59).

Bubbling Brown Sugar transports a young black couple, Jim and Ella, and a white man, Charlie, from the 1970s to an earlier era in the century. They find themselves in a speakeasy. When a black character, Sage, is told by a waiter that they do not serve Negroes, Sage responds that he does not "eat or drink Negroes" (10). The protagonists enjoy a strolling routine and watch newcomers of all types getting down at the Harlem subway station and taking the A train to Harlem. They taste the flavor of a Sweet Georgia Brown routine; meet Bumpy, a numbers racketeer at the Savoy; and then "get to listen to JIM JAM JUMPIN' JIVE at Small's Paradise." The sights and sounds they have experienced transform their outlook on life.

CRITICAL RECEPTION

Only a few of Loften Mitchell's works have received serious critical attention. *A Land Beyond the River* received generally favorable reviews. Brooks Atkinson admires the play for its characterization and humor, but finds it lacking in its plot construction: ". . . thanks to the vigorous characterizations, it is human and likable. Despite the seriousness of its theme, it flares into comedy repeatedly" (15). Francis Herridge lauds it for "humorous detail, an accurate ear for language, a fine sense of theater, and a message that develops logically from the actions" (50). According to Samuel A. Hay, "What distinguishes *A Land Beyond the River* are Mitchell's specially designed spirituals and sounds. . . . Negro spirituals enliven the drama and magnify the theme" (90). Mitchell notes the use of sound for "character illumination" (*Black Drama* 180). However, C. W. E. Bigsby describes the work as "morality play" in which characters personify virtues and vices, and the victory of good over evil is assured (141). While Bigsby considers its action to be melodramatic, and characters unidimensional, he finds it "both moving and powerful" (145). William R. Reardon and Thomas D. Pawley write, "The strength and courage of Layne shine forth in this drama and assure Mitchell of a lasting place in the role of dramatists who have recorded the black heritage" (132).

James V. Hatch commends *Star of the Morning* for its close adherence "to the facts and the characters of history" (619). Robbie Jean Walker remarks, "In *Star of the Morning*, a tribute to actor Bert Williams, Mitchell acknowledges the debt owed to pioneer actors who often compromised pride to keep open opportunities for cultural expression in the theater" (505).

Darwin T. Turner hails *Tell Pharaoh* as "'eloquent theatre-at-the-lectern' history of black people," in which Mitchell "reached his artistic heights" (567). Walker writes, "*Tell Pharaoh* poignantly depicts the realities of a population finally acknowledging their disappointment in the environs once deemed as the promised land" (505). Bob Wilcox, reviewer for KDHX Theatre, writes that the play traces the suffering of the enslaved Africans and their search for the freedom and the community they had known in Africa, finally finding something of each in Harlem at its best" (par. 3).

Ja A. Jahannes calls *Bubbling Brown Sugar* "a nostalgic tribute to the entertainers of Harlem from the early 1920s to the 1940s" (212). Gwendolyn E. Osborne describes the work as "a mystical, rhythmical musical which recreates over 25 years of Harlem life and nightlife" (34). Ottis L. Guernsey, Jr. writes, "*Bubbling Brown Sugar* was the first musical revue to explore the history of black music on Broadway and in Harlem" (345).

Black Drama: The Story of the American Negro in the Theatre is, says Jahannes, a "seminal work" that "brilliantly portrays American theater as a mirror of American society," and will serve "as a possible catalyst" for a revolution that is needed to rid white America of self-complacency and a spurious sense of superiority (210). Darwin T. Turner states that *Black Drama* is "an invaluable informal history of blacks in the New York theatre" (566). In *Voices of the Black Theatre*, Jahannes observes that each of the seven black pioneers "tells his or her story of a proud people determined to offer the best of theater to America; each attests to the indomitable will of black Americans to see their people portrayed in noble and realistic terms (210). Edward Mapp writes of *Voices of the Black Theatre*, "Never have the voices of black theater been heard more effectively" (308).

BIBLIOGRAPHY

Dramatic Works by Loften Mitchell

Ballad for Bimshire. 1963. First produced in New York.
Ballad of the Winter Soldiers. 1963. First produced in New York.
The Bancroft Dynasty. 1946. First produced in New York.
Blood in the Night. 1946. First produced in New York.
Bubbling Brown Sugar. New York: Broadway Play Publishing, 1985.
Cartoons for a Lunch Hour. 1978. First produced in New York.
The Cellar. 1952. First produced in New York.
The Final Solution to the Black Problem in the United States; Or, The Fall of the American Empire. 1970. First produced in New York.
A Gypsy Girl. 1982. First produced in Pine Bluff, Arkansas.
"A Land Beyond the River." *The Black Teacher and the Dramatic Arts*. Ed. William R. Reardon and Thomas D. Pawley. Westport: Greenwood, 1970. 301–396.
Miss Waters, To You. 1983. First produced in New York.
The Phonograph. 1961. First produced in New York.
Shattered Dreams. 1961. First produced in New York.
Sojourn to the South of the Wall. 1973. First produced in New York.
"Star of the Morning: Scenes in the Life of Bert Williams." *Black Drama Anthology*. Ed. Woodie King, Jr. and Ron Milner. New York: New American Library, 1971. 575–639.
Tell Pharaoh. New York: Broadway Play Publishing, 1986.
The Walls Came Tumbling Down. 1976. First produced in New York.

Literary History and Criticism and Other Cited Works by Loften Mitchell

Black Drama: *The Story of the American Negro in the Theatre*. New York: Hawthorn, 1967.
Voices of the Black Theatre. Clifton: White, 1975.

Studies of Loften Mitchell's Dramatic Works

Abramson, Doris E. *Negro Playwrights in the American Theatre, 1925–1959*. New York: Columbia University Press, 1969.
African American Registry. "Loften Mitchell, a Theatrical Icon." 3 May 2003. <www.aaregistry.com>.
Atkinson, Brooks. Rev. of *A Land Beyond the River*, by Loften Mitchell. *New York Times* 29 Mar. 1957: 15.
Bigsby, C. W. E. "Three Black Playwrights: Loften Mitchell, Ossie Davis, Douglas Turner Ward." *The Black American Writer*. Vol 2. Baltimore: Penguin, 1971. 137–144.
Chaney, Sandy. "After 45 Years, Pioneer of Civil Rights Is Cleared." *Washington Post* 11 Oct. 2000: A3.

Guernsey, Otis L., Jr. *The Best Plays of 1975–1976*. New York: Dodd, 1976. 344–345.

Gussow, Mel. "Loften Mitchell's Theatrical Legacy." *New York Times* 23 May 2001: C19+.

Hatch, James V., ed. Introduction to Loften Mitchell. *Black Theatre U.S.A.: Forty-Five Plays by Black Americans, 1847–1974*. New York: Free, 1974. 618–652.

Hatch, James V., and Omanii Abdullah, comps. and eds. "Mitchell, Loften." *Black Playwrights, 1823–1977: Annotated Bibliography of Plays*. New York: Bowker, 1977. 165–166.

Hay, Samuel A. *African American Theatre: An Historical and Critical Analysis*. 1994. Cambridge: Cambridge University Press, 1998.

Herridge, Frances. Rev. of *A Land Beyond the River*, by Loften Mitchell. *New York Post* 29 Mar. 1957: 50.

Jahannes, Ja A. "Loften Mitchell." *Afro-American Writers after 1955: Dramatists and Prose Writers*. Vol. 38 of *Dictionary of Literary Biography*. Ed. Thadious M. Davis and Trudier Harris. Detroit: Gale, 1985. 208–214.

"Loften Mitchell." *Contemporary Black Biography*. Vol. 31. Detriot: Gale, 1995. 128–130.

Mapp, Esward. Rev. of *Voices of the BlackTheatre*, by Loften Mitchell. *Library Journal* 1 Feb. 1975: 308.

Mueller, Michael E. "Mitchell, Loften." *Contemporary Authors New Revision Series*. Vol. 26. Detroit: Gale, 2002. 280–282.

Osborne, Gwendolyn E. Rev. of *Bubbling Brown Sugar*, by Loften Mitchell. *Crisis* (Jan. 1977): 34.

Peterson, Bernard L., Jr. *Contemporary Black African Playwrights and Their Plays: A Biographical Directory and Dramatic Index*. Westport: Greenwood, 1988. 344–347.

Phelps, Shirelle, ed. "Mitchell, Loften." *Who's Who Among African Americans, 1996/97*. New York: Gayle, 1997.

Ploski, Harry A., and Ernest Kaiser, ed. "Loften Mitchell." *Negro Almanac*. New York: Bellwether, 1971.

Reardon, William R., and Thomas D. Pawley. *The Black Teacher and the Dramatic Arts*. Westport: Greenwood, 1970.

Redding, Saunders. "Literature and the Negro." *Contemporary Literature* 9 (Winter 1968): 130–135.

Rev. of *Voices of the Black Theatre*, by Loften Mitchell. *Choice* (Jan. 1976): 1457.

Rush, Theressa Gunnels, Carol Fairbank Myers, and Esther Spring Arata. "Mitchell, Loften." *Black American Writers Past and Present*. Vol. 2. Metuchen: Scarecrow, 1975. 549–551.

Sheffer, Isaiah. Rev. of *Black Drama*, by Loften Mitchell. *Nation* (Aug. 1969): 151.

Turner, Darwin T. "Mitchell, Loften." *Contemporary Dramatists*. Ed. James Vinson. 3rd ed. New York: St. Martin's, 1982. 564–566.

Walker, Robbie Jean. "Mitchell, Loften." *The Oxford Companion to African American Literature*. Ed. William L. Andrews, Frances Smith Foster, and Trudier Harris. Oxford: Oxford University Press, 505–506.

Wilcox, Bob. Rev. of *Tell Pharaoh*, by Loften Mitchell. 8 May 2000: 11 pars. 21 June 2003 <http://www.kdhx.org/reviews/tell_pharaoh.html>.

BARBARA MOLETTE
(1940–   )

Gwendolyn S. Jones

BIOGRAPHY

That Barbara Molette is a talented artist is evidenced by the range of positions she has held in theater. Foremost, she is a playwright. And as a professor of playwrighting, she considers her "role to be one of fostering a community of writers that learn to use language that enables discussion and criticism of scripts and articulation of their imaginations as dramatic discourse" (personal interview). Molette is also well-known as director, actress, costume designer in theater and film, wardrobe mistress, makeup artist and designer, theater technician, writer, consultant, and lecturer, with more than eighty-five productions to her credit. This experience was gained at colleges and universities and at such venues as the Frank Silvera Writers' Workshop, the Negro Ensemble Company, the University of Iowa Opera Workshop, the Asolo Theatre Festival, the Des Moines Community Playhouse, and the Atlanta University Summer Theatre.

In higher education, Molette has taught courses in fine arts, drama, mass communications, humanities, and composition at such colleges and universities as Spelman College, Florida Agricultural and Mechanical University, Clark College (Clark Atlanta University), Texas Southern University, Towson State University, Baltimore City Community College, and Morgan State College. Administrative positions include coordinator of funded proposals, director of Arts-in-Education Programs for the Mayor's Advisory Committee on Art and Culture in Baltimore, director of Writing Across the

Curriculum at Baltimore City Community College, associate director of Summer Drama Workshops cosponsored by Spelman College and the National Endowment for the Arts, and drama coordinator for Upward Bound at Florida Agricultural and Mechanical University. Positions in teaching and in administration provided opportunities for travel and study in West Africa, Egypt, Italy, and Canada.

Membership in professional associations includes such organizations as the National Conference on African American Theatre, where she served as president (1989–1991); Dramatists Guild of America, Inc.; National Association of Dramatic and Speech Arts; Audience Development Committee (AUDELCO); and Sigma Tau Delta, International English Honor Society.

Barbara Molette, a native of Los Angeles, California, where she was born in 1940, largely credits her mother for her interest in theater. While a child, she was enrolled in drama classes, attended plays, and appeared in movies. Molette admits that she "grew up in the theater" (personal interview). With majors in art and history, she earned the bachelor of arts degree, with highest honors, at Florida Agricultural and Mechanical University in 1966. Molette was further influenced in theater by her husband, Carlton Molette. She was encouraged to enroll in courses in drama, her first, at Florida State University where Carlton was enrolled; she pursued graduate study and earned the master of fine arts degree in drama. Barbara and Carlton have collaborated as playwrights since 1969. In addition, they have produced scholarly papers, workshops, articles, and a book, *Black Theatre: Premise and Presentation*, now in its second edition. In recognition of Barbara Molette's dedication, commitment, and high level of professionalism, the University of Missouri–Columbia, where she earned the doctor of philosophy degree in theatre and mass communications, honored her with the Distinguished Alumna Award in 2000.

Barbara Molette retired from Eastern Connecticut State University, in Willimantic, with the rank of professor emerita of English in May 2002. During her tenure there, she served as associate chair, then as chair of the Department of English. Since retiring, she is a volunteer in community activities and has another play in progress.

MAJOR WORKS AND THEMES

Barbara Molette's plays have been produced Off Broadway and at such venues as the Negro Ensemble Company; the Free Southern Theatre; black theatre companies in Washington, DC, Houston, and Memphis; and college and university theaters. Plays have been published by Dramatists Play Service and in anthologies, including *Black Writers of America: A Comprehensive Anthology* and *Center Stage: An Anthology of Twenty-One Contemporary Black American Plays*.

With middle-class black urban families as characters, her plays treat the impact of white values on black society. Unspoken is the need to develop a black identity. According to Elizabeth Brown, Molette writes protest drama or drama of accusation (21). This type of drama fosters black consciousness and the characters distance themselves from white society. "These plays center on violent verbal and physical confrontation between blacks and whites" (Brown 9). In *Rosalee Pritchett*, the main characters are middle-class blacks; however, the blacks are portrayed with negative images, another characteristic of drama of accusation. The central message is that "educated . . . blacks are . . . leading meaningless lives when they . . . identify with whites and show no empathy for people of their own race" (52). The wives and husbands in this play are characterized as assimilationists because they have middle-class values, and they try to deny their black identity; the women, Rose and her friends Doll, Belle, and Dorry, are intentionally portrayed with negative images; they are destroying racial pride. For example, they separate themselves from blacks who are less fortunate than they are and make negative comments about them. The play, in fact, attacks blacks who do not associate with blacks they consider to be lower class. Their lives are meaningless because they try to model their lives after middle- and upper-class whites and want to be accepted by them. Brown's idea is that some of Molette's plays suggest that blacks should disassociate themselves from the decadent white society and its values.

In other plays, Molette also expresses the idea of black consiousness. As in *Rosalee Pritchett*, the settings are frequently in southern cities. In *Booji Wooji*, a black attorney attempts to make "the system" work for black people. The play details the difficulties he encounters with both blacks and whites. In *Dr. B. S. Black*, set in a southern city, the main character is a con artist. It is based loosely on Molière's *Dr. in Spite of Himself*. It has been produced in Atlanta, Washington, DC, and Memphis. In *Noah's Ark*, Noah is a college professor and a pacifist. His son, Daniel, is to be inducted in the army during a period of wars in Africa. Noah wages his own nonviolent war. These are middle-class blacks who live in an urban locale in the South.

Fortunes of the Moor was produced by Abibigroma, the NationalTheater Company of Ghana. This presentational African performance style is characterized by the use of grotesque masks and energetic dancing. *Fortunes of the Moor* is based on a part of the last line of *Othello*; hence, the title. It has also been referred to as the sequel to *Othello*. The story line is that a baby boy was born to Othello and Desdemona and raised by nuns following the death of his parents. Because of the battle for custody between Desdemona's powerful family and African-born Othello's noble Moorish family, the play makes political and social statements as it addresses cultural difference, religion, and slavery. It has been produced widely and received a $5,000 production grant from Rites & Reason Theatre at Brown University.

CRITICAL RECEPTION

Plays by Barbara Molette receive favorable responses, as evidenced by the diverse venues in which they have been produced. Further, they receive favorable notice from their peers. Richard Barksdale and Keneth Kinnamon describe *Rosalee Pritchett* as a "timely and moving comment on the ever-changing social values of Black America" (824). They see it as a play that provides insight into "the impact of white values on Black society" (824). These critics announce that *Rosalee Pritchett* received excellent notices.

In a competition sponsored by WMAR-TV, *Perfect Fifth* won third place and was produced by Arena Players of Baltimore. *Perfect Fifth* was also produced in New York and Rhode Island, at Western Michigan University, at the Connecticut Repertory Theatre, at the National Theatre Company of Ghana, at the Ohio State University, at the University of Louisville, and at the University of Pittsburgh.

Another indication of their positive reception is the appearance of acclaimed actors in her productions. *Dr. B. S. Black* was produced at Just Us Theatre in Atlanta with Samuel L. Jackson in the title role. *Presidential Timber*, with Paul Winfield reading the part of the president of Pemberton State University, met with enthusiastic response at its first reading. This first reading was part of the New Plays at High Noon series at the National Black Theatre Festival in Winston-Salem, North Carolina. A comedy, *Presidential Timber* has been selected for inclusion in the New Federal Theatre 30 Play Reading Series.

BIBLIOGRAPHY

Dramatic Works by Barbara Molette

Booji Wooji (with Carlton Molette). First produced at Atlanta University Summer Theatre, 1971. Title shortened to *Booji* when aired on KPRC-TV in Houston in 1982.
"*Dr. B. S. Black*" (musical version, with Charles Mann and Carlton Molette). *Encore* 13 (1970): 12–99. First produced at Atlanta University Summer Theatre, 1972.
"*The Escape; or A Leap to Freedom* (with Carlton Molette). Adapted from the play by William Wells Brown. First produced at Texas Southern University, 1976.
Fortunes of the Moor (with Carlton Molette). First produced in New York by the Frank Silvera Writers' Workshop, 1995.
"*Noah's Ark*" (with Carlton Molette). *Center Stage: An Anthology of Twenty-One Contemporary Black-American Plays*. Ed. Eileen J. Ostrow. Oakland: Sea Urchin, 1981. 177–196. First produced by Morehouse-Spelman Players, 1974.

Perfect Fifth. First produced by WMAR-TV and the Arena Players as a teleplay, Baltimore. Produced as a stage play by Arena Players in August 1988.

Presidential Timber, (with Carlton Molette). First read at the National Black Theatre Festival in Winston-Salem, North Carolina, 2001.

"Rosalee Pritchett" (with Carlton Molette). *Black Writers of America: A Comprehensive Anthology.* Ed. Baskdale, Kenneth and Keneth Kinnamon. New York: Macmillan, 1972. 825–836. First produced in Atlanta by Morehouse-Spelman Players, 1970; published by Dramatists Play Service.

Studies of Barbara Molette's Dramatic Works

"Barbara Molette." <http://www.ecsu.ctstateu.edu/depts/english/molette.html>.

Barksdale, Richard, and Keneth Kinnamon, eds. *Black Writers of America: A Comprehensive Anthology.* New York: Macmillan, 1972. 824–835.

Brown, Elizabeth. "Six Female Black Playwrights: Images of Blacks in Plays by Lorraine Hansberry, Alice Childress, Sonia Sanchez, Barbara Molette, Martie Charles, and Ntozake Shange." Diss. Florida State University, 1980.

Faculty Profile from News & Notes, the Newsletter for African American Studies. <http://www.ucc.uconn.edu/~aasadm03/malprefi.html>.

Hoehn, Doug. "Good Fortune." Columbus AlivewireD Theatre. http://www.alivewired.com/1998/19980304/theatre.html>.

Kaye, Phyllis Johnson, ed. "Barbara Molette." *National Playwrights Directory.* Waterford: O'Neill Theatre Center, 1977. 217.

Kinsman, Clare D., ed. "Molette, Barbara Jean." *Contemporary Authors: A Bio-Bibliographical Guide to Current Authors and Their Works.* Vol 382. Detroit: Gale, 1975. 45–48.

"Kuntu Presents Fortunes of the Moor March 22–April 7." *Pitt Campaign Chronicle: Briefly Noted.* <http://www.pitt.edu/media/pcc010226/briefs.html>.

Metzger, Linda, ed. "Molette, Barbara Jean." *Black Writers: A Selection of Sketches from Contemporary Authors.* Detroit: Gale, 1989: 409–410.

Molette, Barbara. Personal interview. 10 Feb. 2003.

"New Molette Play Read at the National Black Theatre Festival." <http://www.artszine.uconn.edu/headlines/headlines_fa2001/>.

"Play by Dramatic Arts Professor Premieres Nov 30 in New York." <http://www.news.uconn.edu/rel9541.htm>.

"Plays Deal with Nazi Germany, Othello Sequel." University of Connecticut Advance. <http://vm.uconn.edu/~advance/02289707.htm>.

Rush, Theressa Gunnels, Carol Fairbanks Myers, and Ester Spring Arata eds. "Molette, Barbara." *Black American Writers Past and Present: A Biographical and Bibliographical Dictionary.* Vol. 2. Metuchen: Scarecrow, 1975. 551.

RICHARD BRUCE NUGENT
(1906-1987)

Linda M. Carter

BIOGRAPHY

Writer and artist Richard Bruce Nugent (also known as Bruce Nugent and Richard Bruce) was born on July 2, 1906, in Washington, DC, to Pauline (née Bruce) and Richard Henry Nugent, Jr. Nugent's parents were not affluent, yet they were members of Washington's elite African American society. Their son attended the city's public schools including Dunbar High School, "the pride of Washington's African American community, staffed with the best and the brightest college graduates of their generation" (Wirth, Introduction 8). At Dunbar, Angelina Weld Grimké* was Nugent's English teacher when he was eleven years old. When Grimké told her class to create a short story, Nugent wrote a love story. He recalls: "The girl was named 'Hymen' and, you know, all of the . . . technical names that struck my fancy. I gave these names to people and to places and to flowers, and Angelina Grimké asked me to read it in front of the class. I did, so proud of my story. *And she never turned a hair*. I became great friends with Angelina Grimké later, and we had many a laugh about that story" (qtd. in Wirth, Introduction 8).

In 1920, when Nugent was thirteen years old, his father died and Nugent, his younger brother, Gary (who later became a famous tap dancer), and his mother moved to New York. There, Nugent worked as an art apprentice, errand boy, bellhop, secretary, and ornamental iron worker and enrolled in art classes at the New York Evening School of Industrial Arts and Traphagen School of Fashion before he told his mother that he would pursue a career as an artist. Mrs. Nugent, concerned that her oldest son did not intend to hold a steady job, sent him to live with his grandmother in Washington, DC, where, in 1925, he met Langston Hughes* at one of Georgia Douglas Johnson's* artistic soirees. The two young men became friends, and Hughes encouraged Nugent's creative endeavors.

Nugent, at the age of nineteen, returned to New York during the Harlem Renaissance's zenith. His first poem, "Shadow," was printed in *Opportunity* in 1925, the same year his first short story, "Sahdji," was published in Alain Locke's *The New Negro*. Nugent's better known short story "Smoke, Lilies, and Jade," identified by Eric Garber as Nugent's "fictionalized self-portrait" (218), was published in 1926 in *Fire!! A Quarterly Devoted to the Younger Negro Artists*, edited by Wallace Thurman.* "Smoke, Lilies, and Jade" is apparently one of the earliest, if not the first, published African American literary works with an explicitly homosexual theme. Indeed, according to Emmanuel Nelson, the story "remains the most defiantly explicit gay text produced during the Harlem Renaissance" (9). Nugent contributed to Thurman's *Harlem: A Forum of Negro Life* (1928) and Dorothy West's *Challenge* (1937) and *New Challenge* (1937), as well as *Trend: A Quarterly of the Seven Arts* (1932, 1933). In the late 1930s, Nugent wrote biographies of other African Americans and other articles for the Federal Writers Project; Claude McKay and Ralph Ellison were his coworkers. In December 1970, Nugent's "Beyond Where the Star Stood Still," a Christmas story, was published in *Crisis*.

As an artist, Nugent was "influenced by Michelangelo, Beardsley, and Erte" (Wirth, "Richard" 16) and was known for his erotic, art deco drawings; *Fire!!* contains two of Nugent's silhouette brush and ink drawings. Additional drawings were printed in Charles S. Johnson's anthology *Ebony and Topaz* (1927). *Opportunity* published many other brush and ink drawings by Nugent during the late 1920s and early 1930s. He also created line drawings (in pen and ink or pencil) as well as works in oils and pastels. Nugent's artwork was exhibited by the Harmon Foundation during the early 1930s. Since the 1970s, his drawings have been included in various periodicals such as *Art Journal*, *Crisis*, *Print*, and *Transition II*, as well as several books.

Nugent was also involved with the performing arts. In 1927, he began acting in Dubose Heyward's Broadway play *Porgy*. After the play left New York, Nugent remained a cast member as *Porgy* toured the United States and Europe until 1930. In 1933, he was a dancer in Hall Johnson's *Run, Little Chillun*. Decades later, Nugent appeared briefly in *Before Stonewall*, a 1984 film documentary about gay history. In addition to Nugent's activities as a writer, artist, performer, and commentator, he, along with Romare Bearden and others, founded the Harlem Cultural Council during the 1960s; the organization sought municipal and federal funds for the arts and played a major role in the efforts to construct a new building for the Schomburg Center for Research in Black Culture.

Nugent outlived most of his Harlem Renaissance contemporaries and his wife of seventeen years, Grace (née Marr), who was "brilliant and beautiful" (Wirth, Introduction 34) and possessed impressive academic and professional credentials. Although she knew that Nugent was gay, she married him in 1952. Grace Nugent continued her career as a nursing administrator until she founded Operation Democracy, a project that attempted to improve social conditions. She died in 1969. Richard Bruce Nugent died on May 27, 1987, of congestive heart failure in New York City. A memorial service was held in July 1987 at the Schomburg Center for Research in Black Culture.

MAJOR WORKS AND THEMES

When Locke asked Richard Bruce Nugent to contribute to the anthology *The New Negro*, he submitted a picture: "a wash drawing of an African girl standing in a hut, the doorway of a hut, apparently jangling her bracelets—which Locke liked very much. . . . He thought it was beautiful and said, 'It looks like a story. Can you write something about it?' And I wrote something called 'Sahdji.' And it appeared in the book with an illustration by Aaron Douglas" (qtd. in Wirth, Introduction 3). Sahdji, young and beautiful, is the favorite wife of Konombju, an East African chief. Although Sahdji loves her husband, her stepson, Mrabo is in love with Sahdji and wants to be with her. Mrabo ". . . could wait . . . his father was getting old . . ." (573). Another young man, "Numbo [,] idolize[s] Mrabo. . . . Numbo . . . would do anything to make Mrabo happy . . ." (573). Numbo, aware that Mrabo is waiting for his father to die, kills him during a hunting trip. Sahdji, grief stricken, throws herself on Konombju's funeral pyre as Mrabo watches. The story ends as "Mrabo stood unflinching . . . but Numbo, silly Numbo had made an old. . . old man of Mrabo" (574). Maxine Sample points out, "'Sahdji,' an African morality tale, condemns murder, not homosexual love" (350). Nugent's short story "is considered by some to be the earliest gay prose text written by an African American due to its allusion to the love of a male warrior for his chief's son" (Patton and Honey 570).

After Locke asked Nugent to create a story based on his drawing, he encouraged Nugent to adapt his first short story for the stage, and Nugent created *Sahdji: An African Ballet* (1925). William Grant Still wrote the ballet music score for the one-act drama. *Sahdji* premiered at Howard University in the late 1920s and was also produced at the Eastman School of Music in Rochester, New York, in the summer of 1932. A chanter interprets the ballet for the audience. He is "an enormous black man, is discernible at the extreme left, who stands stationary throughout the ballet. . . . From time to time, making only gestures with his spear, he chants in a booming singsong voice, the African proverbial sayings which are indicated for his role. All other action is dance pantomime" (389).

The suggestion of homosexuality in the story "Sahdji" is replaced with adultery in the drama *Sahdji*. In the story's second paragraph, Nugent writes of Sahdji's love for her husband; however, in the play, Nugent does not state that Sahdji loves the chief. When Konombju goes on the hunting expedition, Mrabo visits Sahdji at Konombju's hut while Numbo stands guard outside the chief's hut in an effort "to screen the lovers from intruders" (393). After Konombju's death during the hunt, an ambivalent Sahdji dances. In his stage directions, Nugent writes, *"Reverential gestures and oblivious abandon alternate as she is torn between her loyalty to the vow of death and her desire for life"* (399). Finally, as Mrabo watches, Sahdji plunges a dagger into her bosom, falls upon her husband's body, and dies. Thus, in the story and the drama, clandestine love leads to tragedy. Sahdji, whether the loving wife in the story or the adulteress in the play, is compelled "by tribal custom and her marriage vows" (Peterson 154) to commit suicide.

CRITICAL RECEPTION

Richard Bruce Nugent is one of the least-known members of the Harlem Renaissance, and his writing, especially *Sahdji: An African Ballet*, has received little scholarly attention. James Hatch is apparently the lone contemporary scholar to offer even a brief critical assessment of the play. He compares *Sahdji* with Thelma Duncan's *The Death Dance* (1923):

Both are tales of love and death in an African village, both use African names for their characters, and both center about a "Medicine Man" and a beautiful female dancer. Both use dance and drums as theatrical and dramatic spectacle. These two plays, to use Locke's phrase, are "adaptations of art-idioms and symbols"; they express an Africa researched more in imagination than in the village. The plays are dramatic parallels to the lyrical African figures drawn by Aaron Douglas who illustrated the printed texts. (16–17)

Peterson summarizes *Sahdji*'s plot and appears to be the only scholar to assert that Nugent wrote the play in collaboration with Locke (154). Venetia Patton and Maureen Honey's *Double-Take* (2001) includes Nugent's story and play. It appears to be the first reprint of *Sahdji* since its publication in Locke and Montgomery Gregory's *Plays of Negro Life* (1927). Thus, Patton and Honey have made Nugent's drama accessible to contemporary readers. Thomas Wirth's *Gay Rebel of the Harlem Renaissance* (2002) includes "Sahdji," the story, but not *Sahdji*, the drama; however, Wirth's introduction makes *Gay Rebel* a valuable source for researchers interested in Nugent's drama as well as his other works. *Gay Rebel* is the first compilation of Nugent's prose, poetry, and drawings; consequently Wirth, as editor, provides an extensive introduction to Nugent for present-day readers. All other secondary sources listed in the Bibliography, with the exceptions of articles by Wirth ("Richard Bruce Nugent," 1985) and Nelson (1995), generally provide concise details about *Sahdji*'s few performances. All secondary sources are excellent starting points for additional studies of Nugent's life and work.

BIBLIOGRAPHY

Dramatic Works by Richard Bruce Nugent

Paupaulekejo (with Georgia Douglas Johnson). 1926. Unpublished.
Sahdji: An African Ballet. 1925. *Plays of Negro Life: A Source-Book of Native American Drama*. 1927. Ed. Alain Locke and Montgomery Gregory. Westport: Negro Universities Press, 1970. 387–400.
Taxi Fare (with Rose McClendon). 1931. Unpublished.

Studies of Richard Bruce Nugent's Dramatic Works

Garber, Eric. "Richard Bruce Nugent." *Afro-American Writers from the Harlem Renaissance to 1940*. Vol. 51 of *Dictionary of Literary Biography*. Ed. Trudier Harris and Thadious M. Davis. Detroit: Gale, 1987. 213–221.
Grant, Nathan L. "Richard Bruce Nugent." *The Oxford Companion to African American Literature*. Ed. William L. Andrews, Frances Smith Foster, and Trudier Harris. New York: Oxford University Press, 1997. 550.
Hatch, James. "Some African Influences on the Afro-American Theatre." *The Theatre of Black Americans: A Collection of Critical Essays*. Ed. Errol Hill. New York: Applause, 1987. 13–29.
Nelson, Emmanuel S. "African American Literature, Gay Male." *Gay and Lesbian Literary Heritage*. Ed. Claude J. Summers. New York: Holt, 1995. 8–12.
Patton, Venetria K., and Maureen Honey, eds. "Richard Bruce Nugent." *Double-Take: A Revisionist Harlem Renaissance Anthology*. New Brunswick: Rutgers University Press, 2001. 570–571. (Note: The short story "Sahdji" (1925) is reprinted on 573–574, and *Sahdji, An African Ballet* (1925) is reprinted on 583–589.)
Peterson, Bernard L., Jr. "Richard Bruce Nugent." *Early Black American Playwrights and Dramatic Writers: A Biographical Directory and Catalog of Plays, Films, and Broadcasting Scripts*. Westport: Greenwood, 1990. 154–155.
Sample, Maxine J. "Richard Bruce Nugent." *African American Authors, 1745–1945: A Bio-Bibliographical Critical Sourcebook*. Ed. Emmanuel S. Nelson. Westport: Greenwood, 2000. 349–352.
Wirth, Thomas H., ed. Introduction. *Gay Rebel of the Harlem Renaissance: Selections from the Work of Richard Bruce Nugent*. Durham: Duke University Press, 2002. 1–61.
———. "Richard Bruce Nugent." *Black American Literature Forum*. 19 (Spring 1985): 16–17.

ROBERT O'HARA
(1970-   )

Johnny Woodnal

BIOGRAPHY

On February 2, 1970, Robert Antonio O'Hara was born to Little O'Hara and Robert Bowman in Cincinnati, Ohio. O'Hara's professional theatrical inclinations did not begin until his undergraduate studies at Tufts University in Medford, Massachusetts, but the seeds of his now representative juxtapositions of theater with historical and political fantasy were planted at an early age. Although his Cincinnati family never directly attempted to cultivate his artist within, O'Hara was staging backyard performances with neighborhood actors in the years before his tenth birthday, while *Ebony and the Six Cool Cats*, his witty take on "Snow White and the Seven Dwarfs," was penned in the sixth grade (Whiting 26). While these forays into the world of theatricality may seem like the elements of a typical American childhood, O'Hara does remember being intrigued by the "rhythm" of words at an early age. When he was young, he would tape record heated conversation at the dinner table in order to study and understand the workings of human conversation; he would even deliberately enrage his southern-accented grandmother, so he could later listen to the rhythms of her angered voice (Che 82).

While O'Hara toyed with this fascination over the nuances and cadences of the human voice, he also struggled with his homosexuality. Prior to leaving his Cincinnati home at the age of eighteen, he found it incredibly difficult to finish reading *The Colored Museum* by George C. Wolfe, O'Hara's future mentor and close friend, because it dealt so openly with issues of homosexuality. O'Hara says of the incident:

I started reading *The Colored Museum* in high school, but I put it down because I didn't like the portrayal of the drag queen. . . . I was in the closet at the time, so that's part of the reason, but I also thought that Wolfe was some awful white man. Later, I found out that he was a black gay man, so I picked it up again in college and discovered that it was brilliant. Not because Wolfe was black or gay, but because it's an obnoxious, tremendous, theatrical and emotive play about identity and acknowledging who you are. After I did that myself, I could appreciate it. (qtd. in Che 82)

This early denial of his sexual identity was certainly made more problematic by a childhood in which "relatives told him that Santa Claus doesn't visit faggots" (Dedds 32). In fact, O'Hara did not come to terms with his homosexuality until after his self-proclaimed "escape" from Cincinnati to attend Tufts University, where he founded the Black Theatre Company that allowed him to write and produce a trilogy of plays that helped him accept his sexuality ("Generation Q" 54). While at Tufts, O'Hara wrote plays that dealt primarily with the issue of homosexuality. He claims, "I finally came out as a result of the plays I was writing. . . . I was dealing with the issue in my work but not acknowledging it in myself. When I finally came out, I was 20, and everyone was like, 'No kidding!' I was the last to know apparently" (qtd. in "Generation Q" 54).

O'Hara's academic life at Tufts is only part of a rather successful schooling résumé. In Cincinnati, he graduated from Walnut Hills High School, "an entrance-exam based college preparatory school" (Zabel 342). Due to his love for the television show *L.A. Law*, O'Hara began his undergraduate career at Tufts, first in political science and then English, in the hopes of continuing his studies in law school, but he remembers switching his major to theater after realizing that he wanted to emulate the acting on the prime-time drama and not the legal rhetoric (Che 82). Upon graduation from Tufts, O'Hara was accepted into the Columbia University Graduate Directing Program, where he graduated with an M.F.A. in 1995. Columbia supplied him with a strong foundation in theater but also offered him an indication of the public reception he could expect when he started producing his plays professionally. Students in the M.F.A. program at Columbia met each semester with their instructors to receive evaluations; this was followed by a meeting with the chair of the program, Arnold Aronson. O'Hara recalls, "After my first semester at Columbia, [Aronson] sits me down and tells me 'Well, we think that you're a bit too focused on homosexuality and African-American issues.' The only thing I could do was laugh" (qtd. in Croal 37). Against Aronson's advisement, he continued to pursue African American and gay themes.

But the personal ideology that emerges in his plays began long before he started writing in a style that many critics view as uncompromisingly political. Recalling a day in high school when he noticed a statement by Martin Luther King, Jr.—"If you have nothing to die for, then you are not really living"—O'Hara began to form his current ideology that "everyone has too much to contribute to die" (qtd. in Werner 25). However, it was not until college that O'Hara began to inquire about his own family's history in order to portray more accurately African Americans on stage:

No, my family did not pass down history, not willingly at least, not in the sense of "what happened with so-and-so." And that was so odd because I would hear, especially in college, those fantastic stories you hear about when you start to acknowledge your history. When I started reading slave narratives in college I thought of calling my grandmother and asking her about her own experiences. She said, "What are you talking about?" She was completely and totally uninterested in discussing it. My making her life fascinating was stupid to her. She just lived it. She had 12 kids and she lived. (qtd. in "Holding History" 28)

Regardless of his family's reluctance to discuss its personal history, O'Hara fell in love with the "the stories that we *invent* about history" (Werner 20). This love of historical fantasy, coupled with the final acceptance of his own homosexuality, led to the creation of a playwright who was destined to be viewed as controversial by both audiences and critics. However, O'Hara does not consider himself overtly political. He believes that the personal is by its very nature political; thus, "just being who I am—an out homosexual, someone who is proud to be black, and an artist who speaks his mind freely—makes me political in some way . . . and I do believe in political consciousness raising, although that's not why I write. I write because I think everybody has stories of significance that they need to tell" (qtd. in Werner 25).

In addition to his training at Tufts and Columbia, O'Hara interned at the Manhattan Theater Club and the Joseph Papp Public Theater (Zabel 343). While at the Public Theater, he worked directly with George C. Wolfe in 1992 (Che 82) as part of a directing residency for Oliver Mayer's *Blade to the Heart* and the Broadway musical *Bring in Da' Noise / Bring in Da' Funk* (Taylor 20). This began a strong business relationship with the theater company that led to a professional New York production of O'Hara's work. While O'Hara understandably lists Wolfe as one of his mentors and role models, he also includes openly gay writers James Baldwin* (Craig 26; "Generation Q" 54) and Paula Vogel (Winn 25) as influential in his own writing.

MAJOR WORKS AND THEMES

Robert O'Hara's most well-known work is his Insurrection trilogy, of which only *Insurrection: Holding History*, the first part of the trilogy, has been published. Each of the three plays deals with what have come to be known as O'Hara's major themes, including homosexuality and African American issues. None of the plays is linked by plot or character, but each is representative of the trilogy thematically.

O'Hara wrote *Insurrection: Holding History* as part of his graduate thesis at Columbia University; however, the play first began to take form when he awoke from a vivid dream of his deceased grandfather, T.J., who asked O'Hara to take him home. O'Hara concluded that his grandfather was referring to the pre–Civil War South (Werner 22) and *Insurrection: Holding History* evolved from the scenario. While at Columbia several years later, O'Hara directed a play, a requirement that all graduate directing candidates at the school must complete. Unlike his colleagues who felt this project to be "the culmination of their graduate school work," O'Hara felt his "thesis would be the beginning of [his] professional career" (Whiting 26), so he wrote and specifically tailored a play to suit his needs as the vehicle that would introduce him to the New York theater community. The play was subsequently directed by Timothy Douglas as a workshop at the Mark Taper Forum in Los Angeles where it won the very first Sherwood Award (Milvy Q13); it was then professionally produced Off Broadway at the Public Theater under O'Hara's own direction in late 1996. The production won not only the John Golden Award for Playwrighting but the most prestigious award a fledgling New York playwright can receive, the Oppenheimer. However, O'Hara was far more pleased with the production as mounted by Charles Randolph-Wright at the American Conservatory Theater (A.C.T.), as O'Hara felt the New York production was plagued by casting problems, timing problems, and hasty cuts made to the script (Taylor 20). The A.C.T. production was made possible after O'Hara was selected by the National Endowment for the Arts/Theater Communications Group Theater Residency Program for a yearlong residency with the San Francisco Theater Company (Werner 22).

The play follows Ron Porter, a gay African American graduate student researching slave revolts for his dissertation. With his incapacitated 189-year-old grandfather T.J., named for O'Hara's own grandfather, Ron travels back in time to the day of Nat Turner's slave rebellion where he finds comedic difficulty reconciling a nineteenth-century slave revolt with his 1990s mentality. Using comedy to open the minds of his audiences, the playwright includes many nontraditional elements to a play dealing with such a bloody rebellion as Turner's, including such popular cultural references as Ron and T.J.'s house landing on top of an evil slave owner in a deliberate allusion to *The Wizard of Oz*. The slaves then break into a rousing musical number, staged with a barefooted tap dance as produced by A.C.T. While this combination of the terrible with the humorous may seem self-defeating, O'Hara's work seems to suggest that the societal views of historical tragedy are often so misguided that comedy is a natural forum in which to present these views. In *Insurrection: Holding History*, he takes the stereotype of the slave worker who rises early to toil in the field all day only to return to bed before repeating the labor again the next day and replaces it with a new version, a slave who not only reads and writes, but laughs and loves. Regarding this endeavor, Hilda Scheib notes, "In examining slavery and the myths surrounding it, O'Hara confidently mixes the audaciously funny with the chillingly stark to create a new vision of history that rests on an acknowledgment that truth is all a matter of perspective" (C2).

Insurrection: Holding History was one of O'Hara's first attempts to portray accurately slave history, albeit in a fictional manner. In the play, he found a way to merge his sense of a prejudicially nostalgic history with his sense of current reality. In an interview with Russell Rottkamp, O'Hara speaks to these contrasting ideals of fiction and reality:

I don't think there's such a thing as objective history. We know the big events but then there's all the in-between. People feel very comfortable saying there's no use talking about slavery anymore because we got through it, we survived, we worked from sun up to sun down [*sic*], there was no laughter, which is just not true. Because I exist! I came from some type of place where people were laughing, if anything, in order to not kill each other. There had to be some joy. (12)

This joy is found in the play when Ron finds love in the arms of a nineteenth-century male slave. By dramatizing the lives of slaves beyond the traditional views of enslavement, O'Hara attempts to offer a more three-dimensional viewpoint of those human beings, often in an extremely nontraditional manner, as with Ron's time-traveling homosexual love affair. In scenarios such as this one, O'Hara succeeds in intertwining his own identity into the fabric of his play. In the same manner that he feels his African American culture must restructure its roots and history, O'Hara has endeavored to do the same for another portion of his past as a homosexual:

Homosexuality has been around since before the ancient Greeks, so it's ridiculous to believe, as some people would have you, that gay people did not exist before Stonewall, and that black people were invented during the civil rights movement. God forbid black *and* gay! Where did the voices and power of our culture come from if they didn't exist before 1969? If I exist now, someone like me had to exist before me or I wouldn't be here. (qtd. in Werner 23)

This sentiment is seen plainly in *Insurrection: Holding History* when T.J. tells Ron "you my future. [Y]ou the one gon' carry my scars" (68).

Brave Blood (1999), the second play in the trilogy, is set in the present and attempts to address how slavery "impacts the family and sexual identity in America" (Zabel 345). The play centers on Ms. Anne, a psychiatrist who tries to rehabilitate the lives of a group of prostitutes by taking them into her home. However, a murder investigation fragments the narration as each character must deliver separate and contradictory testimonies. As O'Hara points out, the only difference between slavery and the women in this play is that these characters "allow themselves to be exploited" (qtd. in Zabel 345). The playwright's efforts in *Brave Brood* revolve around the ownership of one's body and the causes of voluntary exploitation.

The third installment of the Insurrection trilogy is entitled *–14: An American Maul* and was written as part of an artist-in-residence program with A.C.T. This play, pronounced "negative fourteen," is set in both the distant past and the near future and involves the creation of a new form of cotton that requires manual labor for its cultivation. The president of the United States then leads a movement to repeal the Fourteenth Amendment, which repeals the tenants of slavery and guarantees citizenship rights to the descendants of slaves while also denying voting rights to criminals, rebels, and traitors.

Part of O'Hara's inspiration to write *–14: An American Maul* was a CBS miniseries based on Thomas Jefferson's affair with slave Sally Hemmings. "I was very concerned that CBS called the mini-series [*sic*] 'Sally Hemmings: An American Scandal,'" says O'Hara, "because one would never think to call Jefferson 'an American scandal'" (qtd. in Sabir 6). This inspirational foundation paved the way for a clause in O'Hara's fictional abolishment of the Fouteenth Amendment scenario: any descendants of slaves who could prove they had presidential blood were not subject to reenslavement. As with his earlier plays, O'Hara attempts to turn his audiences' preexisting beliefs about a situation upside down. With no openly gay characters, *–14: An American Maul* acts as a meditation on history by focusing on the repercussions of society taking for granted its preconceived notions about history and what it accepts as fact. O'Hara's typical juxtaposition of contrasting ideas is also present in the title of *–14: An American Maul*. The play on words brings together the ideas of a horrific attack in *maul* and a traditional American staple in the homonym *mall*. O'Hara deliberately ties something American society believes to be harmless and benign with a word that connotes an intentional and gruesome act of violence. As seems representative of all his work, the playwright believes "great plays should choke you. I don't think you should be able to digest them easily" (qtd. in Winn 26).

CRITICAL RECEPTION

The most widely produced play by Robert O'Hara is the first in his trilogy, *Insurrection: Holding History*. While productions have been mounted fairly consistently since its initial incarnation at the Public Theater in New York, the critical reception of that show did not bode well for the play. Of the Public Theater production, Peter Marks of the *New York Times* claimed, "It seems appropriate that the play . . . has been staged on a set that resembles a map: the show is all over it" (C1). While applauding O'Hara's intentions of "toying with the accepted notions about history, race and sexual identity," Marks concluded that "there has got to be a more direct route to this nugget of wisdom than the circuitous one Mr. O'Hara has chosen" (C1).

Similarly, Howard Kissell of the *New York Daily News* did not care for the comedic touches O'Hara put on the Turner Rebellion. "Treating this somber event largely with a cartoon sensibility is, of course, outrageous," Kissell asserted. "It is balanced by an underlying sense that the contemporary blacks O'Hara depicts, with their mindless hip-hop mentality, have forgotten Turner's legacy" (53). Michael Feingold of the *Village Voice* saw promise in the young playwright's work when he declared that "it was probably unwise of the Public Theater to put such unseasoned and muddled work in front of the public, but nurturing and encouraging a talent of this breadth was a wise move; two or three plays down the pike, he will probably produce something masterful" (89). Ironically, however, Jonathan Mandell wrote disparagingly of the play for *Newsday*, the publication that bestowed the prestigious Oppenheimer Award upon O'Hara for the same production that Mandell claimed was "in sum, too much," claiming that at "nearly two hours . . . it winds up seeming too long to pay attention to this anarchic mix of styles, tones, themes and ideas" (B21). There were, nevertheless, a few critics who were enthusiastic about O'Hara's production at the Public. One was Alexis Greene of the *Star-Ledger* who stated "O'Hara forges a spirited, coherent production" (75).

While critical reception in the popular press was less encouraging than what a new playwright would hope for his first endeavor, the literary world lauded O'Hara's initial effort. Pulitzer Prize–winning playwright Tony Kushner asserts that the play "is a wild, thrilling ride down one of history's darkest, scariest corridors. . . . Through comedy, poetry and pure chutzpah, he teaches us all over again how to be truly frightened and appalled. This is a gorgeous, fresh and vital play from a very exciting playwright" (qtd. on *Insurrection* book jacket). In the preface to the publication of *Insurrection: Holding History*, Shelby Jiggetts-Tivony applauds O'Hara's use of *The Wizard of Oz* motif to explore the tension between the two dreamworlds of leaving and staying. Jiggetts-Tivony also comments on how O'Hara appears to be the culmination of his predecessors, including George C. Wolfe and Tony Kushner. She avows that "in *Insurrection*, the gay fantasia on national themes and the colored museum of Black stereotypes collide and merge" (v), alluding to Kushner's *Angels in America* and Wolfe's *The Colored Museum*.

While O'Hara's initial foray into the professional world of theater was extensively reviewed, his subsequent productions, although produced in various venues, have been less visible in the press. In an interview with *San Francisco Bay View* reporter Wanda Sabir in March 2000, O'Hara said, "I have a relationship with A.C.T. and the Public. Most of the black theaters do not call me. Most of the regional theaters do not call me—for various reasons,

I'm sure. I don't know if I'm writing the plays they're used to doing or that they're interested in doing" (7).

Regardless of the degree of his plays' prominence in the regional and New York theater arenas, O'Hara seems poised to maintain a long career in the arts. Shortly after *Insurrection: Holding History* premiered, Martin Scorsese signed him to write a screenplay based on the autobiography of Richard Pryor, in addition to a second screenplay he has written for the Hollywood production company Fineline about Admiral Mike Boorda (Milvy Q13). O'Hara vows that he loves the theater most of all and continues to write plays; he has even written a musical version of the epic poem *Beowulf* with composer Eric Schwartz. His professional credits and his harshest critics seem equally convinced that Robert O'Hara will continue to produce theatrical art long enough to sustain a healthy and masterful career.

BIBLIOGRAPHY

Dramatic Works by Robert O'Hara

Brave Brood. Produced at Reverie Production, New York, 1999. Also produced at the Transparent Theater, Berkeley, California, 2001.

Dreamin' in Church and Genitalia. Produced by the Worth Street Theater Company, at the Tribeca Playhouse, as part of *Snapshots 2000*, New York, October 2000.

Insurrection: Holding History. New York: Theatre Communications Group, 1999. MFA Directing Thesis. Produced at the Oscar Hammerstein II Center for Theater Studies, School of the Arts, Columbia University, April 1995. Workshop production produced at Center Theater Group/Mark Taper Forum New Work Festival, December 1995. World premier produced by George C. Wolfe at the Joseph Papp Public Theater/New York Shakespeare Festival, November 1996. West Coast premiere produced at the American Conservatory Theater, main stage, January 1998.

–14: An American Maul. Produced at the American Conservatory Theater, M.F.A. program production. February 2000.

Studies of Robert O'Hara's Dramatic Works

Che, Cathay. "*Holding* Out." *Time Out New York* 21–28 Nov. 1996: 82.

Craig, Pat. "This Time, O'Hara Throws Himself at the Constitution." *Contra Costa Times* 3 Mar. 2000: 26.

Croal, N'gai. "Rebellion with a Cause: *Insurrection* at the Public." *Theater Week* 2 Dec. 1996: 30–37.

Dedds, Richard. "Robert O'Hara's Latest Insurrection." *Bay Area Reporter* 24 Feb. 2000: 32.

Feingold, Michael. "Time Release." *Village Voice* 24 Dec. 1996: 89.

"Generation Q." *The Advocate* 19 Aug. 1997: 54.

Greene, Alexis. "'Insurrection' a Trip Back to Troubled Times." *Star-Ledger* 12 Dec. 1996: 75.

"Holding History." *A.C.T. Stagebill* (Jan. 1998): 27–37.

Jiggetts-Tivony, Shelby. Preface. *Insurrection: Holding History*. New York: Theatre Communications Group, 1999. iii–vi.

Kissell, Howard. "Getting a Rise Out of Nat Turner." *New York Daily News* 12 Dec. 1996: 53.

Kushner, Tony. Book Jacket. *Insurrection: Holding History*. New York: Theater Communications Group, 1999.

Mandell, Jonathan. "A Musical-Comedy Version of Slavery." *Newsday* 13 Dec. 1996: B21.

Marks, Peter. "Of Slavery and Sex in a Time Warp." *New York Times* 13 Dec. 1996: C1.

Milvy, Erika. "Playwright O'Hara a Slave to His Work." *Press Democrat* 11 Jan. 1998: Q13.

Rottkamp, Russell. "Interview: Robert O'Hara." *Q San Francisco* (Jan. 1998): 12.

Sabir, Wanda. "An Interview with Playwright Robert O'Hara." *San Francisco Bay View* 8 Mar. 2000: 6–8.

Scheib, Hilda. "Robert O'Hara: 'Insurrection: Holding History.'" *Marin Independent Journal* 16 Jan. 1998: C1–C2.

Taylor, Belinda. "*Insurrection: Holding History*." *Callboard* (Jan. 1998): 20–21.

Werner, Jessica. "A Love Affair with History." *A.C.T. Stagebill* (Jan. 1998): 20–25.

Whiting, Sam. "Robert O'Hara Makes His Place in History." *San Francisco Examiner and Chronicle* 4 Jan. 1998: 26.

Winn, Steven. "Dialogue from Two Playwrights." *San Francisco Examiner and Chronicle* 4 Jan. 1998: 25–26.

Zabel, Darcy A. "Robert O'Hara (1970–)." *Contemporary Gay American Poets and Playwrights*. Ed. Emmanuel S. Nelson. Westport: Greenwood, 2003: 342–348.

OYAMO (1943–)

Rochell Isaac

BIOGRAPHY

Playwright, Charles F. Gordon, was born in Elyria, Ohio, to Earnest and Bonnie Gordon. Soon after his birth, the family moved to Lorraine, Ohio. While attending Admiral King High School, Gordon wrote for the school newspaper. He also wrote poems and stories during that time period. Gordon caused quite a stir in school because of his outrageous sense of humor. However, he also loved reading and writing and playing alone in the woods.

After graduating from high school in 1962, Gordon worked a number of jobs to earn money for college. In 1963, he enrolled at Miami University at Oxford, Ohio. Two and a half years later, he would drop out because of the school's conservative atmosphere and because of his frustration with the curriculum. Gordon would then serve in the United States Naval Reserve while actively engaging in antiwar demonstrations and voter registration drives in the South. He would then join the Black Theatre Workshop in Harlem—an appendage of the New Lafayette Theatre—after deciding he could make more of a social impact as a playwright.

Gordon adopted the name OyamO because his real name was entirely too similar to that of another playwright, Charles Gordone,* who penned the play *No Place To Be Somebody* (1970) and won a Pulitzer Prize for it. The name OyamO was coined by neighborhood children when Gordon lived in Harlem in the late 1960s. The children (re)created the name from an alma mater T-shirt that read "Miami University of Ohio." It was Gordon who capitalized the last letter to attract attention. OyamO would return to school, specifically the College of New Rochelle, earning a B.A. in 1979. Later, in 1981, he would earn an M.F.A. from the Yale University School of Drama.

To date, OyamO, has successfully managed two careers: playwright and professor. He is the author of thirty plays, a good number of which have been produced in New York City. His plays have been presented at numerous theaters: the New York Shakespeare Festival's Public Theatre, Penumbra in St. Paul, the Manhattan Theatre Club, the Lorraine Hansberry Theatre of San Francisco, Theatre Emory in Alaska, the Yale Repertory Theatre, Festival des Amériques in Montreal, Frank Silvera Writers' Workshop, the Frederick Douglass Creative Arts Center, the Eugene O'Neill National Playwrights Center, BACA in Brooklyn, the Goodman Theatre in Chicago, the Arena Stage in Washington, DC, the Philadelphia Theatre Company, the Karamu House in Cleveland, and many others.

Early in his career, during the 1980s, OyamO taught as an adjunct professor and guest lecturer at numerous colleges and universities including the College of New Rochelle, Emory University, Princeton University, and at the University of Iowa Playwright's Workshop. In 1989, he began teaching at the University of Michigan and eventually became an associate professor of theatre and playwright in residence of the university. His awards include a Guggenheim Fellowship (1973), Rockefeller Foundation Playwright-in-Residence grants, (1972, 1983), New York State Council of the Arts Fellowships (1972, 1975, 1982, 1985), Ohio Arts Council Award (1979), McKnight Foundation Award (1984), Berrilla Kerr Award (1984), National Endowment for the Arts Fellowships (1985, 1992), Yale University School of Drama Molly Kazan Award (1980), and numerous other award nominations in Los Angeles, Chicago, and Washington, DC. He is a member of the New Dramatists, the Dramatists Guild, PEN (the National Association of Literary Writers), the Ensemble of Studio Theatre, the Eugene O'Neill Playwright Center, and the Writers' Guild of America East. OyamO has also been a member of the professional theater panel of the National Education Association.

MAJOR WORKS AND THEMES

One of OyamO's first notable publications is *The Breakout* (1969). As the title suggests, the drama centers on the search for independence and freedom of its two protagonists, Slam and Feet. Set in the 1970s, the two characters find out who really murdered Malcolm X. His most critically acclaimed play, *I Am a Man* (1995), chronicles the story of T. O. Jones, president of the black sanitation workers' union. The workers' repeated requests for better working conditions have been repeatedly ignored, and so the play begins with the horrifying incident that ignited Jones to lead his workers to strike. The black garbage men were not allowed to work when it rained and were not allowed to sit with the whites in the sheltered areas. As a result, they were forced to sit in the back of the garbage truck. Two men were crushed to death when lightning struck the faulty garbage compressor. The incident compounded the disrespect and humiliation often felt by the black workers. They had no job security as they often lost their jobs to white applicants. In addition, they were forced to be on a probationary period, which really meant that they were forced to pay the foreman to keep their jobs. So the men feel they have nothing to lose when Jones enters ready to lead them on a wildcat strike.

Jones is portrayed as a heroic but humane figure. He remains focused on his cause even when it would cost him his family. He has to address the many demands and concerns of a condescending mayor, other union organizers, and of the workers. The strike becomes larger than life and brings Martin Luther King, Jr. down to Memphis to offer support. King would be assassinated there. With King's death, Jones feels the world closing in on him. He questions his political standing:

Martin Luther King died fah a eight cent raise?" . . . All these weeks of striking. All them peepas killed or hurt! All the marchin' and jailin' and beatin's! All that starvin' and prayin' and downright cryin'! King dead! Murdered! What we git in return? One piece of paper and eight bright, shiny pennies. Not even thirty pieces of silver! Eight pennies and a maybe! Ain't a damn thing change! In twenty, twenty-five years, when things cool down, the city gon' break that union. The sanitation men were sold back to slav'ry and dey come here axing' me if it's all right. (23)

Though Jones is disheartened, the sanitation workers remained faithful to him and their cause. The play ends with Jones being told that he is the only person from whom the workers will accept the order to return to work.

I Am a Man is based on historical events. The play reenacts the Memphis sanitation strike of 1968, which culminated in massive riots and the assassination of Martin Luther King, Jr. The walkout forced to the forefront the issues that the civil rights and labor movements were attempting to address. The idea for the play came to OyamO after reading Joan T. Beifuss's *At The River I Stand*, a factual account of the Memphis strike. OyamO became extremely interested in the union president and began doing research on the man. Historically, King's assassination made Jones obscure. After the strike he was forced out of the union and ended up living alone in his pickup truck. In the play, however, Jones's story remains the focus. OyamO is adamant that *I Am a Man* is not about King or the civil rights movement but about Mr. Jones (Snyder 49).

One of the most striking elements of the play was the language with its glaring differences in dialogue among the characters. Critic Lloyd Rose, in his review of the play, insists that "it's great to hear so many of the speaking styles that are—across class, race and geography—the American voice" (C8).

Mr. Jones only had an eighth grade education and his language reflected his background. OyamO is aware that Jones had a problem with language but maintains that "he [Jones] was quite expressive, but his metaphorical, syntactical, and rhythmic arrangements of the English language were nonstandard and subject to condescending derision" (OyamO, *"Kick Ass"* 99). Jones's vernacular left him open to the ridicule of educated blacks and whites alike. OyamO further suggests that one of the reasons that Jones may have lost leadership of the strike was because of language:

The language Jones spoke played off of standard English; it engaged it but was not committed to its rules and definitions. His language was full and rich in its silences and intuitive nuances and it metaphorically expressed the fundamental human needs of a desperate group of lowly workers. His language reminded me of the improvisational technique of jazz. His syntax and usage syncretically combined to form a hybrid oral expressionism that aptly conveyed meaning and emotion and valuable information. But Jones' nonstandard language rituals were not acceptable to others and therefore, he was pushed further into the background. Eventually, he lost the leadership of the strike and the union to those others. He perished in obscurity. (99).

It was important for OyamO to emphasize the ordinary and everyday men who rose to the occasion to bring about extraordinary circumstances and change. Language here becomes political, especially when placed in a historical context where blacks were denied the right to read and write.

OyamO's other works include *The Resurrection of Lady Lester* (1981). The drama is described as a "poetic mood song" and was inspired by the life of Lester Young, the famous saxophonist. In *Fried Chicken and Invisibility* (1988), the protagonists William Price and Winston McRutherford discuss their experiences as African Americans. Price is convinced that blacks should adopt invisibility as a means for survival. The drama *In Living Color* (1992) celebrates song and dance and focused on Gullah-speaking African Americans. The play explores the people's attempt to evolve without losing their culture. *Let Me Live* (1991) dramatizes the lives and crimes of eight black prisoners. The penitentiary system becomes a reflection of the real world with all of its negative conditions and social injustices for blacks. *Famous Orpheus* (1991) is based on the legend of the mythical lovers Orpheus and Eurydice and the film adaptation of the story *Black Orpheus*. The drama blends myth and reality to dramatize the story of the lovers.

A consistent theme explored in OyamO's works is the evolving culture of black people toward attaining a measure of political, financial, and cultural freedom. His plays also examine America's class structure and clearly advocate for political efficacy. Jasmin Lambert notes:

Not unlike the plays of August Wilson, OyamO's work blends the African and African American narrative voice with elements of surrealism, expressionism, and realism— as well as with music, dance, and poetry. His characters include well known historical figures, such as Lester Young and Martin Luther King Jr., as well as unknown men and women, the common man or Everyman searching for meaning amid the mixed messages of racism and the mythology of the American Dream. (241)

In writing about the writing process and his motivation, OyamO himself admits that:

. . . The life that playwriting comes from is part of that effort to be free. The playwright is attempting to free himself and his people in whatever way he can. But the playwright by himself cannot be freer than the people.

I try to work toward the accomplishment of the ideal of freedom through writing plays which seek to eliminate the many confusions that hinder Black people. And I deal with questions that are crucial to blacks. (*"Kick Ass"* 99).

CRITICAL RESPONSE

OyamO's work, unfortunately, has not received much academic attention. Jasmin Lambert's short essay offers a general overview of OyamO's life and work. The only other substantial scholarly piece on his plays is Addell Austin Anderson's two-page entry in *Contemporary Dramatists*. She notes the lyricism that characterizes OyamO's dramatic vision and his seamless juxtaposition of myth and reality. "His gift for the use of languages," Anderson states, "evokes an intense emotional impact, while creating vivid visual images" (545).

BIBLIOGRAPHY

Dramatic Works by OyamO

The Advantage of Dope. 1971. Produced in Buffalo, New York.
Angels in the Men's Room. 1992. Produced in New York.
The Breakout. Produced in Waterford, Connecticut, 1972; New York, 1975.
Chumpanzees. 1970. Produced in New York.
Crazy Niggas. 1975. Produced in Napanoch, New York.
Distraughter and the Great Panda Scandal (musical). 1983. Produced in Atlanta.
An Evening of Living Colors (music by Olu Dara). 1988. Produced in Trenton, New Jersey, 1988; New York, 1989.
Every Moment. 1986. Produced in San Francisco.
Famous Orpheus. 1991. Produced in New Brunswick, New Jersey.
Fried Chicken and Invisibility. 1988. Produced in New York.
His First Step. 1972. Produced in New York.
I Am a Man. 1995. Performed at the Arena Stage, Washington, DC.
In Living Color. 1992. Produced in New York.

The Juice Problem. 1974. Produced in Waterford, Connecticut.

The Last Party. 1970. Produced in New York.

Let Me Live. 1991. Produced in New York.

The Lovers (also director). 1971. Produced in New York.

Mary Goldstein and the Author. 1979. Chicago: Third World Press, 1989.

The Negroes. 1970. Produced in New York.

Old Black Joe. 1984. Produced in San Francisco.

One Third of a Nation (adaptation of a play by Arthur Arent). 1991. Produced in Fairfax, Virginia.

Outta Site. 1970. Produced in New York.

The Place of the Spirit Dance. 1980. Produced in New Haven, Connecticut.

The Resurrection of Lady Lester. 1981. Produced in New Haven, Connecticut, and New York.

Return of the Been-To.1988. Produced in New York.

Sanctuary (sketches). 1992. Produced in New York.

Singing Joy. 1988. Produced in New York.

The Stalwarts. 1988. Produced in New York.

A Star Is Born Again (for children). 1978. Produced in New York.

The Temple of Youth (for children). 1987. Produced in New York.

The Thieves. 1970. Produced in Seattle.

Willie Bignigga. 1970. Produced in New York.

Other Cited Material by OyamO

"*Kick Ass* Taking on the Language Controllers." *Village Voice* 1 Dec 1992: 99.

Studies of OyamO's Dramatic Works

Armstrong, Linda. "*I Am a Man*: Powerful Close-Up of That Memphis Mess." *Amsterdam (NY) News* 29 May 1993: 36.

Anderson, Addell Austin. "OyamO." *Contemporary Dramatists*. Ed. Thomas Riggs. 6th ed. Detroit: St. James, 1999. 545–546.

James, Helen Marie. "OyamO, Black Man, Artist, the Challenge." *Amsterdam (NY) News* 10 July 1976: D-16.

Lambert, Jasmin. "OyamO." *Dictionary of Literary Biography* Ed. Christopher J. Wheatley. Vol. 102. Detroit: Gale, 2002: 240–242.

Rose, Lloyd. "*I Am a Man*: A Strike for Justice." *Washington Post* 10 Mar. 1995: C8.

Snyder, Jim. "Playwright with a Wild Side." *Chronicle of Higher Education* 41 (14 Apr. 1995): 49.

SUZAN-LORI PARKS
(1964–   )

Sharon M. Brubaker

BIOGRAPHY

Born in Fort Knox, Kentucky, Suzan-Lori Parks, daughter of a United States Army colonel, spent her formative years in six states prior to attending high school in Germany. A precociously early writer, Parks began crafting stories at the age of five. She spent her early adolescent years in the former West Germany, where she attended German schools rather than American institutions for children of military personnel. However, it was not until 1983, while an undergraduate student at Mount Holyoke College, in South Hadley, Massachusetts, that Parks came to the realization that writing plays should be her life's work. In a 1983 creative writing class with James Baldwin,* Parks was encouraged to pursue playwriting. It was while working on a short story titled "The Wedding Pig" for a creative writing class, that Baldwin posed the question to Parks, "Why don't you try writing plays?" (Garrett 22). "Someone I respected was telling me to what to do—in a good way," she says, "It wasn't some Whosey-Whatsit who runs La Fuddy Duddy Playhouse in 'Whosey-Whatsitville'" (qtd. in Garrett 22). It was Baldwin's suggestion that inspired Parks to write her first play, *The Sinners' Place*, during her senior year. The play, while earning Parks recognition in the English Department, was rejected production by the Theater Department on the grounds that "You can't put dirt on stage! That's not a play!" (Garrett 22).

Mary McHenry of the college's English Department softened the early rejection. McHenry gave Parks a copy of Adrienne Kennedy's* *Funny House* *of a Negro* (1962). The adventurous Kennedy, along with Ntozake Shange,* who devised the "choreopoem" as theater text, showed Parks she could do anything she wanted on stage. Parks also learned from her favorite fiction writers—William Faulkner, Virginia Woolf, and James Joyce—that she could do anything she wanted with language, and that "high character and feeling needn't be sacrificed at the high altar of formal experimentation" (Garrett 24). A cum laude B.A. in German and English from Mount Holyoke in 1985 was followed by advanced study at the Yale University School of Drama and a stint in London studying acting. Married to musician Paul Oscher, bi-coastal Parks maintains residences in Brooklyn, New York, and Venice, California. Dual careers as both a playwright and an educator find Parks currently at the Audrey Skirball Kernis Theater Projects, at the California Institute of the Arts in Valencia, as director, a position she has held since 2000. She has served as guest lecturer and as writer in residence in some of the top drama departments on American campuses.

Throughout her distinguished career, Parks has been the recipient of numerous awards. The most recent of which was the 2002 Pulitzer Prize for Drama, for *Topdog/Underdog*. Others include the *New York Times* Most Promising New Playwright Award (1989); a National Endowment for the Arts grant (1990) and Playwriting Fellowship (1990–1991); a New York Foundation for the Arts grant (1990); a Rockefeller Foundation grant (1990); two Obie Awards: in 1990, for Best Off-Broadway Play for *Imperceptible Mutabilities in the Third Kingdom* and in 1996 for *Venus*; the Whiting Writers' Award (1992); a W. Alton Jones grant, Kennedy Center Fund for New American Plays (1994); a Ford Foundation grant (1995); the Leila Wallace/*Reader's Digest* Award (1995); the California Institute of the Arts Alpert Award in Drama (1996); the PEN–Laura Pels Award for Excellence in Playwriting (2000); a Guggenheim Fellowship (2000); and a MacArthur Foundation Fellowship (2001).

"Interview with Suzan-Lori Parks," by Shelby Jiggetts, reveals precisely what playwriting means to Parks. Writing plays, according to Parks, is "about space." "The more I think about plays, I think plays are about space. Plays are about space to me. Plays are about space, and, say, fiction is about place. I think that one of the things that led me to writing plays is the understanding I have inside about space. Because I moved around so much when I was younger" (309). Moving around as a child, to Germany, Texas, Kentucky, and California, as a military officer's child, enabled Parks to have varied cultural experiences. Other than the continual movement in her formative and adolescent years, the most important constant in Parks's background, which is endemic to her career as a playwright, would be music. Again with respect to Parks's musical tastes, diversity is the key: ". . . Musicals like the *Sound of Music* or *Oklahoma*, you can't beat them. I mean, just the idea of people, you know in costumes. . . . I love that whole thing" (309). Music in fact has become an integral part of Parks's most recent plays. *Fucking A* (2000; published as *F...A*) has original songs written by Parks, and there is no mistaking the rap or, more aptly described, jazz riffs, which are the "three-card monte" mantras spoken by Lincoln and Booth in *Topdog/Underdog* (2001). When asked about the influence of music on her writing, Parks responded, "I listen to a lot of music, different kinds of music for each piece. *The Last Black Man* was jazz. . . . For *Venus* it was opera . . ." (Jiggetts 309).

Beginning with her first play, *The Sinners' Place*, and continuing with her most current, *Fucking A*, Suzan-Lori Parks is a playwright who challenges the notion of the historical construction and context of the African American experience. "The real jungle is the jungle within, just empowering [our]selves," Parks says in an interview with Angeli R. Rasbury, upon winning the 2001 Pulitzer Prize (par. 17). Controversy found in Parks's *The Sinners' Place* carries through successive plays. *The American Play* (1995), *In the Blood* (1999), *Fucking A*, (2000), and *Topdog/Underdog* (2001) contain deliberate references and allusions to American history (for example, the assassination of President Lincoln). The effect these events have on persons of all ethnicities and genders becomes an underlying, albeit tacit, theme running throughout Parks's canon. *Imperceptible Mutabilities in the Third Kingdom* (1989) and *Venus* (1996) equally as inclusive have a more distinctly African American background with respect to subject matter. Parks's first novel, *Getting Mother's Body*, was published to critical acclaim in May 2003; she is currently at work along on *Hoopz*, a stage musical about the Harlem Globetrotters.

MAJOR WORKS AND THEMES

The plays of Suzan-Lori Parks dramatize the subtle and complex influences forming identity, both individual and collective. "I didn't aspire to get to Broadway—I aspired to be a playwright, not because I saw a lot of women writing plays, but because I love plays and I think of myself, while I am a black woman, I am also a writer" (Rasbury par. 3). Language, the power of words, has been important for Parks from the outset. During the time she spent in Germany as an adolescent, Parks gained a critical, almost estranging, perspective on language itself, and therefore also on identity and culture (Garrett 24). Parks's drama is not a drama of polemics. And she does not write with a specific, or indeed any, theatrical audience in mind. She writes as much for her love of language as for the people who have led to her plays. "I write from the gut, or the balls. I don't have balls, but I know someone who does. That's tacky, I know, but I write from the gut. I think theater should come from there. Especially because it is life . . ." (Jiggetts 312). Instinct, intuition, call it whatever you like, Parks's theater is a theater of emotion. However, she does not provide any sort of road map in her writing. Given a visual and verbal overload of images, one may experience the theater of Suzan-Lori Parks on an emotional level, an intellectual level, or both simultaneously. Meditations on history, identity, and culture, Parks's plays deconstruct simultaneously the mythic experience of black America and the history of America. Through theatrical poetic language that relies on the musical techniques of repetition and revision, Parks creates works that are controlled exegeses of the American experience. The language used is musical and subversive, influenced by Euripides as well as by such divergent musical genres as jazz and opera.

Parks's first play produced in New York City, *Betting on the Dust Commander*, opened in 1987. Beginning and ending with identical scenes, Lucius and Mare narrating a double-frame slideshow, *Betting on the Dust Commander* is an exploration of language and relationships. Betting on someone other than one's self to come through becomes a question of both survival and manipulation. Images of horse racing ("Mare" the name of one of the characters, is also the name for a female horse) and weddings makes the connection between betting, horse racing, and marriage poignant and humorous.

Imperceptible Mutabilities in the Third Kingdom, Parks's second play, won the Obie Award as Best Off-Broadway Play of 1989. Written over a span of three years, *Imperceptible Mutabilities* is divided into four parts and requires a large or doubled cast. Faraway places—Timbuktu, France, Africa, the mythic "third kingdom"—along with forced separation and the longing for home pervade Parks's writing and in particular *Imperceptible Mutabilities*. African American identity and history—in particular how African American identity was created, the roles of memory and history in the formulation of this identity, and concepts of gender, and the roles of women as nurturers and as disenfranchised—are the thematic elements in *Imperceptible Mutabilities*. Written in four parts and a reprise, this play is nonnarrative, experimental, and satirical. Part 1, "Snails," shows three black women as a white naturalist observes them through a camera hidden in a replica of a giant cockroach hidden in their living room. In Part 3, an old black woman, an ex-slave, remembers her life as resembling the painful extraction of teeth. Two white children (black actors in whiteface) stand at her bed for pictures. Running throughout the play are black and white images, ones traditionally associated with photography, a process that selects and subsequently embalms. The most accessible narrative occurs in Part 4, "Greeks (or the Slugs)." Sergeant Smith, separated from his family, returns home having lost his legs while saving a boy, having finally earned the distinction (the loss of his legs) that will merit a photograph to record the moment.

The Death of the Last Black Man in the Whole Entire World features several fictional stereotypes, among them the "Black Man with Watermelon," who is enslaved, chased, beaten, and lynched, but who continually reappears on stage to tell his story. In *The American Play*, which premiered in New York City in 1995, Parks creates a protagonist who grows to adulthood obsessed with the life and death of President Abraham Lincoln. Parks dubs this protagonist the "Foundling Father," who works as a carnival sideshow attraction complete with whiteface paint—a reversal of the early-twentieth-century minstrel shows in which white comedians wore blackface paint to denigrate African Americans. For a small sum, arcade visitors can take a shot at the Foundling Father with a toy cap gun. When the Foundling Father disappears (in the second act), his wife listens for sounds of her husband while her young son digs for artifacts of his missing father. Just as in Part 4 of *Imperceptible Mutabilities*, a faithful wife and child wait for the head of the family and create their own history.

Venus, Parks's next work, was a collaboration with avant-garde theater director Richard Foreman. Produced in 1996, *Venus* is the fictionalized account of the curious case of Saartjie Baartman, a South African Khoi-San woman brought to England in 1810 as a sideshow attraction and named the "Venus Hottentot" due to her exaggerated female form, specifically an exaggerated, enormous posterior. Parks's play addresses the furor the sideshow aroused in London, where slavery was illegal. In *Venus*, Saartjie eventually escapes to Paris, where the Baron Docteur falls in love with her, but has plans to dissect her after she dies. In *Venus*, Parks uses a female protagonist to examine historical gaps in African American history. Like the Foundling Father in *The American Play*, the Venus Hottentot finds recognition in a sideshow. From Miss Saartjie Baartman's decision to leave Africa to make her fortune in England to her indenture in the freak show to her rescue and ultimate betrayal, this play by Parks is more accessible because the narrative follows conventional chronology. *Venus* won Parks her second Obie Award.

Under the auspices of the New York Shakespeare Festival in 1999, Parks's next work, *In the Blood*, had its premier. This comic–tragic drama is about a homeless single mother named Hester La Negrita and her five children. The character of Hester is based on two beleaguered heroines of literary history: Bertold Brechts's Mutter Courage and Hester Prynne, the doomed sinner in Nathaniel Hawthorne's *The Scarlet Letter*. Hester La Negrita and her five children live under a bridge; the word *slut* is scrawled on a wall in the background. Hester has nothing: no money and not enough food to feed herself or her family. All she possesses is her children, to whom she is fiercely loyal. She is exploited by all whom she comes in contact with: the community doctor, the father of one of her children; the street corner preacher, also father of one of her children; and her welfare caseworker. Hester is cheated and used by everyone. Ultimately, in the last act, Hester is driven to commit a violent act, the brutal murder of one of her own children that ultimately destroys her conscience. "The world of *In the Blood* is very much one of Parks' own creation, an imaginative, compelling setting that, though it may have been inspired by (Bertolt) Brecht's work, is refreshingly free of the didacticism of his plays. Like Hester Prynne, Parks' Hester wants to make her own way in the world" (Keating D04).

Fucking A, written in 2000, continues the imagery associated with Hawthorne. However, the "scarlet A" in *Fucking A* represents an abortionist rather than an adulteress. At the Public Theater in New York City on March 2003, *Fucking A* premiered three years after its debut in Houston by the Infernal

Bridegroom Ensemble. Set in a dystopia of the future, *Fucking A* is about an abortionist, Hester Smith, who tries to win the freedom of her imprisoned son, Monster. Monster has been imprisoned for twenty years, since age five, for stealing a piece of meat from a rich family. Betrayed by a little girl who grows up to be The First Lady, Hester pays all of her earnings to a freedom fund to purchase the right to have a picnic with her son. "Ms. Parks calls *Fucking A* a Jacobean revenge tragedy. It's a bloody work, with Hester on stage sometimes covered with her patients' blood . . ."(Smith 24). *Fucking A* is the story of the divisions of genders, classes, races, and generations, set in an indeterminate future. "I'm deep into deep transgression," Ms. Parks explains, referring to her unprintable title and her dark subject matter (qtd. in Smith 24).

Topdog/Underdog, Parks's next play, premiered at the Joseph Papp Public Theatre in 2001 moving to Broadway's Ambassador Theatrer in April 2002. Lincoln, who once was a skilled player of three-card monte, works in an arcade shooting booth costumed as Abraham Lincoln, paralleling Parks's Foundling Father in *The American Play*. Booth, Lincoln's brother, a skilled shoplifter, ridicules his brother's job and tries to convince him to return to a more lucrative career as a three-card monte player. Resenting his brother Lincoln's natural talent, Booth's bitterness breeds aggression, which leads to an inevitably violent finale. On April 9, 2002, Parks was announced as that year's winner of the Pulitzer Prize for Drama for *Topdog/Underdog*, which is the only play by an African American woman, aside from one-woman shows, to reach Broadway since Ntozake Shange's *for colored girls who have considered suicide/when the rainbow is enuf*, which opened in 1976. The play is also a rare example of a woman writing drama featuring only male characters.

Only one of Parks's plays, *Venus*, is based on historical fact. The others are pure poetic invention. Characters struggle and suffer, but are also seen through the lens of a pervasive, absurdist, tragic sense of irony. Parks does not employ in any of her plays a realistic version of African American speech. Rather, like Shange, she crafts a theatrical poetry reminiscent of black dialectic forms. In keeping with the tradition of James Joyce's language use in *Dubliners*, a language he heard and remembered, what Parks does is capture the rhythm, tone, and color of African American speech.

Over the past three years, Parks's work has changed radically. New works—*Topdog/Underdog*, *In the Blood*, and *Fucking A*—do not truly look backward, even though loosely based on historical personages. These plays instead look forward: toward individual and psychologically motivated acts of violence that take place on stage (unlike in the history plays). Parks said in 1994:

. . . Forced separation, longing and the longing for home, for the missing, for the distant and the dead, pervade her writing; Part Four of *Imperceptible Mutabilties* centers around a black army sergeant separated from his family. Reducing this recurring motif to psychology or biography obscures the more important matter of how it works as a formal principle: Parks' is a drama of longing and echoes. Every play I write is about love and distance. And time. . . . And from that we can get things like history. (qtd. in Garrett 25)

The theater of Suzan-Lori Parks deftly reflects and refracts social imagery in American and African American culture and history. Her works reveal the role that drama must play in shaping and propagating assumptions about race and culture. Emotionally engaging characters such as Hester in *Fucking A* and Lincoln in *Topdog/Underdog* find themselves in symbolic or allegorical situations in which humor is mixed with tragedy. In *Venus*, written in 1996, Parks chooses to ignore common conventions of stage realism, exposing the ambivalent depictions of racism, sexism, and economic oppression. In contrast, *In the Blood* presents audiences and critics with a more naturalistic meditation on social responsibility and the treatment of the most indigent. Parks's signature use of gritty colloquialisms and provocative stagecraft illuminates contemporary issues. In creating compelling stories and characters, Parks's deep explorations challenge audiences to reconsider assumptions about themselves as well as others. Shelby Jiggetts, in a 1996 interview, used the word *multidirectional* to describe Parks's drama. Parks's response: "Exactly, so you can fill in the blanks. You can do it now by inserting yourself into the present. You can do it back then, too" (Jiggetts 317). Multidirectional drama, depicting the African American experience, impacts theatergoers and critics alike. Filled with images that can and do horrify (for example, the ending tableaux of *Topdog/Underdog* where Booth is cradling the body of his dead brother, Lincoln), Parks's drama is one of paradox, specifically African American in conception, but universal in its message and appeal.

CRITICAL RECEPTION

Critical reception of Suzan-Lori Parks's work ranges from laudatory, in particular for recent works such as *Topdog/Underdog* and *In the Blood*, to "challenging" for earlier works, specifically *Venus*. Jean Young asserts in an essay in the *African-American Review*, "Saartjie Baartman [the main character in *Venus*] is an accomplice in her own exploitation" (699). Contrasting views of Parks's oeuvre commend her ability to depict racism and its legacy. In *Venus* and previous works, points out *American Theater* contributor Shawn-Marie Garrett, "Parks has dramatized some of the most painful aspects of the black experience: Middle Passage, slavery, urban poverty, institutionalized discrimination and racist ethnographies. Yet even as her plays summon up the brutality of the past, they do so in a manner that is, paradoxically, both horrific and comic— irresistibly or disrespectfully so, depending on your point of view" (22).

Topdog/Underdog won enthusiastic responses from critics, culminating in its being awarded the 2002 Pulitzer Prize for Drama. *Christian Science Monitor* reviewer Iris Fanger describes it as "a cross between a hip-hop riff and a Greek tragedy; as entertaining as the former and as gripping as the latter" (19). Comparing *Topdog/Underdog* to a classic of African American literature, Ralph Ellison's 1952 novel *The Invisible Man*, *New York Times* critic Ben Brantley describes the play as a new twist on the biblical Cain and Abel story: "Brotherly love and hatred is translated into the terms of men who have known betrayal since their youth . . . and who will never be able to entirely trust anyone, including (and especially) each other. Implicit in their relationship is the idea that to live is to con" (E1). "I think she is truly original," director George C. Wolfe tells interviewer Don Shewey. "A lot of people are talented and smart and gifted, and that's exciting. Not a lot of people are original. Every time she and Caryl Churchill and Sam Shepard write a play, they throw themselves into the truth of the play and a world emerges. We find ourselves fully engaged, our minds, our hearts and our spirits. Even in the presence of devastation, there is possibility—and vice versa" (Shewey, "Suzan" par. 1).

Praise for Parks's work has always been accompanied by complaints that her plays are obscure, impenetrable, pretentious, even infuriating. Interviewed at the theater prior to the final dress rehearsal for *Topdog/Underdog*, Parks talked with her typical breeziness about the plays' origins: "I was thinking about *The American Play*, one day in 1999[,] and I thought, 'Oh, man, I should just—that'd be cook, two brothers, Lincoln and Booth.' Ha, ha, ha, it's funny. To me, it's funny" (Shewey, "Suzan" par. 1). Theater reviewer Robert Brustein's critique of *Topdog/Underdog*, "A Homeboy Godot," written after Parks was awarded the Pulitzer, best illustrates the seemingly contradictory opinions that exist about Parks's oeuvre in general, and in particular about *Topdog/Underdog*:

. . . This play was not my first choice for the award. [Brustein is on the Pulitzer Prize committee for drama.] It is far from Parks' most ambitious writing. . . . I was glad I had read the script first. Watching it cold might have made me register a dissent. . . . Frustration drove me back to the text. . . . I was glad to find the play perfectly coherent with the author's diction displaying the perfect pitch that the actors diction lacked. . . . Parks has written this play in the style of black vaudeville, the homeboy equivalent of *Waiting for Godot*. Like her previous work, it is a non-didactic theatricalization of the African-American condition. (25).

Parks is highly conversant with the twentieth-century avant-garde literary scene—in particular James Joyce, Gertrude Stein, and Samuel Beckett. ". . . The Great Emancipator or a white supremacist? Suzan-Lori Parks refuses to choose, embracing the ambiguities," writes *New York Times* critic Joshua Wolf Shenk in "Beyond a Black—and—White Lincoln" (AR5). Reviewing Parks's Pulitzer Prize–winning *Topdog/Underdog*, Shenk captures in a few words the major problem with Parks's plays, that she refuses to choose, and in fact does embrace and cultivate the ambiguities. On Abraham Lincoln, a central character in two of Parks' plays, *Topdog/Underdog* and *The American Play*, Shenk comments, "It is like Lincoln created an opening with that hole in his head . . . we've all passed through into it now, you know, like the eye of a needle. Everything that happens from 1865 to today has to pass through that wound . . ." (AR5). When asked by Shenk if the same is true with whites and blacks, Parks answers, "Yes, I think it shifts back and forth more than we're willing to admit, I think it's constantly in flux, any case moment by moment" (AR5). Lincoln, the great emancipator, is given a different history by Parks. According to Shenks's review, if Lincoln is a god and was in fact a white man, Parks as an African American playwright does not feel excluded from this American mythology. Parks not only gives a fresh interpretation to the character of Abraham Lincoln, she also has pragmatic reasons for her affinity for Mr. Lincoln. Asked directly by Shenk if she felt excluded from the "American (white) mythology," Parks's response was "No, I've gotten two plays out of it" (AR5).

It is critic Robert Brustein's opinion that Parks's latest offerings are more acceptable both thematically and linguistically than her earlier works, particularly works like *Imperceptible Mutabilities*, *Pickling*, and *Betting on the Dust Commander* (25). "Riffing" on Hawthorne, in a play about abortion set in a former colony turned dystopia, *Fucking A* is Parks's most recently produced Broadway play, debuting at the Public Theater in March 2003. "Tough-Minded Playwright Chooses a Title Too Tough to Ignore" is *New York Times* reviewer Danita Smith's extensive commentary on this play. The first question posed to Parks by Smith concerns the choice of Parks's "unprintable" title: "Why give your new play a title that no mainstream newspaper is ever going to print?" Parks responds: "The title is what led me to the play. . . . It's what led me to the play . . . if they don't print it, that's o.k. So what? Big deal" (24). According to Smith, the title is "typical Parks—independent, confident, won't be pinned down" (25). The play incorporates songs composed by Parks, the music a cross between Kurt Weill and the blues. However, most interesting, according to Smith, is Parks's creation of a "special language" for the play, labeled simply by Parks "talk": "Talk, which the actors speak intermittently (super titles translate it for the audience). It is mostly when they are talking about vaginas. 'Die Aban-nazip' means abortion" (25).

Fucking A is a play of metaphors, grounded in the dusty earth of west Texas in the early 1960s, filled with details about poor blacks of that era when the richest person in town was often the funeral director and the beauty parlor was the center for gossip (Smith 24). Pointing out similarities between *Fucking A* and William Faulkner's *As I Lay Dying*, Smith shows once again the paradox that is Suzan-Lori Parks, someone who is simultaneously in and out of the mainstream of contemporary theater. Parks's college writing teacher, James Baldwin,* predicted in his final evaluation that his student would go on to great things. According to Garrett in her essay for

American Theater, Baldwin noted of Parks that she is "an utterly astounding and beautiful creature who may become one of the most valuable artists of our time"(qtd. in Smith 24).

The dramas of Suzan-Lori Parks affirm the importance of the role of minority cultural perspectives in enriching and enlightening society. Rich in metaphor, based on history and personal experience, Parks's drama crosses boundaries of gender, race, and class. The dramas of Suzan-Lori Parks are visceral and imbued with the emotional intensity and intellectual curiosity found in all persons, regardless of gender or ethnicity.

BIBLIOGRAPHY

Dramatic Works by Suzan-Lori Parks

The American Play. New York: Dramatists Play Service, 1995.

"*Betting on the Dust Commander*." *The American Play and Other Works*. New York: Theater Communications Group, 1995. 73–90.

"*The Death of the Last Black Man in the Whole Entire World*." *Theater* (Summer–Fall) 1990: 16–34. Also published in *The American Play and Other Works*. New York: Theater Communications Group, 1995. 99–132.

"*Devotees in the Garden of Love*." *The American Play and Other Works*. New York: Theater Communications Group, 1995. 133–156.

F...A. 2000. New York: Theater Communications Group, 2001.

"*Imperceptible Mutabilities in the Third Kingdom*." *The American Play and Other Works*. New York: Theater Communications Group, 1995. 1–23.

In the Blood. 1999. New York: Dramatists Play Service, 2001.

"*Pickling*." *The American Play and Other Works*. New York: Theater Communications Group, 1995. 91–98.

Topdog/Underdog. New York: Theater Communications Group, 2001.

Venus (with Richard Foreman). 1996. New York: Theater Communications Group, 2001.

Studies of Suzan-Lori Parks's Dramatic Works

Bernard, Louise. "The Musicality of Language: Redefining History in Suzan-Lori Parks's '*The Death of the Last Black Man in the Whole Entire World*.'" *African-American Review* 31.4 (1997): 687–699.

Brantley, Ben. "Not to Worry, Mr. Lincoln." *New York Times* 8 Apr. 2002: E1.

Brustein, Robert. Rev. of *The Death of the Last Black Man in the Whole Entire World*, by Suzan-Lori Parks. *New Republic* 206.15 (1992): 29–31.

———."On Theater—A Homeboy Godot." *New Republic* (2003): 25.

Coleman, Wendy R., and Stacy Wolf. "Rehearsing for Revolution: Practice, Theory, Race, and Pedagogy (When Failure Works)." *Theater Topics* 8.1 (1998): 13–31.

Dixon, Kimberly D. "An I am Sheba me am (She be doo wah waaaah doo wah) O (au) rality, Textuality and Performativity African-American Literature's Vernacular Theory and the Work of Suzan-Lori Parks." *Journal of American Drama and Theater* 11.1 (1999): 49–66.

Druckman, Steve. "Suzan-Lori Parks and Liz Diamond: Doo-a-diddly-dit-dit." *TDR—The Drama Review* 39.3 (1995): 56–75.

Elam, Harry J., Jr., and Alice Rayner. "Unfinished Business: Reconfiguring History in Suzan-Lori Parks's 'The Death of the Last Black Man in the Whole Entire [*sic*] World.'" *Theater Journal* 46.4 (1994): 447–462.

Fanger, Iris. "Pulitzer Prize Winner Shakes Off Labels." *Christian Science Monitor* 12 Apr. 2002: 19.

Frieze, James. "Imperceptible Mutabilities in the Third Kingdom: Suzan-Lori Parks and the Shared Struggle to Perceive." *Modern Drama* 41 (Winter 1998): 523.

Garrett, Shawn-Marie. "The Possession of Suzan-Lori Parks." *American Theater* 17.8 (2000): 22–26, 132–134.

Heilpern, James. "'Foundling Father' Honest Abe Just Can't Find Honest Work." *New York Observer* 8 Apr. 2002: 214.

Hurwitt, Robert, "'*Topdog/Underdog*' Is Worthy of Pulitzer." *San Francisco Chronicle* 9 Apr. 2002: 24.

Jiggetts, Shelby. "Interview with Suzan-Lori Parks." *Calloo* 19.2 (1996): 309–317.

Keating, Douglas J. "'*In the Blood*': Modern Hester." *Philadelphia Inquirer* 1 Jan. 2003: D04.

Morales, Donald M. "Do Black Theatre Institutions Translate into Great Drama?" *African-American Review* 31.4 (1997): 633–677.

Rasbury, Angel R. "Women's Enews Pulitzer Prize Winner Parks Talks about Being a First." 11 Apr. 2002: 17pars. 3 June 2003. <http://www.now.org/eNews/april2002/041102parks.html>.

Ryan, Katy. "No Less Human": Making History in Suzan-Lori Parks's 'The American Play.'" *Journal of Dramatic Theory and Criticism* 8.2 (1999): 81–94.

Shenk, Joshua Wolf. "Beyond a Black—and—White Lincoln." *New York Times* 7 Apr. 2002: AR5.

Shewy, Don. "George C. Wolfe: Public Service." 15 Dec. 1997: 23 pars. 3 June 2003 <http://www.donshewey.com>.

———."Suzan-Lori Parks Turns towards Naturalism." 22 July 2001: 1 par. 3 June 2003 <http://www.donshewy.com>.

Smith, Dinitia. "Tough-Minded Playwright Chooses a Title Tough to Ignore." *New York Times* 16 Mar. 2003: 24–25.

Solomon, Alisa. "Signifying on the Signifyin': The Plays of Suzan-Lori Parks." *Theater* 21.3 (1990): 73–80.

West, Stan. "Tip-Toeing on the Tightrope: A Personal Essay on Black Writer Ambivalence." *African-American Review* 32.2 (1998): 285–291.

Wilmer, S. E. "Restaging the Nation: The Work of Suzan-Lori Parks." *Modern Drama* 43.3 (2000): 442.

Young, Jean. "The Re-Objectification and Re-Commodification of Saartjie Baartman in Suzan-Lori Parks's '*Venus.*'" *African-American Review* 31.4 (1997): 699–708.

Zoglin, Richard. "Moving Marginal Characters to Center Stage." *Time* 19 Feb. 2001: 62.

LOUIS STAMFORD PETERSON (1922–1998)

James L. Hill

BIOGRAPHY

A native of Hartford, Connecticut, Louis Stamford Peterson, Jr. was an actor, playwright, television and movie screenwriter, educator, and a talented pianist. Born on June 17, 1922, he was one of three sons of Louis Peterson, Sr. and Ruth C. Peterson, both of whom worked as employees of a local bank. Peterson grew up in a predominantly white section of Hartford that consisted mainly of immigrant families, and his childhood friends were mostly Swedish, Scottish, Italian, and Irish. Hartford was "a pleasant place in which to grow up," he remembered, a place where "there were never any awful destructive incidents as today when Negroes move into white neighborhoods in some places" (Carter 87).

After graduating from Bulkeley High School in Hartford in 1940, Peterson conformed to his parents' wishes that he attend college, enrolling in Morehouse College in Atlanta, Georgia. At Morehouse, he began his acting career, playing roles in several college productions, including *Murder in the Cathedral*, *Prometheus Bound*, *The Family Portrait*, *The Cherry Orchard*, and *Shadow and Substance*. Though initially interested in music, he graduated with a B.A. degree in English in 1944 and received the Benjamin Brawley Award for Excellence in English in his senior year. His interest in acting led him to enroll in the Yale University School of Drama, where he studied stage techniques during the school year 1944–1945. The next year Peterson enrolled in New York University to pursue his interest in acting; and during this period, he began working as an actor in and around New York City, landing his first lead role in the Blackfriars premiere of Edwin Bronner's *A Young American*. In 1947, he received his M.A. degree from New York University and appeared on Broadway in Theodore Ward's *Our Lan'*.

From 1948 to 1949, Peterson continued his professional preparation as an actor with Stanford Meisner at the Neighborhood Playhouse School of the Theatre in New York. By this time, however, he had already begun to have doubts about his career as an actor, and he still wanted to write plays. Since his first attempts at playwriting were unsuccessful, prompting him to seek additional professional training, Peterson enrolled in 1950 in a playwriting class taught by Clifford Odets at the Actors Studio, where he also took additional acting lessons with Lee Strasberg. Odets, well-known for his realistic plays, took a personal interest in Peterson and became his mentor. Subsequently, when he joined the national tour of *The Member of the Wedding* in September 1951, Peterson began writing his first and best known play, *Take a Giant Step*, which he completed in 1953. On July 21, 1952, he had married Margaret Mary Feury, and the next year, he persuaded a group of young producers to option his play for Broadway.

After a successful tryout in Philadelphia, *Take a Giant Step* opened on Broadway on September 24, 1953, at the Lyceum Theatre in New York and ran for seventy-six performances. Louis Gossett, Jr., then a high school senior and basketball player, was selected from 445 applicants to play the lead. Other cast members included Estelle Hemsley, Frederick O'Neal, Estelle Evans, Dorothy Carter, Pauline Myers, and playwright Frank Wilson. In 1956, *Take a Giant Step* was revived in an Off-Broadway production that ran for 264 performances, with black playwright Bill Gunn in the lead and Beah Richards, Godfrey Cambridge, Rosetta LeNoire, and Raymond St. Jacques as cast members.

After *Take a Giant Step*, Peterson completed an unpublished play about his experience in the Connecticut tobacco valley; however, he was unable to get the play produced. Fortunately, for Peterson, the social and political forces of the late 1950s conspired to create favorable conditions for African Americans interested in writing for movies and television, and he was prepared to make his mark. Although he had achieved initial success in the theater, Loften Mitchell* concluded, Peterson was unappreciated as a dramatist and turned to more profitable television and movie writing (Mitchell 166).

Peterson's first script, *Padlocks*, was a full-length television drama produced on the CBS series *Danger* in 1954, with James Dean in the lead. In 1954, he also wrote *Class of 1958*, a drama sequel to *Take a Giant Step* that explores the difficulties of a young man in college. Although the script is clearly a sequel to *Take a Giant Step*, Goodyear Theatre produced it on NBC with an all-white cast. Two years later, Peterson followed with *Joey*, another full-length television drama produced by the Goodyear Theatre, starring Anthony Perkins and Kim Stanley. *Joey* was also selected as one of the best teleplays in

1956 and nominated for an Emmy Award. Peterson later sold *Joey* to Hollywood for an enormous sum, but unfortunately his teleplay was never filmed. In 1957, Peterson collaborated with Alberto Lattuada in writing *The Tempest*, a television version of the play; and he coauthored the film script of *Take a Giant Step* with Julius Epstein. The film, released in 1958, featured ballad singer Johnny Nash as Spencer, Ruby Dee as Catherine, and other members of the original Broadway cast. Peterson's other film and television credits include *The Emily Rossiter Story*, a full-length television script produced on the NBC *Wagon Train* series in 1957; *Hit and Run*, an episode for the popular television series *Dr. Kildare*; and the 1970s film *The Confessions of Nat Turner*.

Peterson's Hollywood success did not come without sacrifice. In 1961, his marriage dissolved, and family problems forced him to return to the East Coast permanently. His second produced play, *Entertain a Ghost*, opened Off Broadway at the Actors Playhouse on April 9, 1962, but closed after eight performances. One year later, Peterson suffered a heart attack and was forced to cease his activities for six months. In 1972, he accepted a position in the Department of Theatre Arts at the State University of New York at Stony Brook, where he began his teaching career, as he later indicated, to support "myself while I worked on things I really wanted to work on" (Delatiner E19). While teaching at Stony Brook, he completed two plays, *Crazy Horse* (1979), which had a limited twelve-run performance beginning on November 8, 1979, at the New Federal Theatre in New York, and *Another Show* (1983), which he produced at Stony Brook. He retired from Stony Brook in 1993, and with Ken Lauber, began cowriting *Numbers*, an interracial play focusing on a black gangster and a Jew involved in the numbers racket in Harlem after World War II. Peterson died of lung cancer on April 27, 1998, in New York.

MAJOR WORKS AND THEMES

Louis Stamford Peterson is best known as the author of the contemporary drama *Take a Giant Step*, a pioneering coming-of-age story that graphically demonstrates the difficulties of a young black adolescent male growing up in a predominantly white middle-class neighborhood in New York and confronting the insidious racism of his teacher and his classmates. When Spencer, the protagonist, questions his teacher's knowledge of slavery and the Civil War, he is expelled from school for two weeks; and his parents, Lem and Mary Scott, are uncompromising in their chastisement of him because they feel that he has acted irresponsibly and may have jeopardized his chances of going to college. The play also focuses on Spencer's loss of his grandmother, his humorous and unsuccessful encounter with a prostitute, and his sexual initiation with a caring and lonely widow. The most striking accounts of racism surface, however, in Spencer's relations with his neighborhood friends who eventually desert him because their girlfriends' parents do not want them associating with blacks. Thus, *Take a Giant Step* addresses several outcomes of racism, including the isolation, fear, and indignities a young black male faces growing up among white youths.

Like *Take a Giant Step*, all but one of Peterson's unpublished plays focus on interracial relations. *Entertain a Ghost*, his second play, is semiautobiographical and the story of an interracial couple. A play within a play, the outer play focuses on a married actress rehearsing a play written by her husband, and the interior play concerns the deterioration of their marriage. Similarly, *Crazy Horse* explores an interracial marriage in the 1950s between a black journalist and a white woman, a relationship obviously based on the author's life. The play emphasizes the disapproval of the marriage by parents on both sides; and at the center of the drama are the emotional conflicts between David and his wife, Kate, and the gradually developing insanity of their young daughter. *Another Show*, Peterson's final play, deviates from the interracial focus of previous plays. It is a story about a college student who commits suicide and the effects of his death on the people closest to him, all of whom feel guilty in one way or another for his demise.

CRITICAL RECEPTION

With the opening of *Take a Giant Step* on Broadway in 1953, African American drama, as Darwin T. Turner observed, came of age professionally (12). *Take a Giant Step* preceded *A Raisin in the Sun* in its Broadway debut by six years and as a Hollywood feature film by two years, establishing Louis Stamford Peterson as a serious dramatist. Critics praised his play as an original and poignant drama. *Take a Giant Step* had successful Broadway and Off Broadway runs. It was, however, as a harbinger of a new kind of African American drama that Peterson's play truly took a giant leap, for it appealed to theater audiences primarily as a "sympathetic, psychologically credible presentation of the emotional problems of a Negro youth reared in a predominantly white neighborhood" (Turner 13). Although the play uniquely addresses the insidious racism of America, Peterson was defensive and even apologetic that it did not attack the more blatant forms of racism and oppression prevalent in the American South (Peck E1). Perhaps the most significant recognition of Peterson's achievement came with the Burns Mantle Yearbook selection of *Take a Giant Step* as one of the best plays of 1953–1954.

While Peterson received significant recognition for his television and movie screenwriting, his subsequent plays failed to attract the critical acclaim of *Take a Giant Step*. Because of unfavorable reviews, *Entertain a Ghost*, for example, was forced to close after only eight performances, and Howard Taubman labeled it a "drab play within a dull one," expressing dismay that Peterson, who had earned well-deserved praise on Broadway a decade earlier, could have even written the play (48). Critics found *Crazy Horse* an arduous adventure for theater audiences, and *Another Show* did not fare much better. Thus, while Peterson continued to write and produce his plays throughout his career, critics generally agree that his reputation as a dramatist rests primarily on *Take a Giant Step*, his only published play.

BIBLIOGRAPHY

Dramatics Works by Louis Stamford Peterson

Another Show. Stony Brook: State University of New York, 1983.
Crazy Horse. Performed at New Federal Theatre, New York, November 8, 1979.
Entertain a Ghost. Performed at Actors Playhouse, New York, April 9, 1962.
Take a Giant Step. New York: French, 1954.

Studies of Louis Stamford Peterson's Dramatic Works

Abramson, Doris E. *Negro Playwrights in the American Theatre, 1925–1959*. New York: Columbia University Press, 1969.
Atkinson, Brook. "Giant Step." *New York Times* 4 Oct. 1953: B1.
Carter, Steven. "Louis Peterson." *Afro-American Writers, 1940–1955*. Vol. 76 of *Dictionary of Literary Biography*. Ed. Trudier Harris. Detroit: Gale, 1986. 86–92.
Delatiner, Barbara. "Playwright Eyes a New Giant Step." *New York Times* 20 Feb. 1983: E19.
Gussow, Mel. "Stage: 'Crazy Horse,' Drama by Louis Peterson, at New Federal." *New York Times* 12 Nov. 1979: C13.
Mitchell, Lofton. *Black Drama: The Story of the American Negro in the Theatre*. New York: Hawthorne 1967. 163–166.
Peck, Seymour. "The Man Who Took a Giant Step." *New York Times* 20 Sept. 1953: E1.
Smith, Virginia Whatley. "Peterson, Louis." *The Oxford Companion to African American Literature*. Ed. William L. Andrews, Frances Smith Foster, and Trudier Harris. New York: Oxford University Press, 1997. 570.
Taubman, Howard. "Theatre: Peterson Work." *New York Times* 10 Apr. 1962: sec. 2, 48.
Turner, Darwin T., ed. *Black Drama in America: An Anthology*. New York: Fawcett, 1971. 12–13, 22.

AISHAH RAHMAN
(1937–   )

Suzanne Hotte Massa

BIOGRAPHY

Born Virginia Hughes, Aishah Rahman was raised by her foster mother, Winnie Feral, in Harlem. Her own mother, who became a widow while still pregnant with Virginia, died of tuberculosis in a welfare sanatorium shortly after leaving her baby with the Ferals. The Ferals, who had emigrated to New York City from Bermuda, found life in Harlem oppressive. Winnie took in foster children to earn extra money and "dominate[d] the household with an unrelenting psychic terrorism" (Rahman, *Chewed* 45). In a dual act of revenge against her boyfriend and Winnie, Hughes escaped her foster mother's clutches by getting pregnant at the age of seventeen and leaving home. She gave up her son, Kelvin, for adoption in 1956. Her memoir, *Chewed Water*, is largely an explanation and apology to her son for making the choice to relinquish him to another family.

Hughes's literary interest began in grade school with her discovery of Langston Hughes,* who she believed was her father. She "was convinced that [his poems] were his secret codes and private messages to" her (Rahman, *Chewed* 83). However, when Hughes enrolled at Howard University, she studied political science, and earned her B.S. in 1968. Following graduation, she began teaching at Queens College, became active in the Congress of Racial Equality, converted to Islam, and changed her name to Aishah Rahman. In 1970, she started writing professionally for the theater, blending her political and literary interests. Her daughter, Yoruba, was born in 1972 while *Lady Day: A Musical Tragedy*, her first play, was playing at the Brooklyn Academy of Music. Since that time, Rahman has devoted her career to writing and teaching. She has taught at Amherst College in Massachusetts, Nassau Community College on Long Island, and Brown University in Providence, Rhode Island, where she is currently a professor in the Creative Writing Program, and editor of *NuMuse*, a journal for new plays, which she founded.

Rahman won the Doris Abramsom Playwriting Award for *The Mojo and the Sayso* in 1988. In addition to receiving the Rockefeller Foundation and the New York Foundation for the Arts Fellowships in 1988, she also received a special citation from the Rockefeller Foundation for dedication to playwriting in the American theater.

MAJOR WORKS AND THEMES

Although Aishah Rahman has written innumerable plays, only three are currently in print: *Unfinished Women Cry in No Man's Land while a Bird Dies in a Gilded Cage*, *Mojo and the Sayso*, and *Only in America*. And for many of her plays, there is no performance data available either. All of Rahman's work, including these three plays, share two motifs that create her signature form. Each play reverberates to the same rhythm as improvisational jazz, something Rahman calls "polytones." And each work deals with a cultural experience of the African diaspora. These often unpleasant experiences showcase the myriad ways in which marginalized people suffer oppression in the hands of the mainstream culture. On this landscape, Rahman creates a variety of scenes.

Unfinished Women is especially close to the jazz motif because Charlie Parker is the "Bird" who "Dies in a Gilded Cage," while the "Unfinished Women," pregnant teens, cry in the Hide-A-Wee home for unwed mothers, a "No Man's Land." The play is a study of contrasts carried to extremes for emphasis. While Charlie Parker is impeccably dressed, the master of ceremonies, Charlie Chan, is dressed in an ill-fitting, tattered tuxedo. While Charlie Parker is dying in Pasha's luxurious boudoir, the unwed mothers are languishing as they make difficult choices in the conventlike Hide-A-Wee home. These contrasts clearly demonstrate the difference between the privileged and the marginalized. Though the characters are relatively flat, Rahman counts on the reverberation of the music to generate emotion, providing exacting staging directions so that the music becomes another character that makes the story cohesive. This play relies more on staging technique and jazz tones than it does on carefully developed characters.

Rahman uses time as a tool to emphasize the squalor of the marginalized soon-to-be mothers. It fluctuates between being stagnant and elastic. Time stands still to accommodate the tension of two disparate scenes, while simultaneously underscoring the hopelessness of both situations. The play hinges on the moment of Parker's death, which is also the moment when the girls must decide the fate of their babies, thus linking death and life, as well. But life for these babies is death. One of the the moms, Midge, calls childbirth "babies murdered into this world" (9), because in 1955, an illegitimate child's life is more closely linked to death, a living hell. By making time stand still, Rahman expands the moment to accommodate the wide range of emotions present in the lives of the characters, thus providing an opportunity for the audience to examine their circumstances, which brings validity to the lives of the disenfranchised.

Charlie Parker is linked with these women because his art is also on the fringes of the mainstream culture. Rahman says that this play "juxtaposes the oppression of the artists and women in American society" ("Tradition" 24). And men, it appears, are the architects of oppression. Wilma, another unwed mom, says: "Secretly, I always wanted to be a man 'cause they can do things and go places. Bird is the man I wanted to be" (21). Later, Paulette bemoans the futility of her decision. If she gives up her baby, she can return to her father's home and "be [his] daughter again" (29). But this choice would only mean that she would be subjected to her father's control. However, she can be free of her father if she keeps her baby. But then she cannot pursue her dreams because she becomes socially stigmatized. As Paulette continues to ponder her decision, she more clearly comprehends the hold men have on women. "I bet a woman first used the word 'love,'" she says. "And that's just what 'love' is. A woman's weakness" (30). Paulette is implying that if a woman could learn to love herself rather than a man, she might be free. So Wilma suggests seeking sexual satisfaction with a woman to avoid the traps men set, viewing them as the culprits of their ruination. "We've been used, hurt, and abandoned by our men," she says (32). Unable to find a way to exist in a man's world, she seeks the comfort in no-man's-land. All of these young women are trapped in a world designed to imprison them.

Mojo and the Sayso is an examination of lives profoundly affected by racial profiling. Awilda and Acts's son, Linus, was killed by a policeman who mistook him for a thief. Three years after the tragic event, Awilda and Acts are still trying to make sense of their lives. As the play opens, we see Awilda and Acts living together in two different worlds. They have learned to avoid conflict, and simply cohabitate, each one lost in his or her own diversion from grief. Acts is in their living room, rebuilding his dream car, while Awilda is searching for her white gloves to complete her pristine churchgoing ensemble. She has become devoted to her church and Pastor Delroy, who is having a memorial for Linus on this day. She finds solace in her belief that as long as Linus is in her memory, he remains alive. Acts, on the other hand, views his car as the vehicle to his dreams, and does not want to dwell on Linus. As Awilda and Acts vocalize their personal reveries, as if in conversation, we learn that they have just received a sizable sum from the city as payment in the wrongful death of their child. But it is money that neither of them wants to touch. Awilda is puzzled: "How do they add up what a ten-year-old boy's life is worth to his parents?" (51). Acts calls the payment "[e]vil. Blood money. Payoff. Hush money" (52). He tells Awilda, "[D]o what you want with it and don't tell me" (52). While Awilda is at church, their other son, Walter, arrives. He had changed his name to Blood after his brother died to demonstrate the level of his anger about the injustices from which he suffers. He and his father discuss the money and various ways in which he feels marginalized and frustrated. He, too, expresses his disgust with the city's pitiful attempt to ameliorate the family's loss: "I hate that money as much as you. It's no treasure. It's no pot of gold after the rainbow" (59). They will not be persuaded to trade Linus's life for any amount of money. The truth is that Linus's death leaves a chasm in their lives that they cannot cross.

In the midst of Acts and Blood's discussion, Awilda returns from church with the pastor in tow. The pastor is an easily recognizable fraud, but Awilda is oblivious to that. He exploits his parishioners, and there are hints that he is probably guilty of pedophilia as well. He has persuaded Awilda to donate the check to his church, so that he can construct a monument for Linus. Blood and Acts, however, can see the pastor for what he is. They terrorize him and order him to strip, revealing that the pastor's attire is merely a costume. Under the pastor costume, he is a vulture, both figuratively and literally. This is the point at which the family's salvation emerges. Once the family is able to see with clarity, they resume real communication and are able to reconcile. The play ends as the family agrees to start a new life, and they exit in the newly completed dream car..

Only in America is a commentary on the power of voice: whose is heard, whose is not, and whose is distorted. Does *Only in America* mean that the right to free speech is only an American privilege? Or does it mean that only in America can a person desecrate that right? These questions are the basis of Rahman's satire.

Cassandra, a woman who understands English but can only speak gibberish, works for Oral. Oral is a man who knows he is required to follow the civil rights laws, but finds endless amusement in what he considers their absurdity, and mocks them. He is completely delighted and thoroughly amused by the irony that he is the head of a government-sanctioned animal rights group. He is laughing while he says to Cassandra that "[o]nly in America will you see a man like me at the head of the A B C, the Animal Bureau of Civil Rights in spite of the fact that I HATE ANIMALS!" (88). Cassandra works with a voice coach, Lilli, who encourages Cassandra to assimilate and become a part of the mainstream culture. However, Cassandra cannot, no matter how hard she tries. Her instinct is to protect herself by not leaving herself vulnerable. But that is not how Oral interprets her actions. Oral considers himself Cassandra's benefactor because he helped to "mainstream" her "despite [her] handicap" (86). Oral is shamelessly mercenary and hypocritical, and boasts to Cassandra about what he considers his triumphant speech before Congress: "Honored Knights. Throw away your Liberal Guilt and rest assured. Anything can be justified as a matter of economics" (87), a statement that further emphasizes his irreverence. Oral is so swept up in his dialogue that by the end of act 1, he is taunting and cruelly denigrating Cassandra with a lewd rap. Oral feels perfectly safe with his despicable behavior because he knows that Cassandra will not make the effort to speak. Again, he laughs as he tells her, "I suppose that if you could speak you would appeal to me for Justice?" (103). His tirade continues in this fashion until Lilli comes to Cassandra's rescue, helping her out of the cage in which Oral has put her.

Meanwhile, Scatwoman, the cleaning woman who provides the jazz background in this play, is scatting and cleaning the office. Lilli follows her lead as she continues her attempts to get Cassandra to speak. Cassandra tries to force a couple of insults out of her mouth and finally succeeds with R-A-P-E. Her first word unleashes a diatribe about male power and the ways in which they use rape to maintain that power. The final message, delivered by Cassandra, is that women must "[i]n known tongues / Speak out!" (116).

Rahman's plays are almost instructions meant to teach people how to rise above oppressive circumstances. Her message is clear: be strong, proud, and courageous, while insisting on ethical treatment.

CRITICAL RECEPTION

Aishah Rahman's plays have generated little critical response. Thadious M. Davis, in the introduction for *Plays by Aishah Rahman*, writes that "Rahman's writing is synonymous with music" (v). Davis continues her praise of Rahman's plays: "She weaves spells of transformation and hope, of continuity and love, perhaps especially of love—of self as well as of family and community—for all human kind besieged by violence and pain, by disappointment and confusion, by oppression and isolation" (v). Indeed, these are ideas that form the tableau of Rahman's work, and inform her subtext.

Alicia Kae Koeger reiterates Davis's assertion that Rahman's *Unfinished Women* "draws upon the structures and conventions of . . . jazz, to provide the framework for its story" (100). "The central core of the play," Koeger continues, "explores the cycle of life, death, and rebirth as it is manifested in the teenagers' lives and in Parker's music. The creativity of childbirth parallels the musician's power to create while the death of the young women's innocence parallels Charlie Parker's death" (103–104). According to Koeger, "jazz is the organized principle for the play's structure," creating "a play that reaches beyond traditional western theatrical conventions" (105). Finally, Koeger states that the "written text merely suggests the final effect in performance" (109). Like jazz, Rahman's plays are meant to be heard and seen.

BIBLIOGRAPHY

Dramatic Works by Aishah Rahman

Chiaroscuro: A Light and Dark Comedy. Unpublished. No production data available.
Lady and the Tramp. Unpublished. No production data available.
Lady Day: A Musical Tragedy. Produced at Chelsea Theatre, 1972.
The Mojo and the Sayso. 1987. New York: Broadway Play Publishing, 1997. Produced at Crossroads Theatre Company, 1987.
Only in America. New York: Broadway Play Publishing, 1997.
Parsley. Unpublished. No production data available.
Public Spaces. Unpublished. No production data available.
Smoke and Mirrors. Unpublished. No production data available.
Tale of Madame Zora. Produced at Ensemble Theater, New York, 1986.
Transcendental Blues. Produced at Frederick Douglass Creative Arts Centre, New York, 1976.
Unfinished Women Cry in No Man's Land While a Bird Dies in a Gilded Cage. 1977. New York: Broadway Play Publishing, 1997. Produced at New York Shakespeare Company, 1977.

Other Cited Material by Aishah Rahman

Chewed Water. Hanover: University Press of New England, 2001.
"Tradition and a New Aesthetic." *MELUS* 16 (Fall 1989–1990): 23–26.

Studies of Aishah Rahman's Dramatic Works

Davis, Thadious M. *Plays by Aishah Rahman*. New York: Broadway Play Publications, 1997.
Koeger, Alicia Kae. "Jazz Form and Jazz Function: An Analysis of *Unfinished Women Cry in No Man's Land while a Bird Dies in a Gilded Cage*." *MELUS* 16 (Fall 1989–1990): 99–111.
Maynard, Suzanne. "1997 Interview with Aishah Rahman." 4 Oct. 1997. 8 Apr. 2003 <http://www.brown.edu/Departments/English/Writing/rahmanmaynard.html>.
Peterson, Janet, and Suzanne Bennett. *Women Playwrights of Diversity: A Bio-Bibliographical Sourcebook*. Westport: Greenwood, 1997.

WILLIS RICHARDSON
(1889–1977)

Harish Chander

BIOGRAPHY

Willis Richardson, the first African American playwright to have a play produced on Broadway, was born on November, 5, 1889, in Wilmington, North Carolina. His father, Willis Wilder Richardson, was a construction worker, and his mother, Agnes Ann Richardson (née Harper), a laundry woman. His father was educated, and he encouraged his young son to read. The identity of his biological parents, however, is shrouded in mystery because some of his relatives believe that a rich white man with the surname "Mckoy" was his biological father, and Agnes Richardson was his grandmother rather than his mother (Gray, *Willis* 8). He enjoyed a relatively happy childhood, not knowing any significant privation. While in Wilmington, he attended Mrs. Moore's "pay school," as he records in his unpublished autobiographical essay "Youth to Age" (Gray, *Willis* 9). The victory of the Democratic white supremacy advocates in the November elections in 1899 led to riots in Wilmington in which sixteen blacks were killed. Consequently, Richardson's father, who voted and actively participated in local politics, left Wilmington, in fear for his life. In "Youth and Age," Willis Richardson writes that he will "never forget" the traumatic effects of the bloody Thursday, November 10 (qtd. in Gray, *Willis* 9).

The Richardson family moved to Washington, DC, in August 1899, where Richardson attended M Street High. Among his teachers was the playwright Mary Burrill, who considered Richardson one of her best students and encouraged his interest in drama.

Upon his graduation, Willis Richardson was offered a scholarship to attend Howard University. However, he could not avail himself of this opportunity because he had to seek full-time employment to help his family financially. In 1911, Richardson was hired as a clerk at the U.S. bureau of Engraving and Printing, Washington, DC. He remained with the bureau for forty-three years, until his retirement in 1954. On September 14, 1914, he married Mary Ellen Jones, another bureau employee, whom he had first met in 1912. He converted to Catholicism, which was his wife's religion. The couple had three daughters—Jean Paula, Shirley Antonella, and Noel Justine.

In March 1916, Richardson saw a performance of Angelina Weld Grimké's* *Rachel* (1920), a "race" play in which a black woman's fear of persecution of her would-be children by whites forces the title character to forgo marriage and motherhood. While watching Rachel, Richardson decided that plays written by African Americans should focus on the black community rather than interracial conflicts, and he resolved that he would write such plays. He then took correspondence courses in poetry and drama from 1916 to 1918. He embarked on his career as a playwright with an essay, "The Hope of a Negro Drama," published in *Crisis*, an NAACP publication edited by Dr. W. E. B. Du Bois, in November 1919. He considered the Irish theater movement "an excellent model" to follow for black playwrights (338), and looked forward to the day when "a company of Negro players with Negro plays" would tour the United States and Europe (339).

His first play, *The Deacon's Awakening* (1920), espousing women's rights, also appeared in *Crisis*. The play was staged the following year in St. Paul, Minnesota, but failed to elicit the attention of the critics. Between 1920 and 1921, four of his plays for children—*The King's Dilemma*, *The Gypsy's Finger King*, *The Children's Treasure*, and *The Dragon's Tooth*—appeared in *The Brownies' Book*, another NAACP publication, also edited by Du Bois. These plays teach "Universal Love and Brotherhood for all little folk—black and brown and yellow and white" (Du Bois 229). Richardson's first notable success came in 1922, when the Ethiopian Art Players of Chicago, on Du Bois's recommendation, asked to perform a Richardson play. He suggested either *The Chip Woman's Fortune* (1923) or *The Broken Banjo: A Folk Tragedy* (1925) to the group, which chose the former, performing it in 1923 in Chicago, Washington, DC, and Harlem. The play also became the first serious black play to be presented on Broadway, when the company performed the play at Frazee Theatre on May 15, 1923.

The Broadway success of *The Chip Woman's Fortune* bolstered Richardson's image. In 1924, the Howard Players performed Richardson's play *Mortgaged*. The Gilpin Players produced his play *Compromise: A Folk Play* in Cleveland, Ohio, in 1925, and then the Krigwa Players produced it in New York the following year. The Krigwa Players also produced his *The Flight of the Natives* in Washington, DC, in 1927. During the 1920s, Richardson also wrote *The Bootblack Lover* (1926), *The House of Sham* (1929), and *The Idle*

Head (1929). Richardson was a member of the literary group the Saturday Nighters, from its inception in 1926 to its disbanding in 1936, that met at the home of Georgia Douglas Johnson* on Saturday nights to discuss members' new works and projects.

At the request of Carter G. Woodson, historian and founder of the Association for the Study of Negro Life and History, Richardson edited the first anthology of plays by black authors, *Plays and Pageants from the Life of the Negro* (1930), aimed at teaching black children black history. In 1935, Woodson again sought Richardson for another book—a collection of plays on black history. The result was an anthology coedited with May Miller,* *Negro History in Thirteen Plays*. Richardson contributed three plays to the first anthology, and five to the second.

During the 1930s, black schools and colleges, as well as church groups, produced Richardson's plays, quite often without obtaining his permission. However, Richardson was piqued when the Howard University Players produced *Compromise* without seeking his permission. He complained to Alain Locke, the company's codirector. Locke, who had helped revise the play by providing a new ending, broke off all relations with him. With the loss of Locke's support, Richardson was unable to have his new works published or produced. Lack of encouragement and appreciation seemed to have sapped Richardson's creativity because for the rest of his life he did not write any plays comparable to his best works of the 1920s and 1930s. Most of his plays are one-act plays. A one-act play, as a distinct art form having its own artistic integrity, became popular around 1890 with the onset of the Little Theatre movement. In the preface to *Representative One-Act Plays by American Authors* (1928), Margaret Gardner Mayorga, holds that a one-act play is a play of "exposition" rather than one of "development" (ix). Richardson wrote eight three-act plays, but to his great disappointment he could not get any of them published or produced.

In 1947, Richardson's family was bereaved as Richardson's youngest daughter, Noel, committed suicide. Also, Richardson's correspondence with Du Bois aroused the suspicion of the federal government, and he was made to sign a loyalty oath to the U.S. government.

In 1956, Richardson reissued the collection of children's plays he had contributed earlier to *The Brownies' Book*, and added new plays to it, under the title *The King's Dilemma: Episodes of Hope and Dream*.

Apart from his fifty plays (twenty-nine of them unpublished), Richardson left behind seven short stories, titled *The Banny Simms Stories*, four of them still unpublished, and a collection of sixty-four poems titled *Victorian Poems*, most of them yet to be published.

In 1974, Richardson was diagnosed with Padgett disease. While he was convalescing in a nursing home, his wife gave away most of his books to a priest. When he returned home, he was shocked to find his treasure trove of books gone. During the last days of his life, he felt unhappy because he felt that the merit of his works had not been recognized by the world. He died on November 7, 1977. Ironically, a fortnight after his death, on November 21, he was posthumously honored with an AUDELCO (Audience Development Committee) Award as an Outstanding Playwright.

MAJOR WORKS AND THEMES

Willis Richardson was the first proponent and practitioner of the black folk play, which challenged the white stereotypical portrayal of blacks as comic or tragic darkies prevalent in the vaudeville jigs and minstrel shows of his time. However, unlike the Irish playwright John Millington Synge's folk plays that deal with their protagonists' conflict with forces of nature, black folk plays deal with the problems faced by ordinary black people, rural or urban. There is, however, a wide difference between black folk plays written by white Americans and by black Americans because they write from different points of view. While it was a white writer—Ridgley Torrence—who began the black folk play movement in his *Three Plays for a Negro Theater*, presented in New York in 1917, he and other white playwrights such as Eugene O'Neill did not write from firsthand knowledge and understanding of black people and, hence, created, in James V. Hatch's words, only "synthetic folk plays" (210–211). It was thus left to the black playwright, Willis Richardson, to write the first genuine black folk play depicting real black people and issues. In his November 1919 *Crisis* essay, "The Hope of a Negro Drama," Richardson lays down his ideas on the goals of black drama and provides a road map of his own future contribution to drama. He holds that "Negro plays" should be much more than mere "plays with Negro characters" and propaganda plays, and that they should show "the soul of the people," emphasizing that "the soul of [black] people is truly worth showing" (338). In another essay, "Propaganda in the Theatre," which appeared in the November issue of *Messenger* in 1924, Richardson writes about the subject matter of black drama: "Every phase of life may be depicted in Negro drama. . . . The lives of the educated with their perfect language and manners may be shown as well as the lives and problems of the less fortunate who still use the dialect" (354). In the same essay, like George Bernard Shaw who proclaimed that he wrote with the explicit purpose of converting the nation to his own opinion, Richardson expresses the view that the stage be used "for the purpose of changing the opinion of the people" (353). Like W. E. B. Du Bois, he sincerely believes in the use of theater as an educational tool.

In his plays for adults, Richardson tackles black issues of the day, such as gender and class discrimination, marriage and family problems, black exploitation of other blacks, racial solidarity, black male unemployment, and requirements for the advancement of the black race. In his plays for children, Richardson teaches lessons in human brotherhood, charity, and democracy. In his history plays, Richardson portrays black heroes as the embodiment of the African and African American ideals and virtues.

In *The Deacon's Awakening* (1920), Richardson deals with the issue of women's rights as Deacon Dave Jones and his friend Sol, in deference to their church's orders, try to dissuade women members of their church from voting. Dave Jones says to his wife Martha, "We don't mean to have the women in our congregation goin' to the polls to vote. Ah believe in a woman's stayin' in her place and not tryin' to fill a man's shoes" (219). When his daughter refuses to give up membership in the Voting Society, Dave Jones threatens to take her out of Howard University, and Sol threatens the same action against his daughter, Eva. Martha Jones then explains that men are wrong if they think that the woman's sphere is limited to the household, and that women are no more than "parts of the house" (212). She clinches her case by arguing that there is no antagonism between the interests of men and those of women, and that, accordingly, men and women should combine their voting power for their common good. Thereupon, Dave Jones and Sol withdraw their opposition to women's voting.

A Pillar of the Church (written in the 1920s; first published in 1996) deals with a woman's right to receive the education of her choice. John Fisher, an extremely religious man who lords over his wife to such an extent that he has "bullied the soul out of her" (33), is upset to learn that his older daughter, May, has won medals for excellence in music and artistic dancing. When the teacher, Miss Knight, visits with the Fisher family to persuade them to enroll their younger child, Geneva, in the same school as May, Mr. Fisher questions the usefulness of teaching dancing and literature, suggesting that he prefers teaching "facts, plain newspaper and Bible" (42). Miss Knight defends her school curriculum, explaining that novels expand the reader's mental horizon (42). Ultimately, Mr. Fisher permits May to continue at her school for another year to finish her education, but refuses to send Geneva to that school, ignoring both her wishes and those of her mother. Geneva can do nothing but accept her father's decision.

The Chip Woman's Fortune (1923) is Richardson's most successful folk play; it is the only play by Richardson that enjoyed the distinction of a Broadway appearance. The need for black self-help and cooperation is at the heart of this play. The Green family faces the prospect of losing the Victrola, their only source of entertainment. Silas Green has purchased the record player on an installment plan, but falls behind in his payments. Upon the Victrola seller's request, the white storekeeper where Silas works furloughs Silas for not making payments on time, and the seller sends his men to repossess the Victrola. While her son, Jim, is away, Aunt Nancy, the chip woman, lives for free with the Greens in exchange for taking care of Liza Green, Silas's ailing wife. Jim is serving time in a penitentiary for beating a white man who had relations with his girlfriend, and beating the girlfriend when he learns of her relationship. During her stay with the Greens, Aunt Nancy has been saving money for her son by selling bits of coal and chips of wood. Silas asks Aunt Nancy to pay him rent for the time she has stayed with his family because he knows that she has hoarded her money. She responds that she has some money, but that it belongs to Jim. Fortuitously, for the Green family, Jim is released the day the merchant's men come to repossess the Victrola. Learning about the Greens' financial problem, Jim gives Silas Green the whole of the $15 he has, but that is not enough. Informed by Silas Green that his mother has some money, Jim asks his mother to dig up her treasure box, and then shares the money with the Greens, permitting them to pay for the Victrola.

The play asks the reader not to judge too harshly a person who has served time in prison. The playwright seems to be in agreement with Aunt Nancy's response to Silas Green's criticism of Jim because of his jail term: "Goin' to the pen ain' nothin'. Some o' the best men in the world's been to the pen. It ain't the goin' to the pen that counts, it's what you go there for . . . the people . . . forgot that the Lord was locked up" (40–41). Jim's generosity to the Greens redeems him.

The Broken Banjo: A Folk Tragedy (1925) highlights the need for black unity and family solidarity. However, unlike *The Chip Woman's Fortune*, in which the family remains together, dissension within the family brings about the destruction of the family. Matt Turner and Emma Turner constantly quarrel about the time Matt spends playing the banjo. Emma complains to Matt, "[Y]ou don't care a thing about nobody or nothin' but that old banjo" (640). Matt, in his turn, complains about Emma's brother, Sam, and her cousin, Adam (640). He even doubts his wife's love for him, telling her, "Ain't nobody likes me but you, and you ain't crazy about me" (640). She responds, "Ah'm thinking for you every minute o' my life, but you don't know it. You never will know till you get in a big pinch" (640). The "big pinch" presents itself soon when Sam and Adam, in a scuffle, break the banjo. The breaking of the banjo leads to the breaking apart of the family through betrayal.

Compromise: A Folk Play (1925) depicts the difficulty blacks experienced in obtaining justice in the post-Emancipation period. Seven years have elapsed since the white man Ben Carter accidentally fatally shot Joe Lee who was hiding in a tree. Carter escaped being called to account by paying only $100. With the money he received for his son's killing, Jim Lee drank himself to death. The Lee family faces another crisis when Ben Carter's son, Jack, impregnates Annie Lee. When Jane Lee confronts Ben Carter to seek justice, Ben Carter, one of the wealthiest white men of the county, responds, "I'll do what's reasonable, but it's got to be fair" (186). Jane Lee says that he should pay for her children, Alec and Ruth, to go to school. He agrees, but later reneges when he learns that Alec has broken Jack Carter's arm to punish him for "ruining" his sister. The play ends with Jane Lee's frantic efforts to save Alec from falling into the hands of Ben Carter.

The Flight of the Natives (1927) gives a lie to the myth of the contented slave. As the play opens, the mulatto slave, Luke, brings the news that the fugitive slave, Slim, has been captured because of Jude's, Marse's favorite slave, betrayal. The slave Mose threatens to beat Jude for his action, but is dissuaded by his wife, Pet, who fears that Marse will retaliate by selling Mose down the river. Marse asks the slave Monk to whip Mose the way he has whipped Slim, but Monk says that his "arm's almost dead from lashin' Slim" (386). Marse then asks Jude to whip Mose, but Jude is too frightened to do it. Marse, therefore, says that he will whip Mose himself, but then announces instead that he will sell Mose down the river the next morning. When Marse leaves, Luke offers a plan that will bring "deliv'rance" to all of them. Dressed as a planter, the light-skinned Luke looks like Marse and poses as a slave owner, while Mose and others act as his newly purchased slaves, who are helping him catch the runaway slave, Slim. As the curtain closes, the slaves, under Luke's command, make a dash to freedom.

The Idle Head (1929) is a folk play about a black man who, refusing to grin and cringe before white people, is unable to obtain employment. Since he stands on his dignity and does not want to compromise his self-respect, he enters white people's houses from the front door. He loses his last job at a club, when he rebuffs a tip from a young man, who says as he throws a quarter at him, "Here, Sambo, here's a tip for you" (236). Without a job, he pawns some jewelry he finds in clothes sent for washing to his mother. He uses the funds to pay his mother's church dues, but he ends the play under arrest because of the telltale pawn ticket in his clothes.

Mortgaged (1924) and *The House of Sham* (1929) are two other important plays that deserve consideration. The first play concerns the Fields brothers, one a slumlord who makes money by exploitation of other black people, the other a research scientist who seeks to uplift the black race through science. The scientist needs funds to send his son to Harvard University, but his rich brother will loan him money only if he agrees to give up his research and obtain a regular job. But before the scientist accepts the money, he receives a letter from a major corporation stating that it has accepted his formula, and will pay him very well. The scientist seems to be speaking for the author when he argues to his brother that "[i]t's not money that's going to make this race of ours respected, but what its men and women accomplish in science and the arts" (113). Here, Richardson seems to support W. E. B. Du Bois's notion of encouraging the talented tenth of the black race as a method for encouraging black advancement. As for *The House of Sham*, it tells the story of the shady deals and sharp practices of Mr. John Cooper to support an extravagant lifestyle for himself and his family. The moment of truth comes when a buyer exposes Cooper for overcharging him in the sale of his house. Cooper's family members are shocked when he confesses that the $500 check his wife has written to compensate the buyer for the overpayment is no good because there is no money in his bank account. To support his extravagant lifestyle, Cooper admits, "I stole and did everything else crooked, and now I'm done for. We're all done for!" (286).

Of Richardson's plays for children, *The King's Dilemma* (1920?) and *The Black Horseman* (1930) are the most important. A favorite among school-children, *The King's Dilemma* employs the elements of fantasy and fairy tale, such as future time, to dramatize the beginnings of democracy in the last kingdom of the world whose white prince chooses to befriend a black boy in spite of the opposition of the king. The prince shows the equality of all of his friends by pointing out that each one of them has his special area of excellence, and that the blood flowing in the veins of each one of them has the same color. The play's message is perhaps best expressed in its own words: "The power of the world belongs to all the people, and no one race shall rule the world again" (234). Ironically, democracy comes only when the king reluctantly yields the government to the people rather than continue a monarchy in which a black man, the prince's friend, would share equal power with the prince.

Set in 204 B.C., *The Black Horseman* shows Carthage's attempted plot to annex East Numidia by offering King Massinissa of East Numidia the hand of Princess Sophonisba in marriage, if he agrees to Syphax's becoming the king of both Numidias. King Massinissa proves himself as a brave and steadfast ally of Rome, who, heeding the wise counsel of the women of Numidia and his counselor Friatus, discovers the treacherous plot of Syphax, and remains the beloved King of East Numidia.

In addition to *The Flight of the Natives*, Richardson contributed five history plays to the anthology *Negro History in Thirteen Plays* (1935). They are *In Menelek's Court*, *The Elder Dumas*, *Attucks the Martyr*, *Antonio Maceo*, and *Near Calvary: An Easter Play for Children*. In the introduction to the anthology, Carter G. Woodson writes about its subject matter: "The Negro is presented as a maker of civilization in Africa, a contributor to progress in Europe, and a factor in the development of Greater America" (v). In the preface to the anthology, Willis Richardson and May Miller* observe, "The writers have not attempted to reproduce definitive history, but have sought to create the atmosphere of a time past or the portrait of a memorable figure . . ." (vi).

In Menelik's Court, set in 1896, Abyssinians successfully repulse the Italian spies' attempts to abduct Princess Zoenda and hold her as a hostage in Italy. When the spies are discovered, Abyssinian Emperor remarks, "Abyssinians are civilized. We do not betray our enemies when they trust us. Our hands are brown and we play a fair game—always above the table" (124). *Antonio Maceo* and *Attucks the Martyr* tell the stories of two fighters for freedom of their countries. The first play dramatizes the assassination of the Cuban freedom fighter Antonio Maceo by Spanish soldiers. With his dying breath, he prophesies that the Cubans will continue to fight for the freedom until victory is won. Set on March 5, 1770, the second play depicts the martyrdom of Crispus Attucks, a fugitive slave in the Boston Massacre. He leads the attack against the British soldiers in Boston, and is the first one to die in the colonists' fight for independence. *Near Calvary* is set on the day of the Crucifixion. While Peter "denied knowing anything about Jesus" (100), Simon, who is "brave and black" carried Jesus' cross on the way to Calvary. In *The Elder Dumas*, set in Paris in 1843, the famous mulatto playwright of the title is charged with stealing other people's ideas and jokes. Even his secretary, Marie, complains that Dumas receives lots of "rubbish" from unknown writers, which "will be polished and painted and sent out under the name of Alexandre Dumas" (69).

CRITICAL RECEPTION

Despite winning initial recognition and fame with the Broadway production of *The Chip Woman's Fortune* in 1923, and enjoying popularity with his history plays among black teachers and students alike, Willis Richardson's plays have received only sporadic critical attention, sometimes no more than a passing comment or remark. That Doris E. Abramson in her *Negro Playwrights in the American Theatre, 1925–1959* (1969) does not include Willis Richardson may be indicative of his declining popularity. Of his folk plays, only two of them—*The Chip Woman's Fortune* and *The Broken Banjo*—have been the focus of black drama critics. In his review of the former, James Corbin praises it for its convincing characterization and writing: "[It] is an unaffected and wholly convincing transcript of every day character . . ." (1). Darwin T. Turner seems to concur with Corbin: "Although it evidences some of the supposedly exotic quality of black life which appealed to Broadway audiences during the 1920s, *The Chip Woman's Fortune* seems realistic in characterization and in language" (25–26). However, C. W. E. Bigsby considers *The Chip Woman's Fortune* "a slight work, a one-act morality play whose characters lack credibility and whose moral is as disturbingly simplistic as the action is punctilious in its threadbare morality" (209). Helene Keyssar compares Richardson's *The Chip Woman's Fortune* and *The Broken Banjo* in their depiction of "the inner life of poor black families" (46). Whereas the latter play reveals the playwright's unswerving "commitment to the revelation of the inner life of black people," she writes, the former play employs a fairy tale technique that hampers the revelation of the inner life of its characters, especially to a white audience (47). Frederick W. Bond remarks about *The Broken Banjo*: "This drama has an interesting plot, story, and theme, and presents a sympathetic discussion of the characteristics of Negro life" (111). Leslie Catherine Sanders observes that "Richardson's impulse is always didactic. He values honesty, loyalty, courage, personal integrity, and industry. [His] plays depict what occurs when misfortune tempts his characters to abandon these virtues" (*Development* 30).

Richardson's anthologies, *Plays and Pageants from the Life of the Negro* and *Negro History in Thirteen Plays*, have received scant critical attention. Christine Rauchfuss Gray in her introduction in the 1993 reprint of *Plays and Pageants* states, "Each play and pageant in this collection reflects Richardson's philosophy regarding the education of African Americans. Each play . . . reveals either a facet of African or African American history or an aspect of the African American experience at the time the play was written" (xxxviii). On the contrary, Benjamin Brawley notes that there is "a sense of unreality" about the subject matter of the works included in the first book because of their setting in the remote past or distant future (284). According to Bernard L. Peterson, Jr., "Richardson's history plays are critically less important than his folk plays" (Foreword xii). According to Darwin T. Turner, Richardson "recreated black heroes of history," and taught the black community to be proud of their character and history" (25).

Last but not least, Peterson observes, "Most of [Richardson's] plays were attempts at realistic treatment of Black life (both contemporary and historical)" on a variety of black concerns of the 1920s ("Willis Richardson: Pioneer Playwright" 362). And Gray concludes, "More than any other African-American dramatist, Richardson contributed to the development of African-American drama during the 1920s. His plays are important for their portrayals of life as many African Americans dealt with it" (*Willis* 110–111).

BIBLIOGRAPHY

Dramatic Works by Willis Richardson

Amateur Prostitute: 3 Acts. Unpublished. No date available.

"Antonio Maceo." *Negro History in Thirteen Plays*. Ed. Willis Richardson and May Miller. Washington, DC: Associated, 1935. 16–21.

"Attucks the Martyr." *Negro History in Thirteen Plays*. Ed. Willis Richardson and May Miller. Washington, DC: Associated, 1935. 29–61.

"The Black Horseman." *Plays and Pageants from the Life of the Negro*. Rpt. with intro. by Christine R. Gray. Jackson: University Press of Mississippi, 1993. 179–218.

Bold Lover. Unpublished. No date available.

The Bootblack Lover: 3 Acts, 1926. Unpublished. First prize in *Crisis* contest for drama in 1927.

"The Broken Banjo: A Folk Tragedy." *The Crisis Reader*. Ed. Sondra Kathryn Wilson. New York: Modern Library, 1999. 48–81. Expanded into three acts in 1965.

The Brown Boy. Unpublished. No date available.

The Chasm (with E. C. Williams). Unpublished. No date available.

"The Chip Woman's Fortune." *Black Drama in America: An Anthology*. Ed. Darwin T. Turner. Greenwich: Fawcett, 1971. 27–52.

"Compromise: A Folk Play." *The New Negro*. Ed. Alain Locke. New York: Boni. Rpt. with a new preface by Robert Hayden. New York: Atheneum, 1969. 168–195.

The Curse of the Shell-Road Witch. Unpublished. No date available.

"The Danse Calinda." *Plays of Negro Life*. Ed. Alain Locke and Montgomery Gregory. New York: Harper, 1927.

The Dark Haven. Unpublished. No date available.

"The Deacon's Awakening." *Crisis* 1.4 (1920): 14–30. Also published in *Black Theatre USA: Plays by African Americans, 1847 to Today*. Ed. James V. Hatch and Ted Shine. Rev. and exp. ed. New York: Free, 1996. 218–230.

The Dope King. Unpublished. No date available.

"The Dragon's Tooth." *The King's Dilemma and Other Plays for Children*. New York: Exposition Press, 1956. 21–35.

"The Elder Dumas." *Negro History in Thirteen Plays*. Ed. Willis Richardson and May Miller. Washington, DC: Associated, 1935. 63–94.

The Fall of the Conjurer. Unpublished. No date available.

Family Discord: 3 Acts. Unpublished. No date available.

"The Flight of the Natives." *Black Theatre U.S.A: Forty-Five Plays by Black Americans, 1847–1974*. Ed. James V. Hatch. New York: Free, 1974. 383–389. Expanded into three acts in 1963.

"The Gypsy's Finger Ring." *The King's Dilemma and Other Plays for Children*. New York: Exposition Press, 1956. 36–64.

The Holy Spirit. Unpublished. No date available.

Hope of the Lowly: A Play in Three Acts. Unpublished. No date available.

"The House of Sham." *Plays and Pageants from the Life of the Negro*. Rpt. with intro. by Christine R. Gray. Jackson: University Press of Mississippi, 1993. 241–291.

"The Idle Head." *Black Theatre U.S.A: Forty-Five Plays by Black Americans, 1847–1974*. Ed. James V. Hatch. New York: Free, 1974. 234–240.

Imp of the Devil. Unpublished. No date available.

"In Menelik's Court." *Negro History in Thirteen Plays*. Ed. Willis Richardson and May Miller. Washington, DC: Associated, 1935. 109–139.

The Jail Bird. Unpublished. No date available.

Joy Rider. Unpublished. No date available.

"The King's Dilemma." *Plays and Pageants from the Life of the Negro*. Rpt. with intro. by Christine R. Gray. Jackson: University Press of Mississippi, 1993. 219–239.

"Man of Magic." *The King's Dilemma and Other Plays for Children*. New York: Exposition Press, 1956. 65–85.

The Man Who Married a Young Wife. Unpublished. No date available.

Miss or Mrs.: A Comedy. 1941. Unpublished.

"Mortgaged." 1924. *The New Negro Renaissance: An Anthology*. Ed. Michael W. Peplow and Arthur P. Davis. New York: Holt, 1975. 113–117.

"Near Calvary: An Easter Play for Children." *Negro History in Thirteen Plays*. Ed. Willis Richardson and May Miller. Washington, DC: Associated, 1935. 95–107.

The New Generation. Unpublished. No date available.

The New Lodgers. Unpublished. No date available.

"The New Santa Claus." The King's Dilemma and Other Plays for Children. New York: Exposition Press, 1956. 86–101.

The Nude Siren. Unpublished. No date available.

The Peacock's Feather. 1928. Unpublished.

"A Pillar of the Church." 1920s. *Lost Plays of the Harlem Renaissance, 1920–1940.* Detroit: Wayne State University Press, 1996. 32–44.

Protest. Unpublished. No date available.

"The Rider of the Dream." Plays of Negro Life. Ed. Alain Locke and Montgomery Gregory. New York: Harper, 1927.

Rooms for Rent. 1926. Unpublished.

Sacrifice (1930). Unpublished.

A Stranger from Beyond. Unpublished. No date available.

Victims (original title: *The Deep Regret*). Unpublished. No date available.

The Visiting Lady. Unpublished. No date available.

The Wine Seller: 3 Acts. Unpublished. No date available.

Studies of Willis Richardson's Dramatic Works

Bigsby, C. W. E. *The Second Black Renaissance Essays in Literature.* Westport: Greenwood, 1980.

Bond, Frederick W. *The Negro and the Drama.* 1940. College Park: McGrath, 1969.

Brawley, Benjamin. *The Negro Genius: A New Appraisal of the Achievement of the American Negro in Literature and Fine Arts.* New York: Dodd, 1937.

Corbin, John. Rev. of *The Chip Woman's Fortune. New York Times* 20 May 1923: sec. 7, 1.

Du Bois, W. E. B. *The Selected Writings of W. E. B. Du Bois.* Ed. Walter Wilson. New York: New American Library, 1970.

Gray, Christine Rauchfuss. Introduction. *Plays and Pageants from the Life of the Negro.* Ed. Willis Richardson. Jackson: University Press of Mississippi, 1993. vi–xli.

———. *Willis Richardson: Forgotten Pioneer of African-American Drama.* Westport: Greenwood, 1999.

Hatch, James V. *Black Theater U.S.A.: Forty-Five Plays by Black Americans, 1847–1974.* New York: Free, 1974.

Hatch, James V., and Omanii Abdullah, comp. and ed. "Richardson, Willis." *Black Playwrights, 1823–1977: Annotated Bibliography of Plays.* New York: Bowker, 1977.

Hay, Samuel A. *African American Theatre: A Historical and Critical Analysis.* Cambridge: Cambridge University Press, 1994.

Houston, Helen R. "Willis Richardson." *The Oxford Companion to African American Literature.* Ed. William L. Andrews, Frances Smith Foster, and Trudier Harris. New York: Oxford University Press, 1997. 632.

Keyssar, Helene. *The Curtain and the Veil: Strategies in Black Drama.* New York: Franklin, 1981.

Mayorga, Margaret Gardner. Preface. *Representative One-Act Plays by American Authors.* Boston: Little, 1928.

Page, James A. *Selected Black American Authors: An Illustrated Bio-Bibliography*. Boston: Hall, 1977.

Perry, Patsy B. "Willis Richardson." *Afro-American Writers from the Harlem Renaissance to 1940*. Vol. 51 of *Dictionary of Literary Biography*. Ed. Trudier Harris. Detroit: Gale, 1987. 236–244.

Peterson, Bernard L., Jr. Foreword. *Willis Richardson, Forgotten Pioneer of African-American Drama*. Westport: Greenwood, 1999. vii–xiv.

———. "Willis Richardson." *Early Black American Playwrights and Dramatic Writers: A Biographical Directory and Catalog of Plays, Films, and Broadcasting Scripts*. Westport: Greenwood, 1990. 21.

———. "Willis Richardson: Pioneer Playwright." *Contemporary Authors*. Ed. Hal May and Susan M. Trotsky. Vol. 124. Detroit: Gale, 1988. 360–362. Originally published in *Black World* 26.6 (1975): 40–48, 86–88.

Rush, Theresa Gunnels, Carol Fairbank, and Esther Spring Arata, eds. *Black American Writers: Past and Present: A Biographical and Bibliographical Dictionary*. Vol. 2. Metuchen: Scarecrow, 1975.

Sanders, Leslie Catherine. *The Development of Black Theater in America: From Shadows to Selves*. Baton Rouge: Lousiana State University Press, 1988.

———. "Richardson, Willis." *Dictionary of the Black Theatre*. Comp. Allen Woll. Westport: Greenwood, 1983. 243–244.

Turner, Darwin T. Introduction to *The Chip Woman's Fortune*. *Black Drama in America: An Anthology*. Greenwich: Fawcett, 1971. 25–26.

Woodson, Carter Goodson. Introduction. *Negro History in Thirteen Plays*. Washington, DC: Associated, 1935. iii–v.

———. Rev. of *Negro History in Thirteen Plays*. *Journal of Negro History* 21 (1936): 73–76.

SONIA SANCHEZ
(1934–   )

Sharon Glazier Hochstein

BIOGRAPHY

Sonia Sanchez was born Wilsonia Benita Driver on September 9, 1934, in Birmingham, Alabama. Her childhood was not to be a carefree one: her mother died when she was only a year old and her grandmother, Elizabeth "Mama" Driver, took on the task of raising Sonia and her sister. Instability and heartbreak prevailed as her beloved grandmother passed away when Sonia was just five, and she was subsequently shuttled between various relatives' homes. When she was nine years old, her father remarried for a third time and took his family north to live in Harlem.

Sanchez earned a B.A. in political science from Hunter College in 1955, and did postgraduate work at New York University. It was during this time that she began her writing career, forming the Broadside Quartet with Don L. Lee, Nikki Giovanni, and Etheridge Knight, whom she later married and had three children with. She continued writing with this group until the early 1970s. For Sanchez, writing and political activism, bolstered by her university studies, were inseparable and mutually supporting. While initially she believed that blacks could and should be integrated into white America, by the mid-1960s she had been influenced by the black Muslim leader Malcolm X, who preached that blacks would never be fully accepted by the white society and therefore should take a separatist stance. In 1971, she converted to Islam and became a member of the Nation of Islam, but left the movement in 1976 because of her perception that women were relegated to subservient roles within that theopolitical organization.

Independent and outspoken, Sonia Sanchez's career is both impressive and inspiring. She has taught at several universities, including San Francisco State, the University of Pittsburgh, Rutgers, City College of the City University of New York, Amherst College, the University of Pennsylvania, Temple University, and numerous scholar-in-residence programs, and has received a plethora of fellowships. Rather than use her role as a writer and teacher as a translator of aesthetics and emotions, she has used her pen and voice as tools to encourage much-needed reform in the educational system from the elementary to the university level. Responding to a curriculum that either ignored or spoke negatively to herself and her people, she cofounded the Black Studies Program at San Francisco State and initiated one of the first seminars on black women in literature in the nation while teaching at Amherst College.

Sanchez is the author of numerous volumes of poetry and several short stories, including some specifically written for children. She has published seven plays, although it is often difficult to obtain them. In addition, she has contributed to a variety of anthologies, and edited and authored the introduction to *Living at the Epicenter: The 1995 Morse Poetry Prize Selected and Introduced by Sonia Sanchez* (1995). Sanchez has been recognized for her prolific writing and activist leadership with a multitude of awards and citations, including the PEN Writing Award (1969) and a PEN Fellowship in the arts (1993–1994), a National Endowment for the Arts Award (1978–1979), the Community Service Award from the National Black Caucus of State Legislators (1981), the Lucretia Mott Award (1984), the Peace and Freedom Award from the Women [*sic*] International League for Peace and Freedom (1986), and the Pennsylvania Governor's Award for Excellence in the Humanities (1988).

MAJOR WORKS AND THEMES

One of Sonia Sanchez's first published plays, *Sister Son/ji*, appears in *New Plays from the Black Theatre*, edited by Ed Bullins.* In the inside flap of the book jacket, Bullins defines the literary mood that prevailed as Sonia Sanchez embarked on her writing career: "We don't want to have a higher form of white art in black-face. We are working towards something entirely different and new that encompasses the soul and spirit of Black people, and that represents the whole experience of our being here in this oppressive land." It was a time of rage and revolution for a people who saw themselves as a nation within a nation. Sanchez's work both mirrors this fury and projects her attempt to ignite her people into taking action to change the status quo. She experiments in bold new forms, using black speech patterns and novel punctuations and stresses to speak directly to her people. Indeed, the very act of using language in this way and pushing it to its outer limits is an act of empowerment, as she not-so-gently, but always lovingly, challenges her people to take ownership of their lives through words and action.

Sister Son/ji simmers on a rolling boil, as Sanchez wastes no words, time, or space in her portrayal of a black woman's reflections on the turning points in her life that correspond to the black female's experience in white America during the twentieth century. She is one woman and yet she represents every black woman, and she is wise for all of her experiences. Time here is knowledge, and the movement of the play is circular, beginning with Sister Son/ji as an old woman, moving backward into her early and later adulthood, and then returning to her old age, with Sanchez using time as the ultimate teacher. She wants to show the audience what was then but is not now, and how they can facilitate change for tomorrow. Sister Son/ji informs us that "today I shall be a remembered Sister Son/ji. today I shall be what I was/shd have been and never can be again. today I shall bring back yesterday as it can never be today. as it shd be tomorrow." (99)

Her story seemingly contains biographical components, as Sister Son/ji attends Hunter College, and an instructor, in a "they-all-look-alike" scenario, cannot manage to remember her name, confusing her with the other two black women in the class. Sister Son/ji/Sanchez is not only humiliated by this event, but feels that her identity as an individual human being has been obliterated. If, like Sanchez, Son/ji had felt that integration into white society was the answer, experiences like this one radicalize her into looking for new answers, by reaching solely for her people, and building their society from their own blood. Son/ji, like Sanchez, is transformed by the voice and message of Malcolm X, and as a recording of him is played on the stage, Son/ji describes him as a "beautiful/blk/warrior/prince" who uses "dagger/words" (102) to spur his people into action, much as Sanchez does.

Their vision is to build a strong and powerful black family unit, replete with young warriors and sisters, who take pride in who they are and therefore will contribute to building a strong black nation. The reality, however, is both age-old and colorblind. For if Sister Son/ji/Sanchez imagines her family spending time together and nurturing their bond, her man goes his own way, spending his time in bars. Here, the disillusionment is very real, and Sanchez, who hitherto has drawn a sharp line between blacks and whites, acknowledges that the gender problem is universal.

Sanchez, ever surprising and unconventional, inserts at this crisis point a poem that laments both her tragic past, as she was separated from her ancestral native land losing her identity in the process, and the barrenness of the relationship with this man/men who have planted the seed but then not stayed around long enough to nurture it. The poem hauntingly blends memory, loss, and longing.

The pivotal climax of the play takes place in a battle scene, where, significantly, Sister Sonji, a lone female fighter among an unseen army, straps a gun and ammunition to her belt and a baby carrier on her back. She goes to do battle against white America so that her children and all black children will win the right ". . . to run on their own land and let their bodies explode with the sheer joy of living" (106). Here, Sanchez metaphorically details all the anger and violence of the race riots during the 1960s. Tragically, her eldest "warrior" is shot down during the battle with the white "fascist pigs" (104), representing both the concrete and the symbolic attempt to murder her people's aspirations for the future.

Sanchez makes it very clear that this is not a war to end segregation and promote integration; rather, their fight is about establishing a strong black community that neither wants nor needs the endorsement or support of white America. In this work as well as in her other plays, she particularly vilifies the participation of white women in this struggle, as she expresses a common fear that the already wandering black man will commit the ultimate travesty not only by sleeping with the enemy, but by further tearing apart the black family unit and thereby damning their future as a people as well. If the white woman wants to contribute to their fight, and here Sister Sonji/Sanchez seems to question her motives, then she advocates sending the woman back to her own people to "liberalize them" (106). The alternative is to slay the black lover who has betrayed his people.

The last vision that we have of Sister Sonji is as a tired old woman living off the state in Mississippi. She has lived a poignant life and waged battles that desperately needed to be fought, and has ". . . dared to pick up the day and shake its tail until it became evening" (107), much as Sanchez is doing even as she writes this play to inspire. But even as her sun sets, Sister Sonji attempts to spur her audience into action, to claim ownership to the struggle of black people and share in the responsibility of their future as a community. She challenges, "Anybody can grab the day and make it stop. Can u my friends? or may be it's better if I ask: will you?" (107).

Sonia Sanchez's sense of urgency and use of her literary works as political inspirations continue in her subsequent plays, as she often examines a common theme from a different angle. In *The Bronx Is Next*, a group of black men are participating in a mission to burn the slums of Harlem, ostensibly not only as a show of rage and rebellion against the white society that has relegated them to the ghetto, but also metaphorically as a way to clear the land of the old ways, and rebuild on their own terms. This is not only an attempt to destroy the slum, but to dismantle the societal, racist hierarchy that created it. Several critics have noted that Larry, Roland, and Jimmy, who are the male characters of the play, correspond with the names of prominent leaders of the black arts movement, signifying that Sanchez also has an angry message to share with that group. The two women depicted in the play, the Old Sister and the Black Bitch, are typical categories that Sanchez uses repeatedly to illustrate the roles that black women are forced into by their male counterparts.

This very short, but equally loaded, work begins with the men clearing the tenants out of the tenements so they may burn them to the ground. The Old Sister, who may be seen as representative of the obsequious black society that has been broken by the white, states that she will not leave without her collected belongings; they are all that she can show for her last forty years of living. In a seeming show of kindness, Charles allows her to return to her apartment to wait it out with her things, and the audience only comprehends after Roland's protests that Charles has given up on her and sent her to her death. Charles and those who have joined him in his mission consider the old unnecessary and disposable—in military terms what would be called "collateral damage." Quite simply, her season has passed and they have no time to wait for her.

As in *Sister Son/ji*, time is essential to the movement of *Bronx*. There is a palpable urgency in getting the people out of the tenements quickly and destroying them as fast as they can. The real danger presented here is not in the blazing of the ghetto set on fire, but of the perils of inaction if the movement does not "grab the day" (*Sister Son/ji*). The fear is that the black community will end up as worn, broken, and obedient as the Old Sister.

While the men are clearing the buildings of their residents, they come upon a white policeman who visits Harlem regularly in order to have sex with a black woman before he returns to his white wife and two boys in suburbia. As they question him about his motives for being in Harlem, he is quick to assert his superior position over them, calling Jimmy "son" (79), and demanding his "right to know" (79) what is happening in the ghetto. Charles corrects him with "You ain't got no rights here" (79), and as White Cop begins to feel cornered, he tries to intimidate them with his power by threatening ". . . you just wait . . . you just wait . . ." (79). White Cop expresses his disgust in how the blacks could live in a filthy slum, stating that every other ethnic group that lived in ghettos managed to make theirs inhabitable and keep some self-respect in the process. Charles retorts, very much on his own terms, that all the other ethnic groups that lived in ghettos were white, and that there is no way that white America is going to let the black community rise up and flourish (80).

It is at this point that a shift in power takes place in the play, for if the white man is not going to allow the black man to rise up and take control of his destiny, then the black man will do it by physically overtaking the whites. Sanchez inverts the power struggle by having the black men pretend that they are white policemen, and White Cop is forced into the role of the black man on the streets of Harlem. White Cop protests, asking, "How would it help—what good would it do?" (80), but it soon becomes very clear exactly what good it will do, as Sanchez uses this scenario to illustrate the injustices, lies, and abuse visited on innocent black men if they dare to be caught walking the streets of their community when some white power figure does not want them there. White Cop/black man tells the black men/white cops that he is running because he is happy, but they do not believe him; they accuse him of stealing and then proceed to beat him unmercifully. This scene, all too familiar to African Americans living in America in the twentieth century, is summarized by Roland, who tells the metamorphosed White Cop, "You ain't shit boy. You black. You a nigger we caught running down the street—running and stealing like all the niggers around him" (81).

But if the object here is to overthrow the black men's oppressors and build a new black community built on respect and mutual esteem, Sanchez makes it clear that the black men are abandoning their women in this process, and, indeed, abusing and demeaning them much as the white man has done to them. The black men bring out a woman who is only referred to as Black Bitch, and proceed to beat down any resistance she gives them in obeying their demands. But as much as they try to exert their power over her, she will not bow to their threats or physical command over her. She defiantly retorts, "Who you? Man. I don't owe no black man no explanations 'bout what I do. The last black man I explained to cleaned me out, so whatever you doing don't concern me 'specially if it has a black man at the head" (81). She has been betrayed, sold out, and left behind in their struggle for equality. Furthermore, she feels that they have used her as a commodity, jumping around ". . . from black pussy to black pussy like jumping jacks" (82), and planting their seeds but then running from the accompanying responsibility.

Her sexual encounters with White Cop, on the other hand, is a necessary survival skill as she receives some payment for her services. In a miserable parallel to his life, she too is trying to raise two sons, but she is poor and alone, and her only hope for them is that, unlike the men that surround her, her sons ". . . will never make a black woman cry in the night" (82). She clearly knows who she is and what her people need, but she is equally sure that the men need their women for guidance and support, and their neglect of them is a tragic mistake for all. She challenges both the men and the audience to think about whom they are and what their goals are, saying: "I know what I am. But all you revolutionists or nationalists or whatever you call yourselves—do you know where you at? I am a black woman and I've had black men who could not love me or my black boys—where you gonna find black women to love when all this is over . . ." (82).

This is no longer her struggle, and she leaves them to their work. Charles and Roland want to escort White Cop to Black Bitch's apartment so that he may apologize, and it is now clear that he is their prisoner and they have no intention of letting him go. Now that he has experienced life as a black man, he feels truly vulnerable and scared, and even as he incredulously screams "But, I'm white! I'm white! No. This can't be happening—I'm white!" (83), the men continue to proceed with the plans to burn the ghetto, and he will ostensibly perish with it. Sanchez asserts here that a few men at the top of the movement are making decisions for all, as Roland questions the wisdom of burning the ghettos, but neither man thinks to defy their leaders, and even as they burn Harlem, announce that "The Bronx is next . . ." (83). Sanchez is indicating here that a male dictatorship, be it the black power movement, or in its voice the black arts movement, cannot possibly represent the interests of its people if it does not allow all to participate in the process and have a say in their future.

This theme of the struggle of black women against the domination of black men is repeated again in *Uh,Uh; But How Do It Free Us?* This play is composed of three separate skits, or groups, poising black women in suppressive situations, leaving the reader echoing the title of the work by asking how the black identity/power/arts movements liberate black women. The skits are separated by dancers who pantomime and interpret the lamentable scene that has just concluded, further intensifying the scene's emotional impact and preparing the viewer for the next skit. The time, that ever-precious and crucial commodity in Sanchez's plays, is now.

In the first skit, two women are sharing one man in a "liberated" relationship. Waleesha, the elder of the two and considered the "first wife," is in the later stages of pregnancy. Nefertia, the more recent addition to the household, is also pregnant, but is not showing yet. Malik, their mate, is a young actor who can only profit from this exploitive situation; his meals are cooked and his home kept for him, he unabashedly requests Nefertia's school check, his ego is stoked by the women's admiration for him and even by their bickering over him, and he has sex with them freely but is just as free to run around without them as he pleases. The women are left at home while he wanders, fighting it out over "their man." Waleesha, pregnant and stuck and in love besides, defends his decision to invite Nefertia into their lives, saying that ". . . since I love him I have to abide by his choice, no matter how unwise it may be" (164). Nefertia scorns the other woman's passivity, yet her jealousy and her youth blind her to her own inferior position in her relationship with Malik. She does not dislike Waleesha because they are incompatible, rather because Malik has set her up to deride the Waleesha by telling Nefertia how boring and unsuitable the older woman is for Malik. Furthermore, he lures the young and naïve woman by telling her that she is his own true love, and that she ". . . saved him from the boredom" of Waleesha (165). Viewing these "kept" women the reader is struck by the fact that the man has divided, and therefore has conquered, the women, and that he has everything to gain by this arrangement, while they have already lost everything. Indeed, one may ask, "But how does it free them?"

In the second group, we see the return of Sister Whore, who along with White Whore, is "entertaining" four black customers and a white one. The men comment on how they found their black ethnicity and became heroes in prison due to such leaders as "Malcolm/man" and "Eldridge/man" (166). The ex-cons, who employ and abuse prostitutes and snort cocaine, are portrayed as being highly regarded in the black community and revered as the ". . . the new breed" (166), while their female counterpart is simply referred to as "Black/bitch" (166). She seemingly does not think that she deserves better, as she simply states, "Ain't got no name. Lost my name when I was eleven years old. I became just a body then so I forgot my name. Don't no-body want to know a Black woman's name anyway" (168). The "brothers" put a collar on her and proceed to "ride" her, as she clearly serves both as their hobbyhorse plaything and as their beast of burden.

The white man, although obviously deluded and psychotic, is unani-mously and unquestionably accepted as their superior, and he announces, "I rule the universe. I am the universe. The universe revolves around me. I am the universe. I am a man" (169). Although the Black Whore muses on the idea that she could be a "beautiful Blk/woman/queen" (170), she has no sense of her own worth and continues to abide by their base image of her. And while she clearly has both brains and her finger on the pulse of her peo-ple, telling the men that ". . . they still hurting, killing, selling dope to our people, and they don't know that instead of having a little bit of the planet, that the planet earth is ours. All ours just waiting to be taken over" (171), she too accepts the fact that the crazy "white dude" is the only viable and capa-ble ruler of the universe. The viewer is left with a shocking image of a muti-lated life ruled by a sadomasochistic white man, and again asks what this power hierarchy does for her—how does it free her?

The closing skit of this play features again one man and two women in a love triangle, this time with a black man attempting to simultaneously con-duct two seemingly exclusive relationships—one with a black woman and one with a white woman. The "sister" has relocated to the West Coast to love her man and build a family with him, and help him in the struggle for black power and expression. She is ready to give him all that she has—her money, her body, and her faith—and naïvely indulges him when he spends evenings out without her, as he is moving up in the movement and she wants to give him the space he needs to grow. In reality, he is spending his evenings with his totally supportive, but equally controlling, white lover. Seemingly liberal and ultramodern, she encourages his relationship with the black woman, telling him that ". . . since you're moving up in the movement out here, you do need a Blk/woman image. She's cute looking. Small. Compact, with a good/growing awareness of what's to be done" (175). To her, the black sister is simply a commodity that her lover needs to succeed. She also bankrolls him, rationalizing that ". . . it's the money that my father got by underpaying Black people for years" (177), but she ironically, and insidiously, uses the money as a means to control a black man, just as her father did. And while she does support the black power struggle, and Sanchez insinuates here that it is to superficially project a progressive image, it is obvious that the white woman wants to control the movement by manipulating him. When she finds out that his black partner is pregnant, she is not only jealous, but also wants to know how having a baby will impede "their" progress in the move-ment. And when she gets really desperate, she leads him to believe that she has attempted suicide, forcing him to abandon his pregnant black partner at a crucial point in her career and to run to her. In the end, he concedes that he is only a man because his white patroness has allowed him to be one, and she coerces him into a symbolic marriage ceremony, where she, God-like, instructs him that he ". . . should have no other woman besides me" (182).

Although both women have indulged and supported him, the white woman can use her money, power, and race to ultimately dominate him. On the other hand, the black woman finds herself in the humiliating position of having raged against the female white "devil" while her common-law husband loved one, and unloved yet pregnant with his child, has nowhere to go. Without any viable choices, she is relegated to the bottom of the power ladder, subservient not only to the white woman and the society that she represents, but to black men as well. He has put her squarely in her place, informing her, "You a black woman bitch. You the same as every Black [*sic*] woman. You were born to cry in the night" (185). The reader must once more ask the question, "How does the black arts/black power movement help black women?" The black sister's only answer to this question seems to be that she will ignore the man's indiscretions and betrayals and continue on alone in the struggle, as she is ". . . the new Black woman" (187). Sanchez's message here seems to be that no matter how large the obstacles and how hurtful the despotic treatment from their men, black women must find the strength and inner power to continue with their quest for freedom.

Yet, Sanchez also seems to believe that at some point black men will realize that their women are precious for more than their bodies, and not only deserve respect, but should be encouraged to take part in the struggle for black freedom and in the black arts movement on equal footing. *Malcolm/Man Don't Live Here No More* is a short play and tribute to Malcolm X that is written for children in verse, in which three female sisters, represented as Malcolm's mother, his wife, and white America, direct the play's action and message. Malcolm's mother presents him as a baby, pure and innocent, but when we see him a few years later as a child in school, he is trying to make sense of the treatment he is receiving from his teachers and the world around him: "why oh why am I patted on the head/ like an animal who is well/fed/ why oh why am I discouraged to be/what I want and know can be me. me. Me" (25).

A chorus of the three women then ask, "malcolm, malcolm where did u go?" (25) and it soon becomes apparent that they have lost the naïve, confused boy to a new Malcolm that is completely disillusioned by the world around him, believing in nothing but himself and his own hatred and rage. "Wite/amurica," carrying both an American and a Confederate flag, wants to make an outward show of sympathy for the troubled youth, self-professing that she gives ". . . justice for the poor . . ."(26), but then throws him into prison. It is there that Malcolm finds Islam and is transformed, and, with his wife, proclaims that their children will have positive lives as they live as free and aware black Muslims (26).

But he is not allowed to live, and it is the sisters who make the audience aware of Malcolm's assassination. They also lead the grieving and then the subsequent encouragement to continue on and persevere in their quest as a tribute to his life. Here, the message to black children is uplifting and inspiring, yet also encourages them never to trust or look at white America as a partner in the search for justice, equality, and peace. "Wite/ amurica" proclaims, ". . . don't they know one man can't change my years/ of rule. for wite/ amurica am I/ & I will never, never, die" (26). The message here to children, both black and white, is that they cannot work together to build a better future and a better world, and if this is truly what Sanchez is communicating, it paints a hopeless and bleak picture for all.

In *Dirty Hearts*, Sanchez also paints a timeless picture of black America's search for equality and respect, and as in many of her other works, the characters are ". . . neither young nor old . . ." (258), signifying the timelessness of this issue. Unfortunately, this play tends to be so oblique at points that Sanchez's exact meaning and intention is often difficult to follow. It is staged as a game of cards called "Dirty Hearts," and is played between two men without any names, a woman who seems to be a Hiroshima survivor called Shigeko, and Carl, who is described as a black businessman. There is also a poet who interrupts the game and speaks in verse about his work and the past, but this section is so enigmatic as to be almost incomprehensible.

The play begins with the two men waiting for the others, and Second Man commenting that there is something yellow and disturbing in the air outside, like a ". . . permanent isolation invading our world" (258). First Man, who is oblivious to the aura, faults the other man for listening to intuition as a woman might. Shigeko enters, and it is revealed that her face is disfigured, that she works as a maid for First Man's wife, and that she longs for her country and for her past that she cannot return to. She is the walking wounded, yet she is also presented as a woman who wishes to heal both her own pain and others, and while she is very conscious of who she is and how she got there, holds no bitterness for those around her.

Carl, the black businessman, arrives last on the scene, and although he reminds the others of his success, power, and clout, when his cards are dealt and he is given the ace of spades, he cannot help but express his sense of betrayal and shock at finding himself the loser, despite all his outward appearance of power. He too has an uneasy feeling that something is wrong, and relates a dream that he had the previous night. He was back in the South and was picked up for vagrancy by the police, and then taken to a country club for questioning, and although he protested that he was from New York, they continued to beat him unmercifully. He began to laugh, knowing that although they could bruise his body, they could not touch his soul. The poet wanders in and, in an eerily cryptic message, reiterates that the nights and their dreams are for the disillusioned.

The men and Shigeko resume their game, but First Man cruelly deals Carl the queen of spades card again, and he responds much as he did in his dream—by laughing hysterically. He then disappears into the street, where we hear him scream in agony. Second Man comments on how benevolent he and his kind have been to men like Carl, and First Man chides him for trying to be so sensitive. He states the they are not responsible for the world's problems, and that only women like his ex-wife and other "bleeding hearts" would try to solve the problems that plague the world. In the meantime, he will enjoy himself and not feel guilty, and exits for an evening with Shigeko. Second Man is left to ponder all of the world's silent misery, and asks, "will there be someone tomorrow to break the quiet?" (256). Once again, Sanchez is challenging her audience to listen to the female intuitive voice of compassion within us, and sound it as a call for social action and change.

CRITICAL RECEPTION

Although much has been written about Sonia Sanchez's poetry, very little scholarly attention has been given to her plays. One can only hope that in the future her plays will elicit serious academic interest.

BIBLIOGRAPHY

Dramatic Works by Sonia Sanchez

Black Cats and Uneasy Landings. First produced at the Freedom Theatre, Philadelphia, 1995.

"*The Bronx is Next*." 1967. *Tulane Drama Review*. Ed. William Irwin Thompson. New York: Grove, 1968. 76–83.

"*Dirty Hearts*." *Break Out: In Search of New Theatrical Environments*. Ed. James Schevill. Chicago: Swallow, 1973. 255–259.

I'm Black When I'm Singing, I'm Blue When I Ain't. First produced at the OIC Theatre, Atlanta, April 23, 1983.

"*Malcolm Man/Don't Live Here No More*." *Black Theatre* 6 (1972): 24–26.

"*Sister Son/ji*." *New Plays from the Black Theatre*. Ed. Ed Bullins. New York: Bantam, 1969.

Uh, Uh; But How Do It Free Us? 1974. *Black Women's Blues—A Literary Anthology*. Ed. Rita B. Dandridge. New York: Hall, 1992.

VICTOR SEJOUR
(1817 – 1874)

Ladrica Menson-Furr

BIOGRAPHY

Born a freedman in New Orleans, Louisiana, on June 2, 1817, Juan Victor Sejour Marcou-Ferrand would make his mark in the dramatic world at the age of twenty-seven with the play *Diegarias*. First produced in 1844, this drama would set the stage for a dramaturgy that would consist of approximately twenty more plays that would be regularly staged in Paris and garner much successful critical reception. Sejour's career as a playwright began, like that of many playwrights, first as a poet and short story writer. His first "successful" poem was written and recited by him at the age of seventeen. This poem, considered to be Sejour's "literary debut" (Daley 7), illustrated his disdain for the pretentiousness demonstrated by the colored Creoles of whom he and his family were akin to as well as his "poetic genius" and gift of satire.

Sejour's father, Juan Franciso Louis Victor Sejour Marcou (a native of Santo Domingo), and mother, a New Orleans Creole named Eloise Phillipe Ferrand, reared Sejour within the bourgeoisie traditions of the colored Creole culture and had him tutored, as was the fashion, by the well-respected black journalist Michel Seligny. At the age of eighteen, Sejour's parents sent him abroad to Paris to complete his academic studies, for, as noted by T. A. Daley, nineteenth-century New Orleans culture offered few opportunities for higher education to its white or colored citizens (7). Thus, it was in Paris where Sejour's poetic and dramatic talents began to flourish unhampered by the racial prejudices of North America, and where he would be greatly influenced by the works of Victor Hugo, Alexandre Dumas, and Ponsard, and through the assistance of the mulatto journalist, abolitionist and editor Cyrille Bisette, who edited the abolitionist journal *La Revue des Colonie*. Bisette would be responsible for introducing Sejour to Parisian literary society through his publication of Sejour's first short story, "Le Multare" ("The Mulatto"), in his journal *La Revue des Colonie* in 1837. Sejour continued to make a name for himself in the literary world, but also forged an important political alliance through the writing of the heroic poem *le Retour de Napoelon*. Written in 1841, this poem not only displayed Sejour's allegiance to his new homeland, France, but also to one of its most celebrated figures, Louis Napoléon (soon to be Napoléon III). This alliance would continue to have a major influence on Sejour's development into a successful dramatist.

Following the success of his first successful play, *Diegarias* (a drama about a Jew persecuted because of his "race"), Sejour presented his second play, *La Chute de Sejan*, in 1849. Ever concerned with the audience's taste and dramatic preferences, Sejour began to alter his dramaturgy to simultaneously subscribe to and anticipate their dramatic tastes. Thus, after 1848, he turned away from poetic and romantic structures and centered on the melodramatic and comedic forms of drama. Sejour's Parisian notoriety grew with this change, and he would become a very familiar and welcome name on the Parisian stage until the 1870s.

Considered to be one the first African American expatriates, Victor Sejour's dramatic career serves as a testament to the genius of the colonial person of African descent both in Europe and America. He should be studied and celebrated as an African American dramatist, for although he came into his notoriety away from home, it was because of the racial climate of nineteenth-century New Orleans culture that he was, in essence, forced to find a place that would welcome his artistry. Although at least three of his plays were performed in his hometown of New Orleans, Sejour's talents were never fully appreciated in the United States as they were in Paris. Sejour only returned home for short visits. He died on September 20, 1874, of tuberculosis. He is buried in Paris.

MAJOR WORKS AND THEMES

Victor Sejour's most important work is *Richard III*. Modeled after his first dramatic influence, William Shakespeare, whose plays were read and performed in New Orleans during his youth, and Alexandre Dumas's *Henri III*, Sejour's *Richard III* again illustrates his interest in historical figures. His version "create[s] a stirring drama out of what might otherwise have been a horrible tragedy":

Sejour's Richard is none the less [*sic*] diabolical, none the less [*sic*] murderous; but the author knew only too well that not much interest could be sustained in a play dominated by a horrible monster. Seizing therefore upon the lovely princess, Elizabeth, whom Richard is bent on marrying or destroying, and on the handsome and chivalrous Richmond of York, who has been forced to flee the country and whom Richard intends to prevent from ever rejoining his fiancée, Sejour conceived a perfect drama: a hero and heroine thwarted in their purpose by the lustful hate of a villain. (Daley 11)

After the successful staging of *Richard III*, Sejour authored, almost exclusively, historical dramas. But his third play, *L'Argent du diable* (The Devil's Money), was the first comedy in his dramaturgy. In this work, Sejour revisits the idea that money is the root of all evil and comically presents the vices of the play's protagonist, the miller Loirot, and his redemption. Critically, Sejour's first comedy met with mixed reviews, but most of the critics felt that Sejour was too talented to waste his time in this form of drama (O'Neill, *Sejour* 38–40). Sejour did not write another comedy until 1859. This play, *Le Paletot brun* (The Brown Overcoat), however, exemplified his movement toward melodrama and was the last comedy he wrote.

Thematically, Sejour constructed his dramas around familial relationships, nationalism, historical personae, and issues usually associated with characters from the nobility. For example, in *La Chute de Sejan*, his second play, he examines a Sejan, minister to the Roman emperor Tiberius, who was killed by the order of the latter for having attempted to seize the supreme power. According to Daley, although Sejour was greatly influenced by writers whose works exemplified the characteristics of realism and naturalism, Sejour "refused to be either a priest or philosopher, or to be much concerned with the social problems of his contemporaries" (13). He did not view his work as propagandistic, but rather as a commemoration of the lives of nobles and their family members.

His interest in family love is exemplified in the plays *Les Volontaires de 1814*, *La Madone des Roses*, and *Les Massacres de la Syrie* in which parental love of a child is often the catalyst for the daring plots. Sejour continues his presentation of love through romantic love between characters, but as noted by Charles Edwards O'Neill, this love "is an idealized, morally directed love" (*Sejour* 28). Sejour's view of love is one that is of the highest and most extreme of human emotions, and thus, in order for it to be pure and just, it must adhere to the moral codes and mores of the society.

Although by today's standards Sejour's themes may seem trite and typical, they allowed him to speak directly to the interests of his audience. His critics may have, at times, found fault with his extreme historicism and romanticism, but audiences continued to attend his plays and revel in their messages.

CRITICAL RECEPTION

Victor Sejour's initial critical reception was favorable. Seldom without an audience, his dramas enjoyed successful premieres and runs, for Sejour, as discussed, constantly sought to understand the tastes of his audience and meet them. Although the themes of the dramas themselves were superficial and centered mainly on the power and abuses of power conducted by the European bourgeoisie, Sejour mastered the art of creating impressive and elaborate scenery and costuming that served as either accoutrements or diversions from the lofty dialogue of his works.

However, after his initial successes, the criticism of Sejour's dramas became markedly mixed. Critics continued to applaude his focus on active and romantic characters and plots, but they began to tire of this form of Sejourian drama, and commented on his "unfulfilled talents" (O'Neill, *Sejour* 81). For example, Sejour's play *Les Aventuriers* came under brutal critical attack for its weak construction. Critic Alexis Rodet, as stated by O'Neill, "praised the cast and scenery, but panned the play 'a drama ill concocted, poorly digested, made of bits and pieces, crumbs from the great masters, picked underneath tables. From Act III on, you don't know where you are'"(*Sejour* 84). Other critics shared Rodet's critique of the drama's faulty structure, but still had to concede that the followers of Sejour would still continue to patronize his work, despite its failures.

Sejour was known for having a work on stage and a work in rehearsals during his heyday; hence, he used the theatrical critiques as the basis for some revisions of his dramas. However, despite the wavering critiques, Sejour's dramaturgy never appeared to change in any drastic way. He continued his focus on romantic, historical, and political themes throughout his career. Despite his early successes, by 1865, Sejour's popularity began to diminish. He collaborated on two plays, *Les Enfants de la Louvre* (1865) and *La Madone des Roses* (1869), with Theodore Barricute, and had a difficult time securing a director for his last two plays, *Cromwell* and *Vampire*.

BIBLIOGRAPHY

Dramatic Works by Victor Sejour

Andre Gerard. Paris: Levy, 1857.
L'Argent du diable. Paris: Levy, 1854.
Les Aventuriers. Paris: Levy, 1860.
La Chute de Sejan. Paris: Levy, 1849.
Compere Guillery. Paris: Levy, 1860.
Diegarias. Paris: C. Tresse, 1944.
Les Enfants de la Louvre (with Theodore Barricute). Paris: Levy, 1865.

Les Files de Charles Quint. Paris: Levy, 1862.
Le Fils de la nuit. Paris: Levy, 1857.
Les Grands Vassaux. Paris: Levy, 1859.
La Madone des Roses. Paris: Levy, 1869.
Le Marquis caporal. Paris: Levy, 1864.
Le Martyr du Coeur. Paris: Levy, 1858.
Les Massacres de la Syrie. Paris: Barbe, 1861.
Les Mysteres du Temple. Paris: Levy, 1862.
Les Noces venitiennes. Paris: Levy, 1855.
Le Paletot brun. Paris: Levy, 1859.
Richard III. Paris: Giraud, 1852.
La Tireuse de Cartes. Paris: Levy, 1860.
Les Volontaries de 1814. Paris: Levy, 1862.

Studies of Victor Sejour's Dramatic Works

Daley, T. A. "Victor Sejour." *Phylon* 4.1 (1943): 5–16.
O'Neill, Charles Edwards, S.J. "Theatrical Censorship in France, 1844–1875: The Experience of Victor Sejour." *Harvard Library Bulletin* 26 (1978): 417–441.
———. *Sejour: Parisian Playwright from Louisiana*. Lafayette: University of Lafayette Press, 1996.

NTOZAKE SHANGE
(1948–)

Carrie J. Boden

BIOGRAPHY

Feminist, poet, playwright, actor, dancer, director, and teacher Ntozake Shange offers a candid look into the psychological and social realities of being a black woman. She accomplishes this by breaking apart language and recrafting it to suit her intent. Shange writes, "I cant count the number of times I have viscerally wanted to attack deform n maim the language that I waz taught to hate myself in/ the language that perpetuates the notions that cause pain to every black child as he/she learns to speak of the world & the self'" (*See No Evil* 21). Shange expresses her distinctly African American voice through the choreopoem, a combination of dance, music, mime, and poetry, which has revolutionized American theater.

Shange, the oldest of four children, was born Paulette Williams on October 18, 1948, in Trenton, New Jersey, to father, Paul T. Williams, a surgeon, and mother, Eloise Owens Williams, a psychiatric social worker (Shange, "With" 317). According to Sandra Richards, Shange enjoyed a culturally rich and materially secure childhood and was exposed to a wide variety of cultural icons including such diverse influences as Dizzy Gillespie, Shakespeare, Chuck Berry, T .S. Eliot, and Countee Cullen ("Ntozake" 379).

Shange's parents were committed to the black community and were interested in the political and social issues faced by people of African descent; however, this liberal tendency was tempered by black, middle-class conservative values. Shange, at age eight, was one of the first black children to integrate the

St. Louis public schools. There she began to write, but the racist attitudes of segregated St. Louis intimidated and silenced her. When Shange was thirteen, the family moved back east to Lawrenceville, New Jersey. In high school, Shange wrote several poems that were published in the school magazine, "but derogatory comments concerning her choice of black subject matter caused her to again abandon this mode of self-expression" (Richards, "Ntozake" 380). Through these experiences, Shange became increasingly aware of the impact of racism and sexism on her self-perception and of the absence of role models for young black women—a theme central to many of Shange's choreopoems and integral to understanding her theatrical works.

After finishing high school, Shange married and went on to Barnard College in New York City where she majored in American studies. In 1966, she separated from her husband, and according to Philip Effiong, this created serious turmoil for Shange:

She could hardly cope with the sense of alienation and bitterness that consumed her after her unsuccessful first marriage and the personal frustrations drove her into a suppressed rage that culminated in a series of suicide attempts. Failing to commit suicide, Shange channeled her anger into student protest, Civil Rights, and Black Liberation Movements. (132)

Although Shange was often despondent and struggled with personal issues during her college years, she excelled academically and graduated from Barnard College with honors in 1970.

In the early 1970s, Shange's Boston and New York activist acquaintances introduced her to Yoruba religions and to the study of tribal dance styles (Effiong 133). In 1971, Shange moved across the country to Los Angeles where she continued both her interest in dance and her formal education. She enrolled in a master's program at the University of Southern California and apprenticed with local dancers, writers, and musicians (Richards, "Ntozake" 380). During these years, Shange began to spend more time researching African American writers such as Claude McKay, Amiri Baraka,* Jean Toomer,* Zora Neale Hurston,* Richard Wright,* Ann Petry, and James Baldwin,* who have heavily influenced Shange's works. It was also during this time that she adopted the Zulu name Ntozake Shange, which translates "she who comes with her own things" and "one who walks like a lion," respectively. The name affirmed her self-reinvention and her new artistic direction (Effiong 132). In 1973, Shange graduated with an M.A. in American studies from the University of Southern California (Bryer 205).

Shange moved to the San Francisco Bay Area where she taught women's studies and humanities courses at a variety of universities including the University of California Extension–San Francisco, Sonoma State College, and Mills College in Oakland. The cultural climate of San Francisco at that time was a nurturing environment for women artists and for people of color. According to Richards:

At this time Shange was reciting poetry with the Third World Collective and was also dancing with Raymond Sawyer and Ed Mock, whose class routines and formal choreography linked specific folk traditions of West Africa and the Caribbean to the vaudeville and street dance traditions of Afro-America. ("Ntozake" 381)

When Shange writes about her San Francisco years, she recounts a time of awakening, arousal, and increased understanding of her own body: "The freedom to move in space, to demand of my own sweat a perfection that could continually be approached, though never known, waz poem to me, my body & mind ellipsing" (*for colored girls* xi). Richards notes "the theme of body and dance as sites of a knowledge whose rhythms constitute poetry is one . . . Shange would return [to] again and again. Its importance is related to her likely exposure at this time to . . . New World African religions" ("Ntozake" 381). During this time, Shange was collaborating with choreographer Halifu Osumare and with musicians and dancers who practiced Santeria. Working with Osumare's troupe, The Spirit of Dance, offered Shange a first glimpse into women's theater. She performed with the group, learned some basics of theater production, and "became imbued with Osumare's confidence in the legitimacy of their own women-centered/African-centered visions" (Richards, "Ntozake" 381).

According to the introduction to *for colored girls*, Shange left Osumare's dance troupe in 1974 to collaborate with Paula Moss, a horn trio called The Sound Clinic, and Jean Desarmes and His Reggae Blues Band. The music, dance, and poetry they created eventually became the choreopoem *for colored girls who have considered suicide/when the rainbow is enuf* (xii). The initial performances were staged in cafés, bars, women studies departments, and poetry centers (xiii). There was a positive response to "the show," as the performers called it, and the *Bay Guardian* touted it as a "must see" event (xiii).

Shange and Moss drove cross-country to present *for colored girls* in New York. Initially, it did not enjoy the same success experienced in California. Shange and the cast worked to shape the work for a New York audience and performed in a number of locations. Oz Scott, brought in to advise Shange, eventually directed the show. In September 1976, *for colored girls* opened at the Booth Theater. This was the beginning in a series of 867 performances, 747 on Broadway (Effiong 133–134). After its extended Broadway run, *for colored girls* toured internationally and throughout the United States.

In 1977, Shange married musician David Murray, and in 1981, Savannah Thulani-Eloisa, a daughter, was born (Richards, "Ntozake" 386). These were the most productive years of Shange's career. It was also in 1977 that Shange followed up her Broadway hit *for colored girls*, with *A Photograph: A Study of Cruelty* (subtitle later changed to *Lovers in Motion*), which opened to mixed reviews. *Photograph* is more conventional than Shange's previous work, and it is best described as a poem-play that explores the intricacies of male–female relationships. In 1978, Shange returned to the choreopoem form with *Spell #7: A Theater Piece in Two Acts*, which centers on the struggles of a group of black artists. Shange's adaptation of Bertolt Brecht's *Mother Courage and Her Children* opened in 1980 at the Public Theater. In Shange's rendition, Mother Courage is an emancipated slave in post–Civil War America. Later that year, another play, *Boogie Woogie Landscapes*, premiered at the Kennedy Center in Washington, DC. Allen Woll notes that this dream-motif piece explores the inner reality of a black girl and was first presented as a one-woman performance in the New York Shakespeare Festival's Poetry at the Public Series (249). Neal Lester claims that Shange's next major production, *From Okra to Greens: A Different Kinda Love Story: A Play with Music and Dance*, "is the most structurally complicated of Shange's theater pieces" (9). This play is taken almost verbatim from an earlier collection of her poetry, *A Daughter's Geography*. In the dramatic version, the poems are divided into two voices, Okra and Greens, and the dialogue unfolds in much the same way as in *for colored girls*. The play portrays a different kind of story as Okra and Greens subvert the typical boy-meets-girl love story as the two meet, fall in love, separate, reconcile, marry, and parent a child within a global context.

In the early 1980s, Shange moved to Houston, Texas, where she was a Mellon Distinguished Professor of Literature at Rice University and an associate professor in the Creative Writing Program at the University of Houston. Shange's *Three for a Full Moon and Bocas* was produced in 1982 at the Mark Taper Forum in Los Angeles. Also in that year, Shange's adaptation of Willy Russell's script *Educating Rita* was produced at the Alliance Theater in Atlanta. Shange's autobiographical novel, *Betsy Brown*, was successfully adapted to the stage and performed at the New York Shakespeare Festival in 1983. In 1987, the unpublished play, *Three Views of Mt. Fuji/A Poem with Music*, premiered at the Lorraine Hansberry Theatre in San Francisco. In 1989, the play *Daddy Says* was published, and Shange returned to the East Coast, where she capitalized on the proximity to the New York arts scene. In 1993, Shange's volume of poetry, *The Love Space Demands*, was adapted for the stage and ran at both the Painted Bride Art Center in Philadelphia and the Crossroads Theater in Trenton, New Jersey.

In 2000, Shange was commissioned to adapt Harriet Beecher Stowe's *Uncle Tom's Cabin* for the stage. In 2002, Shange was a visiting professor at the theater school at DePaul University and a visiting artist at Brown University. Shange collaborated with the famous South African group, Lady Smith Black Mambazo, on a musical, *Nomathebu*, which was presented at the Kennedy Center in Washington, DC, and Chicago's Steppenwolf Theater. In 2003, as a visiting professor at the University of Florida, Shange completed a new choreopoem, *Lavender Lizards and Lilac Landmines*, which premiered at the University of Florida in the spring and subsequently toured several cities throughout the United States.

Shange's many awards include a 1977 Obie, Outer Critics Circle, AUDELCO (Audience Development Committee), and *Mademoiselle* awards for *for colored girls*, as well as Tony, Grammy, and Emmy nominations. Shange also received an Obie for her adaptation of *Mother Courage and Her Children*. In 1981, Shange's collection, *Three Pieces*, won the *Los Angeles Times* Book Review Award for Poetry. In that same year, Shange was granted a Guggenheim Fellowship and the Medal of Excellence by Columbia University. Shange has also been the Mellon Distinguished Professor of Literature at Rice University, the artist in residence at Villanova University, the writer in residence at Maryland College of Art, and a visiting professor at the University of Florida. Additionally, Shange has taught at various institutions across the country, including Sonoma State College, Mills College, Rice University, City College of New York, Douglass College, and the University of Houston (Bryer 205).

MAJOR WORKS AND THEMES

In her first major theatrical work, *for colored girls who have considered suicide/when the rainbow is enuf: a choreopoem*, Ntozake Shange translates the intense personal pain of growing up black and female into a collage of vignettes in verse form that together mold a black feminist manifesto celebrating both the intricacies of being a black woman and the strength gleaned from living with double oppression in a hegemonic society. The piece captures the density of women's lives, and in the foreword to *for colored girls*, Shange gives a history of the progression of the work as it metamorphosed from a poetry piece with dance performed at bars and cafés, into a choreopoem, and eventually into a full-blown Broadway production. For Shange, recognizing *for colored girls* as a choreopoem was a matter of trust in her voice and vision. Shange recounts, "I acknowledged that the poems & the dance worked on their own to do & be what they were. As opposed to viewing the pieces as poems, I came to understand these twenty-odd poems as a single statement, a choreopoem" (*for colored girls* xiv).

The choreopoem is characterized by its unique storytelling form that integrates a combination of poetry, song, music, prose, dance, and mime into a nonlinear narrative form. Shange often uses stream of consciousness in her theater pieces, and she urges black playwrights to abandon European theater models and move toward African traditions that include storytelling, rhythms, and dance. She suggests that black playwrights forsake the conventions of straight theater for a decade of their careers so their work with unconventional forms will flourish (Woll 248–249). The choreopoem, as Neal Lester points out, combines elements that "outline a distinctly African American heritage—to arouse an emotional response in an audience" (3).

When *for colored girls* was first introduced to Broadway audiences, it was like nothing they had previously experienced in American theater. *for colored girls* struck a chord as the audience embraced this avant-garde piece that at the time was unique in terms of both form and subject matter. The choreopoem opens with seven characters in tableau vivant before they collectively celebrate a common culture, regardless of their dispersed geographical locations across the United States. The women revel in the sounds of Motown rhythm and blues music of the 1960s and bask in the beauty of their bodies as they dance the pony, the swim, and other popular dances. The mood of the piece, like the rhythms of women's lives, ebbs and flows from despair to exaltation tracking the coming of age of black girls from teenage experimentation to twentysomething motherhood. The first character to speak, Lady in Yellow, recounts her decision to lose her virginity on the evening of her high school graduation as a rite of passage in becoming a "grown up." She embraces her own budding sexuality and gloats that she could not "stop grinnin" after her first sexual encounter (10).

There follow a series of vignettes that shift the tone of the piece. Against the Afro-Latin beat of Willie Colon, Lady in Blue speaks about how she came to love being black through her connection to music and dance. The women explode into the meringue and the bomba as they forge an impromptu celebration of the vitality of their bodies. This celebration is briefly interrupted by a dark mood as Lady in Red speaks of breaking up with her boyfriend through a note listing his shortcomings and inconsiderate behavior. However, the convivial spirit is rekindled as the women again respond by breaking into dance and listing their various reasons for dancing in the face of adversity. In the midst of the dancing, there is an abrupt lighting change, and the ladies react as if they have been struck; the conversation shifts to acquaintance rape. The tone becomes increasingly labored as each woman contributes to the conversation. Here and throughout the work, women share commonalities that blend into one statement representative of the experiences of an urban black girl.

In the next segment, Lady in Blue shares the story of having an abortion while Lady in Purple, Sechita, describes the degrading nature of her work as an exotic dancer who performs for good old boys in Natchez, Tennessee. Sechita is perhaps the best crafted poem in the series as the character, through dance and the continued intonation of variations of the phrase "sechita/ egyptian/ goddess," takes on the multifaceted roles imposed on women throughout history. She is naïve, wise, detached, and loving, both a slut and a deity: "Through sound, rhythm, and repetition, through what the Yorubas of West Africa term *ase*, or the power to make things happen . . . she strives to call into being that primordial spirit who presides over the perpetuation of life" (Richards, "Ntozake" 383). Through Sechita, the human and the divine merge among the least likely of circumstances in the sobering and sanguine story of an exotic dancer.

Several vignettes include experiences with men that function simultaneously as reality and metaphor. A young girl in St. Louis discovers Toussaint L'Overture through a summer reading project and coincidentally meets a boy named Toussaint Jones, who becomes the L'Overture of her daydreams. A woman who has learned that sex equals power chooses promiscuity and seduction as a safer life choice than intimacy. The women share betrayal by men and the loss of love. This series of vignettes ends with the characters uniting in a common determination to be loved for who they are, and in chorus they express appreciation for their bodies, their personalities, and their own unique beauty.

In the next poem, Lady in Green merges humor and despair in the story of a breakup as she infuses the blues like refrain "somebody almost walked off wid alla my stuff" (52) into this list poem. The stuff in the poem constitutes her self and her culture as represented by her physical body—arms, legs, and feet, her spirit—mouth, voice, and quick wit, as well as her sexuality—crotch and thighs. On a more innocuous level, her stuff also includes her material possessions—clothes, records, and food. The other ladies respond by listing the apologies that some men would contrive in this situation. Lady in Blue declares that she does not need more apologies, and she details the ways in which she will become more like an insensitive man in relationships and "wont be sorry for none of it" (54). She takes responsibility for her own actions and demands would-be future partners to do the same instead of perpetually being sorry for repeated wrongs.

At this point, *for colored girls* segues into the saga of Crystal and Beau Willie Brown. Unlike the previous male characters, Beau Willie is more developed as the audience is aware that he is traumatized from a tour of duty in Vietnam. As the piece chronicles several years of Crystal's struggle with single motherhood, poverty, and domestic violence, it is apparent that Willie is as much a victim of his own choices as of the larger racist society. It is also obvious why Crystal secures a restraining order against Beau Willie and forbids him to see their children, Naomi and Kwame. While Beau Willie is separated from his family, he schemes about how he can win them back, marry Crystal, support the family with veteran's benefits, and succeed as the man of the house. One night, Beau Willie defies the restraining order, and he appears apologetic and humble so Crystal allows him to see the children. Beau Willie kicks the screen out of the window and holds the kids hostage five stories above the street while insisting that Crystal marry him. As the neighbors scream in horror, Crystal cannot respond either quickly or loudly enough, and Beau Willie drops the children to their deaths.

Crystal's lack of self-assertion and loss of personal voice is central to this piece. At the moment of Beau Willie's ultimatum, Crystal looses her ability to speak on behalf of her children or herself. Presumably from the confidence she has gained by uniting with the other characters, Crystal regains her voice as she reveals her personal history to the group. Integral to the characters' collective endeavor to rise from personal tragedy and societal oppression is their voicing of their stories. Crystal confesses moments of complete self-hatred and reveals the stages she moved through beyond dysfunction to finally find God in herself. The other women repeat this mantra to themselves softly and tentatively until it becomes an emphatic life-affirming declaration. Lady in Brown then dedicates the choreopoem to colored girls who have considered suicide but "are movin to the ends of their own rainbows" (67), an homage to black womanhood despite the double binds of racial and gender oppression.

Shange's *A Photograph: A Study in Cruelty*, later published as *A Photograph: Lovers in Motion*, is deeply disturbing yet ultimately hopeful. *Photograph* chronicles the relationships of Sean David, a photographer, and his three lovers, Claire, Nevada, and Michael. Characteristic of Shange's style, *Photograph* incorporates poetry, music, and dance into a poem-play that expounds on the themes of self-exploration and the emotional exploitation of others. Sean believes that he can capture the essence of life in motion when, in fact, as a photographer, he does just the opposite. A photograph captures stasis, not movement, and this idea is central to understanding Sean as a character paralyzed by his "own economic and social status as a black person, caught perpetually in the act of becoming rather than being a great photographer" (Lester 151).

Sean identifies with Alexandre Dumas, the famous nineteenth-century French writer, who was a flagrant womanizer and an outcast in French society; Sean, emotionally abandoned by his father, also relates to Dumas's bastard son who avidly and vengefully sought his father's approval. For Sean, the act of photographing the world around him is a form of objectification. His camera is a "weapon by which he avenges his own perceived lowly position as a black male in a racist society" (Lester 147). Sean struggles with a distorted definition of manhood. In the simplest sense, Sean defines manhood as his ability to have psychological and physical power over women; acting on this distortion, he prides himself on his ability to handle three women at the same time. Controlling women is so fundamental to Sean's sense of being that he is willing to psychologically exploit and physically assault women in order to maintain control.

Each of the three female characters represents a specific stereotypical expectation of female sexual identity. Claire is a numinous being full of her own sensuality and sexuality. Claire prides herself on her promiscuity, and as a model believes that her body is a commodity to be traded. However, Claire's bisexuality and unwillingness to be in a monogamous relationship threaten Sean's masculinity. This sense of danger reveals "a part of Claire's psyche that welcomes . . . abuse as foreplay to intimacy" (Lester 144). Philip Effiong points out that Claire's "encounters with love, art, disenchanting dreams, sex, and frustrations are also synonymous with Claire's struggles to express her bisexuality" (163).

Unlike Claire, who uses her body as her primary asset, Nevada lives in the realm of the intellect. She is an attorney and the epitome of an intelligent, well-educated, and upwardly mobile professional. She pays Sean's rent and buys camera equipment for him, and despite her keen skill as a lawyer, Nevada allows herself to be emotionally and financially manipulated by Sean. Nevada is aware of Sean's feelings for her and of his relationships with other women; still, she wants to be the only woman in his life. She continues to offer financial support to Sean, convinced that he can fulfill her emotional needs. At the very least, she believes she can bribe Sean for his love until a more viable partner emerges.

Michael, a dancer, is a stark contrast to both Claire and Nevada, and Sean's relationship with Michael is markedly different from his other relationships. Michael, a female character with a traditionally male name, works as Shange's mouthpiece as she touts a reality where heterosexual relationships can be healthy and enhance the spiritual well-being of both parties. It is through Michael that Sean discovers his sense of self, and it is Michael who guides and encourages Sean to pursue his artistic ambitions. At the end of the play, presumably through a transformation due to his relationship with Michael, Sean announces his love for her. Although many critics consider this ending disingenuous or too romantic, Shange argues that the larger theme of the poem-play hinges on Sean's ability to learn to love. Furthermore, the characters have to find their own remedies for their own situations. Shange writes, "[this is] why i'm doubly proud of *a photograph: lovers in motion/* which has no cures for our 'condition' save those we afford ourselves" (*See No Evil* 24).

In *Spell #7: A Theater Piece in Two Acts*, the characters explore onstage and offstage role playing while Shange experiments with various theatrical conventions and notions associated with masks, the most remarkable of these the idea that people differ dramatically in their public and private selves. The play-within-a-play structure incorporates a giant blackface minstrel mask to depict how blacks, particularly black artists, are oppressed by racism in America. Shange again employs elements of the choreopoem as the work is nonlinearly structured, utilizes dance to suggest points of connection, and sustains an improvisational effect. The characters are a group of black actors exasperated by the lack of available and acceptable roles for people of color in a white-dominated theater industry. Lou, the magician, emcee, and trickster figure, embodies the troupe of the minstrel show as he promises to "cure" the desire for whiteness and cast a "black magic" spell so that all under its control will love being black.

When, through Lou's spell, all are transported behind the minstrel mask, the audience sees the characters offstage as their guard is let down and they relax and have a drink at a favorite bar. In this locale, the characters are free to enact stories that are meaningful both metaphorically and literally and to transmit often unseen realities of black culture. Unlike the structured and prescribed roles the characters are forced to play in white society, the stories the characters choose to tell among themselves are episodic and unconventional. For example, two of the stories they recount are those of Fay and Lily. The more mundane story of Fay is of a woman who lives in Brooklyn and is looking to have a good time during a night out on the town without being labeled a whore; the more surreal tale of Lily discloses fantasies about brushing treasures from a full head of luxurious hair. In another narrative, Alec demands a national holiday where all whites will acknowledge past wrongs and apologize for the havoc wreaked upon African Americans. In the telling of these stories, the actors use varying degrees of imagination to cope with the realities of living in an oppressive society and to reveal their deepest fantasies.

The two most developed narratives in the piece, those of Sue-Jean and Maxine, are placed at the end of each act. At the conclusion of the first act, the tragic portrait of Sue-Jean, a desperate woman who gives birth to a child named Myself, leaves the audience veritably speechless. Sue-Jean longs to provide a better life for her child, and she desperately wants to nurture and protect him. However, as Myself grows and becomes increasingly autonomous, Sue-Jean kills the child and drinks his blood. Symbolically, this act represents the attempt to maintain the meaningfulness and purposefulness inherent in initial stages of motherhood, where Sue-Jean celebrates the merging of infant and self. On another level, this act also echoes earlier generations of slave women who killed their children rather than condemn them to a life of involuntary servitude; in this instance, Sue-Jean spares her child from the desperation and hopelessness of life in the urban jungle.

The story of Maxine at the end of act 2 is equally disturbing. When Maxine is a child, she is convinced that epidemics such as polio and social problems such as child abuse only affect whites because she has never seen blacks included in public service announcements. However, as Maxine grows older, she learns that blacks too are prone to disease and "unnatural acts." As a contrary form of atonement, Maxine buys a piece of gold jewelry for her ostentatious collection as she learns of each unsavory act committed by a black person. Through the ritual of taking something "pure" from Africa, Maxine believes she cleanses her reality and is atoning for the sins of wayward African Americans. In this fable, Shange uncovers a clear conflict of class and behavioral norms within the black community.

Like other of Shange's works, the major crises in *Spell #7* are not resolved within the action of the play. Rather, the cure that we "afford ourselves" is the work of the individual members of the audience, and ultimately, the larger society. Sandra Richards points out that "because Sue-Jean's and Maxine's stories are marked by a pain almost beyond resolution, Lou interrupts to reassure audiences that they will indeed love his black magic" ("Ntozake" 387). Lou's affirmation of loving being colored enables the characters and audience to live and define themselves as they wish, and they are free to depart from the descending minstrel mask and from the auspices of Lou's spell. This spell empowers blacks to overcome oppression in the most important way, by having free minds in the face of the resistance they encounter in a racist society.

In one of Shange's most experimental and provocative works, *Boogie Woogie Landscapes*, a black woman's psyche is revealed through conscious and subconscious episodes in a dreamscape comprised of imagistic monologues. While thematically similar to *for colored girls*, *Boogie* probes deeper into the psychological realities of a black woman's experiences. While the physical setting of the choreopoem is Layla's bedroom, the landscape alluded to in the title is the internal terrain of Layla's psyche where boogie woogie music echoes and punctuates the rhythms and pace of her dreams.

Shange incorporates the impressionistic techniques of symbolic colors, dream imagery, surreal structure, improvisation, and skewed temporality into the framework of *Boogie*. The choreopoem closely resembles a dream; at first glance the work appears as a disordered, episodic, and incomplete sketch of the substantial victimizations and victories of a single character. However, these seemingly chaotic pieces beg to be connected, untangled, and interpreted by the audience in the intuitive realm.

Like *for colored girls*, *Boogie* chronicles Layla's coming of age from childhood perceptions of reality to painful adult experiences. Shange suggests that black girls deal with the discovery and acceptance of race before coming to an awareness of gender roles and discrimination. As Layla reveals personal fears through dream sequences and fragments, her struggles are recognizable to the audience as universal issues that are easily politicized and transferred to social realities. Layla self-defines as "grey" because she is both physically black and a participant in a predominantly white culture. In this sense, Layla considers herself a "hazard to definitions" (115). In the course of *Boogie*, Layla overcomes the dual victimization of race and gender and perceives herself as a Jesus figure who is the architect of her own salvation.

Shange's next major work, *From Okra to Greens: A Different Kinda Love Story: A Play with Music and Dance*, is feminist love story set amid global turmoil and social injustice. This work has appeared in several venues and forms. The choreopoem was first produced in 1981 under the title *Mouths*. Later that same year, a section of the work titled *It Has Not Always Been This Way: A Choreopoem* was produced at the Symphony Space Theater. In March and April 1982, *It Hasn't Always Been This Way* and *Mouths: A Daughter's Geography* were presented in Los Angeles at the Mark Taper Theater Lab. Additionally, virtually every poem in *Okra* appears verbatim in Shange's collection of poetry, *A Daughter's Geography*.

The title signifies Shange's variation on the theme of the boy-meets-girl love story. In Shange's work, Okra exists as an independent and self-sufficient woman before she meets Greens. The play is candid, if not graphic, in the specific portrayal of the sexual encounters between the two characters and the more generalized sexual escapades of "some men" and the women they victimize. Shange depicts a paradoxical situation as "some men" in the poems prefer the idea of controlling a woman through denying her pleasure rather than relishing a complete moment of unity when, through female orgasm, the woman surrenders to her partner willingly. Shange also outlines some men's "mythic notion of impregnating women as a sign and determinant of their manhood" (Lester 239). Apparently, these men are unaware of the possibility of loosing their place in a woman's life to technology in the roles of both financial and sexual provider. These ideas are integral to Shange's feminist vision as *Okra* unravels the cultural mythology that women who are comfortable in their bodies and who consider themselves sexually and intellectually liberated are inferior to their male counterparts.

In the progression of the choreopoem, Okra and Greens fall in love, date and marry, split because of Greens's infidelity, reconcile, and eventually conceive and raise a child. This redefinition of the "typical" relationship sequence and of "happily ever after" is not the only way that Shange lives up to her promise of a different kind of love story. Okra and Greens, both poets, are continuously writing about social realities, including inequities from the lack of funding initiatives for black and poor missing children to restraints often imposed on nations by a postcolonial presence to the peoples around the globe who are separated linguistically but are united in fighting "the same old men" (54). Shange extends the parenting metaphor from the insular world of Okra and Greens's marriage to a global context. Lester points out that "as persons of color, Okra and Greens are not politically or culturally privileged to disconnect themselves from a global community or oppressed people of color" (262). The choreopoem ends with the honeymoon-like merging of Okra and Greens with the wind, the sun, and the sea. The oppositional forces—male and female, water and light—unite in a ceremony in which the insatiable sea who "want[s]s it all" licks the toes of the characters (56). In this merging of worlds, Okra and Greens commit to personal and global solidarity while cooled by the ocean and warmed by the watchful eye of the sun.

CRITICAL RECEPTION

Ntozake Shange has been both celebrated and condemned as controversies over her use of theatrical form, language, and politics abound. One of the recurring criticisms of Shange's works is her virtually exclusive depiction of black artists and her apparent middle-class bias. Robert Staples aggressively argues that Shange "put[s] down [black] working culture without really understanding" it and contends that Shange's narrow focus is due to the fact that she is "middle class, raised away from the realities of the black experience and tend[s] to see [class differences] as pathological in the same way that whites view us [blacks]" (32). Neil Lester adamantly rejects this criticism of Shange and contends that her "upper middle-class childhood . . . moved her toward greater race consciousness and fuller awareness of her historical connectedness with those who [do] not necessarily have her . . . background" (191).

Another issue critics raise about Shange is her unconventional approach to theater. Some critics, such as John Simon, contend that Shange has yet to write a "real play." Simon argues that Shange is "something besides a poet but she is not . . . a dramatist" (57). Richard Eder insists that Shange's works are "roughly structured and stylistically unrefined" ("Papp" 11). Other critics praise Shange for her commitment to experimentation. Sandra Richards points out that Shange's modification of conventional theatrical styles is rooted in significant literary traditions. Like Antonin Artaud's "Theatre of Cruelty" and Amiri Baraka's "Black Revolutionary Theatre," Shange exhibits "a locus for emotionally charged, eruptive forces which assault social complacency to expose victims who, nevertheless, contain within themselves seeds of their own regeneration" ("Conflicting" 76). Effiong adds that Shange's avant-garde approaches to theater have ritualized her drama and given audiences and actors new personal and spiritual insights: "This ritual approach to black drama, a concept promoted in the 1960s, borrows and reapplies the sacred, spiritual, and communal significance of traditional African performance in a new setting" (168).

Shange's unique use of language has dazzled literary and theater critics. Y. S. Sharadha praises the real and immediate dimension of Shange's works. Sharadha contends that Shange "manipulates language to achieve raw emotion like passion, rage, anger, resentment, ecstasy, and pain" (24). Effiong considers Shange a gifted and unique voice who is able to attend to the tenuous work of combining dance, poetry, and movement to "express her views on the effects of racism, sexism, poverty, and spiritual decay on women, Blacks, relationships, art, and life's energies" (167).

Many, such as Mary DeShazer, have noted Shange's striking representation of the black female experience. DeShazer points out that Shange's works allow women of color to "assert their very presence . . . become warriors raging against their own invisibility" (87). Sharadha praises Shange for putting "her finger on the pulse of black women's lives in contemporary urban society" (24) while Effiong argues that "Shange makes pronounced contributions to the Black Aesthetic and its efforts to break down conventional walls" (167). Effiong continues:

Shange assists in expanding the Black literary focus on racial and cultural identity so that it embraces a sexual revolution. Having lost faith in the ability of men to respond effectively to female subordination, she furnishes the American stage with not just a significant Black presence but a feminine one too. (167)

These critics place Shange in a literary tradition including such greats as Alice Childress and Lorraine Hansberry,* who "have brought to the American stage a multiplicity of images of female heroines and have not confined themselves to such limiting images of black women as immoral, promiscuous, wanton, frigid, overbearing, or pathetically helpless" (Sharadha 10).

On the whole, Shange's works aspire to define an African American female identity and to preserve a cultural voice. Shange's structural and representational depictions demonstrate that "while she confronts critical themes and raises fundamental questions, she also mourns the loss of an indigenous culture whose vibrancy is dependent on rhythmic and religious precedents. It is a culture that her theatre strives to recover" (Effiong 168). While Shange sets her plays in mostly contemporary urban environments, she also acknowledges the impact of history on the ethnic and cultural traditions: Shange constructs "an ethnic theatre [that] is born out of historical conflict. At the heart of its beginnings is the quest for identity" (Sharadha 9).

for colored girls opened to both favorable and scathing reviews. Many established male critics were outraged by Shange's portrayal of black men as uncaring, violent, and oppressive. The most widely held criticism of *for colored girls* is the lack of positive male–female relationships represented in the piece. In a particularly controversial poem, the characters describe their perceptions of almost universal experiences with acquaintance rape. Nancy Gray points out that this has been considered an indictment of black men and that Shange has been criticized for "writing such scenes; she has been named a traitor to her people for speaking of the divisions . . . for connecting the divisions within herself to those between men and women who have together been victims of oppression" (143). Despite the fact that *for colored girls* was often criticized within certain sectors of the black community, it was a great commercial success among the principally white Broadway audience. Richards points out the irony of this situation and claims that *for colored girls* enjoyed critical success precisely because the predominantly white male critics were not threatened by Shange's work: "White male critics . . . could celebrate a newly discovered humanity with black women . . . [while] feeling not the least bit threatened . . . as [they were] . . . by the earlier Black Arts plays of Amiri Baraka and others" ("Ntozake" 385).

Despite the fact that some criticized Shange's portrayal of blacks, others took pride in and closely related to Shange's work. Alan Rich hones in on some black audience's positive reaction to *for colored girls* and claims that this reception is probably a combination of pride in a captivating play coupled with the effect of the relatively new phenomenon of a respected play on Broadway depicting black life (qtd. in Lester 22). Rich's sentiment is echoed by Jessica Harris who dubs *for colored girls* a "theatrical milestone" in accurately and respectfully presenting black life on the stage (qtd. in Lester 22).

In contrast to focusing on *for colored girls'* commercial success, other critics concentrate on Shange's use of language. Houston Baker praises

Shange for her knack of expanding meaning by her use of virgules, "which are traditionally employed to separate alternatives such as *either/or*," but in Shange's case are "deployed to *summon* alternatives and to avoid closure" (qtd. in Olaniyan 127). Shange explains this when she writes that "I can't let you get away with thinking you know what I mean. . . . After all, I didn't mean whatever you can just ignore. I mean what you have to struggle with" (qtd. in Olaniyan 18). Carol Christ praises Shange for writing in genuine black women's language and claims that "Shange must re-create the language of her experience, a language which . . . has almost never been spoken" (101). Christ describes Shange as "a gutsy, down-to-earth poet . . . [who] gives voice to the ordinary experiences of Black women in frank, simple, vivid language, telling the colored girl's story in her own speech patterns" (97).

The last theme in the critical literature about *for colored girls* is Shange's impact on American theater. Lester points out:

While broadening existing forms of Westernized American theater, she affords people of color and women alternative possibilities for existence, working an ideal where one's potential for development as a complete individual assuming his or her rightful place in the social and world order is not dictated by race or gender, or by Eurocentric ideals. (267)

Other critics view *for colored girls* as liberating for black women as well. James Hatch describes *for colored girls* as "the greatest change of image for black women" on the American stage (xi), and Mel Gussow writes that "each articulate actress invests her scenes with herself . . . it is the closeness, the intimacy, and the specificity of the revelations that make the play so tangible and so poignant" (200). It is also this freedom of expression that is bestowed on the audience through the performance of *for colored girls*. In comparison, *Photograph* was largely unsuccessful and received mostly negative reviews. Some critics, such as Simon, offer fierce assessments of the work:

A Photograph . . . , calls itself a "poemplay." What is a poemplay? Something, evidently, that is neither poem nor play, but hopes that the poetry experts will let it pass as a play, while the drama critics will assume it to be poetry. Actually it is neither. It is exactly the same drivel as Miss Shange's previous *for colored girls*." (58)

Similarly, Martin Gottfried echoes Simon's remarks and contends that "*A Photograph* is a play and a series of poems, but unfortunately, it is never both. . . . Shange is a wonderful poet, but she is not yet a playwright and does not create playable characters" (42). Gottfried goes on to claim that the piece does not cohere. In another scathing review, Dean Valentine claims that in *Photograph* "intelligibility stops. I have not the faintest notion of how the multitudinous vignettes that comprise the play are related" (42).

Other critics tend to be intensely negative about thematic concerns. Richards criticizes the lack of sociohistorical context, the gratuitous emotions exhibited by the characters, and the gender roles of the women who service men while leaving their own needs largely unattended: "Glimmering in the work may be the theme of the artist who virtually destroys himself in the process of creating, but because the writing allows the public no easy access, it fails to suggest how the characters' pain is on some level our own ("Ntozake" 386). Another point of contention is *Photograph*'s potentially sentimental ending. Lester points out that "the ending seems appropriate if we accept the sincerity of Michael and Sean's professions of love. Yet the motives for Sean's commitment to Michael remain unclear" (170). Shange resists this criticism and insists that *Photograph* is generally about "the ways people exploit each other emotionally," but more importantly, it is about "the possibility of learning love" (Shange, "Future" 70).

In addition to the structure, plot, and theme, critics focus on Shange's intentional manipulation of the English language. In response to harsh criticisms about her destruction of the English language, Shange responds:

[T]he man who thought I wrote with intentions of outdoing the white man in the acrobatic distortions of english was absolutely correct . . . yes/ being an afro-american writer is something to be self-conscious abt/ & yes/ in order to think n communicate the thoughts n feelings I want to think n communicate/ I haveta fix my tool to my needs/ I have to take it apart to the bone/ so that the malignancies/ fall away/ leaving us space to literally create our own image. (*See No Evil* 21)

Positive assessments of the work, such as Edith Oliver's claim that in *Photograph* Shange's "own poetic talent and passion carry the show, and her characters are . . . flesh and blood" (48), are less plentiful. The most positive criticisms of Shange's work come from Sharadha, who claims that the spiritual journeys of the female characters in the play are meaningful because they can be linked to six stages of growth that roughly parallel developmental stages in Gustav Freytag's *Pyramid* (103–104).

Shange's *Spell #7* (1978) was received with mostly positive criticism despite its refusal to conform to the standards of mainstream theater. Critics who are negative about the piece suggest it is perhaps an unfinished work rather than condemn it as irrevocably flawed. Christopher Sharp refers to *Spell #7* as "a workshop production, . . . a fecund garden that badly needs trimming" (109). Richard Eder suggests that *Spell #7* is an "uneven work . . . it is a talented and often beautiful work, excitingly performed; and there is reason to hope that if it continues to evolve, it will become a remarkable one" ("Dramatic" C13).

Lester praises Shange for reenlisting the choreopoem form and expanding the subject matter beyond the scope of the issues present in *for colored girls*. He points out, "While *for colored girls* consciously emphasizes a black feminist voice, *Spell #7* focuses on the subtle and overt manifestations of racism in America" (81). He also argues that through "embracing some aspects of racist stereotypes, Shange shows that the status of a description is not as significant as how it functions and what it does socially and psychologically within an individual" (82–83). Similarly, in an interview with Lester, Laurie Carlos accentuates Shange's efforts to destroy racial stereotypes that inhibit black performers: "What Zake is bringing to the stage— legitimate and complex black experience—is not new to black people, but new to the American stage" (109).

Barbara Christian focuses on Shange's character Sue-Jean and the notion of contrariness. Because Sue-Jean is "othered" as abnormal in terms of race and gender, she has limited opportunities. In this character, Shange creates an archetypal mother figure with a vengeful streak. Like Medea, Sue-Jean kills her child, named Myself, and "makes actual the suicide which many women symbolically experience in sublimating their own identities to those of their children" (qtd in Sharadha 99). Lester concludes that *Spell #7* is not only about individual tragedies such as Sue-Jean's but is overwhelmingly about the social realities of being black in modern America: "It . . . demonstrates the need for individual fantasy as a tool for survival in a bigoted society" (7). *Spell #7* also shows the "definitive need for racially segregated experience to dispel oppressive and often internalized myths about black culture and celebrates positive aspects of black identity" (Lester 7).

Many critics of Shange's *Boogie Woogie Landscapes* compare it to *for colored girls* and draw parallels between the two pieces. Sharadha points out that Shange creates a space where a "black female's conscious and subconscious desires are visibly personified. While resembling *for colored girls* most in content and subject matter, this play moves deeper into a black female's psychological identity" (113). Lester expands on this assessment with claims that "*Boogie* resumes the study where *for colored girls* ends, revealing what is at the core of a black girl's innermost existence" (215). Lester asserts that as a companion piece to *for colored girls*, *Boogie* is "more complicated structurally, more theatrically complex, less idealistic philosophically, less naturalistic performatively, and more entertaining theatrically" than Shange's previous works (215). Effiong concentrates on the differences and notes that "unlike *colored girls* . . . the characters here are not only women; men are present and interact with the women, and there are also occasional instances of actual dialogue" (142). Effiong also sees this as a gradual shift from the "choreopoem to other models" while Shange begins to explore additional themes and forms (142).

Like Shange's other works, a main criticism of *Boogie* as well as Shange's next major published play, *From Okra to Greens: A Different Kinda Love Story*, is the dramatic structure. Judith Martin argues that in *Boogie* "Ntozake Shange's litany of complaints . . . [has] no dramatic point of view" and that the work is "lacking [in] organization" (n.p.). Martin also argues that Shange does not fulfill her own definition of the play as one night of dreams. Joseph McLellan contends that Shange's use of dream motif as a structural device is ineffective and that the dream sequences give Shange an opportunity to "empty out her notebook of any odds and ends that might be passed off as dreams or memories (that is to say, anything in the world) without thought or structure, coherence or continuity)" (C6). Lester defends the dream motif and points out that the advantage of this device is that it "frees Shange from an artificially ordered portrayal of a human mind at work, even when one's body and consciousness are at complete rest" (176). Similarly, *Okra* is heavily criticized for its structure. Lester points out that "a potential problem with this piece lies with its coherence as Shange endeavors to rework an entire volume of poems into a single play" (224). Although there are obvious structural difficulties, Lester praises *Okra* for offering "a black woman's view of both romantic bliss and turmoil amid rampant political and social injustice" (270).

As a feminist writer offering a candid look into what it means to be female and black, Shange has been applauded, disparaged, and often misunderstood, especially in "her portrayal of black men on the stage" (Lester 273); however, her works continue to present a context in which blacks struggle together to "secure political, social, and economic gains" (Sharadha 10). Although she is best known as a playwright, Shange has studied music and dance, directed productions, and performed in jazz and music ensembles (Woll 248). Throughout the span of her nearly thirty-year career, Shange has continued to produce poems, children's books, short stories, cookbooks, novels, dramas, essays, and other pieces. Her works are vehicles to preserve her individual, political, cultural, and artistic identities. As a significant voice in American theater, Shange presents a holistic vision of theater that is at once personal and political, aesthetic and spiritual, specific and universal. In this vision, or choreopoem, past traditions and future norms collide as the lines between genres blur, and self, other, political, personal, poetry, dance, music, and movement merge.

BIBLIOGRAPHY

Dramatic Works by Ntozake Shange

Betsy Brown. 1983. Unpublished.
Black and White Two-Dimensional Planes. 1979. Unpublished.
Carrie. 1981. Unpublished.
"Daddy Says." *New Plays for the Black Theater.* Ed. Woodie King, Jr. Chicago: Third World, 1989.

Educating Rita. 1982. Unpublished.

for colored girls who have considered suicide/when the rainbow is enuf : a choreopoem. New York: MacMillan, 1977.

From Okra to Greens: A Different Kinda Love Story: A Play with Music and Dance. New York: French, 1985.

Lavender Lizards and Lilac Landmines. 2003. Unpublished.

The Love Space Demands. 1993. Unpublished.

Mother Courage and Her Children. 1980. Unpublished.

Mouths. 1981. Unpublished.

Negress. 1977. Unpublished.

Nomathebu (with Lady Smith Black Mambazo). 2002. Unpublished.

A Photograph: Lovers in Motion. New York: French, 1981.

Plays, One. London: Methuen Drama, 1992.

Spell #7: A Theater Piece in Two Acts. New York: French, 1981.

Three for a Full Moon and Bocas. 1982. Unpublished.

Three Pieces: Spell #7, A Photograph: Lovers in Motion, Boogie Woogie Landscapes. New York: St. Martin's, 1981.

Three Views of Mt. Fuji/A Poem with Music. 1987. Unpublished.

Uncle Tom's Cabin. 2000. Unpublished.

Other Cited Material by Ntozake Shange

"Future Subjunctive: Shange's New Song." *Horizon* 20 (Sept. 1977): 70.

See No Evil: Prefaces, Essays, and Accounts, 1974–1983. San Francisco: Momo's, 1984.

"With No Immediate Cause." *Nature's Ban: Women's Incest Literature.* Ed. Karen Jacobsen McLennan. Boston: Northeastern University Press, 1996. 317–320.

Studies of Ntozake Shange's Dramatic Works

Bond, Jean C. *"for colored girls* Who Have Considered Suicide." *Freedomways* 16 (1976): 187–191.

Brown, Elizabeth. "Ntozake Shange." *Dictionary of Literary Biography.* Detroit: Gale, 1985.

Brown-Guillory, Elizabeth. *Their Place on the Stage: Black Women Playwrights in America.* Westport: Greenwood, 1988.

Bryer, Jackson R., ed. "Ntozake Shange." *The Playwright's Art: Conversations with Contemporary American Dramatists.* New Brunswick: Rutgers University Press, 1995. 205–220.

Carney, Sean. *Artaud, Genet, Shange: The Absence of the Theatre of Cruelty.* Ottawa: National Library of Canada, 1994.

Christ, Carol P. *Diving Deep and Surfacing: Women Writers on Spiritual Quest.* Boston: Beacon, 1980.

DeShazer, Mary. "Rejecting Necrophilia: Ntozake Shange and the Warrior Re-Visioned." *Making a Spectacle: Feminist Essays on Contemporary Women's Theater*. Ed. Lynda Hart. Ann Arbor: University of Michigan Press, 1989. 86–100.

Eder, Richard. "Dramatic Poetry." *New York Times* 4 June 1979: C13.

———. "Papp Proves Less Is More." *New York Times* 2 Apr. 1978: 11.

Effiong, Philip. *In Search of a Model for African-American Drama: A Study of Selected Plays by Lorraine Hansberry, Amiri Baraka, and Ntozake Shange*. Lanham: University Press of America, 2000.

Geis, Deborah R. "Distraught Laughter: Monologue in Ntozake Shange's Theater Pieces." *Feminine Focus: The New Women's Playwrights*. Ed. Enoch Brater. New York: Oxford University Press, 1989. 210–225.

Gottfried, Martin. "Theater: Playmaking Is Not Enough." *Saturday Review* 18 Feb. 1978: 42.

Gray, Nancy. "Communities of Diversity: Ntozake Shange, E. M. Broner, Monique Wittig." *Language Unbound: On Experimental Writing by Women*. Chicago: University of Illinois Press, 1992. 133–176.

Gussow, Mel. "Stage: *colored girls* on Broadway." *New York Times Theater Critics' Reviews* 37 (1976): 200.

Hatch, James. Foreword. *Contemporary Black American Playwrights and Their Plays*. Ed. Bernard L. Peterson, Jr. Westport: Greenwood, 1988. ix–xii.

Keyssar, Helene. "Rites and Responsibilities: The Drama of Black American Women." *Feminine Focus: The New Women Playwrights*. Ed. Enoch Brater. New York: Oxford University Press, 1989. 226–240.

Kosseh-Kamanda, Mafo. *Ntozake Shange*. University of Minnesota. 2000. 24 Apr. 2003. <http://voices.cla.umn.edu/authors/SHANGEntozake.html>.

Lester, Neal. *Ntozake Shange: A Critical Study of the Plays*. New York: Garland, 1995.

Martin, Judith. "A Scattered Landscape." *Washington Post* 27 June 1980: n.p.

McLellan, Joseph. "Bungled *Boogie*: Ntozake Shange's Lower-Case Editorials." *Washington Post* 20 June 1980: C6.

Mitchell, Carolyn. "'A Laying on of Hands': Transcending the City in Ntozake Shange's *for colored girls who have considered suicide/when the rainbow is enuf*." *Women Writers and the City: Essays in Feminist Literary Criticism*. Ed. Susan Merrill Squier. Knoxville: University of Tennessee Press, 1984. 230–248.

Olaniyan, Tejumola. *Scars of Conquest/Masks of Resistance: The Invention of Cultural Identities in African, African-American, and Caribbean Drama*. New York: Oxford University Press, 1995.

Oliver, Edith. "The Theatre: Off Broadway." *New Yorker* 2 Jan. 1978: 48.

Peters, Erskine. "Some Tragic Propensities of Ourselves: The Occasion of Ntozake Shange's *for colored girls who have considered suicide/when the rainbow is enuf*." *Journal of Ethnic Studies* 6 (1978): 79–85.

Peterson, Bernard L., Jr. "Notzake Shange." *Contemporary Black American Playwrights and Their Plays: A Biographical Directory and Dramatic Index*. Westport: Greenwood, 1988. 417–421.

Richards, Sandra L. "Conflicting Impulses in the Plays of Ntozake Shange." *Black American Literature Forum* 17 (1983): 73–78.

———. "Ntozake Shange." *African American Writers*. Ed. Valerie Smith. New York: Scribner's, 1991. 379–393.

Sharadha, Y. S. *Black Women's Writing: Quest for Identity in the Plays of Lorraine Hansberry and Ntozake Shange*. New Delhi: Sangam, 1998.

Sharp, Christopher. "*Spell #7: A Geechee Quik Magic Trance Manual.*" *New York Theater Critics' Reviews* 40 (1979): 109. Also published in *Women's Wear Daily*, 4 June 1979.

Simon, John. "Fainting Spell." *New York Magazine* 30 July 1979: 58.

———. "Theater. A Touch Is Better Than None." *New Yorker* 16 Jan. 1978: 58.

Staples, Robert. "The Myth of Black Macho: A Response to Angry Black Feminists." *Black Scholar* 10 (1979): 24–33.

Valentine, Dean. "On Stage: Theater of the Inane." *New Leader*, 2 Jan. 1978: 29.

Watson, Kenneth. "Ntozake Shange." *American Playwrights since 1945: A Guide to Scholarship, Criticism, and Performance*. Ed. Phillip C. Kolin. Westport: Greenwood, 1989. 379–386.

Woll, Allen, ed. "Ntozake Shange." *Dictionary of Black Theatre: Broadway, Off-Broadway, and Selected Harlem Theatre*. Westport: Greenwood, 1983. 248–250.

TED SHINE
(1931 –   )

Joyce Russell-Robinson

BIOGRAPHY

Theodis "Ted" Shine was born in Baton Rouge, Louisiana, on April 26, 1931. Shortly after his birth, his parents, Theodis Wesley and Bessie Herson Shine, and he moved to Dallas, Texas, where Ted grew up. Shine attended the public schools in Dallas, and after graduating from high school he enrolled at Howard University, in Washington, DC. Shine's writing talents were soon discovered by Professors Owen Dodson* and Sterling Brown, though Dodson, who intuited early on that satire and comedy were Shine's forte, proved to be more of a nurturer and mentor than did Brown. Because of Dodson's early mentoring, Shine's strength as a comedic-satiric playwright are artfully employed and are quite visible in almost all of his plays.

Shine at first saw himself as a writer of tragedy. Fully expecting to pursue a career as a writer in that area, he abandoned that plan when for one full year Dodson gave him no feedback on *My Mother Came Crying Most Pitifully*, a play Shine wrote in 1952—his second year at Howard. Dodson returned the play to Shine and ordered him to go "sit on a park bench and read it" (Fletcher 38). After doing so, Shine realized that he was indeed more gifted at writing satire and comedy.

My Mother Came Crying Most Pitifully was the twenty-one-year-old's first attempt at writing a long play. It had been preceded by *Cold Day in August*, which was first performed at Howard in 1951. Two other one-act plays had also been performed in 1951: *Sho Is Hot in the Cotton Patch* and *Dry August*. Each of these three performances received much praise and critical acclaim.

After earning a B.A. in 1953, Shine received a Rockefeller grant that enabled him to study at the Karamu House in Cleveland, Ohio. (*Karamu* is a Swahili word meaning a place of joyful gathering.) In 1955, Shine concluded his studies in Ohio and went on to serve two years in the army. After that, he enrolled in the playwriting program at the University of Iowa, and in 1958, he was awarded an M.A.

Shine's long teaching career began in 1960 when he went to Dillard University in New Orleans as an instructor of English and drama. In 1961, he joined the faculty of his alma mater, Howard, where he remained until 1967. From there, he went to Prairie View A & M University in Texas, where he taught and chaired in the Drama Department until he retired in 1998. Just a year or so after joining the faculty of Prairie View A & M, in 1969 to be specific, Shine began pursuing his Ph.D. at the University of California at Santa Barbara. His terminal degree in theatre was awarded in 1973. Shine also has been an adjunct professor at the University of Texas in Austin.

A service-oriented individual, Shine has held memberships on many boards and commissions, among them the Board of the Texas Nonprofit Theatres; the Panel of the Texas Commission on the Arts, which he chaired; and the Community Arts Panel of Cultural Arts of Houston. He has also been a member of the Southwest Theatre Conference. As a member of that organization, Shine once chaired the playwriting program of the conference, which was designed to promote playwriting in colleges and universities in the Southwest.

Although Shine has written primarily for stage production, there was a time when he might have chosen to write for television, or film, which undoubtedly would have been more financially beneficial. From 1969 to 1973, while Shine was engaged in his doctoral studies, he wrote more than sixty television scripts for the Maryland Center for Public Broadcasting. The television series *Our Street* was directed by Shine's good friend Whitney J. Le Blanc whom he met at the University of Iowa when both were graduate students. *Our Street* was enormously popular and "[b]rought [Shine] two subsequent invitations to conduct workshops in writing for the stage and screen. In 1972, Shine and Le Blanc visited Indiana University in conjunction with a live television studio production of *Idabel's Fortune*" (Fletcher 28). *Idabel's Fortune*, first produced in 1969, is one of the few plays by Shine in which white characters appear and have substantial roles. In 1973, Shine and Le Blanc appeared in a television interview on Kentucky Educational Television. The interview, titled "Morning, Noon, and Night on Our Street," followed a Kentucky production of Shine's *Morning, Noon, and Night* (1964).

When asked in a 1973 interview why he decided not to pursue a career as a television or film writer, Shine, who chose to remain a university professor, responded:

I enjoy teaching and working with young people. I also wanted stability and security in my life. The theatre, writing—the arts are too uncertain. Although I enjoyed doing the *Our Street* scripts, I don't know if I would have enjoyed being there during the actual shooting of the scripts. . . . It would have been a good time to get into television since they were beginning to employ more blacks at that time in various areas, but I was concerned with security. And I had a genuine interest in the students; my first obligation was to them. (LeBlanc 38)

Shine's decision to remain a professor has hindered his creation of more plays. He himself has stated that meetings, reports, teaching, and directing assignments have interfered with his creative and writing processes. "When I do have time to write something," he said, "someone manages to interrupt my train of thought. I cannot work in the office anymore because someone is always knocking on the door" (qtd. in LeBlanc 39).

While Shine is an important and respected playwright in American and African American theater, he has never had a play produced on a Broadway stage. But for him, having a play on Broadway does not necessarily equate to success, although, he admits, a Broadway hit would be economically rewarding. What matters first and foremost for Shine is getting the play produced, whether by a black university, a white university, or by a community theater company. Shine also believes that Broadway "accepts only so much Blackness and this is especially so if the work is a non-musical" (LeBlanc 35). Broadway, however, has not eluded Richard Wesley, one of Shine's former students who in 1978 saw his *The Mighty Gents* open at the Ambassador Theater.

Even though Shine cannot count a Broadway show as one of his numerous accomplishments, New York has been kind to him in other ways. In February 1970, three of Shine's one-act plays were produced Off Broadway at Tambellini's Gate Theatre under the title of *Contributions*. The plays were *Contribution* (1967), *Plantation* (1970), and *Shoes* (1969).

Many individuals have influenced Shine's work. In addition to Dodson, William Reardon and Oscar G. Brockett, two of Shine's professors at the University of Iowa, encouraged him. Reardon was especially helpful in teaching Shine structure and discipline. And, Shine says, the works of Langston Hughes* and Lorraine Hansberry* have also been influential (LeBlanc 41). Shine's use of humor to call attention to the verities of black life, for example, is similar to what one sees in Hughes, though Hughes's humor is of a softer kind. Hansberry's *A Raisin in the Sun* (1959) is a play that Shine has always admired because it "was the perfectly structured play when he first read it" (LeBlanc 40), and he still feels the same way now.

Shine has received many prestigious honors and awards. He was the recipient of the Brook–Hines Award for Playwriting (1970); he was a member of the Kennedy Center for the Performing Arts Task Force and Black Producing Theatres (1977); and he served as an adjudicator for the

Lorraine Hansberry Playwriting Award, sponsored by the American Theatre Association (1980–1981).

Although Shine officially retired from Prairie View A & M on August 10, 1998, he remains a vital part of that university, teaching and directing on a part-time basis.

MAJOR WORKS AND THEMES

For many African American viewers, or readers, Ted Shine's themes mirror their own life themes or those of some other individual whom they may know. Encounters with racism, struggles for recognition and empowerment, and the frustrated pursuit of economic success are quickly recognized. Shine's characters are simply trying to "make it" the best way they can. Often, however, their methods border on the bizarre, and sometimes approach the macabre. Jilting lovers, psychotic preachers, wayward busboys, cunning caregivers, and murderous old women, are some of the types of characters one finds in Shine's work. Although critics and scholars are usually quick to point out that Shine's plays are comical, one should remember that the comedy is not always light and laughable. Instead, it may be heavy and incongruous with the popular definition of comedy.

Epitaph for a Bluebird (1958) has been labeled a comedy-farce and depicts a young woman mourning the death of her father. She falls in love with a soldier who abandons her after she becomes pregnant. Not much to laugh about there! And there is even less to laugh about in *Morning, Noon, and Night* (1964), although it has been described as a comedy, with elements of tragedy and humor.

Morning, Noon, and Night, one of Shine's more memorable plays having a religious theme, centers on Gussie Black, an evil grandmother with a prosthetic leg. She has plans to make her grandson into a preacher who can make money for her. Gussie's plans, however, do not include the boy's aunt Ida Ray. She is in the way, so Gussie kills her by poisoning her food. Hence, *Morning, Noon, and Night* is a critique of black religion, or more precisely, a critique of how one black family relies on preaching and religion for their livelihood.

Shoes (1969) is a lesson in values and aims to expose the immorality of drugs, alcohol, and theft. The play further attempts to discourage murder. Among the characters are three teenage boys—Travis, Ronald, and Marshall—who are employed by a Dallas country club. An older man, Mr. Wisely, has helped one of the boys, Ronald (called Smokey), save his earnings. When Mr. Wisely and Smokey disagree on how the money should be spent, the teenager pulls a gun on the older man, demands his money and leaves. While there are comical moments in the play, their presence is minimal. Nor are these moments of comedy likely to cause outbursts of laughter.

For example, when Smokey and his friends discuss using their money to purchase items like a Pierre Cardin shirt and a $90 Barracuda raincoat, the audience may chuckle, but in a sad kind of way. Spending money on these kinds of pricey items seems foolish and suggests misplaced values on the boys' part.

Charlene, an African American housekeeper is among the characters in *Idabel's Fortune* (1969). She is also the caregiver for Idabel, the white woman named in the title. Idabel is old, dying, and confined to her wheelchair. She has promised her wealth (her fortune) to Charlene in exchange for lifelong care. As Idabel is nearing her death, Charlene notifies Idabel's two surviving relatives, a niece and her husband. The relatives arrive thinking that they will inherit Idabel's fortune but are disappointed by the news that there is nothing for them. Then, Charlene boards the evening train and leaves—with Idabel's fortune. For some viewers, Charlene's actions may suggest deception, while for others, wit and cunning. Although different audiences may not view Charlene in the same way, most would agree that in this play a conflict exists between the black family and the white one even though the conflict at first is quite subtle. It is also clear that here Shine is flirting with an old African American survival technique: trickery and artful manipulation. Charlene has tricked the whites by making them wrongly assume that she is loyal to them.

Flora's Children (1969) is about a black woman who, with her four children, must survive on welfare checks. *Hamburgers at Hamburger Heaven Are Impersonal* (1969) concerns a schoolteacher who becomes romantically involved with a maniac in Dallas. Clearly, there is not much to laugh about in either of these two cases.

Of Shine's many plays *Contribution* (1967) is the most popular and the one most often performed. The play takes as its focus an old black southern woman and her grandson, a college student whose "contribution" to the civil rights movement does not come close to matching his grandmother's. Although Mrs. Grace Love may not participate in demonstrations and sit-ins, she makes her contribution by poisoning the actual food of the whites who have caused trouble. Explaining the murder of Sheriff Morrison, Grace says:

I gave peace [to him]. Sent him to meet his maker! Sent him in grand style too. Tore his very guts out with my special seasoning! Degrading me! Callin' me "nigger!" Beating my men folks! . . . I'm a tired old Black woman who's been tired, and who ain't got no place in this country. You talk about a "New Negro"—Hell, I was a New Negro seventy-six years ago. (21)

Plantation (1970), based on the real life of a staunch segregationist from Louisiana, has been described as a difficult play to perform because the actors do not always know how to portray the characters. In *Plantation*, the white protagonist comes home to discover that his wife has given birth to a black son. Shine describes the play as a farce concerned with "the absurdity of racism and bigotry" (LeBlanc 41). He also states that for him one of the best productions of *Plantation* occurred at the Karamu House. The play was performed by an all-black cast with the white characters done in whiteface.

Comeback after the Fire (1969) centers on Sally Starr, an evangelist who is trying to "come back" after falling from grace because of a tent fire during a revival. Many of her former congregants hold her responsible for the damages they suffered. The community wants nothing to do with her. Hence, Sally's plans for a comeback do not come to fruition.

Another one of Shine's important plays is *The Night of Baker's End* (1974), in which the spotlight is on a male character. In most of Shine's other plays, females are at the center. In *The Night of Baker's End*, Reverend Baker, a grandfather, is obsessed with making and selling "Blessed Oil." This play is a drama, although, as in many of Shine's other plays, there is a tinge of humor. The audience may laugh when, for example, they see just how obsessed Rev. Baker is with his Blessed Oil and its presumed magical powers.

Herbert III, first performed in 1975, has been widely received in foreign countries. It has been produced in several cities in England, including London. And, it has been translated into Yugoslavian (LeBlanc 40). A mother's anguish of not knowing the whereabouts of her son makes the message of the play universal.

The thematic refrain of Shine's plays is African Americans (often in the South) toiling and eking out an existence, frequently by less than admirable means. Whatever humor there is tends to exist purely for comic relief. For racism, phony preachers, invalids dumped out of wheelchairs (*Idabel's Fortune*) and murder are never laughable. Never. However, there is something eerily funny about a grandmother who at one moment sweetly sings church songs but who at the next boasts of poisoning her White enemies and "leaving their bodies for maggots" (*Morning, Noon, and Night* 8).

CRITICAL RECEPTION

Although Ted Shine's plays remain popular with university and regional companies, especially in the South, his plays have not really caught on like those of, say, August Wilson.* Even Shine's best-known play, *Contribution* (1967), has not yet been included in standard textbooks for schools, colleges, and universities. One or two of his plays have been included in a few specialized anthologies for courses in African American literature or drama. But even those anthologies are around thirty years old or more.

In 1970, William Brasmer and Dominick Consolo included *Contribution* in *Black Drama: An Anthology*. It also appears in *Black Theater U.S.A.: Forty-Five Plays by African Americans: The Early Period*, an anthology that Shine coedited with James V. Hatch. *Black Theater U.S.A.* originally appeared in

1974 but was revised and expanded to two volumes in 1996. *Contribution* appears in Volume 2 of the expanded anthology; *Herbert III* appears in the 1974 version.

Critical and scholarly treatments of Shine and his plays are sparse. Again, whatever treatments there are are the products of decades past. In 1980, Shine's Howard University mentor, Dodson, wrote "Who Has Seen the Wind? Part III." His article, totally positive, appeared in *Black American Literature Forum*. *Sho Is Hot in the Cotton Patch* (1950), *Contribution* (1967), *Shoes* (1969), *Idabel's Fortune* (1969), and *Morning, Noon, and Night* (1964) are among the works discussed. In these and in other Shine plays, Dodson says that "we feel the brooding evil/squat of society and racial tension over his characters" (57).

Dodson sees *Sho Is Hot in the Cotton Patch* as an overall theme for all of Shine's plays. The action takes place in a YWCA kitchen in the South. There is no cotton patch. But there are black workers—laboring under the solitary white worker, a dietician whose name is Miss Shelton. She and the other workers are intimidated and controlled by Carrie, the cook, who has invented a "Mis' Weaver," and threatens them by calling Mis' Weaver's name when the workers fall out of line. Carrie is killed when she accidentally falls on her own knife. Her body is dragged offstage to an enormous meat grinder. Dodson suggests that seeing the evil Carrie carried off to the grinder is, for some, funny. Yes, audiences may delight in seeing the evil one receive her comeuppance. But it must be remembered that Shine's objective is not necessarily to create laughter. He is instead concerned with exposing the wretched working conditions of a group of black southerners who still must labor under the eyes of drivers and overseers, though they appear as dressed-up, modern, citified characters.

One of the most thorough treatments of Shine was done in 1985 by Winona L. Fletcher. In her article, appearing in *Afro-American Writers after 1955*, she mentions *Entourage Royal* (1958) and notes that it was Shine's first attempt at writing a musical. Whether it was completed Fletcher does not say. She says only that the work is structured around a family of gypsies who invade a southern community. Their intention is to take all of the community's possessions. But that does not occur because the gypsies are overtaken by the love they find in the community. Fletcher does say, however, that Shine did complete two musicals. He wrote and produced *Good News* in 1956 for troop entertainment in Germany, and *Jeanne West*, which was written in 1968.

Brief treatments of Shine appear in *The Encyclopedia of African American Culture and History* (1996) and in the *The Oxford Companion to African American Literature* (1998). In a Web site, Della Dameron-Johnson discusses *Comeback after the Fire* (1969). These three sources seem to be the only ones in the last ten years to offer even a peek at Shine and his huge body of work.

When *Contributions* (*Contribution*, *Plantation*, and *Shoes*) opened in New York, the reviews in the *New York Times* were mixed. Walter Kerr, for example, praised Shine for his "low-key sauciness" and his "uncanny knack for being warm-hearted and blood-curdling at once" (qtd. in LeBlanc 33). The comments of another *Times* critic, Clive Barnes, were a bit more stinging:

Ted Shine is a new black playwright with a great eye for a funny situation. His actual writing as yet is not nearly so smooth as his sense of the ridiculous is acute. . . . He is an interesting newcomer who writes from the heart with a brash and bitter humor. (qtd. in LeBlanc 39)

In conclusion, it is fair to say that Shine has been overlooked by the scholarly community. Although he has written more than thirty plays, partnered with Hatch to produce what remains an important anthology of African American plays, and had plays performed in New York, Shine and his works have not been the subject of very many scholarly studies. This neglect is unfortunate, as this important playwright was a pioneer in the black arts movement of the 1960s. Similar to one of his best-known characters who did her part to bring about change—though bizarre her actions may have been—Shine, in his own way, helped bring about change in black theater. Let us be reminded that—like Mrs. Grace Love, who went about her work silently, quietly—Ted Shine too has quietly, but surely and profoundly, gone about his work. He too, let us all remember, has certainly made his "contribution."

BIBLIOGRAPHY

Dramatic Works by Ted Shine

Ancestors. 1986. Unpublished.
Baby Cakes. 1981. Unpublished.
Bat's Out of Hell. 1955. Unpublished.
The Coca-Cola Boys. 1969. Unpublished.
Cold Day in August. 1950. Unpublished.
Comeback after the Fire. 1969. Unpublished.
"Contribution." 1967.
Contributions: Three Short Plays. New York: Dramatists Play Service, 1972.
Death Row (work in progress).
Deep Ellum Blues (ballet). 1986. Unpublished.
Dry August. 1951. Unpublished.
Entourage Royal (musical). 1958. Unpublished.
Epitaph for a Bluebird. 1958. Unpublished.
Flora's Children. 1969. Unpublished.

Going Beserk. *Encore* 27 (1984): 32–44.

Good News. 1956. Unpublished.

Good Old Soul. 1983. Nashville: Tennessee State University Press, 1984.

Hamburgers at Hamburger Heaven Are Impersonal. 1969. Unpublished.

Idabel's Fortune. 1969. Unpublished.

Jeanne West (musical). 1968. Unpublished.

Miss Victoria. 1965. Unpublished.

Morning, Noon, and Night. 1964. *The Black Teacher and the Dramatic Arts*. Ed. William Reardon and Thomas D. Pawley. New York: Negro Universities, 1970.

The Night of Baker's End. 1974. Unpublished.

Old Grass. 1983. Unpublished.

"Plantation." Contributions: Three Short Plays. New York: Dramatists Play Service, 1972.

Pontiac. 1967. Unpublished.

A Rat's Revolt. 1959. Unpublished.

Revolution. 1968. Unpublished.

"Shoes." 1969. *Contributions: Three Short Plays*. New York: Dramatists Play Service, 1972.

Sho Is Hot in the Cotton Patch. 1951. *Encore* 9 (1966): 18–24. Later produced as *Miss Weaver* at St. Mark's Playhouse, New York, 1968.

The Woman Who Was Tampered with in Youth. 1980. Berkeley: Sea Urchin, 1980.

Studies of Ted Shine's Dramatic Works

Carter, Steven R. "Ted Shine." *The Oxford Companion of African American Literature*. Ed. William Andrews, Frances Smith Foster, and Trudier Harris. New York: Oxford University Press, 1997. 658–659.

Dameron-Johnson, Della. *The Role of the Black Female Preacher as Religious Leader in Black Drama*. 11 Dec. 1999. 3 June 2003 <http://www.umes.edu/breakerbar/djohnson.html>.

Dodson, Owen. "Who Has Seen the Wind?: Part III." *Black American Literature Forum* 14.2 (1980): 54–59.

Fletcher, Winona. "Ted Shine." *Dictionary of Literary Biography*. Ed. Thadious M. Davis and Trudier Harris. Vol. 38. Detroit: Gale, 1985. 250–259.

LeBlanc, Whitney. "An Interview with Ted Shine." *Studies in American Drama, 1946–Present* 8.1 (1993): 29–43.

Schilling, Peter. "Ted Shine." *Encyclopedia of American Culture and History*. Ed. Jack Salzman, David Lionel Smith, and Cornel West. Vol. 5. New York: Simon, 1996. 2428–2429.

ANNA DEAVERE SMITH
(1950–)

Kimberly Rae Connor

BIOGRAPHY

Anna Deavere Smith was born on September 18, 1950, in Baltimore, Maryland, the eldest of five children in a family that was solidly middle class. Although a mimic as a child, she pursued theater because she was "interested in social change," and unwittingly ended up in acting class where she was "stunned at how the process of acting was about transformation." Part of her exploratory personality she attributes to growing up during the "experiment" of integration. Being a product of integration, she learned that the world can be an indifferent place and that even in the communities of the academy and the theater where she is most at home, "the dominant culture decides when we will be hidden and when we will be seen" (Lewis 62).

As a playwright and performer, Smith has, over the past two decades, created a body of theatrical work that she calls *On the Road: Search for American Character*. Smith creates the pieces by interviewing people in select locales and later performing them using their own words. As she describes it, her goal "has been to find American character in the ways that people speak" *Fires* xxiii).

Smith attended Beaver College and earned an M.F.A. from the American Conservatory Theatre but developed the method that would lead to *On the Road* as exercises to teach students. First produced as a play in New York at Cleare Space in 1982, *On the Road* was developed after college when Smith made her way to New York. It was there, while supporting herself with sporadic appearances on soap operas, that Smith began conducting acting workshops and developing her method. She began approaching people she encountered who resembled participants in her workshop, hoping they would agree to be interviewed so her students could use their words. In exchange, the interviewees were invited to see themselves performed.

Smith persisted in employing the interviewing technique, but rather than asking a troupe of players to create each character, she began to assemble one-woman shows in which she would play all the parts herself. From these simple exercises, her ambition evolved into an enterprise wherein she seeks to "capture the personality of a place by attempting to embody its varied population and varied points of view in one person—myself" (C. Martin 48).

A devout student of Shakespeare, Smith's fascination with his plays led to her understanding how the spoken word works in relationship to a person's psychology and the psyche of the times. The goal of *On the Road*, therefore, is to create a kind of theater "that would have a different relationship to the community than most of the theatre I was seeing. It would be a kind of theatre that could be current . . . capture a moment and as quickly as possible give that moment back to the people" (Kaufman G11).

Fires in the Mirror: Crown Heights, Brooklyn, and Other Identities was Smith's first large-scale attempt to give a moment back to the people and extend *On the Road* to address a specific event. Preceding this were several other plays Smith staged, including *Aye, Aye, Aye, I'm Integrated* (1984), *On Black Identity and Black Theatre* (1990), and *From the Inside Looking In* (1990). First performed at the Joseph Papp Public Theatre in New York, *Fires in the Mirror* explores the 1991 clash between Jews and blacks in that New York community. A runner up for the 1993 Pulitzer Prize, the play earned her Obie, Drama League, and Drama Desk awards. It was broadcast on PBS as part of *The American Playhouse* series.

Twilight: Los Angeles, 1992, examined the civil unrest following the Rodney King verdict. First produced at the Mark Taper Forum in Los Angeles, Smith received two Tony nominations as well as Obie, Drama Desk, and Outer Critics Circle awards and two NAACP Theatre Awards. A film adaptation of *Twilight* premiered at the 2000 Sundance Film Festival and was broadcast on PBS in 2001 as a presentation on the series *Stage on Screen*. In 1997, she also edited with Elaine H. Kim and Dui-Young Yu a volume titled *East to America: Korean American Life Stories*, inspired in part by her experiences with Korean Americans in Los Angeles whom she interviewed for *Twilight*.

Smith's most recent play, *House Arrest: A Search for American Character in and around the White House, Past and Present*, explored the mythic role that the presidency has played throughout American history. The play was first produced, with Ms. Smith and a cast, at the Arena Stage in Washington, DC, in 1997. As part of her preparation for writing the play, Smith spent time in Washington, DC, and, on the 1996 campaign trail, talking with a wide range of political players, historians, and journalists. In 2001, Smith published *Talk to Me: Listening Between the Lines*, based on her observations and impressions of her time in Washington, DC, and on the road.

Funded by the Ford Foundation (where Smith served in 1997 as its first artist in residence), Smith founded and directed the Institute on the Arts and Civic Dialogue, held during the summers of 1998–2000 at Harvard University, where in 2000 she debuted the play *Piano*. In 2002, Smith used her interviewing technique to help assemble, with editor Annie Thoms, a theatrical response by the students at Stuyvesant High School to the attacks of September 11 *With Their Eyes: September Eleventh—The View from a High School at Ground Zero*.

In film, Smith has played roles in *Dave*, *Philadelphia*, and *The American President*. She also appears on the television programs *The West Wing*, *The Practice*, and *Presidio Med*. In addition to her theatrical awards, in 1996, Smith was awarded the prestigious MacArthur Foundation "Genius" Fellowship. Smith is currently a professor at the Tisch School of the Arts at New York University.

MAJOR WORKS AND THEMES

Anna Deavere Smith identifies her early goal for the *On the Road* series as having a traveling troupe of actors based on the model of the Free Southern Theatre. She also cites as influences Ntozake Shange,* Allen Ginsberg, and George Wolfe, while also pointing to a Johnny Carson interview as critical to the development of her approach to character. Others have connected her work to Brechtian theater, Cubist visual art, West African rituals, Faith Ringgold's story-quilts, talk shows, and oral histories such as Studs Terkel's. Smith's choice of *On the Road* as the title for her enterprise elaborates and extends two familiar endeavors associated with the same title—the novel by Jack Kerouac and the television program created by Charles Kerault. But she goes beyond the exploratory hedonism of Kerouac, the nostalgia of Kerault, and the reportage of Terkel to investigate in her theater fundamental issues of identity that underlie all these investigations.

Smith also aligns with several African American aesthetic traditions. Like a folk artist, she creates out of what is available, using "found objects" like dialogue culled from interviews or basic elements of wardrobe. She takes the lives that society would throw away or ignore and through creative arrangement invests them with value. Like a quilt maker, she creates a verbal patchwork of pieces that she sews together with her own constant bodily presence. But despite the temptation to surrender the everyday use of these quilts to become museum pieces, her plays retain their intended function, becoming a cover that envelops in intimate conversation characters and audience members who most likely would never share the same room together. And like a jazz musician, Smith adopts an improvisational style as each performance of *On the Road* and each subject matter she tackles improvises on the theme of identity and difference. She adds or subtracts characters to suit the needs of particular audiences or her own evolving ideas so that each performance is unique and cannot be fully duplicated. Like jazz compositions, her performances are, by definition, always works in progress.

While developing her theater, Smith encountered Constantin Stanislavsky, the founder of the method-acting technique and applied some of his theories. But she objected to aspects of Stanislavsky's technique in which objectives—little and super—are graphed with straight lines and arrows. Smith came to appreciate that method acting locks identity into place instead of letting it breathe and transform. Method acting and psychological realism require actors to look inside themselves and build a character through their experiences. To Smith, this kind of exercise is narcissistic and prevents her from creating a theatrical form that is socially engaged.

In resisting the linear through-line, she refined her method and began to see her thought processes as more organic and circular. Remembering her grandfather's words, "that if you say a word often enough it becomes you," Smith believes her power as an artist comes from not just what people tell her but how they tell her something that makes a whole-soul impression on her psyche, an experience she describes as becoming "possessed, so to speak, of the person" (qtd. in C. Martin 51).

How this transference might be accomplished Smith explains by speech-act theory: "Theatre is action, but in the beginning was the word. And the word was all. And speech is action. Theatre is action. . . . The way action happens in the theatre is through the propulsion of words. The text is spoken to push action forward" (qtd. in Lewis 58). Smith appreciates a concept central to speech-act theory—that words do things and actions say things. Furthermore, she observes that the power of the speech of people backed up by crowds can frighten people, as they did in Crown Heights and Los Angeles. People with the power of the word know that their words cause action and so theater is speech as action, but in a context where individuals have agreed to participate in a communal language.

In both *Fires in the Mirror: Crown Hieghts, Brooklyn, and Other Identities* and *Twilight: Los Angeles, 1992*, Smith tried to display authentically the apparent ethnicity of people as a way to underscore the basic humanity of people in all their difference. Smith's efforts in both these endeavors are directed not just at observation but also at solution, to get people where she finds herself: engaged. Smith is trying to present a standard of truth that is not actual in a metaphysical sense, but representational in a contextual sense. By drawing our attention to different perspectives on truth, she also shows us what is possible in terms of social justice and action. By facilitating a radical empathy, she enables the viewer a transformative slippage across socially produced identities of race, nation, gender, and class. Or as she expresses her intent in the introduction to *Fires in the Mirror*: "The spirit of acting is the travel from self to the other" (xxxvi).

The musings of A. M. Bernstein—an MIT physicist whom Smith interviewed and portrays in *Fires in the Mirror*—are especially pertinent. Imagining the idea of a mirror large enough to reflect accurately the true nature of the universe, he describes how if you want to focus on the stars without getting caught in a circle of confusion, you need a telescope big enough to gather in a lot of light. Gathering enough light to see through a dark scene becomes the metaphor for Smith's enterprise in this piece. To underscore the relevance of these metaphors of reflection, the set for *Fires in the Mirror* was highlighted with mirror fragments in which the audience was reflected. Large screens were also used to project the characters' names, and halfway through the piece, a montage of photographs taken during the riots was shown. These technical adaptations are part of Smith's entire theatrical enterprise that is aimed at casting as much light as possible.

Fires in the Mirror concerns the racial conflict that erupted in the Brooklyn neighborhood of Crown Heights in August 1991. Smith interviewed six hundred people in just eight days—two months after the violence abated—and from the gathered recollections, she crafted her performance. Blacks and Jews had clashed following a car accident in which a Jewish van driver—steering one of the cars in a procession carrying the Lubavitcher Hasidic *rebbe* believed by his followers to be the Messiah—ran a red light, hit another car, and swerved onto the sidewalk. The car struck and killed a young black child, Gavin Cato, and seriously injured his cousin. Further aggravating the situation in the minds of the black residents were rumors that the children had been left lying on the sidewalk while a private Jewish ambulance helped the driver and his passengers.

That evening, a group of young black men fatally stabbed Yankel Rosenbaum, a twenty-nine-year-old Hasidic scholar from Australia. The three-day riots that followed were a culmination of years of resentment between the Orthodox Jewish sect and Crown Heights's black majority. Blacks cited white racism as playing a critical role in the conflict. Many believed that the Lubavitchers had received preferential treatment in the community from police and other city agencies and they reported that some Lubavitchers threatened and harassed them. According to Jews, black anti-Semitism also played a role, as they cited reports that they were frequent victims of black street crime and verbal abuse such as "Heil Hitler" and "Kill the Jews."

The conflict also reflected the pain, oppression, and discrimination these groups have historically experienced outside their own communities. Many in the Crown Heights black community were Caribbean immigrants who faced discrimination owing to their color and their national origin. And the Lubavitchers—members of a 250-year-old messianic Hasidic sect that fled the Nazi genocide in Europe—were particularly vulnerable to anti-Jewish stereotyping because of their religious style of dress and insular community. The resulting trials—in which no one directly involved was convicted of a crime—and the media coverage that polarized the people involved made it difficult, as Anna Deavere Smith writes, "for people to develop an understanding of the Crown Heights situation that acknowledges the experiences of all people involved" (*Fires* xiv).

In accordance with her notion of adapting concepts of American character, Smith structures her text in such a way that issues related to character and identity formation are investigated in a circular fashion, from the general to the particular. The first two sections, "Identity" and "Mirrors," offer broad and speculative reflections on not just identity but how one sees or discerns the reality in which identities are constructed. From there, Smith locates specific issues of "Hair," "Race," "Rhythm," and "Seven Verses" (a biblical allusion) to structure the dialogue pertaining to how the African Americans and Jews of the community come to describe and define themselves and each other. The drama concludes with the unambiguous "Crown Heights, Brooklyn, August 1991" section that offers different perspectives on the actual events and their meanings.

As the drama moves from general reflection to the specific issues that led to the incident documented, the audience confronts more difficult discussions of specific racist attitudes and the "reification of those ideas" (Laris 119). It is only the continuity of Smith's presence that undercuts the authority of one group over another or of one individual over another. Functioning like a diviner through whom many voices travel, all the characters speak together while their presence and words, as Carol Martin observes, "mark the absence and silence of the two people around whom the drama revolves, Gavin Cato and Yankel Rosenbaum" (46).

The role language plays in both advancing and obstructing conflict resolution is also articulated by Robert Sherman, a city bureaucrat who was not at all surprised by the episode in Crown Heights. His observations of the community reveal not a simple cultural conflict or black/Jewish dichotomy but what he calls a "soup of bias—prejudice, racism, and discrimination" (64). This murky soup is the result, he claims, of "lousy language," that does not clearly identify the complexity of the social problems American society faces.

It is this "lousy language" that Smith attempts to rehabilitate while also not denying its presence and effect. Carmel Cato, the father of the child who was killed and the final character portrayed by Smith, most overwhelms one with his ability to use language as a way to focus in on the locus of identity. By ending his comments with a description of the circumstances of his birth—being born feet first, which he believes makes him a "special person" who cannot be overpowered—Cato's speech is structured "in the way classical drama is structured. It crosses different worlds, different feelings, and articulates his view of his existence in a really short span of time" (Lewis 64). There is also an African element to this structure that by ending with reflections on birth affirms the myth of eternal return where the cycle of life renews itself, suggesting that even out of the ashes of Crown Heights, a new mode of existence could rise.

Sonny Carson, who recognizes "tonight by nighttime it could all change for me," alludes that a new existence might rise. "I'm always aware of that, and that's what keeps me going today and each day" (105). Carson's comment anticipates the new perspective offered by *Twilight: Los Angeles, 1992*, another title ripe with metaphoric possibilities. Twilight is the chosen name of one of Smith's characters, Twilight Bey, who hoped to organize a truce between the gangs of Los Angeles and whose poetic interpretation of his name gave Smith the idea for her title. The concept of twilight is both the introduction to and the coda for the limbo Smith explores in this drama, while the character Twilight Bey himself functions like a surrogate for Smith's voice—one who speaks or communicates across seemingly insurmountable lines of hierarchy and difference. The metaphoric potential of twilight paradoxically recalls a time of danger and obscured vision, but also one of liminality and creativity. In *Twilight*, the bright light of fires reflected in a mirror becomes the dim light of a day ending, revealing new truths about identity but also new ambiguities.

Like *Fires in the Mirror*, *Twilight* brings the political into the realm of the personal. The effect of the individual personality—along with her ethnic history and economic status—is given an importance that neither media nor history books customarily elaborate. Also like *Fires in the Mirror*, *Twilight* concerns a recent social uprising that generated national attention. In 1992, Los Angeles came to experience some of the worst violence in U.S. history as the result of a protracted sequence of perceived injustices. In the spring of 1991, Rodney King, a black man, was severely beaten by four Los Angeles police officers after a high-speed chase in which King was pursued for speeding. A nearby resident videotaped the beating from his balcony, and when the tape was broadcast on national television, there was an immediate outcry from the community. The next year, when the police officers who beat King were tried and found not guilty, the city exploded with fury over the surprising verdict. Three days of burning, looting, and killing followed the announcement.

The role "lousy language" plays in social discourse becomes apparent again in how these events are perceived and described. "Riot," "uprising," and "rebellion," have all been used to denote the events of April 1992. But as Smith points out in her introduction to the drama, "beneath this surface explanation is a sea of associated causes" (xviii). A declining economy, a growing hostility between the police and people of color, and the increased development of marginalized ethnic communities all contributed to the pre-existing tension. These factors and others reveal that the story of race in America is much larger and more complex than a story of black and white, involving not just a variety of ethnic divisions, but divisions within ethnic groups themselves.

Twilight presented a multidimensioned challenge to Smith and her entire theatrical enterprise. The dispersed geography, the layered economic classes, and the multiple ethnic associations complicated her search for identity and put at risk her notions of how theater could function to clarify social problems. Furthermore, the proximity of Hollywood—whose major industry is enchantment—presented an ironic context for a play that so clearly is intended to make people uncomfortable. In preparing *Twilight*, Smith became more aware of "how little there is in culture or education that encourages the development of a unifying voice" (xxv).

The absence of a unified voice is illustrated in the set Smith designed—a haphazard clutter of chairs and tables in front of a large undecorated gray-wall backdrop. At the center of the wall was a recess that became, variously, a television split screen, a hodgepodge of graffiti, or an office window. Like *Fires in the Mirror*, Smith structured the testimony of *Twilight* in sections, giving each a thematic title, usually drawn from the conversation of one of her characters but also evocative of more universal circumstances. "The Territory" offers general assessments of the conditions that led to the uprising. "Here's a Nobody" traces different reactions to the beating of Rodney King and the resulting trial of the police officers involved. "War Zone" gives graphic renditions of the uprising itself, while "Twilight" and "Justice" deal with the aftermath and attempts to rebuild the community actually and psychologically.

The play concludes by circling back to the same issues raised in the prologue by the sculptor Rudy Salas when he traces a familial history of minority victimization. From his grandfather who died resisting "gringos" in Mexico to his own son, a Stanford student who was harassed by the police for no apparent offense, Salas shows by his own family's experience that oppression and resisting it have become a kind of tradition in American life. He also enunciates the fear felt by both people of color and whites about the other and how this fear descends into hate on the part of both the oppressor and the oppressed. Despite his own uncle's reminder that "to hate is to waste energy and you mess with the man upstairs" (3), hate remains because fear has not been eliminated, only disguised by "masks" people put on in order to resist any interaction with the other.

In his stunning final speech, Twilight Bey discourses about his name, probing both language and life and embodying the aspect of twilight when its harder to see, but when more creativity is allowed because you have to participate more. He chose his name because it reflected his temporal habits and to signify his position in the community as one who possessed "two times the wisdom" or twice the light of wisdom. His assessment of the events in Los Angeles resonates with others' as he perceives society stuck in limbo. But he is aware that "to be a true human being I can't forever dwell in darkness, I can't forever dwell in the idea of just identifying with people like me and understanding me and mine" (255).

House Arrest premiered not with Smith playing all the roles as she did before but with a group of twelve actors of different genders and races playing across lines of race, age, and gender to become Bill Clinton, Thomas Jefferson, Sally Hemings, celebrities, journalists, prison inmates, and academicians, among a vast array of historical and contemporary figures. It is an epic view of the presidency through the legacies of slavery and sexual misconduct with profound implications for our understandings of the operations of power. The play is an ambitious attempt to renarrate U.S. history and interrogate presidential power and the role of the press. The play unfolds in multiple registers, juxtaposing historical material, interview excerpts, music, dance, and video.

Thematically, *House Arrest*'s point of view is revisionist history, highlighting the legacy of slavery and the complex intertwining of race, sexuality, and power that have been part of American democracy since the founding of the Republic. We see Thomas Jefferson engaged in sexual intercourse with Sally Hemings in ways that recall the Clinton–Lewinsky story. One production also featured a fashion show of Jefferson and Hemings, O. J. Simpson and Nicole Brown, among other couples, in a theatrical lampooning of presidential privilege and interracial liaisons. Also present was a restaging of the Lincoln–Douglas debates as a kind of circus with actors walking among the audience in the proceedings with applause and laughter signs to signal the audience how to respond.

House Arrest was a significant development in Smith's work because she chose in this play to extend the earlier work in several ways. She makes use of several sources of textual material (historical documents, a conventional fictive play that framed the action in the Arena Stage version, first-person narrative/direct audience address, and the interview-based text she used before). Video and television also were central characters, echoing the play's themes of media surveillance and saturation. For example, actors reenacted the Lincoln assassination as the Magruder tapes of the Kennedy assassination were screened on the other side of the stage. An omnipresent prison guard sat off to one side during much of the action, watching commercials and sitcoms. Dance was also featured prominently in *House Arrest*, setting it apart from *Fires in the Mirror* and *Twilight*. Choreographed pieces framed several scenes. Finally, the scope of the play extended far beyond the analysis of a single contemporary urban crisis to encompass centuries of U.S. history presented in nonlinear juxtaposition.

CRITICAL RECEPTION

Overall assessments of Anna Deavere Smith's method are enthusiastic. *Newsweek* hailed Smith as "the most exciting thing in American theatre" (Knoll 62), and the *New York Times* has called her "the ultimate impressionist: she does other people's souls" (qtd. in "Anna" par. 4). Richard Hornby has observed how her work has also reinvigorated the concept of a "regional" theater further empowering those traditionally distanced from mass influence. John Lahr asserts of Smith's work "in this heroic undertaking, she is conducting one of the most sophisticated dialogues about race in contemporary America" (90). He continues: "In making the audience hear the characters, Smith is also showing it how to listen to the strangers in its midst. She creates a climate of intimacy by acknowledging the equality of the other" (93).

Fires in the Mirror and *Twilight* have evoked near unanimous praise. Carol Martin describes Smith's performative language as "conjuring" and her method as that of a "spirit doctor" who "brings ancestors or other spirits in contact with the living—in the presence of the community of the audience" (45–46). Richard Schechner writes of how Smith's way of working is less like that of a "conventional, Euro-American actor," but more like an African, Native American, or Asian "ritualist" or "shaman" (63). He goes on to explain that he observes Smith working "by means of a deep mimesis, a process opposite to that of 'pretend.' To incorporate means to be possessed by, to open oneself up thoroughly and deeply to another being" (64). As Schechner describes her method, Smith composes her performances much as a ritual shaman might investigate and heal a diseased patient. By closely consulting with the "patients"—opening to their intimacy and listening and looking closely at those whom she interviews—Smith goes beyond the process of interviewing to create a more spiritual encounter. She shows respect and looks and listens with empathy, a sensibility Schechner describes as "going beyond sympathy . . . the ability to allow the other in, to feel what the other is feeling" (64).

The philosopher and theologian Cornel West, in his introduction to *Fires in the Mirror*, reaffirms the role imaginative empathy plays in Smith's dramas when he observes how they "force us to examine critically our own complicity in cultural stereotypes that imprison our imaginations . . ." (xvii). For West, Smith demonstrates how art can constitute an empowering public space because she functions as a citizen who knows that we cannot address problems of ethnic strife "without a vital public sphere and that there can be no vital public sphere without genuine bonds of trust"; and she functions as an artist who knows that "public performance has a unique capacity to bring us together—to take us out of our tribal mentalities—for self-critical examination and artistic pleasure" (xxii). Jennifer Drake observes that in *Twilight*, "Smith's interest in performing the eloquent stutters and missteps that together create American character(s) offers one democratic alternative to the colonialist performance history of ethnographic display" that characterizes other theater works because "*Twilight* attempts full representation even as it critiques the possibility of full representation" (166).

House Arrest was received with much more ambivalence than Smith's earlier works. Although Dorrine Kondo describes the play as a "multicultural symphony and a demystification of power" (81), when the play premiered in Washington, DC, Lloyd Rose claimed it played like a "first draft," that required a different set of expectations on the part of the audience than the first two plays did. While still "good stuff," Rose believed the play needed to be "edited to advantage" to tighten the multiple narrative strands (C1). Still, overall assessments of Smith's success as a dramatist point to her ability to create a dialogue and to offer "an invitation to, as she has said 'negotiate the differences'" (Laris 119).

BIBLIOGRAPHY

Dramatic Works by Anna Deavere Smith

Aye, Aye, Aye, I'm Integrated. Produced American Place Theatre, New York, 1984.
Fires in the Mirror: Crown Heights, Brooklyn, and Other Identities. New York: Anchor, 1993.
From the Inside Looking In. Produced Eureka Theatre, San Francisco, 1990.
House Arrest: A Search for American Character in and around the White House, Past and Present. 1997. New York: Dramatists Play Service, 2003.
On Black Identity and Black Theatre. Produced Crossroads Theatre, New Brunswick, New Jersey, 1990.
On the Road: Search for American Character. Produced Cleare Space, New York, 1982.
Piano. Produced Harvard University, Cambridge, 2000.
Twilight: Los Angeles, 1992. New York: Anchor, 1994.
With Their Eyes: September Eleventh—The View from Ground Zero. Ed. Annie Thoms. New York: Bt Bound, 2002.

Studies of Anna Deavere Smith's Dramatic Works

"Anna Deavere Smith." *American Repertory Theatre Online*. 5 Oct. 1999: 4 pars. 10 Dec. 2002 <http://amrep.org/people/anna.html>.
Bernstein, Robin. "Rodney King, Shifting Modes of Vision and Anna Deavere Smith's *Twilight: Los Angeles, 1992*." *Journal of Dramatic Theory and Criticism* 14.2 (2000): 121–134.
Connor, Kimberly Rae. "Negotiating the Differences: Anna Deavere Smith." *Imagining Grace: Liberating Theologies in the Slave Narrative Tradition*. Urbana: University of Illinois Press, 2000: 194–238.
Davis, Thulani. "Anna Deavere Smith." *BOMB* 41 (1992): 40–43.
Drake, Jennifer. "The Theatre of the New World (B)orders: Performing Cultural Criticism with Coco Fusco, Guillermo Gomez-Pena, and Anna Deavere Smith." *Women of Color: Defining Issues, Hearing the Voices*. Ed. Diane Long Hoeveler. Westport: Greenwood, 2001: 159–173.
Ede, Lisa, and Andrea Abernethy Lunsford. "Crimes of Writing: Refiguring 'Proper' Discursive Practices." *Writing on the Edge* 11.2 (2000): 43–54.

Guinier, Lani, and Anna Deavere Smith. "Rethinking Power, Rethinking Theatre." *Theater* 31.3 (2001): 31–45.

Harris, Hilary. "Failing 'White Woman': Interrogating the Performance of Respectability." *Theatre Journal* 52.2 (2000): 183–209.

Hornby, Richard. "Regional Theatre Comes of Age." *Hudson Review* 46.3 (1993): 529–536.

Kaufman, Joanne. "Anna Deavere Smith: Passion Plays." *Washington Post* 25 Apr. 1993: G1, G11.

Knoll, Jack. "Fire in the City of Angels." *Newsweek* 28 June 1993: 62–63.

Kondo, Dorinne. "(Re)Visions of Race: Contemporary Race Theory and the Cultural Politics of Racial Crossover in Documentary Theatre." *Theatre Journal* 51.1 (2000): 81–107.

Lahr, John. "Under the Skin." *New Yorker* 28 June 1993: 90–93.

Laris, Katie. "*Fires in the Mirror: Crown Heights, Brooklyn, and Other Identities.*" *Theatre Journal* 45 (Mar. 1993): 117–119.

Lewis, Barbara. "The Circle of Confusion: A Conversation with Anna Deavere Smith." *Kenyon Review* 15.4 (1993): 54–64.

Martin, Carol. "Anna Deavere Smith: The Word Becomes You." *Drama Review* 37.4 (1993): 45–62.

Martin, Victoria. "The Personal Voice: Anna Deavere Smith at Mark Taper Forum." *Artweek* 24 (22 July 1993): 5.

Richards, Sandra. "Caught in the Act of Social Definition: *On the Road* with Anna Deavere Smith." *Acting Out: Feminist Performances*. Ed. Lynda Hart and Peggy Phelan. Ann Arbor: UMI, 1993: 35-53.

Rose, Lloyd. "*House Arrest*: Too Early Release." *Washington Post* 7 Nov. 1997: C1.

Schechner, Richard. "Anna Deavere Smith: Acting as Incorporation." *Drama Review* 37.4 (1993): 63–64.

Simon, Dawne E. V. "29 Characters in Search of Community." *Ms* 3 (Sept./Oct. 1992): 67.

Stanyton, Richard. "A Fire in a Crowded Theatre." *American Theatre* 10.7–8 (1993): 20–22, 72–75.

Snead, James. *White Screens: Black Images*. New York: Routledge, 1994.

Thacher, Zachary. "American Rhythms: An Interview with Anna Deavere Smith." *Intermission* 29 (Feb. 1996): 8–9.

Wald, Gayle. "Anna Deavere Smith's Voices at Twilight." *Postmodern Culture* 2 (1994): 1–17.

West, Cornel. Introduction. *Fires in the Mirror: Crown Heights, Brooklyn, and Other Identities*. By Anna Deavere Smith. New York: Anchor Books, 1993. iv–xii.

Witonsky, Trudi. "Twilight Conversations: Multicultural Dialogue." *Asian American Studies: Identity, Images, Issues, Past and Present*. Ed. Esther Mikyung Ghyman. New York: Lang, 2000: 217–229.

EULALIE SPENCE
(1894–1981)

Yvonne Shafer

BIOGRAPHY

Born on the island of Nevis in the British West Indies, Eulalie Spence spent her early years on her father's sugar plantation. Unhappily, it was destroyed in a hurricane and, seeking employment, her father moved the family to the United States. Her father was unable to find regular work and Spence grew up in poverty in Brooklyn, New York. Later, she said that she was actually unaware of the poverty, but keenly aware that West Indians were unwelcome. Modeling herself on her mother, Spence became a strong, independent figure often creating female characters of the same type. Her niece remembered her as, "prim, proper and ultracorrect in her speech and dress, yes—but she was gentle, generous and loving and the backbone of a family of seven girls" (qtd. in Perkins 105).

Although the Spence family was poor, the playwright had the advantage of growing up in a supportive, loving atmosphere. Her mother often read to her and she became interested in writing as a child. She was also fortunate in receiving an unusually fine education for a woman at that time. She attended the New York Training School for Teachers and followed that with courses at the Ethiopian Art Theatre School in 1924. She continued her education both at the College of the City of New York and Columbia University. At Columbia she had the good fortune of studying with Pulitzer Prize winner Hatcher Hughes. All her life she manifested a great desire to learn, and even after she became a teacher, she went on to earn a B.A. in speech from Teacher' College in 1937 and an M.A. in speech from Columbia University in 1939.

Spence had a long and productive teaching career in which she pursued her interest in theater. She taught speech and directed the student dramatic society at Eastern District High School in Brooklyn. She directed the students in plays she wrote and plays by other playwrights. In later life, she remembered with great pleasure the many talented students she taught, including Joseph Papp. Studying with Spence must have contributed to his appreciation of Shakespeare, as well as his unconventional attitudes, particularly in the aspect of interracial casting.

Spence never married, but she found pleasure in the company of her sisters' children. Instead of raising a family, she devoted herself to her own eduction, followed by an active life involved in theater. She wrote fourteen plays and several screenplays and directed plays. From 1926 until the demise of the Krigwa Players, she wrote plays and participated in their play production. Unlike many of the early black playwrights, she was determined that her plays should be produced. In 1928, she wrote an article for *Opportunity* opposing the writing of plays to be read only:

I have seen plays written by our Negro writers with this caption: To be Read, not played!

A play to be read! Why not a the song to be read, not sung, and the canvas to be described, not painted! To every art its form, thank God! And to the play, the technique that belongs to it. (qtd. in Perkins 105)

Although her plays were not commercially produced or in any way part of mainstream American professional theater, Spence directed them as a part of her active participation in community theater. She took a strong interest in other emerging playwrights, directing plays by Eugene O'Neill and others. As one of the founders of the Dunbar Garden Players in the late 1920s, she directed plays at the St. Marks Church on lower Second Avenue in New York. Although not a member of the Harlem Renaissance, she had contacts with contemporary writers such as Zora Neale Hurston* and she corresponded with Alain Locke at Howard University.

At the end of her long life Spence could look back on many full years devoted to teaching and theater. She had directed her sisters Doralyne and Olga in her own plays and she coached Doralyne when she assumed the leading role (previously played by Rose McClendon) in the Broadway production of *In Abraham's Bosom*. Through her many activities she served as a role model to her students and to aspiring playwrights.

MAJOR WORKS AND THEMES

Eulalie Spence was a determined woman and knew very definitely the kind of plays she could write and wanted to write. She worked with

W. E B. Du Bois but declined his insistent advice that she "use her excellent writing skills for propaganda" (Peskins 106). Growing up in Brooklyn, she had no personal experience of the subjects he wanted to press upon her. She stated that "her rationale for avoiding propaganda issues was that she knew nothing about lynchings, rapes, nor the blatant racial injustices in this country" (qtd. in Perkins 106). Although her father had difficulty finding employment, her family was not subjected to the sort of actions present in the plays of Georgia Douglas Johnson* and May Miller,* which are set in the South. Spence concluded that she would write folk dramas that essentially provided fun and entertainment.

At the age of twenty-six, Spence wrote her first play, *Being Forty* (1920). Although never published, it was performed in 1924 by the National Ethiopian Art Players at the Lafayette Theatre. Two years later, *Foreign Mail* not only won the second prize in a *Crisis* contest, but was published in 1927 by the prestigious publishing company Samuel French. In 1926, Spence wrote another play, *The Starter,* which was also published in 1927 and was widely produced by amateur groups throughout the country. The play tied for third prize in an *Opportunity* contest in 1927. This is a simply staged, one-act play set on a park bench in Harlem with two main characters. An enthusiastic and romantic young man has made up his mind to propose to his girlfriend. Quite interestingly, she is more realistic and down to earth than he is, and much more cautious. In a surprise ending, his idealism is undermined by her views about finances and responsibilities in marriage and he decides not to propose. The development of the clear-headed woman's character is an interesting element in the play.

Although far from a grim play, *The Starter* is certainly not merely "fun and entertainment." The next play, *Her* (1927) had even stronger elements of darkness and social commentary. Described as a mystery play in one act, it is a play of the supernatural in which an avaricious white man is punished for his cruelty to his Filipino wife by her reappearance as a ghost. Also present is the realistically developed picture of the disempowerment of women who are foreign or black. The simple story is revealed largely through the characterization of Martha. She has been victimized by both the white landlord, Kinney, and her layabout husband. Although she suffers from back trouble, she earns money for the rent and food by ironing for "very old families" (132). Her description to a pair of potential renters of Kinney's brutal treatment of his wife (which caused her to hang herself) is followed by her description of the appearance of the ghost: "Ah jes seen John Kinney walkin' down the stairs with *Her*! She had him by the hand an' she was laughin'!" (140). The interesting characters and the element of the victimization of women leading to vengeance on the persecutor gives added meaning to a familiar type of ghost story. The play was produced by the Krigwa Players in January and April at the 135th Street Library Theatre in Harlem.

In the same year, 1927, the Krigwa Players produced Spence's *Fool's Errand*. This is a satire on gossiping zealots in a church who suppose that there is a scandal in the offing because they find baby clothes hidden in the home of a young girl and her parents. Maza is the innocent girl, and suffers the reproaches of the "hard, fanatical, relentless" women of the church (124) and her violent father. The play is an effective mixture of comedy and violence that ends in a surprise as it is Maza's mother who is pregnant. The play is enhanced by songs in which the women reveal their outlooks and songs that satirize them for their repressive behavior. After the successful first production, the play was performed as part of the National Little Theatre Tournament in New York City, winning the Samuel French prize of $200. The play was published by French and was presented by many little theater groups.

Spence's play *Undertow* is a very grim Strindbergian play of hate and thwarted love between a man and his wife and a woman who bore his illegitimate child. The wife, Hattie, has turned entirely against her husband because he fell in love with Clem, a light-skinned black woman, when Hattie was pregnant. She says to Clem, "Ah was soft 'nuff, when yuh fust stepped on me. Ef Ah's hard now, 'tis yo' fault" (114). The play is filled with surprisingly frank language for the time; for example, she calls Clem a dirty-minded whore. The title of the play indicates the unavoidable power of past passions that still lie beneath the surface and will suck the three into renewed tragedy.

Hot Stuff is a surprisingly sordid depiction of the squalid lives led by many African Americans in Harlem. With a slight story line, the play is essentially a picture of vivid characters trying to maintain an existence by cheating and conning one another. The central figure is Fanny who lives an amoral, careless life as a numbers runner, a salesperson for stolen clothing, and a prostitute. She has a husband and a lover and is willing to sleep with a Jewish peddler in order to get an ermine coat. Her husband discovers them and beats her but she is so hardened by life that she considers she still got a good bargain for the coat.

A number of Spence's plays were never published or produced. One very odd event is the history of a play she wrote in 1934 called *The Whipping*. Far from "fun or entertainment," it depicts the story of a black southern woman who is whipped by the Ku Klux Klan. The play was not produced, but Spence sold it as a screenplay to Paramount Pictures for $5,000. In the film, renamed *Ready for Love* [!], the African American characters in the South are replaced by Puritans in the North who dunk their victim in a pond. Ironically, Spence claimed this was the only money she ever made from her writing for the theater (Peterson 179). In this and other plays, she seems to have gone into greater depths than she initially intended. Her strong interest in characters who are victimized by circumstances, who suffer rejection, and who are hardened by an indifferent society give a strong texture and interest to all of her plays.

CRITICAL RECEPTION

Elizabeth Brown-Guillory is one of many critics who claim a high place in the history of American women playwrights for Eulalie Spence. She called Spence "a daring and vociferous woman playwright who might one day be credited with initiating feminism in plays by black women" (*Their Place* 4). Writing about *Hot Stuff*, she noted that the play written in the 1920s seems very much related to events of today:

Spence seems to be mirroring a society in which blacks do what they have to do in order to survive and to secure material things. Some of them, like John Cole, place all of their trust in the numbers game, hoping to win enough to make ends meet. Some prostitute their bodies in order to live and to have the finer things in life. What permeates the play is a sense of urban poverty and the con games that are enacted in order to survive in a fast-paced, uncaring world. (*Wines* 40–41)

James Hatch and Ted Shine, discussing *Undertow*, conclude that Spence "may be one of the first to write black characters into a non-racial plot" and that some people might say that the characters are really white, only "painted black," while others would praise her for enlarging the sphere of black experience on the stage (192).

Long forgotten as a playwright, Spence is just beginning to be discussed and her plays are now being anthologized. Given the opportunity, she could have developed into a major playwright. As it is, she was surprisingly successful with her one-act plays. She won the respect of her peers through her own personal conduct and through the talent she displayed. Bernard Peterson describes her as a "pioneer playwright and drama director of the 1920s and 1930s" (178). Brown-Guillory emphasizes the significance of Spence's pioneering efforts in which she was "unwelcome in the commercial theatre of the period" (*Their Place* 4). Speaking of Eulalie Spence and other long-ignored playwrights, she comments, "These authors are crucial to any discussion of the development of black playwriting in America because they provide the feminine perspective, and their voices give credence to the notion that there was a 'New Negro' in America" (4).

BIBLIOGRAPHY

Dramatic Works by Eulalie Spence

Being Forty. Unpublished.
"Episode." *Wines in the Wilderness: Plays by African-American Women from the Harlem Renaissance to the Present*. Ed. Elizabeth Brown-Guillory. Westport: Greenwood, 1990. 51–60.

"Fool's Errand." *Black Female Playwrights: An Anthology of Plays before 1950*. Ed. Kathy A. Perkins. Bloomington: Indiana University Press, 1989. 119–131.

Foreign Mail. New York: French, 1927.

Her. *Black Female Playwrights: An Anthology of Plays before 1950*. Ed. Kathy A. Perkins. Bloomington: Indiana University Press, 1989. 132–140.

"Hot Stuff." *Wines in the Wilderness: Plays by African-American Women from the Harlem Renaissance to the Present*. Ed. Elizabeth Brown-Guillory. Westport: Greenwood, 1990. 43–50.

"The Starter." *Plays of Negro Life*. Ed. Alain Locke and Montgomery Gregory. Rpt. ed. Westport: Greenwood, 1971. 21–26.

"Undertow." *Black Female Playwrights: An Anthology of Plays before 1950*. Ed. Kathy A. Perkins. Bloomington: Indiana University Press, 1989. 107–118.

The Whipping. 1934. Unpublished.

Studies of Eulalie Spence's Dramatic Works

Brown-Guillory, Elizabeth. *Their Place on Stage: Black Women Playwrights in America*. Westport: Greenwood, 1992.

———, ed. *Wines in the Wilderness: Plays by African-American Women from the Harlem Renaissance to the Present*. Westport: Greenwood, 1990.

Hatch, James V., ed., and Ted Shine, consult. *Black Theater, U.S.A.* New York: Macmillan, 1974.

Perkins, Kathy A. *Black Female Playwrights: An Anthology of Plays before 1950*. Bloomington: Indiana University Press, 1989.

Peterson, Bernard L., Jr. *Early Black American Playwrights and Dramatic Writers*. Westport: Greenwood, 1990.

Shafer, Yvonne. "Eulalie Spence." *American Women Playwrights, 1900–1950*. New York: Lang, 1997. 271–283.

WALLACE THURMAN
(1902 – 1934)

Linda M. Carter

BIOGRAPHY

Wallace Henry Thurman, journalist, editor, literary critic, novelist, short story writer, playwright, and poet, was born on August 16, 1902, in Salt Lake City, Utah. The son of Oscar and Beulah Thurman, he was raised by his maternal grandmother, Emma Jackson, and attended public schools in Salt Lake City and studied at the University of Utah as well as the University of Southern California. While in Los Angeles, Thurman wrote a column for the *Pacific Defender*, a local African American newspaper, and worked at a post office where he met Arna Bontemps,* who like Thurman, was beginning his writing career. Thurman published and financed the *Outlet*, a literary magazine, for six months before moving to New York in 1925.

In New York, Thurman held a variety of editorial positions. He was a reporter and editorial writer for Theophilus Lewis's *Looking Glass* prior to his aPointment as managing editor of A. Philip Randolph and Chandler Owen's magazine, the *Messenger*. During his brief tenure at the *Messenger*, Thurman published the works of other young Harlem Renaissance authors such as Bontemps, Langston Hughes,* Zora Neale Hurston,* and Dorothy West, as well as his own writing. His articles were also published in periodicals such as *New Republic*, *Independent*, *Bookman*, and *Dance Magazine*. When Thurman was hired as the *World Tomorrow*'s circulation manager, he was the first African American hired in an editorial position at the magazine. Thurman also worked on McFadden Publications and Macaulay Company's editorial staffs; at Macaulay, he was promoted to editor in chief. As with Thurman's employment at the *World Tomorrow*, he was the first African American to hold such positions at McFadden and Macaulay.

Thurman was a spokesperson for the Harlem Renaissance's younger members. In 1926, he edited *Fire!! A Quarterly Devoted to the Younger Negro Artists*. *Fire!!* was a manifesto of the younger generation as they focused on art rather than propaganda, refused to write exclusively about the African American middle class, and sought literary independence from organizational publications such as the National Association for the Advancement of Colored People's *Crisis* and the Urban League's *Opportunity*. In 1928, Thurman edited *Harlem: A Forum of Negro Life*, a magazine that featured the works of older, established writers as well as younger authors.

In 1929, Thurman's first novel, *The Blacker the Berry: A Novel of Negro Life*, was published; among the issues focused on are intraracial prejudice, self-hatred, and homosexuality. That same year marked the debut of *Harlem: A Melodrama of Negro Life in Harlem*, a play he cowrote with William Jourdan Rapp, a white writer. One year later, Thurman and Rapp wrote a second play, *Jeremiah the Magnificent*. In 1932, Thurman published two more novels: *Infants of the Spring*, a satirical account of the Harlem Renaissance that Mae Gwendolyn Henderson describes as Thurman's "autobiographical novel" (159), and *The Interne*, a work cowritten with the white author Abraham Furman, in which Thurman focuses on the activities of a metropolitan hospital. He wrote two screenplays: *Tomorrow's Children* (1934) and *High School Girl* (1935). Thurman, using pen names such as Ethel Belle Mandrake and Patrick Casey, was a ghostwriter for books and magazines, including *True Story*.

Thurman's personal life was not as successful as his professional life. He frequently experienced melancholy due to health problems and other reasons. His 1928 marriage to Louise Thompson ended after six months. Thurman, diagnosed with tuberculosis, was hospitalized during the final six months of his life. Ironically, he was a patient at City Hospital's Incurable Ward on Manhattan's Welfare Island, the facility that he exposes in *The Interne*. Wallace Thurman died on December 21, 1934, at the age of thirty-two. According to Dorothy West, his death "caused the first break in the ranks of the 'New Negro'" (227) while Henderson asserts that Thurman's "life itself became a symbol of the New Negro movement. Thurman had made his entrance into the Renaissance at the height of the movement. His life, brilliant and turbulent as it had been, ended after the Renaissance came to a close" (170).

MAJOR WORKS AND THEMES

Wallace Thurman and William Jourdan Rapp created *Color Parade*, a dramatic trilogy: *Harlem, Jeremiah the Magnificent*, and *Harlem Cinderella*. *Harlem*, Thurman's most well-known play, opened on Broadway on February 20, 1929, at the Apollo Theatre on 42nd Street. As Bernard Peterson points out, the building is "not to be confused with the Apollo Theatre in Harlem" (184).

On April 29, 1929, *Harlem* was relocated to the Times Square Theatre on 42nd Street. After 93 performances, the show was closed. A road company performed *Harlem* in Los Angeles and Chicago and returned to Broadway's Time Square Theatre on October 21, 1929, for sixteen performances.

Harlem is based on Thurman's short story, "Cordelia the Crude," that was published in *Fire!!* (1926). For the Broadway production, Thurman "provided the story and dialogue, and . . . Rapp shaped the play" (Woll 76). In the three-act melodrama, Pa and Ma Williams as well as their offspring have recently moved from South Carolina to Harlem seeking relief from poverty and racism. However they encounter the grim realities of urban life. The Williams family lives in a five-room apartment; in order to supplement their incomes, the parents rent rooms to boarders and hold Saturday night rent parties. The couple is quickly disillusioned with city life. Pa Williams, realizing that living in Harlem has not met his expectations, states, "Dey ain't nothin' for a nigger nowhere. We's the doomed children of Ham" (qtd. in Abramson 36). Ma Williams is a religious woman and does not condone drinking and dancing although she and her husband, like so many other residents in Harlem during the Renaissance, are forced to hold rent parties out of economic necessity. Ma Williams worries about Harlem's effects on her children. She is most concerned about Cordelia, her older daughter. During her family's rent party, Cordelia leaves with Roy, who operates a gambling house and a numbers racket. They go to his apartment, where later that evening, Roy is murdered by his partner, Kid. Cordelia's former boyfriend, Basil, arrives at the apartment to take her home. Instead, he is framed for Roy's murder. Cordelia returns home and is about to leave with Kid when white gangsters, looking for Kid, arrive. Cordelia leaves her home without Kid and states that she will make the world notice her. *Harlem* ends as Cordelia's distraught mother cries, "Lawd! Lawd! Tell me! Tell me! Dis ain't the City of Refuge?" (qtd. in Abramson 37). Peterson asserts that *Harlem* contains a number of themes prevalent in Harlem Renaissance literature such as "the devastating effect of the Depression on the black family; the color and ethnic prejudices among blacks; the migration of blacks from the South to find a better life; and the portrayal of Harlem as both a romantic, wild, and exotic playground and as a den of debauchery . . ." (183).

Harlem was Thurman's most successful play. The three-act melodrama, *Jeremiah the Magnificent*, which is centered around Marcus Garvey's back-to-Africa movement, was staged at least once while *Harlem Cinderella*, also known as *Black Cinderella*, was never completed. Thurman's third play focuses on color prejudice among African Americans. As of this writing, Thurman's plays remain unpublished.

CRITICAL RECEPTION

When *Harlem* opened on Broadway in 1929, it "skyrocketed its author to overnight fame. *Harlem* was an immediate hit, the most successful play of the period written by a black playwright" (Henderson 161). Wallace Thurman's drama has generated a variety of critical commentary. At least two members of the Harlem Renaissance have expressed an appreciation for *Harlem*'s innovations. Langston Hughes, while acknowledging that Thurman's play was "considerably distorted for box office purposes, [opines that *Harlem*] was nevertheless, a compelling study—and the only one in the theater—of the impact of Harlem on a Negro family fresh from the South" (235). Theophilus Lewis, in a 1929 review of *Harlem*, describes Cordelia as an immoral, determined woman who victimizes men rather than become their victims (132). Lewis writes that *Harlem*'s characters "are not abnormal people presented in an appealing light but everyday people exaggerated and pointed up for the purposes of melodrama. This is a sound orthodox theatrical practice, and if *Harlem* proves to be as profitable as it is entertaining other playwrights will be encouraged to adopt its methods with the result that Negro drama will be changed from an aberrant to a normal form . . ." (132). More recently, Peterson has recognized Thurman's pioneering effort. Although a number of critics (Bond 1940; Isaacs 1947; Mitchell 1967; Scott 1985; Walden 1997) have focused on *Harlem*'s realistic aspects, Peterson identifies the play as "the first realistic portrait of Harlem to focus on its seamier aspects, including gambling and playing the numbers, rent parties, drinking, racketeering, prostitution, and murder" (13).

Venetria Patton and Maureen Honey point out that *Harlem* was "the source of controversy among the Harlem intelligentsia for its bold portrayal of a prostitute: noted African American literary critic Benjamin Brawley and W. E. B. Du Bois found the play . . . offensive and alarming" (520). Skinner complains that *Harlem* "exploits the worst features of the Negro and depends for its effects solely on the explosions of lust and sensuality" (514). Sharon Hall and Dennis Poupard write, "The play *Harlem*, some reviewers maintain, is exploitive in that it overemphasizes the vice and squalor of ghetto life. Yet others view the work as an honest, albeit melodramatic depiction of the problems of unemployment, racial bias, and overcrowded housing" (444). It appears that the controversy continues to the present day. Is *Harlem* an honest portrayal or exploitation of African American urban life? It is hoped that Wallace Thurman's first drama will finally be published; and thereby, contemporary readers will be able to form their own opinions of *Harlem*.

BIBLIOGRAPHY

Dramatic Works by Wallace Thurman

Harlem: A Melodrama of Negro Life in Harlem (with William Jordan Rapp). 1929. Unpublished.
Jeremiah the Magnificent (with William Jourdan Rapp). 1930. Unpublished.

Studies of Wallace Thurman's Dramatic Works

Abramson, Doris E. *Negro Playwrights in the American Theatre, 1925–1959*. New York: Columbia Unverisity Press, 1969.

Bond, Frederick W. *The Negro and the Drama*. Washington, DC: Associated, 1940.

DeKane, Carol L. "Wallace Thurman." *Black Writers: A Selection of Sketches from Contemporary Authors*. Ed. Linda Metzger et al. Detroit: Gale, 1989. 545–547.

Draper, James P., ed. *Black Literature Criticism: Excerpts from Criticism of the Most Significant Works of Black Authors over the Past 200 Years*. Vol. 3. Detroit: Gale, 1992.

Hall, Sharon K., and Dennis Poupard, eds. *Twentieth-Century Literary Criticism*. Vol. 6. Detroit: Gale, 1982. 444–451.

Henderson, Mae Gwendolyn. "Portrait of Wallace Thurman." *The Harlem Renaissance Remembered*. Ed. Arna Bontemps. New York: Dodd, 1972. 147–170.

Hughes, Langston. *The Big Sea*. New York: Knopf, 1940. New York: Thunder's Mouth, 1986.

Isaacs, Edith J. *The Negro in the American Theatre*. 1947. College Park: McGrath, 1968.

Klotman, Phyllis R. "Wallace Henry Thurman." *Afro-American Writers from the Harlem Renaissance to 1940*. Vol. 51 of *Dictionary of Literary Biography*. Ed. Trudier Harris and Thadious M. Davis. Detroit: Gale, 1987. 260–273.

Lewis, Theophilus. "If This Be Puritanism." *Opportunity* (Apr. 1929): 132.

Mitchell, Loften. *Black Drama: The Story of the American Negro in the Theatre*. New York: Hawthorn, 1967.

Patton, Venetria K., and Maureen Honey, eds. "Wallace Thurman." *Double-Take: A Revisionist Harlem Renaissance Anthology*. New Brunswick: Rutgers University Press, 2001. 520–521.

Peterson, Bernard L., Jr. "Wallace Thurman." *Early Black American Playwrights and Dramatic Writers: A Biographical Directory and Catalog of Plays, Films, and Broadcasting Scripts*. Westport: Greenwood, 1990. 182–184.

Scott, Freda L. "Black Drama and the Harlem Renaissance." *Theatre Journal* 37 (1985): 426–439.

Skinner, R. Dana. "The Play: *Harlem*." *Commonweal* 6 Mar. 1929: 514.

Van Notten, Eleonore. *Wallace Thurman's Harlem Renaissance*. Amsterdam: Rodopi, 1994.

Walden, Daniel. "'The Canker Calls . . . ,' or, the Short Promising Life of Wallace Thurman." *Harlem Renaissance Re-Examined*. Ed. Victor A. Kramer and Robert A. Russ. Rev. ed. Troy: Whitson, 1997. 229–237.

West, Dorothy. "Elephant's Dance." *The Richer, the Poorer: Stories, Sketches, and Reminiscences*. New York: Doubleday, 1995. 215–227.

Woll, Allen. "*Harlem*." *Dictionary of the Black Theatre: Broadway, Off-Broadway, and Selected Harlem Theatre*. Westport: Greenwood, 1983. 76.

EUGENE (JEAN) PINCHBACK TOOMER (1894-1967)

Emma Waters Dawson

BIOGRAPHY

Eugene (Jean) Pinchback Toomer was born December 26, 1894, in Washington, DC, as the only child of Nathan and Nina Pinchback Toomer. His mother was the daughter of Pinckney Benton Stewart Pinchback, who was a former lieutenant governor of Louisiana during Reconstruction and former U.S. senator. His father, the illegitimate mulatto son of a wealthy white North Carolina landowner, left the family with debts a year after his marriage to Nina and shortly after Toomer's birth.

Bacon Street, where the Pinchbacks resided, recalled the Old South and "an aristocracy—such as never existed before and perhaps never will exist again in America—midway between the white and black world" (Lewis 60). An affluence that included life in a wealthy white neighborhood, replete with African American domestics serving the family, lasted until the senator's gambling at Saratoga and other eastern racetracks forced the family to relocate to New Rochelle, New York, in 1904, where the elder Pinchback had received a patronage slot in a New York Customs House. The annual salary of $10,000, however, barely sustained the family due to Nathan's continued gambling. Nina remarried in 1905, again over her father's objections, to a "poor white . . . known to posterity only as Coombs" (Lewis 61). Still, the Pinchback family moved to Brooklyn after Nina and her new husband relocated there. Four years after remarrying, Nina Pinchback died due to complications following an appendectomy, ending Toomer's life as a white youth and contributing to his unhappy childhood and growing sense of insecurity. The family relocated to Washington, DC, to an African American neighborhood not far from Howard University, where, for the first time in his life, Toomer lived in an African American world, despite his ancestry being mixed and racially complicated—though in some part African. By physical appearance, Toomer was white. During this period of his life, his uncle Bismarck, who had dropped out of Yale Medical School, taught him how to read books critically. Toomer also attended Dunbar High School for an elite, publicly financed education, which he completed in three years, despite negative effects to his health from sexual indulgences, withdrawal from friends, and reclusive brooding at home. In adolescence, Toomer established a pattern of pursuit for new interests, enthusiasm about their fruition, frantic cultivation of the new project, and a despondent anxiety about fear of failure—a pattern destined to repeat itself in almost all of Toomer's future endeavors.

Because the family's finances did not permit it, Toomer could not attend Yale like his uncle Bismarck. He then briefly majored instead in agriculture at the University of Wisconsin in 1914, withdrawing after one semester. Returning to Washington, DC, Toomer became a bon vivant in the bohemian circle of Washington, DC, artists and theater people, where he assisted his uncle Bismarck in managing a theater. This experience he undoubtedly creatively adapted to his later sketch of Dorris in "Theatre" in the second section of *Cane* (1923) and to the semidramatic structure of "Kabnis" in the third section of the work. In 1915, Toomer spent a hasty stint at Massachusetts College of Agriculture during the fall semester, dropping out to attend American College of Physical Training in Chicago in February 1916. Despite his enrollment in six institutions, Toomer never became a serious degree candidate. Disconcerted, he read psychology and George Bernard Shaw, whom he later credited with having made him "aware of literary style and having introduced him to the intellectual life" (Turner, *In a Minor Chord* 9). According to Darwin Turner, "While chasing many gleams, he had read extensively in atheism, naturalism, socialism, sociology, psychology, and the dramas of Shaw" (*In a Minor Chord* 10). In a relatively short period, Toomer sold Ford cars, taught physical education near Milwaukee, rode rails to Washington, DC, and hitchhiked to New York. A versatile individual, he learned to play piano; he also hoboed, developed as a bodybuilder, and welded in New Jersey shipyards "in order to gain among the working classes the practical experience which he considered necessary to his work as a socialistic reformer" (Turner, *In a Minor Chord* 9).

Around 1920, Toomer denied his African American ancestry, claiming that his grandfather pretended to be of African ancestry in order to gain personal profit in Louisiana during Reconstruction. He even stated, "I do not know whether colored blood flows through my veins. . . . I am of no particular race. . . . I am of the human race, a man at large in the human world preparing a new race" (Barksdale and Kinnamon 501). By 1924, he had abandoned black writing in favor of more didactic and philosophical work—perhaps predicted by the personae of Kabnis and Lewis in the third dramatic section of *Cane*. Toomer succumbed to a state of psychological disarray; in a quest of elusive principles of unity, he, along with several other intellectuals, turned to the philosophies of F. Matthias Alexander, P. D. Ouspensky, and George I. Gurdjieff, a Russian who combined elements of yoga, religious mysticism, and Sigmund Freud into a system called "unitism." The Gurjieffian philosophy emphasized personality and essence as two aspects of human beings. According to the philosophy, personality shaped by people's social environment is superficial; strong personality hides essence, which is the true nature and core of being. Gurdjieff, therefore, proposed to help people find the essence. For Toomer, the philosophy promised the possibility of being and personal unity. He taught the Gurdjieffian message in Chicago and New York, where some of his pupils included major figures of the Harlem Renaissance: Wallace Thurman,* Aaron Douglass, and Nella Larsen. He also taught Margery Latimer, a white writer whom he married in 1932, but who died in childbirth the following year. In 1934, Toomer married his second wife, Margery Content, who was also white.

After *Cane*, he continued to write, but he had difficulty getting published. His scantily published output, however, obscures that he produced a small body of dramatic works—most before the publication of *Cane*. Eventually, readers and critics forgot about him. The rediscovery and republication of *Cane* in the 1960s, thanks to scholars and critics such as Robert Bone, Darwin T. Turner, and S. P. Fullinwider, led to Toomer's great role in the canon of African American literature. Toomer's body of work includes two novels, two books of poems, a collection of stories, books of nonfiction, two books of aphorism, a half dozen plays, three of which were written in the early 1920s.

In essence, Toomer's dramas, like the other creative genres, reflect the vast dilemmas he experienced as a young man largely shaped by his environment. His perceptions were altered by his quest for meaning, attempted in various sources: the vanishing black peasant life in the South and the Freudian mysticism of George Ivanovitch Gurdjieff. Finally, in the 1940s, he sought meaning in the Society of Friends when he turned to the Quaker faith for spiritual sustenance. He died on March 30, 1967. Toomer had much earlier summed up his life: "Perhaps . . . , our lot on this earth is to seek and to search. Now and again we find just enough to enable us to carry on. I now doubt that any of us will completely find and be found in this life" (Turner, *The Wayward* 500).

MAJOR WORKS AND THEMES

While critics and scholars credit Jean Pinchback Toomer with heralding the beginning of the Harlem Renaissance with the publication of *Cane* in

1923, he also attempted success as a playwright for over ten years. Darwin Turner notes of Toomer's affinity toward development as a playwright, "Almost unknown, however, is his struggle to succeed as a dramatist. For more than a decade Jean Toomer experimented with dramatic form and technique in order to blend social satire with lyric expression of [the] modern . . . quest for spiritual self-realization" (Turner, "Failure" 377). *Natalie Mann* (1922), Toomer's first drama, similar to *Cane*, advocates freedom of the young, middle-class African American woman. In this regard, the play foresees the middle-class character Esther in *Cane*. The middle-class status of Esther and Natalie alienates them from both the whites and working-class poor in the Sparta, Georgia, setting. However, Natalie, unlike Esther, is freed from the constraints of middle-class rules and reliance on someone else through the central character in the play, Nathan Merilh. The sacrificial aspect of his character, a Christlike representation of Toomer himself, permits Natalie to achieve autonomy after her defiance of social convention in her cohabitation with Nathan in New York. Nathan's collapse at the conclusion of a dance ritual affirms Natalie's autonomy. Whereas Esther loses her fragile grip on reality in the sketch in *Cane* when the drunken Barlo rejects her romantic overture, Natalie comprehends Nathan's spirituality in his ultimate sacrifice of himself. To achieve such dramatic effect, Toomer created characters as types in imitation of the German expressionistic playwrights. Another character type, Mertis, a contrast to Natalie, however, closely parallels Esther. Despite engagement in teaching, social work, and the struggle for civil rights of African Americans, her independence from social constraints proves futile. These diversionary activities, expanding to a relationship with Nathan's friend Law, prove futile: "Her search begins too weakly and too late; she dies from chill" (379).

In addition to *Natalie Mann*, Toomer wrote *Balo*, a one-act sketch one year before the publication of *Cane*. It was published and performed by the Howard Players in 1924. Similar to "Kabnis," the third section of *Cane*, it emphasizes the separation of the middle-class blacks from their emotions. In this regard, similarities exist between Toomer's depiction of the southern rural women and the urban women, respectively, in the first and second sections of *Cane*. However, in *Balo*, white Christianity functions as a primary divisive force. Set during cane-harvesting season, *Balo* features an African American farmer and prospective preacher, Will Lee, and his sons, Tom and Balo, who work tirelessly during a depressive crop season, despite the elder's apparent thrift during more prosperous preceding periods. In his work ethic and other areas, Will Lee does not differ from Jennings, his white neighbor. Toomer describes the Jenningses as ". . . a poor white family . . . who would, but for the tradition of prejudice and coercion of a rural public opinion, be on terms of frank friendship growing out of a similarity of occupations and consequent problems. As it is, there is an understanding and bond between them little known or suspected by northern people" (qtd. in Krasny 356).

Separating the races and inhibiting behavior, cultural ignorance dictates decorum and conduct in this environment. During the play's progressions, other characters, including friends and relatives, arrive. Uncle Ned, who resembles Father John of "Kabnis," suggests a disruptive, religious persona in that his accompaniment with Sam disturbs the ensuing card playing. In their interpretation of religion, the gathering consider card playing and the presence of Father John conflicting and disrespectful; consequently, they look toward Will, the aspiring preacher, for appropriate guidance and conduct. At this point, the excitedly religious and devoted Balo reminds them of the fears they associate with spiritual conviction when he shouts an outburst to God and begs for mercy on his sinful soul. Still, after this animated display of passion, the high-spirited atmosphere of the party reemerges to be subdued by Uncle Ned's discourse on the entrapment of sin and the need for healing. At this point, Balo accelerates the rate of his previous spiritual outburst, and he screams as though possessed, "Jesus, Jesus, I've found Jesus. One mo' sinner is a-comin' home" (285). In "sheepishness and guilt" (286), the card players file out as Uncle Ned embraces the zealously crying Balo.

Before the action of the play, Jennings confesses to Will his observation about Balo. He states, "Saw Balo there a while back actin' like he was crazy. An' what do yer think he said? An' kept on repeatin' it. 'White folks ain't no more'n niggers when they gets ter heaven (Laughs)'" (277). Despite his commonality with the Lees in economic conditions and other areas, Jennings cannot perceive Balo's prophecy. Nevertheless, regardless of his animated nature, Balo, unlike Jennings, recognizes the oneness of humankind, not withstanding differences such as race. The Lees and the Jenningses cannot have an open and free friendship because of preconceived social and racial limitations, established by the same white culture fostering the Western perception of Christianity.

In "Kabnis," Toomer also grapples with humanity's concept of God, black religion, and Christianity, as well as issues relating to race and color. Unlike the first two sections, comprised of a series of short stories or vignettes and lyrical poems depicting primarily black women in the rural South and the urban settings of Washington, DC, it is a drama divided into six sections and focuses on a male figure Ralph Kabnis, a teacher at a Georgia girls' school. As the first section opens, Kabnis sits alone in his cabin in Sempter, Georgia, a portrait based on Toomer's own experience in Sparta, Georgia, as a visiting superintendent during 1922. Feeling estrangement and homesickness for his home in Washington, DC, Kabnis questions God as he pleads with Him not to torture him with the beauty of the landscape and culture:

There is a radiant beauty in the night that touches and . . . tortures me. Ugh. . . . Whats beautiful there? Hog pens and chicken yards. Dirty red mud. Stinking outhouse. Whats beauty anyway but ugliness if it hurts you? God, he doesn't exist, but nevertheless He is ugly. Hence, what comes from Him is ugly. Lynchers and business men, and that cockroach Hanby, especially. (83)

In addition to Kabnis, other characters include the principal of the school, Samuel Hanby; a shopkeeper, Fred Halsey; a fellow teacher and northern militant opposing segregation, Lewis; Layman, a "tall, heavy, loose-jointed Georgia Negro, by turns teacher and preacher, who has traveled in almost every nook and corner of the state and . . . knows more than would be good for anyone other than a silent man" (86); an old man and former slave Father John; and three women, Stella, Cora, and Carrie Kate, Halsey's sister. The second section of "Kabnis" centers on a conversation between Halsey, Layman, and Kabnis as they debate their differing views about race. Kabnis attacks both Halsey and Layman, for he feels that their views about race and black religion are as distorted as the cruelty of whites and the simplicity of blacks in this rural setting. Layman observes, "Nigger's a nigger down this away, Professor. An only two dividins: good an bad. An even they aint permanent categories. They sometimes mixes um up when it comes t lynchin . . ." (86).

On black religion, Layman notes that he has also studied the behavior of the community, observing its apparent hypocrisy:

An its th worst one in th community that comes int th church t shout. . . . You take a man what drinks, th biggest licker-head around will come int th church an yell th loudest. An th sister whats done wrong, an is always doin wrong, will sit down in th Amen corner an swing her arms an shout her head off. Seems as if they cant control themselves out in th world; they cant control themselves in church. (89)

The third section emphasizes Kabnis's feelings about Samuel Hanby as a symbol of the then-prevailing image of the black southern principal as an enemy of the black people, reaffirming Kabnis's description of him in the first section as a cockroach, for he fires Kabnis when he unexpectedly catches him drinking with Halsey. In firing him, Hanby treats Kabnis's conduct as a threat to the race in stating that the school was founded and maintained at the expense of others and that its "purpose is to teach . . . youth to live better, cleaner, more noble lives. To prove to the world that the Negro race can be just like any other race. It hopes to attain this aim partly by the . . . examples set by its instructors" (93). Kabnis must leave the school because of his drinking, but Lewis also plans to leave because of philosophical differences, illustrated most poignantly in his description of Father John, whom he tauntingly describes as a slave boy taught to read the Bible by a former mistress and a black man who saw Jesus in the ricefields and then began preaching. Section six ends "Kabnis" the morning after Kabnis, Halsey, and Lewis spend the night in the "hole," the basement of Halsey's shop, with Stella and Cora at a party for Lewis's departure. Ironically, despite the perception that Father

John is blind and deaf, he mumbles and talks for the first time, similar to the drunken Barlo in the sketch of "Esther" in *Cane* and Balo in *Balo*: "Sin . . . S . . . Th sin whats fixed . . . (Hesitates). . . . upon th white folks. . .—f tellin Jesus—lies. O the sin th White folks 'mitted when they made th Bible lie" (115). While Carrie is moved to tears, Kabnis contemptuously declares that Father John is an "old black fakir" (116), ending the drama in his questioning the world at his perception of its ultimate contradictions and paradoxes.

Characteristic of his personal demeanor and artistic endeavors, Toomer abandoned writing plays for a few years after "Kabnis" appeared in *Cane*. He then wrote *The Sacred Factory* (1927) as an Expressionistic drama, further exploring the disintegration of humanity. In the vein of expressionism, so familiar to American critics and audiences of the time, Toomer used for the first time a nonrepresentational stage set: three chambers not separated by walls but divided by pillars. Religion, similar to the roles of Balo and Father John and other minor characters in "Kabnis," functions in a crucial role as the central chamber separating the proletariat and the intellectual class. The tedious, unproductive, profitless, mechanical life cycle of a proletariat family and the opposing intellectual, spiritual battles, frustrating and defeating the middle class, operate as robots. First, the proletariat pantomime their lives, illustrating marriage, work, eating, and sleeping and their subsequent repetition. These activities follow with the birth of children, their departure from home, the death of the husband, mourning by the woman, and then her death. Mechanical beings, the proletariat have no interests, expectations, optimism, or alternative.

The intellectual class, represented by the names John and Mary, give birth to an inquisitive child wondering where she is. The chorus responds in ridicule to the mother's imaginative answer that she is on "a little speck of dust on a great elephant full of stars" (qtd. in Turner, "Failure" 383). The physician-husband argues with the wife when the child asks additional questions about life and God and then accuses the wife of desiring a liaison with a new husband. Knowledge, belief, and morality function as drugs of destruction that the chorus responds to with chant and dance in their praise of the drugstore for its dispensation of art, science, and religion. Like Ralph in "Kabnis," the husband ignores the appeal of religion and God. The wife, sacrificially and physically, remains with her husband, despite spiritual separation, because of her child. In the final act, the chorus praises both the joy of and the aversion to war. The husband acknowledges that the first marital estrangement developed from the conflict between his intellect and her emotion. Manifestation of the conflict results in his dedication to pleasure, called "God" by humans. The chorus rejects pleasure and kneels and worships the Madonna. The confused child enters the central chamber and seats herself when John refuses to die because he has not lived. Despite *The Sacred Factory's* affinity to plays shown to New York audiences in 1927, such as Eugene O'Neill's *The Emperor Jones*, Toomer failed to find a producer for the play.

The Gallonwerps (1928), first rejected by publishers as a novel, was rewritten as a play for gigantic marionettes. It emphasizes Toomer's thesis "that the world is a puppet-show manipulated by a master puppeteer" (Turner, "Failure" 384). Earlier in the century, designer-director Gordon Crag had proposed the use of gigantic marionettes as a means to transcend the limitations of human actors. In the play, worldly Prince Klondike of Oldrope tricks people in such a way "that they enjoy being tricked" (384). He plots and succeeds in his plan to steal Little Gasstar from the nurse after helping Wimepime Gallonwerp assemble an audience to listen to the philosophical ideas of her husband, Wistwold. He later returns to the Gallonwerp home to take both the wife and husband with him. Observing the play's heavy reliance on satiric caricatures and quips, Turner describes the drama as an example of the "ego's rescue of the id from the superego" (385). Readily apparent in *The Gallonwerps* is Toomer's immersion in Gurdjieffian philosophy, for the character types in the drama represent the merging of the emotion and intellect into one individual. The play, however, failed to be produced, as was the fate of *A Drama of the Southwest* (1935), based on Toomer's experiences in New Mexico. Though he continued to write dialogue, Toomer abandoned his efforts to write drama for stage production. His saturation in philosophical and psychological doctrines was not attractive to the uninformed reader or audience, a fact affirmed with the rejection of an attempted magazine sale of a brief drama of modern humans as late as 1947. The wife in the unidentified play preoccupies herself with meetings, while the deserted husband seeks company with a sympathetic robot.

CRITICAL RECEPTION

Jean Pinchback Toomer's legacy to African American literature has received steady critical acclaim since the republication and rediscovery of *Cane* in 1975. However, the corpus of book articles, journal articles, dissertations, and full-length books written about Toomer as playwright remains a vacuum. Few journal and book articles exist. Most notable among them is the text *Jean Toomer: A Critical Evaluation* (1988), edited by Therman B. O'Daniel. In this collection of critical essays, a chapter of three short essays explores Jean Toomer as playwright. An article by Michael J. Krasny essentially links the play *Balo* to the poetry and sketches in *Cane* as an intense dramatization of Toomer's concern with "the forces which inhibit, pervert, and destroy innate spirituality" (357). Similarly, William J. Goede concentrates on "Kabnis" in its unique role of offering the first portrait of an African American writer in American literature, emphasizing specific problems Toomer faced as an African American writer (360). The final essay in the chapter, by Darwin Turner, aptly titled "The Failure of a Playwright," scrutinizes Toomer's unknown struggle to receive acclaim as a dramatist. It is the most comprehensive discussion to date, for he examines all of Toomer's dramatic ventures, beginning with the first drama, *Natalie Mann* (1922), and spanning to a brief mention of a satirical drama that Toomer wrote in 1947. A cursory summary of Toomer's career as a playwright sadly identifies *Balo* as the only play produced on stage, although Turner notes that both "Kabnis" and *The Sacred Factory* share characteristics of Theater of the Absurd that proved rather productive for Samuel Beckett, Eugene Ionesco, Jean Genet, and Edward Albee. Turner's final assessment is that Toomer predates Theater of the Absurd, where perhaps he may have found an appreciative audience (386).

The *MLA Bibliography* lists only seven essays assessing the work of Jean Toomer as playwright. They include three that examine the early plays: Frederic L. Rusch published an article in *MELUS*, which discusses both *Natalie Mann* and *Balo*; Onita Estes-Hicks's essay in *SAGE* praises the work in Toomer's glorification of the essence of feminine emotions; and Elon A. Kulii notes in an article about "Kabnis" in *The Language Quarterly* the correlation between genre, the physical, and the black proletariat concept of the law. One rare discussion noting similarities between other playwrights is Robert Cooperman's article "Unacknowledged Familiarity: Jean Toomer and Eugene O'Neill." Such sporadic analyses about Jean Toomer as playwright signal that with little exception much of the valuable work to have appeared thus far devotes itself to *Cane* and its application to other genres rather than drama. Even an earlier work by Blyden Jackson and Warren French discusses *Cane* in the context of its form, despite a focused analysis of "Kabnis." Perhaps, Robert H. Brinkmeyer accurately assesses Jean Toomer as playwright in his essay in the *Southern Quarterly*, for Toomer failed to impress on his generation his genius as a playwright: "Despite imaginative techniques, occasionally striking characterizations, and frequently brilliant dialogue, Toomer failed to sell his . . . drama to producers of his generation" (Turner, "Failure" 386).

BIBLIOGRAPHY

Dramatic Works by Eugene (Jean) Pinchback Toomer

"Balo." *Plays of Negro Life*. Ed. Alain Locke and Gregory Montgomery. New York: Harper, 1927. 269–286.

"The Gallonwerps." *The Wayward and the Seeking: A Collection of Writings by Jean Toomer*. Ed. Darwin T. Turner. Washington, DC: Howard University Press, 1980. 202–241.

"Kabnis." New York: Boni and Liveright, 1923. New York: Liveright, 1975; 1993. *Cane: An Authoritative Text, Background, Criticism*. Ed. Darwin T. Turner. 1988. New York: Norton, 1993. 81–116.

"Natalie Mann: A Play in Three Acts." *The Wayward and the Seeking: A Collection of Writings by Jean Toomer*. Ed. Darwin T. Turner. Washington, DC: Howard Univeristy Press, 1980. 243–325.

"The Sacred Factory: A Religious Drama of Today." *The Wayward and the Seeking*: A Collection of Writings by Jean Toomer. Ed. Darwin T. Turner. Washington, DC: Howard Univeristy Press, 1980. 327–410.

Collections of Eugene (Jean) Pinchback Toomer's Dramatic Works

Jean Toomer: A Critical Evaluation. Ed. Therman B. O'Daniel. Washington, DC: Howard University Press, 1988.

A Jean Toomer Reader: Selected Unpublished Writings. Ed. Frederik L. Rusch. New York: Oxford University Press, 1993.

The Wayward and the Seeking: A Collection of Writings by Jean Toomer. Ed. with intro. Darwin T. Turner. Washington, DC: Howard UP, 1980.

Studies of Eugene (Jean) Pinchback Toomer's Dramatic Works

Barksdale, Richard, and Keneth Kinnamon. *Black Writers of America: A Comprehensive Anthology*. New York: Macmillan, 1972.

Benson, Brian Joseph, and Mabel Mayle Dillard. *Jean Toomer*. Boston: Twayne, 1980.

Brinkmeyer, Robert H., Jr. "Wasted Talent, Wasted Art: The Literary Career of Jean Toomer." *Southern Quarterly: A Journal of the Arts in the South* 20.1 (1981): 75–84.

Cooperman, Robert. "Unacknowledged Familiarity: Jean Toomer and Eugene O'Neill." *The Eugene O'Neill Review* 16.1 (1992): 39–48.

Dawson, Emma Waters. "Eugene (Jean) Pinchback Toomer." *African American Authors, 1745–1945*. Ed. Emmanuel S. Nelson. Westport: Greenwood, 2000. 408–417.

Dorris, Ronald. "Early Criticism of Jean Toomer's *Cane*: 1923–1932." *Perspectives of Black Popular Culture*. Ed. Harry B. Shaw. Bowling Green: Popular, 1990.

Estes-Hicks, Onita. "*Natalie Mann*: Jean Toomer's Feminist Drama of Ideas." *SAGE: A Scholarly Journal on Black Women* 5.1 (1988): 21–24.

Foley, Barbara. "Jean Toomer's Washington and the Politics of Class: From 'Blue Veins' to Seventh-Street Rebels." *Modern Fiction Studies* 42.2 (1996): 289–321.

Goede, William J. "Jean Toomer's Ralph Kabnis: Portrait of the Negro Artist as a Young Man." *Jean Toomer: A Critical Evaluation*. Ed. Therman B. O'Daniel.

Washington, DC: Howard University Press, 1988: 359–375.Also published in *Phylon* 30 (Spring 1969): 73–85.

Jackson, Blyden, and Warren French. "Jean Toomer's *Cane*: An Issue of Genre." *The Twenties: Fiction, Poetry, Drama.* Ed. Warren French. Deland: Everett/Edwards, 1975. 317–333.

Jones, Robert B. *Jean Toomer and Selected Essays and Literary Criticism.* Knoxville: University of Tennessee Press, 1996.

Kerman, Cynthia Earl, and Richard Eldridge. *The Lives of Jean Toomer: A Hunger for Wholeness.* Baton Rouge, Louisiana University Press, 1988.

Krasny, Michael J. "Design in Jean Toomer's *Balo*." *Jean Toomer: A Critical Evaluation.* Ed. Therman B. O'Daniel. Washington, DC: Howard University Press, 1988. 359–375. Also published in *Negro American Literature Forum* 7.3 (1973): 103–104.

Kulii, Elon A. "Literature, Biology and Folk Legal Belief: Jean Toomer's *Kabnis*." *Language Quarterly* 25.3–4 (1987): 5–7, 49, 54.

Larson, Charles R. *Invisible Darkness: Jean Toomer and Nella Larsen.* Iowa City: University of Iowa Press, 1993.

Lewis, David Levering. *When Harlem Was in Vogue.* New York: Oxford University Press, 1981.

McKay, Nellie Y. *Jean Toomer, Artist: A Study of His Literary Life and Work, 1894–1936.* Chapel Hill: University of North Carolina Press, 1984.

Rusch, Frederik L. "Jean Toomer's Early Identification: The Two Black Plays." *MELUS* 13 (Spring–Summer 1986): 115–124.

Turner, Darwin T. "The Failure of a Playwright." *Jean Toomer: A Critical Evaluation.* Ed. Therman B. O'Daniel. Washington, DC: Howard University Press, 1988. 377–386. Also published in *CLA Journal* 10 (June 1967): 308–318.

———. *In a Minor Chord: Three Afro-American Writers and Their Search for Identity.* Carbondale: Southern Illinois University Press, 1971.

———. *The Wayward and the Seeking.* Washington, DC: Howard University Press, 1980.

JOSEPH A. WALKER
(1935–   )

Emmanuel S. Nelson

BIOGRAPHY

A distinguished figure in African American theater, Joseph Walker was born to working-class parents in Washington, DC, in 1935. His father, Joseph Walker, was a house painter; his mother, Florine Walker, was a housewife. Walker's interest in theater began while he was an undergraduate student at Howard University, where he received his bachelor's degree in philosophy and drama in 1956. Shortly thereafter he entered the United States air force as a second lieutenant. Although he excelled in his military career, he grew increasingly uneasy with his duties as an air force officer and decided to return to civilian life to pursue a career in writing. He received an honorable discharge in 1960, and three years later, he earned his master's degree in fine arts from the Catholic University in Washington, DC. For the next few years, he taught English at a high school in the nation's capital and subsequently at the City College of New York. While in New York, he immersed himself in the city's large and lively theater scene. He began to act and choreograph.

Walker's first play, *The Believers*, opened in New York City's Garrick Theater on May 9, 1969. It was largely ignored by the critics. His second produced work, *The Haranguers*, opened at St. Marks Playhouse, also in New York City, on December 30, 1969; it received several but mixed reviews. But three years later, when *The River Niger* was staged at St. Marks Playhouse, Walker gained national attention. The play won numerous awards including a Tony, an Obie, the Black Rose, and the Drama Desk Award. A successful movie based on the play was released in 1976. Though Walker has written eight plays, *The River Niger* remains his best and most widely produced work.

Walker is married to Dorothy Dinroe, a musician. They currently live in Washington, DC, where Walker is a professor of drama at Howard University.

MAJOR WORKS AND THEMES

Joseph A. Walker's theatrical projects center around his insightful explorations of the black male experience in contemporary United States. The rage and rebellion of the activist 1960s inform his worldview and lend a sharp edge to his dramatic texts. His early work, *The Haranguers*, presents some of the themes he would explore with greater skill and precision in his later plays. Unconventional in its structure, *The Haranguers* has four seemingly unrelated units: a prologue, an episode, and two one-act plays. The prologue, set in Africa, pivots around a father's terrifying decision. Rather than allow his son to be captured and taken in a slave ship across the Atlantic Ocean to a life of captivity in America, he murders him. The episode that follows the prologue is set in the United States at the height of the black power movement of the late 1960s. A young African American activist, rather than watch his son grow up in a viciously racist society, decides to kill him. These two segments of the play highlight a central idea that resonates in Walker's works: slavery that violated Africa has left an enduring legacy that continues to maim the lives of contemporary African Americans. The third section of *The Haranguers* focuses on an interracial couple. A young black man is in love with a wealthy white woman whose father is violently opposed to their marriage. The young lovers plot to kill the racist father but their scheme is exposed by a disloyal black friend of the couple. The male protagonist is killed, but during his dying moments, he pleads with his pregnant girlfriend to raise their child as a revolutionary who will fight for social justice. The last segment of the play centers around an elderly African American man who holds three hostages—a white man, a white woman, and a black male—and forces them to listen to his diatribes against all whites and assimilationist blacks. When he tries to execute the black captive, the latter overpowers and shoots him dead. All four sections of the play examine the overwhelming sense of powerlessness that the black male experiences in a society that refuses to acknowledge fully his personhood. His efforts to gain some measure of control over his life are often thwarted by racist whites and their assimilationist black collaborators.

Walker's next two plays—*Ododo* (1970) and *Yin Yang* (1973)—premiered at St. Marks Playhouse. Both were theatrically nontraditional works and neither generated much enthusiasm. *Ododo* is a musical revue with elaborate dance routines and spectacular costumes; it attempts to re-create onstage a miniaturized version of the entire African American experience. This ambitious project, though visually arresting at times, does not entirely succeed in achieving its goal. In *Yin Yang*, Walker broke new theatrical grounds. At times a hilarious meditation on the theme of good versus evil, the play centers around a verbal confrontation between God and Satan. Both cosmic characters are played by sassy black women. Conceptually the play is provocative but in its execution it failed to realize fully the comic as well as philosophical possibilities of its plot.

It was *The River Niger*, a play that opened in New York City in late 1972, that made Walker a major award-winning playwright. Though not an autobiographical work, it draws generously from Walker's own life experiences. At the center of the play is a multigenerational family living under one roof in Harlem. The matriarch of the family is Wilhelmina Brown, a black woman who takes inordinate pride in her relatively light complexion and her part–Native American ancestry. John Williams, her middle-aged son, and Mattie Williams, his wife, live with her. The primary crisis in the play, however, is precipitated by John and Mattie's son, Jeff, who comes home after being dishonorably discharged from the United States Air Force. His father had hoped that a career in the military would save his son from the crime-ridden, drug-infested streets of Harlem. He is devastated by his son's failure and even more so when Jeff, upon his return home, reconnects with a street gang of which he was once a member.

John, unable to cope with his own and his son's troubles, retreats into heavy drinking to numb his feelings while his long-suffering wife remains steadfastly loyal to him. Soon, however, John emerges as a "heroic" figure. When Jeff and his friends are betrayed by one of the gang members, a betrayal that is sure to land Jeff in jail—John decides to take revenge. His confrontation with the disloyal gang member results in a shootout in which both men die. But moments prior to his death, John takes the blame not only for the death of the disloyal gang member but also for the offense that Jeff and his friends allegedly committed. The father's selfless love ensures his son's safety; his dying gift redeems Jeff. Aptly, Walker dedicates his play to "underrated black daddies everywhere."

Though the father–son relationship is at the heart of the play, Walker also deals with a variety of other themes. Among the play's many characters, there is Dr. Dudley Stanton, a self-hating black physician from the West Indies, who embodies the most degrading elements of colonized consciousness. There is Ann Vanderguild, a young black South African nurse, who is romantically involved with Jeff. Her father's antiapartheid activism has landed him in prison and her siblings have fled the country to escape the South African government's repression. Both Dudley Stanton and Ann Vanderguild—two characters who are damaged in different ways—allow Walker to explore one of his key concerns: the racial memories, spiritual affinities, and unifying experiences of Africans and the members of the African diaspora.

Walker's diasporic consciousness and commitment surface in his most recent play, *District Line*, first produced in 1984. The action of the play takes place in Washington, DC, and centers around six taxi drivers. Five of them are men; three are black and the other two are white. The sixth is an African American woman. One of the black characters is a professor at Howard University who works part time as a taxi driver to provide a comfortable life for his family. In this play too, there is an African character: one of the drivers is a South African whose antiapartheid militancy has resulted in his forced exile. Walker, who had once worked briefly as a taxi driver in Washington, DC, explores a typical day in the lives of the six drivers. He does so with humor and penetrating insight. The extended conversations among the drivers provide an occasion for Walker to examine the changing dynamics of race relations in urban centers of the United States.

CRITICAL RECEPTION

Joseph A. Walker's early works did not garner many favorable reviews in mainstream venues. The racial anger that informs those works perhaps makes many middle-class white viewers less than comfortable. Feminist critics too find his work rather offensive. Addell Austin Anderson, in her fine overview of Walker's life and works, relentlessly foregrounds the misogyny that she sees in many of his plays. While acknowledging that many of Walker's "black male characters are deftly drawn and complex," Anderson insists that his "portraits of black women . . . rarely escape the limitations of stereotypes" (718). Even in *The River Niger*, a play that has several women characters of different ages and backgrounds, Anderson argues, the women seem monodimensional and preoccupied largely with serving "their men's needs with little concern for their own desires and ambitions" (718). Anderson sees no shift in Walker's representation of women; even in his recent works, they uniformly "appear to be gratuitous . . . and remain stereotypes" (718).

The best piece of scholarship that has been published so far on Walker's work is Anthony Barthelemy. Like Anderson, Barthelemy points out that in Walker's plays, especially in *The River Niger*, the "pervasive hostility towards women, whether it is active or passive, becomes impossible to deny or overlook" (786). But Barthelemy situates this misogyny in its larger ideological and literary contexts. *The River Niger*, according to Barthelemy, is a conscious and contestory response to Lorraine Hansberry's* classic drama *A Raisin in the Sun*. The "antifeminist agenda" (786) of Walker's play then is intentional because Walker is responding to Hansberry's allegedly unflattering portrayal of black male characters in her work. After acknowledging and addressing Walker's sexism, Barthelemy proceeds to offer a perceptive and provocative interpretation of *The River Niger*.

BIBLIOGRAPHY

Dramatic Works by Joseph A . Walker

Antigone Africanus. 1975. Unpublished.
The Believers. 1968. Unpublished.
District Line. 1984. Unpublished.
The Haranguers. 1969. Unpublished.
The Lion Is a Soul Brother. 1976. Unpublished.
"*Ododo*." *Black Drama Anthology*. Ed. Ron Milner and Woodie King, Jr. New York: New American Library, 1971.
The River Niger. New York: Hill, 1973.
Yin Yang. 1973. Unpublished.

Studies of Joseph A. Walker's Dramatic Works

Anderson, Addell Austin. "Joseph A. Walker." *Contemporary Dramatists*. Ed. Thomas Riggs. 6th ed. Detroit: St. James, 1999. 717–718.
Barthelemy, Anthony. "Mother, Sister, Wife: A Dramatic Perspective." *Southern Review* 21.3 (1985): 770–789.
Cooper, Grace. "Joseph A. Cooper." *Dictionary of Literary Biography*. Ed. Thadious M. Davis and Trudier Harris. Vol. 38. Detroit: Gale, 1985. 260–264.
Cooper, Theodore G. "Development of Black Theatre through the Black Playwright." *Onstage* 3 (1973): 3–5.
Fontenot, Chester J. "Mythic Patterns in *River Niger* and *Ceremonies in Dark Old Men*." *MELUS* 7.1 (1980): 41–49.
Lee, Dorothy. "Three Black Plays: Alienation and Paths to Recovery." *Modern Drama* 19 (1976): 397–404.
Peterson, Maurice. "Taking Off with Joseph Walker." *Essence* 4 (Apr. 1974): 55.
Taylor, Clarke. "In the Theatre of Soul." *Essence* 5 (Apr. 1975): 48–49.
Washburn, Martin. Rev. of *The River Niger*, by Joseph A. Walker. *Village Voice*. 14 Dec. 1972: 41.

DOUGLAS TURNER WARD
(1930–)

Kristina A. Clark

BIOGRAPHY

Douglas Turner Ward, the only child of Roosevelt and Dorothy Ward, was born on May 5, 1930. The Wards lived on a plantation in Burnside, Louisiana, for eight years. Ward's three aunts also lived with him in Burnside. One aunt died while he was still very young; the other two worked as domestics in the town. Ward later patterned the two female domestics in his first play, *Happy Ending*, after these two aunts. Ward and his parents then moved to New Orleans where Roosevelt and Dorothy ran a tailoring business out of their home. Ward was a bright boy and excelled at school, especially in reading and writing at Xavier University Preparatory, a black Catholic high school. Ward decided at a young age that he wanted to become a writer. After high school, he attended Wilberforce University in Xenia, Ohio, where he majored in journalism. He stayed at Wilberforce University for a year. He then transferred to the University of Michigan on a football scholarship in 1947, but lost the scholarship after a knee injury. Though he was determined to dedicate himself to academics after the loss of his scholarship, he attended classes sporadically and concentrated more on leisure reading than on assignments. He spent two turbulent years at college before deciding he was destined for more and moved on to pursue a better life in New York City.

At the end of his yearlong enrollment at the University of Michigan, in 1948, Ward moved to New York City where he worked part time as a journalist for the *Daily Worker*. While employed by the *Daily Worker*, Ward was free to explore his political views in writing. It was during this time that he decided to pursue his theatrical ambitions. He believed that in order to write good plays one must first understand the actor. In 1955, he enrolled at Paul Mann's Actors' Workshop where he remained for the next three years. During his time at Paul Mann's Actors' Workshop, he continued to hone his ability as a dramatist while working alongside such notable black actors as Sydney Poitier and James Earl Jones. While studying at the Actors' Workshop, Ward met Diana Hoyt Powell. They married in 1966 and had two children.

In 1967, Ward coestablished the Negro Ensemble Company (NEC), with fellow dramatists Robert Hooks and Gerald S. Krone. Ward advocated the need for a theater that would address the black experience in an article entitled "American Theatre: For Whites Only?" that he wrote for the *New York Times* in 1966. In this article, Ward called for Negroes and whites alike to dedicate them to the pursuit of African American drama. The article resulted in a $1.2 million grant from the Ford Foundation with which the NEC was created and was able to run for the next three years. Ward worked as a director for the NEC, while he continued to act and write drama.

During his work as actor, director, producer, and writer, Ward won many notable awards. In 1966, for example, he won the Verona Desk Award and an Obie Award for Drama. These awards were followed by the Lambda Kappa Nu citation in 1968. In 1969, Ward won a series of awards including a special Tony Award, League of American Theatres and Producers, and Brandeis University Creative Arts Award for *Happy Ending* and *Day of Absence*. He won additional awards for acting, such as the Vernon Rice Desk Award in 1969 and an Obie Award, and the Village Voice Award for his work in *The Reckoning*. In 1973 and 1974, Ward received recognition for producing and his work in the NEC: these awards included the Margo Jones Award, a Tony nomination, and a nod for best supporting actor in *The Reckoning*. In addition, Ward received the *Ebony* Black Achievement Award in November 1980 for his work and performance with the NEC. Thus, Ward has been widely recognized for his exemplary role in the advancement of African American drama.

Since the publication of *Brotherhood* in 1970, Ward's only work as a playwright has been in the production of a play called *The Redeemer*, which was performed in 1979 but never published. Ward has dabbled in the craft of playwriting since the 1970s but has invested most of his time in the running of the Negro Ensemble Company. He has continued to be a dedicated producer and director at the NEC helping many other African American playwrights find outlets for their craft.

MAJOR WORKS AND THEMES

In 1965, Douglas Turner Ward produced his first two plays, *Happy Ending* and *Day of Absence*, Off Broadway, with the aid of Robert Hooks at St.

Mark's Playhouse. Both plays were later published together under the title *Two Plays* in 1966. *Happy Ending* is a cunning satire aimed at the sometimes symbiotic relationships between whites and their African American servants. The play opens with two black women, Ellie and Vi, sitting at a kitchen table crying about a terrible misfortune that had taken place that day. Their nephew, Junie, enters the scene and is horrified to learn that the reason for his aunts distress is the impending divorce of their employers, the Harrisons:

Here we are—Africa rising to its place in the sun wit' Prime Ministers and other dignitaries taking seats around the international conference table—us here fighting for our rights like never before, changing the whole image, dumping stereotypes behind us and replacing 'em wit' new images of dignity and dimension—and I come home and find my own aunts, sisters of my mother, daughters of my grandpa who never took crap off no cracker even though he did live on a plantation—DROWNING themselves in tears jist 'cause boss man is gonna kick boss lady out on her nose . . . !!! (14)

Junie is shocked when his aunts respond to his tirade by informing him that everything he has is owed to the Harrisons' wealth and marriage. Junie receives his upper-class clothes from the wardrobe of Mr. Harrison because they both wear the same size suits. The food his aunts serve him every morning, noon, and night comes from their ordering extra for their own kitchen each time they order food for the Harrison kitchen. The furniture that decorates both their apartment and that of Junie's mother and father is the result of Ellie and Vi's taking the old Harrison furniture and giving it to the poor: themselves. After the revelation of this shocking news Junie takes a place beside his aunts at the kitchen table where he too begins to weep at the news of the Harrisons' divorce. The play ends with the reconciliation of the Harrisons and their asking Ellie to watch their children while they go out to celebrate the special occasion. Ellie agrees to watch the children, but only at an extortionist price. Junie, Ellie, Vi, and Ellie's husband, Arthur, celebrate their own good fortune in the Harrison reconciliation by toasting the Harrisons with a bottle of the white couple's own champagne.

Day of Absence offers an even more startling criticism of the race relations between whites and their Negro servants than *Happy Ending*. *Day of Absence* is a play with almost exclusively white characters and is meant to be performed as a "reverse minstrel show"; it is to be performed by black actors or whites, if possible, wearing whiteface paint. The play is set in an "unnamed Southern town of medium population on a somnolent cracker morning" (36). The white townspeople find themselves increasingly uneasy as the morning goes by; however, they are unable at first to identify the cause of their anxiety. As the play goes on, the townspeople slowly come to the realization that all the African Americans of the town are missing. What follows is absolute bedlam: couples are unable to tend to their children or cook a meal, offices fall to ruin without black gophers and secretaries, telephone calls cannot be placed, and all the whites are left in a state of complete confusion. The mayor when questioned on the gravity of the "absentee nigra situation" replies: "But speculating on the dark side of your question—if we don't turn some up by nightfall, it may be all over. The harm has already been done. You see the south has always been glued together by the uninterrupted presence of its darkies. No telling how unstuck we might get if things continue on like they have" (70). The play ends with the reappearance of the town's Negro citizens after the whites have existed twenty-four hours in a state of utter panic. Rastus, the only black character in the play, steals the stage in the play's final scene by uttering that he has no idea what happened the previous day because he has no recollection of missing a day. *Day of Absence* is a play much like *Happy Ending*; both detail the power that the blacks exercise in their subtle way in the service of whites.

Both *Happy Ending* and *Day of Absence* are commentaries on the relationships between black domestics and their white masters. Ward presents his audience with the stark reality of race relations in these two plays. Critic Gail Stewart comments on Ward's depiction of the servant–master relationship in *Day of Absence*: "*Day of Absence* is one of the most revolutionary plays written by an American black, for Ward depicts the enormity of the contribution of blacks to American life and in the same stroke the enormity of the exploitation that blacks have historically suffered" (302). Ward uses his supreme gift of satire to reveal to his audience a real American problem while keeping the tone of the play light enough to encourage free thought on the subject. According to William Couch, Jr.:

Douglas Turner Ward's *Day of Absence* and *Happy Ending* superbly combine thesis with theatre farce, establishing a real and sometimes half surreal, world in which whites get their comeuppance from black folks whose sardonic cunning is mordant proof that they, like people in general, though less than angels are far more than fools. Mr. Ward's effects derive chiefly from his access to a brand of realism that is geared to the tempo and style of the absurd theatre. (xxi)

Ward uses the same satirical tone in his third play, *The Reckoning: A Surreal Southern Fable*, which was produced at St. Mark's Playhouse, in New York City in September 1969; it was published in 1970 by Dramatists Play Service. *The Reckoning* took on a much darker tone than either of Ward's earlier works. The play begins with a discussion between a black pimp, Scar, and his black prostitute and significant other, Baby. They speak street lingo that is hard to follow for some readers, but what finally emerges is that they are going to blackmail the state governor who just happens to be one of Baby's clients. At the same time that Baby and Scar are plotting their blackmail scheme, Governor is sitting in his office ruminating on his feelings toward his people, and "the nigras." He gives a speech to the audience that is a parody of Martin Luther King, Jr.'s famous "I Have a Dream" speech, in which Governor expounds on the consequences of letting the black man gain the same rights as white individuals. Governor concludes his speech with the importance of stopping a lone black man's pilgrimage to the capital as a revolutionary act in the hopes of equal treatment for those of his race. This is the end of what Ward calls "Movement One." It is important to look at the idea of different parts of the play being called movements and the overall meaning of the word. Movement One can be seen as a demonstration of a "movement" to keep the African American race down, whereas Movement Two concludes with the retraction of Governor's speech and the subsequent "victory" of Scar and the other blacks over the stereotypical southern white man in power.

Movement Two takes place in Governor's office, where he is approached by Scar and Baby, who are also accompanied by his supposed loyal servants, Josh and Missy. Scar presents Governor with photographs of Governor's rendezvous with Baby. Scar demands not only money from Governor, but he also demands that Governor let the lone revolutionary black man make his way to the capital unmolested. Governor does not want to comply with the wishes of his undesirable black underlings, but in the end feels no choice in the matter. Governor speaks to the crowd outside his office and defends the pilgrimage of the solitary black man in an offhand way, saving his own reputation while still living up to his part of the bargain with Scar. This is an impressive play for many reasons, perhaps the most startling of these being the use of corrupt tactics by Scar and his followers in order to fight the corruption of Governor.

Ward's last published play, *Brotherhood*, was first performed by St. Mark's Playhouse in March 1970; it was published later that same year by Dramatists Play Service. *Brotherhood* is a short satire on race relations that makes quite an impact. It is a play about Tom and Ruth Jason, a white suburban couple, who entertain two black friends, James Johnson and Luann Johnson, for an evening in their home. The play opens with Tom and Ruth rushing frantically about the house covering up pieces of furniture and other miscellaneous objects in an effort to have their home redecorated by the time the Johnsons arrive. When the Johnsons finally do arrive at the Jasons, they are presented to us as middle-class Negroes visiting white friends of the same social standing. However, they are wearing evening attire, whereas the Jasons are still dressed in their work clothes. This is the first hint the reader receives that not all is well in this quaint suburban home.

As the play moves on, the Johnsons are constantly commenting on the decor of the Jason's quickly redecorated home. Tom and Ruth defend their odd choices by passing off their hurried designs as fashions of the time. James and Luann comment appropriately, but the sense that something is off in the house prevails no matter how relaxed they try to make themselves. James searches for an ashtray only to be told that he may flick his cigarette ashes on the floor, while Luann is made to go outside in order to use the bathroom. Ward's play keeps the audience off their guard and wondering until the very end. Only after the Johnsons leave their hosts' residence is the audience allowed to see the Jason living room in its entirety. What is revealed is a hideous show of plantation-style decorating.

Tom and Ruth uncover "a grotesque menagerie of Negro plantation statuettes: crimson-lipped, white eye–rimmed jockeys, bandannaed mammies, bare-assed ash-tray blacks, ebony pissing–stanced lamps, and a staggering profusion of diverse artifacts of 'Niggerphalia'" (16). The Jasons have even gone to the trouble of locking their two children away in a closet to keep them from singing racist songs like "Eeny Meeny" and "Little Black Sambo." The fact that the Jasons even considered allowing James and Luann into their home with such artifacts of slavery and racist prejudice in their home is sickening, a point that Ward foregrounds toward the end of the play. The last scene of the play focuses on the Jasons on their way back to their own residence. The audience is made privy to the notion that the Jasons too are phony characters and hold the Johnsons in as much contempt as is possible to muster. They have endured the strange evening at the Jasons only to live up to appearances and without any real interest in befriending the white couple. The last time the audience sees the Johnsons they are discussing taping back together a check that the Jasons had given them for their children, which the Johnsons had torn into pieces as an act of false bravado in front of the Jasons. In the end, we are left with the notion that neither couple is really any better than the other; they are both racist, but seek to hide their feelings however possible.

In *Brotherhood*, Ward's tone is more satirical than in his previous plays. While still allowing the audience to make up their minds about which race is more corrupt, Ward presents the audience with some harsh images. *Brotherhood* is clearly a play about the secret lives of people. People of every race have secrets in their lives; Ward shows us this with his great satirical skill. Not only does he expose the Jasons' secret racism, but he also shows his audience the pretentious aloofness of the Johnsons. Like all of Ward's plays, *Brotherhood* encourages audiences to think about racism critically and confront their own inner demons.

Gail Stewart asserts about Ward's last published play that "the satire of *Brotherhood* is darker than in Ward's other plays. It underlines the falseness of facile 'brotherhood' manners and implies strongly that pretense supplies no solution to radical differences between blacks and whites" (302). In this play, Ward reveals to his audience the concept of brotherhood. He shows brotherhood to be an entity that only exists within the confines of race and does not transcend racial boundaries to extend its limits to the human race. The Johnsons and the Jasons claim a false brotherhood to one another based on the fact that they both belong to the same species; however, they clearly show that their brotherly alliance to one another is just for show and extends only to people they consider their own "kind." Ward gives great insight in this play into the consequences of false displays of "brotherhood."

CRITICAL RECEPTION

Critics have had mixed responses when considering Douglas Turner Ward's early work. *New York Times* critic George Wellwarth in reviewing Ward's first two plays, *Happy Ending* and *Day of Absence*, accuses Ward of writing "about the master–servant relationship as if it still existed and present[ing] us with the ironic paradox of the servant superior to the master" (E12). Ward defended such criticism of his plays: "Stereotypes have changed—from Stepin Fetchit to a menacing black militant hiding behind every lamppost—but they are still stereotypes. As for the servant–master relationship, it exists; you can see it on the street corners in the Bronx where women shape up for jobs as domestics" (E12). Most critics, however, have found Ward's one-act plays on race relations as interesting commentaries on the interdependence of people despite cultural differences. William Barrow of *Negro Digest* comments, "Both plays [*Happy Ending* and *Day of Absence*] are comedy satires, with sharp, jagged teeth, drawing their substance and their thrust from the bitter-sweet reality of race relations as seen from the bottom side of the coin" (2). In addition, Wilfrid Sheed in *Commonweal* comments on Ward's transcendence of race in *Happy Ending*: "Mr. Ward's message that the servant is finally corrupted as much as the master might not come so gracefully from a white playwright. But these are not raceplays in the usual sense; race is treated mainly as a local aspect of universal institution" (440). Ward shows his audience that corruption exists in all peoples. Ward's next two plays, *The Reckoning: A Surreal Southern Fable* and *Brotherhood*, have faced the same sort of mixed criticism.

Critics have mixed responses to the subjects that Ward presents to his audience in his play *The Reckoning*. One argument that critics make regarding *The Reckoning* is that the language Ward uses can in some ways inhibit the message he is trying to convey. According to critic Stephen M. Vallilo, "Some reviewers also had difficulty understanding the black dialect mentioning that the blacks responded to the play while whites sat bewildered, and, although some black critics appreciated Ward's approach and his use of language, others criticized him for failing to offer better black role models than a pimp and a whore" (269). Vallilo goes on to comment on the lack of morals found in the play: "Both characters are morally bankrupt—opposite sides of the same coin—but in this play Scar has the advantage. He is able to reverse the usual order and victimize the white man. The con man exploits the other man's weak spot" (269). Ward shows both black and white characters in this play to be corrupt, once again leaving judgments for the audience to make based on their own views of race and corruption. Overall, the criticism visited on *The Reckoning* is harsher than that for *Happy Ending* or *Day of Absence*. One can only attribute this to the denser subject matter and complex views on racism that are present in *The Reckoning*, which in the other plays appear under the guise of satire.

Ward's last published play, *Brotherhood*, has received much less criticism than his previous works. Critics tend to overlook some of the implications of *Brotherhood* since it is such a short and strange satirical play. Clive Barnes, a writer for the *New York Times*, expresses that "*Brotherhood* is probably more of a dramatic metaphor than a play. . . . It is a stark and startling accusation of racism against white and black alike. . . . Ward plays no sides. He looks at our two nations with an unvarying yet compassionate eye" (C12). This is the sentiment of all of Ward's plays. He tends never to give more sympathy to one race or the other, but criticizes both races equally by making them look equally as foolish on stage. It is this selective objectivity that gives Ward his power as an African American playwright of the twentieth century.

BIBLIOGRAPHY

Dramatic Works by Douglas Turner Ward

Brotherhood. New York: Dramatists Play Service, 1970.
Happy Ending and Day of Absence: Two Plays. New York: Okpaku, 1966.
The Reckoning: A Surreal Southern Fable. New York: Dramatists Play Service, 1970.

Studies of Douglas Turner Ward's Dramatic Works

Barnes, Clive. "Theatre Review." *New York Times* 18 Mar. 1970: C12.
Beauford, Fred. "The Negro Ensemble Company: Five Years against the Wall." *Black Creation* 3 (Winter 1972): 16–18.
Barrow, William. "Douglas Turner Ward." *Contemporary Authors Online*. Gale, 2001: 4 pp. 23 Apr. 2003 <http://www.galegroup.com/pdf/facts/ca.pdf>.
Couch, William, Jr., ed. *New Black Playwrights*. New York: Bard/Avon, 1970.
"Douglas Turner Ward." Interview. *Blackstage* (Jan.–Feb. 1974): 1–9, 37–40.
Harris, Trudier. *From Mammies to Militants: Domestics in Black American Literature*. Phildelphia: Temple University Press, 1982. 143–154.
Harrison, Paul Carter. *The Drama of Nommo*. New York: Grove, 1972.
Peavy, Charles D. "Satire and Compory Black Drama." *Satire Newsletter* 7.1 (1976): 40–48.
Peterson, Maurice. "Douglas Turner Ward." *Essence* (June 1973); 44–45, 75.
Ribowsky, Mark. "'Father' of the Black Theatre Boom." *Sepia* 25 Nov. 1976: 67–78.
Sheed, Wilfred. "The Stage: Masters and Servants. *Commonweal* 8 July 1966: 440.
Stewart, Gail. "Douglas Turner Ward." *Twentieth Century American Dramatists*. Vol. 7 of *Dictionary of Literary Biography*. Ed. John MacNicholas. Detroit: Gale, 1981. 300–304.
Vallilo, Stephen M. "Douglas Turner Ward." *Afro-American Writers after 1955: Dramatists and Prose Writers*. Vol. 38 of *Dictionary of Literary Biography*. Ed. Thadious M. Davis and Trudier Harris. Detroit: Gale, 1985. 264–270.
Wellwarth, George. "Theatre Review." *New York Times* 30 Dec. 1970: E12

SAMM-ART WILLIAMS
(1946–   )

Rochell Isaac

BIOGRAPHY

Samm-Art Williams was born in Burgaw, North Carolina, to Valdosia and Samuel Williams. Though his parents were separated by the time he was four, Samm-Art, nevertheless, grew up in a close-knit family and community. He and his mother lived next door to his uncle, grandfather, and aunt. He attended Burgaw Elementary School and C. F. Pope High School.

While Samm-Art knew at an early age that he wanted to be a writer, he perhaps did not think his dream would be realized. However, fate seemed to have conspired against him. His mother, an English teacher at C. F. Pope High School, also headed the Drama Department. Valdosia Williams recognized and fostered her son's interest. She guided her son's reading, introducing him to the works of countless black writers; James Weldon Johnson and Langston Hughes* being two of his favorites. It was she who presented her son with all of Shakespeare's works and provided him with the opportunity to perform in the plays she directed. Samm-Art refers to his mother as his "first real influence in terms of drama" (qtd. in Harris 284). She made him read just about everything of literary value including Edgar Allan Poe. To date, Williams believes that "The Raven," one of Poe's poems, was his greatest influence, "in seeing the bird, I saw what a great thing it was to be able to work on a person's mind with words" (qtd. in Gale Group par. 4).

Upon graduating from high school, Samm-Art attended Morgan State College in Baltimore. He majored in political science as he intended to become the civil rights attorney that his family wanted him to become. The civil rights movement had opened doors to blacks, and black students everywhere were being pressured to succeed and to move into stable careers. Though Samm-Art continued to write during his years at Morgan State, nothing serious was happening with his writing.

However, after graduating in 1968, Samm-Art moved to Philadelphia, where he joined the Freedom Theatre. He would continue to secretly write poetry even as he studied acting and theater. The experience with the Freedom Theatre would later provide for his entry into New York theater. As Trudier Harris notes, it was not until Samm-Art's arrival in New York in 1973 that he found an environment that provided support for his desire to become a writer (285). Though he went to New York to become a writer, he had to do some acting to pay the rent. His first part in a play was in Ken Eulo's *Black Jesus* in 1973. He auditioned for the Negro Ensemble Company (NEC) in 1974, but was initially rejected. However, the occasion proved to be an important one. Samm-Art had managed to meet the right people. He was able to join the Playwrights Workshop of the NEC, where he performed in many productions even while he continued to write. Later, the NEC would produce a number of his plays, including *Welcome to Black River* (1975), *The Coming* (1976), *A Love Play* (1976), *The Frost of Renaissance* (1978), *Brass Birds Don't Sing* (1978), and *Home* (1979).

MAJOR WORKS AND THEMES

Home (1979) is arguably Samm-Art Williams's most successful work. The play received a Tony nomination and a Drama Desk nomination, won a John Gassner Playwriting Medallion, and was selected best play of 1979–1980 in the Burns Mantle Yearbook. Williams received the Outer Critics Circle Award for Best Play (1980–1981), the Governor's Award from North Carolina, the NAACP Image Award, and the AUDELCO (Audience Development Committee) Recognition Award. The play was first produced Off Broadway at St. Mark's Playhouse Company, by the Negro Ensemble, but would later run for ten months on Broadway at the Cort Theatre. The success of the play led Williams to be compared to other major playwrights, including, Charles Gordone* for his play *No Place to be Somebody* (1969) and to Lonne Elder III* for *Ceremonies in Dark Old Men* (1969). Both plays were also major triumphs for the respective playwrights. As Trudier Harris notes, the "production of *Home* made Williams the hottest black playwright in America" (284).

The community in *Home* is modeled after the community of Burgaw, North Carolina, where Williams grew up. The play started out as a poem that addressed the reverse migration of black people from the North to the South. The idea apparently came to Williams as he rode a bus from New York to North Carolina. People were returning home to the South and pretending to their relatives that they were "living it up" up North. However, Williams knew the reality was that people were struggling up North just as they struggled down South (Harris 289).

Home introduces us to Cephus Miles, a North Carolina farmer. Cephus finds himself imprisoned for his refusal to serve in the military during the Vietnam War. He is released from prison five years later, only to learn that he has lost everything, including the farm that his grandfather left him. Cephus migrates to a large city in the North where he loses his job when his convict past is revealed. From there, his life spirals down to one of dependence on drugs, alcohol, and welfare. He has already been humiliated by Pattie Mae, who promised to marry him, yet marries someone else when she goes away to college. The silver lining in the play comes when Cephus receives a letter from his aunt assuring him that an unknown benefactor has purchased his old farm and has invited him to come home. Cephus returns home to the South (Crossroads, North Carolina) and is shocked by the changes that have taken place. The audience learns that it is the estranged Pattie Mae who has bought back Cephus's farm. Pattie Mae is now divorced and has returned to Cephus. Despite his embarrassment regarding his life, the two decide to rebuild their relationship. The play has a happy ending and the audience is led to believe that the two will live happily ever after. Cephus's prayers have been answered. Throughout the play, Cephus repeatedly calls on God for deliverance, but he is convinced that God is vacationing:

I believed in God! . . . I gave him my life, my soul, my breathing, my sight, my speech. All of me I gave to him. I believe in him totally until he took a vacation to the sun-soaked, cool beaches of Miami, while I needed his help and love in the hot sticky tobacco fields of North Carolina. . . .

God. I want to speak with God. No . . . no I don't have the wrong number. I know his number. This is Cephus Miles. Cephus . . . he knows me. We're friends. Miami . . . on vacation? I need him now Miss. No! Don't hang up. (3–4)

Society had failed Cephus and Cephus had failed Cephus. His only chance at recovery was to return to the essence of his spirituality and to home. In her review of *Home*, Marilyn Stasio insists that the play "calls us back home— even against our better judgment" (30).

Interestingly enough, only two other actors—both female—appear in the play. The two actors alone portrayed numerous characters in Cephus's life as he reminisces in a rocking chair on the front porch. The title of the play signifies a person's roots and community. It also serves as a source of hope when there is nothing left to be hopeful about. The play was praised for its structure and narrative style. I myself was struck by its blend of humor and poignancy.

Williams has also managed to complete a body of representative works with some plays still unpublished. *Welcome to Black River* (1975), Williams's first play, is a portrayal of two families, one black one white, living in North Carolina during the 1950s. The families are connected secretly by blood, and circumstances force them to renegotiate their roles in one another's lives. The play dramatizes the poverty, racism, and exploitation that the black family is forced to endure. Williams would revisit this North Carolina community years later in *Home. Do Unto Others* (1976) is a story of deceit, crime, and the revenge of a housewife who manages to escape the death trap set in motion by her husband, a numbers racketeer. In *The Coming* (1976), God appears and converses with a skid-row bum in the form of unsavory characters, including a prostitute, a slave, and a dope addict. *A Love Play* (1976) examines the motives of four women who decide to become lesbians. It is a conscious choice after looking at their failed relationships and the quality of men available to them. *Brass Birds Don't Sing* (1978) tells the story of two sisters, Donia and Freida. The sisters were rescued by an American soldier from a Lebensborn breeding camp in Poland during World War II. However, the sisters' past follow them into their new lives in the United States. Despite the unspeakable acts endured by the sisters, a reporter continues to follow them revealing their past.

The Sixteenth Round (1980), originally titled *Pathetique*, centers on Jesse, a boxer, who fears for his life because he has thrown a fight. Lemar, the executioner, finds Jesse in a deteriorated state and realizes that Jesse will die soon whether he kills him or not. The play is comprised of a series of conversations accompanied by Tchaikovsky's "Pathetique." *Friends* (1983) circles around a woman, Amanda, who lives with both her husband and boyfriend, both blind men. The men are unaware of each other's identity until the end of the play. *Bojangles* (1985) is based on the career of tap dancer Bill "Bojangles" Robinson. In *Eyes of the American* (1985), the conflicting values of West Indian blacks and African Americans are highlighted. The play is set on an unidentified Caribbean island with two male protagonists. *Cork* (1986) deals with the choices made by black minstrels in the early 1800s. Though these early entertainers perpetuated negative stereotypes of black people, Williams pays them tribute. He recognizes that these minstrels paved the way for future black actors. The title refers to the burned cork used by some minstrels to blacken their faces in caricature (Morgan E11). *Eve of the Trial* (1986) was Williams's contribution to an anthology of Anton Chekhov stories, *Orchards*, adapted for theater. Williams is also the author *of Frost of Renaissance* (1978).

More recently, Williams wrote *The Dance on Widow's Row* (2000), a comedy, that focuses on four old and rich widows. All four women live on the same street and between them have buried nine husbands. Foul play is suspected. The wives have inherited property, insurance, and pensions from their dead husbands' estates. Nevertheless, the women are still not averse to marriage as they are planning to hold a party and invite eligible widowers and divorced men. *Conversations on a Dirt Road* (2002) is the story of a poor and middle-aged farmer who inherits property when his father dies. He wants to sell the property but his desire is met with resistance and disapproval from his brother and the community. The play brings to the forefront questions about the importance of historical memory.

A number of Williams's works are yet unpublished. In *Kamilla* (1975), a woman is forced to admit to her sexual preference by her dream consciousness. *The Last Caravan* (mid-1970s) is a musical that revolves around the search for virility by an aging male protagonist. He goes to a hoo-doo woman to cure his impotency. His virility is restored, though the remedy given to him is only a placebo. Other unproduced works include *Something from Now* (1974), *Break of Day Arising* (1976), *We Three and Me* (1979), *Panty Raid* (1982), *Flowers of Winter* (1982), and *Woman of the Town* (1986). Williams continues to rework a number of his plays as he is unsatisfied with the end results.

Several major themes seem to compound Williams's works, including racial and identity politics, pride, sexuality, humor, the importance of community, and recognizing the essence of our humanity. Williams somehow manages to force his audience to deal with the issues that he has presented them with. At the core of Williams's work is a focus on the individual. Harris argues that Williams tends to see and look for the redeeming qualities in people. He goes on the premise that human beings are innately good but are often negatively impacted by the environment (286). Williams's desire to focus on the individual and not the issue stems in part from his belief that black playwrights of the 1960s did not accurately portray black life in America. Black militants were portrayed as universally good, while the black middle class was portrayed as snobbish. Older blacks were alienated, as they were considered to be Uncle Toms. Williams appears to be arguing that those distortions will be historically detrimental to black people. He centers his plays on human beings because as Williams says:

I am more interested in how the human being approaches the issue instead of trying to write about the issue itself because we really know what the issues are in this life regardless of what we're talking about, whether it's marriage, whether it's segregation, whether it's the Air Force, the Army, whether it's nuclear war. We know the issue. I'm really more or less interested in how, and I hope that eventually when somebody goes back to read all these plays, they will say, well the man chronicled how folk thought about certain issues. That's really where my interest is, because I think that history will give an accurate account of nuclear war, you know, so I try not to make an overt stand on that. I would like to see a character make his stand on what he things about it because that way I think I can get into the humanness of people, and that's really where my head is. (qtd in Harris 287)

Samm-Art Williams's style of writing has been compared to that of major authors of American fiction and poetry, including Mark Twain and Vachel Lindsay. *New York Times critic* Mel Gussow, in his review of *Home*, maintains that "Mr. Williams seems closer to the spirit of Mark Twain. If Twain were black and from North Carolina, he might have written like Samm-Art Williams." In addition, Gussow clearly recognizes Williams's way with words. He notes that "Mr. Williams is clearly in love with words, which in his hands become a rolling caravan of images. Occasionally, he stops for rhyming interludes, talking blues, which remind one somewhat of Vachel Lindsay's tympanic incantations" (C12). Williams's sense of humor is very apparent in the language of his works. This may very well show the author's outlook on life as well as his optimism: "My whole life and my work is based on hope. It might be a desperate situation, and seemingly hopeless, but you have got to have tried" (Gale Group par. 4). Most of Williams's protagonists have faced trying situations and have been tested. The journey that ensues is both necessary and mandated by fate and circumstances.

CRITICAL RECEPTION

Samm-Art Williams's career is not limited to that of a playwright. In addition to his plays, he has worked in television and film as both an actor and a writer. His work has been well received, as proven and shown by his sterling career. He was awarded a Guggenheim Fellowship and a National Endowment for the Arts Fellowship and has even been nominated for two Emmy Awards. In fact, he is one of only a few African Americans to achieve the level of success that he has in television and theater. After the success of *Home*, Williams began writing scripts for the screen: *John Henry* for Showtime, *Badges* and *Lenny's Neighborhood* for CBS, *Solomon Northup's Odyssey* for PBS, and *With Ossie and Ruby* for Ruby Dee and Ossie Davis. He has written episodes of *Miami Vice, The New Mike Hammer, Cagney and Lacey, Kneeslappers, Mackron*, and countless other programs. He has worked as executive producer for *Martin, Good News*, and *The Fresh Prince of Bel Air*, and coproducer of *Hanging with Mr. Cooper*. As an actor, Williams has appeared in films—*Dressed to Kill, Blood Simple*, and *Huckleberry Finn*—and on television—just to name a few, *The Women of Brewster Place, Race to the Pole*, and *Cook and Perry*; he has also appeared in soap operas, for example, *Search for Tomorrow*. Williams also played the role of a slave rebel in *Denmark Vesey*, a 1985 American Playhouse documentary.

Currently, Williams is still writing for both for television and theater and will continue to do so. He continues to write everyday for three to four hours in the morning and for yet another hour in the evening (Harris 290). The body of work that he has managed to accumulate and produce is truly amazing, and Robbie Jean Walker attests to this saying that "the entire corpus of Samuel Arthur Williams' activities in defining the moral and political contours of our diverse society will no doubt secure his place in American theatre and culture" (780).

It is important to note that Williams credits his success to his writing ability. "Experience and imagination are two things a writer must have and a certain amount of fearlessness. Writing is extremely important. Directing is technical, but writing is skill. For getting into film and television, writing is extremely important, because ultimately you want to produce. That's where the power lies. When you come from the ranks of writers, you have power" (qtd. in Blanchet and Epps par. 7).

BIBLIOGRAPHY

Dramatic Works by Samm-Art Williams

Bojangles. Produced Shubert Theater, New York, 1985.
Brass Birds Don't Sing. Produced Stage 73, New York, 1978.
The Coming. Produced Billie Holiday Theatre, New York, 1976.
Conversations on a Dirt Road. Produced St. Louis Black Repertory Company, 2002.
Cork. Produced Courtyard Theatre, New York, 1986.
The Dance on Widow's Row. Produced Harry De Jur Playhouse, New York, 2000.
Do Unto Others. Produced Billie Holiday Theatre, New York, 1976.
Eve of the Trial. Produced Lucille Lortel Theatre, New York, 1986.
Eyes of the American. New York: French, 1986. Produced Theatre Four, New York, 1985.
Friends. Produced Billie Holiday Theatre, New York, 1983.
The Frost of Renaissance. Produced Riverside Church, New York, 1978.
Home. Produced St. Mark's Playhouse, New York, 1979; and Cort Theatre, New York, 1980.
A Love Play. Produced St. Mark's Playhouse, New York, 1976.
The Sixteenth Round. Produced Theatre Four, New York, 1980.
Welcome to Black River. Produced St. Mark's Playhouse, New York, 1975.

Studies of Samm-Art Williams's Dramatic Works

Armstrong, Linda. "Samm-Art 'On Widow's Row.'" *Amsterdam (NY) News* 22–28 June 2000: 21.
Blanchet, Geri and Arnie Epps. Press Release for Samm-Art Williams. *New Jomandi* 2002: 8 pars. 8 Jan. 2003 <http://www.jomandicom/news.html>.
Gale Group. "Samm-Art Williams." *Contemporary Authors Online*. Biography Resource Center, 2003: 12 pars. 20 Jan. 2003 <http://www.galenet.com/servlet/Bio/RC>.
Gussow, Mel. "Stage: Samm-Art Williams' 'Home.'" *New York Times* 20 Dec. 1979: C12.
Harris, Trudier. "Samm-Art Williams." *Afro-American Writers after 1955: Dramatists and Prose Writers.* Vol. 38 of *Dictionary of Literary Biography*. Ed. Thadious M. Davis and Trudier Harris. Detroit: Gale, 1985. 284–290.
Mapp, Edward. *Directory of Blacks in the Performing Arts*. Metuchen: Scarecrow, 1990.

Morgan, Thomas. "Minstrel: The Myth and Men." *New York Times* 27 Dec. 1986: E11.

O'Haire, Patricia. "Samm-Art Takes 'Widow's' Walk." *Daily News* 26 June 2000: 32.

Peterson, Bernard L., Jr. *Contemporary Black American Playwrights and Their Plays: A Biographical Directory and Dramatic Index*. Westport: Greenwood, 1988.

Stasio, Marilyn. "You Can Go 'Home' Again with Samm-Art Williams." *New York Post* 8 May 1980: 30.

Walker, Robbie Jean. "Samm-Art Williams." *The Oxford Companion to African American Literature*. Ed. William Andrews, Frances Smith Foster, and Trudier Harris. New York: Oxford University Press, 1997. 779–780.

AUGUST WILSON
(1945–   )

Karen C. Blansfield

BIOGRAPHY

August Wilson was born Frederick August Kittel on April 27, 1945, on Bedford Avenue in Pittsburgh, the fourth of six children and a child of mixed parentage. His mother, Daisy Wilson, was black, while his father, Frederick Kittel, was a white German immigrant baker who was frequently absent and eventually abandoned the family. His mother subsequently married David Bedford, who proved far more influential in Wilson's life than his biological father. Cramped with his family into a two-room apartment, Wilson grew up in a racially mixed ghetto area known as the Hill District that would figure prominently in his dramatic work, with most of his plays being set in Pittsburgh.

Daisy Wilson, whom August adored and whose surname he later adopted, supported the family with janitorial jobs and welfare checks, working hard to ensure that her children would have a good education and social opportunities. She kept many books in their home, and Wilson learned to read at the age of four. Wilson attended both parochial and public schools, but he was taunted and ostracized, especially when he was the only African American student in the class, and at the age of fifteen, he dropped out permanently when his high school teacher accused him of plagiarizing a term paper about Napoléon. To keep his mother from finding out what he had done, Wilson spent his days at the public library, immersing himself in reading and developing an impressive self-education. Wilson has referred to this time as his "learning years," noting that he read "everything and anything that I could get my hands on," from anthropology to fiction to furniture making (Fitzgerald 14). Wilson subsequently worked a series of menial jobs, including gardener, porter, cook, and sheet metal worker, and he frequented the streets of the Hill, listening to stories, observing characters, and absorbing the rhythms and vernacular of the language that would later shape his drama.

Some pivotal events occurred in 1965, which was also the year Wilson's natural father died. Wilson moved to a rooming house in Pittsburgh, an environment that would be reflected in his play *Joe Turner's Come and Gone*. He bought his first typewriter as well as a record player, and perhaps most importantly, he discovered the blues when he chanced upon a 78-rpm record by Bessie Smith—which, as has often been noted, he played twenty-two times nonstop. In the blues, which informs much of his drama thematically and structurally, Wilson discovered a culture central to African American life. He continued to write poetry and short stories, while getting to know other writers and political activists. In 1968, he and his friend Rob Penny cofounded Black Horizons Theatre, where Wilson directed one of Penny's plays. The following year, Wilson's stepfather died. Wilson married Brenda Burton, although the marriage would only last until 1972. In 1970, his daughter Sakina Ansari was born.

It was in the 1970s that Wilson began writing plays, mainly one acts, and in fact, it was not until 1976 that he saw his first professional production— Athol Fugard's *Sizwe Bansi Is Dead*—an experience that further prompted him toward playwriting. He was encouraged in this endeavor by his friend Claude Purdy, director in residence of the Penumbra Theatre in Minneapolis, which mounted Wilson's early works and which has, over time, produced more of his plays than any other theater in the country. The Penumbra gave Wilson his first professional production in 1981, *Black Bart and the Sacred Hills*, which had originated as a poem. Wilson had moved to St. Paul in 1978, where he wrote children's plays for the Science Museum in Minneapolis and later worked as a cook for a social organization, Little Brothers of the Poor. The separation from his Pittsburgh roots is what really forged Wilson as a playwright and what "enabled me to hear the voices and to recognize and respect them. And that freed me up" (Whitaker 84). Even much later in his career, Wilson would say, "I carry Pittsburgh with me wherever I go" (Whitaker 82). During this time, Wilson won a Jerome Fellowship from the Playwright Center in St. Paul for his script of *Jitney* and was also sending plays to Connecticut's Eugene O'Neill Theater Center. When *Ma Rainey's Black Bottom* was accepted by the center's National Playwrights Conference, Wilson's career was about to take off.

In 1982, Wilson traveled to Connecticut for the staged readings of his play, where he met Lloyd Richards, artistic director of the conference as well as dean of the Yale Drama School and artistic director of the Yale Repertory Theatre. Richards, who had in 1959 shepherded Lorraine Hansberry's* *A Raisin in the Sun* to Broadway, recognized the latent genius in Wilson's work, and the two gradually developed a working partnership that has become almost legendary. Richards served as mentor and advisor to Wilson, as well as staging the first productions of his works before guiding them to national stature. Their collaboration lasted well into the 1990s, when Wilson began working primarily with director Marion McClinton.

After a production at the Yale Repertory Theatre in April 1984, *Ma Rainey's Black Bottom* moved to Broadway in October, winning the New York Drama Critics Circle Award for Best Play as well as a Tony Award nomination, establishing Wilson as a major new voice in American theater. Following this notable debut, Wilson's career and reputation rose rapidly in the ensuing two decades, earning him the status as one of America's most important dramatists and its foremost black playwright. Unfortunately, his beloved mother died in 1983, and while she had been able to attend one of her son's productions, she was not to see his meteoric ascent to fame—and fortune.

In 1987, *Fences*—after productions at the Yale Repertory Theatre and Chicago's Goodman Theatre—opened in New York to stunning success, featuring James Earl Jones in the lead role of Troy Maxson. Among its many honors, the play won the Pulitzer Prize; four Tony Awards, including one for Best Play; and the Drama Critics Circle Award. The following year, *Joe Turner's Come and Gone*, which had premiered at the Yale Repertory Theatre in 1986, opened on Broadway, garnering another Tony nomination for Best Play and again winning the New York Drama Critics Circle Award. It also endowed Wilson with the unusual honor of having two plays running simultaneously on Broadway. In 1990, Wilson earned his second Pulitzer Prize—only the seventh dramatist to attain this honor—with *The Piano Lesson*, which opened in April and won numerous other awards, including a Tony for Best Play and the Drama Critics Circle Award.

However, 1990 also signaled some major changes in Wilson's personal life. His second marriage, to social worker Judy Oliver, ended in divorce, and Wilson moved from St. Paul to Seattle, where he has lived ever since. In 1994, he married costume designer Constanza Romero, with whom he has one daughter, Azula Carmen Wilson, born in 1997. Meanwhile, his presence on Broadway continued: *Two Trains Running* opened in 1992, winning the American Theatre Critics' Association Award, Drama Critics Circle Award, and a Tony nomination for Best Play. Then came *Seven Guitars* in 1995, after productions at the Goodman Theatre and Boston's Huntington Theatre Company. It won two Outer Critics Circle Awards, a Drama Critics Circle Award for Best Play, and other honors. That same year, Wilson presented the keynote address at the National Conference of the Theatre Communications Group, a speech that was to spark controversy for its strident separatist views and that was to define Wilson as a cultural nationalist. In his speech, Wilson attacked the notion of color-blind casting and deplored the lack of black professional theaters in the country. The most outspoken critic of Wilson's remarks was Robert Brustein, artistic director of the American Repertory

Theatre, whose charges included the point that Wilson's own plays had achieved success through mainstream white theater as well as that rejecting color-blind casting would have denied prominent roles to many black actors. The following year, Wilson and Brustein held a debate at New York's Town Hall, moderated by Anna Deavere Smith,* which was billed by some as "the fight of the century."

Three more plays followed. In 2000, *Jitney* had its New York premiere and was awarded eight Vivian Robinson AUDELCO (Audience Development Committee) Awards, and in a 2002 London production, it won the Laurence Olivier Award for Best Play. *King Hedley II* opened in New York in 2001, earning Tony nominations for Best Play and Best Director, though it had an unusually short run of only twelve weeks. Wilson's latest work, *Gem of the Ocean*, has been staged at the Goodman Theatre and the Mark Taper Forum in Los Angeles, though as of this writing, the New York premiere has not been scheduled.

Other awards that Wilson has earned on his journey to stardom include a Guggenheim Fellowship, Rockefeller Playwriting Fellowships, a Whiting Foundation Writers Award, a McKnight Fellowship, and a Bush Fellowship, as well as memberships in the American Academy of Arts and Sciences and the American Academy of Arts and Letters; he also has some two dozen honorary degrees. In 1996, the William Inge Festival in Independence, Missouri, devoted its season to Wilson's work; Penumbra Theatre in St. Paul, Minnesota, did the same for its 2002–2003 season; and New York's Signature Theatre will devote its 2005–2006 season to Wilson's oeuvre. Additionally, Wilson moved into yet another career in 2003 when he performed a one-man show at the Seattle Repertory Theatre as part of its Festival of New Works, and he has plans to develop this performance further.

Director Marion Isaac McClinton, in his introduction to *Jitney*, writes, "August Wilson is the griot, our Homer, our Shakespeare, our grandfather sitting on the front porch telling us the stories that we need to know" (8). As one of the most produced American playwrights and the first African American to be a constant presence in mainstream theater, Wilson has established himself as a major and unique voice in contemporary drama.

MAJOR WORKS AND THEMES

August Wilson's body of work is perhaps the most ambitious undertaking in American theater: a cycle of ten plays (nine of them now completed) that chronicles the cultural history of African Americans in the United States through the course of the twentieth century. Each work is set in a specific decade, featuring characters who are influenced and shaped by the social, cultural, and political environments of the particular era in which they live. (In this sense, Wilson has often been compared to Eugene O'Neill, who also initiated cycles of plays, though he fell far short of completing any.) Wilson's plays tend to be long and are based on dialogue rather than action or visual effects, characteristics that have drawn some criticism, although offstage events are often central to the action and—as in Greek drama—are all the more powerful for being unseen.

Wilson has frequently said that he writes only for himself, though he does take audience dynamics into consideration, but he also acknowledges aesthetic motives. "What I am trying to do is put Black culture on stage and demonstrate to the world—not to White folks, not to Black folks, but to the world—that it exists and that it is capable of sustaining you. I want to show the world that there is no idea or concept in the human experience that cannot be examined through Black life and culture" (qtd. in Whitaker 80).

Wilson has explicitly cited as key influences what he calls "my four B's: [artist] Romare Bearden; Imamu Amiri Baraka, the writer; Jorge Luis Borges, the Argentine short-story writer; and the biggest B of all: the blues" ("How to Write a Play" 5). Overt manifestations of these influences include *The Piano Lesson* and *Joe Turner's Come and Gone*, both inspired by Bearden paintings; *Ma Rainey's Black Bottom*, based on the famed blues singer; *Two Trains Running*, whose title comes from a blues song; and the mystical ending of *The Piano Lesson*, as well as the ghosts that pervade that play—and others—echoing the surrealism of Borges's work.

Wilson's plays invoke racial memory and heritage as well as a sense of community, and they are infused with poetic imagery and the supernatural. Filled with storytelling, the plays are noted for their strong sense of place, their authentic vernacular and dialogue—often racy and raunchy—as well as for their long, powerful monologues. Each play has only a single setting—a recording studio, a boardinghouse, a backyard, a cab station, a restaurant, and others—that provides the environment in which family and friends play out such themes as love, betrayal, integrity, dignity, and duty. And while his plays expose the oppression, abuse, and rejection that African Americans have endured in this country, they are never polemical (though the short historical prologues Wilson sometimes appends can be a bit incisive). The characters in Wilson's plays define themselves by their own racial heritage as well as by racism, and despite their economic and social hardships, they carry themselves proudly. Wilson's plays often feature characters who are slightly off balance mentally and act as a kind of comic relief, such as Hambone in *Two Trains Running*, obsessed with obtaining a ham for a job he'd done a decade earlier, and Gabriel in *Fences*, whose wartime head injury has left him rather childlike and fully convinced that he is the angel Gabriel. Such characters, as well as other elements in the dialogue and the characters' attitudes toward themselves and each other, temper the angry, hostile undercurrent of Wilson's plays and imbue them with humor, a sense of renewal, and the possibility of better days to come.

The first play Wilson wrote, *Jitney* (which was rejected by the O'Neill Conference), did not reach Broadway until 2000, although it had premiered in 1982 at Pittsburgh's Allegheny Repertory Theatre and had received many subsequent stagings. It is also the only play Wilson actually wrote in the decade in which it takes place. Set in *"a gypsy cab station"* in 1977, *Jitney* depicts the daily lives of cab drivers working in a dilapidated office that is threatened with impending demolition, ostensibly to be replaced by much-needed housing but more likely to go the way of neighboring buildings—boarded up and abandoned (11). The company is run by a stalwart man named Becker who is proud of doing work that contributes to the community and is determined to fight the land developers. "We ain't just giving rides to people," he says. "We providing a service. That's why you answer the phone 'Car service.' You don't say Becker's Cabs or Joe's Jitneys. . . . I want everybody to pull their weight and provide the service that's expected of us" (86). He also acts as a father figure, deflecting the bickering that often breaks out among the characters, although he is unable to assuage the relationship with his own son, Booster, who has just been released from a twenty-year prison sentence for murdering a white woman.

Jitney sets the stage for the central themes and techniques that define all of Wilson's subsequent plays. It is peopled by a variety of quirky characters, such as Turnbo, who cannot keep his nose out of other people's business, and the money-grubbing Fielding, always nipping at a bottle when no one is looking. All have their own tales, which are told through direct monologue or through stories recounted by other characters. The play also demarcates its historical framework through allusions to the Vietnam War, the demise of neighborhoods and the rise of inner-city slums, and increased opportunities for blacks to attend college and own homes, as well as through specific details such as the types of cars being driven. Furthermore, the play establishes a note of hope and renewal not only through Becker's determination to save the building, but also through the connection that Booster finally finds after his father's sudden death. The closing words of the play as Booster answers the phone, "Car service," suggest that he will try to carry on his father's heritage and dreams (96).

It was Wilson's second play, *Ma Rainey's Black Bottom*, that catapulted the writer to success. Based on the real-life "Mother of the Blues," celebrated recording star and mentor to Bessie Smith, the play takes place on a March afternoon in Chicago 1927—the only of Wilson's plays not set in Pittsburgh—and is perhaps the fullest expression of the blues as a primary influence on Wilson's drama. As he writes in the prologue, this is "music that breathes and touches. That connects. That is in itself a way of being, separate and distinct from any other" (xvi). Ma Rainey herself defines its black identity: "White folks don't understand about the blues. They hear it come out, but they don't know how it got there. They don't understand that's life's way of talking. You don't sing to feel better. You sing 'cause that's a way of understanding life" (76).

Ma Rainey's Black Bottom examines the exploitation of black artists in a recording industry dominated by whites, yet it also incorporates Ma Rainey's own manipulation of her band to attain her objectives—most notably, a faithfulness to her brand of blues over the emerging and more popular swing style. The central conflict is between Ma Rainey, a dynamic and domineering prima donna, and the hot-headed trumpet player Levee, the youngest band member, who rebels against what he considers "jug band" music, dreams of forming his own band, and insists on playing his upbeat version of the play's title song. The tension leads to the kind of explosive climax common to Wilson's plays that prompted one critic to praise his "gift for the seat-edging theatrical and thrillingly, mysteriously dramatic . . ." (Barnes, "Piano Lesson" 317). Furthermore, the delayed entrance of the main character, more than halfway into act 1, establishes this sense of suspense from the outset.

Perhaps Wilson's two best-known (and most anthologized) plays are those that won him Pulitzer Prizes: *Fences* and *The Piano Lesson*. Set in 1957, when "the hot winds of change that would make the sixties a turbulent, racing, dangerous, and provocative decade had not yet begun to blow full" (xviii), *Fences* centers on the stubborn, bitter figure of Troy Maxson, a garbage collector who resents having been denied the opportunity to play professional baseball because of his color. This is one of Wilson's most autobiographical plays, since his own stepfather, like Troy, had hoped for a career in sports, ended up in prison for years, and spent the remainder of his life in a menial job.

Two central conflicts shape *Fences*: that between Troy and his son, Cory, who aspires to a football career, and that between Troy and his long-suffering wife, Rose, who has stood by Troy for eighteen long years, despite his faults and shortcomings. Because of the discrimination in sports he suffered, Troy refuses to let Cory accept a college athletic scholarship, unwilling to recognize the opportunities increasingly available to blacks since Jackie Robinson broke the color barrier, and perhaps jealous that Cory would be able to achieve the dream denied to him. His insistence that Cory keep his job at the A&P or learn a trade, even as Rose tries to make him see that times are changing, deepens the gap between Troy and his son and ultimately becomes unbreachable. He causes a similar divide from Rose through his affair with another woman that produces a pregnancy. When the mother dies in childbirth, Troy brings the baby home, and though Rose agrees to raise her, she also affirms the dissolution of their marriage. "From right now . . . this child got a mother," Rose says, in perhaps the play's most poignant moment. "But you a womanless man" (79). *Fences* offers a powerful illustration of the changing opportunities for blacks that took root in the 1950s as well as of the inability of men like Troy to accept such possibilities and the resulting generational gaps. The title refers not just to the backyard fence Troy is building for Rose but to the social, economic, and cultural barriers blacks faced, as well as the boundaries that separate characters and ultimately destroy relationships. But there are also positive aspects in the hurdles that are overcome and in the prospect that the baby, Raynelle, will grow up in a new, more racially generous world.

The connection between past and present is more haunting and ghostly in *The Piano Lesson*, set in 1936 and inspired by Bearden's painting *Piano Lesson*. In this play, the piano is the central character and source of contention in the Charles family, descendants of slaves whose owners had bought the instrument—the price being two of the Charles' slaves. Boy Willie wants to sell the piano to buy the land in Mississippi on which their ancestors had toiled, but his sister Berenice refuses to part with it because it depicts the family's heritage. Long ago, their great-grandfather, also named Boy Willie, had carved onto the piano intricate images of the family and relics of their lives. The slave owner had only asked Boy Willie to carve the faces of the two Charles slaves who had been traded for the piano—the great-grandfather's wife and young son—because the master's wife missed them, but having done that, Boy Willie went on to sculpt a much more extensive totemic heritage. The piano came into the Charles family's possession when, after the slaves were freed, Berenice and Boy Willie's father stole it (and was subsequently killed), feeling that whoever owned the piano still owned the family. Because the piano tells the story of the family's ancestry, Berenice wants to keep it, while Boy Willie's desire to sell it represents his assertion over the whites both in profiting financially and in claiming the land that had enslaved them.

Joe Turner's Come and Gone was also inspired by a Bearden painting, *Mill Hand's Lunch Bucket*, and also contains spiritual and supernatural elements, such as African folklore and a conjure man with the power to "bind" people who have been separated. The play is set in 1911 when, as Wilson writes in his prologue, "the sons and daughters of newly freed African slaves wander into the city," alone and "cut off from memory" (iv), seeking new identities and better lives. The setting is a boardinghouse run by Seth and Bertha Holly that acts as a kind of way station for these uprooted people. The character of the title, Joe Turner—an actual historical figure who was the brother of Tennessee's governor at the time—never appears in the play, but his absence creates a powerful presence. Long after Emancipation, Turner captured and enslaved black men for a period of seven years each, and the play's title refers to a song sung by women whose men have been taken.

One of those victims, Harold Loomis, arrives at the boardinghouse with his eleven-year-old daughter, Zonia. He has been searching for his wife, who had left when Harold was enslaved by Turner. Bynum, the conjure man, says that Loomis has lost his song; indeed, Loomis is described as a man *"unable to harmonize the forces that swirl around him . . ."* (14), and the theme of the lost song is central to the play. Bynum recounts a supernatural story about how he rediscovered his, choosing "the Binding Song" that gave him the power to be "a Binder of What Clings" (10). Loomis engages Rutherford Selig, a white man known as the People Finder, to locate his wife; when he does, Loomis is finally able to say good-bye to her—because she had not waited for his freedom—and to begin a new life, "*Having found his song, the song of self-sufficiency, fully resurrected, cleansed and given breath . . .*" (93–94).

The desire to forge a new future also informs *Two Trains Running*, set in 1969 against the backdrop of assassinations and the demise of the civil rights movement. Indeed, Memphis's restaurant, where the play takes place—and which is slated for demolition—sits across the street from a funeral home, and a sense of death and turmoil permeates the play through the hordes that gather to view the body of the late Prophet Samuel, a popular preacher, and to attend a Malcolm X rally. Aside from these referencs, though, no specifics set the play in its time frame as clearly as some of Wilson's other works. Stefan Kanfer considers *Two Trains Running* to be "fatally sealed from the actual world," with no mention "of Vietnam, the youthquake, Martin Luther King Jr., the Kennedys, or any other global personalities or events" ("Two" 21).

While blacks have made some social and economic inroads by this time, racial injustice still prevails, and the notion that violence is the only recourse rumbles through the play in references to using guns for power and burning buildings for insurance money. Wilson has remarked that the title reflects two central ideas in the play "that have confronted black America since the Emancipation, the ideas of cultural assimilation and cultural separatism" (Pettengill 208). The element of the occult is also present, most notably in the figure of Aunt Ester, a kind of oracle said to be 322 years old and who, while never seen in the play, helps bring about the healing, hope, and liberation that ends the play.

Like Wilson's other plays, *Seven Guitars* is infused with the spirit of the blues linguistically and thematically, and with this play, Wilson again presents a central character who is a musician—Floyd "Schoolboy" Barton, who is on the verge of success. Set in 1948, the play addresses African American life in the post–World War II era, when blacks are still second-class citizens despite serving their country, and "history is viewed with blacks as the spiritual center" (Taylor 20). The structure of *Seven Guitars* is unusual, beginning and ending on the day of Floyd's funeral, with the intermittent scenes all in flashback. Having had one hit record, Floyd is planning to return to Chicago at the invitation of producers and wants his former girlfriend Vera to accompany him, even though he had abandoned her for another woman, a transgression he attempts to amend. In the end, Vera agrees to marry him. In a further reference to the blues, the character of Hedley—age fifty-nine and dying of tuberculosis—had been nicknamed "King" by his father in honor of the legendary jazz trumpeter "King" Buddy Bolden, and Hedley dreams that Bolden will return from the dead and provide him money for a plantation.

Bolden's spirit does not return, but some characters from *Seven Guitars* do resurface in *King Hedley II*, whose title character is the son of the prior play's Hedley. Like his father—in temperament as well as behavior—Hedley II committed what he felt to be a justified murder, and in the play, he has just been released from prison for this crime, a fight in which Hedley himself was physically disfigured. Returning to Pittsburgh, he schemes with a friend to sell stolen goods, ostensibly planning to use the profits to start a legitimate business. Other characters include Hedley's hard-edged wife Tonya, who is determined, against Hedley's wishes, to abort their child. Having already borne a daughter when she was only seventeen, and who is now herself a single mother, Tonya refuses to perpetrate the cycle of poverty and despair or to bring into the world yet another black youth who will be gunned down. Set in 1985, *King Hedley II*—like Wilson's other plays—addresses the disenfranchisement of African Americans, this time in the Reagan era when no supply-side economics have trickled down to the black community. Still, at least one critic considered *King Hedley II* to be "the first play in the cycle that does not feel strongly informed by the specifics of its time," noting that the world of the play "feels insular, timeless and unmoored from the real currents of the era"—a comment similar to Kanfer's critique of *Two Trains Running* (Isherwood 76).

Wilson's latest play, *Gem of the Ocean*, set in 1904, also involves the return of a character from previous plays: the mystical Aunt Ester from *Two Trains Running* and *King Hedley II*. But whereas she was an offstage presence in those dramas, in *Gem of the Ocean* she is a visible and powerful character, an ancient women who represents black America's links to its cultural roots and whose age corresponds to the number of years Africans have been in America. She also, Wilson acknowledges, "has become increasingly important to my way of thinking. . . . She has emerged for me as the most significant persona of the cycle" (qtd. in Gener 66).

Gem of the Ocean concerns the encounter between Aunt Ester and Citizen Barlow, a troubled and spiritually bereft man—like so many of Wilson's characters—who breaks into Aunt Ester's home, hoping "to get his soul washed" through her (Gener 21). She emerges in the play "as a mythic figurehead, an African-descended conjurer who inherits the mantle of power from her great-grandmother" and through whom "spirituality and belief can bridge the Atlantic gap between America and Africa, between life and afterlife, between the earthly and the superearthly" (Gener 67).

CRITICAL RECEPTION

In the two decades since August Wilson burst on the theatrical scene with *Ma Rainey's Black Bottom*, he has come to be considered one of the most important and prominent playwrights in America, and one who transformed the Great White Way into a venue for African American drama. His wealth of awards certainly reinforces this view, and the fact that four major revivals of his first Broadway play were staged in 2003—including another Broadway production—"further consolidates the belief that Wilson has spawned a veritable industry of his own . . ." (Gener 22). With *Fences*, William Henry acclaimed that "the American stage has not heard so impassioned and authentic a new voice" since the emergence of David Mamet ("Righteous" 320). And by the time *Seven Guitars* reached Broadway in 1996, Stefan Kanfer would write, "By now praise seems beside the point. Better simply to state that no other playwright has so skillfully portrayed the heritage and experience of an ethnic group in 20th-century America" ("Seven" 23). In addition, the spiraling number of books, articles, and reviews about the playwright and his work attests to the ever-increasing scholarly as well as popular interest in Wilson's drama.

Critical response to Wilson's work has generally been positive, although there have been plenty of mixed reviews as well as unabashed criticism, often for the tediousness and length of some plays (*King Hedley II*, for example, was pared down to about three hours by the time it reached Broadway, and *Seven Guitars* ran over four hours at its initial reading). Some of this variation can be attributed to Wilson's notoriety for prodigious revision as his plays work their way through regional theaters to Broadway, so that different critics may see very different versions of the play. Other criticisms have included imbalance among acts, weakness of plot, and a preponderance of monologues. Still, even critics who fault the structure of a play as a whole often note the striking, rich quality of individual scenes. Frequently, too, commendation is directed toward the leading actors, such as James Earl Jones, Theresa Merritt, and Charles Dutton. Aspects of Wilson's plays that are consistently lauded include the keen awareness of his characters' bonds to their African heritage as well as their sense of displacement in white America, his powerful storytelling ability, and the musicality and authenticity of the language. "He has the ear of a recording angel," wrote Kanfer. "I doubt if there is another author in America, or for that matter Europe, who has so faithfully reproduced the speech patterns and attitudes of a people" ("Seven" 23).

Wilson's Broadway debut garnered mainly praise, not only for the play itself but for the appearance of a new and powerful voice. *Ma Rainey's Black Bottom* was applauded for its insightful examination of racism in America, its blend of humor and suffering, and its use of what would become standard Wilson motifs: music and monologues. Frank Rich observed that "Wilson sends the entire history of black America crashing down upon our heads" ("Wilson's" C1), while Seymour Simon, in one of the few negative reviews, "felt Wilson had promise but didn't deliver a real drama" (qtd. in Shafer, *August* 32).

Wilson's two Pulitzer Prize–winning plays received curiously differing critical response. *Fences* was highly praised, with most criticism tempered by an overall positive review. John Beaufort found it "a work of exceptional depth, eloquence, and power" ("Fences" 318), while Clive Barnes suggests that Troy Maxson "will be remembered as one of the great characters in American drama" ("Fiery" 316), citing the play as "the strongest, most passionate American dramatic writing since Tennessee Williams" (317). Edwin Wilson said the play demonstrates how the playwright "can strike at the heart, not just of the black experience, but of the human condition" (317). While some critics desired more action, Richard Hornby notes that "like Chekhov, Wilson always keeps the plot subtly moving forward" ("Theatre" 470). The few negative criticisms include David Lida's complaint that plot turns are "achingly melodramatic" and the final scene "dismal" (321), while Thomas Disch harshly charges that the play had been overhyped, with the press treating it as "a kind of coronation ceremony" for the playwright (517).

The Piano Lesson, in contrast, while garnering much praise, also "received more hostile criticism than earlier plays," such as Robert Brustein's charge that it was "long and poorly written, and totally lacking in poetry" (Shafer, *August* 37). Many critics found the ending unsatisfactory, considering it too mystical, melodramatic, or unclear. But the wealth of positive response includes Frank Rich, who called it "joyously an African American play," yet one in which "the presence of white America is felt throughout" ("A Family" C13).

Wilson's subsequent plays have received similar mixtures of primarily positive response—focusing on his theatrical genius, the universality of his themes, his engaging mixture of naturalism and wonder, and his steady improvement in technique—tempered with the usual criticisms of structure, length, and troublesome conclusions. *Seven Guitars*, for instance, was described by one critic as a "sparkling play" that has "a powerful resonance," though to some degree, it "romanticizes black community life . . ." (Heilbrunn 42), while another critic wrote, "In its refusal to sentimentalize the past, *Seven Guitars* gives its cultural tradition new life on stage" (King, "World" 46). William Tynan calls it "[p]art bawdy comedy, part dark elegy, part mystery" but notes that it "loses its potency as it reaches its climax . . . tangled in a confusing thicket of mysticism and subplots" (71). Similarly, *Two Trains Running* was praised as "one of [Wilson's] most graceful and urgent plays" (Pressley 15) as well as "a vivid and uplifting tone poem" (Henry, "Two" 65), but also as "an airless, plotless work, full of follow-the-dots sociology and entry level symbolism" (Kanfer, "Two" 21).

Critical response to Wilson's latest work, *Gem of the Ocean*, remains to be seen. But of its Goodman Theatre premiere, Chris Jones remarked, "It's a powerful beginning to a singular series of works" and noted that, as the first play in Wilson's decade-long cycle—set in 1904—"one cannot help but think about how it will change the context of the works that followed" (39). Indeed, once the full cycle is completed, new evaluations of the works as a complete picture will undoubtedly be undertaken. And speculation is no doubt already underway as to what the future holds for August Wilson the playwright, once his magnum opus is finished.

BIBLIOGRAPHY

Dramatic Works by August Wilson

Black Bart and the Sacred Hills. Performed St. Paul, Minnesota, 1981.

Fences. New York: New American Library, 1986.

Fences and Ma Rainey's Black Bottom. Harmondsworth, Eng.: Penguin, 1988.

Fullerton Street. Unpublished.

Gem of the Ocean. Premiered Goodman Theatre, Chicago, April 18–May 24, 2003. Also produced Mark Taper Forum, Los Angeles, July 20–September 7, 2003.

"The Janitor." *Short Pieces from the New Dramatists*. Ed. Stan Chervin. New York: Broadway Play Publishing, 1985.

Jitney. New York: Overlook, 2001.

Joe Turner's Come and Gone. New York: New American Library, 1988.

King Hedley II. Premiered Pittsburgh Public Theater, 1999.

Ma Rainey's Black Bottom. New York: New American Library, 1985.

The Mill Hand's Lunch Bucket. Produced New York, 1983.

The Piano Lesson. New York: Penguin, 1990. Originally published in "August Wilson's *The Piano Lesson*." *Theater* 19.3 (1988): 35–68.

Seven Guitars. New York: Penguin, 1997.

Three Plays. Pittsburgh: University of Pittsburgh Press, 1991.

Two Trains Running. New York: Dutton, 1992. Originally published in "August Wilson's *Two Trains Running*." *Theater* 22.1 (1990–1991): 40–72.

Other Cited Material by August Wilson

"The Ground on Which I Stand." Keynote Address to Theatre Communications Group National Conference 26 June 1996. *The Ground on Which I Stand*. New York: Theatre Communications Groups, 1996. Also published in *American Theatre* 13.7 (1996): 14–16+.

"How to Write a Play Like August Wilson." *New York Times* 10 Mar. 1991: sec. 2, 5.

"I Want a Black Director." *New York Times* 26 Sept. 1990: 25A.

Studies of August Wilson's Dramatic Works

Anderson, Addell Austin. "August Wilson." *Contemporary Dramatists*. 6th ed. Detroit: St. James, 1993. 753–754.

Anderson, Douglas. "Saying Goodbye to the Past: Self-Empowerment and History." *CLA Journal* 40.4 (1997): 432–457.

Arkatov, Janice. "August Wilson: His Way." *Los Angeles Times* 7 June 1987: 35–36.

"August Wilson." *Contemporary Literary Criticism*. Vol. 39. Detroit: Gale, 1986. 275–282.

"August Wilson." *Contemporary Literary Criticism*. Vol. 50. Detroit: Gale, 1988. 266–271.

"August Wilson." *Contemporary Literary Criticism*. Vol. 63. Detroit: Gale, 1991. 446–459.

"August Wilson." *Contemporary Literary Criticism*. Vol. 118. Detroit: Gale, 1999. 370–422.

"August Wilson." *Current Biography*. New York: Wilson, 1987. 607–610.

"August Wilson." *Drama Criticism*. Vol 2. Detroit: Gale, 1992. 469–490.

Baker, Houston. A., Jr. *Blues, Ideology, and Afro-American Literature*. Chicago: Univeristy of Chicago Press, 1984.

Barbour, David. "August Wilson's Here to Stay." *Theater Week* 18 Apr. 1988: 8-14.

Barnes, Clive. "Fiery 'Fences.'" *New York Post* 27 Mar. 1987. Also publsihed in *New York Theatre Critics' Reviews* 48.5 (1987): 316–317.

———. "O'Neill in Blackface." Rev. of *Joe Turner's Come and Gone*, by August Wilson. *New York Post* 28 Mar. 1988. Also publsihed in *New York Theatre Critics' Reviews* 49.5 (1988): 320–321.

———. "'Piano Lesson' Hits All the Right Keys." *New York Post* 17 Apr. 1990. *New York Theatre Critics' Reviews* 51.5 (1990): 325–326.

———. "'Trains' Doesn't Run." *New York Post* 14 Apr. 1992: 138.

Barnett, Douglas O. "Up for the Challenge." "Forum: Plowing August Wilson's 'Ground': Four Commentaries on the Cultural Diversity Debate." *American Theatre* 13.10 (1996): 60–61.

Beaufort, John. "'Fences' Probes Life of Blacks in '50s." *Christian Science Monitor* 27 Mar. 1987. Also published in *New York Theatre Critics' Reviews* 48.5 (1987): 318–319.

———. "New Chapter in Wilson's Saga of Black Life." Rev. of *Joe Turner's Come and Gone*, by August Wilson. *Christian Science Monitor* 30 Mar. 1988: 21.

Bergeson, Eric, and William W. Demastes. "The Limits of African-American Political Realism: Baraka's *Dutchman* and Wilson's *Ma Rainey's Black Bottom*." *Realism and the American Dramatic Tradition*. Ed. William W. Demastes. Tuscaloosa: University of Alabama Press, 1996. 218–234.

Bigsby, C. W. E. *Modern American Drama, 1945–1990*. Cambridge: Cambridge University Press, 1992.

———. *Modern American Drama, 1945–2000*. Cambridge: Cambridge University Press, 2000.

Birdwell, Christine. "Death as a Fastball on the Outside Corner: *Fences*, Troy Maxson, and the American Dream." *Aethlon: The Journal of Sport Literature* 8.1 (1990): 87–96.

Bissiri, Amadou. "Aspects of Africanness in August Wilson's Drama: Reading *The Piano Lesson* through Wole Soyinka's Drama." *African American Review* 30.1 (1996): 99–113.

Bloom, Harold, ed. *August Wilson: Bloom's Major Dramatists*. Broomall: Chelsea House, 2002.

Blumenthal, Anna S. "'More Stories Than the Devil Got Sinners': Troy's Stories in August Wilson's *Fences*." *American Drama* 9.2 (2000): 74–96.

Bogumil, Mary L. "'Tomorrow Never Comes': Songs of Cultural Identity in August Wilson's *Joe Turner's Come and Gone*." *Theatre Journal* 46.4 (1994): 463–476.

———. *Understanding August Wilson*. Columbia: University of South Carolina Press, 1999.

Brown, Chip. "The Light in August." *Esquire* (Apr. 1989): 116–126.

Bruni, Frank. "From the Wings, A Prayer: A Black Troupe Improvises." *New York Times* 12 Feb. 1997: C9+.

Brustein, Robert. "The Lesson of 'The Piano Lesson.'" *New Republic* 21 May 1990: 28-30.

———. *Reimagining American Theatre*. New York: Wang, 1991.

———. "Subsidized Separatism." *New Republic* 19 and 26 Aug. 1996: 39–42. Also published in *American Theatre* 13.8 (Oct. 1996): 26–27+.

Ching, Mei-Ling. "Wrestling against History." *Theater* 19.3 (1988): 70–71.

Clark, Keith. "August Wilson." *American Writers Supplement VIII*. New York: Scribner's, 2001. 329–353.

DeVries, Hilary. "August Wilson: A New Voice for Black American Theatre." *Christian Science Monitor* 16 Oct. 1984: 29–30.

———. "The Drama of August Wilson." *Dialogue* 1 (1989): 48–55.

———. "A Song in Search of Itself." *American Theatre* 3.10 (1987): 22–25.

———. "Theater's Godfather Reaches Entr'acte." *New York Times* 30 June 1991: sec. 2, 1.

DiGaetani, John L. "August Wilson." *A Search for Postmodern Theater: Interviews with Contemporary Playwrights*. Westport: Greenwood, 1991. 275–284.

Disch, Thomas M. Rev. of *Fences*, by August Wilson. *Nation* 18 Apr. 1987: 516–517.

Elam, Harry J., Jr. "*Ma Rainey's Black Bottom*: Singing Wilson's Blues." *American Drama* 5.2 (1996): 76–99.

Elkins, Marilyn, ed. *August Wilson: A Casebook*. New York: Garland, 1994.

Euell, Kim. "Wilson's Worlds through African Eyes." *American Theatre* 20.5 (2003): 22–23.

Fitzgerald, Sharon. "August Wilson: The People's Playwright." *American Visions* 15.4 (2000): 14–19.

Freedman, Samuel G. "A Voice from the Streets." *New York Times Magazine* 15 Mar. 1987: 36+.

Gates, Henry Louis, Jr. "Department of Disputation: The Chitlin' Circuit." *New Yorker* 3 Feb. 1997: 44–55.

Gener, Randy. "Ma Rainey and Aunt Ester Sing Their Own Songs in August Wilson's Grand Cycle of Blues Dramas." *American Theatre* 20.5 (2003): 20–24, 66–67.

Gerstle, Alan. "Not Radical Enough." "Forum: Plowing August Wilson's 'Ground': Four Commentaries on the Cultural Diversity Debate." *American Theatre* 13.10 (1996): 59.

Glover, E. Margaret. "Two Notes on August Wilson: The Songs of a Marked Man." *Theater* 19.3 (1988): 69–70.

Goldman, Jeffrey. "Think of History as One Long Blues Tune: August Wilson." *Dramatics* 61.8 (Apr. 1990): 12–17.

Grant, Nathan L. "Men, Women, and Culture: A Conversation with August Wilson." *American Drama* 5.2 (1996): 100–122.

Gussow, Mel. "Fine-Tuning 'The Piano Lesson.'" *New York Times* 10 Sept. 1989: sec. 2, 19+.

Heard, Elizabeth. "August Wilson on Playwriting: An Interview." *African American Review* 35.1 (2001): 93–102.

Heilbrunn, Jacob. "Bus Boy." Rev. of *Seven Guitars*, by August Wilson. *New Republic* 27 Oct. 1997: 42.

Henry, William A. III. "Righteous in His Own Backyard." Rev. of *Fences*, by August Wilson. *Time* 6 Apr. 1987. *New York Theatre Critics' Reviews* 48.5 (1987): 320–321.

———. "Two Trains Running." *Time* 27 Apr. 1992: 65–66.

Herrington, Joan. *I Ain't Sorry for Nothin' I Done: August Wilson's Process of Playwriting*. New York: Limelight, 1998.

Hornby, Richard. "New Life on Broadway." *Hudson Review* 41.3 (1988): 512–518.

———. "Theatre: Our Middle-Aged Avant-Garde." *Hudson Review* 40.3 (1987): 465–472.

Isherwood, Charles. Rev. of *Fences*, by August Wilson. *Hudson Review* 40.3 (1987): 470–472.

———. Rev. of *King Hedley II*, by August Wilson. *Variety* 7 May 2001: 76.

Johann, Susan. "On Listening: An Interview with August Wilson." *American Theatre* 13.22 (1996): 22.

Jones, Chris. "Gem of the Ocean." *Variety* 5 May 2003: 39.

Kanfer, Stefan. "Seven Guitars." *New Leader* 3 June 1996: 23.

———. "Two Trains Running." *New Leader* 4 May 1992: 21.

Killen, Tom. "Black Theater Triumphant." *World and I* (Dec. 1987): 236–239.

King, Robert L. "Recent Drama." Rev. of *The Piano Lesson*, by August Wilson. *Massachusetts Review* 29.1 (1988): 87–97.

———. "World Premieres." *North American Review* 280.4 (1995): 44–49.

Kleiman, Dena. "'Joe Turner,' The Spirit of Synergy." *New York Times* 10 May 1986: 11C.

Lahr, John. "Been Here and Gone." *New Yorker* 16 Apr. 2001: 50.

Lida, David. "'Fences'—A Review." *Women's Wear Daily* 27 Mar. 1987. Also published in *New York Theatre Critics' Reviews* 48.5 (1987): 321.

Lieb, Sandra R. *Mother of the Blues: A Study of Ma Rainey*. Amherst: University of Massachusetts Press, 1981.

Little, Jonathan. "August Wilson." *Twentieth Century American Dramatists*. Vol. 228 of *Dictionary of Literary Biography*. Ed. Christopher J. Wheatley. 2nd ser. Detroit: Gale, 2000. 289–305.

Lyons, Bonnie. "An Interview with August Wilson." *Contemporary Literature* 40.1 (1999): 1–21.

McClinton, Marion. Introduction. *Jitney*. By August Wilson. New York: Overlook, 2001. 7–8.

McDonough, Carla J. *Staging Masculinity: Male Identity in Contemporary American Drama*. Jefferson: McFarland, 1997.

McKelly, James C. "Hymns of Sedition: Portraits of the Artist in Contemporary African American Drama." *Arizona Quarterly* 48.1 (1992): 87–107.

Miller, Russell. "On a Napkin in a Coffee Shop, Life Is Written (A Play, Too)." *New York Times* 3 June 1992: 1C.

Mills, Alice. "The Walking Blues: An Anthropological Approach to the Theater of August Wilson." *Black Scholar* 25.2 (1995): 30–35.

Mordecai, Benjamin. "The August Wilson Experiment: Buying Time." *American Theatre* 3.10 (1987): 26.

Moyers, Bill. "August Wilson." *A World of Ideas*. Ed. Betty Sue Flowers. New York: Doubleday, 1989. 167–180.

———. "August Wilson's America." *American Theatre* 6.3 (1989): 12–17+.

Nadel, Alan, ed. *May All Your Fences Have Gates: Essays on the Drama of August Wilson*. Iowa City: University of Iowa Press, 1994.

Nunns, Stephen. "Wilson, Brustein, and the Press." *American Theatre* 14.3 (1997): 17–19.

Oliver, Edith. "Boarding House Blues." Rev. of *Joe Turner's Come and Gone*, by August Wilson. *New Yorker* 11 Apr. 1988: 107.

O'Neill, Michael C. "August Wilson." *American Playwrights since 1945: A Guide to Scholarship, Criticism, and Performance*. Ed. Philip C. Kolin. Westport: Greenwood, 1989. 175–177.

Palmer, Don. "Interview with August Wilson: He Gives a Voice to the Nameless Masses." *Newsday* 20 Apr. 1987: 47.

Pereira, Kim. *August Wilson and the African-American Odyssey*. Urbana: University of Illinois Press, 1995.

Peterson, Bernard L., Jr., ed. "August Wilson." *Contemporary Black American Playwrights and Their Plays*. Westport: Greenwood, 1988. 505–506.

Pettengill, Richard. "The Historical Perspective: An Interview with August Wilson." *August Wilson: A Casebook*. Ed. Marilyn Elkins. New York: Garland, 1994. 207–226.

Plum, Jay. "Blues, History, and the Dramaturgy of August Wilson." *African American Review* 27.4 (1993): 561–567.

Pointsett, Alex. "August Wilson: Hottest New Playwright." *Ebony* (Nov. 1987): 68–74.

Powers, Kim. "An Interview with August Wilson." *Theater* 16.1 (1984): 50–55.

Pressley, Nelson. "'Two Trains Running' Chugs on Plenty of Steam." *Washington Times* 12 Jan. 1996: 15.

Rich, Frank. "August Wilson Reaches the '60s with Witnesses from a Distance." Rev. of *Two Trains Running*, by August Wilson. *New York Times* 14 Apr. 1992: 139–140.

———. "Panoramic History of Blacks in America in Wilson's 'Joe Turner's Come and Gone.'" *New York Times* 28 Mar. 1988: C15.

———. Rev. of *Fences*, by August Wilson. *New York Times* 27 Mar. 1987: C31.

———. "A Family Confronts Its History in August Wilson's 'Piano Lesson.'" *New York Times* 17 Apr. 1990: C13+.

———. "Wilson's 'Ma Rainey's' Open." *New York Times* 12 Oct. 1984: C1.

Rosen, Carol. "August Wilson: Bard of the Blues." *Theater Week* 9.43 (1996): 18–35.

Roudané, Matthew. *American Drama since 1960: A Critical History*. New York: Twayne, 1996.

Rush, Theresa Gunnels, et al. "August Wilson." *Black American Writers Past and Present: A Biographical and Bibliographical Dictionary*. Vol. 2. Metuchen: Scarecrow, 1975. 779.

Saunders, James Robert. "Essential Ambiguities in the Plays of August Wilson." *Hollins Critic* 32.5 (1995): 2–11.

Savran, David. *In Their Own Words*. New York: Theatre Communications Group, 1988. 288–305.

Schechner, Richard. "In Praise of Promiscuity." "Forum: Plowing August Wilson's 'Ground': Four Commentaries on the Cultural Diversity Debate." *American Theatre* 13.10 (1996): 58–59.

Shafer, Yvonne. *"August Wilson: A New Approach to Black Drama." Zeitschrift für Änglistik und Amerikanistik* 1 (1991): 17–27.

———. "Breaking Barriers: August Wilson." *Staging Difference: Cultural Pluralism in American Theatre and Drama*. Ed. Marc Maufort. New York: Lang, 1995. 267–285.

———. "An Interview with August Wilson." *Journal of Dramatic Theory and Criticism* 4.1 (1989): 161–174.

———, ed. *August Wilson: A Research and Production Sourcebook*. Westport: Greenwood, 1998.

Shannon, Sandra G. "Blues, History, and Dramaturgy: An Interview with August Wilson." *African American Review* 27.4 (1993): 539–559.

———. *The Dramatic Vision of August Wilson*. Washington, DC: Howard University Press, 1995.

———. "From Lorraine Hansberry to August Wilson." *Callaloo* 14.1 (1991): 124–135.

———. "The Good Christian's Come and Gone: The Shifting Role of Christianity in August Wilson Plays." *Melus* 16.3 (1989–1990): 127–142.

———. "The Long Wait: August Wilson's *Ma Rainey's Black Bottom*." *Black American Literature Forum* 25.1 (1991): 136–146.

———. "The Role of Memory in August Wilson's Four Hundred Year Autobiography." *Memory and Cultural Politics: New Approaches to American Ethnic Literatures*. Ed. Amritjit Singh, Joseph T. Skerrett, Jr. and Robert E. Hogan. Boston: Northeastern University Press, 1996. 175–193.

———. "A Transplant That Did Not Take: August Wilson's Views on the Great Migration." *African American Review* 31.4 (1997): 659–666.

Smith, Philip E. *"Ma Rainey's Black Bottom*: Playing the Blues as Equipment for Living." *Without the Dramatic Spectrum*. Ed. Karelisa V. Hartigan. Lanham: University Press of America, 1986. 177–186.

Staples, Brent. "'Fences': No Barrier to Emotion." *New York Times* 5 Apr. 1987: 1.

———. "Spotlight: August Wilson." *Essence* (Aug. 1987): 50–51+.

Stone, Les. "Wilson, August." *Contemporary Authors*. Ed. Hal May and Susan M. Trosky. Vol. 122 Detroit: Gale, 1988. 484–485.

Taylor, Regina. "That's Why They Call It the Blues." *American Theatre* 13.22 (1996): 18–23.

Tynan, William. "Seven Guitars." *Time* 6 Feb. 1995: 71.

Usekes, Cigdem. "'We's the Leftovers': Whiteness as Economic Power and Exploitation in August Wilson's Twentieth-Century Cycle of Plays." *African American Review* 37.1 (2003): 115–125.

Wang, Qun. *An In-Depth Study of the Major Plays of African American Playwright August Wilson: Vernacularizing the Blues on Stage*. Lewiston: Mellen, 1999.

Weales, Gerald. "American Theater Watch, 1984–1985." *Georgia Review* 39.3 (1985): 619–628.

———. "American Theater Watch, 1987–1988." *Georgia Review* 42.3 (1988): 592–604.

Weber, Bruce. "Sculpting a Play into Existence." *New York Times* 24 Mar. 1996: 7H, 9H.

Weeks, Jerome. "August Wilson Sings the Blues." *Dallas Morning New*s 18 Oct. 1992: 1C.

Wessling, Joseph H. "Wilson's *Fences*." *Explicator* 57.2 (1999): 123–127.

Whitaker, Charles. "Is August Wilson America's Greatest Playwright?" *Ebony* (Sept. 2001): 80–86.

Wilde, Lisa. "Reclaiming the Past: Narrative and Memory in August Wilson's *Two Trains Running*." *Theater* 22.1 (1990–1991): 73–74.

"Wilson, August." *Contemporary Authors*. Ed. Hal May. Vol. 115. Detroit: Gale, 1985. 477.

"Wilson, August." *Contemporary Authors*. Ed. Susan M. Trosky. Vol. 42. Detroit: Gale, 1994. 477–479.

Wilson, Edwin. "Theater: Wilson's 'Fences' on Broadway." *New York Theatre Critics' Reviews* 48 (1987): 317–318. Originally published in *Wall Street Journal* 31 Mar. 1987.

Wolfe, Peter. *August Wilson*. New York: Twayne, 1999.

X, Marion. "Out on a Limb, Reaching Back." "Forum: Plowing August Wilson's 'Ground': Four Commentaries on the Cultural Diversity Debate." *American Theatre* 13.10 (1996): 60.

CHARLAYNE WOODARD
(1955–   )

Christine M. Lemchak

BIOGRAPHY

Acclaimed actress of television, stage, and screen and now accomplished playwright, the multitalented Charlayne Woodard was born into a lively and gifted family in Albany, New York, on December 29, 1955. The oldest of five children, she credits her family as her personal and professional inspiration and foundation. Woodard remains close to her large extended family. She recalls that "[t]wice a month on Sundays . . . her family, which includes 25 first cousins, would gather 'to entertain Granddaddy. The loudest one got the floor'" (qtd. in Komaiko 1). It was these memorable Sunday afternoons that provided Woodard with the ideas for her plays.

As a playwright, Woodard, a voracious reader, claims to be a product of her studies. She mentions such puissant authors as Toni Morrison, Truman Capote, Jamaica Kincaid, Gloria Naylor, and Eudora Welty, as leading forces in her development as an artist (Komaiko 2). She also acknowledges one of her high school drama teachers, John Velie, as a person who taught her more than how to move about the stage effortlessly; he taught her the dynamics of creating and re-creating oneself for the benefit of the stage as well as the individual. The ability to alter one's persona with clarity and feeling takes more than a change of costume. A successful stage actress must convince the audience of her authenticity by drawing them into a *different* world, an imaginary world. This lesson seems to be one that Woodard has learned very well.

In 1977, after graduating from the Goodman School of Drama in Chicago where she was classically trained, Woodard "took $2000 and her violin and headed to New York City" (Peterson and Bennett 356). With a handful of monologues and a head full of idealism, Woodard began to make the rounds of auditions. She quickly won her first part in a revival of *Hair*, to be followed by a coveted role opposite Nell Carter in *Ain't Misbehavin'*. Because of her outstanding performance, Woodard went on to be nominated for "both a Tony and a Drama Desk" Award (Peterson and Bennett 356). After a decade of success acting in a number of plays, Woodard and her husband, screenplay writer Alan Harris, moved to Los Angeles in 1989. It was here that she began to expand her acting capabilities and took on the competitive venue of television and film. After several years of success playing myriad roles from daytime's *Days of Our Lives* to primetime's *Chicago Hope* to the made-for-TV movie *Run for the Dream: The Gail Devers Story*, Woodard felt compelled to return to her roots in the theater (Peterson and Bennett 356).

Because of her years spent in the more relaxed atmosphere of various film and television sets, Woodard became known for her entertaining storytelling abilities. She reminisced, "On the set for [the movie] *Eye for an Eye* . . . I told Sally Field a little story. She responded with, Ooohh. Then on location for *The Crucible* . . . we were on a little road in the country. . . . I started at the beginning of the story and kept going . . . people wanted to hear the rest of the story" (qtd. in Komaiko 1). It was these early experiences that brought Woodard to the conclusion that her life in Los Angeles was good for both her personal and her professional growth. It was when she was at the Actors' Studio in Los Angeles that she first put pen to paper. When unable to find an acting partner for a scene, she began to compose feverishly her own scenes by typing out her many memories from her colorful childhood ("Charlayne Woodard" par. 6).

After encouragement from friends, Woodard decided in 1993 to move forward with her first one-woman play *Pretty Fire* and had it staged at the Fountainhead Theatre in Hollywood. Opening to solid reviews, the play was then "moved to New York by the Manhattan Theater Club and taken by Seattle Rep" ("Charlayne Woodard" par. 10). In 1995, while in Seattle to perform her play, Woodard again provided the behind-the-scenes entertainment for the director and crew. Seattle Rep artistic chief, Daniel Sullivan, recounted, "[Charlayne] tells wonderful stories. . . . I'm attracted to her willingness to look at herself and her past and find those essential anecdotes that reveal her life and her character" (qtd. in Berson 3). It was after hearing Woodard's lively narratives involving her aunt Beneatha that Sullivan felt compelled to urge her to write another play. It was out of these conversations that Woodard's second one-woman play, *Neat*, was born.

Neat very quickly became a hit in Seattle, New York, and Los Angeles (Berson 3). With two successful plays and a bank of solid reviews, Woodard prepared to take a much-deserved rest. However, her supporters had other ideas. Again, Sullivan, from Seattle Rep, approached her to write another play. Woodard asserted, "The next script I write will be for more actors than just me" (qtd. in Berson 3). This idea, however, was not destined to be. Because of her passionate and happy recollections of her first years in New York in the 1970s, Sullivan convinced Woodard to once again compose a one-woman rendition of those turbulent years (Berson 3). It was at this time that Woodard wrote her third one-woman play, *In Real Life*. After a successful run in Seattle, *In Real Life* moved to the Mark Taper Forum in Los Angeles in July 2001 (Berson 3).

Charlayne Woodard has often been criticized for creating characters who seem to be so real that they are unreal. Skeptics have wondered how true to her family and experiences she has been. To those who scoff at the blatant and sometimes surreal intrafamily connectedness of her characters, Woodard has been known to retort, "We're loud. We do everything with everything we've got. My family gave me joie de vivre. Sometimes people don't think those plays are real. If they traveled to Albany they'd see" (qtd. in "Charlayne Woodard" par. 7).

MAJOR WORKS AND THEMES

Charlayne Woodard did not set out to be a playwright; it was the encouragement of friends and the memories of the theatrical racism that she encountered on Broadway that pushed her to create her own roles of substance. Calling to mind her first experiences in New York, Woodard describes her break into Broadway as a commingling of euphoria and frustration: "Basically, when people saw I was a black woman who could hold a tune, I was immediately pushed into musicals" (qtd. in Berson 1). The role of a singing, dancing black woman, however, was not enough for Woodard. She had come to New York "to do the real stuff, about who we are in our hearts" (qtd. in Berson 1). Overriding the good-natured pressure from friends, Woodard cites her dissatisfaction with the availability of substantial female parts as the prevailing motivation for creating her biographical one-woman plays: ". . . when there is nothing there, what do you do? You find yourself saying, 'I better go in there and create something.' And you do" (qtd. in Berson 3).

Woodard's first undertaking as a playwright culminated in her first of three one-woman plays, *Pretty Fire*. Tracing the events of her life from birth to age eleven, *Pretty Fire* is comprised of five progressively telling vignettes. The play appropriately opens with "Birth," in which Woodard brilliantly creates the first, harried moments of her life. Literally born into her mother's hand in their bathroom at home, she was a mere pound and a half at birth. With her second vignette, "Nigger," Woodard presents her first encounter with the ugliness of racism. During her tender years at grammar school, she was jeered with a racial slur during a track race. The experience was both eye opening and life altering for the young, innocent Woodard. Juxtaposed with her pleasant experiences in the classroom, Woodard's portrayal of the incident is particularly poignant. In her third vignette, "Pretty Fire," the inspiration for her title, Woodard again masterfully juxtaposes the lazy, hot, and humid summers she spent with her grandparents in the South and the horrifying cross burning she witnessed in their neighborhood. Looking at the horrid display of racism, the young Woodard is struck by a mixture of fear and wonderment regarding the "pretty fire." The fourth vignette, "Bonesy," recounts in chilling detail an incident of attempted rape. An older boy of questionable reputation in Woodard's neighborhood tries to assault her sexually. Woodard's disturbingly vivid performance brilliantly conveys both the confusion and the ugliness of the experience. In her final vignette, "Joy," Woodard brings to a close both her play and her childhood years. Rich in animation and spirituality, the final scenes depict her fulfillment of her grandmother's dying wish. Wanting all of her grandchildren to experience God's hand, Woodard's grandmother wishes for them to join the church choir. With "Joy," Woodard passionately recreates her first church solo.

Composed as an annex to *Pretty Fire*, Woodard's second one-woman play takes a closer look at a personal family relationship from her youth, that of her aunt Beneatha. Initially, Woodard had wanted to ask some of her fellow actors to take part in the play; however, once again, Daniel Sullivan, her friend and past director, convinced her that she was the only one who could bring *Neat* to the stage in a heartfelt and passionate manner (Berson 1). The play's namesake, Aunt Neat, was mentally challenged owing to an accidental poisoning during infancy that went untreated for several hours because the local hospital tended to "whites only." After her grandfather's death, Woodard's grandmother, "Mamma," and aunt Neat come to live with her and her family in Albany. Initially embarrassed, the teenage Woodard would have preferred to keep Aunt Neat a family secret. Her aunt, however, ends up being one of her greatest inspirations. As Woodard declares, *Neat* is the culmination of "my coming of age because of Aunt Neat's existence in my life" (qtd. in Komaiko 1).

The play follows Woodard's adolescence from age twelve to age eighteen. *Neat* becomes the vehicle for which Woodard brings to life the many trials and tribulations of growing up during the 1960s. From the attempts to tame her unstylish, unruly hair to the police beating of two hundred black students at a peaceful school gathering, Woodard recreates in *Neat* the 1960s through the eyes of a teenage girl. Broken into scenes by a lone piano in the beginning that builds to a full gospel choir, it is her childlike aunt Neat who pushes Woodard to discover her African ancestry and all that it means to be a black woman. The play ends with an epiphany for Woodard that is both horrifying and beautiful. As she witnesses her aunt Neat gently spread her imaginary wings and seemingly float over the edge of a steep cliff, Woodard moves from terror to a quiet knowing. Her aunt had done as she had always hoped. For just a moment, she had soared with the birds on the gentle breeze.

Woodard's most recent one-woman show is entitled *In Real Life*. It was with this play that she hoped to present the universal struggles and ideals that many young people experience in their lives. "It's about this young woman's journey and what I think we all go through in our twenties. . . . We believe we're immortal at that age and ready to step into the jaws of hell" (qtd. in Berson 2). Although some of her family members make brief appearances, the backdrop for Woodard's telling play is no longer her family or her childhood; it is simply she and New York City. Once more, she brilliantly reproduces the potpourri of people she encountered as she made her transition to big-city life.

Based on her first few years after her arrival in New York, Woodard works to transport her audience from her first experiences in the city to the dusty life of the backstage theater to one of her first auditions for Ntozake Shange's* play *for colored girls who considered suicide/when the rainbow's not enuf*. It is after this particular audition that Woodard first encounters some of the absurdity of Broadway. She is discounted as an option for a role because, as the director retorts, she didn't "have the stuff to be a colored girl" (qtd. in Stasio 43). To him, she did not appear to have "suffered one day in [her] entire life" (qtd. in Phillips 1). The senseless remark and its irony were not lost on Woodard. However, it was the 1970s, and "a time when black actors, [Woodard] says, were in great demand on Broadway—as long as they could 'sing, dance, and make people happy'" (qtd. in Kelly-Saxenmeyer par. 4). A particularly poignant moment in the play occurs when Woodard re-creates an incident of piercing pain that happened after her opening night performance for *Ain't Misbehavin,'* which earned her a Tony nomination. During the celebration, she is confronted by her father who remarks, "I couldn't stand to see you like that. . . . I can't stand to see any black person give it up like that, just to entertain somebody" (qtd. in Phillips 1).

The material of *In Real Life*, however, is not entirely weighty. Woodard's talents for characterization are utilized to the fullest once again. Her representations of a drug addict friend—mixed with priceless impersonations of her, at times arrogant, *Ain't Misbehavin'* costar Nell Carter—are impressively graphic. Woodard's passionate energy does not relent during her performance. She brings to a close her last one-woman play with as much artistic gusto and skillful narration as her first two.

It is reported that Ms. Woodard, along with pursuing her acting endeavors, is continuing to write plays, but this time she is embarking on new subject matter: "She firmly says no more one-person plays" ("Charlayne Woodard" par. 25). One of her plays in progress is tentatively entitled *Women Like Us* and is going to encompass the lives of Woodard's friends in New York City. As she declares, "I'm done with the family" (qtd. in "Charlayne Woodard" par. 25). Although no plot has been revealed, the second of Woodard's plays in progress is said to be entitled *I Came to Live Out Loud* (Peterson and Bennett 356).

CRITICAL RECEPTION

Charlayne Woodard's plays have been well received by both audiences and critics across the country almost without exception. Her booming voice, animated gestures, and dynamic delivery all add up to a captivating presence. She is to the stage as Norman Rockwell is to the canvas: sincere and real.

Woodard's *Pretty Fire* opened in Los Angeles in 1992 at the Fountainhead Theatre. Quick to receive critical acclaim, the play earned both an "NAACP Theatre Award for Best Play and Best Playwright, and a Los Angeles Drama Critics' Circle Award" ("Charlayne Woodard's" par. 3). As the enthusiastic reviews continued, the seats filled and the play was moved to the Manhattan Theatre Club in 1993. As the *Los Angeles Times* noted in 1992, Woodard's *Pretty Fire* is "a rare autobiographical tour-de-force so lustrous it seems to reinvent the whole solo-acting genre" (qtd. in "Charlayne Woodard's" par. 9). With sold-out performances across the country, Woodard's first one-woman play was a resounding success. Her characterizations were hailed as both heartfelt and genuine, a night of pure entertainment for audiences. Michael Greif, one of the play's artistic directors, remarked, "'Pretty Fire' is a powerful story of how a family's love of beauty, song and justice helped shape a remarkable human spirit" (qtd. in "Charlayne Woodard's" par. 6).

When questioned about the development of her second one-woman play, *Neat*, Woodard revealed that she is not a follower of the conventions of a playwright. Because of her strong acting background, she says, "I create from an actor's point of view, not a writer's. . . . I need to hear and see people reacting to my stories before I can [write them down]" (qtd. in Berson 3). Woodard's second play was as well received as her first. Opening to notable reviews, *Neat* was destined to follow the illustrious paths of its predecessor. With "sold-out runs at Manhattan Theatre Club, where it was nominated for an Outer Critics' Circle Award, Seattle Repertory Theatre and Mark Taper Forum," Woodard's play "was awarded the prestigious Irving and Blanche Laurie Theatre Vision Award" ("Charlayne Woodard's" par. 10).

Woodard's third, and she maintains last, one-woman play, *In Real Life*, continues the momentum her first two plays established. Hailed as pure and effortless, Woodard's presence is charismatic and her performances are eminent. *Los Angeles Times* theater critic, Michael Phillips, pronounced that in her latest play "Charlayne Woodard deftly glides through tales of her stage career. . . . [She] is pure pleasure in performance . . . with her own power supply—you could warm your hands on her smile" (1). With full audiences and lively reviews, Woodard does not seem to be slowing down. As her successes mount, she continues to strive as a playwright and an actress. Concerning Woodard's personal performance, Phillips expressed his admiration: "Without getting grandiose or sanctimonious, Woodard's solo—one woman's look back at where she was half a lifetime ago—is positively symphonic" (1). Anne Kelly-Saxenmeyer, theater critic for the *Santa Monica Theatre*, considers

Woodard's talents as a playwright and an actress to be awesome: "Her voice . . . is stunning, and she's an expressive physical presence, sculptural one moment, wobbly and comic the next. Absolutely charming all the way around" (par. 5). Once again, Woodard seems to have created with breathless reality a play of poignant slices of time, which clearly depict the many universal truths that encompass a "real life."

BIBLIOGRAPHY

Dramatic Works by Charlayne Woodard

In Real Life. Not yet released.
Neat. Dir. Stuart K. Robinson. Produced L.A. Theatre Works, 2000.
Pretty Fire. Dir. Stuart K. Robinson. Produced L.A. Theatre Works, 1999.

Studies of Charlayne Woodard's Dramatic Works

Berson, Misha. "Charlayne Woodard One On One." *American Theatre* 17.10, (2000): 1–3.
"Charlayne Woodard Creates Plays From Stories about Her Family." *Jam*. 19 Mar. 1997: 26 pars. 16 Sept. 2002 <http://www.canoe.ca/JamMoviesArtistsW/woodard_charlayne.html>.
"Charlayne Woodard's Award-Winning 'Pretty Fire' Has Its San Diego Premiere at La Jolla Playhouse on July 28." *La Jolla Playhouse News*. 28 July 1999: 13 par. 12 Apr. 2003 <http://www.lajollaplayhouse.com/news/fireopen.htm>.
Kelly-Saxonmeyer, Anne. "Woodard's Performance Is Perfect." *Santa Monica Mirror*. 3.8 (2001): 7 pars. 16 Sept. 2002 <http://www.smmirror.com/volume3/issue8/woodards_performance_is.asp>.
Komaiko, Leslee. "Story on the Set: Charlayne Woodard Has Been Telling Her 'Neat' Stories Since Childhood." *Los Angeles Downtown News*. 5 Jan. 1998: 8 par., 1–2 8 Sept. 2002 http://losangelesdowntown.com/archive/store/1998/OLD/ent086.html>.
Peterson, Jane T., and Suzanne Bennett, eds. "Charlayne Woodard." *Women Playwrights of Diversity*. Westport: Greenwood, 1997. 356–357.
Phillips, Michael. "Pleasures of 'Real Life.'" *Times Theater Review*. 31 July 2001: 1 pp. 17 Sept. 2002 <http://events.calendarlive.com/top/1,1419,L-LaTimes-Print-X!ArticleDetail-39533,00.html>.
Stasio, Marilyn. "In Real Life: A Theatre Review." *Variety* 388.10 (2002): 43.

RICHARD WRIGHT
(1908–1960)

Robert Felgar

BIOGRAPHY

Much of the material for the stage version of *Native Son* can be found in Richard Wright's childhood and youth. He was born near Natchez, Mississippi, in 1908, a time when black people in the South faced huge obstacles to their chances in life. In his autobiography, *Black Boy*, he recounts numerous incidents that taught him that he, like Bigger Thomas, the play's protagonist, was expected by whites to entertain only the most modest of ambitions. Just as Bigger knows he will never fly an airplane, so Wright knew he was not going to grow up to become a doctor or a lawyer. Largely self-educated and from a poor, unhappy family, which Wright's father abandoned, Wright nevertheless managed to do what Bigger was unable to do, namely, overcome his environment. Rejecting the South's judgment of him, he left in 1927 for Chicago, where he became interested in communism and worked for the Negro Federal Theatre.

In 1938, he published *Uncle Tom's Children*, a collection of short stories that included "Big Boy Leaves Home," which focuses on a group of young black males who also encounter white power as Bigger and his gang do. Two years later, Wright published the source for the stage version of *Native Son*, the novel of the same name. In his essay "How Bigger Was Born," he noted that Bigger was indeed a native son of America, an inevitable product of a racist environment, a theme that play retains. Why Wright himself did not become a Bigger Thomas is at least partially explained in *Black Boy*, published in expurgated form in 1945: it reveals a potential Bigger who transmutes fury into art, whereas the character Bigger accidentally kills a white woman out of uncontrollable fear of being discovered in her bedroom.

After World War II, Wright moved with his second wife and their first child to France, which served as a home base for his frequent trips to other European countries and to Africa; two books, *Black Power* (1954) and *White Man Listen!* (1957), results of his trips to Africa, can be used as the context for one of his two radio plays, *Man, God Ain't Like That . . .* , in that they present Wright's theory of what can happen when traditional African values engage with those of an imperialist West that has carved Africa up into colonies. Wright eventually came to see Bigger as part of a global framework that oppressed the nonwhites of the world.

His other radio play, *Man of All Work*, while based on a true story, may also reflect his experience growing up in a family in which a husband and father was not willing to perform any kind of work to support his family, as the protagonist in the play is. *Man of All Work* reveals Wright's personal knowledge of how discrimination against black men makes it difficult for them to be the sole breadwinners of their families.

MAJOR WORKS AND THEMES

Written in collaboration with a white playwright, Paul Green, *Native Son (The Biography of a Young American): A Play in Ten Scenes*, is based on Richard Wright's most famous novel, *Native Son*. It appeared on Broadway in 1941 under the direction of Orson Welles and was a popular and critical success. Wright and Green rely on the techniques of naturalism and symbolism to display some of Wright's key themes: injustice, racism, violence, and oppression. Bigger Thomas represents the product of America's racial hatred—an angry black man who accidently kills Mary Dalton (Daltonism is a form of color blindness) when he fears he is about to be discovered in her bedroom by Mrs. Dalton. Wright revises the bedroom scene in *Othello* to reflect the horror of American racial experience. Other character names also serve as emblems of thematic concerns: Mr. "Max" hints at Marx and the class struggle; Clara "Mears" (Bigger's girlfriend) suggest that she was merely an exploited black woman (Bigger uses her as a shield from the police bullets); and "old man Dalton" (the rat that lives in the Thomases' one-room tenement apartment) suggests that his human namesake devours his black victims. Because Wright's naturalism requires an emphasis on environmental determinism, Bigger is very much a product of poverty, ignorance, racism, and limited opportunity, but he cannot be accounted for completely by his background, as the final scene implies.

In addition to revealing Wright's reliance on naturalism and symbolism, the stage version of *Native Son* also proves his debt to traditional dramatic technique in its effective use of foreshadowing, irony, and melodrama. When Bigger kills old man Dalton with a skillet, we are being presented with a foreshadowing of what will happen to Bigger himself when the police chase him down for killing Mary Dalton. During his interview with Mr. Dalton for the position of chauffeur, Mr. Dalton tells Bigger, "Now . . . about this reform school business. Just forget about it. I was a boy myself once, and God knows I got into plenty of jams" (44). Mr. Dalton's "jams" turn out to be the killing of his own daughter in Bigger's case. Wright's effective use of melodrama can be seen in his use of the ubiquitous white cat and in the glowing furnace in which Mary is incinerated, although the earring she was wearing when smothered gives Bigger away.

Wright's other two plays, *Man of All Work* and *Man, God Ain't Like That* . . . , were misunderstood when they were published in *Eight Men* because it was not known then that they were radio plays rather than short stories, like the other five short stories in the collection (one piece, "The Man Who Went to Chicago," is an autobiographical sketch). *Man of All Work* relies on symbolism and irony to convey Wright's themes that black men have had to perform many different kinds of work to support their families and that passing for women has been one of them. To meet the last two payments of his mortgage, a black husband and father named Carl Owens takes a job as a maid under his wife's name, Lucy Owens. His white employers, the Fairchilds, are deceived until Mrs. Fairchild shoots and wounds Carl–Lucy after accusing him of making a pass at her husband, which leads to his exposure as a male. The play anticipates contemporary interest in cross-dressing and gender-bending, as it examines the links between sex, gender, race, and economics. Wright has a lot of fun laughing at the white family's hypocritical respectability—especially in light of Carl–Lucy's tight-knit black family and Mr. Fairchild's making a pass at Carl–Lucy, when he is passing as a woman. These thematic concerns are adumbrated by Carl's being a professional cook and a skilled giver of child care: his wife says, "You did it [burping the newborn] as well as I could" (112). Wright suggests that Carl is a man, in the sense of someone who puts his family first, whether or not he is wearing a dress.

Wright's third play, *Man, God Ain't Like That* . . . , examines Western cultural imperialism; it also registers the disastrous effects of Christianity's contact with traditional African religion: an American painter named John Franklin and his wife, Elsie, bring Babu, a young African, back to Paris, where he mistakenly concludes that John is Jesus. By killing John, Babu believes he will be able to have what whites have—buildings, airplanes, and so on. In a resonant, prospective irony, John mocks Elsie's concern that the African might eat them: "Ha, ha! Elsie, these savages think we're gods" (156). Wright also relies on irony to hold the play together when he has the inspector of police opine that Babu "had no motive whatsoever for committing the crime" (182).

CRITICAL RECEPTION

The dramatized version of *Native Son* was a critical success, although there were a few dissenting voices. In his review for the New York *Daily News*, Burns Mantle rated it very highly (8), and Walcott Gibbs said it was "one of the few satisfactory dramas of this unfortunate season" (34). The reviewer for the *New York Times*, Brooks Atkinson, described the stage version of *Native Son* as "realism with psychological overtones" (9). Joseph Wood Krutch, on the other hand, criticized the play as an inferior version of the novel (417). But Samuel Sillen contended that it was faithful "to the original" and achieved "independent vitality in the new medium" (28). The reviewer for the *New York World-Telegram* was extremely positive in his assessment, describing it as "a stark melodrama, touched by the hand of genius" (Whipple 14). When the play moved to Brooklyn, the reviewer for the *Brooklyn Eagle* was unusually enthusiastic about it, claiming there "is beauty in the play and force and vividness and a rich reality that few plays can boast" (Pollock E6).

Unfortunately, the reviews of *Man, God Ain't Like That . . .* and *Man of All Work*, both of which first appeared in print in *Eight Men*, were written by critics who thought Richard Wright was experimenting with new techniques for writing short stories. Irving Howe wrote that "there a few embarrassingly bad experiments with stories written entirely in dialogue" (18). Richard Gilman said the "two experiments—stories written entirely in dialogue—are painful to read" (131). He would be correct if his assumption were true, but the two radio plays did not receive fair treatment at the time of publication, 1961, because they were not read as plays.

BIBLIOGRAPHY

Dramatic Works by Richard Wright

"*Man, God Ain't Like That . . .*" *Eight Men*. 1961. New York: HarperCollins, 1989.
"*Man of All Work*." *Eight Men*. 1961. New York: HarperCollins, 1989.
Native Son (The Biography of a Young American): A Play in Ten Scenes (with Paul Green). New York: Harper, 1941.

Studies of Richard Wright's Dramatic Works

Atkinson, Brooks. "'Native Son.'" *New York Times*. (6 Apr. 1941: sec. 9, 1.
Draper, Muriel. "Citizen Welles." *Direction* 4 (Summer 1941): 9–14.
Gibbs, Walcott. "Black Boy." *New Yorker* 17 (5 Apr. 1941): 33–34.

Gilman, Richard. "The Immediate Misfortunes of Widespread Literacy." *Commonweal* 74 (28 Apr. 1961): 130–131.

Howe, Irving. "Richard Wright: A Word of Farewell." *New Republic* 144 (13 Feb. 1961): 17–18.

Krutch, Joseph Wood. "Minority Report." *Nation* 152 (5 Apr. 1941): 417–418.

Lee, Lawrence. "Evident Art Diluted by Uncontrollable Anger." *Chicago Sunday Tribune Magazine* 22 Jan. 1961: 4.

Mantle, Burns. "'Native Son' Stirs Audience to Emotional Pitch at the St. James." *Daily News* (NY). 25 Mar. 1941: 8.

Pollock, Arthur. "Playthings: Messrs. Wright, Green and Welles Make 'Native Son' a Little Epoch." *Brooklyn (NY) Eagle* 30 Mar. 1941: E6.

Redding, Saunders. "Richard Wright's Posthumous Stories." *New York Herald-Tribune Book Review* 22 Jan. 1961: 33.

Rosenthal, John. "Native Son: Backstage." *Theatre Arts* (June 1941): 467–470.

Sillen, Samuel. "Bigger Thomas on the Boards." *New Masses* 39 (8 Apr. 1941): 27–28.

Whipple, Sidney B. "Native Son Stark Drama Stamped with Genius." *New York World-Telegram* 25 Mar. 1941: 14.

MARVIN X
(1944–)

Michael E. Idland

BIOGRAPHY

Born Marvin Ellis Jackmon on May 29, 1944, in Fowler, California, Marvin X attended high school in Fresno at Edison High School. An individual involved with education on many fronts, he attended Oakland City College (now Merritt College) from which he received an associate's degree in 1964. Here, Marvin X forged a relationship with follow students Huey P. Newton and Bobby Seale, the founders of the Black Panther Party. Marvin X furthered his education, earning a bachelor's degree in English at San Francisco State College (now San Francisco State University) and a master's degree, also in English, from the same institution. His own teaching career is one of great breadth, ranging from the grammar school level to the university level. He has taught at such colleges and universities as Fresno State University, San Francisco State University, the University of California (Berkeley and San Diego), the University of Nevada at Reno, Mills College, Laney College, and Merritt College. One of his most significant marks on the black arts movement of the 1960s was the establishment of Black Arts/West (subsequently named The Black House), a theater in San Francisco's Fillmore district, which he founded along with playwright Ed Bullins* in 1967. The theater was deliberately established in the vein of Amiri Baraka's* Black Arts Repertory Theatre/School in Harlem. Having survived a dangerous period of drug abuse, Marvin X presently heads the Recovery Theatre (cofounded by Marvin X and Geoffrey Grier), also in San

Francisco, which is mostly staffed by, and produced for the betterment of, recovering addicts.

Marvin X's work is not to be assessed independently from its social context. He is indeed a key figure in the black arts movement; and the black arts movement, it must be remembered, is a major artistic component in the black liberation movement. Amiri Baraka, in whose footsteps Marvin X followed when founding Black Arts/West, states, "The Black Arts was significant because it sought to articulate and structure a black institution that could express and create the committed black art we knew must come to exist, side by side with and as a form of the Black Liberation Movement itself" (232). In accordance with this ideology, Marvin X sought not to create art to be appreciated merely for its aesthetics, an approach some argue is a perpetuation of an elitist social structure, but to strive toward the betterment of his own people—that is, the North American African people. Hence, Marvin X's drama and his politics must be considered in unison. Perhaps this is best symbolized by the fact that, for a time during the beginning of Black Arts/West's establishment, the building served as a headquarters for the Black Panther Party as well as a venue for the performing arts. During this time, the controversial Eldridge Cleaver—critic, activist, and writer—became a party member and was present at the headquarters. He and Marvin X (along with Huey P. Newton) developed a comradeship, which eventually became estranged; this is discussed in Marvin X's play *One Day in the Life*.

Having embraced the Muslim religion, Marvin X found himself the victim of racial and religious prejudice and injustice. Like other followers of the Nation of Islam, headed by Elijah Muhammad, the most famous of whom was Muhammad Ali, Marvin X vehemently refused induction into any of the United States armed forces during the Vietnam War. Tried and convicted, Marvin X traveled to Honduras via Canada while awaiting sentencing but was arrested and brought back to the United States. In extremely passionate, grounded, and articulate diction, Marvin X delivered a sharp statement in the form of a legal summation during his retrial. This summation was subsequently published in the *Black Scholar*. Of his forced return, Marvin X lashes out, "I was recently kidnapped in a conspiracy between the United States of America and the bootlicking neocolonial government of Honduras, and returned to the hells of North America" ("Black" 9). Speaking as a victim of religious discrimination, he cites one of numerous bans placed on him from teaching:

I attempted to teach in your so-called educational institution known as Fresno State College, but after being given a classroom, after having my courses approved by the college, after some 70 poor, Black and Chicano students registered for my classes—the school discovered I was a Muslim and obtained a court order to remove me from the classroom. Even before going to court, your governor,

Ronald Reagan, demanded that I be removed by any means necessary. So there is no future for me in America. ("Black" 10).

He further points to racial injustice that denies African Americans their basic rights by arguing, "If this were not true, I would not be in this court-room today, nor would the jails and prisons of America be filled with black men and women whose so-called 'crimes' are the direct result of the politi-cal–economic crimes of the United States of America, which has exploited our minds and bodies for the past 400 years" (Marvin, "Black" 8).

That Marvin X's revolutionary politics remains unchanged becomes ev-ident in his recent commentary on the American invasion of Iraq in 2003. He writes in his unpublished essay, "The New Nat Turner: Hasan Akbar" (a copy of which he e-mailed to me) about the violent actions of Hasan Akbar, a soldier in the United States Army who allegedly tossed a number of grenades into tents occupied by high-ranking American officials. In that piece he suggests, "Yes, we are the real threat to American security because we have no social security for ourselves, so why should our oppressors of 400 years feel secure? If every black man would just attempt to do what Hasan Akbar did, we would be offered reparations, including land and suf-ficient resources for the next 100 years." Such ideological and social radi-calism informs his theatrical work as well.

Considering theater to be a didactic platform, Marvin X intends his plays to serve an educational purpose. He explains the theory behind this purpose in an essay titled "The History of Drama as Therapeutic Educa-tion." He argues that the first-known examples of drama are African and were used to teach the African ritual of resurrection so that Egyptians would learn the proper way from their present lives to the afterlife. He notes that the "ancients" presented the proper model for manhood and womanhood in the form of drama, and it was through participation in these dramas that the young were trained to become positive men and women. Because these dramas corrected any problematic areas in the pupils' lives, Marvin X appreciates the ability of ancient African drama to heal an individual and even a people. This philosophy propels Marvin X's Recovery Theatre. Speaking of the drama currently being performed there and of the drama of the black arts movement as a whole, Marvin X force-fully declares, "Yes, in the original African manner, drama prepared North American African youth for the adulthood of revolutionary action. Drama came full circle—returned to its ancient roots as myth-ritual theatre, a heal-ing/educating/liberating vehicle" ("History" par. 9). Indeed, the plays of Marvin X, in addition to their artistic sophistication, do help foster a heal-ing process; they inform the audience of the urgency of the contemporary social crisis, invite critical engagement with compelling political issues, and encourage meaningful action toward fundamental transformation of American Society.

MAJOR WORKS AND THEMES

Marvin X's first play that placed him in the thick of the black arts movement is titled *Flowers for the Trashman* (also produced with an alternate title, *Taking Care of Business*). Concise and powerful, the one-act play takes on important issues embedded in the social strife of African Americans (particularly African American males) in the United States in the 1960s; it rings of truth and relevance today as it did then. The play is set in an unidentified jail cell, and the audience views the majority of the action through the bars of the cell. The play's protagonist, Joe Simmons, an African American college student, finds himself in jail with Wes, whom the playwright describes as "his hoodlum friend" (541). Although the implied action that precedes the opening scene is rather ambiguous (probably by design for a broad statement), it becomes known that the two have been put in jail after an altercation with the police. Apparently, Wes, on his way home with Joe from a dance they had attended, directed harsh words to the police after the police nearly ran Wes and Joe down in their patrol car. Little more is revealed about their legal situation, but another young black character, named only as Negro, is thrown into the jail cell for allegedly stealing a white woman's purse—an accusation that he flatly denies, chiefly, because he is already on parole and therefore would face serious legal consequences if found guilty of another crime.

The overt presentation of black males unjustly held in the prison system speaks literally to the disproportionate percentage of black males in American jails and prisons and metaphorically to the oppressive society of captivity that Marvin X sets out to expose. Equally important is Marvin X's exploration of the devastating effects of internalized racism and the psychic damage it does. For example, recalling the words of a black woman about his father, Joe reiterates that "you can't depend on no nigger, you know that" (548). This theme of ethnic self-loathing reappears several times as Joe and Wes, who clearly do like each other, are driven to hateful words toward each other by the frustration their unjust circumstance generates. However, once a white man is present in the cell, apprehended for an unidentified charge, Joe turns his aggression toward him: "You scared of us niggers, Charlie? Why you scared? You made me, baby. Think on that. You made me. I'm your creation. You defined me, told me my limits, my possibilities. Yeah, everythin' I believe in: God, the devil, democracy, all that bullshit, you gave to me, gave to me outta the kindness of your heart" (552–553). Joe's rhetoric reminds one of Malcolm X's language. But, always speaking directly to his audience, Marvin X crafts Joe's character to encompass more than the militant attitude of Malcolm X. Joe also reveals a more passive or nonviolent attitude toward blatant racist discrimination that may represent a philosophy more like that of Dr. Martin Luther King, Jr. when he attempts to calm an irate Wes, who has just been called "nigger" by the jailer. Such delicate incorporation of references to known figures of the struggle for black freedom not only confirms the breadth of thought informing Marvin X's writing but makes clear to the audience that the play and its message are to be taken as part of that struggle.

Another such figure effectively referenced is the prolific novelist, essayist, and playwright James Baldwin.* Baldwin's role in this play, however, points to the largest issue at hand in *Flowers for the Trashman*—the identity of the black family—rather than at the conflict between races. Speaking of Baldwin, Joe says, "Yeah, I think he's pretty cool; he's honest. He's a writer that wants to be a man; that's what I want to be, a man" (555). Throughout the play, Joe is very concerned with his own manhood and that of his recently estranged father, a vendor of flowers to whom the title refers. This grappling with manhood in relation to fathers is at play also with Wes, who has never seen his father. Again, with a pulse on the life of his people, Marvin X examines what was often referred to as the "crumbling" black family. At the time of *Flowers for the Trashman*, sociologists, when commenting on the condition of African American families, maintained that many African American fathers, owing to economic racism, were unable to provide sufficiently for their families and, thus, lost both self-respect and the respect of their families for the fathers. Such is the case with Joe's father, who is never directly present in the play although he is spoken of (and to, during a telephone call) in each scene. Joe's father is spoken of harshly by Joe and other characters because of his struggling business selling flowers. Although Joe seems to understand that social and economic circumstances are responsible for his father's hardships, he is caught in a paradox and retains great anger toward him, citing his lethargic work habits and broken promises. While speaking to his father on the phone to request his help in bailing him out, Joe says to him, "Hell, man, don't nobody respect you. . . . I heard niggers talkin' about you. Don't make no difference who it was. Naw it doesn't, not if they were tellin' the truth. . . . Man, you ain't shit. That's right—you're not shit—no, not a goddam thing. Ah, go to hell; just take a merry ride to hell" (551). Ironically, Joe's father dies en route to bail Joe out from jail. Joe is crushed and is jolted into a dazed but cathartic moment with respect to his issues of hatred and manhood. He addresses Wes, but is speaking to himself and the audience, and concedes, "He was a man, wasn't he? I was his son. . . . That's why I gotta start doin' something—I wanna talk to ma sons" (558). The revelation suggests a need for communication in the midst of racial struggle and a need for loyalty, familial solidarity, and action.

Marvin X speaks more directly from a Muslim perspective on race relations in America in his play *The Black Bird (Al Tair Aswad)*. A structurally simpler and more succinct play, the entirety of the action consists of a dialogue between two young black sisters, aged six and seven, and a young black man, a writer approximately twenty-six years old. The young girls are meeting their neighbor, a follower of the Nation of Islam, for the first time and are engaged by the basic Muslim ideas of black identity. The man tells the girls that he is their brother because they have the same father, Allah. They question this, and it is explained to them: "He's the leader of our people—the Black people. The white folks have a leader and we have a leader. They have a president—Nixon—and we have a president, Elijah Muhammad" (112). Similar exchanges reveal to the girls that their last name cannot be Jones, "a white man's name"; "the white man is the devil"; "Heaven is on Earth," rather than in the sky; and that their parents are living in a hell characterized by hard work with little pay. Before the two sisters leave, the young man tells them a story about a black bird, which is an allegory about Allah's children. In the young man's allegory, which comprises what is nearly the majority of the play's text, a black bird lives in a cage in a white house and prefers his master's way of life, his songs, and his food to those of other birds. The master, who has become rich by exploiting the bird for his singing and tricks, leaves the bird's cage open in confidence that it will not fly away. Despite repeated attempts by other birds to convince the black bird to fly away to freedom, he will not leave. Even when the white house catches fire, it takes another bird's physical force to remove the bird and fly him to a new home of freedom. The girls promise not to be "black birds," and before the girls leave the young man's apartment, he teaches them a simple Muslim exchange: "As-Salaam-Alaikum—that means peace be unto you. You say: Wa-Alaikum-Salaam [and on you be peace]" (118).

In addition to offering a clear, if simplified, rendition of the teachings of Elijah Muhammad with respect to the necessity for North American Africans to break free from the imposing and oppressing white power structure, *The Black Bird* can also be interpreted as an exercise in recruitment to Islam. Scholars of Islam in the United States confirm that entertainment, such as drama and song, has been widely used as a recruitment tool for the Nation of Islam. Such recruitment may take place in any number of places ranging from bars to college campuses—addressing the people of each establishment with appropriate language that can be understood. Therefore, teaching through question and response in combination with storytelling would be ideal for the recruitment of young children such as the ones in *The Black Bird*. Knowing that Marvin X writes drama to educate and help his people, one must assume that the play itself is meant to explain to the audience—on all intellectual levels—the very same lesson that is explained to the girls in the story.

Marvin X's most recent production, *One Day in the Life*, performed by his Recovery Theatre, explores his own addiction to crack cocaine and the catastrophic impact it had on his life and on the lives of many of his loved ones. Much longer than his previous work, it completely breaks from traditional dramatic form to achieve maximum educational effect. Available as a taped performance through Black Bird Press, the action of the play is interspersed with lectures from Marvin X to the audience in which he comments on the dreadful condition of addiction in the context of a racist society. Marvin X's abilities as an orator and his professorial skills are unmistakable, and the audience, which can be heard on the recording, is extremely engaged by his message.

The play opens with a very forward, lengthy, and intentionally irritating scene depicting a younger Marvin X and a female character, listed as Crack Ho, involved in an exchange of crack cocaine for oral sex. Clearly indicative of some addicts' denial, each character ironically fires insulting remarks at the other for his or her sad condition. The exchange is successfully delivered in large part as comedy, but this relates directly to the racial struggle—a parallel that is easily overlooked. For this reason, considering that the play is being performed for an audience primarily composed of recovering African American addicts, the inherent hypocrisy and paradox of such individuals unwilling to fight the drug crisis in their community is complex and requires the eloquent explication from the playwright and professor. He lectures to the audience:

Think about this . . . with all the professors that we [Africans in America] have, all the doctors, all the engineers, all the preachers on every fucking corner, why is the dope man the number one employer of our youth coast to coast? Think about that. You mean to tell me that all these niggers with all these brains, with all these degrees can't figure out a creative way to employ our youth, but the dope man can? . . . That's pitiful! (21)

After allowing this harsh fact to set in, Marvin X gives a brief and humorous account of his time in the "nut house." Always with a racial objective, he uses this to set up his audience for a powerful call for action from the black community. He says what is needed is "an ass-whopping. You need a black bullwhip over your black ass. Do you understand?" (23). Marvin X seems to be pointing to what he perceives to be inaction and indifference among many African Americans to the crisis in their communities.

The play proceeds similarly in a series of flashbacks to Marvin X's past, followed by speech from Marvin X himself. The flashbacks show his troubled relationships with his children, his "woman," his peers, his people, and himself. The culmination of the action is a flashback to Marvin X's last encounter with his dear friend Huey P. Newton in a crack house in Oakland. During this meeting the two are in the presence of a young black male involved with drug dealing, and the two men discuss their revolutionary days dating back to their school days at Oakland City College. At this point, the stage is set to expose what is arguably the main problem impeding significant progress in the black liberation movement. It is widely argued that a void of leadership in the African American communities has developed, and, as a consequence, the youth of those communities, the people most apt to take action against their social restraints, have been left with no role models from which to learn and draw inspiration toward that action. As the founder of the Black Panther Party and a major playwright from the black arts movement sit in front of this young boy high on crack, the audience must agree with this claim at the moment. Although Newton's character says that the black youth needs ideology, the young boy understandably lashes out at the two fallen figures: "You niggers is dope fiends. You ain't no revolutionaries, so don't say shit to me about no program. . . . You some punk bitch niggers. When you get your shit together, we'll have some respect for you, but until then, don't say shit to us about no revolution! . . . Don't be no walking contradiction, my niggers!" (32). Here, the audience must recognize the matured and humbled voice of Marvin X, as a playwright, who transcends the condition of ethnic shame in order to educate and lift the very people that he and his contemporaries had temporarily abandoned. The play is also punctuated by a series of tragic deaths: Marvin X's female companion, from cancer; his son, from suicide; Newton, because of murder; and his parents, who passed away while Marvin X was still on crack. The play speaks to the horror of drug addiction in the African American communities as well as the racism that at least partly produces and sustains it. However, *One Day in the Life* is also a motivational and educational celebration of recovery from such horror.

Having emerged from the physical and emotional constraints of drug addiction, Marvin X forges forward once again in continuation of his work to better the lives of his people. His people, now, are not only North American Africans but also people who suffer from addiction, especially those who fit into both categories. He remains an active writer of drama, poetry, critiques, and essays, and maintains a Web site called *Marvin's World* (www.marvinx.com), which contains information on the Recovery Theatre, recent writings, events, Black Bird Press, and contact information including an active e-mail address, which he checks regularly. From this modern platform, he takes a proactive approach to informing those in contact with him over the Internet of developments in his work and in the work of others striving toward freedom and equality for the African American people. His drama has made a significant mark on American theater and the black arts movement in particular. A vehicle for his people, his plays are a voice of identity and intellect, oppression and resistance, rage and reason. It is an eloquent and urgent voice that needs to be heard.

CRITICAL RECEPTION

Criticism of Marvin X's plays is extremely limited. The playwright himself has asserted that this can be, in large part, attributed to racism. Of *One Day in the Life*, he claims with certainty that if it were written by a white person instead of himself, it would be on Broadway or at least have significant corporate sponsorship ("Racism" par. 11). However, this does not mean that his work is unpopular. Lorenzo Thomas, in his entry on Marvin X in the *Dictionary of Literary Biography*, explains that "his work did not receive substantial critical comment even in the journals of the black arts movement, yet [his work] continues to be highly praised by word of mouth" (183). Indeed, the great popularity of his best-known work, *Flowers for the Trashman*, can be measured only in the widespread attention it received at its time from "growingly politicized audiences in the black community" in addition to the high praise Marvin X received (Thomas 180), after writing the play, from other respected African American playwrights such as Ed Bullins and Amiri Baraka. For example, Baraka highlights the importance of *Flowers for the Trashman* (referred to as *Taking Care of Business*) in his "Black Theater in the Sixties." Recalling a Black Communications Project in 1967, which he headed, Baraka says that "we sent a black theatre/poetry tour up and down the West Coast that included Bullins' *How Do You Do?*, Marvin X's *Taking Care of Business*, *The First Militant Preacher* by Ben Caldwell, my own *Madheart*, [and] *Papa's Daughter* by Dorothy Ahmad" (234). The necessity to present Marvin X's play is confirmed by Ed Bullins in an interview with Marvin X in which he alludes to Black Arts/West and explains, "There was no Black theatre to do your plays in then. If you were in San Francisco, as we were, you knew there was nobody to do *Flowers for the Trashman*. Black people had to come together and create our own theatre" (ix). Such narrow but weighty praise is fitting for the play, which is aimed specifically at the African American community and, by the very nature of its content, discourages positive attention from writers and critics who are members of the empowered class of which Marvin X is so critical.

The simpler play *The Black Bird (Al Tair Aswad)* earns negative criticism from Thomas. He calls it "transparently propagandistic but quite effective when staged" (182). Apparently taken with the religious component of this play along with other works (including the poetry) of Marvin X, Thomas contests Marvin X's prowess in contributing to social change. He claims, "Although Marvin X emerged form an extremely politicized era and enthusiastically confronted the issues of the day, his work is basically personal and religious and remains most effective on that level" (184). To this end, Amiri Baraka, in an interview titled "Islam and Black Art" with Marvin X, states that "that's what art is supposed to be about: to collect that Divinity, to show its existence, to praise it and damn things that are seemingly trying to throw themselves against it. The artist's words, the signs, the symbols, the artifacts are magic things; they're supposed to be able to suggest the presence of Allah" (148).

Among Marvin X's plays, *One Day in the Life* certainly deserves greater attention in major venues than it has received. Among the sparse reviews of the play is one by Steven Winn, a theater critic for the *San Francisco Chronicle*. Winn acknowledges that Marvin X's intended message is larger than an account of his own drug addiction, and, in consideration of the play's form, he concludes, "The private drama of addiction, with its staggering social cost, doesn't lend itself to neat dramatic formulas. Soap opera, farce, didacticism, naturalism and even a healthy skepticism about recovery itself are part of the mix" (par. 8). The critic, however, argues that the play does not depict the arduous process of recovery. Yet, Winn implicitly (and perhaps unconsciously) acknowledges the production's success as a means of recovery when he concedes that "this Recovery Theatre production has the overtones of a 12-step meeting" (par. 8). Due in significant part to the strong performances from The Recovery Playaz but in chief to the wonderfully complex and honest script, what cannot be overlooked is the play's power. Of this, Winn writes, "'Life' has the absorbingly raw authority of a documentary" (par. 9). Undoubtedly, the play's effectiveness, in Marvin X's eyes, shall be determined not by critical reviews but by the number of recovering addicts it helps or saves and by the degree to which people's consciousness of the need for African American struggle against oppression is heightened.

BIBLIOGRAPHY

Dramatic Works by Marvin X

"*The Black Bird (Al Tair Aswad): A One-Act Play*." *New Plays from Black Theatre*. Ed. Ed Bullins. New York: Bantam, 1969. 109–118.
Come Next Summer. Produced Black Arts/West, San Francisco, 1966.
"*Flowers for the Trashman*: *A One Act Drama*." *Black Fire: An Anthology of Afro-American Writing*. Ed. Amiri Baraka and Larry Neal. New York: Morrow, 1968. 541–558.
In the Name of Love. Oakland: Laney College Theatre, 1981.
One Day in the Life. Oakland: Black Bird, 2001.
Resurrection of the Dead. Produced Your Black Educational Theatre, San Francisco, 1972.

Other Cited Material by Marvin X

"Black Justice Must Be Done." *Black Scholar* 2.8 (1971): 8–11.
"The History of Drama as Therapeutic Education." *Marvin's World: Home of Recovery Theatre and Black Bird Press*. 3 Nov. 1999: 21 pars. 1 Mar 2003 <http://www.marvinx.com/news3791.html#drama>.
Marvin's World: Home of Recovery Theatre and Black Bird Press. Home Page. 13 May 2003 <http://www.marvinx.com>.
"The New Nat Turner: Hasan Akbar." E-mail from the author, 23 Mar. 2003.
"Racism and Recovery." *Marvin's World: Home of Recovery Theatre and Black Bird Press*. 30 Apr. 2000: 18 pars. 1 Mar. 2003. <http://www.marvinx.com/new 3791.html#racism>.

Studies of Marvin X's Dramatic Works

Baraka, Amiri. "Black Theatre in the Sixties." *Studies in Black American Literature II: Belief vs. Theory in Black American Literary Criticism*. Ed. Chester J. Fontenot and Joe Weixlmann. Greenwood: Penkevill, 1986. 225–237.

Baraka, Amiri. Interview. "Islam and Black Art: An Interview." *Black Arts: An Anthology of Black Creations*. Ed. Ahmed Alhamisi and Harun Kofi Wangara. Detroit: Black Arts, 1969. 144–158.

Bullins, Ed. Interview. *New Plays from Black Theatre*. Ed. Ed Bullins. New York: Bantam, 1969. vii–xv.

Thomas, Lorenzo. "Marvin X (Marvin E. Jackmon, Nazzam Al Fitnah Muhajir, El Muhajir)." *African American Writers after 1955: Dramatists and Prose Writers*. Vol. 38 of *Dictionary of Literary Biography*. Ed. Thadious M. Davis and Trudier Harris. Detroit: Gale, 1985. 177–184.

Winn, Steven. "'Day' a Searing Account of Addiction." *San Francisco Chronicle* 7 Dec. 1998: 9 pars. 28 May 2003 <http://sfgate.com/cgi-bin/article.cgi?file=/chronicle/archive/1998/12/07/DD92875.DTL>.

SELECTED BIBLIOGRAPHY

Abramson, Doris E. *Negro Playwrights in the American Theatre, 1925–1959*. New York: Columbia University Press, 1969.

Archer, Leonard C. *Black Images in American Theatre*. Nashville: Pageant, 1973.

Bond, Fredrick W. *The Negro and the Drama*. Washington, DC: Associated, 1940.

Brown, Sterling. *Negro Poetry and Drama and the Negro in American Fiction*. 1937. New York: Atheneum, 1969.

Brown-Guillory, Elizabeth. *Their Place on the Stage: Black Women Playwrights in America*. Westport: Greenwood, 1988.

Craig, E. Quita. *Black Drama of the Federal Theatre Era: Beyond the Formal Horizon*. Amherst: University of Massachusetts Press, 1980.

Fabre, Genevieve. *"Drumbeats, Masks, and Metaphor." Contemporary African American Theatre*. Cambridge: Harvard University Press, 1983.

Harrison, Paul Carter, Victor Leo Walker II, and Gus Edward, eds. *Black Theatre: Ritual Performance in the African Diaspora*. Philadelphia: Temple University Press, 2002.

Hay, Samuel A. *African American Theatre: A Historical and Critical Analysis*. New York: Cambridge University Press, 1994.

Hill, Errol, ed. *Theatre of Black Americans: A Collection of Critical Essays*. 2 vols. Englewood Cliffs: Prentice, 1980.

Isaacs, Edith. *The Negro in the American Theatre*. New York: Theatre Arts, 1947.

Keyssar, Helene. *The Curtain and the Veil: Strategies in Black Drama*. New York: Franklin, 1981.

Mitchell, Loften. *Black Drama: The Story of the American Negro in the Theatre*. New York: Hawthorn, 1967.

Molette, Carlton W., and Barbara J. Molette. *Black Theater: Premise and Presentation.* Bristol: Wyndham Hill Press, 1986.

Sampson, Henry T. *Blacks in Blackface: A Sourcebook on Early Black Musical Shows.* Metuchen: Scarecrow, 1980.

Toll, Robert C. *Blacking Up: The Minstrel Show in Nineteenth Century America.* New York: Oxford University Press, 1974.

Williams, Mance. *Black Theatre in the 1960s and 1970s: A Historical-Critical Analysis of the Movement.* Westport: Greenwood, 1985.

Woll, Allen. *Black Musical Theatre: From "Coontown" to "Dream Girls."* Baton Rouge: Louisiana State University Press, 1989.

INDEX

Aldridge, Ira, 1–6
Alexander Plays, The, 275–276
Alice in Wonder, 127, 128
All White Castle, 83, 86
Amen Corner, The, 8, 11–12, 141
Angelo Herndon Jones, 237–238, 243
Another Show, 349, 351
Author's Evening at Home, The, 149
Autobiography of Malcolm X, The, 8

Baba Chops, 179
Baccalaureate: A Drama in Three Acts, 47
Bakair, La, 58
Baldwin, James, 7–16, 141, 211, 233, 388, 507
Balo, 443–444, 448
Baptism, The, 23
Baraka, Amiri, 17–32, 57, 78, 79, 94, 134, 142, 211, 291, 297, 388, 504
Bayou Legend, 144, 145
Bayou Relics, 56, 57, 59
Being Forty, 431
Believers, The, 451
Birth of a Blues!, 83, 84
Black Arts Movement, 57, 79, 506
Black Bird, The, 507–508, 511

Black Doctor, The, 3, 5
Black Girl, 172–175
Black Panther Party, 64, 504, 509
Black Picture Show, 202, 204–205
Black Power Movement, 64, 80
Bloodrites, 27
Blancs, Les, 210, 212, 214
Blue Blood, 254, 256, 257–258
Blue-Eyed Black Boy, 254, 255–256
Blues for an Alabama Sky, 98, 99
Blues for Mister Charlie, 8–11, 12–13
Blue Vein Society, The, 262
Bojangles, 467
Bonner, Marita, 33–39, 212, 254
Bontemps, Arna, 40–44, 239, 435
Boogie Woogie Landscapes, 397, 403
Booji, Wooji, 313
Boucherie, La, 58
Bourbon at the Border, 98
Boy & Tarzan Appear in a Clearing, 26
Branch, William Blackwell, 45–50
Brave Blood, 325–326
Break of the Day, The, 58, 60, 62
Breakout, The, 331–332
Breath, Boom, 116, 119, 120, 121
Broken Banjo, The, 363, 366
Bronx Is Next, The, 374–377

Brotherhood, 457, 460–461, 463

Brothers, The, 103, 104–105, 107

Brown, John, 48–49

Brown, William Henry, xii, 1

Brown, William Wells, 51–55

Brown-Guillory, Elizabeth, 56–63, 151

Bubbling Brown Sugar, 302, 307, 308

Bullins, Ed, 64–77, 79, 94, 211

Bury the Dead, 89

But Never Jam Today, 91

Cage Rhythm, 117–118, 121

Caldwell, Ben, 78–87

Cane, 442

Carroll, Vinnette, 88–95

Catnap Allegiance, 116, 117

Cellar, The, 302–303

Ceremonies in Dark Old Men, 154, 156, 157–159, 161–164, 465

Chain, 97

Charades on East Fourth Street, 156, 159, 161, 164–165

Checkmates, 294, 296–297

Chip Woman's Fortune, The, 359, 362–363, 366

Christchild, 174

Chute de Sejan, La, 383

Clara's Old Man, 65

Class of 1958, 348

Cleage, Pearl, 96–101

Cold Day in August, 408

Collins, Kathleen Conwell, 102–108

Color Struck, 248, 249

Comeback after the Fire, 413

Come Down Burning, 117, 121

Compromise: A Folk Play, 359, 360, 363–364

Confession Stone, The, 144

Conjure Man Dies, The, 42, 168–170

Contributions, 410, 414, 415

Cooper, J(oan) California, 109–114

Corthron, Kia, 115–124

Cotton Comes to Harlem, 130

Crazy Horse, 349, 351

Cristophe's Daughter, 285

Croesus and the Witch, 89, 189

Cruz Bothers and Mrs. Malloy, The, 103

Cut Out the Lights and Call the Law, 174

Daddy, 73–74

Dante, 19

Davis, Ossie, 125–132, 173

Day of Absence, 457, 458–459, 462

Deacon's Awakening, The, 359, 362

Death of the Last Black Man in the Whole Entire World, The, 339–340

Dent, Thomas Covington, 133–139

Diegarias, 382, 383

Digging Eleven, 117, 120

District Line, 454

Divine Comedy, 141, 143

Dodson, Owen, 140–147

Don't Bother Me, I Can't Cope, 89, 91, 93, 189, 190–191, 193

Douglass, Frederick, 48–49, 127, 129

Do Unto Others, 467

Dr. B. S. Black, 313, 314

Drinking Gourd, 210

Dry September, 409

Duet for Three Voices, 97

Dunbar-Nelson, Alice Moore, 148–153

Duplex, The, 72

Dust to Earth, 185

Dutchman, 19, 22, 24, 28–29, 57

Eighth Ditch, The, 18

Elder, Lonne, III, 154–166, 465

Electronic Nigger, The, 65

Entertaining a Ghost, 350–351

Epitaph for a Blue Bird, 411

Escape, The, 52–53, 54

Escape to Freedom, 127, 128, 129

Essentials, 97

Evening with Dead Essex, An, 275

Everytime It Rains, 111

Experience, or, How to Give a Northern Man a Backbone, 52–53, 54

Eyes of the American, 467

Fabulous Miss Marie, The, 70, 71–72

Faith, Hope, and Charity, 262

Family Portrait, or My Son the Black Nationalist, 81–82, 85

Famous Orpheus, 333

Fences, 474, 478–479, 482–483

Fires in the Mirror, 418, 420, 421–423, 424, 426

First One, The, 249

First Step to Freedom, A, 172

Fisher, Rudolph, 167–171

Flight of the Natives, The, 364, 365

Floating Bar, 18

Flowers for the Trash Man, 506, 507
Flyin' West, 98, 99
Fools Errand, 432
Force Continuum, 119, 120
for colored girls who have considered suicide/when the rainbow is enuf, 174, 341, 389, 393–394, 397, 400–401
Fortunes of the Moor, 313
Franklin, J. e., 172–176, 190
Frederick Douglass, 254
Free and Easy, 42
Fried Chicken and Invisibility, 333
From Okra to Greens, 397–398, 403–404
Front Porch, 240
Fucking A, 340–341, 342, 344–345
Funnyhouse of a Negro, 266, 267, 269–270, 279, 336–337

Gallonwerps, The, 447
Garden of Time, 141, 144, 145
Giovanni's Room, 8
Golden Slippers, 168
Gold Piece, The, 233
Gone Are the Days, 129
Gone White, 150, 151
Good News, 97
Gordone, Charles, 177–181, 330, 465
Gordone Is a Muthah, 178
Gospel Glory, The, 241
Graham, Shirley, 182–187
Grant, Micki, 89, 188–195
Graven Images, 285
Great Day, The, 249
Great Goodness of Life, 17, 26
Grimké, Angelina Weld, 196–199, 254, 283, 316, 359
Gunn, William Harrison, 200–207

Hansberry, Lorraine, 106, 127, 155, 208–216, 410, 473
Happy Endings, 456, 457–458, 462
Harlem, 436
Haranguers, The, 451, 452
Harlem Renaissance, 34, 41, 43, 129, 151, 211, 248, 253, 307, 317, 318, 435, 436, 438, 442
Harriet Tubman, 285
Hawaiian Idyll, An, 149
Her, 431–438
Herbert III, 413, 414
Hill, Leslie Pinckney, 217–222

Home, 465–466, 467
Home Boy, 72
Homosexuality, 8, 19, 23–24, 142, 227–229, 318, 319, 321–322
Hopkins, Pauline Elizabeth, 223–225
Hospice, 97, 99
Hot Stuff, 432, 433
House Arrest, 425, 426–427
House of Sham, The, 364–365
How Now?, 110
Hughes, Langston, 34, 41, 42, 43, 110, 127, 129, 183, 209, 226–246, 290, 352, 410, 435
Hurston, Zora Neale, 34, 43, 110, 173, 183, 227, 233, 247–252, 254, 388, 435
Hymn for Rebels, 97

I Am a Man, 331–332
Idle Head, The, 364
I Gotta Home, 185
Imperceptible Mutabilities in the Third Kingdom, 339, 340, 344
In Abraham's Bosom, 430
Inner Blk Blues, 135, 137, 138
In New England Winter, 69–70
In Real Life, 493, 495, 496
In Splendid Error, 48–49
Insurrection: Holding History, 323–325, 326–328
In the Blood, 340, 341
In the Midnight Hour, 103, 105–106
In the Wine Time, 65, 66–69
Isabel's Fortune, 412, 414
It Has No Choice, 65
It's Morning, 184, 185

Jazz-set, 297
Job, The, 81
Joe Turner's Come and Gone, 479
Johannas, 202, 204
Johnson, Georgia Douglas, 34, 253–259, 284, 431
Joy to My Soul, 239, 240
Jubilee: A Cavalcade of the Negro Theatre, 42
June and Jean in Concert, 268, 277
Junkies Are Full of Shh . . ., 27
Just a Little Mark, 57, 60, 61–62

"Kabnis," 444–446, 448
Karamu House, 238

Kelley, Samuel L., 260–264
Kennedy, Adrienne, 265–282, 336
Killing of Kindness, 111
King Hedley II, 481, 482
King, Martin Luther, Jr., 8, 104, 130, 261, 323, 332, 506
King of Soul, The, 83
King's Dilemma, The, 360, 365
Kissing Rattlesnakes Can Be Fun, 156

Lady Day: A Musical Tragedy, 353
Lancashire Lad, A, 268
Land Beyond the River, A, 257, 302, 305–306, 307–308
Late Bus to Mecca, 97
Leonidas Is Fallen, 128
Lesson in Dead Language, A, 272, 273
Life by Asphyxiation, 118
Life in the Streets, 142
Little Black Sambo, 183
Little Ham, 238–239, 240, 241
Little More Light Around the Place, A, 179
Loners, 112
Looking for Jane, 103
Losing Ground, 103, 104, 107
Loved to Death, 111

Malcolm/Man Don't Live Here No More, 379–380
Mam Phyllis, 59–60, 61
Man, God Ain't Like That, 499, 500, 501
Man of All Work, 499, 500, 501
Ma Rainy's Black Bottom, 473, 474, 476, 477–478, 481–482
Marcus in the High Grass, 202, 204
Maria, 198
Marry Me, Again, 57, 59
Medal for Willie, A, 46–47
Mighty Gents, A, 410
Militant Preacher, 79
Miller, May, 34, 254, 255, 283–288, 431
Milner, Ron, 79, 85, 289–299
Mine Eyes Have Seen, 149, 151
Miscegenation, 53
Missing Sister, 58
Mission Accomplished, 82
Mitchell, Loften, 257, 300–310
Mojo and the Sayso, The, 353, 354–355
Molette, Barbara, 311–315
Monster, The, 290
Morning, Noon, and Night, 411

Morning in the South, A, 254, 257
Mortgaged, 359, 364
Mother, The, 111
Motherhood 2000, 268
Movie Star Has to Star in Black and White, A, 264, 265, 268
Mulatto: A Play of the Deep South, 234–235, 243
Mule Bone, 223, 235–236, 238, 242–243, 250, 251
My Mother Came Crying Most Pitifully, 408

Natalie Mann, 443, 448
Native Son, 499–500, 501
Neat, 492–493, 494
Night of Baker's End, The, 413
No Place to Be Somebody, 178, 179–180, 330, 465
Not One of a Kind, 111
Nugent, Richard Bruce, 227, 254, 316–320

Ododo, 452–453
O'Hara, Robert, 321–329
One Day in the Life, 504, 508–510, 511–512
One for the Money, 111
One Hour or Forever, 112
One Scene from the Drama of Early Days, 224
Only in America, 353, 355–356
Only the Sky Is Free, 103
On the Road: Search for American Character, 417, 419
OyamO, 330–335
Owl Answers, The, 268, 274

Padlocks, 348
Parks, Suzan-Lori, 336–346
Peculiar Sam; or the Underground Railroad, 224–225
Perfect Fifth, 314
Peterson, Louis Stamford, 347–351, 483
Phonograph, The, 302
Photograph: Lovers in Motion, A, 394–395, 401–402
Phyllis, 190
Piano Lesson, The, 479
Pill Hill, 261–263
Pillar of the Church, A, 362

Plantation, 416, 412–413, 415
Plumes, 256
Polk Country, 250, 251
Pot Maker, The, 34, 35–36, 37
Prayer Meeting, or the First Militant Preacher, 80, 81, 84, 85
Pretty Fire, 492, 493–494
Prodigal Daughter, The, 172, 173, 175
Prodigal Sister, The, 190
puppetplay, 97
Purlie Victorious, 127, 128–129, 130
Purple Flower, The, 34, 36, 37–38, 212

Rachel, 197–198
Racism, 4, 10, 13, 22, 117, 173, 190, 279, 305, 342
Rahman, Aishah, 352–357
Raisin in the Sun, A, 130, 155, 208, 209, 211, 213–214, 410, 473
Rat's Mass, A, 272–274
Reading, The, 103
Reckoning, The, 459–460, 462
Resurrection of Lady Lester, The, 333
Resurrection of Life, 20
Rhinestone, 202, 205
Richardson, Willis, 34, 254, 358–370
Richard III, 383–384
Riding the Goat, 284, 285–286
Riot Sale, or Dollar Psyche Fade Out, 80–81
Ritual Murder, 137, 138
River Niger, The, 452, 453, 454
Rosalee Pritchett, 313, 314

Sacred Factory, The, 446, 448
Sahdji: An African Ballet, 318–320
Sanchez, Sonia, 175, 371–381
Saving Grace, 57, 61
Say What You Willomay, 111
Scottsboro, Limited, 236, 237, 243
Seeking the Genesis, 116, 118
Sejour, Victor, 382–386
Seven Comes Up and Seven Goes Down, 156
Seven Guitars, 480, 482
Shange, Ntozake, 174, 175, 337, 387–407
Shine, Ted, 408–416
Shining Town, The, 143
Shoes, 410, 411, 414, 415
Sho Is Hot in the Cotton Patch, 409–414

Sign in Sidney Brustein's Window, The, 210, 212, 213
Simply Heavenly, 232, 240, 241
Sister Son/ji, 372–374, 375
Slave's Escape; or the Underground Railroad, 224
Sleep Deprivation Chamber, 268, 278
Slide, Glide the Slippery Slope, 119
Smith, Anna Deavere, 417–428, 475
Snapshots of a Broken Doll, 59, 61
Sojourner Truth, 285
Somebody Almost Walked Off with All My Stuff, 57
Somnia, 119
Son Come Home, A, 65
Song of Survival, 135, 137
Soul Gone Home, 239–240, 241
Spell #7: A Theater Piece in Two Acts, 395–397, 402–403
Spence, Eulalie, 429–434
Spirit House, 19, 29, 79
Splash Hatch on the E Going Down, 118, 119–120
Star of the Morning, 302, 306, 308
Starter, The, 431
Step Lovely Boy, 89, 189
St. Louis Woman, 41, 42–43
Stragglers in the Dust, 286
Sun, 267
System, Suckers, Success, 112

Take a Giant Step, 348, 349–351
Taking Care of Business, 506, 511
Taking of Miss Janie, The, 74–75
Tambourines to Glory, 241
Tell the Pharaoh, 307, 308
Three Plays by Ed Bullins, 65
Throw Thunder at This House, 174
Thurman, Wallace, 227, 435–439, 442
To Be Young, Gifted, and Black, 210, 212, 213–214
Toilet, The, 19, 23–24, 58
Tom-Tom, 184, 185
Too Hep to Be Happy, 111
Toomer, Jean, 34, 388, 440–450
Top Dog/Under Dog, 337, 338, 341, 342–343
Top Secret, or a Few Million after B.C., 82–83, 86
Toussaint L'Ouverture, 217, 219–221
Track Thirteen, 185

Trumpets of the Lord, 90–91
Twilight: Los Angeles, 1992, 418, 420, 423–424, 426
Two Trains Running, 480

Uh, Uh; But How Do It Free Us?, 377–380
Undertow, 432, 433
Unfinished Women Cry in No Man's Land while a Bird Dies in a Gilded Cage, 353–354, 356
Unintended, The, 111
Ups and Downs of Theophilus Maitland, The, 89, 92, 189
Urban Transitions: Loose Blossoms, 293, 297

Venus, 340, 341
Vici Kid, The, 168

Wake Up Lou Riser, 117
Walker, Joseph, 451–455
Ward, Douglas Turner, 155, 456–463
Waring: A Theme for Linda, The, 290
Weight of Clay, 112
Welcome to Black River, 446–467
What the Wine-Sellers Buy, 290, 291, 292–293, 295–296
What Use Are Flowers?, 210

What Was the Relationship of the Lone Ranger to the Means of Production, 26
When Ancestors Call, 58, 60, 62
When Hell Freezes Over, I'll Skate, 93
When the Jack Hollers, 41, 239
Where the Dewdrops of Mercy Shine Bright, 174
While Older Men Speak, 103
Whipping, The, 432
White Chocolate, 262
Who's Got His Own, 290, 291, 295
Wife of His Youth, The, 262
William and Ellen Craft, 254, 256–257, 258
Williams, Samm-Art, 464–471
Wilson, August, 472–490
Women Like Us, 495
Woodard, Charlayne, 491–497
World of Ben Caldwell, 79, 85
Wright, Richard, 388, 498–502

X, Malcolm, 8, 11, 267, 331, 371, 373, 379, 506
X, Marvin, 64, 79, 503–513

Yin Yang, 452, 453
Your Arms Too Short to Box with God, 89, 91–92, 93, 94, 189, 191–192, 193

ABOUT THE CONTRIBUTORS

KAREN C. BLANSFIELD is adjunct assistant professor in the Department of Dramatic Art at the University of North Carolina at Chapel Hill. In addition to dozens of scholarly articles and reviews, she has authored two books: one on O'Henry, the other on William Sydney Porter.

CARRIE J. BODEN is assistant professor of English at Friends University in Wichita, Kansas.

LEAN'TIN L. BRACKS is an associate professor of English and African American literature at Fisk University. She is the author of *Black Women Writers of the Diaspora* (1997).

JUSTIN BRODEUR is a graduate student in English at the State University of New York at Cortland.

SHARON M. BRUBAKER is a doctoral candidate at Temple University and teaches multicultural drama at Drexel University.

LINDA M. CARTER is an associate professor of English at Morgan State University. Author of over thirty articles on African American literature and culture, she has coedited four books.

STEVEN CARTER is a professor of English at Salem State College. He is the author of *Lorraine Hansberry's Drama: Commitment Amid Complexity* (1993), which won an American Book Award in 1993. He is also the author of *James Jones: An American Literary Orientalist Master* (1998), as well as dozens of scholarly articles.

HARISH CHANDER is a professor of English at Shaw University, North Carolina. He has contributed chapters to various reference volumes on African American and postcolonial literatures.

KRISTINA A. CLARK is a graduate student in English at the State University of New York at Cortland.

KIMBERLY RAE CONNOR is the author of *Conversions and Visions in the Writings of African American Women* (1994), *Imagining Grace: Liberating Theologies in the Slave Narrative Tradition* (2000), and dozens of articles on African American literature and multicultural pedagogy. She teaches at the University of San Francisco.

EMMA WATERS DAWSON is professor of English and associate dean of the College of Arts and Sciences at Florida A&M University–Tallahassee.

ROBERT FELGAR is professor of English and chair of the English Department at Jacksonville State University. He has published three books on Richard Wright: *Student Companion to Richard Wright* (2000), *Understanding Richard Wright's "Native Son"* (1998), and *Richard Wright* (1988).

CRISTI A. FOX is a graduate student in English at the State University of New York at Cortland.

DEBORAH GLEASON-RIELLY holds an M.A. in English and teaches multicultural literature at a high school near Syracuse, New York.

KIMBERLY K. HARDING is associate professor of theatre arts at Florida A&M University–Tallahassee.

RHONDA HARVEY is a recent recipient of an M.A. in English from the State University of New York at Cortland.

JAMES L. HILL is professor of English and assistant vice president for Academic Affairs at Albany State University, Georgia.

SHARON GLAZIER HOCHSTEIN teaches English as a second language at the State University of New York at Morrisville.

VALLERI ROBINSON HOHMAN is assistant professor of theatre arts at the University of Arizona at Tucson. Her research focuses on the early relationship between Russian and American theater artists and audiences.

HELEN R. HOUSTON is professor of English at Tennessee State University–Nashville. She is the author of *The Afro-American Novel, 1965–1975* (1977) and coauthor of the teacher's guide to the *Norton Anthology of African American Literature* (1997).

MICHAEL E. IDLAND is a graduate student in English at the State University of New York at Buffalo.

ROCHELL ISAAC is adjunct assistant professor of English at Long Island University.

YMITRI JAYASUNDERA is assistant professor of English at Prairie View A&M University. Her research centers on ethnic American and postcolonial literature.

GWENDOLYN S. JONES is professor emeritus of English at Tuskegee University. She has published extensively on the women writers of the Harlem Renaissance.

LEELA KAPAI is professor of English at Prince George's Community College in Maryland.

CHRISTINE M. LEMCHAK is lecturer in English at the State University of New York at Cortland.

ROBIN JANE LUCY is assistant professor of English at Eastern Michigan University.

LAVERNE LUSTER is associate professor of English at Albany State University in Georgia.

JESSIE N. MARION holds a master's degree in English education and teaches multiethnic literature at a high school in Johnson City, New York.

SUZANNE HOTTE MASSA, who has published on Gwendolyn Brooks, Sojourner Truth, Jamaica Kincaid, and Italian American authors, teaches multiculture literature at a high school for at-risk students in Ithaca, New York.

LADRICA MENSON-FURR is assistant professor of English at the University of Memphis.

FREYA M. MERCER is a graduate student in English at the State University of New York at Cortland.

CHANDRA TYLER MOUNTAIN is associate professor and chair of the Department of English at Dillard University. Her research work centers on women writers of the African diaspora.

EMMANUEL S. NELSON is professor of English at the State University of New York at Cortland. The author of over fifty articles on various international literatures in English, he has edited a dozen reference volumes including *African American Autobiographies* (Greenwood, 2002), *African American Authors, 1745–1945* (Greenwood, 2000), and *Contemporary African American Novelists* (Greenwood, 1999).

TERRY NOVAK is associate professor of English at Johnson and Wales University in Rhode Island. She has published several scholarly articles on African American women authors.

YOLANDA W. PAGE is assistant professor of English at Dillard University. Her research interests include the dramaturgy of August Wilson, gay and lesbian literature, and popular culture.

LOUIS J. PARASCANDOLA is associate professor of English at Long Island University's Brooklyn campus. His publications include an edition of the writings of the Harlem Renaissance author Eric Walrond and a monograph of the Victorian novelist Captain Marryat, as well as three editions of Marryat's novels.

JOYCE RUSSELL-ROBINSON is professor of English at Fayetteville State University in North Carolina.

YVONNE SHAFER is professor of English at St. John's University. She has published books on August Wilson, Henrik Gibson, and Eugene O'Neill.

JOEL SHATZKY is professor of English at the State University of New York at Cortland. A playwright and novelist, he is coeditor of *Contemporary Jewish-American Novelists* (Greenwood, 1997) and *Contemporary Jewish-American Dramatists and Poets,* (Greenwood, 1999).

TARSHIA L. STANLEY is assistant professor of English at Spelman College.

KARL L. STENGER is associate professor of German at the University of South Carolina–Aiken. He has published several articles on African American literature.

ABOUT THE CONTRIBUTORS

Loretta G. Woodard is associate professor of English at Marygrove College in Detroit. She has published widely on African American women authors.

Johnny Woodnal recently received his M.A. in English and currently teaches multicultural writing at a high school near Boston.

Darcy A. Zabel is assistant professor of English and vice chair of the Religion and Humanities Division at Friends University in Wichita, Kansas.